AMERICAN

US Army ribbon and medal awarded to those who served in the American Theater during World War II.

**Hershel "Woody" Williams established the Gold Star Families Memorial Monuments in many communities.**

## Dedication

This book is dedicated to all those American military personnel and American civilians who guarded our borders and shores during World War II. Their voluntary selfless efforts, courage, and sleepless nights throughout the war protected our country from imminent attack and permitted America to liberate Europe and Asia. As with all World War II veterans, we humbly salute you. May future generations forever reflect on and honor your extraordinary patriotism and sacrifices with unrelenting gratitude.

I want to dedicate this book to Hershel "Woody" Williams, the last living Medal of Honor Recipient from World War II. Woody received the Medal of Honor for his bravery as a Marine in the Battle for Iwo Jima, saving the lives of many others in his unit. He spent his lifetime helping the American public. Woody spent many years doing what he loved to do, supporting their families as a VA counselor. In 2005, he established the Woody Williams Foundation, which built many Gold Star Families monuments throughout the country. With approximately 60 projects currently underway, the Woody Williams Foundation will have a footprint in about 40 states. Woody realized that families of those lost defending the country are often overlooked and that memorials are needed to honor them and the fallen. It is an honor and a privilege to know him. He has done so much for veterans and their families. Woody has said, "I've had a number of people tell me, 'Now I know my loved one will not be forgotten.'"

*Anyone interested in establishing a Gold Star Family Memorial for their community can contact the Woody Williams Foundation. For more information on Woody Williams and the Gold Star Families Monuments, please visit* www.woodywilliams.org.

*"During World War II, never has the United States faced such a threat to her national existence. Never had this country faced so many insurmountable problems at one time."*
**General George Marshall, US Army Chief of**
**Staff**

*"The opportunity to secure ourselves from defeat lies in our own hands."*
**Sun Tzu, The Art of War**

# Acknowledgments

**M**y greatest appreciation to the World War II veterans and civilians *for* their detailed accounts of their experiences. Without their interviews, much of this history addressing enemy attacks on America off our coasts and on American soil would never have been preserved.

Thank you to the following World War II veterans: Pearl Harbor survivors Frank Schimmel and Joe Lockard, Putty Mills of Santa Barbara, California, and Mel Surofsky. Thank you to the Gray brothers, Jim and Caroll, who all recalled their house shaking from U-boat-produced explosions. Thank you to Bee Haydu and Karina Anderson for their interviews. Thank you for support from all Navy, Army, Air Force, Merchant Marines, Coast Guard personnel, and civilians Carol Dillon (who witnessed many German attacks) and James Rubin. Thanks to Vicki Lokken of Santa Barbara, California, who led me to local interviews, Steph and Joe Bigley for their support on the World War II Homefront in North Carolina, and Wilbur Jones for all his work on North Carolina World War II history. Thanks to Rebekah Slonim and Rachel Lane for their transcriptions of World War II veterans and civilian interviews. And to Orion Zangara, a successful artist in his own right, for his outstanding drawings and cover for this book.

My most sincere gratitude for the support and assistance of the following people and organizations: Library of Congress, Veterans History Project; Tim Nenninger and Nathan Patch of the National Archives and Records Administration; Louella Large, past President of the Sons and Daughters of Pearl Harbor Survivors, for her permission to publish excerpts of her presentation on the Pearl Harbor attack; Deidre Kelly. Thank you to the Friends of Old Ft. Stevens, Oregon, Santa Barbara Library Archives, Brookings History Museum, Army Heritage Center, and the US Army Corps of Engineers Office of History.

Thanks to the NPS World War II Homefront San Francisco; War in the Aleutians NHP, Alaska; Pearl Harbor National Memorial Park, Hawaii; NPS Ocracoke Island, North Carolina; Susan Gold of the Beaches Museum Jacksonville Florida; Portsmouth New Hampshire Library/Archives, Brooklyn, New York. A big thank-you to the Graveyard of the Atlantic Museum and the Ocracoke Island Historical Society. The Smithsonian Institute, Washington DC, also provided great material. And a special thanks to Ilana Sol for her permission to use interview excerpts from her documentary, *On Paper Wings.* We cannot thank enough Russ Shrine and the great people at the Mid Atlantic Air Museum. The Museum occupies a division of the Reading, PA Airport and includes active restored aircraft from the era as well as hosting WWII Weekend. It was all started by World War II Vet and pilot Eugene Shrine. Over the past 30 years, the annual weekend event has provided many WWII Vets to meet with the public. I am grateful to have met them through MAAM.

My most significant appreciation to those who led the way and inspires us today, including Woody Williams, the last surviving World War II Medal of Honor recipient. Woody received the Medal of Honor from President Truman for his extraordinary bravery in defeating the enemy at Iwo Jima and saving many American lives. My appreciation also goes to the "Dean of World War II Historians" Dr. Gerhard Weinberg. Dr. Weinberg was a refugee from Germany, and after immigrating to America, he served in the Army in the occupation of Japan. His many classic award-winning volumes are currently used throughout the world for World War II studies. My discussions with him were a real inspiration. Other outstanding World War II historians who have had a similar impact are Richard Frank, Rick Adkinson, Alex Kershaw, Donald Miller, Allen Millet, Mark Felton, Bert Webber, and Ed Offley.

And an extra special thanks and appreciation goes to my wife of 40 years, Lisa. Through her unending support and encouragement, she helped me attain my goal of keeping WWII history alive for future generations.

# PREFACE

Several years ago, I started a non-profit group, WW2 History Archive, which is to interview and record the history of our last remaining World War II veterans. The stories I have recorded defy imagination and surpass the narratives of captivating novels in their drama and compelling nature. I was fortunate enough to interview hundreds of World War II veterans who served our country in the massive overseas theaters of war. Future volumes will be presented with these remarkable veterans' interviews in the context of the history in which they participated.

It has been gratifying to interview these heroes who recall the attacks on our coasts during World War II and present them here in the context of these forgotten events. In teaching World War II history, I emphasize two fundamentals usually overlooked in hindsight. These basics are that the Allies could have lost the war and that an invasion of the US was inevitable but for the US Marines, Sailors, Soldiers, and Airmen who took the fight to the enemy. Underscoring these premises are the attacks that did occur in the states and territories of American sovereignty. Although not decisive in the overall outcome of the war, the Axis attacked America. On the East Coast, within sight of land, many would die, resulting in more killed than were at Pearl Harbor.

In my presentations to various audiences on the history of the Second World War, I noticed audiences familiar with World War II history were unaware of the extent of attacks on America. People would converse in great detail regarding the war. Thoughtful questions were asked regarding the Pacific or Europe Theaters but received surprised reactions regarding our own country's historic World War II episodes. Few realized that five-thousand civilians were killed within American waters and the Navy Armed Guard on civilian ships. Very few of those attacked were US Navy, and none were warships. Hundreds of hundreds of people witnessed many sinkings on the beaches of the East Coast. Thousands more Merchant Marines and passengers would struggle in lifeboats at sea and suffer from starvation, dehydration, and exposure to the elements.

Although the Merchant Marines were not considered part of the military, their casualty rate (not the number of casualties) exceeded that of all service branches other than the US Marines. The number of Americans killed, wounded, or missing persons were not nearly on the scale of the tens of millions of deaths across Europe or Asia. Nevertheless, the American Eastern seaboard and Caribbean waters were the most dangerous sea lanes in the world in 1942.

This volume aims to address the often-forgotten history of the time when America experienced the Second World War as disastrous attacks occurred here at home. World War II is the most significant event in human history. Indeed, it was the largest war in which nearly every country would have decided with whom they were aligned. The War was a sequence of well-connected wars. This book is the only single volume, to my knowledge, that outlines the American Theater of World War II, including Hawaii, Alaska, the West Coast, and the East Coast, and combines oral history with a graphic-novel style. It outlines the breadth of the American Theater. Our hope is it will stimulate greater interest and reading on the American and Overseas Theaters during some of the most complex events in modern world history, World War II.

# INTRODUCTION

The Japanese attack on Pearl Harbor, Hawaii, could have been the Japanese Imperial Navy and Army's stepping stone to the American mainland. After the occupation of the Aleutians, it would have then been possible for the Japanese Imperial Army to advance through Alaska and Canada to the American West Coast. Japanese airbases established within the range from the American mainland would enable bombing raids on US West Coast cities.

Americans were taken from Alaska as prisoners of war. Half of these American prisoners would never return, dying a horrible death in the camps, along with the American military POWs. Nearly 600 soldiers and sailors gave their lives in Alaska, preventing the Japanese from advancing to our West Coast. Unfortunately, many of these personal histories of the survivors were never told.

To the casual observer, the lives lost and the wounded in the American Theater pales compared to the conglomerate of perhaps up to 80 million or more killed in World War II. From a textbook perspective, these casualties in America, the majority that happened in the first six months of the war, are portrayed as somehow insignificant. To view through that narrow lens neglects the understanding of the traumatic and distressing experiences of Americans who faced the most significant threats in our nation's history right here in America. Here lies the value of oral history: interviewing actual witnesses and participants who were here on the Homefront. While interviewing eyewitnesses, one begins to understand how they experienced the events first-hand. All were astonished to face hostile powers on our shores, hitting them so close to their own home while praying for their husbands, fathers, and brothers serving overseas in harm's way.

4

Those killed in the American Theater, compared to the 400,000 Americans total killed in the war, may in hindsight, appear to be anomalies of World War II. This mistaken view of hindsight history denies insight into those terrifying and unique experiences Americans faced, some of which are still with us to attest to today's unimaginable. Lives were lost in America in World War II, and just one life lost was one too many.

In the early months of the war, the outlook for the Allies looked as if there was one disaster after another. By early 1942, Germany had successfully occupied nearly all European countries that had not joined the Axis powers voluntarily. Nazi Germany invaded the Middle East and occupied most of industrialized Russia. Germany achieved the unthinkable, and that is, it conquered much of the industrial world in the Eastern Hemisphere. England was in shambles from German air bombing assaults, with 15% of London's population killed. Along with other major British cities, the total number the Germans killed by bombing in the UK was 60,000.

Japan dominated Asia and attacked or occupied many US sites in the Pacific. On April 9, 1942, 15,000 Americans and 60,000 Filipinos surrendered on the Bataan Peninsula of the Philippines after holding out for three months. A month later, another 11,000 US and Filipino soldiers surrendered on Corregidor Island in Manila Bay, capping the biggest capitulation of US military forces in US history. The defeat resulted in the largest surrender since Union Forces did so to the Confederacy in 1862 at Harpers Ferry, Virginia, during the Civil War. By the spring of 1942, America had experienced its worst defeats in history, and it was facing the most significant threat ever to our Homeland. Unimaginable today, these horrific events weighed heavy on the minds of Americans.

In the early part of the war, the Germans and Japanese attacked America directly. By clever use of their aircraft carriers and submarines as airplane hangars, the Japanese had conquered the previous limitations of aircraft range. They could reach Alaska and the Western US Coast.

On the Eastern US Coast, Germany did not possess such an aircraft carrier fleet as the Japanese did. Therefore, they could not yet use airpower to attack American military bases or civilian targets. However, the Nazis had an even more effective means of sinking tankers, freighters, and other ships of the East Coast: The *Underseeboot*, otherwise known as the U-boat. These German stealthy maneuverable submarines were small enough to approach their prey, fire torpedoes, and quickly disappear before an Allied bomber was called in. The German U-boats got so close to the East Coast that they used the lights on the American shore to spot the silhouette of the victim ship, whose lights were off in anticipation of the enemy U-boat. Thousands would die, and hundreds of ships would be sunk on the American East Coast, often in sight of observers on the beaches.

Tough times were the order of the day. By 1942, families in America had already begun to lose loved ones to the enemy at Pearl Harbor, the Philippines, China, southeast Asia, Burma, and the Marshall Islands, Rubal at the *Battle of the Coral Sea* from May 4-8, 1942. The deep sentiment of the times was that Armageddon was upon us, and it was understood as a final judgment of who will dominate civilization. And for America, all of this happened just in the first six months of the war.

The title of this book, *America Under Attack: The Secret History of World War II,* implies that many of the attacks were kept secret during the war. It is much more challenging to declassify than to classify information in the US government. Most Americans at that time were not aware of the landings of the Japanese balloon bombs and the extent of the German attacks on our East Coast shipping vessels during the war. However, as these events became declassified many years after the war, the impact of their importance was diminished since we were then living in a safe Post-War Era. Much of the details of these events are still not found, and many of the accounts of the balloon bombs and U-boats may have been lost to history. A massive effort should be made to locate more of this history in local libraries and museums. Through descendants of Merchant Marines and civilians, more information could be learned. It is assumed that all events of World War II are no longer classified and readily available. However, this may not always be the case. At the National Archives in College Park, MD, World War II documents are so extensive that I suspect they have not all been analyzed. More research should be done to uncover stories and details on warfare, spying, espionage, and sabotage during World War II from the National Archives and other official sources.

The public's assumption that World War II would be fought here within the United States has been largely neglected in history. In a recent interview in December 2021 by the WWII Roundtable of Central Pennsylvania, the last living Medal of Honor Recipient of World War II, Woody Williams, recalled the assumption nearly everyone had that the war would be here in America. Woody recollected his thoughts during his enlistment. "So, I elected to be discharged from the Civilian Conservation Corps and came home. It was on a train, and they sent us back to West Virginia. I had not reached my 18th birthday, but I still wanted to be in the Marines. I didn't know anything about war. I didn't realize at the time that I would not stay in the United States of America. I thought all of us who were entering were joining to protect our country and our freedom, and it wasn't until I got into boot camp in May 1943 that I learned we are not going to fight the war in America."

# PROLOGUE: DEFENDING THE HOMELAND

## UNITED STATES MILITARY

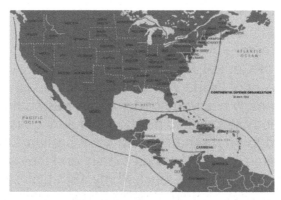

*The five areas of the country were designated as Army Defense Commands.*

Army Defense Commands in coordination with the US Navy included five major Army Commands: Western, Central, Eastern, Southern, and the Caribbean. No doubt, the mainland of the United States was next in line for an enemy attack. The government and the public counted the days until the eventual bombings would arrive from Germany or Japan. How could America plan to defend itself? The nation was divided into five Defense Commands by the Army. All five had ocean access and were vulnerable to Axis attacks by sea and air. About half of the states resided on the waters or could be approached from the Atlantic Ocean or the St. Lawrence Seaway.

**Western Command:** Alaska and Hawaii and the West Coast and other Pacific Islands were under the Western Command. In terms of square miles, the Western Command's jurisdiction was actually the largest area in size, i.e., the Pacific.

*WWII era map showing military bases in the North Eastern United States*

**Eastern Command:** The Eastern Command was the closest to Germany and its fleet of hundreds of U-boats, so naturally, it was the most significant concern. The Germans had plans to attack the US from the air and sea, which was taken very seriously. America's defense against the Germans at sea was primarily due to the Army or Navy bombers. The Eastern Command extended from Maine to Florida, and with many major cities to contend with, its' jurisdiction had the most significant complexity. Having the most extensive industrial base, the area was also a target for German bombing and sabotage. The Eastern Command also supported the defense of eastern Canada, Greenland, and Iceland.

**The Central Command:** The Central Command was responsible for the central states and the Great Lakes. German U-boats attacked twenty-three ships in the St. Lawrence River and killed hundreds of people. The St. Lawrence River empties into Lake Ontario, which connects the Great Lakes throughout the mining and industrial centers of the country. The shipping lanes obscured in the Great Lakes were vital to keep safe during the war.

The heavy mining and industrial belts of the Great Lakes Region offered ample opportunity for Germany's dexterous U-boats. These sinkings created panic among both Canadians and Americans. The possibility of further penetration by the submarines was genuine.

**The Southern Command:** This command included the Gulf of Mexico, swarming with U-boats and American oil tankers. New Orleans and Florida were particularly struck with sinkings from the Germans. The Texas Coast and Mexico were very vulnerable. Texas had a good share of military installations.

**The Caribbean Command:** The Caribbean Command protected Puerto Rico and the Panama Canal. The Panama Canal was a target of the Japanese at the beginning of the war, with Puerto Rico being fired upon by German U-boats. The Caribbean Command's mission was to protect our island neighbors and South America. The American Theater, in practice, comprised basically of the Western Hemisphere. Hundreds of ships from many nations were sunk off the Caribbean Islands and in South America, concentrating on the oil-producing Aruba area.

## US NAVY ATLANTIC AND PACIFIC FRONTIERS

In America, the first half of 1942 was a bleak year. Following the unthinkable attack on Pearl Harbor in December 1941, the US Navy's main worry was preventing the destruction of its remaining significant fleet, including its aircraft carriers along with their aircraft. Most naval assets were in the Pacific, including Hawaii, Guadalcanal, the Philippines, New Guinea, the Coral Sea, and many other locations in the Pacific. There were not enough naval assets to defend the East or West Coasts. The British Empire couldn't spare any warships to even defend itself in fighting Japan since it was already severely involved in combat with the Nazis in North Africa and the *Battle of the Atlantic*. Some of the warships Britain did send to our East Coast to protect American lives were sunk by the Germans with many casualties. During the war, the US NAVY Eastern Sea Frontier (EASTSEAFRON) was a United States Navy Operational Command responsible for the coastal waters from Canada to Jacksonville, Florida, extending out for a nominal distance of two hundred miles. The commander of a Sea Frontier had control and responsibility for convoys within its defined area, had its vessels for convoy use or other uses as determined by the commander, and worked closely with the US Army Air Force in defense of the frontier. Usually, offices of the US Navy and US Army Air Force officers assigned to the frontier had their offices side-by-side to create effective two-way communications that expedited reaction to reports of enemy presence. In addition to providing escorts for convoys within its frontier, the Sea Frontier was responsible for sea-air rescue, harbor defense, shipping lane patrol, minesweeping, and air operations.  The commander of the Eastern Sea Frontier, until the closing months of 1943, was Vice Admiral Adolphus Andrews, whose operational orders could only be appealed to Chief Admiral Ernest King.

The United States Marine Corps, although usually thought of as the fighting force in the Pacific, trained and prepared for an actual invasion by the Japanese on the West Coast and by the Germans on the east coast. The buildup was extensive on Marine Bases in 1942 on the West and East Coast. The Marines fought the Japanese in Hawaii and Alaska and throughout the Pacific. The US Marines had the highest casualty rate of all US Military Services; the Pacific War would never have been won without the United States Marines. Their iconic flag raising of Mt. Suribachi on Iwo Jima is an enduring symbol of their tenacity and patriotism in World War II. Not enough can be said about the United States Marines. They would fight on a Japanese-occupied island. After taking it, the

Marines still living were brought to the next island to do the same again and again.

## US NAVY ARMED GUARD

United States Navy Armed Guard units were established to provide defensive firepower to Merchant ships in convoy or Merchant ships traveling alone. This was done because of the constant danger from enemy submarines, surface raiders, fighter aircraft, and bombers. Because of the shortage of Allied escort vessels, it was necessary to provide the Merchant vessels with some measure of protection.

The Armed Guards did not have enough firepower to counter the submarine threat before a ship was torpedoed. Navy Armed Guards were provided with a limited number of depth charges with little effect. The Guard saved lives by assisting the Merchant Marines who had to abandon ship. As a result, the Navy Armed Guard and the Merchant Marine often acted as one entity and built a unique relationship in military history. It was a strange assignment for Navy men to be on a civilian ship without any Navy infrastructure and all of its defense, security, communications, and support.

## US MERCHANT MARINE

The United States Merchant Marine refers to the organization that sails and runs freighters and tankers, both federally or privately owned Merchant vessels. The civilian mariners and the Merchant's vessels are managed by the government and private sectors. They engage in commerce or transportation of goods and services in and out of the navigable waters of the United States. The Merchant Marine primarily transports cargo and passengers during peacetime. The Merchant Marine can be an auxiliary to the United States Navy in war or national emergency. It can be called upon to deliver military personnel and material for the military. Master is the title for Captain; Seamen and Able-bodied seaman are lower ranks.

Today, Merchant Marine officers may also be commissioned as military officers by the Department of Defense. The federal government currently maintains fleets of merchant ships via organizations such as the Military Sealift Command (part of the U.S. Navy) and the National Defense Reserve Fleet, which the United States Maritime Administration manages. In World War II, the Merchant Marine was critical to winning the war.

These mariners, civilians with the US Merchant Marine, hauled vital war cargo for the Allies. They were the supply line that provided virtually everything the Allied armies needed to fight on foreign battlefields. These seamen had no military standing or government benefits, but they possessed unusual courage. Many gave their lives for their country.

Surviving a U-boat attack often meant running a gauntlet of dangers, including fire, explosions, icy water, sharks, flaming oil slicks, and long odysseys in open lifeboats. "You were taking a chance, that's for sure," recalled Jack Rowe, a Merchant Mariner from tiny Gwynn's Island in Mathews County, Virginia. "But a lot of people were taking chances. You couldn't just say, 'Why me?' Someone had to step up."

Standing lookout on a Merchant ship was nerve-racking, especially around dawn and dusk, when the colors of the sea and sky merged into a gray haze, and any ripple of motion or flash of color might be the plume of a torpedo. "Occasionally, a man will get the jitters and will be noticed walking the deck at night when he should be asleep," recalled Mariner Raymond Edwards. Once a torpedo struck, every moment became precious and every decision irreversible. "Even two seconds could mean the difference between life and death for any member of the crew. Running in the wrong direction might cut a sailor off from all means of escape. Jumping overboard at the wrong spot or at the wrong instant might easily cost a life. If a sailor is lucky enough to be alive after a torpedo hits his ship, it takes quick thinking and fast action to get him off the ship and into a lifeboat. Many are saved by sheer luck."

The U-boat was particularly unforgiving to Merchant Mariners. The Merchant Marine suffered a higher casualty percentage rate than most other military branches, losing 9,300 men, many losses occurring off the East Coast in 1942. Enemy attacks killed over two hundred even before Pearl Harbor and the Declaration of War by Germany. Most Merchant ships sailed US waters with little protection, except the Navy Armed Guard. The Armed Guard was courageous and saved many lives. Unfortunately, there were limited options available for the Armed Guard after a torpedo hit a ship to keep the ship or the attacking U-boat. The crew of the sinking boat was grateful to have assistance in manning lifeboats.

## US COAST GUARD

Today, the US Coast Guard is a branch of the US Armed Forces, charged with enforcing US Maritime Laws and ensuring the safety of the Nation's ports and waterways. In World War II, this unusual military branch performed some remarkable feats.

World War II completely redefined America's military. In the years immediately preceding the United States' entry into the war and over the subsequent four years and eight months of fighting, the Coast Guard's responsibilities grew exponentially. To support the cause, the Coast Guard expanded to a record high of more than 170,000 men and women serving in uniform, with nearly 250,000 personnel serving throughout the war. The Coast Guard watched and defended the shores by various boats and patrolled up and down beaches on horseback and foot with search canines. Two hundred and fourteen Coast Guardsmen were killed.

## EMERGENCY EVACUATION AND A "SHORT SNORTER"

An enormous cooperative effort developed between the US Army and civilians to execute a massive evacuation of coastal cities. From the Teaneck, New Jersey, Joe Bigley, Sr. left college to join the Army after the Pearl Harbor attack. In 1942 he was assigned to the vast effort to evacuate the hospitals, schools, and other defenseless facilities in Hoboken, Jersey City, and other vulnerable towns. The institutions and operations were relocated to New Jersey and Pennsylvania sites further inland. Joe Bigley, Sr., also operated advanced radar devices to locate U-boats secretly roaming close to shore.

The Army was serious about the possibility of a German air or sea attack on New Jersey just across the Hudson River from New York. The metropolises comprised vital war industries easily accessible from the Atlantic Ocean.

All members of Joe's company signed a dollar bill, called a "short snorter." For sport, it was a common practice during the war. A signatory could challenge one of their fellow soldiers to produce it. If he could not, the next round of drinks was bought by the soldier or sailor who should have had it handy.

Over seventy years later, Joe Bigley Jr. would receive an e-mail from a New Yorker neither he nor his father ever knew. This Manhattan resident received a "short snorter" randomly in his change and recognized it as a relic of WWII. He then began searching the legible names signed on the bill. Fortunately, Joe Sr. wrote legibly enough that his name could be read. After contacting anyone with the last name Bigley, the New Yorker found the right Joe Bigley, Jr. Joe confirmed it was his dad's signature. The "short snorter" was immediately sent to him for safekeeping.

## PROTECTING WASHINGTON DC

Protection of the nation's capital was at the forefront of the country's defense. The anticipation of the enemy bombing the Nation's Capital was so feasible that bunkers were built underground beneath the White House. Tunnels with hidden exits were completed downtown for the emergency escapes that our leaders prayed would never materialize. Plane spotters with anti-aircraft guns scanned the skies for the inevitable German or Japanese Bomber. Many of the Washington DC elderly residents I have known recalled a frantic and hectic Nation's Capital like never seen since. And in the middle of all the chaos just after Pearl harbor: If we are bombed, what would become of our "Charters of Freedom"? The Constitution,

Declaration of Independence, the Magna Carter, the Gettysburg Address. In the middle of the night on 26 December 1941, the Secret Service took possession of the Founding Documents and secured them on a particular government guarded train. It was an unnerving 675-mile journey for the government agents through West Virginia, Ohio, and finally, Fort Knox, TN. No one except the President and a few select cabinet members knew where the foundation of the American system was being hidden. While the founding documents were now safe, the residents of Washington continued to look skyward and hoped Armageddon would pass them by.

## CIVILIANS IN ACTION

During World War II, civilians had to step forward and form civilian support to the Army, Navy, and Air Force since the military was not yet large enough to carry out the necessary protection of the Homeland while fighting in Europe and the South Pacific.

*The Hooligan Navy: Officially called the Coastal Picket Patrol or Corsair Fleet*

"Hooligan" means a "typically young guy who participates in a boisterous or aggressive activity, especially as part of a group or gang." Because these seafaring men were not members of the Navy or Coast Guard, they were jokingly referred to as "Hooligans," a term no longer used in the American lexicon.

In the early days of World War II, the Navy was in desperate need of ships to monitor the coastal seas for U-boats and to rescue survivors of assaults. Alfred Stanford of the Cruising Club of America persuaded the Coast Guard those private citizens could help by contributing several sailing ships to the mission. On May 4, 1942, the Navy ordered the Coast Guard Reserve to create the Coastal Picket Patrol.

The Coastal Picket Patrol arose from a public, Navy, and media debate about whether sailing boats might be effective in anti-submarine operations. Vessels had to be able to sail in the open ocean for up to two days. The boats would be equipped with machine guns, depth charges, and a radio. The Masters (i.e., Captains) on the boats were required to be knowledgeable about sailing, while the crew comprised Boy Scouts, college students, and beachcombers.

On a Navy drill on August 13, 1942, ten Army aircraft flew along the Massachusetts Coast to test the Air Defense Network. No military ship or Navy shore station picked up the incoming possible hostile jet. The only ones that saw and reported them were the four Picket Patrol boats.

On September 15, 1942, the *Edlu II*, a Picket Patrol boat, patrolled south of Montauk Point, Massachusetts. Then a U-boat surfaced about 100 yards away. Then the U-boat skipper came close enough to engage with machine guns; it suddenly crash-dived and fled the area. In another case, a German captain surfaced his U-boat close to a Picket boat, walked out onto the deck, and screamed in perfect English, "Get out of here, you guys!" A "Hooligan" boat, *Zaida,* was stranded in a winter gale off the coast of New England for three weeks before being discovered and saved.

The Coast Guard also bought or leased numerous yachts from local boaters in the early days of the war and outfitted them with guns and a Coast Guard crew. Many wealthy people donated their boats for use in the Hooligan Navy, including JP Morgan and others.

One of the 20th century's most well-known and well-loved American authors, Ernest Hemmingway, went beyond the call of duty by donating his yacht to the cause. Hemmingway went out on his yacht off Florida and Cuba (he had houses in both locations) with explosives to find and sink U-boats. His concept was accepted and supported by the US Navy. The Navy even supplied Hemmingway with explosives and support. The idea that a yacht would be a threat to U-boats totally escaped the captains of these German submarines. Hemingway's experiences would lead him to write *Islands in the Stream*, an autobiographical novel.

Recipient of the 1956 Nobel Prize for literature and the Pulitzer Prize (only a few authors have ever won both), Hemmingway was not an ivory tower philosopher. Few people of any background have had as many adventures and wartime experiences.

Hemmingway spent his life in the center of WWI, the Spanish Civil War, several fronts in World War II, even the Cold War, and adventures in Asia and Africa. He was one of the few Americans in China during the Japanese invasions. As a freelance journalist, he traveled by his own choice. As a seriously injured WWI veteran, Hemmingway later wrote *Farewell to Arms* about the war. He was passionately involved with bullfighting, big-game hunting, and deep-sea fishing, and his writings reflected it. He visited Spain during their Civil War and described his experiences in the bestseller, *For Whom the Bell Tolls*.

Due to health issues, Hemmingway was not permitted to join any branch of the service in World War II, but he demanded to be in on the first wave at Normandy as an Army Journalist. He was only permitted to view the invasion from a ship that had shells exploding nearby. When allowed to go ashore, he went behind enemy lines, without Army oversight, and organized resistance to the Nazis. His actions helped to save Allied lives. The United States Army awarded him the Bronze Star, the highest award a civilian can receive. Few civilians have ever received the Bronze Star. This rare civilian award is not widely known, even in military circles. During the Cold War, while living in Havana, Hemmingway met with Fidel Castro in 1959, when he first came to power. This was Hemmingway's attempt to moderate the dictator's attitude toward the United States.

Ernest Hemmingway passed away in 1961 with few regrets. His life reads like a series of his novels, but his story was more than that. It was imperfect yet a remarkable inspiration.

"The world breaks everyone, and afterward, many are strong at the broken places." Ernest Hemmingway

*Civil Defense Corps*

**The United States Civil Defense logo in World War II:**
The triangle emphasized the three-step Civil Defense
philosophy: prevention, mitigation, and response. The symbol
has become an international symbol to identify workers of any
civilian humanitarian agency.

Today, America's defense comprises the Army, Navy,
Marines, Air Force, Space Force, and the Coast Guard, each
branch's respective reserves. National Guard units are state
agencies with federal funding and training. Department of
Homeland Security and other civilian agencies provide a
component of America's overall defense. Today, civilians who
the government does not employ typically would not act on their
own to defend the country.

However, during World War II, which was arguably the
greatest of all crises America ever faced, the government
asked for as many immediate volunteers as possible. Over ten
million people took the challenge. These volunteers were a
large portion of the population. Most men had enlisted or were
drafted into the military. Women were tasked with working at
defense plants.

The concept of Civil Defense is not well known today. Late in the 20th century, the term and practice of Civil Defense fell into disuse. Official government "Emergency Management" and "Homeland Security" terms have replaced them. While these local and federal agencies saved lives, there has been an overreliance, which disempowers the public, causing them to be disengaged from confronting potential threats.

After the United States entered World War II, preparedness for potential air or sea attacks was characterized by significantly greater use of Civil Defense. The term "Civil Defense" implies the utilization of civilians rather than military or government employees, yet possibly with some government assistance.

The Civil Defense worker's compensation was the understanding that they were defending the country. Many were working full-time jobs in war-related industries. Many of them placed their children in daycare, so they could spend one "day off" a week sky watching and identifying planes as friend or foe. Preparing for eventual attacks, community air raid shelters were built, and emergency supplies were stocked.

These organizations worked together to mobilize the civilian population in response to the threat. The Civil Defense Corps, run by the Office of Civil Defense (OCD), organized approximately ten million volunteers to prepare for the attacks. They trained to fight fires, decontaminate after chemical weapon attacks, provide first aid, and other functions.

Although they were volunteers, the Civil Defense Corps still needed its workers to be organized and trained. Before the Pearl Harbor attack, President Roosevelt's Council of National Defense was reactivated, and the Division of State and Local Cooperation was created to further assist the Council's efforts. The Civil Defense of World War II began as a continuation of World War I. New York Mayor Fiorello LaGuardia initially headed the OCD, and he was in charge of promoting protective measures and elevating national morale.

There were many specialized functions, and each had a separate focused organization. These technical functions included air raid wardens, auxiliary firefighters, auxiliary police, emergency food, and housing personnel, Christian chaplains, Jewish chaplains, air patrol workers, decontamination specialists, demolition experts, fire watchers, instructors, medical corps, drivers, messengers, nurse aides, rescue squads, road repair crews, and utility road squads. Members of these Civil Defense organizations wore insignias on their helmets and armbands to identify their specialty. The OCD symbol was a white triangle inside a blue circle. Specialist armbands displayed a unique insignia within the OCD symbol.

The Civilian Voluntary Service organized various volunteer efforts, including scrap drives, a public program of gathering discarded or unused items made of materials needed by the Defense industry, such as rubber tires, metal pots and pans, and nylon hosiery. Other positions included victory speakers (people who gave speeches on government policies), victory gardens (small private gardens planted in backyards or public places such as parks to supplement the production of food by commercial farms), and neighborhood block leaders (individuals who took responsibility for overseeing the war effort on a single city block). The duties of a neighborhood block leader included explaining government programs that required the residents' cooperation (such as rationing), finding salespeople for war bonds and war stamps, checking on housing needs, and recruiting women for openings in local war factories.

Many people gained a sense of contributing to the war effort by participating in the movement. People got involved by taking classes on emergency preparedness. First aid classes were made available to hundreds of thousands of civilians, and courses on how to survive air raids were highly popular. By the summer of 1942, there were eleven thousand local defense councils and more than seven million volunteers. By July 1943, there were twelve million registered volunteers.

The Civil Defense established a network of civilian volunteer airplane spotters whose duty was to thwart any Axis attack such as that had occurred in America at Pearl Harbor. From lonely observation posts throughout the coastal defense areas, the Army Air Forces Ground Observer Corps, numbering about 1,500,000 volunteers, maintained a vigilant and continuous watch on the skies over America to see that no hostile planes approached unnoticed. The Fighter Command set up this Volunteer Air Defense System with the assistance of the American Legion, the OCD, and other agencies, and it established a new pattern of scouting.

Phil Jackson of Pennsylvania recalled as a teen his pursuit as a "spotter" who could save lives. "After school and on Saturdays, friends and I would climb to the top of the spotting tower, and with our binoculars, we'd try to identify any incoming planes as friend or foe." Germany and Japan knew spotters were watching, which probably deterred an air attack.

Thirty-four women from the Women's Airforce Service Pilots (WASP) would lose their lives ferrying newly-built planes throughout the US on a very tight schedule. The WASPs were not a military organization. Though they flew Army and Navy planes, they were a civilian-supported organization that trained women to fly planes for the war since men pilots were in very short supply. Flying was only permitted within the US. In 1988, the government decided to classify the WASPs as military personnel. WASPs would begin to receive benefits forty-seven years later after they served.

**Love and Duty:** "We all liked to fly. We felt so honored and privileged to be able to be flying military aircraft. If you were flying on your own, you were paying for your own time in those days. You could never have afforded to fly an attack aircraft. It was a two-way street. We were doing our patriotic duty, and at the same time, we were doing something we loved to do."

**The Requirements:** "You had to have had a minimum of 35 flying hours on your own before you were accepted. Originally, they wanted you to have more hours, [but] they weren't able to get enough volunteers, so they finally reduced it to 35 hours. I had been taking flying lessons, so I did get my 35 hours in when I applied."

**Aviation Is Here to Stay:** "I looked into night courses, all in New Jersey, at the New York College of Engineering, and they had a course on aviation. I thought, 'Aviation is here to stay; I think I'll take that!' After the course, I was all excited and said, 'Maybe I'll take a lesson and see what it's all about.' The first time I was up, I was hooked."

**A Couple of Flames:** "The first time that I was soloing [in a particular plane], I set out, and as I was pretty close to where I was supposed to make my first landing, smoke started coming out of the exhaust, including a couple of flames. I was scared. I could pull my parachute and crash, and then there is going to be an inquiry, and then I might be washed out of the program. I called because I was pretty near where I was supposed to be and asked for an emergency landing. The magnetos had gone bad. I stayed with the airplane."

I highly valued my interview with Bee. She has written a book on her World War II Homefront history, *Letters Home, 1944-1945*. She has been instrumental in helping to establish the WASP Museum in Sweetwater, Texas.

## CIVIL AIR PATROL (CAP)

Although the Japanese attack initially caused federal authorities to focus on the West Coast, another threat emerged on the East Coast and the Gulf of Mexico. German U-boats started operating within a few hundred yards of the East Coast shoreline, often sinking merchantmen and tankers at the rate of two a day. The US Navy was spread too thin to be everywhere at the same time along the 1,200-mile Eastern Sea Frontier, ranging from Halifax to the Florida Keys. Nor did the Army Air Force (AAF) have enough aircraft to screen the coast and provide adequate early warning to ships. Using civilian pilots and their private aircraft for such a hazardous mission was a measure of desperation. It was a considerable risk, but there was no viable alternative. By the end of the war, sixty-four Civilian Air Patrol (CAP) members had lost their lives directly defending the American mainland. Ninety CAP aircraft were also lost at sea.

The initial flights were reconnaissance missions only, consisting of a pilot and an observer with a donated maritime radio. They operated as far as 150 miles from shore, and the crew only overwater gear consisted of Kapok life vests. The volunteer pilots received $8 a day, and the ground crew members received $5 to cover gas and maintenance. Volunteers ranged from garage mechanics to millionaire sportsmen, farmhands, and even grandfathers. Private plane owners donated their planes without financial compensation, as did commercial airlines.

Whenever a patrol spotted a U-boat, the crew broadcast its' position to merchant ships in the area and the Navy and AAF. The CAP plane then stayed with the U-boat to vector in any intercepting forces as long as possible. The patrols also radioed in reports of tankers and merchant ships that had been hit and the position of survivors in the water.

In May 1942, one patrol sighted a U-boat sitting on the surface. Not knowing the aircraft was unarmed, the U-boat crew tried to execute a crash dive, but it was hung up on a sandbar. The CAP pilot circled the U-boat for more than half-hour, but it finally managed to work loose and get away just before the land-based bombers reached the target. Shortly after that incident, CAP planes carried bombs and depth charges slung from jury-rigged external racks.

CAP claimed its first U-boat kill on July 11, 1942, when Captain Johnny Haggins and Major Wynant Farr, flying a Grumman G-44 Widgeon armed with two depth charges, bombed a U-boat they had been shadowing for three hours, just as it came up to periscope depth. The resulting oil slick and surface debris seemed to confirm the kill, and for many years after the war, the claimed kill was credited to CAP.

## AMERICAN RED CROSS

The American Red Cross was prepared for the attack on Americans. They helped American POWs and refugees even though Japan and Germany obstructed humanitarian help from the Red Cross. Millions of Red Cross volunteers provided comfort and aid to Armed Forces members and their families at home. On the Home Front, Red Cross workers served in hospitals suffering from severe medical staff shortages, produced emergency supplies for war victims, collected scraps, ran victory gardens, and maintained home nutrition, first aid, and water safety training programs.

Overseas, Red Cross workers served as field directors, providing compassionate support for the troops they accompanied and operating clubs for the Armed Forces. They were also attached to military hospitals, hospital ships, and hospital trains.

At the peak of the Red Cross wartime activity in 1945, 7.5 million volunteers and 39,000 paid staff provided service to the military. The Red Cross served 16 million military personnel throughout the war, including one million combat casualties. By the time World War II ended in September 1945, the American public had contributed over $784 million to support the American Red Cross. Nearly every family in America contained a member who had served as a Red Cross volunteer, made contributions of money or blood, or was a recipient of Red Cross services.

## AIR WARDEN CORPS

*ABOVE: Seattle's Boeing military plane manufacturing plant is camouflaged to look like a residential neighborhood from the air.*

The Air Warden Corps was officially ten thousand strong, but it was likely more considerable than that. It's nearly impossible for someone not living at the time to grasp the public's vulnerability. Every town in America prepared for air attacks. Even a tiny insignificant lamp lit inside someone's house at night could give the enemy a target. Air Wardens could frequently be yelling, "Put that light out!"

In addition, many cities piled sandbags against the glass of buildings. Many volunteers, including Air Wardens, often camouflaged war industry buildings.

## WAR BOND DRIVES

Remarkable with all that the military and civilians did for the war effort, they also financed it. Very few of the population were well-off, considering they had just emerged from a 12-year-long depression. People saved their small change to buy war bonds. Today it is difficult to imagine the dire economics of the time. However, some Americans did benefit from the war economically. Consequently, it took World War Two to bring some of the nation out of economic tragedy.

Perhaps nothing represents the community-minded patriotism of the US Home Front in World War II better than the War Bond Drives. A Bond Drive was a campaign whereby celebrities, sports figures, and politicians spoke to the public about buying War Bonds – but the heroes in uniform were the most convincing in this endeavor. The War Bonds sold in the US helped the government raise about $185 billion, about $3.3 trillion in today's dollars. Over 84 million Americans bought Bonds, nearly 75% of the adult population. There was a nationwide effort to advertise the Bonds, ranging from sports events to radio show promotions. The purchase of the Bonds was primarily linked to patriotism and to people feeling that they were doing their part in the war effort. The holder would redeem them at a high-interest rate for that era. The government relied on the public to finance it beyond the usual taxation, which is unimaginable in the present. Today's economy is strikingly different since massive financial institutions control much of the government's debt.

**WAR BONDS**

*RUBBER DRIVES, PAPER DRIVES, AND SCRAP DRIVES*

Enemy conquests cut off supplies of necessary raw materials such as tin and rubber, and the need for products made from these materials skyrocketed due to the war. Nearly a hundred percent of rubber came from Asia. Several tons of rubber were needed just to build one aircraft. With so much of these unused materials in homes and on farms, the War Production Board encouraged scrap drives throughout the war.

Rubber was vital for war use, and acute shortages affected the United States from early in the war. From June 15-30, 1942, the United States held a nationwide Rubber Drive. People contributed old or excess tires, raincoats, hot water bottles, boots, and floor mats. In exchange, they received a penny a pound. Although 450,000 tons of scrap rubber were collected, the used rubber that was collected was found to be of poor quality.

Metal shortages were also critical. In 1942, citizens searched through their homes, farms, and businesses for metal. Homemakers donated pots and pans, farmers turned in farm equipment, and children sacrificed their metal toys. Many people removed bumpers and fenders from their cars for the war effort. Communities melted down Civil War cannons and tore down wrought iron fences, sacrificing their history for their future. Even WWI cannons and other military equipment were donated and melted down.

These drives were often significant community events with performers, speeches, and opportunities to throw your scrap metal at a bust of Hitler. Competitions were held to see which town, county, and state produced the most scrap, and the winners boasted of their feats. These drives had mixed results. Used aluminum was helpful in aircraft. However, tin, steel, and copper were easily melted down and reused.

The use of tin packaging was significantly reduced during the war due to alternative packaging materials and the rationing of canned goods. However, consumer use of tin continued throughout the war, and this irreplaceable resource needed to be recovered. Most communities collected tin cans once a month. In some towns, people placed boxes of cleaned and crushed tin cans by the curb for collection, and other cities had major collection sites. Youth groups, especially the Boy Scouts, were highly involved in these drives.

The need for paper also increased during the war. The military's love for paperwork could be blamed, but the military also used lots of paper packaging for supplies. On the civilian side, paper packaging had replaced tin for many products. A Paper Drive in mid-1942 brought in so much paper that mills were inundated and called for a stop. However, by 1944, an acute paper shortage existed, and government and industry were grateful to the American public for their efforts.

The lumber industry was also hard-hit by the workforce shortage caused by the draft. Lumberjacks went on strike, demanding a higher meat ration, which they did not receive. Many of these men left for higher-paying jobs in the defense industry.

Publishers found their paper allotment cut by 15 percent. Newspapers, magazines, and books were printed on fewer pages with thinner paper and narrow margins. Paperback books were introduced in 1939, which also used less paper. However, more scrap paper was needed.

The children of America stepped up their efforts. The Boy Scouts and local schools organized regular Paper Drives, often coordinated with the tin can drives. The War Production Board started the Paper Troopers Program, designed to sound like "paratroopers" to involve more schoolchildren in the effort. Participants received arm patches and certificates for collecting specific amounts.

Scrap Drives were a vital part of the American war effort. While not all scrap materials proved helpful, many of these scraps provided a small yet significant source of the material. These drives galvanized the Home Front and made each individual, even children, feel like a crucial part of the war effort.

## THE FARM INDUSTRY AND VICTORY GARDENS

The economy was completely different in the early 1940s compared to today. Americans depended greatly on American farmers and other primary industries. Farmers were forced to produce significantly more food as the war progressed. The American military located overseas increased the demand for these goods. The farm labor crisis increased, particularly for fruit and vegetable growers who relied on migrant workers. The nation briefly went from the highest unemployment in US history to a severe labor shortage!

Fifteen million men and women were drafted into the military throughout the war. There were only 73 million people in the workforce at the time. Over 20% of the pre-war workforce were now serving in the military rather than working in civilian jobs. The country required new methods of accomplishing its goals. Many new workers came from farms, as defense plants hired and paid high salaries.

These factors put a strain on agriculture, which was one of the leading industries in the economy before the war. Farmers first dealt with the situation by setting their wives and children to work. Some, like Kelly Holthus, who was ten years old at the time, when he was put on a tractor, shown how to drive it, and then was told, "you're in charge now." He was so proud to be working to save the family during the war years. Unlike the Depression years when there was nowhere to sell produce at a high enough price, prices were going up, but there weren't enough workers!

### The Women's Land Army

One of the unknown civilian groups of the World War II Homefront was the crucial role the many women and minors plowed the ground, planted the seeds, cultivated the plants, and harvested much of the nation's crops from 1942 through 1945. Food would have been even scarcer without their contributions, both at home and on the fighting fronts. In addition, the physical well-being of the combat forces would have been less, and America's allies would have suffered greater privations. Rationing, price controls, and dietary changes designed to meet food shortages would have been harder to bear. Food would have been scarier if it hadn't been contributed, both at home and on the battlegrounds.

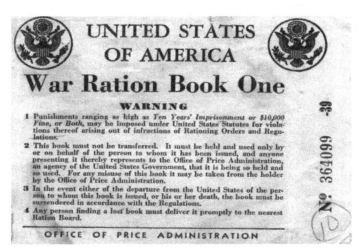

Americans were asked to make sacrifices in many ways. Rationing was only one of the ways that Americans contributed to the war effort.

When the United States declared war after the attack on Pearl Harbor, the government created a system of rationing, limiting the number of specific goods that a person could purchase. Supplies such as gasoline, butter, sugar, and canned milk were rationed because they needed to be diverted to the war effort. War also disrupted trade, limiting the availability of some goods. For example, the Japanese Imperial Army controlled the Dutch East Indies (today's Indonesia) from March 1942 to September 1945, creating a shortage of rubber that affected American production.

On August 28, 1941, President Roosevelt's Executive Order 8875 created the Office of Price Administration (OPA). The OPA's primary responsibility was to place a ceiling on most goods' prices and limit consumption by rationing.

Americans received their first ration cards in May 1942. The first card, War Ration Card Number One, became known as the "Sugar Book," for one of the commodities Americans could purchase with their ration card. Other ration cards developed as the war progressed. Ration cards included stamps with drawings of airplanes, guns, tanks, aircraft, ears of wheat, and fruit, which were used to purchase rationed items.

The OPA rationed automobiles, tires, gasoline, fuel oil, coal, firewood, nylon, silk, and shoes. Americans used their ration cards and stamps for household staples, including meat, dairy, coffee, dried fruits, jams, jellies, lard, shortening, and oils. Only three gallons of gas per week was permitted per vehicle. With the typical gas mileage capability of a car at that time, three gallons would seem enough only for an emergency. Engine parts and tires were nearly unobtainable.

As they did during the Great Depression, Americans learned to do without. Sacrificing certain items during the war became the norm for most Americans. It was considered a common good for the war effort, and it affected every American household.

*The Gold Stars and Blue Stars Displayed in Windows*

Parents and spouses would hang a Blue Star in their windows to show each son, daughter, husband, or father active in the military during the war. The Gold Star represented those who were killed in action defending our country. One could drive into residential neighborhoods and main streets in any town and see the stars posted in the windows. Neighbors and other community-minded people would stop by a house when they saw a Blue or Gold Star and ask if they could help the family in some way. It was a stark reminder to all of the very high price of freedom.

An astounding 405,399 Americans lost their lives in the military in World War II. Assuming there were about a half dozen family members for each service member killed in the military, there were about 2.5 million Gold Star family members resulting from World War II. In addition, there were hundreds of thousands of Gold Star family members from WWI still around at that time. This remarkable number does not consider those seriously wounded in both wars and the impact on their families. For America, this was far from the norm. A newly arrived dystopian world had been initiated. This was what the period from 1917 to 1918 and 1941 to 1945 was often forgotten in America: the effects on our Veterans and their families from the World Wars.

## Western Union

The worst attacks on the people of the United States were the losses of life as a result of the war, whether in the US or overseas. The Gold Star Families were the family members that lost husbands, fathers, and sons.

Delivering Western Union telegrams was a significant event in the life of Jimmy Rubin. He recalled being a Western Union delivery boy when he was only fifteen years old, early in the war. The houses in his town were like many homes in America, comfortable but not extravagant. His town was one of those small American towns where nearly everyone knew each other. A lot of people were related. Today, few realize the Western Union Company delivered employees' difficult position during America's wars. Western Union employees deserve a lot of credit for dealing with it.

Jimmy was just fifteen-years-old when a Western Union delivery boy from 1941 to 1942. "I had been delivering telegrams on my bike for a year. It was a great job. You had to keep your uniform neat and clean. I knew most of the people I delivered to. I would get a wave and got a 'Hi, Jimmy' from nearly everyone I passed. I even got tips. The news was usually good, like marriages, babies being born, and business. Then came the war. All of a sudden, people didn't wave; they looked away, even ran away. Especially if they had the Blue or Gold Star in their window. At first, I was very confused, but I began to understand after glancing at a few of those telegrams. I'll never forget the one that said, 'The Secretary of the Army regrets to inform you that your son Kevin was killed in action on Guadalcanal' I got the idea.

Later it was other South Pacific Islands, North Africa, even before Europe. People somehow had to take their anguish out on someone, and I was there. I could almost hear them saying,

'Don't stop here! Don't stop here!' And I thought, who else was seeing all this with parents breaking down, young mothers with kids at their side and falling to the ground after reading the gram'. The government didn't give details, just that the love of their life is suddenly gone, dead, that's it. It was a shock for a 15-year-old. I grew up fast. I wondered who else saw all this. I wondered how long it would last. I used to try to run away before they read the gram', but it was too late. Some of the families I knew well. One kid killed in the war was a good friend in the Boy Scouts. I had to hand the telegram to his mother. It was a very heart-wrenching situation. It was too much, so I quit. When I joined the Army the following year, I sure knew what I was fighting for!"

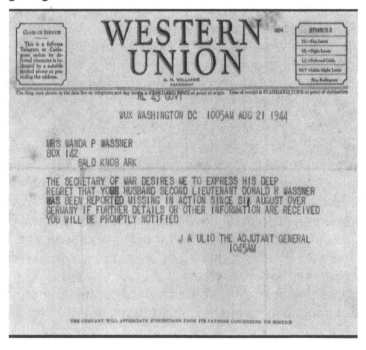

*Karina Anderson,*
*A Real-Life Rosie the Riveter*
**Proudly Served on the Home Front**

**A Mother Desperate to Get Off Welfare:** "I graduated from high school when I was 17. My dad deserted the family, and I promised my mother I would get a job where I could make enough money to take her off welfare. She was so ashamed of being on welfare. So, when I turned 18, I left the job I had, which was child care. I took care of two children. But then I went to the place where you went if you wanted to put in an application for Fairchild Aircraft. I took a week's training with some other ladies on second shift. We weren't used to being on second shift. Eventually, we went to work. We were given a toolbox, an air gun, and bars they used on the other side of the rivet."

**Communication in the Factory:** "I had to learn a code because the other person bucking the rivet—I couldn't see her. If I made the rivet too flat the first time, she would hit twice, and that meant, 'Hit it again.' She was making the rivet on the other side where I couldn't see her so that it wouldn't go through the metal. If it had to be taken out, she'd hit once, and if it was okay, she'd hit twice."

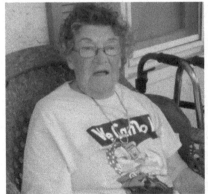

**Hot Rivets:** "When I was doing some of the riveting, it had to be riveted with heat. They brought this to us in a cupcake pan, and if there wasn't frost on it, we had to send them back. Then the metal was softer, and we could buck it easier."

**She Was Drilling in My Leg:** "We all had to wear pants. We couldn't wear skirts. If the man in charge wanted to say something to us, he'd pull on our pants leg [instead of saying something]. It was so noisy that I [eventually] lost about two-thirds of my hearing. [One day,] he pulled on my pants leg, and I turned my head sideways. It was too late. The lady underneath didn't have a buddy on top to keep the people away from where she was drilling, and she was drilling in my leg. The drill was so tiny I didn't even bleed. They took me down to the caring center and washed it off, and put a Band-Aid on it. They said, 'You want to go home?' I said, 'It doesn't hurt, and I have worked up there that I have to finish.' When they advertised Rosie the Riveter, it said, 'We can do it.' I had to do it, so I did."

**Patched Pants:** "One day, I was working on the wing of a [plane]. The average person would think that there wasn't anything in the wing. There were a lot of wires in the wing, and they had to have something to hold them. I called [the thing holding them] a thingamabob. The whistle blew, and I was stuck. I don't know. The foreman came by and said, 'Karina, didn't you hear the whistle?' I said, 'I can't get out.' He said, 'I'll pull on your hands, and you push with your feet.' I could feel myself coming loose, and after a while, I came out. So did the seat of the pants. I patched them and was back the next day with my patched pants."

*Above: Technology played an enormous role in World War II.*

*The world's first electronic computer is shown. Designed and built at the secret campus Bletchley Park, England, it broke what was thought to be unbreakable: the German Enigma Code.*

Before the war, many new technologies were under development. But the war accelerated forward a whole new generation of technologies. Among the most profound changes from the war were technological advancements, but they would not solely result in military applications. Germany began the Space Age on October 10, 1942, by sending a V-2 Rocket over 50 miles in the sky; that distance is considered outer space by NASA. The Nazis had plans for a space program, venturing to the moon and beyond.

The computer revolution began at Bletchley Park in the UK. The first electronic microwaves and the understanding of the atomic and sub-atomic world in nuclear science led to the development of the lifestyle we have today. Satellites, the internet, telecommunications, and the technology we take for granted began their development due to the intense push during the war to make leaps and bounds in science and technology. Thousands of less dramatic but critical inventions and applications were developed at lightning speed. These less-visible developments have had profound implications for an ongoing improvement of everyday machines, both in low and high tech alike. In many countries, mechanical, electrical, and electronic implementations were advanced decades ahead in a short number of years. After the war, the technological breakthrough would create an economic boom in the US and even in Germany and Japan. Understanding air flight, ocean conditions, and energy technologies pushed the world ahead to a higher standard of living. Medicine also made huge strides during the war; antibiotics were one of the most sweeping medical technology applications that gained momentum, but there were many others. The competition during the war was, to a marked degree, based on its technological development and the implementation of those developments on a sufficient scale.

We are still experiencing an ongoing technology boom. We have grown so accustomed to continuous technological innovation in the US that we just assume it will always continue.

# ATTACKS ON THE WESTERN AMERICA

## HAWAII

December 7th,1941
*A DATE THAT WILL LIVE IN INFAMY*

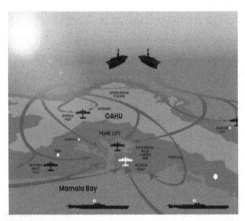

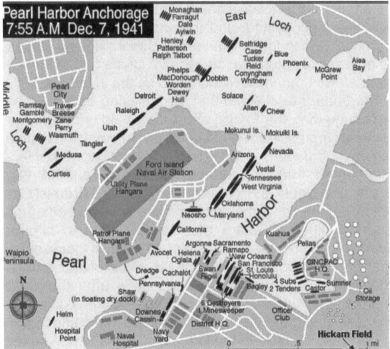

*The Japanese intelligence was obviously good. Japanese maps were found after the war with great detail of "battleship Row" above.*

There is likely no other military event in American history that had such profound consequences as the Japanese attack on Pearl Harbor. The attack also changed world history. It would be impossible to address the attack completely in this volume. Here we only provide a glimpse and some highlights of this extraordinary event. There are many authors who have produced excellent books about this since 1941.

In hindsight, there were many warnings, and since the attack, there has been plenty of blame to go around. One of the most commonly asked questions was why the Japanese did it? And why were the US Navy and Army not more prepared?

At the beginning of 1937, the invasion of China by the Imperial Japanese Army (IJA) was not originally authorized by the Japanese government. Once the takeover was successful, and after several assassinations of civil leaders, the civilian government consented, and the Japanese military took more control. It was an ideal situation for Japan, having slave labor and accessible natural resources that China had in Manchuria. This area was renamed Manchukuo by the invaders.

The Japanese claimed that the resulting economic growth from conquering the Pacific and Asia would bring them out of the Great Depression and establish a vast empire. Hirohito, the Emperor of Japan, was worshipped as a god. He was, according to tradition, the descendant of a 2000-year-old dynasty (the oldest and longest-lived). Army Extremist General Hadicki Tojo became the prime minister. He and other military leaders decided to attack the United States to control the Pacific and eliminate the US as a potential deterrent to its expansion. The hope was that the US would call for a truce and negotiate an agreement to resume trade after the attack as other countries Japan attacked had done. Some colleges in the Japanese government correctly observed that going to war with the US could be futile in the long run. At that time, Japan was already at war with China and Southeast Asia, and it was in combat with many other nations, including the United Kingdom. Since the 1930s, those in the Japanese government who were opposed to the war plans of expansion were either removed or assassinated.

The Japanese military was undefeated in all of its 2000-year history. Their military was well-trained, highly-skilled, and disciplined, and they followed the Samurai Warrior Code of Bushido. The Bushido Code valued honor before defending their own lives, and they would fight to the death. To a Japanese soldier, it was unthinkable to surrender, and as a result, the United States had few opportunities to take Japanese prisoners of war.

The Japanese had surveyed Pearl Harbor and the American military bases in Hawaii for years. Takeo Yoshikawa, an experienced Japanese Naval Ensign, arrived in Hawaii nine months before the attack. He was employed as a cover by the Japanese Foreign Ministry using an alias while working for the Imperial Japanese Navy. He provided continuous and thorough updates on US Navy deployments, arrivals, and departures from Pearl Harbor, the centerpiece of US Naval operations in the Pacific. Yoshikawa was scrupulously careful not to carry a camera, maps, or documents, and he never jotted down notes on what he observed on his outings around Hawaii.

Yoshikawa was the perfect man for the mission. He had a solid naval background, having graduated in 1933 from the Japanese Naval College. He also attended torpedo, gunnery, and aviation programs in the Imperial Japanese Navy. In addition, he served as a code officer aboard a cruiser. Then he worked for three years in Tokyo with the Imperial Japanese Navy's British Affairs Section before expressing an interest in working abroad as an agent. That led to his assignment in Hawaii, working for Japan's Foreign Ministry as a cover agent.

Even though Yoshikawa did not have diplomatic immunity, he was not officially linked to the Imperial Japanese Navy. Otherwise, he would have been known almost immediately to the American counter-intelligence officials as a cover agent. Only Nagao Kita, the new Consul in Hawaii, and Vice Consul Okuda, who had done some prior spying in Hawaii, were aware of Yoshikawa's true role in providing Japan with updates on the US Navy. These updates transmitted to the Japanese included the number, location, and schedules of the American ships.

By December 7, 1941, Japan had occupied China for nearly ten years and had already defeated the British and Dutch in Asia. Germany had occupied most of Europe for almost two years, and it was in the process of standing off with the Soviet Union. Besides the US and the United Kingdom, much of the militarized and industrialized world was under the Axis Powers.

On December 7, 1941, Admiral Yamamoto, the Commander of Japan's Naval Fleet, masterminded the surprise attack on Pearl Harbor utilizing 363 aircraft. During the two hours of bombing, 2343 American soldiers and 68 civilians were killed, and 1272 were wounded. Over half of those, 1177 sailors, were killed on the USS *Arizona* alone. The Japanese sunk 4 American battleships, destroyed 188 aircraft and damaged 150 planes. These totals included a large portion of the American military assets in the Pacific at that time.

Japan's planning of the December 7 attack was meticulous and well-coordinated, and it was designed with the highest degree of careful study. The strategy was bold and comprehensive. The tactics were sound. Admiral Yamamoto, Commander of the Japanese Combined Fleet, conceived the plan in the spring of 1941. This plan needed the element of surprise. At that time, Japanese diplomats were in Washington negotiating to ease strained relations, so the US would not expect an attack while talks were in progress.

By October, the Japanese Army and Navy plans were completed. They bombed Pearl Harbor in Hawaii on December 7, 1941, and they invaded Thailand, the Malay Peninsula, and the Philippines. Vice Admiral Nagumo was the Commander of Japan's six largest carriers, two fastest battleships, two cruisers, and several destroyers and tankers. Their aircraft torpedoes were modified with wooden fins to be used successfully in the shallow waters of Pearl Harbor. The Pearl Harbor attack was tested during the September War Games in remote Japanese waters, and final adjustments were made.

In mid-November, the first element of the Japanese Task Force was made up of twenty submarines, including five subs that carried a 2-man, 2-torpedo midget sub piggyback. These submarines slipped away from Japan's West Coast and prepared to take a round-about route to Hawaii. On November 26, the main force of 30 ships, including all six of Japan's aircraft carriers and 400+ airplanes, left from their North Coast. They maintained radio silence and blackout. They stayed far from shipping lanes. Before dawn on December 7, the subs were in position south and west of Hawaii. At 6:00 am, the main force reached its launching point 220 miles north of Pearl Harbor. At the time, America's aircraft had not been flying surveillance to the north. The first wave of the 183 Japanese aircraftAt the, divided equally among fighters, torpedo planes, dive-bombers, and high-level bombers, left their mother ships, flying toward Pearl Harbor, Hawaii.

As dawn came, the bright sun began to climb over Hawaii's horizon, bringing a glow to the clouds. It seemed like a typical Sunday. On Battleship Row off Ford Island in the middle of the Harbor, seven big battlewagons gently swayed at anchor in an orderly column, and ninety other warcraft were at adjacent anchorages. It was a fantastic sight. At Hickam, Wheeler, and other nearby Army, Navy, and Marine airfields, some three hundred planes were lined up in neat rows to facilitate guarding them against possible sabotage. In other words, we were sitting ducks for the Japanese.

"Tora! Tora! Tora!" Those famous Japanese code words, meaning "Charge!" were transmitted and sent to Tokyo. At 7:55 am on December 7, 1941, the first attack wave came hurtling in from the sea. The Japanese made a surprise attack on Pearl Harbor. Against all common sense and unpredictable odds, the Japanese Task Force caught the Americans unaware. In that terrible instant, the dawn was transformed into the "...date which will live in infamy..." as President Roosevelt so aptly put it. The cutting edge of the assault, Torpedo planes raced toward the American anchored fleet. A torpedo slammed into the cruiser *Raleigh,* and another put a hole in the cruiser, *Helena.* However, the American battleships were Japan's prime targets. Torpedoes hit the Arizona, West Virginia, and Oklahoma battleships in rapid succession. The *California* was hit with two torpedoes within seconds of each other. Dive-bombers swooped down, dropping 250 kilo of explosives. The *Arizona* took a bomb in the starboard quarterdeck, and the *Tennessee* took one forward. The high-level Japanese planes began releasing their 850 kilo bombs.

The torpedo that ripped into the *Raleigh* jolted an ensign out of his bunk. He rushed on deck in his red pajamas, and within minutes, he had a gun crew firing a three-inch battery. He was one of the first, of what was a growing number of batteries, firing on the attackers. Japanese planes flew in all directions, but each knew their assignment and performed very well.

As the Japanese planes flew by, everyone was in disbelief, and many remained that way even as the bombs were being dropped. As the aircraft flew by, it was easy for the American soldiers to see the Rising Sun insignia, and they knew it was the Japanese. One could hear, "Japanese! Man your stations! This is war!"

Military wives were at home. Some were still sleeping, while others were preparing breakfast, getting ready for church, or tending to their families as explosions sounded on Ford Island. One Japanese pilot described the US Fleet as looking "so beautiful, just like toys on a child's floor, something that should not be attacked at all." But other Japanese pilots who had dropped torpedoes had no such feelings and felt the splash in the water. They said that "a torpedo streaking for a battleship was just like a dragonfly laying eggs in the water." A strafing of bullets killed 10 out of 11 sailors manning one five-inch gun. The lone survivor of this disaster grabbed a shell, set it in the tray, rushed to the other side of the gun to ram the shell home, leaped into the pointer's seat, and fired the gun. He got off three shells before a bomb blast blew him over the side.

At 8:02 am, machine gunners onboard the *Nevada* shot down a Japanese torpedo plane. The battleship's gunners downed a second plane one minute later, but it had already released its torpedo, ripping a giant gash in *Nevada's* port bow. The *West Virginia*, by now having been struck by three torpedoes, was in danger of capsizing. Captain Mervyn S. Bennion, who was on the bridge, ordered counter-flooding to stabilize the vessel when shrapnel ripped his stomach. He refused medical aid so other men could be treated, and he remained at his post, giving orders to stabilize the ship and fight flames that had broken out. Unfortunately, Captain Bennion died on the bridge. A third torpedo hit the *Oklahoma*, and then a fourth. The port was leaning so severely that it was clear nothing could save it from turning over completely. The senior officer directed the crew to climb out on the starboard rail and work their way up the hull as the vessel rolled over. Some hundred sailors ended up perched on the bottom of the overturned battleship.

Chief Davis was on his way from his bunk aboard the *Ralph Talbot* to the shower room in a state of nature when he happened to look out a port. He saw two torpedoes heading toward the *Utah* as it was hit and then exploded. As the attacking planes pulled up, Davis recognized the Rising Sun insignia. He then rushed for the destroyer's Combat Information Center to get communications and gun control in action. A sailor standing on the *Oglala* pointed and said to his Captain, "There's a torpedo coming!" The captain knew he could do nothing about it because the ship was moored. The torpedo went under the *Oglala* and struck the *Helena* scoring a double hit for the Japanese. The *Oglala's* log recorded the scene graphically. The torpedo "exploded under the bottom on the port side. The force of the explosion lifted up the fireroom floor plates and ruptured the hull on the port side. Fireroom started flooding rapidly, and personnel secured fires, closed water-tight doors, and abandoned the fireroom."

The *Helena's* log reported a "series of three heavy explosions were felt nearby. At about 07:58, the ship rocked by a violent explosion on the starboard side." A torpedo sped under the repair ship, *Vestal,* and "tore the bottom out of the Arizona, in Chief Crawford's words." The Japanese pilot who torpedoed the *West Virginia* listed his plane so he could watch the torpedo hit. He is reported to have said, "It was indeed a great sight." A Zero pilot admitted that the American counter-attack was more rapid and fierce than expected, but it did not seem systematic. Rather it appeared to be carried out at random to eliminate fears. Hulbert, a sailor aboard the destroyer that was moored at the submarine base, claimed it "shot down a Japanese torpedo plane." The destroyer-seaplane tender, *Thorton*, located across the dock, confirmed this claim.

The *Nevada* was preparing to get underway when a torpedo struck her port bow. Acting as the *Nevada's* Air Defense Officer, Taussig was at his battle station when a missile went through his thigh and hit the ballistics computer in front of him. In shock, he felt no pain. He observed that his left foot had lodged under his left armpit in a detached way. Despite all efforts to remove him to a battle dressing station, he refused to leave and insisted on the continuation of fire on enemy aircraft.

This promising young officer survived but spent the rest of World War II in the hospital, recovering from his wounds received at Pearl Harbor. Very few ships could retaliate as promptly and effectively as the *Nevada*. Just imagine the frustration of the men on the minesweeper, *Grebe*, as they prepared to fight back:

"Main battery, consisting of two .30 caliber Lewis machine guns, eleven Springfield repeating rifles model 1906, and six US Navy pistols. Except for pistols and rifles, all ammunition had been turned into the Ammunition Depot. Sent messengers in search of ammunition. Served out all available small arms to officers and men. Issued steel helmets and gas masks to all hands."

By the time they completed this exercise, the first wave was over. Leo F. Storm, an 18-year-old mess cook on board the destroyer-minesweeper, *Perry*, was washing dishes in the galley. When the Japanese struck, he ran to his station on a .50 caliber machine gun, only to find the guns "under wraps and all gummed up with heavy preservative grease." No one was more upset than the captain aboard the Antares as a fighter plane circled low to strafe. The pilot "grinned one of those typically arrogant Japanese grins of the time," and the captain shook his fist at him. He was so mad because his only weapons, two machine guns, could not be elevated. He cried out to one of his seamen, "Throw a spud at him!" The man replied despairingly, "I'm sorry, Captain, but I don't have anymore."

The Japanese credited Petty Officer Noboru Kanai, a crack bombardier, with the astounding hit that sank the *Arizona*. Those US Naval personnel, hiding behind the *Oklahoma's* anti-roll keel, were looking directly at the *Arizona*. "There was an awful blast and a terrific concussion, but the force was upward instead of out. The foremast tilted forward took a crazy angle, and the ship went down immediately. They could see parts of bodies in the foremast rigging." The explosion was one of the largest ever recorded by any country up until that time.

To Fink, aboard the *St. Louis*, "the explosion of the *Arizona* seemed almost unreal. The explosion seemed to have a focal point, with huge red flames shooting from all angles. It was the most horrifying thing I have ever seen." Twenty-one-year-old Lloyd Coole was in the *Arizona's* number 3 turret when he felt the ship bounce and shake like a leaf. The blowers began discharging smoke and gas. "I crawled out of there in a hurry." The ship was a mess. Wounded soldiers were lying all over the place. He saw one man crawling around without any clothes because they had been blown off. He fell into the water and drowned. Coming down the main mast of the *Arizona*, a man was seen walking around with arms outstretched, blindly groping his way, with severe burns that had temporarily deprived him of sight. A big husky cook was sitting on deck, staring blankly at the stump where his leg had been blown off, watching his life pump out through severed arteries. Charred bodies lay everywhere. Those on the *Vestal* could see men on the *Arizona* walking on the deck and burning alive. They had their helmets on, and their clothes were all seared off. They were only recognizable because of their helmets. They were a ghostly crew as they walked out of the flames, and then they just dropped dead.

Tons of debris rained down on the *Vestal's* deck. "On part of the ship, there were legs, arms and heads of men, all sorts of bodies were lying around our ship." The Captain of the *West Virginia* was on the bridge. He suddenly doubled over and moaned. He had been hit in the stomach, probably by a large piece of shrapnel, and he was seriously hurt. A Chief Pharmacist Mate named Leak was caring for him the best he could. Hoping to move him to a safer place, he hurried off. He returned with Mess Attendant 2nd Class Doris Miller, a towering black man who was well-known throughout the ship, being the *West Virginia's* heavyweight boxing champion. When the fire broke out on part of the bridge, the captain had to be moved. Shortly thereafter, the captain died.

Ensign Victor Delano rounded up another officer, a seaman, and Doris Miller to man two idle machine guns on the conning tower. He meant for Miller to handle the ammunition while others did the firing. Miller was completely untrained with the weapon, but he seized one of the guns anyway. Miller appeared to be enjoying himself for the first time since winning the heavyweight title. So impressed with Miller's courage, coolness, and initiative, his superior officer recommended him for the Navy Cross. On May 27, 1942, Admiral Chester W. Nimitz pinned the award on Miller, the first African American to receive such high tribute in the Pacific Fleet in World War II.

Scores of others were trapped below the ship in air bubbles within an upturned hull. For those trapped in one dispensary, they stood in water up to their necks, with only a narrow bubble of air to sustain them. They had only one flashlight, which they used to relieve the tension when blackness became unbearable. Hallucinations set in, and time became meaningless. The air became foul, and the oxygen depleted. They were hardly able to breathe, they became sleepy, and their hands and feet were numb. They took turns diving beneath the water in the compartment, searching the bulkhead for a way of escape. Finally, a short husky seaman popped out of the water, excited because he had found a porthole. It was at this point the crewmen realized the ship was upside down.

Their escape strategy was for one man to hold the porthole while the others went out. It was no small feat for an American-sized male to squirm through a hole only 14 inches in diameter. The oil on the water lubricated their bodies. Some sailors stripped naked to get through. They all made it with one exception, the husky seaman, who found the porthole was too small to fit through. In the end, he was left alone in the darkness, a certain death. The last sailor who slipped through said he heard an animal cry of anguish that reverberated in his ears. He would hear that cry for years to come.

Shortly after the *Oklahoma* turned over, a bomb struck deep in the *Arizona*, detonating its forward magazine with a tremendous explosion. According to a report from Japan's Attack Commander, a massive column of dark red smoke rose to 1000 meters. Even in his plane several miles away from the Harbor, the shockwave was felt. The *Arizona* was mortally wounded, but it was a fighter. It took three hours and a total of eight bombs, besides the initial torpedo that had struck it before she finally settled beneath the surface to become the watery tomb for more than 1000 crew members.

At a Pearl Harbor Survivors reunion, USS Arizona survivor Lauren Bruner recalled, "All hands-on deck, man your battle stations, this is not a drill! You see these planes coming in – they were coming in shooting! I was lucky. I was hit twice in the leg, and the Japanese warplanes hit the ship hard with several bombs. I and five others were located on the anti-aircraft gun director's platform above the bridge when the forward powder magazine blew. All of us were very badly burned. Machine Repairman, 2nd Class Joe George saved our lives right then and there. George spotted the six of us. We had no way to escape the burning ship. Joe George realized the desperate situation of the six of us on the *Arizona* and threw a line over to us, which was against his Commander's orders. We secured the line on the *Arizona,* and each of us climbed hand-over-hand over to the USS *Vestal,* even though we were severely burned. To this day, I don't know how we did it."

A sailor on the *California* was standing on the bridge when a 250-pound bomb smashed through the deck. The *California* and the *West Virginia* later limped into the shipyard for repairs, costing more than $300 million in today's dollars. Another sailor in the *Nevada's* Plotting Room ended up several decks below water when the battleship sank. He and a dozen other men escaped several long hours later via a tube leading into a conning tower.

The sneak attack that had changed Pearl Harbor into Hell's Vestibule was wreaking similar havoc ashore. Servicemen rushing back to their bases and civilians evacuating areas under attack congested traffic on Pearl Harbor Road. Sugarcane fields were on fire. A mother sat holding her child as her husband ran up the path toward her. She watched in shock as shrapnel killed both her child and husband. Three hundred and sixty-three Japanese planes attacked Pearl Harbor, Hickam Field, and the Scofield Barracks that day.

Machinist's Mate First Class Robert R. Scott, among fifteen other sailors, was awarded the Medal of Honor for acts of valor on that day by refusing to leave his flooding battle station within the depths of the USS *California*, declaring to the world, "This is my station, and I will stay and give them air as long as the guns are going."

The history of the bombing of Pearl Harbor, including events that led up to it and the aftermath, is so vast and compelling that it could not be all covered here. Our future publication will cover more of the dynamics of this seminal event in 20th-century America.

*ABOVE: The USS West Virginia and behind her the USS Tennessee.*

The 1177 Sailors and Marines killed on the USS Arizona were over half of all service personnel killed at Pearl Harbor. Today the USS Arizona memorial can be visited, built on top of the *Arizona*. It is one of the most moving memorials in the world.

Eighty years later, oil and air bubbles can be seen coming to the surface from the sacred tomb. Nearly all those killed on the Battleship remain in their silent final resting place. Standing above them and looking down into the ship is a unique experience, indeed. History is preserved and portrayed well by the National Park Service at Pearl Harbor.

## *Four hours of opportunity may have been lost.*

Some in the US Navy knew Japan's submarines were near, even before the attack on Pearl Harbor. Japanese submarines close to shore were spotted four hours before the attack, but no alert was given to personnel at Pearl Harbor.

The Japanese min submarine was an ingenious invention. The purpose of the innovative mini-sub was to move into the Harbor with such stealth that the moored battleships would never recognize them. The unsuspecting size of the sub allowed it to maneuver quickly and get into the Harbor.

Shortly after midnight on the "date which will live infamy," the first of the five Japanese mini-subs were released seven miles from the entrance to Pearl Harbor after riding piggyback on a conventional submarine. The Nissan men inside the submersibles knew they were on a suicide mission. The one-man mini-sub was so small it was called a human torpedo. When the USS *Condor*'s Quartermaster reported the periscope sighting to the destroyer USS *Ward* not long after the launch of a fifth mini-sub, it became a disastrous day for the Japanese mini-subs men. The USS *Condor,* the USS *Ward*, and a Japanese mini-sub would meet four hours before the Pearl Harbor attack. The USS *Ward* got within 50 yards of the suspicious boat and opened fire at 6:45 am, sending the mini-sub to the bottom of the sea.

At 6:51 am, the USS *Ward* reported that "we have dropped depth charges upon a sub operating in the defensive sea region. We have engaged, fired at, and placed depth charges aboard submarine operating in defensive sea area." Although it was the opening fire of the Pacific War, no extra preparations were made at Pearl Harbor. The tiny Japanese mini-sub was never recovered, despite years of searching in the waters near Pearl Harbor. Robert Ballard, the man who discovered the Titanic, gave up the search.

In 2002, researchers from the University of Hawaii's Hawai'i Undersea Research Laboratory (HURL) aboard the research vessel, *Ka'imikai-o-Kanaloa,* believed they had discovered the 78-foot, two-man Japanese mini-sub that the USS Ward sank three to four miles off the coast of Pearl Harbor on December 7, 1941. This was the location and description that the Navy later confirmed. Those who tried to reject USS *Ward* Commander Outerbridge's sinking story were proven wrong sixty-one years later, early in the morning in 2002.

After the attack, a Japanese mini-sub washed ashore on the beach near Bellows Field, Hawaii. Torpedoes were also fired from the sea, according to American sailors. One of the mini-subs sent a signal in morse code to its mother submarine, stating it had successfully torpedoed an American ship. Which ship was torpedoed has never been determined.

Four mini-subs ended up at the bottom of the sea, either sunk by American ships or due to mechanical failure, but the fifth was doomed from the start due to a malfunctioning gyroscope. As it attempted to breach Pearl Harbor submarine nets, it became stranded on a coral reef. The crew was struck unconscious after being hit by depth charges from the American destroyer, USS *Helm.* Around midnight, Ensign Kazuo Sakamaki awoke from a concussion and foul gases aboard his ship, which had drifted to the other side of Oahu. Sakamaki scuttled his malfunctioning mini-sub by detonating an explosive and diving overboard.

Sakamaki washed up on Bellows Field Beach when the fuse failed to ignite. His crewmates drowned. Later, he awoke to see US Army Sergeant David Akui, who happened to be of Japanese-American descent, staring down at him. Akui took

Sakamaki as America's first World War II prisoner of war. It has been widely overlooked that the first American to take an axis prisoner of war was a Japanese American soldier.

Because the impact was so devastating, the Japanese Navy assumed one of the mini-subs fired the torpedo that sank the USS *Arizona*. In truth, the massive explosion was caused by an implausible direct hit on the shiproom's ordinance stockpile. The subsequent explosion was one of the largest in all of military history up to that point.

In Japan, the nine Japanese submariners who perished were hailed as heroes and were given posthumous promotions. On the other hand, Sakamaki faced nothing but scorn from his fellow citizens for failing to commit Hari-Kari Suicide.

*ABOVE: Japanese Miget Sub being transported on the back of a larger submarine.*

*Through RADAR, the US Army was aware an hour before the attacks that the Japanese were going to bomb Pearl Harbor. However, the US Army did not announce this discovery to their troops.*

## THE RADAR STATION DETECTED JAPANESE PLANES AN HOUR BEFORE THE ATTACK

I have been fortunate to have personally interviewed the first men who knew that hundreds of Japanese planes were headed to Pearl Harbor and would commence the attack very shortly after that. Knowing one hour beforehand could not have prevented the attack, but it would have bought time to prepare for a more effective defense. Their foresight of this impending attack was due to radar's new mysterious technology.

The five men who held this incredible position were George Elliot, Joe Lockard, Joe McDonald, Dick Schimmel, and Kermit Tyler. I interviewed Joe Lockard and Dick Shimmel several times, and I met with George Elliot and Joe McDonald. They all went over to Pearl Harbor on the same ship, and they later found out they were on the same unit that involved something new for the military, which was land-based RADAR.

They were all members of one of America's first Radar Units. It was tasked with watching over Pearl Harbor and its vicinity on December 7th, 1941. Joe Lockard was training George Elliot at the Opana RADAR station. It was located on the northern side of Oahu Island. Peral Harbor, Hickam Field, Wheeler Field, Fort Shafter, and Scofield Barracks are on the southern side and central area of the Island. The team monitored the RADAR screen for incoming planes.

Joe McDonald and Dick Schimmel were best of buddies. Their stations were at the Information Center several miles away at the Fort Shafter Army Base. The RADAR stations would call in with any sightings from their screens. There were several radar stations spread throughout Hawaii. However, this particular pair, Joe Lockard and George Elliot at Opana, were on the only radar installation that detected the incoming Japanese planes.

*George Elliot:*
*The first person to see the Japanese planes on RADAR.*

Pvt. George Elliot was the first to see the Japanese planes 137 miles away on the radar. He was training under Pvt. Joe Lockard. "At 07:02 am, I was sitting at the controls while Joe Lockard peered over my shoulder and instructed me on how to detect planes. Suddenly, the largest images either of us had ever seen appeared. I asked him what it was. He thought the unit had either malfunctioned or was giving us a false reading. He looked over the equipment and determined it was working ok. We believed the blip to be a large group of aircraft approaching us quickly from 3 degrees east and approximately 137 miles out to sea. I suggested to Lockard that we should notify our Information Center.

"There were two direct telephone lines connecting our radar station to Fort Shafter: a tactical line that linked us directly with the plotters at the Information Center and an administrative line. I tried the tactical line, but no one answered. I then used the administrative phone, which was answered by the switchboard operator, Private Joseph McDonald. He informed me that the five plotters and the Historical Information Plotter at the Information Center had already left for breakfast. I nervously explained what we'd seen, and I asked him to get someone in charge to call us back as soon as possible.

"At 07:20 am, a lieutenant rang back, and Lockard took the call. The lieutenant knew that a dozen B-17s were due from San Francisco from the same direction as our mystery blip. In fact, he had listened to Honolulu radio station KGMB broadcast Hawaiian music early that morning so that the bombers could tune their directional finders. The Japanese attack planes were now honing in on that same frequency. 'Well, don't worry about it,' Lt. Kermit Tyler told Lockard on the phone."

"Lockard again wanted to shut down the Radar Unit," said Elliot, "but I insisted that we keep it operational because I still wanted instruction on using the oscilloscope and the incoming flight presented a perfect opportunity. We continued to track the aircraft until they were approximately twenty-two miles from the Oahu coastline and disappeared behind the permanent distortion of the surrounding mountains at 07:39 am.

"Five minutes later, the truck showed up to replace us with Privates Hodges and Lawrence. They came to take us back to Kawailoa for breakfast. About halfway back to Kawailoa, we passed a truck full of GIs speeding towards Opana. We honked our horn, slowed down, and asked what the truck was doing, but they just blew their horn and rushed past. This shocked us, along with the fact that they were all outfitted with backpacks and wearing World War I doughboy-style helmets!"

"We arrived at Kawailoa to see a group of soldiers gathered around and staring up at the sky. It was here that we learned about the attack on Pearl Harbor. Lockard and I just stared at each other, and at that moment, we knew that the flight we tracked at Opana really was the Japanese attack force!"

OSCILLOSCOPE BC-403-B      RECEIVER TROMBONE

SPARK GAP
GA-4

RECEIVER
BC-404-/

SPARE
RECEIVER

SPARE
WL 530'S

SPARE
450 T.H.

SPARE
PARTS KIT

RECTIFIER
REMOTE
CONTROL

AZIMUTH
SPEED
CONTROL

AZIMUTH MOTORS START-STOP SWITCH

*ABOVE: The equipment that Private Elliot and Lockard were operating when they saw the signals of the first wave of Japanese planes on their way to bomb Pearl Harbor. The planes were seen on the oscilloscope.*

*Joe Lockard:*
*The second person to see the Japanese planes on radar.*

**In Search of Glowing Tales:** "On August the 16th of 1940, I joined the United States Army. I joined because a friend of mine's older brother had just come back from a tour of duty in the Philippines with glowing tales that we teenagers really soaked up. I arrived at Honolulu, Oahu, Territory of Hawaii, on December the 10th, 1940. While we were in port, a group of Signal Corps officers came aboard, recruiting for a new company they were forming in Oahu, named Signal Company Aircraft Warning Hawaii. I joined them—I was thoroughly sick of the ship by then. We had no equipment. They started school to teach us radiophysics and field communications procedures. In July, the first of our equipment arrived. The frequency of the units [that arrived] was 100 megacycles. In September, we participated with the Navy in a test. We were able to detect planes taking off from the carriers at 80-some miles distant out in the sea."

**Just Before the Day That Will Live in Infamy:** "The unit that I had been stationed at Headquarters was at the same time moved to Opana Ridge. It is a spur of the Koʻolau Range on the north side of the Island. The unit was put there near

Thanksgiving [of 1941]. On December 7, we were going to have a program of operation from 4 am to 7 am. I was assigned to that job, along with George Elliot. George was new to the company. So, there would just be the two of us that day. Normally, there would have been a three-man crew, but since it was Sunday, they just assigned two."

**The Day That Will Live in Infamy** At 7:02 am (Pvt. George), Elliott sat down and began turning the (radar) controls. (Pvt. Joseph) Lockard leaned over his shoulder and started explaining the various echoes or blips. Suddenly, a blip flashed on the screen far more significant than anything than Lockard had ever seen before. He shoved Elliott aside and took over the controls himself.

"I told him there was nothing wrong with the radar set. It just might be a huge squad of Jap planes! They're coming from the West - the direction of Japan! "The pair went into an action mode as they had never done before in their lives. Their minds were overtaken by the sudden lighting up of the screen. All else ceased to exist but the glow of two hundred fighter planes on their screen.

"At 7:06 am, Elliott tried the headphones that connected directly with one of the spotters in the Information Center. The line was dead, but he finally got through to the switchboard operator, Pvt. Joseph McDonald. McDonald took the message to the Lieutenant. Helpfully, he explained that it was the first time he had ever received anything like this. 'Do you think we ought to do something about it?'

**Receiving Information**: "Any echoes, or targets, that you received appeared as little blips on the line. The line often looked like a row of grass, and targets would just be taller blades of grass. I stayed on [after 7 am] and kept it running. A huge blip or echo appeared on the screen. I had never seen anything like it! I thought that maybe something was wrong with the equipment. I did a check, and there had to be something there. It had to be aircraft because of the speed at which it moved. We watched it and tracked it. Normally, the man operating the scope could swing the antenna back and forth. He would turn a dial just below the scope, and that dial was graduated in miles. He would do that and call out to the plotter, who had before him a map of the Islands. We continued to plot it."

**He Wasn't Impressed:** "George called the Information Center and got the switchboard operator, and he asked him if there was anybody there. The operator found a second lieutenant and brought him to the phone. I told him excitedly what an unusual event I was seeing, but he wasn't impressed. He told us to forget it. I argued with him a little bit, but I couldn't do too much with the difference in our rank. We plotted it all the way in until 20 miles. At that point, we lost it. We would get inference from the background. There was nothing we could do. The truck came, we shut the equipment down, and got on the truck [to go back to our living quarters]."

'Hey, Mac!' (Lockard) protested when McDonald told him that the Lieutenant said everything was all right. Then Lockard asked to speak directly to Lieutenant (Kermit) Tyler. 'Tyler remembered that the (US) carriers were out. There might be (US) Navy planes. These also might be (US Army Air Corps) Flying Fortresses.'"

**Billows of Black Smoke:** "On the way down the highway— the coastal highway—we passed another truck driving madly back toward the radar with the rest of our crew onboard. They were yelling and waving their arms. We couldn't understand what they were saying, but we could see huge billows of black smoke in the direction of the Harbor. We knew something had happened. When we got back [to our living quarters], we were told that the Japanese had attacked. We knew instantly that what we had plotted those planes. All 180 planes were as one big obstacle [on the radar].

He wanted to show the screen to the fellows. It was frustrating for Joe. Alone again in the plotting room, Lt. Tyler had no qualms about the Opana message. Although he didn't know it, on one count at least, he (Lt. Tyler) was right in that some B-17s were coming in from the mainland. At this very moment, twelve of the big bombers were approaching from the Northeast.

But the planes that showed upon the Opana screen were a little less to the East, far more numerous, and infinitely closer. Japanese Commander Mitsuo Fuchida knew they must be nearly there---they'd been in the air now for almost an hour and a half. Tyler assumed the planes were friendly. He told Lockard, "Well, don't worry about it." Sixteen years later, Lockard said that "Pvt. McDonald was still uneasy, and as (he) left the building, he suddenly stuck the original Opana message in his pocket.

"Elliott had already located the blip on the plotting board: 137 miles to the north, 3 degrees east. We did everything we could to warn them, but they did not respond."

## George Elliot:
### The first person to see the Japanese planes on RADAR.

Pvt. George Elliot was the first to see the Japanese planes 137 miles away on the radar. He was training under Pvt. Joe Lockard. "At 07:02 am, I was sitting at the controls while Joe Lockard peered over my shoulder and instructed me on how to detect planes. Suddenly, the largest images either of us had ever seen appeared. I asked him what it was. He thought the unit had either malfunctioned or was giving us a false reading. He looked over the equipment and determined it was working ok. We believed the blip to be a large group of aircraft approaching us quickly from 3 degrees east, and approximately 137 miles out to sea. I suggested to Lockard that we should notify our Information Center.

"There were two direct telephone lines connecting our radar station to Fort Shafter: a tactical line that linked us directly with the plotters at the Information Center and an administrative line. I tried the tactical line, but no one answered. I then used the administrative phone which was answered by the switchboard operator, Private Joseph McDonald. He informed me that the five plotters and the Historical Information Plotter at the Information Center had already left for breakfast. I nervously explained what we'd seen, and I asked him to get someone in charge to call us back as soon as possible.

"At 07:20 am, a lieutenant rang back and Lockard took the call. The lieutenant knew that a dozen B-17s were due from San Francisco from the same direction as our mystery blip. In fact, he had listened to Honolulu radio station KGMB broadcast Hawaiian music early that morning, so that the bombers could tune their directional finders. The Japanese attack planes were now honing in on that same frequency. 'Well, don't worry about it,' Lt. Kermit Tyler told Lockard on the phone."

"Lockard again wanted to shut down the Radar Unit," said Elliot, "but I insisted that we keep it operational because I still wanted instruction on using the oscilloscope and the incoming flight presented a perfect opportunity. We continued to track the aircraft until they were approximately twenty-two miles from the Oahu coastline and disappeared behind the permanent distortion of the surrounding mountains at 07:39 am.

"Five minutes later, the truck showed up to replace us with Privates Hodges and Lawrence. They came to take us back to Kawailoa for breakfast. About halfway back to Kawailoa, we passed a truck full of GIs speeding towards Opana. We honked our horn, slowed down, and asked what the truck was doing, but they just blew their horn and rushed past. This shocked us, along with the fact that they were all outfitted with backpacks and wearing World War I doughboy-style helmets!"

"We arrived at Kawailoa to see a group of soldiers gathered around and staring up at the sky. It was here that we learned about the attack on Pearl Harbor. Lockard and I just stared at each other, and at that moment, we knew that the flight we tracked at Opana really was the Japanese attack force!"

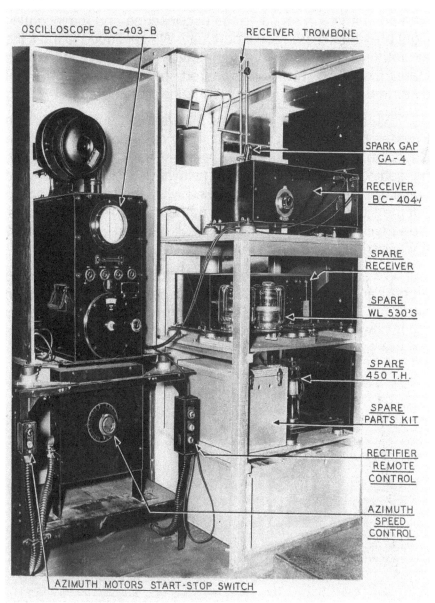

OSCILLOSCOPE BC-403-B  RECEIVER TROMBONE

SPARK GAP
GA-4

RECEIVER
BC-404-/

SPARE
RECEIVER

SPARE
WL 530'S

SPARE
450 T.H.

SPARE
PARTS KIT

RECTIFIER
REMOTE
CONTROL

AZIMUTH
SPEED
CONTROL

AZIMUTH MOTORS START-STOP SWITCH

*ABOVE: The equipment that Private Elliot and Lockard were operating when they saw the signals of the first wave of Japanese planes on their way to bomb Pearl Harbor. The planes were seen on the oscilloscope.*

*Joe Lockard:*
*The second person to see the Japanese planes on radar.*

**In Search of Glowing Tales:** "On August the 16th of 1940, I joined the United States Army. I joined because a friend of mine's older brother had just come back from a tour of duty in the Philippines with glowing tales that we teenagers really soaked up. I arrived at Honolulu, Oahu, Territory of Hawaii, on December the 10th, 1940. While we were in port, a group of Signal Corps officers came aboard, recruiting for a new company they were forming in Oahu, named Signal Company Aircraft Warning Hawaii. I joined them—I was thoroughly sick of the ship by then. We had no equipment. They started school to teach us radiophysics and field communications procedures. In July, the first of our equipment arrived. The frequency of the units [that arrived] was 100 megacycles. In September, we participated with the Navy in a test. We were able to detect planes taking off from the carriers at 80-some miles distant out in the sea."

**Just Before the Day That Will Live in Infamy:** "The unit that I had been stationed at Headquarters was at the same time moved to Opana Ridge. It is a spur of the Koʻolau Range on the north side of the Island. The unit was put there near

Thanksgiving [of 1941]. On December 7, we were going to have a program of operation from 4 am to 7 am. I was assigned to that job, along with George Elliot. George was new to the company. So, there would just be the two of us that day. Normally, there would have been a three-man crew, but since it was Sunday, they just assigned two."

**The Day That Will Live in Infamy** At 7:02 am (Pvt. George), Elliott sat down and began turning the (radar) controls. (Pvt. Joseph) Lockard leaned over his shoulder and started explaining the various echoes or blips. Suddenly, a blip flashed on the screen far more significant than anything than Lockard had ever seen before. He shoved Elliott aside, and took over the controls himself.

"I told him there was nothing wrong with the radar set. It just might be a huge squad of Jap planes! They're coming from the West - the direction of Japan! "The pair went into an action mode as they had never done before in their lives. Their minds were overtaken by the sudden lighting up of the screen. All else ceased to exist but the glow of two hundred fighter planes on their screen.

"At 7:06 am, Elliott tried the headphones that connected directly with one of the spotters in the Information Center. The line was dead, but he finally got through to the switchboard operator, Pvt. Joseph McDonald. McDonald took the message to the Lieutenant. Helpfully, he explained that it was the first time he had ever received anything like this. 'Do you think we ought to do something about it?'

**Receiving Information**: "Any echoes, or targets, that you received, appeared as little blips on the line. The line often looked like a row of grass, and targets would just be taller blades of grass. I stayed on [after 7 am], and kept it running. A huge blip or echo appeared on the screen. I had never seen anything like it! I thought that maybe something was wrong with the equipment. I did a check, and there had to be something there. It had to be aircraft because of the speed at which it moved. We watched it and tracked it. Normally, the man operating the scope could swing the antenna back and forth. He would turn a dial just below the scope, and that dial was graduated in miles. He would do that and call out to the plotter, who had before him a map of the Islands. We continued to plot it."

**He Wasn't Impressed:** "George called the Information Center and got the switchboard operator, and he asked him if there was anybody there. The operator found a second lieutenant and brought him to the phone. I told him excitedly what an unusual event I was seeing, but he wasn't impressed. He told us to forget it. I argued with him a little bit, but with the difference in our rank, I couldn't do too much. We plotted it all the way in until 20 miles. At that point, we lost it. We would get inference from the background. There was nothing we could do. The truck came, we shut the equipment down, and got on the truck [to go back to our living quarters]."

'Hey, Mac!' (Lockard) protested when McDonald told him that the Lieutenant said everything was all right. Then Lockard asked to speak directly to Lieutenant (Kermit) Tyler. 'Tyler remembered that the (US) carriers were out. There might be (US) Navy planes. These also might be (US Army Air Corps) Flying Fortresses.'"

**Billows of Black Smoke:** "On the way down the highway—the coastal highway—we passed another truck driving madly back toward the radar with the rest of our crew onboard. They were yelling and waving their arms. We couldn't understand what they were saying, but we could see huge billows of black smoke in the direction of the Harbor. We knew something had happened. When we got back [to our living quarters], we were told that the Japanese had attacked. We knew instantly that what we had plotted those planes. All 180 planes were as one big obstacle [on the radar].

He wanted to show the screen to the fellows. It was frustrating for Joe. Alone again in the plotting room, Lt. Tyler had no qualms about the Opana message. Although he didn't know it, on one count at least, he (Lt. Tyler) was right in that some B-17s were coming in from the mainland. At this very moment, twelve of the big bombers were approaching from the Northeast.

But the planes that showed upon the Opana screen were a little less to the East, far more numerous, and infinitely closer. Japanese Commander Mitsuo Fuchida knew they must be nearly there---they'd been in the air now for almost an hour and a half. Tyler assumed the planes were friendly. He told Lockard, "Well, don't worry about it." Sixteen years later, Lockard said that "Pvt. McDonald was still uneasy, and as (he) left the building, he suddenly stuck the original Opana message in his pocket.

"Elliott had already located the blip on the plotting board: 137 miles to the north, 3 degrees east. We did everything we could to warn them, but they did not respond."

*Kermit Tyler:*
*The third person to know through radar about the several*
*hundred Japanese aircraft headed to Pearl Harbor.*

Driving to work in the black pre-dawn hours of December 7, 1941, Lt. Kermit Tyler turned on the radio to listen to some music. It was a random act that would change the course of history.

Lt. Tyler was about to begin his 4 am shift at the Information Center at Fort Shafter Army Base in Honolulu when he tuned into local radio station KGMB. Elliot and Lockard reported their findings to the Information Center at Fort Shafter, where all but two of the staff had gone to breakfast. This was Lt. Tyler's second day at the Information Center. He was just learning. Initially, he was a pilot with the 78th Pursuit Squadron at the Army Air Force's Wheeler Field.

After getting the initial report of approaching aircraft, Lt. Tyler reasoned what they saw on RADAR. He believed it was a group of B-17 bombers due in that morning from San Francisco. Elliot and Lockard went to the Information Center at Fort Shafter, where all but two of the employees had gone to breakfast, to report their findings. He also recalls a pilot acquaintance informing him that KGMB only played music at night so that pilots might use the radio beam to aid navigation.

Lt. Tyler famously instructed the Opana Radar operators "not to worry about it" using those two pieces of information. There is no reason to believe if the Lieutenant had tried to alert all military installations, the attack would have been routed. However, more preparation would likely have been made with an hour's warning.

Kermit Tyler was the executive officer of the 78th Pursuit Squadron, United States Army Air Forces. On December 7, 1941, Tyler was the officer in charge of the communication center at Fort Shafter. Years later, he would recall:

"I got a call at 7:15 am, or thereabouts, from the radio operator. They had a huge blip, indicating a larger number of airplanes. He thought his equipment was breaking down or something because it was so large. Periodically, well, they would send B-17s, like in bunches of about a dozen airplanes. So, I thought, well, they must be the B-17s. As a matter of fact, the base operations officer was in the tower at Hickam [Field], and the base commander was down there with various other officers awaiting the arrival of the B-17s. So once I sized all this up, I thought, 'It has to be the B-17s.' And so, I said, 'Don't worry about it.'"

Tyler was, of course, badly mistaken. While there was a flight of twelve B-17s scheduled to arrive from California that morning, the radar operator saw the Japanese heading inbound to attack.

"I hadn't the slightest doubt that it was anything but friendly aircraft. I couldn't believe that they would be able to travel 6,000 miles, a huge force—70-odd ships, to move all those secretly and attack us, and then have the great good luck to have somebody like me there to say, 'Oh well, don't worry about it.' I mean, somehow, I felt that I was destined to be the one to do that; I don't know why."

Tyler was not alone in his error. Instead, his mistake was part of a much greater US intelligence effort that left the United States and Pearl Harbor somewhat vulnerable that day.

*Joe McDonald:*
*The fourth person who knew that incoming Japanese aircraft*
*were heading to Pearl Harbor.*

Pvt. Joseph McDonald started his shift at 5 pm on December 6, 1941. The Information Center was connected with five radar sites from various locations on Oahu. The people at the Center had been on alert for a few weeks. The rumor was that the alert was called because the Japanese Navy could not be located. This rumor was true, so the alert was canceled just before December 7. Why this was done was never determined from the Navy Board inquiries. Joseph McDonald operated the switchboard at 6 pm. Most of the time, he was alone at the switchboard. At 4 am on December 7, the plotters entered the Information Center. The radar plotters were scheduled to operate between 4 am, and 7 am. General Short thought that was the most likely time that an attack could take place. The Center had a large table with a map of Hawaii. The plotters would move arrows on the table to designate planes picked up by the radar sites. The radar sites had a direct line to the plotters.

At 7 am, the plotters exited the Information Center and headed for breakfast. Joseph McDonald's orders were scheduled until 6 am. It was a Sunday, and Joseph stayed on duty beyond his time until his replacement ate breakfast at 7 am. Joseph thought that he was in the Center alone. Shortly after 7 am, the switchboard buzzed. He inserted the plug into the phone and answered. It was the Northern Radar Station from Opana. An excited voice that he could hardly hear asked if the plotters were still around. McDonald said, "No." The voice from Opana said, "There are a large number of planes coming in from the north 3 points east." Joseph replied, "I am not sure what to do. There is nobody here." At that point, the connection was broken. (Pvt. George Elliott made this call.)

McDonald looked at the clock to time the message and saw a lieutenant from the Air Corps sitting at the plotting table. He walked in and said, "I just received a call from Opana reporting a large number of planes coming in from the north 3 points east." The Lieutenant said that there was nothing to get excited about. McDonald returned to the switchboard and called the man back on the Opana Radar Unit. McDonald relayed the Lieutenant's lack of concern. The voice at Opana was coming in stronger now. He recognized the voice as his friend Joseph Lockard. Pvt. Lockard was excited and stated that a large number of planes were heading fast towards Oahu. "Hey, Mac. There is a heck of a big flight of planes coming in, and the whole scope is covered." McDonald told Joseph Lockard to hold on. McDonald, infected by his friend's excitement, again returned to the plotting table. McDonald said, "Sir, this is the first call that I have ever received like this. This sounds serious! Do you think that we ought to do something about it? Shall I call back the plotters?"

McDonald was sure that it was severe. He knew that the Lieutenant was inexperienced in the Information Center's operations as it was only his second day there. McDonald was pretty sure that it was serious. Several times he grabbed the line for Wheeler Field. McDonald then thought that he could be court-marshaled for going around the Lieutenant. Who would listen to a private anyway? At about 7:45 am, McDonald's replacement arrived.

McDonald was exhausted after working over 14 hours, yet the communication from Opana kept gnawing on his mind. He thought that he would call Wheeler from the Orderly Tent. He passed by the Orderly Tent and saw the Sergeant using the phone. He returned to his tent to tell his tent mate Pvt. Richard Schimmel, "Shim, the Japs are coming". McDonald sat on his bunk and recounted the call from the Opana radar. A few moments later, they could hear the drone of planes.

Their tent was on a hill overlooking Pearl Harbor. Finally, they could see the planes coming over. There were a lot of them, and they seemed to play follow- the the-leader. They were flying in single file. Finally, the lead plane dived, and the others followed. They could hear the loud roar of explosions and see the black smoke. A radio was playing in a nearby tent. The music stopped, and a frantic voice said, "All cars keep clear of Pearl Harbor! Pearl Harbor is under attack by the Japanese."

McDonald and Schimmel ran to get a better view on top of the Mess Hall. They could see planes diving on Pearl Harbor and Hickam Field. The explosions kept getting worse. Everybody was stunned. Some guys were getting dressed and running out of their tents with their pants half down. Everybody seemed to be running in different directions. Confusion ruled as the torpedo planes flew overhead. The planes were so low that some threw stones at them.

All of the ammunition was locked up. The rocks became their only weapon. Anti-aircraft guns from the 64th C.A. across the street tried to knock down the oncoming planes. They came so close that it knocked Schimmel and McDonald down to the floor from the Mess Hall roof. They ran to their tent, got their guns and gas masks, and headed to the Information Center. They worked throughout the day, answering the calls.

**"From the radar unit, we knew the attack was coming an hour beforehand, but no one would listen."**

Dick Schimmel was a Radar Operator with the newly-formed radar unit "Signal Company Aircraft Warning Hawaii." He served as a plotter and switchboard operator at the Operations Center.

**About the radar installation:** "Radar was given to us on August the 14th of 1940, from England. I was enlisted into the Army on August the 28th. When the guy said to me, 'OK, we're going to send you here for signal aircraft warning,' I said, 'What is that?' The guy said, 'Don't ask me.' [This was] the recruiting man in Philadelphia. This all happened a year before the war started. We put up the first radar units ever put up—United States or anywhere. That was all by hook or crook. We didn't know much about it. It was like an erector set. They painted the base different colors to match the thing that held them. The red would match the red; the green would match the green. And that's how we did it. We had two or three of them by that time."

**An ambiguous place for a radar unit:** "We never had an insignia. We were part of the Army Air Corps, and then we weren't in the Army Air Corps. Then we were supposed to go with the Navy, and they were supposed to put us somewhere else. Then the war started, and we never got an insignia—still. To me, it isn't right, but that's the way it goes."

**Growth of radar unit:** "We started out with fifty people at the most, and all of a sudden, we exploded into so many different people as we were putting up the radar unit."

**On his job responsibilities:** "You name it, I did it. I had so many different jobs. Right before the war started, they had this place at Fort Shafter—an old building—and they refurbished it, and they made it into an Information Center. I was painting the wood so the bugs couldn't come in. I helped put up a radar unit. Whatever they needed, I was there. I also worked the switchboard. All the calls that came in had to go through me."

**Warning about the Pearl Harbor attack:** "Joe McDonald was the guy that was on then [at the Information Center] had relieved me. Joe McDonald was the guy who got the message from Radar Observer Joe Lockard. I was the fifth person to know the Japs were coming. But the first to see it was the guy George Elliott —you know, Joe [Lockard] didn't actually pick them up on radar. It was another guy by the name of Elliot, and he picked him up and he asked Joe Lockard to call there for help. He called Joe twice to look at it. If there was one plane, you'd see a little blip. But when you see a whole bunch of them—he said the whole screen was loaded. That's why he called in. There was some confusion because they had planes coming in from the States. Those bombers or whatever they were. Well, they were coming from the West. The American planes were coming from the East."

**The Japs are coming:** "So then he called into where we were, where Joe McDonald and I worked. Every time they picked up something, they would send it in to us. There was a table, maybe with five or six people sitting there, with headphones on from each radar unit. The first guy to pick it up told Joe Lockard, and then Joe Lockard went and called McDonald. Now Joe McDonald, I, and Lockard all went over in the same ship. We all knew each other pretty well. But then Joe went and took it into the Lieutenant, and then he came back out, he came down, and when he came, the first thing he said to me, he said, 'Hey, Schim, the Japs are coming.' Well, we could see the planes flying. All of sudden we see black smoke hit the ship. That was a big thing there. But Joe McDonald was the third guy to know about it, and the Lieutenant was the fourth guy."

**Dick Schimel's Famous Note**

"Mac wrote down exactly what Joe Lockard said and handed it to our Lieutenant. After Mac told me what happened, I knew this was going to be really big, so I copied Mac's note by hand, word-for-word. I still have it (my handwritten copy) and bring it to Reading, PA (World War II Weekend) every June. The original note (Mac's) he had to turned over to the Roberts' Commission. You know, the Roberts Commission was Chief Justice Roberts, the first instigation into the Pearl Harbor attack.

**About Joe Lockard getting credit:** "Joe got credit because, between the two of them (Elliot and Lockard), when he called into Joe McDonald about it, Joe just mentioned Lockard's name. Well, what happened after the war started— the kid (George Elliot) who really picked it up, he must have written his father, and his father wrote his congressman, and then I don't know what the hell they gave him. I think they made him a staff sergeant or something out of it."

**After they got the news:** "Then it was up to us to look at it, and see what it is, and then we had to report it to somebody higher than us, which was a lieutenant, whoever was on duty at that time. And he had to decide what to do. [The lieutenant] was new too."

**About the lieutenant in charge:** "[The Lieutenant's] name was Lieutenant Tyler. He was the guy that was in charge of the

Information Center, where I was working at the time. There's where we had the real big plotting table.

**Never seen before:** They said that screen was loaded. When you had one blip, it was just like a finger sticking up. But it was like a whole hand. The Lieutenant didn't know what the hell he was doing. He thought it was the planes coming in from California. They were coming from a different direction. A PFC could find that out. He was young; he was new. "[The Japanese] hit [with a midget sub] at 4:00 in the morning. They didn't do anything with it. Didn't call the alert. When they sank that submarine, if they would have had that notified, all of the services would have been on the lookout—it might have been a different story."

**On the Japanese:** "One thing about the Japs, they practiced that thing so much. How to fly, how to go so low. They couldn't go much lower than that, or the explosion would have hurt them. They were smart pilots. They knew their job. The Japanese were trying to cripple our ships. They were all tied together too close."

**During Pearl Harbor:** "I was at Fort Shafter, the Information Center. Where we were, we could look over, and we would see the planes flying, but then, we wouldn't see anything, and all of a sudden, we see black smoke. I saw the bombs falling; I saw the planes flying, I've seen the black smoke as the bombs fell. I couldn't decipher the bombs because of the distance I was— five miles or whatever it was. They were smaller than I would notice in the sky, but then when they would hit the ship, I would see the black smoke coming up on the ship. Some of the planes flew right over our heads. Where we eat—it was like a picnic thing. I and Joe McDonald, we went and crawled up to the top and laid up there and looked to get a better view. A couple flew over us; we got out of there pretty fast. You never know if they have a machine gun; they could pick you right out. They flew right in between Schofield Barracks—the one side and the other side."

**A close call:** "They [the Japanese] came over [to where I was working], they dropped one [bomb]. They would have liked to find us. We were right next to Tripler General Hospital—the old one. Actually, our Information Center—we built it on a dump. And the one bomb dropped in the middle of the dump. We were very lucky. They would have liked to have found us."

We criticize from the vantage point of hindsight history. Other questions should be asked rather than trying to blame the Army or Navy. Why did FDR move the Pacific Fleet to Pearl Harbor? Did the Departments of Navy and Army Headquarters in Washington do all they could to warn and protect Pearl Harbor, Scofield Barracks, Hickman Field, and the surrounding vicinity?

*ABOVE: Dick Shimmel's famous notebook with the original notes he took on December 7th, 1941. Dick brings it with him to World War II events.*

*ABOVE: Joe McDonald stands on the left, like everyone else present, was in total shock. Dick Schimmel holds the famous note he wrote to document what transpired just one hour before the attack.*

His historic note was subpoenaed by the Government's Roberts Commission, investigating the events. It was useful in understanding what transpired that day. Dick brought the note with him to many commemoration events since the war. I recall him displaying it at the 75th Anniversary of the attack at Pearl Harbor. It was one of the most significant artifacts from that day.

The entire foundation of the use of radar during WWII and the Cold War has its beginnings in these events. The British gave the invention to the US in 1941 under an agreement to share technology. R-a-d-a-r (from **R**adio **D**etection **a**nd **R**anging) is said to have won World War II. Without it, the British would have never been able to win the *Battle of Britain*. The devices would indicate the number of German bombers and their direction. The Allies had an edge throughout the war due to its extensive use.

*The Invention that Changed the World: How a small group of Radar Pioneers Won the Second World War and Launched a Technological Revolution* by Robert Buderi illuminates the remarkable history of the development of radar, often by non-scientists during World War II. Microwaves would help win the war and eventually lead to much of the advanced technology we enjoy today.

*December 7th, 1941. Never before has the US military been so caught off guard in a most extreme enemy wartime attack.*

## NIIHAU:
### A unique story on a unique Hawaiian island

Niihau is an indescribable paradise located in the furthermost western part of the Hawaiian Islands. This dreamlike setting leaves natives and rare visitors spellbound, even in Hawaii. The Island sustains wild Polynesian boar and hybrid sheep. Limited hunting is available for wild eland, wild aoudad (Barbary sheep) and wild oryx. Niihau Island is the only place where Hawaiian is the dominant language. English has long ago dominated the rest of Hawaii.

Niihau has been privately owned since 1858 by the Robinsons, an American family from New England. When it was purchased from the King of Hawaii, Robinson made a solemn vow to always protect the native population and avoid modern society from overwhelming or erasing their authentic culture. To this day, the family has done well with both promises. Only residents are permitted on the island. Niihau is often referred to as "The Forbidden Island."

December 7, 1941

An Island resident, Howard Kaleohano, of native Hawaiian descent, talked to his horse, getting a few beys. The animal quite suddenly appeared spooked. It became clear why the animal became agitated. A 10-ton Japanese warplane blasted through Howard's fence. The aircraft commenced its dive with a loud earthen thump, just missing Howard's house. Like a wounded bird of prey, the fire machine brought the unconscious pilot (Pilot Shigenori) to a final impact. Howard instinctively ran over to the pilot and yanked him out of his seat. However, Howard and anyone else on the Island had no idea about Oahu's Pearl Harbor attack. He instinctively took possession of the pilot's papers and pistol and promptly hid them.

"Are you Japanese?" Shigenori inquired, now that the pilot had awakened. Howard made a significant comeback. "No, I'm an American," he said. Howard recognized Shigenori and his jet as Japanese.

The pilot, Shigenori, was taken to the home of the Island's only Japanese couple, Yoshio and Irene Harada. All the natives on the Island treated the pilot with courtesy and respect, even throwing him a party later that afternoon. Islanders Ishimatsu Shintani and Yoshio Harada (both Nisei, born in the US) exchanged only a few words in secret with the pilot in Japanese.

The pilot pleaded with Howard to return his papers and pistol, which he had been assured would not fall into American hands. The documents contained the entire Pearl Harbor attack plan and codes, and other secret information that would be valuable to American intelligence. Yoshio and Irene Harada decided to assist the pilot in retrieving his papers and fleeing.

Niihau didn't have any power or telephones, but the people on the Island heard a radio report about the Pearl Harbor attack later that night on a battery-operated radio. A Nisei Islander, Shintani also sided with the Japanese pilot. He tried to bribe Harold with approximately $200 in cash (about $3,700 in today's dollars), which was significant for most people.

Yoshio Harada physically overpowered the guard. Yoshio's wife, Irene, played music on a phonograph to drown away the noises of a struggle between the lone guard at the Harada's residence. The guard was then held captive in a warehouse; after that, Yoshio Harada could steal a shotgun and recover the pilot's pistol. Armed, the pilot Shigenori and Yoshio marched to Harold's house to get the secret papers.

Many people couldn't believe that Yoshio Harada, a long-time friend, and neighbor who had been living among them for almost three years, could become so violent and side with the enemy. The women and children of the Island fled to tunnels, thickets, and distant beaches.

Shigenori tried unsuccessfully to contact the Japanese military via the plane's radio. Yoshio Harada removed one of the two 7.7 mm machine guns onboard the Japanese fighter plane and some ammunition. He then torched the plane and proceeded to Harold's house. Harold was nowhere to be found, so Yoshio Harada set Howard's house on fire in a final effort to destroy Shigenori's secret papers.

At the same time, to save the Islanders, Ben Kanahele and his wife, Ella, attempted to steal the two 7.7 mm machine guns hidden at the Haradas' house. However, Harada and Shigenori were there, surprised Ben and Ella, and held them at gunpoint, threatening to kill them.

Harada yelled at Ben, in no uncertain terms, that if Harold were not found, the pilot would kill him and everyone else on Niihau. Ben and his wife knew they had no choice, so they lunged at them when Shigenori transferred the shotgun to Harada. Shigenori subsequently took his handgun from his boot, but Ella grabbed his arm and brought it down, disabling him from firing at her husband.

Harada dragged her away from the pilot, who then fired three shots into Ben, nearly killing him. But Ben Kanahele was so strong that even after being shot three times at the close range, he picked up the pilot and threw him into a stone wall. Ella hit the pilot with a rock, and Ben stabbed his throat with his hunting knife. Harada then turned the shotgun on himself and committed suicide.

Later that day, Irene Harada and Ishimatsu Shintani were taken into custody, and Ben Kanahele was sent to Waimea Hospital on Kauai. Ben received the Medal of Merit and the Purple Heart, a rare honor for a civilian who never was in the military.

Lieutenant General Robert C. Richardson presented Ben Kanahele with the award on August 15, 1945, at Army Headquarters, Fort Shafter, Honolulu, for his contribution to defending his homeland. The song "Niihau, No How!" written by composer R. Alex Anderson was in response to the incident. It was played at the ceremony when Ben received these medals for his heroism. then

Anderson is well-known for writing the song "*Mele Kalikimaka*," the most famous Hawaiian Christmas tune.

Irene Harada was released in June 1944, even when the war with Japan was still intensely ongoing. She was never charged with any crime and moved to Kauai, the closest island to Niihau.  In a 1992 interview with a Japanese television station, Irene said she felt sorry for the pilot and wanted to help him.

Niihau Islander Shintani and the Haradas' acts were documented in an official Navy report dated January 26, 1942. "The fact that these Niihau Japanese, who had previously shown no anti-American tendencies, came to the pilot's aid when Japanese domination of the Island appeared possible indicates[s] [the] likelihood that Japanese residents previously believed loyal to the United States may aid Japan if further Japanese attacks appear successful," wrote report author Navy Lieutenant C. B. Baldwin. Shintani was permitted to return to Niihau and was never prosecuted nor made any amends.

Despite these events, Hawaii's Japanese population was loyal to America, and few were interned or relocated. No similar incidents occurred in Hawaii after the Niihau events. None involving Japanese from Japan (Issei) or those of Japanese descent born in their parent's adopted country (Nisei). A small fraction of Hawaiian residents (Issei or Nisei) was sent to the mainland, but only those who the authorities had reason to suspect. American Nisei joined the US Army and made contributions to the highly decorated 100th Battalion/442nd Infantry Regiment in Europe. Two-thousand six hundred Hawaiian Nisei volunteered for the Army in World War II.

Approximately 33,000 Japanese-Americans served in the US military during World War II.

### Post-War

In Hashihama, Imabari, Ehime Prefecture, Japan erected a 12-foot (3.7 m) granite cenotaph in Shigenori's honor when it was still believed that he had perished on the day of the attack, December 7, 1941. Shigenori's remains were regarded as an unknown Japanese soldier for many years. It was not until 1956 that the circumstances of his death were revealed to his family, and they claimed his ashes. Engraved on the column is what was believed: "Having expended every effort, he achieved the greatest honor of all by dying a soldier's death in battle, destroying both himself and his beloved plane. His meritorious deed will live forever." In June 2017, the pilot's *nafuda* (a set of seven wooden sticks that carried the names of colleagues), the identifying markings of his Zero aircraft, and his administrative command were returned to his family in Japan.

The remains of the Japanese Zero aircraft and the tractor used to travel to the boat landing are on permanent display on Ford Island in Pearl Harbor. The 2006 novel *East Wind, Rain* by Caroline Paul also tells the story of the incident. A film entitled *Enemy Within* was released in theaters in 2019.

JAPANESE SUBMARINES HEAD TO THE US WEST COAST

The following lists the nine Japanese submarines and their locations from December 1941 through 1942: Cape Blanco, Oregon (*I-9*), San Diego, California (*I-10*), San Francisco Bay, California (*I-15*), Cape Mendocino, California (*I-17*), Los Angeles Harbor, California (*I-19*), Estero Bay, California (*I-21*), Monterey Bay, California (*I-23*), Strait of Juan de Fuca, Washington (*I-26*), Southern California (*I-25*). The sightings and subsequent sinkings of American vessels have been well documented.

JAPANESE SUBMARINES HEAD TO THE US WEST COAST

The following lists the nine Japanese submarines and their locations from December 1941 through 1942: Cape Blanco, Oregon (*I-9*) San Diego, California (*I-10*) San Francisco Bay, California, (*I-15*), Cape Mendocino, California (*I-17*), Los Angeles Harbor, California (*I-19*), Estero Bay, California (*I-21*), Monterey Bay, California (*I-23*), Strait of Juan de Fuca, Washington (*I-26*), Southern California (*I-25*). The sightings and subsequent sinkings of American vessels have been well documented.

# ALASKA

*Insignia of the World War II US Army Alaska Defense Command*

# Attacks on Alaska in WWII

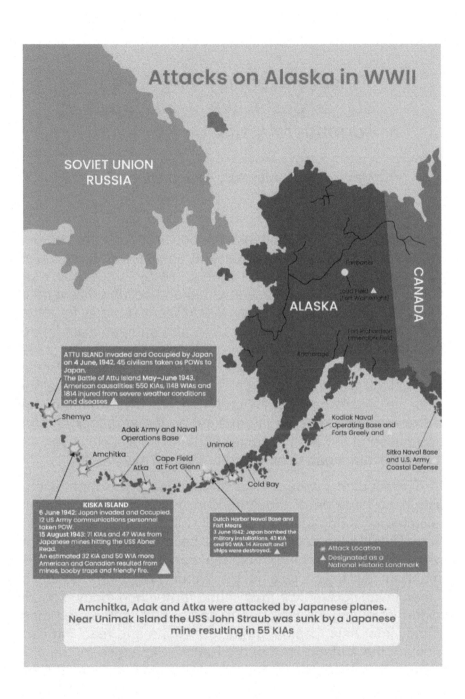

SOVIET UNION
RUSSIA

CANADA

ALASKA

Fairbanks

Cold Field
(Fort Wainwright)

Fort Richardson
Elmendorf Field

Anchorage

ATTU ISLAND Invaded and Occupied by Japan on 4 June, 1942. 45 civilians taken as POWs to Japan.
The Battle of Attu Island May–June 1943. American causalities: 550 KIAs, 1148 WIAs and 1814 injured from severe weather conditions and diseases ▲

Shemya

Adak Army and Naval Operations Base

Amchitka

Atka

Cape Field at Fort Glenn

Unimak

Cold Bay

Kodiak Naval Operating Base and Forts Greely and

Sitka Naval Base and U.S. Army Coastal Defense

**KISKA ISLAND**
6 June 1942: Japan invaded and Occupied. 12 US Army communications personnel taken POW.
15 August 1943: 71 KIAs and 47 WIAs from Japanese mines hitting the USS Abner Read.
An estimated 32 KIA and 50 WIA more American and Canadian resulted from mines, booby traps and friendly fire. ▲

Dutch Harbor Naval Base and Fort Mears
3 June 1942: Japan bombed the military installations. 43 KIA and 50 WIA. 14 Aircraft and 1 ships were destroyed. ▲

■ Attack Location
▲ Designated as a National Historic Landmark

Amchitka, Adak and Atka were attacked by Japanese planes.
Near Unimak Island the USS John Straub was sunk by a Japanese mine resulting in 55 KIAs

*"Once the enemy had taken out our outposts, we would have to surrender Alaska."*

*Maj. Muktuk Marston, Commander Alaskan Territorial Guard*

In June 1942, the unthinkable occurred; Japan bombed American bases in Alaska and invaded and occupied several American Alaskan islands. Many Americans were not aware that the Japanese invaded and occupied several of Alaska's Aleutian Islands during World War II. Largely forgotten in World War II history, the invasion and partial occupation of the Aleutian Islands of Alaska was the only time a foreign power occupied an area in the United States since Great Britain invaded the US in the War of 1812. For those who knew at the time, the psychological effect on Americans was profound. The US government kept the information on the air attack and the occupation of the islands secret from the public. However, the media still managed to print and broadcast the events.

The Aleutians were a potential bridge for the Japanese to use in an invasion of the American mainland. Such thinking reflected what Brigadier General Billy Mitchell, Father of Military Aircraft, told Congress in 1935: "I believe that in the future, whoever holds Alaska will hold the world. I think it is the most important strategic place in the world." While the notion of Japan invading America may sound far-fetched today, keep in mind that during the war, Japan had already conquered most of industrial Asia, capturing much of China and reaching over much of the surface area of the Pacific. Japanese forces also seized control of Southeast Asia and Burma. The Imperial Army would have kept going west to join with Germany in the Middle East if not for Britain's and America's four-year-long struggle against them in that region.

Few if any World War II events happened in isolation. The narrative of World War II in Alaska is intertwined with the Battle of Midway and the Japanese intentions to attack Western Canada and the United States.

The Battle of Midway in June 1942 does not get the respect it deserves in history. It has been a part of the United States since 1867, like Hawaii. Oxford University considers the Battle of Midway Island one of the two most important battles of the 20th century, the other being The Battle of Stalingrad. Midway was a significant turning point in the Pacific War. With little under twenty-six square miles of land, it is located in the Pacific, and it is almost the most westward of the 1200-mile Hawaiian Island chain.

Because of its position, the island was crucial throughout the war. Refueling of aircraft and ships from Asia to North America was required. Moreover, the Japanese hoped they could shoot down some of the thousands of American planes given to the Soviets through the Alaska/Siberia air route. dubbed the "ALSIB."

It is possible that the Japanese invasion aimed to eventually provide Japan with aircraft range to the US mainland. A worst-case scenario for Japan would be that having control of the Aleutians would create another barrier between Japan and the US. They would start their conquest of Alaska's Aleutian Islands simultaneously as the Battle of Midway. A 1200-mile chain of volcanic islands stretching from mainland Alaska to Russia was a constant war zone in 1942. Both Dutch Harbor and Fort Mears Army Base, the largest population in the region, were the first targets for the Japanese. These two military outposts were the Aleutian Islands' sole defenders.

After their triumph at Pearl Harbor, the Japanese were looking to consolidate their victories in the Pacific while simultaneously fending off any potential US attacks on their home islands. While the bulk of the Japanese Navy sailed to attack the American Pacific fleet in the Battle of Midway, a smaller force of two aircraft carriers, destroyers, cruisers, and submarines sailed to the frozen north to invade Alaska.

Dutch Harbor and Ft. Meers were bombed on June 3, 1942, killing at least 25 soldiers. The Japanese invasion of Attu Island began on June 7, 1942, when the Third Special Landing Force (with 550 Japanese Naval men) stormed ashore at Attu and Kiska. More Japanese troops arrived over the next several months, increasing the entire occupying force to approximately 5,640 soldiers and 1,170 civilians.

*ABOVE: The bombing of Dutch Harbor and Ft Meers was significant as the first air attack on the US since Pearl Harbor. Admiral Kakuta ordered his aircraft carriers to launch their strike, which was made up of 12 A6M Zero fighters, 10 B5N Kate high-level bombers, and 12 D3A Val dive bombers which took off from the two carriers Ryūjō and Jun'yōin to strike at Dutch Harbor.*

## Dutch Harbor, Alaska

After two days of bombing, damage to Dutch Harbor after the Japanese raid was severe. Many buildings were destroyed, and at least 25 servicemen were killed in the barracks.

This was the beginning of the Japanese attack on Alaska. On June 3, 1942, seventeen Japanese aircraft carried out a bombing raid on Dutch Harbor and Ft Mears, the most significant American Navy and Army installation in the Aleutians. The sky appeared like a swarm of Japanese bombers, and then Japanese Zero aircraft returned the following day, destroying the Base's oil storage tanks and part of its hospital. This resulted in the killing of more people, including military personnel and civilians. The Japanese aircraft hit barracks, warehouses, oil storage tanks, planes on the ground, ships in the harbor, and ammunition dumps.

Harrel Chancellor Interview:

"My outfit arrived at Dutch Harbor about midnight on June 2. We were quartered in a barracks about a half-mile inland from 'Navy town' on the Harbor. I got my platoon up at 3:30 the next morning (June 3) to go to the dock to unload our equipment. The Japanese attacked at daylight while we were aboard the USS *President Fillmore*. Japanese planes were bombing and strafing Fort Mears and the Naval Air Station for about two or three hours. I saw one fighter plane cripple the PBY mail plane as it was taking off across the Harbor."

"I worked my platoon back to our barracks at Fort Mears after taking cover under the Navy Theater for thirty minutes. We took cover in foxholes and hillsides near our barracks. The enemy planes were bombing Fort Mears. They hit just about every other building. Luckily my barracks was skipped, but the Engineering Barracks was hit on one side, and the Officer's Club was struck on the other. We had a lot of dead and injured. My platoon was covered in their foxholes". I lost only one man who was cut by shrapnel. He was not deep enough in the foxhole."

"The bombing and strafing attack caused quite a lot of damage. The Japanese didn't seem to have any specific targets. They hit barracks, warehouses, oil storage tanks, planes on the ground, ships in the harbor, and ammunition dumps."

"We had a few hours of calm, but they attacked us again the next evening (June 4). This attack was much the same as the day before, with one exception. Most of the troops had dispersed from the Fort Mears area to the hills and shoreline at Captain's Bay, where they dug in. Some of the enemy fighter planes strafed the hills and the shoreline."

"My company was dug in on Hill 400, where I had machine guns on the rim of a 50-foot cliff. One made two passes by our position, spraying sand over myself and four of my men. We waited for more attacks, but none came."

"In addition to my unit, one battalion of the 4th Infantry was at Dutch Harbor as well as an artillery unit. In fact, the artillery fired one round in front of our ship and one behind it as we entered the Harbor. Years later, when I had a drug store, I was filling a prescription for a man named Tom Kirkland when one of us mentioned the Aleutians".

"In the conversation, I mentioned the firing on us, and he said, 'I know, I was the one pulling the lanyard on the gun that fired on you.' He said they were on alert of a possible Jap attack, and the Command had changed the password and hadn't notified our ship. He said we identified just before he was about to fire a third round right in the middle of our ship. I'm glad they didn't". The bombing demonstrated that Japanese secret intelligence was very good about the exact location of US Military bases.

## ATTU ISLAND:

*Alaskan Native Americans were killed and taken as Japanese POWs.*

Alaska Natives are the indigenous people of Alaska. These Native Alaskan tribes include the Aleut, Inuit, Tlingit, Haida, Tsimshian, Eyak, and several northern Athabasca cultures. Natives in Alaska number about 119,241 people (as of the 2000 census). Today, there are two hundred and twenty-nine federally recognized Alaskan villages and five unrecognized Tlingit Alaskan Indian tribes. Many members of these ethnic groups saw death and destruction in Alaska during World War II. Some of these people were taken as prisoners of war (POW) and shipped to Japan, where at least half of them died in captivity. All were prepared to fight if the invasion continued East.

Stretching from Asia to North America, the Aleutian Islands, and the nearby Alaska Peninsula are the home of the Aleuts. Russians introduced the term "Aleut," which originates from the Koryak or Chukchi languages of Siberia. The term *"Aleut"* also appears to have been quickly adopted by the Aleut people.

Aleut comes from the Russian word *"Aleuty."* The Aleut, known as Unangan or Unangas, translates as "we the people." The homelands of the Aleuts include the Aleutian Islands, the Pribilof Islands, the Shumagin Islands, and the far Western part of the Alaskan Peninsula. The natural marine environment defined subsistence, lifestyles, and cultures more than 8,000 years ago.

Nick Golodoff, 2015

When Nick Golodoff was six years old, he and his family were taken from Attu, Alaska, to Otaru, Hokkaido Island, Japan, where they were held captive until the end of World War II. He was ten years old when he returned. More than half of his people, the Aleuts of Attu Island, were killed by the Japanese. He became a prisoner of war at just six years old. He was among the dozens of Unangan Attu residents swept away to Hokkaido and one of only twenty-five to survive.

Nick has written down and documented his memories. Brenda Maly, his granddaughter, transcribed and collected them. The project chronicles the history of four Unangan villages were left vacant after their evacuations and relocations during World War II. These villages were never resettled in Attu after the war. They have been published in his book *Attu Boy*.

On June 7, 1942, the Aleutians were heading home from church when the war fell upon them and permanently changed their lives. Hundreds of Japanese soldiers screamed and fired machine guns as they marched across the hill above the local school. "The muck was flying up from the gunshots," Nick said. As the Imperial Forces came into town, Golodoff, who was six years old, remembers running down the hill with his friend, fleeing Japanese soldiers firing at him. He then realized that

Japanese adult soldiers were trying to kill him and other children.

The Japanese Forces sent the forty-two Attu inhabitants to Otaru, Hokkaido Island, in September 1942, where they lived until the war ended. Many of them perished as a result of hunger and famine. The twenty-five Aleutians who survived were unable to return to their old hamlet. As numerous young people were, those not hospitalized or sent to boarding school relocated to Atka Island.

*ABOVE: Six-year-old Nick Golodoff and his friend were chased down the hill on their way from the church that Sunday morning by Japanese invaders firing at them during the invasion of Attu Island.*

*BEST FRIENDS OF THE ALEUTS:*

### Charles and Etta Jones

For decades, little information was available regarding Charles and Etta Jones' final days on Attu as World War II struck the Aleutian Islands. But Etta's niece, Mary Breu, published the book, *Last Letters from Attu,* which gives remarkable insight into their unique lives.

*ABOVE: Charles Jones, a 60-year-old radio operator and weather observer, was married to Etta Jones, a 62-year-old teacher and trained nurse with their pride and joy, puppy huskies.*

They worked for the Territory of Alaska, serving the native peoples. The couple lived on the island of Attu, in a little hamlet built upon small frame houses near Chichagof Harbor. At the time of the Japanese takeover, the Attu population was just about forty people. Charles and Etta were the only non-natives living on the Island. The rest of the people living there were Aleuts. At that time, no other town or settlement existed on Attu.

The Aleuts could maintain their frail existence by fishing, catching foxes, and weaving baskets, just as they had done for thousands of years. Charles Jones's radio, which he used to communicate with Dutch Harbor, missionaries, government patrol boats, and small fishing ships, was the only direct contact the locals had with the outside world.

In 1897, Charles moved to Seattle to attend Puget Sound University. When the Klondike Gold Rush erupted the following year, he set out for the Chilkoot Pass to join the gold hunting adventure. Initially, he wrote about the food costs, his outfit, and the life of a baker in the Yukon Territory for his hometown newspaper in Washington State. Then he vanished for more than two decades, working on multiple mining claims but never abandoning the country.

While at Tanana on the Yukon River (located about in the middle of the Yukon Territory), Charles met Etta, a New Jersey girl trained as a teacher and nurse. She had gone with her sister to the wilds of Alaska, but her sister didn't stay long. When Charles saw Etta working at the post office, it was love at first sight.

They married on April 1, 1923, mushing off on a dogsled to a trapper's cottage for their honeymoon. At the time, they were both forty-two years old. Mary Breu chronicles the Joneses' journeys across Alaska in the following years. They were sent to remote communities such as Kipnuk and Old Harbor, where they attended one and two-teacher schools, teaching the Yupik people. Etta and Charles would say they learned more critical lessons from the Yupik than the natives probably learned from the Jones.

On the lengthy, rainy boat voyage from Kodiak Island, the Joneses saw the US military presence at Dutch Harbor. With a boat, he could read currents and navigate shoals, and with hand tools, he could build a house and run any generator. He designed and built his own radio and obtained his operator's license. According to Breu, Etta described Charles as a great man and a great partner.

In 1941, they were relocated to the village of Attu by an Alaskan agency to support the Unangas. Before destroying the radio, he yelled, "The Japs are here!"

On the lengthy, rainy boat voyage from Kodiak Island, the Jones saw the US military presence at Dutch Harbor. But they did not for a moment believe the Japanese would be interested in their remote location on the tip of the Aleutian Island chain, even after the Pearl Harbor attack. Because Attu was small and far distant, they thought it was insignificant. However, they sure got a rude awakening! Before the Japanese invaded, Attu was a secure, friendly, and peaceful place to live, despite the harsh weather and slow-monthly mail delivery. The few visitors they received called it heaven. The sea and tundra had plenty of fish, wildfowl, and fruit. The proceeds from the sale of fox fur were dispersed to all residents, young and old. The money was utilized to build houses, fishing boats, and white dress clothes for the children to wear on Sundays when they went to the beautiful Orthodox church.

Charles had barely finished delivering a weather report to Dutch Harbor when the Japanese bombing began. Before destroying the radio, he yelled, "The Japs are here." Until Japan surrendered three years later, those were the last words any citizen of Attu spoke to American officials. Attu was closer to Asia and eastern Russia than the United States mainland. It's about 2000 miles from the US mainland but only 500 miles from Japan. The Joneses were aware of the attack on Pearl Harbor because of Tokyo radio broadcasts.

Fishing was their primary source of food. Bird hunting was done with 22s or shotguns, but bows and arrows were also used. Fighting a thousand-strong Japanese army would have been foolish to do compared to only forty people who lived on Attu. The Attu residents were rounded up, and their homes were searched and ransacked.

Since the Joneses were Americans, they were scrutinized even more closely. Charles was separated from his wife, interrogated, tortured, and then shot in the head. Two Japanese soldiers brought Etta into the school to show her Charles' body, covered in blood. Etta Jones was taken as a civilian prisoner of war and sent to the Yokohama Concentration Camp in Japan together with other US Navy sailors seized by the Japanese on Kiska Island. The Aleuts were held captive in Otaru, Hokkaido, Japan. Etta was lucky enough to be one of the few concentration camp survivors.

*ABOVE: Note in the background that residents of Attu are terrified as the Japanese Imperial Army (JIA) raises their flag with the rising sun icon over Attu, an American sovereign territory.*

## THE FIRST BANZI CHARGE IN WORLD WAR II OCCURRED DURING THE BATTLE OF ATTU:
*Americans were stabbed in their sleeping bags. May 1943*

*ABOVE: Temporary American/Canadian cemetery containing people who died at the Battle of Attu.*

The first Banzai Charge of World War II occurred on Attu. It was the last major battle of the war in Alaska. It gave American soldiers a terrifying taste of Japanese tactics that would become commonplace as American troops fought across the Pacific and Asia. Inconceivable unless being personally there, it involved a mass charge attack from the Japanese forces without concern for their casualties, with yells of "Banzai."

In military terms, the "Banzai Charge" is entirely different and distinct from military charges of European or American origin, such as Pickett's Charge at Gettysburg. In those cases, the tactic was calculated for success. The Japanese Banzai Charge was a last-ditch effort, with the ultimate purpose of suicide, as their Bushido Code commanded. The Banzai Charge was the most feared component of battle with the Japanese. The Banzai Charge on Attu Island is said to have included one of the largest numbers of Japanese personnel of any single advance.

"Banzai," meaning literally, "may you live ten-thousand years." Today, it is used in Japan like the term "Hurray" used in the US. The term is no longer associated with warfare or suicide. Initially, the word was part of the expression "Tennoheikabanzai" meaning "long live the emperor."

By nightfall on May 28, the majority of the American troops were prepared for the decisive assault on Chichagof Harbor. The following morning, General Landrum resolved to complete the battle of Attu with an all-out assault.

When the invasion arrived, Colonel Yamazaki still had approximately 1,000 soldiers capable of bearing weapons out of 2,300 men on hand. His troops would escape out of Chichagof Harbor, killing as they went, to reach the US artillery position on a neighboring hill through Clevesy Pass. He seized the massed howitzers, turned them on the Americans in Massacre Valley, and held them off until the Japanese Imperial Navy (JIN) and the Japanese Imperial Army (JIA), who were miles away, could assist.

The Japanese soldiers who were too severely injured to walk were offered the option of killing themselves with handguns or receiving a fatal injection of morphine. The walking wounded were instructed to arm themselves and accompany them. Few weapons and ammunition were available, and some soldiers were armed simply with bayonets tethered to sticks.

Yamazaki led his troop up the valley around 3 a.m. They attacked the American 32nd Regiment's Company B in the valley and a portion of the 17th Regiment's Company L on top of a hill. This Japanese assault began quietly, with bayonetting Americans while they were in their sleeping bags. Suddenly there was a barrage of gunfire, with grenades bursting all over the place. Company B's befuddled survivors scattered, some sprinting barefoot through the freezing mud.

A tented US Army aid station was overrun by the Japanese, who slaughtered the doctors and those injured in their beds.

Yamazaki's men, however, were engulfed in a state of mass panic. They started shouting and rushing about aimlessly, splitting off into little groups. A couple of the Japanese just sat amid the Americans they had recently murdered, gorging themselves on American food.

The central mass of Japanese soldiers remained together and made it to Clevesy Pass. They smashed into the Division's US Army. The engineers there had formed a defensive line after being alerted by the gunshots below. Even civilian cooks and bulldozer drivers battled with any weapons they could find. Remarkably, the men were able to halt the Japanese in the Pass.

To the Americans, Yamazaki's men's odd conduct became even more insane. After failing to kill enough Americans to prevail, the Japanese resorted to self-destruction. They mostly did this self-destruction with grenades, which they held on their foreheads, breasts, and bellies. The valley was filled with headless, handless, scooped-out bodies at first light. The mass suicide is even more astounding, considering Americans were well-known to be compassionate toward their enemy POWs. The few Japanese who were taken prisoner were taken to hospitals, fed well, and generally well cared for.

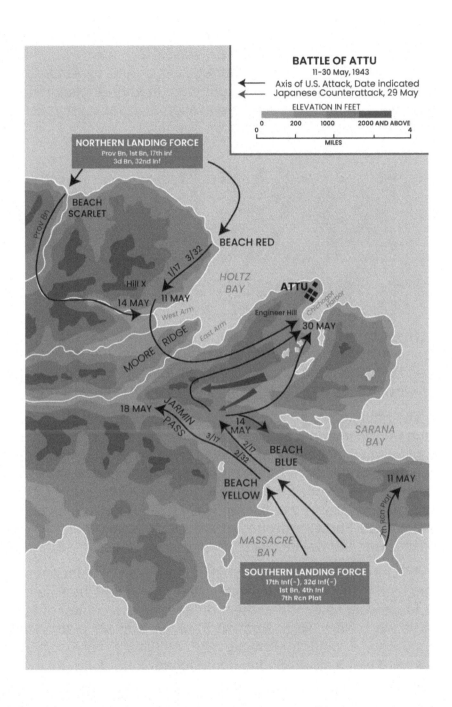

**BATTLE OF ATTU**
11–30 May, 1943

← Axis of U.S. Attack, Date indicated
← Japanese Counterattack, 29 May

ELEVATION IN FEET

| 0 | 200 | 1000 | 2000 AND ABOVE |

0                            4
MILES

**NORTHERN LANDING FORCE**
Prov Bn, 1st Bn, 17th Inf
3d Bn, 32nd Inf

BEACH
SCARLET

Prov Bn

BEACH RED

1/17   3/32

*HOLTZ
BAY*

Hill X

14 MAY   11 MAY

*West Arm*

MOORE   RIDGE

*East Arm*

**ATTU**

*Chichagof Harbor*

Engineer Hill   30 MAY

18 MAY   JARMIN

PASS

3/17   2/17

2/32

14
MAY

BEACH
BLUE

*SARANA
BAY*

BEACH
YELLOW

11 MAY

7th Rcn Plat

*MASSACRE
BAY*

**SOUTHERN LANDING FORCE**
17th Inf(−), 32d Inf(−)
1st Bn, 4th Inf
7th Rcn Plat

119

*OPERATION LANDCRAB:*

*Operation Landcrab was the retaking of Attu by American Northern and Southern Landing Forces. In May-August 1943, the Japanese were eventually encircled, a classic approach, but at a very high cost to American troops.*

*The first conquest of enemy-occupied territory in the Pacific War was American sovereign land. The battle had a special meaning to the US Army since they were fighting to take back American territory.*

The battle for this Aleutian Island was one of the bloodiest in the Pacific in terms of the proportion of soldiers killed. Only twenty-eight Japanese men survived the combat, and nearly all Japanese forces were dead. Around 550 American soldiers were killed in action, 1148 were wounded in battle, and 1814 were injured due to weather or illness. Despite the terrible weather, US Forces surrounded Attu and Kiska in early 1943 and imposed a naval blockade around the islands.

A three-hour battleship combat erupted when the Japanese attempted to breach the blockade in late March, but the smaller US Force was able to fend them off and reclaim control of the sea lanes. Navy Rear Admiral Thomas Kinkaid eventually announced a plan to remove the Aleutian's now-isolated Japanese residents as Spring approached.

After a long bombing campaign, *Operation Landcrab* commenced on May 11, 1943. American troops fought the

Japanese in mountain passes and on desolate hilltops across Attu's swampy environment for the following three days. Yamasaki's men benefited from their excellent defensive positions, even though the US Force had superior numbers regarding Air and Naval support. From their elevated vantage point, they could pound the Americans with machine gun and mortar fire or hurl grenades below.

The weather in the Aleutians was, as usual, a formidable foe. The freezing rain and howling winds affected the GIs greatly, the bulk of whom were not outfitted with cold-weather gear, resulting in thousands of cases of trench foot, frostbite, and gangrene.

In mid-May, the Battle of Attu came to a head when the out-manned Japanese fled to positions near Chichagof Harbor, allowing the American Northern and Southern Forces to join forces. Over the next two weeks, the US pushed forward to reclaim the overrun territory, gradually encircling the Japanese in the Island's Eastern portion. Victories were sometimes counted in yards in these confrontations, which were vicious and violent.

American Forces occupied the high ground in Chichagof Valley in the evening hours of May 28, commanding three key hills: Fish Hook, Buffalo, and Engineer. The Americans planned to bombard the Japanese Forces the next day when they were forced to the sea. When the Americans landed on Attu, Colonel Yamasaki, the Japanese commanding officer, had 2,600 able-bodied soldiers. Yamasaki chose to make a risky advance rather than surrender, which was considered dishonorable.

The Japanese soldiers would attack the Americans at their weakest position, Engineer Hill, and capture their artillery to use against them.

They would then sweep across the Island to Massacre Bay, loot the enemy's supplies, and hide in the highlands until reinforcements arrived. Most Japanese soldiers viewed the strategy as an opportunity for an honorable death.

"What a nightmare, a whirlwind of noise, uncertainty, and looming deadlines," Capt. George S. Buehler reflected on May 29, 1943.

Engineer Hill had a modest number of non-combatant Forces stationed on it. They swiftly prepared a defense consisting of doctors, engineers, and service personnel who began throwing hand grenades at the Japanese under the direction of General Archibald V. Arnold.

The Japanese were unfazed, and fierce hand-to-hand combat broke out as the defenders fought for their lives. The tide turned when the 50th Engineers arrived and used bayonets and rifle butts to drive the assailants back, stopping them from reaching the critical cannon.

Even though the combat went on all day, the Japanese could not mount another concentrated onslaught. Later in the day, Colonel Yamasaki was killed while leading another wave up Engineer Hill. The Battle of Attu would be the Aleutian campaign's most important fight.

**Pvt. William Argyl Anderson, Company K, 32nd Infantry Regiment, 7th Infantry Division**

"During the American invasion's first wave, we boarded the ship again and set sail towards the Bering Sea. The seas were treacherous, with strong waves and the danger of Japanese submarines. We were all ordered to get below decks as the alarm went out, and we could hear our ship launching depth charges. We couldn't do much except hold on as the sea nausea worsened. Suddenly we halted, and while the ship was rolling, we went down the rope ladder and into a landing craft with our weapons in hand. We decided to go to the beach. It was the beginning of May 1943".

"We arrived on two unforgiving, barren islands with only permafrost, fog, terrible weather, and Japanese troops to deal with after the horrible seasickness that most of the men had on the Bering Sea. We walked away from the shore, up the hill, and then climbed down the rope ladder. The ship was rolling, some of the men didn't make it, ending up in the ice-cold water. They froze to death right away. Well, that's war, death, real death. We went up the hill away from the beach, and I later learned we had landed at Holtz Bay, H-O-L-T-Z, and was pinned down by artillery fire. I was in a shallow foxhole and survived the first day. The shooting stopped. We moved on, and within the next day or two, we were caught out in the open. Airplanes appeared overhead and were strafing and dropping bombs".

"The Japanese appeared overhead and were strafing and dropping bombs. Now, this is either the second or third day. We were out in the open, crossing a valley between the beach and the mountains. The mountains are in the background. Me and another soldier were in a bombed-out crater, and I asked him to look up at the planes and see if he could see the Rising Sun on the wings. We looked up together, and I saw it was an American plane bombing us by mistake. A brave soldier took a banner and placed it on the ground to show we were Americans. For several more days, we moved higher into the mountains. It was snowing. We weren't dressed for walking in ice water, we only had leather shoes, and our feet soon became frostbitten. Well, we had two islands; it was a chain island that belonged to the United States. It's territory to the United States. It was taken from us and occupied by the Japanese. Our objective was to take it back from them."

The Commander of the Alaskan Theater was Simon Bolivar Buckner, Jr. His father was Confederate General Simon Bolivar Bucker and a good friend of Gen. Ulysses Grant. General Buckner Jr. successfully planned and executed the Battle of Attu and chased out the Japanese from Kiska Island. Consequently, he has promoted to Commander of the 10th Army but was killed in the Battle of Okinawa in 1945. He was the highest ranking American serviceman killed in World War II.

*Joe Martinez:*
*Attu, 1943 Received the only Medal of Honor in World War II*
*in the North American Theater.*

Joe Martinez was determined to do something huge to save Americans from the evil that had swept across the world. On May 17, 1942, he did what he set out to do. After the Japanese attack on Pearl Harbor, Joe joined the Army, and although Alaska was not his favorite of places, nor was he even familiar with colder climates, he trudged ahead, never knowing what would come next. He thought to himself "It's going to be a long war, but we don't think about that, just one day at a time. If I don't make it back, just know that it was fate and I did what I knew had to be done."

Company K went in search of the Japanese units that were uncomfortably larger than their own. But if his Unit didn't stop them, then who would? Attu Island is a part of America we are here to take back it. He planned on being back home for Christmas, just like they all talked about every day. The outcrops had a lot of places to hide. If they could get the

Japanese out of the rock outcroppings, the company would have an advantage of a two-sided flanking. But their only choice was to climb up over the protective ridge and find the insidious enemy. They understood all too well that the Japanese were waiting for them.

The hill was very steep and contained abrupt sheer cliffs. Joe was always ready and resolute, never waiting for life to happen. He resolved to the reality that if you don't do it, it just won't happen on its own. He could never wait for someone else to do what needed to be done, and this time was no different. The blasts were distinct, but Joe knew that to save his fourteen buddies, he couldn't just echo the typical talk of caution. He climbed the rocky slope, which was not even a trail. The men could feel the presence of the Japanese nearby. It seemed like it took all day; maybe it would be nightfall before they even got over the top. Other companies were doing the same, but Company K couldn't see them. Just the small group of ten.

Some men would be wondering what so few of them were doing slipping into the mouth of death; all of the men were. But Joe always appeared relaxed, calm, and confident, as he knew just where the Enemy would be and what to do once he spotted them. His buddies couldn't believe he even made it to that crest without being killed. Out of the blue, Joe rushed up until he was in the lead.

And we should remember, Joe was a Private, but he was determined to protect his company of fellow soldiers from enemy fire. A higher rank may have more privileges, but the level of command doesn't always determine the soldier's courage or audacity and perhaps not always the commitment as Joe had. As Private Joe Martinez stared down the other side of the rocky mound, his buddies felt the *Crack! Crack! Crack!* They looked; it was Joe firing. He just took out a number of the enemy dug into a kind of foxhole. His buddy yelled to him, 'Hey, Joe watch out! Joe, be careful!' They couldn't believe he wasn't hit then and there. He had an angel looking out for him! Whoever saw that kind of guts? Pure guts and total courage.

As Private Joe Martinez stared down the other side of the rocky mound, his buddies felt the *Crack! Crack! Crack!* It looked and it was Joe firing away. He just took out several enemy soldiers that were dug into a kind of natural foxhole. He had an angel looking out for him!

Silence. This time, a lot of it. A silence and then a *Ratatatataj!* He did it again. He kneed out another group of enemy soldiers. He hit what he meant to shoot but was lucky to be standing there. His brothers tried not to approach the next 300 yards too fast, but the group did anyway. They did it against all instinct. It was the last thing they wanted to do…then they took sniper fire and let them have it back. Slowly, they approached, minute by minute, holding their breath. In front of them was the last thing they ever wanted to see. Then and there was Joe Martinez, lying on the ground. Joe died the next day.

Those that made it back would never forget it as long as they live. What a man he was to give his life so they could live. Who would do that courageous act for his fellow soldiers? Private Joe Martinez attained the highest American Military Honor anyone in the military could receive. As indicated in the Medal of Honor citation, his bravery demonstrated just how extensive an impact one soldier can have. His courage led a pathway through the Japanese stronghold leading to securing this section of the Island. He was the first Hispanic to receive the Medal of Honor in World War II; he was the only American to earn the Medal of Honor for action on US soil outside Pearl Harbor.

His citation for his Medal of Honor reads:

"*For conspicuous gallantry and intrepidity above and beyond the call of duty in action with the enemy. Over a period of several days, repeated efforts to drive the enemy from a key defensive position high in the snow-covered precipitous mountains between East Arm Holtz Bay and Chichagof Harbor had failed. On 26 May 1943, troop dispositions were readjusted and a trial coordinated attack on this position by a reinforced battalion was launched.*

"*Initially successful, the attack hesitated. In the face of severe hostile machine gun, rifle, and mortar fire, Pvt. Martinez, an automatic rifleman, rose to his feet and resumed his advance. Occasionally he stopped to urge his comrades on. His example inspired others to follow. After a most difficult climb, Pvt. Martinez eliminated resistance from part of the enemy position by BAR fire and hand grenades, thus assisting the advance of other attacking elements. This success only partially completed the action. The main Holtz-Chichagof Pass rose about 150 feet higher, flanked by steep rocky ridges and reached by a snow-filled defile. Passage was barred by enemy fire from either flank and from tiers of snow trenches in front. Despite these obstacles, and knowing of their existence, Pvt. Martinez again led the troops on and up, personally silencing several trenches with BAR fire and ultimately reaching the pass itself. Here, just below the knifelike rim of the pass, Pvt. Martinez encountered a final enemy-occupied trench and as he was engaged in firing into it he was mortally wounded. The pass, however, was taken, and its capture was an important preliminary to the end of organized hostile resistance on the island.*"

*ABOVE: Photographed by Don Morfe, August 26, 2000*
*Pvt Joe P. Martinez Burial Site, Ault Cemetery in Ault,*
*Colorado*
*Block 2, Section 15, Lot 1*

## KISKA
*PFC Charlie House and the ten-man Army Metrological Team during the Japanese Invasion*

June 1942

The day Charlie heard about the attack on Pearl Harbor, he went downtown to enlist in the Navy. It didn't matter that he didn't know what it would be like or what he would have to endure. Charlie pushed ahead for his country by learning a new radio communications system, as that would be a meaningful and crucial contribution to the war effort. He imagined being in the South Pacific, transmitting essential details of the enemy's location while saving hundreds of American lives. So, he was surprised when he received his typed-official travel orders to proceed to Dutch Harbor, Alaska. Upon his arrival, he saw Army barracks bombed by the Japanese. He had to stay in the barracks as others did. He was right next to the building where fellow soldiers were suddenly cut down and burned up in a second. War was then absolute, not a newspaper article. It meant death and destruction. "The one state of mind I could not fathom was being dead."

Charlie was assigned to a U.S. Areological Detail in a Communications Shack, the only structure on Kiska Island. All ten of his fellow soldiers lived and worked here. They would report all American or Japanese activities. On Kiska Island at 7:15 am, the sound of silence thickened, and the fog and soggy earth surrounded him. His whole body was shaken. The blast entered the Communications Shack. Instantaneously Charlie's Communications team jaunted out of the Shack. They were suddenly lying in the snow. Charlie hid with a gray blanket that he was clever enough to grab on his way out. His buddies had no choice but to surrender to the Japanese. But Charlie and a few other sailors had that one stroke of luck. It appeared; that fleeting moment when a chance for a break was there, and they took a chance. But not looking back, he expected to be shot in the back at any moment. They separated and ran toward the fog. Charlie stayed low to the ground and ran faster than he knew possible. He survived for an entire month on small plants, and he used the sheet to camouflage himself. After surviving weeks, he was finally caught, taken as a POW, and sent to Japan. Charlie was lucky; he survived the camps and was released at the war's end.

Charlie House interview:

"During this time, I observed the glass cases covering the wind recording instruments breaking from Japanese bullets. As I ran from the building, the first light observed many Japanese landing craft moving up the inner Harbor with machine guns blasting away from their bows. AG2c Turner, who had been outside for a couple of minutes, suggested that we spread out and move up the hill toward the low clouds for cover. As we spread and moved, the Japanese would shoot at us. We would drop down, and they would train on another moving target. The tracer bullets looked like baseballs curving toward us in this early morning light. Luckily for us, we could dodge the tracer, and because of the distance, the tracers had been lighter and higher than the regular bullets, which I could see hitting the dirt short of their mark".

"In about 300 yards, we reached the fog cover and were not visible to the gunners. I scrambled madly up the hill until overcome by exhaustion and lay on the ground for a rest. The sound of footsteps seemed to be closing in. I pressed my ear to the ground and listened to the rhythmic beat, and realized it was my heartbeat. Reason took over, and I analyzed my situation. I was alone, not warmly dressed, but had grabbed a couple of gray blankets as I ran outside".

"The Japanese were landing in force, and I would assume that they would knock out our facilities and leave, so I knew to evade them until they left Kiska. For that day, I moved next to some gray rocks and covered myself with gray blankets, and I did not make a move until darkness. During the day, there was some shooting in different places and a few planes flying around by afternoon. A summer day in Alaska is very long, especially when one is alone, in danger, and your whole world has just pulled out from under you. The goal for the first night was to locate some of the food, a gun and some ammunition that was stashed in a ravine a couple of miles southeast of my present position. "

*Operation Cottage August 1943 Retaking of KISKA-200 Casualties, 71 KIAs*

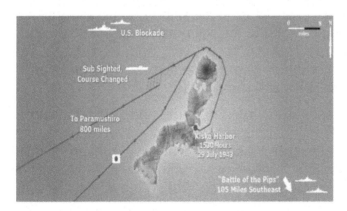

*Upon hearing through apparent intelligence channels of the American invasion, Japan retreats, and the US takes possession of Kiska.*

On August 18, 1943

USS *Abner Read* (DD 526) was on patrol off Kiska Island, Alaska. Although the Japanese had already evacuated Kiska, they left behind sea mines. USS *Abner Read* struck one such mine in the dead of night, and the force of the explosion blew the stern off the ship. The stern quickly sank, taking the lives of 71 crew members and leaving another 47 wounded.

Despite the surprise, shock, and loss of so many of their shipmates, the surviving crew members of the USS *Abner Read* displayed extraordinary courage and determination in saving their ship from the catastrophic damage that, by all rights, should have sunk their entire ship. But the USS Abner Read crew refused to go down without a fight. The crew's absolute refusal to give up their ship, no matter what, inspires the Sailors who serve our Nation today.

Some of the most extreme fog in the world is common in the Aleutians. The "Battle of the Pips" was an attempt to navigate this intense fog by the US Navy Task Group 16.22 under the command of Rear Admiral Griffin, with the *Mississippi* and *Idaho* One of the Battleships upon what was believed to be a Japanese warship. Still, it could never be ascertained due to the intense Alaska fog. A "pip" refers to a small skiff, indicating that there weren't any large ships present, not that a skiff was involved.

*The Alaska Scouts:*
*Castner's Cutthroats.*

A 65-man battalion known as the Alaska Scouts, dubbed Castner's Cutthroats, was one of America's secret armed troops active in the Alaskan War. The Cutthroats were a group of hunters, trappers, surveyors, and frontiersmen entrusted with gathering intelligence while remaining self-sufficient in the harsh Alaskan landscape. The squad was notorious for its loose adherence to military rules. It was led by Captain Robert H. Thompson and Lt. Earl C. Acuff, both collegiate football stars. Individual members of this battalion were given the option of using .22 pistols, bolt-action hunting rifles, or the widely available Army-issued Garands (semiautomatic M-1 rifles) as standard issued guns. Giving this preference for a weapon was unusual in the Army.

Trapper Nelson Packs held their minimum supplies, and their clothes were a mix of Army-issued and Alaskan cold-weather gear with no insignia. On May 11, 1943, the order was given for *Operation Landcrab* to retake Attu, with Kiska being the second target. The Cutthroats were the first to go!

They paddled to Attu in rubber boats, launched from submarines offshore. Their purpose was to conduct reconnaissance for the central large Army Invasion Force. They quickly took up positions and drew enemy fire while being outmanned a hundred to one. The Cutthroats lost one of their members during this first engagement.

The entire fifteen-thousand-man American Offensive Force was able to establish a beachhead. But the peace was short-lived. The Japanese had built emplacements on high terrain. The weather was bitterly cold, with fog, snow, and rain conspiring to slow down American progress and resupply. Nearly one thousand Americans were killed and an estimated 3000 injured in the Battle of Attu. Many succumbed to frostbite, sickness, and Japanese booby traps.

Weather was critical in warfare, but in Alaska, it could determine the survival of an Army. Even the D-Day Normandy landings on 6 June 1944 had been postponed due to the Allied weathermen predicting massive squalls and storms. In the days of World War II, no technology existed to observe and predict the Earth's weather patterns as it does today. Teams of military meteoritic specialists were deployed to combat theaters to ascertain the next day's conditions. However, surprises seemed to materialize overnight throughout Alaska, often impeding the next day's strategy. At times the weather was the greatest enemy of the Aleutians.

If you'd call a native American that wasn't from the north an "Eskimo," they may find it offensive since they don't belong in that group at all. But for, the native people that actually *do come* from the very northern hemisphere in America, Greenland, Northern Canada, Alaska, and Russia, all fall under the broad group called "Eskimo." I understand some have disputed the term "Eskimo."

This includes the groups of the Inuit, Iñupiat, Yupik and sometimes also the Aleut. It's a terminology used to categorize all these groups into one. Like the terminology British includes smaller groups of Welsh, Scottish and English, a term stemming from the islands' name, the British Isles.

The ATG, at times, refers to native Alaskans, who could be Eskimos (various groups) or Native Americans that may not have originated in the northern climate. There were some whites in the ATG as well. Maj Marvin Martson refers to "Eskimos and Indian villages." He was very sensitive to the cultures of the various people he worked with. After the war, he lobbied the state and federal governments for minority rights in Alaska as a territory and as a state. He wrote about these issues in his book, *Men of the Tundra*.

*The Sound of Silence:*
*Thanks to the Eskimo and Native Guard*
*Alaskan Territorial Guard*

*ABOVE: Major Marvin "Muktuk" Marston, Commander of the Alaskan Territorial Guard "Securing the outposts, one hundred and fifty-four Eskimo and Indian villages were key to the Japanese success. Once the enemy took the outposts, we would be forced to surrender all of Alaska to them.". Muktuk is the Eskimo term for whale blubber the Major could never get enough of and was therefore given that nickname.*

The Alaskan Territorial Guard (ATG) consisted of volunteers who didn't need any supervision of their fiercely defended areas. These men and some women knew this land well. This was where they were born and raised. If the JIN did decide to invade, it would find no regular US Army or Navy defense but would be up against an armed populous. Rumors traveled fast through fishing boat sailors of American, Canadian, Russian and Japanese origin. The Japanese probably knew the Alaskan population was well-armed which deterred them from invading the mainland of Alaska from the Bering Sea.

The ATG even shot down eighteen Japanese balloon bombs threatening their homeland. And these were shot down by rifle only. The only other case of such a Japanese weapon being shot down was over California by an AFF fighter plane. It was not with a rifle. This feat was repeated on eighteen occasions, demonstrating the remarkable ability of the native Alaskan to shoot with incredible accuracy. It also reflects their tenacity in defending their land.

According to an official roster, 6,368 unpaid volunteers from 107 villages across Alaska were enrolled, and a paid staff of 21. The ATG brought together members of the many ethnic groups for the first time in a collaborative effort: Aleut, Athabaskan, White, Inupiaq, Haida, Tlingit, Tsimshian, Yupik, and others. Many members of the troops were designated as expert sharpshooters. Sniping was the best defense if a Japanese contingent landed on their shores. The people worked hard to be prepared for this eventuality.

In the Postwar Era, the Alaskan Territorial Guard was often assumed to be just another State National Guard. Nothing could be further from the truth. Unlike the National Guard, the ATG was not paid a cent, yet many Eskimos and Native Americans volunteered to safeguard their homeland.

There were at least twenty-seven female ATG members. Member ages ranged from 12 to 80 years old at the time of enrollment, with both extremes of ages occurring mostly in sparsely populated areas. Members of the ATG served as volunteers because they were either too young or too elderly to be drafted during World War II. According to one estimate, over 20,000 Alaskans engaged in ATG reconnaissance or support actions.

Although the Army appealed to Native Alaskans to defend the area, many volunteered before being asked. Major Marston was in charge of dogsled operations into hundreds of miles of vast wilderness, often without a road or trail and in complete darkness. His mission was to arm the Native Peoples, who he held in the highest regard. He was delivering piles of rifles and ammunition and information to the closest radio communication outlet, which was usually hundreds of miles away.

It was not hard to lose your life in the territory in those days. There were endless hazards in traveling by dogsled, the least of which was finding your destination in the endless plains of blinding snowdrifts or getting lost in the blackness of night. Unlike today, there was very little in the way of patrols or communications.

The arduous dogsled team was headed by the diehard Alaskan Husky, Blackie. These trusty super dogs were unlike any others had ever seen before. Even if it meant compromising their safety, the sled dog's loyalty was unshakable. Marston's year-long aim was to visit every community. He had no means of locating many villages except a rough map and compass. If the trail had been traveled, Blackie might find it, even if covered by two feet of snow. Martson, like the villagers he was traveling to, relied on whale and fish for survival. Some villages had a few white settlers; others had never seen a white person before.

Marvin "Muktuk" Marston gets his name from the Eskimo word "muktuk," which means "whale blubber." Even though women were enlisted in violation of restrictions, the men didn't seem to mind at all. "Some people [women] are capable of firing a rile as good as any man," exclaimed ATG Veteran Sgt.1st Class Sam Jackson. Maj Martson wholeheartedly agreed that some women were very good with a rifle, and there was no reason not to include them.

Maj. Marston was tasked with visiting all 153 Eskimo settlements in the state and recruiting individuals for the new Army mission when Japanese troops attacked the Aleutian Islands in June 1942.

The Alaskan Natives were trained in Army tactics after being recruited so that they could defend the territory in case of an invasion. They fashioned fake weapons out of barrels and wood to trick Japanese planes passing overhead. Nighttime darkness was imposed across the communities to prevent an enemy attack. The villagers would see planes they could not identify. They were assumed to be Japanese recon planes by the Army. Air traffic was sparse, and those who did fly were typically known over the villages. This was apparently secret history of America under attack in WWII.

As a young man, Sgt. 1st Class Jackson helped keep windows covered at night so that light could not be seen outside. "They urged us to keep to our training because it would save our lives," Jackson said of his Army instructors, who provided the scouts with rifles, uniforms, snowshoes, and other items.

Years later, Maj. Marston stated in his book, "*Men of the Tundra: Alaska Eskimos at War,*" that scouts were critical in protecting the territory surrounding the Lend-Lease Air Route. The US used to transfer aircraft to its Russian ally.

The scouts were finally recognized for their service and given veteran status when President George W. Bush signed a bill into law in 2000, directing his Defense Secretary to grant honorable discharges to Alaskan Natives who were the ATG. The Alaska Department of Military and Veterans Affairs organized a task force to educate and assist former military members, their families, and dependents on how to get the benefits.

Soon thereafter, funds were set aside by the federal government to ensure that thousands of Alaskans who volunteered to defend the area were recognized. As statues and plaques began to be unveiled across the state in 2012, a group of US military veterans in neighboring Bethel used the money to build a memorial park to remember the Alaska Territorial Guard soldiers.

A former Army sergeant who served in the Vietnam War, Stanley Rodgers said he is related to at least seventy former Alaska Territorial Guard members. He was born and raised in Bethel, Alaska. He claimed that those relatives would tell him stories about Japanese ships off the coast of the Bering Sea or spies who had landed. They would quietly slip onto the shore and scout. Those Japanese landings remained secret from the public.

Rodgers asserted that "Everyone was a sentry," he said. He claimed that if the Japanese had invaded, they would have faced heavy resistance in a hostile environment. "They would have never made it. [The Alaska Territorial Guard] would have beaten them back."

As he stood next to a monument of an Eskimo Scout in Bethel, observing a wall of plaques within the memorial park, Rodgers said the site isn't just to memorialize what the scouts did. Still, it should also inspire future generations to sacrifice for their country.

*UNIMAK AND SANAK ISLAND: The SS John Straub killing 55 men and sunk on April 19, 1944*

SS John Straub's Merchant Ship was a 7,176-ton Liberty class, a U.S. Maritime Commission Emergency Cargo Vessel.

These were designated EC2-S-C1 ships, built and completed on November 27, 1943. Hundreds were completed by the Kaiser Shipbuilding Company and the Oregon Shipbuilding Corp. Shipyard in Portland, Oregon, for the US Maritime Commission. It was assigned to the Alaska Steamship Company in Seattle, Washington.

On April 19, 1944, the unescorted SS *John Straub* was en route from Seattle, Washington, to the Aleutians with 25,000 barrels of diesel, 9,000 barrels of high-octane aviation fuel, and other supplies. The ship had a crew of 68 men on board, consisting of 41 Merchant Mariners and 27 Navy Armed Guards. There was also one passenger onboard, making sixty-nine members on the ship.

The SS *John Straub* was hit by a torpedo fired by Japanese submarine *I-180* about a hundred miles east of Dutch Harbor, Alaska. As a result of this hit, the ship broke in two. The ship's forward section sank in about two minutes, while the ship's rear didn't sink until about fourteen hours later. The explosion caused forty Merchant Mariners, fourteen Navy Armed Guards, and one passenger to perish. Only two Merchant Mariners and thirteen Navy Armed Guards managed to escape the disaster. Japanese submarine *I-180* was sunk one week later, on April 26, 1944, by the USS *Gilmore* (DE-18).

*Adak Island, Amchitka Island, Atka Island, and Buldir Island*

The Japanese discovered the presence of US Forces on Adak Island on the 30th of September. Single Japanese bombers attacked Adak Island early in the morning on the 1st and 2nd of October. However, no American deaths occurred. Amchitka and Atka Islands runway construction were bombed. Runways were being constructed while under Japanese fire. According to the US Army Corps of Engineers, entire asphalt plants were built on each of the Islands, with runways being a thousand feet long. The Japanese had landed on these Islands to survey them, and a small Japanese vessel was sunk off Adak Island in early 1942.

In June 1942, US troops landed on Adak and set up operating bases. Adak is an Aleutian Island 200 miles from Kiska. After building an airstrip in only two weeks, they started frequent bombing flights over Kiska and Attu.

The North Pacific's rain, strong waves, and fog made it impossible for planes to fly safely, while ground soldiers were exposed to high winds and bone-chilling cold. In January 1943, when US troops seized the island of Amchitka, they were struck by a "williwaw," a strong Alaskan storm that destroyed or stranded many of their ships.

Even on warm days, the weather was often too extreme to operate in. "There was a gauge to measure the wind," Dashiell Hammett, a writer who served as a US Army corporal in the Aleutians, wrote. "But it only measured up to 110 miles per hour, which was not always enough."

In 1988, the remains of a World War II soldier were found on Buldir Island, a very desolate Alaskan island. In Wisconsin, the relatives of this soldier, Cpl. Carl E. Houston prepared for a solemn homecoming forty-three years after he disappeared. The exact cause of his death is unknown, but he is listed as a World War II casualty. There was a weather and observation station on Buldir, a volcanic island that lies between Attu and Kiska Islands. Japanese invaders may have killed him.


### The ALCAN HIGHWAY

A huge highway was built to facilitate the movement of troops, military vehicles, and supplies of all kinds from the US. It was called the Alaskan-Canadian highway or the ALCAN. It begins at the junction with several Canadian highways in Dawson Creek, British Columbia, and runs to Delta Junction, Alaska. When it was completed in 1942, it was approximately 1700 miles long. African American Regiments, the 93rd, 95th and 97th were part of the seven construction regiments of the Army Corps of Engineers tasked with the project. It took over 10,000 men to build the most difficult highway in America over steep mountain passes.

## The SOVIET CONNECTION

It would be an omission if I did not mention the Alaskan-Siberian Route (ALSIB) route and the tremendous transfer of extensive military hardware, medical supplies and food from the United States to the Soviet Union during the War. Much of it moved through this route and the North Atlantic to the Arctic Circle. In both cases, many American lives were lost in the transportation. U-boats attacked many ships in the North Atlantic, while pilots would crash over Alaska and Siberia due to unpredictable weather conditions. Russian military historians now concede that the extent of the American Lend-Lease assistance to the Soviet Union during the war was considerable. In their view, the Lend-Lease Program had many positive aspects, one of which was delivering aircraft via the Alaskan-Siberian Route (ALSIB).

In the early months of the war with Germany, the Red Air Force was virtually decimated. However, the Soviet aircraft industry moved a large number of its plants, allowing the Air Force to oppose German pressure on the retreating Red Army. As the Red Air Force was reorganized and expanded throughout the war, Lend-Lease supplies were likewise bolstered. Over fourteen thousand Lend-Lease aircraft contributed significantly to the Soviet war effort. It is believed that the American Lend-Lease Program supplied around 12% of all aircraft in the Soviet Union.

*World War II US Army Western Defense Command insignia.*

# CALIFORNIA

*BELOW: A Newspaper headline following the Night of Panic in San Francisco*

*"They were enemy planes. I mean Japanese planes."*

*General DeWitt, Commander of the US Army Western Defense Command, December 9, 1941*

*"There was an actual attack," Brigadier General William Ord Ryan.*

Marshall Law was in effect on the West Coast. State and civilian municipal governments didn't have any legal power over the military. Lieutenant General John L. DeWitt came to

San Francisco's City Hall on the 9th, just days after the Pearl Harbor assault, to address an emergency meeting of the city's Civil Defense Council.

Brigadier General William Ord Ryan, commander of the IV Interceptor Command, confirmed DeWitt's allegations of Japanese planes flying over the city. "It was a genuine attack," Ryan explained.

Despite being spread hundreds of miles over Western Command, his fighter aircraft was the only defense against any air assault. "A big fleet has been spotted approaching the Golden Gate. It wasn't a practice run for an airstrike. It was the real deal. The plane came in from the water and then circled back.

"You don't send aircraft up until you know what the adversary is doing and where they are going," Ryan said when asked if his interceptors had gone up to confront the invaders. "And you don't send planes up in the dark until you know what you're doing."

Out of the Army's restricted number of three-star generals, DeWitt was the highest commander in the West, responsible for the defense of the 1,300-mile coastlines of the three Pacific coastal states and the more than 6,000-mile coastline of the Territory of Alaska. Only 48 hours ago, the Japanese attack on Pearl Harbor shocked and enraged the country, but many on the West Coast were particularly traumatized.

Ryan's statement that the IV Interceptor Command had no idea what the adversary was up to apart from flying over the West's second-largest city nor what his command was up to did little to submerge popular fears. Ryan kept his planes grounded on several occasions, most notably several months later on the night of February 24-25, 1942, when "1,400 rounds from antiaircraft guns met mystery airplanes" flying over Los Angeles with no interceptors.

*ABOVE: As San Francisco braces for the attack, aircraft sound detectors sweep the sky. Anti-Aircraft Weapons are tested.*

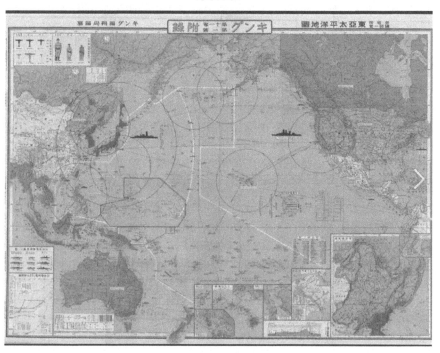

*ABOVE: Japanese plans to attack the United States, showing the occupation of the Aleutian Islands and Hawaii before attacking California, Oregon, and Washington. Map manufactured by the Gunki Company of Japan, as written on the center top line.* Before the Japanese invasion of much of China, Southeast Asia, Indonesia, and a great area of the Pacific islands, this is an early map.

Sighting of the Japanese Submarine I-25

According to the Daily Breeze story, a young fisherman on a barge one mile off Redondo Beach Municipal Pier thought he heard motors nearby that night. At the same time, a lookout stationed in Palos Verdes Estates reported a submarine periscope 4,000 yards off the Redondo Beach Pier. "Around midday on Christmas Day, Gun Battery F, stationed at the end of the Redondo Beach Pier, started firing its 175mm cannon where the submarine was reported to be sheltering."

The submarine chaser, *Amethyst*, rushed up from San Pedro, immediately joining the gunners, while a Navy dive-bombing squadron swooped in from Los Alamitos Air Station. From land, air, and water, they bombarded their target. The relentless shelling shook people's homes as they ate their holiday dinners. Many others thought a full-fledged assault was about to begin. According to the 1991 account, the "Army said the submarine was probably sunk and rewarded Battery F with an official commendation."

Don Young, a historian who resided in Rancho Palos Verdes for twenty-four years, asserts that there was no submarine. "What onlookers mistook for a periscope turned out to be a chimney on the roof of a sinking fishing boat."

Dennis Shanahan depicts the subject in *Old Redondo: A Pictorial History of Redondo Beach, California.* "It would be encouraging if the study could establish Battery F's claim to fame, that they fought an enemy ship," says the researcher. It would have been better if there was confirmation that there wasn't a Japanese submarine two miles out near the deep-sea trench, with its commander peering ashore through the rain, debating whether or not to bring the war home to America.

The best assessment was that Japanese submarines were spotted off the coast in December 1941, but they did not return to Japan to file reports on their conduct. It's plausible that something like this happened.

Following the attack on Pearl Harbor, the Japanese submarine *I-17* headed to a patrol post off the coast of Cape Mendocino. The USS *Emidio*, a 6912-ton General Petroleum tanker, cruised from Seattle, Washington, to San Pedro, California.

In the early afternoon of December 20, 1941, the Japanese submarine *I-17* fired five 14 centimeters (5.5 in) shells at the USS *Emidio* tanker. The tanker was within sight of shore, and the survivors used lifeboats to reach the Blunt Reef lightship. The tanker sank on rocks off Crescent City, California, and stayed there until 1959, when it was demolished. Imperial Japanese submarines were strategically stationed around the West Coast of North America in locations thought to be most suited for attacking trade routes utilized by American commercial ships.

Near the international border between the United States and Canada, the Japanese submarine *I-26* was at the Strait of Juan de Fuca in Washington. It sunk the USS *Coast Trader* six months after the Pearl Harbor attack. Official records show that the *I-25* went from its normal Pacific Northwestern Theater of Action, as mentioned above, to at least as far south as Point Arguello on the California coast.

Ships sunk or damaged by Japanese submarines in early 1942 were the *Barbara Olson (escaped)*, *Agwiworld* (escaped), *Emidio* (sank), *Somoa (escaped)*, *Montebello(sank)*, *Absaroka (damaged)*, *Larry Doheny(sank)*, *Mauna Ala,* USAT *General Gorgas*, and *Idaho* (damaged),*Ft Camosun (sank)*, *Connecticut* (damaged), *Dorothy Phillips* (damaged), *H.M. Storey* (escaped, sank later),*Camden (sank)*, *John A. Johnson (sank)*, *Rockford (damaged)*,and sunk a Soviet *L-16* submarine just of the Oregon Coast.

## The SS Emidio, Cape Mendocino, CA

The SS *Emidio* was sailing in ballast from Seattle, Washington, en route to San Pedro, California.

The SS *Emidio* was found off Cape Mendocino on the early afternoon of December 20, 1941, immediately attacking with its 14cm deck gun. Realizing that the situation was futile, Captain Farrow of the SS *Emidio* raised a white flag and ordered to abandon ship. Ignoring the surrender, the Japanese Submarine *I-17* continued firing from its deck gun, blasting three crew members who were lowering a lifeboat overboard. Four crew members remained on board including a radio operator and three engineers. The *I-17* fired a torpedo which struck the engine room and killed two of the engineers and injured the third. In total, the *I-17* hit the tanker with five shells from its 14 cm deck gun and one torpedo killed five crew members.[1]

A Catalina flying boat of 44 Patrol Squadron attacked *I-17* with depth charges, but the submarine dove and escaped. The United States Coast Guard cutter *Shawnee* rescued the remaining 31 survivors who had rowed 16 hours to Humboldt Bay. The abandoned tanker drifted north and broke upon the rocks off Crescent City. The bow drifted into the harbor, where it lay until scrapped in 1959. The remains of the hull are still in the harbor, near a commemorative plaque. The site has been declared a California Historical Landmark #497.

## Absaroka, Palos Verdes

On Christmas Day, 1941, the Japanese submarine *I-19*, under the command of Lieutenant Commander Narahara Shogo, torpedoed and missed the lumber schooner *Barbara Olson* steaming toward San Diego.

Later that day, off Point Fermin near San Pedro, the *I-19* fired a torpedo and damaged the McCormick Steamship Company's 5,695-ton American lumber carrier *Absaroka*. The steamship was towed and beached at Fort MacArthur. The sub chaser USS *Amethyst* (PYC-3), on patrol off the Los Angeles Harbor entrance, dropped depth charges at the *I-19*, but without effect.

In the January 26, 1942 issue of Life magazine, movie actress Jane Russell was featured in the full-page "Picture of the Week," standing in the tremendous hole in *Absaroka*'s hull created by the Japanese torpedo. In the picture, she is holding a poster that warns: "A slip of the lip may sink a ship," with the words "may sink a ship" crossed out and the words "may have sunk this ship."

ALL THE NEWS ALL THE TIME

LARGEST HOME-DELIVERED CIRCULATION
LARGEST ADVERTISING VOLUME

MAdison 2345
The Times Telephone Number

IN THREE PARTS — 36 PAGES

Part I — GENERAL NEWS — 20 Pages

TIMES OFFICE
202 West First Street

# Los Angeles Times

# ARMY SAYS ALARM REAL

| U.S. Flyers Reap Indies Victories | Storm Grows Over Delay in Alien Ouster | INFORMATION, PLEASE *(Editorial)* | Five Deaths Laid to Raid Blackout | Roaring Guns Mark Blackout |
|---|---|---|---|---|
| Sink Two Transports and Destroy Three Planes; MacArthur Breaks Lull by Successful Attacks; American-British Airmen Blast Foe in Burma | Telegraphic Pleas Sent to Obtain Ueging Action; | In view of the considerable public excitement and concern aroused by yesterday morning's supposed enemy air raid over this area and its spectacular official accompaniments, it seems to The Times that more specific public information should be forthcoming from government sources on the subject, if only to clarify their own understanding statements about it. The first-hour blackout was ordered by the Army's 4th Interceptor Command and the ensuing heavy and long con- | Traffic Accidents and Heart Attacks Take | Identity of Aircraft Veiled in Mystery; No Bombs Dropped and No Enemy Craft Hit; |

## The "Battle" of Los Angeles

Shocking stories appeared on the front page of the Los Angeles Times the next day.

Hundreds of people in Los Angeles observed dozens of planes and a hundred lights in the night sky. Army anti-air defenses went to an all-out blast of everything they had. It was not a real battle on the 23rd of February 1942, at least not as far as anyone can tell today. There were no Japanese planes or plane parts discovered.

According to Army Chief of Staff George Marshall, who addressed a memo to President Franklin D. Roosevelt, stating that the planes were real, but the bombs themselves had not been discovered. It is now assumed that the shells hitting houses that night were stray American anti-aircraft casings. The Army, as well as journalists, questioned a large number of witnesses. Lights in the sky were seen by US Army personnel and civilian observers.

When George and Ann Watson awoke in the early morning hours at their Santa Monica home, they were astonished and perplexed to find what had heard burst nearby. A large cannon shell was buried in our driveway. It was a huge crater. The shell was buried three feet into the soil. They thought, "this is a Japanese bombing!" "Is it going to go off and kill all of us?" Ann recalled "A dazzling flash caught my attention, followed by a hissing sound." As a burning odor permeated the room, George recognized there was a bomb on the driveway. When the officers arrived, they discovered an unexploded bomb in a dug-out shell.

Large shards of whirling fire also destroyed the Selas Sakellaris residence at 1730 W 43rd Place in Santa Monica. Their bedroom wall had collapsed. A shocking blast cut at least four sections of their house. After being stunned by the attack on Pearl Harbor, the Sakellaris family assumed that Los Angeles was under Japanese shelling.

Goldie Wagner was carrying milk to her company's regular customers that morning. She slammed on the brakes without warning as a vehicle without headlights arrived in front of her. Headlights were forbidden in order to deny any enemy aircraft from having a night target.

"The planes were the enemy," according to Army Chief of Staff George Marshall, a Five-Star General who wrote in an emergency memo to President Franklin D. Roosevelt. The military didn't have any planes in the air, and not a single commercial plane could be verified. In any case, commercial planes would never fly in a squadron formation as was witnessed. No tangible evidence was even found to determine the origin of the lights in the sky that night. One theory, although never proven, is that the Japanese had no intention of bombing at first, but they were testing the reaction of the anti-aircraft response to plan for future bombings.

The "Battle of Los Angeles" is commemorated every year on February 23rd at Fort MacArthur in San Pedro, California. A few eyewitnesses speak to the audience about the events of 1942, World War II music and dinner are provided.

*Santa Barbara Area, California, attacked on February 23, 1942.*

*The Ellwood Oilfield in Goleta, CA, under attack from Japanese Submarine I-17, terrified many residents.*

The Real Thing.

The Imperial Japanese Navy submarine *I-17* patrolled north of Oahu during the attack on Pearl Harbor on December 7, 1941. Around sunset on February 23, 1942, the *I-17* arrived just north of Santa Barbara. It surfaced and fired its deck gun at the Tideland's oil-production facilities grouped along the coast on the Ellwood Oil field. The field had several oil wells in production at the time. The target did not appear to have any strategic military significance for the Japanese to bomb. However the psychological impact on the public was huge.

At 7:15 pm, the *I-17*, commanded by Captain Kozo Nishino, started shooting at the shore. Locals in Goleta, California, reported sixteen to twenty-nine shells being fired, with at least three of them hitting near the oil refinery. A well that was approximately 1,000 yards inland had its rigging and pumping equipment damaged, but no further damage was done.

That Sunday evening, Nobukiyo Nishino, a lieutenant on the *I-17* (a big ocean-going Imperial Japanese Navy submarine with a range of 6,000 miles between refueling stops) came to a halt in front of Ellwood Field around 7:00 pm on February 23, 1942. Nishino ordered the deck gun ready to be fired. Its crew aimed just beyond the shore at a Richfield aviation fuel tank and opened fire about 15 minutes later. The first rounds hit near a storage facility. A deadly sound!

Most of the oilfield workers had gone home for the day, but a skeleton staff on duty heard the rounds shot by the I-17. One man noticed the *I-17* off the coast. Still, they assumed it was an internal explosion. G. Brown, an oilfield worker, later told reporters that the submarine appeared to be so large to him that he thought it was a cruiser or destroyer until he noticed only one gun was firing.

Nishino quickly directed his soldiers to the second storage tank. As the Japanese shells continued to rain around them, Brown and the others called the sheriff. The shells missed their target due to firing on a submarine buffeted by waves in the dark.

Laurence Wheeler, the proprietor of Wheeler's Inn, immediately called the Santa Barbara County Sheriff's Office after one of the rounds sailed over his property. He was told that the Army Air Force was already on their way with a deputy sheriff, but no one had arrived.

A derrick and a pump house were demolished by Japanese shells, and the Ellwood Pier and catwalk were damaged. The gunners stopped firing after 20 minutes, and the submarine drifted away. The number of explosive shells launched was estimated to be between 12 and 25. Even though he only did minor damage, Lt. Nishino had accomplished his goal of instilling dread along the American West Coast.

J.J. Hollister III was ten years old when he was startled by the sound of a distant cannon while listening to one of President Franklin D. Roosevelt's "fireside chats." "We heard a whistling noise and a thump as a projectile hit near the home in a matter of seconds," Hollister recalls. Bright flashes near an oilfield on the beach startled the family outside their Winchester Canyon home. "An odd whistling and caterwauling" were heard after some of the gunfire, according to Hollister. "It was a horrifying noise."

*Rutledge "Putty" Alexander Mills, Goleta Resident*

*Photo by Rafael Maldonado, Santa Barbara News-Press*

*"Putty" would serve in Europe and the Pacific in the 331st Artillery Battalion of the 86th Infantry Division.*

When I interviewed Rutledge Alexander Mills (nicknamed "Putty") on August 25. 2020, he was buoyant as always, and his memory was as clear as if World War II had been yesterday. He spoke of his incredible life and unique experiences. At 17 years old, "Putty" had an exciting life in Hollywood, building movie sets and meeting some of the biggest stars at the time, such as Gabby Hayes, Roy Rogers, Dale Evans, and many others.

On the night of February 23, 1942, around 2 am, just weeks before moving to Hollywood, "Putty" was fast asleep at his parents' house when suddenly "all hell broke loose and I was within stone's throw of the terrifying shelling."

He continued, "We really couldn't tell what was going on until the next morning. No one was really sure what was happening. We heard loud sounds. Everyone was so tense and stressed out due to the recent horrific attack on Pearl Harbor just a few months earlier. I was right in the middle of the shelling of Ellwood vicinity. I heard the explosions all around me. I clearly heard shells hitting the ground and hitting fences. People were all confused and didn't really know what to think. People wondered, 'Was it a Japanese attack?' I think they just knew it was just that. I recall the flashes and strange noises."

The next morning, the residents of Goleta met their worst fears. It was indeed a Japanese attack on their hometown.

"Japs had monitored the Coast for decades, but few actually landed unexpectedly. I believe some spies did land over the years to recon. I believe FDR and the government knew Japan was getting ready for a war with us. From Southern California up the whole Coast to Canada and Alaska to the tip of the Aleutian Islands, the Japanese were taking measurements and observing our shoreline. And on February 23, 1942, World War II was going on right here near Santa Barbara!

"After I graduated from Santa Barbara High School during the war, I applied to be a fighter pilot. At the time, most kids idolized fighter pilots, and I was ready to take the two-day test to become one of them. Out of two million people in the military, the officer told me that I had the best scores; I guess I was pretty good. By the time my training was over, the war was just about finished. I never actually got to fight in the sky. I was assigned to the 331st Artillery battalion of the 86th Infantry Division. We were in Europe around the time of the Battle of the Bulge. I was then assigned to the Philippines for the last year of the war as cleanup, but we still took ground fire every day from enemies."

"Putty" now lives in Santa Barbara, where he loves the magnificent views and his family's ranch. A gray go-cart-looking vehicle with a NASA emblem on the front stands near his barn to the untrained eye. As he spoke, he disclosed that this was the Lunar Rover prototype he constructed for American astronauts to practice driving before their journey to the moon in 1972 during the Apollo 17 mission.

"NASA spent $41 million for four lunar rovers," "Putty" claimed, pleased that he saved the government millions of dollars. "I constructed two of them that the astronauts trained with, using leftover military materials that cost approximately $2,000 apiece," he added.

*George Goman, Navy Intelligence Officer, Southern California*

In a letter discovered by the Santa Barbara library in their files and sent to me, George Goman described his experience at Goleta. This is the only document found that includes a sighting several days before a Japanese sub was discovered on the Santa Barbara Coast. We are very grateful to the Santa Barbara Library and Archives for providing us with this letter that reflects valuable hidden history of the Santa Barbara attack. Research will be ongoing with regard to Mr. Tompkins or Frank Prince. This letter has never been previously published to the best of my knowledge. The George Gorman letter states that "five or six days before the attack, I witnessed a submarine surface." This sighting was previously undocumented.

George W. Goman

736 North Doheny Drive

Los Angeles, California 90069

August 23rd, 1965.

Dear Mr. Tompkins,

Thanks for your interesting letter and thank Frank Price for me please. I have written a brief account of the incident in an as yet unpublished book of memoirs mostly about Madison Square Garden and a series of espionage cases I worked on in The Pacific later than 1943.

The lady you mention was a pest and unreliable with a wild imagination as I remember her.

In the first place the shelling took place directly opposite the building of the Barndall Oil Company at Ellwood, West of Goleta. It was on the final evening I believe of a three-day Washington's Birthday holiday and the important thing—almost surely the reason for the time selected—was that it was during the broadcast of an important fireside chat of President Roosevelt's.

As Frank has told you I'm sure, a large part of our job up there was to establish anti-submarine lookouts along the coast of Venture and Santa Barbara Counties. In some places we actually had towers erected. One of the employees at Barndall Oil, as I recall he was a sort of office manager, acted as our lookout in that area. In fact, I appointed himself myself several weeks earlier. This man lived on the premises in a very small house as I remember it and was intelligent and anxious to help. The Barndall Company's dock is directly on an unusually deep channel, which goes right to the shore there and this very dock was used in pre-World War One days for Japanese tankers to load oil from the field to take back to Japan. Some years ago, I read an account in a New York paper of a story told by the captain of the submarine, which did the shelling, telling that he'd been a member of one of those tankers' crews and knew the whole area intimately. He confirmed that the shelling had been to coincide with Roosevelt's speech. I had this clipping and may still have it but as I write this tonight I can't find it. If I come across it, I'll have a copy made and send it to you.

About 6 or 7 days prior to shelling I had a phone call from the Barndall lookout, that he had just seen a submarine surfaced right off his dock with men on deck and a big cannon very clearly outlined. He said that he had called two other employees and they'd all seen the sub and that about two minutes later it started to move off and quickly submerged. I jumped in my car at about 11 A. M., right after getting the call after asking someone in the office, possibly Frank Price, to check with San Diego by phone or teletype and see if it was one of our subs and let me know at Barndall. By the time I got there, there was nothing to be seen but I interviewed all three men and knew their story was accurate. I'd brought along a book of whole page drawings of Jap subs and all three immediately identified one type as what they'd seen, a very big submarine by the way, with a five-inch gun mounted on deck. While I was there the office called me to say that no U. S. Navy sub had been in the area.

I went back to the office and spoke to San Diego myself, giving the type of vessel and all details. The Barndall lookout promised to keep a sharp eye out for any further visitations and around five o'clock the same afternoon I had a call from Naval Headquarters at San Diego, that two planes had been sent up to look everything over thoroughly and they had seen several gray whales, which regularly migrate South at that time of year and that must have been what my lookout saw. I knew this was ridiculous but there wasn't much I could do.

About three days later around four or five P. M., the Barndall man called me again that the sub was on the surface in the exact same spot in broad daylight again and he was looking at it through a window as he spoke to me and others were there with him, one man, who had been there the other time and another employee. He said about five officers and men could be seen plainly on deck. He reiterated that the sub was at least 200 feet long. Gray whales seen along the coast are usually ten to 20 feet long at the most, I think. I went up there again with someone from the office and the others spoke to San Diego of course. The sub was still in sight when I arrived but the light was bad and there was nobody on deck apparently and I could just barely see the gun and after less than a minute it moved out of sight in the dusk. Maybe the arrival of my car with lights was the reason. However, there was absolutely no doubt about the nature of the ship.

Finally on the evening of the shelling I was dining at Pete's on Chapalla Street in Santa Barbara, where I went almost nightly (Casa de Sevilla), when the police station called me that my man at Barndall was on the phone and a submarine was shelling Ellwood. I ran out of the restaurant and drove really fast and made the eight or more miles in record time. The Santa Barbara Police seemingly didn't understand or didn't believe or didn't care because nobody from there did anything about it at all. As I neared Ellwood, I heard firing and saw smoke through patches of light on the road. At that time everyone was using blackout lights and almost no cars were out at night but it wasn't completely dark and I used my headlights because of the emergency.

I pulled into Barndall and everyone had left including my friend. The firing had just ended and the sub was not in sight. I walked into the building and called someone on my staff and ordered everyone back to the office and then I reached the supervisor and told her it was an emergency and they gave me a special operator. I called San Diego and in about five minutes, Admiral Ralston Holmes, the commandant of the 11th Naval District was on the line. Various senior officers spoke to me and planes and ships were dispatched and then the admiral called back and said that a unit of artillery was being sent to Ellwood immediately and would be there in an hour or so. Various admirals and captains called me from Washington and even the commandant in Chicago and the Captain of the Port at Long Beach and naturally my senior Naval Intelligence officers in San Diego and Los Angeles.

One of the men from our office came up to stay at the phone while I went out with the Barndall lookout, who returned as soon as the shooting was obviously over and he and I, two highway patrol officers and a deputy sheriff then covered most of the beach front and across the highway as well and found several shell holes but only one derrick was partially destroyed and no serious damage resulted but we found two five-inch dud shells in perfect condition. So, when we returned and reported back, the Navy said a demolition team would be sent up and that nobody should be allowed near the shells.

At about four A.M. after guards had been posted by me and by the sheriff's office and highway patrol I returned to the office and I believe Frank Price and I had a late snack at an all-night place on State Street.

After a short nap, I showered, stopped at the office, and went back to Ellwood. No military or anyone else had arrived. But in daylight we went out again and located every single shell hole. I forget the exact number, possibly fifteen or more plus the duds.

Around Ten A. M. the Navy demolition team arrived from San Diego and took the duds with them. I had a good look at them when they said it was safe. There were clear Japanese markings on the shells.

Around noon the large artillery detachment came in and camped on the grounds. They made a great display as though they were arriving just in time to save the day but the truth is the sub had left for Japan the night before after the shelling according to the later testimony of the officer previously mentioned. The artillery remained there a day or two and them [sic] moved to another site semi-permanently nearer Goleta center as I recall it and brought in one really enormous gun. I read later that the officer commanding the original detachment had been given a commendation for his action in connection with the shelling although he arrived on the scene 17 or 18 hours after it was over and a complete report listing every shell hole and every detail had been sent to San Diego by myself. Naturally that report would give you lots of names, times, details of all kinds that I can't remember anymore. Maybe after this long somebody in The Pentagon could get Naval intelligence to release it but I don't believe it. I'd like to see it myself. It was long and detailed, dictated to a marvelous stenotype yeoman in our office in Santa Barbara.

Oh, one other thing, just two days earlier, after the second sub sighting, I had been given a real going over by the operations office of ComEleven [the Navy intelligence unit], who told me not to bother them further with the submarine stories, that the whole coast was full of whales and that was what all of us were seeing.

Several high-ranking officers came up to see the results of the firing and the dock and channel and I continued to get calls for details from other admirals and captains for a day or two. The Commandant sent his son-in-law up as a new assistant for me after first sending for me to meet him the day after the shelling. I didn't stay on much longer. The notoriety caused me to be called to work on a spectacular—but never publicized—spy case elsewhere and through all this I became friendly with the powers that ran Naval Intelligence in Washington and they sent me to the duty I'd requested in The Pacific where about three weeks after arrival I became aide and Flag Lieutenant to Commander Service Force Southwest Pacific Force (soon afterward 7th Fleet). By the way the shelling took place in February 1942, not 1943 as in your letter. In February 1943 I was enroute to Sydney in charge of a detachment of Naval Officers on a brand-new U. S. transport.

All the other rumors and gossip about more than one sub and failure of various branches of the service or other lookouts ever sighting submarines are untrue.

As for the Jap signal lights, our Naval Intelligence Office in Santa Barbara was deluged with calls for months about local japs signally [sic] their ships and planes but I don't believe any of it. I was in the raids on Santa Maria and Guadalupe, when we picked up all the members of the Japanese war societies, whose names were on the contribution lists, one of our Naval Intelligence procedure and reliable too. But these people weren't signaling in my opinion. The only real Jap agents were the couple working for a very well-known Santa Barbara doctor in the Riviera section, who had an enormous arsenal, photos of every railroad bridge in the county, every highway bridge and quite new Jap propaganda war films smuggled in from Mexico. This couple were sent to the dangerous alien center at Missoula, Montana.

I was out of carbon paper and didn't make a copy of this letter. If you can have it copied by any process, I'd appreciate it very much for my own file. I hope this has been helpful and I'm most anxious to see your finished book as I lived in Santa Barbara and Montecito, had good friends in Goleta and have close friends in Hope Ranch now and please let me know if there's anything else I can help you with.

Sincerely,

George Goman

## RESIDENTS' ACCOUNTS

Ruth Pratt: "I was home alone with the children that night. my husband had been away, training with the Civil Defense Home Guard. I really got uncontrollably jittery; I suppose it was shock. I was working away, and all of a sudden, I heard the explosions. Bang-bang! Aimed at those storage tanks, deck guns from only a mile offshore missed their mark. We didn't know if any Japanese had come off of the submarine or not. I was so petrified that once the shock set in on me, I saw more Japanese looking in the windows at me that night. Of course, there was nobody anywhere near me. It was just to let us know they could come that far."

J.J. Hollister,

"And then we heard the sound of something shrieking through the sky. There was probably about a two-mile spread between where that flash was taking place and where we were hearing the shells land behind our house. After we learned about the fact of a Japanese shelling, we were more concerned than we were before, of course. My father handed out rifles to all the ranchers up in the canyon to defend ourselves. We really felt we had to defend ourselves from an invasion."

The crater of a five-inch shell, nearly big enough to hide a Jeep, was big enough for all America to see. The film of the Jeep in the crater was shown on weekly newsreels at the movie theaters. Before television or the internet, weekly newsreels would be shown before a film began. Still photos of the war were very limited in the press. Newsreels were the only source of video. Even a 5 or 10-minute film per week of the latest war news was often the sole reason for attending a movie in a theater.

Godwin Pelissero, Goleta resident:

Godwin kept an unexploded shell in his home for decades. This is the only known such Japanese shell fired on America. "This shell is the only one of the twenty-five that were fired that never exploded because it landed in a newly irrigated field of alfalfa."

The Japanese submarine fired about twenty-seven rounds. Moments later, it dived underwater and ran silently out to sea. But it accomplished its mission, and that is, to terrorize the American public.

## A Japanese Submarine at Bodega Bay, California.
## Mel Surofsky, Military Intelligence Police

A secret history of World War II discovered in the Library of Congress. The following was obtained from the Veterans History Project. The citation for this interview is in the Citations section of this volume.

World War II Veteran Mel Surofsky explained that "in September of 1944, the Army received a call from the California Highway Patrol to investigate suspicious activity going on at Bodega Bay which was eleven miles from Two Rock Ranch. Three MPs and myself took a Jeep to Bodega Bay, and what we saw was enough to warrant me sending the Jeep back with one of the MPs to get back up from the Base. We saw a small submarine unloading boxes on to a rubber boat and bring it ashore. They carried the boxes into two bungalows that were near the beach. It took about 45 minutes for three truckloads of MPs and troops to arrive at [from] Two Rock Ranch.

"Until the shooting started, we were not certain if they were Japanese. We lost two of our men and four were wounded. We killed eight Japanese and fourteen surrendered. The FBI sent a 'Black Mariah' to transport the prisoners to San Francisco. We were ordered by our Base Commander as well as the FBI, not to broadcast what happened. However, when I went to town, everyone was already appraised of the skirmish."

Two Rock Ranch was a secret Army telecommunications center that monitored Japanese transmitting during the war. I have asked the FBI Information Management through the Freedom of Information and Protection Act (FOIPA) and I have requested the National Archives to locate any information on this event. In the future, if we obtain any new information, we will include it and republish the book.

We have tried to locate anyone in Petaluma who could corroborate the incident, since Mel Surofsky said the event was well-known in the town. An older member of that community had heard of the story, but he had not seen any direct evidence nor any Japanese. It is not surprising that civilians could not provide testimony to the event since none were present per Mel's description. Given that there were no other known witnesses to the event, another source may be in government files. More research needs to be done on the incident as described.

## OREGON

*ABOVE: A rare attack on a US Army Base and right on the Oregon Coast "Until the shooting started, we were not certain if they were Japanese"*

*ABOVE: Fort Stevens, Oregon. Today a State Park, was an Army base for many years as well as during World War II. On June 21, 1942 Ft. Stevens was attacked by Japanese Submarine I-25.*

### The Japanese submarine attack on a US Army Base.

Fort Stevens appears as a historic site with a Civil War era underground cavern-style structure. All the more astonishing is that this US Army installation was attacked during World War II. In the middle of the night, the Japanese submarine *I-25* fired 25 shells at the fortress.

Americans on the West Coast were vulnerable at a time when Japanese submarines and aircraft carriers could bring death and destruction to the USA. What real defense was there? All the air-raid wardens could do from San Diego to Seattle and from Canada to Alaska were to look up and wait for enemy planes. Civilians as well as soldiers stood watch night and day, peering and gazing at the Pacific for hours. To catch a Japanese submarine and call for the bomber would save lives. Enemy submarines stalking the shores! Who would have thought this nightmare could have actually happened just months ago?

Their watch was justified again when on June 21, 1942, a Japanese submarine attacked the Army Installation in Fort Stevens. Fort Stevens is situated on the mouth of the Columbia River in the northwest corner of Oregon. The original purpose of this Army installation was to protect the river from Confederate commerce raiders such as the CSS *Alabama*. Incredibly, the Confederate raiders would sail around South America to get to the West Coast with the hope of occupation. But the Civil War was over before Fort Stevens was fully operational.

Fort Stevens was named for a former governor and congressional delegate of Washington Territory, Isaac I. Stevens , who was killed in 1862 at the Battle of Chantilly, Virginia. After WWI and prior to World War II, the last major addition to the Fort had been the construction of 10-inch "disappearing" gun batteries. These huge cannons installed on hinges would fold onto the concrete floor and remain unseen on its perimeter. Although considered a frightful weapon during the Spanish-American War, the disappearing guns were obsolete in the wake of Pearl Harbor.

*Eyewitnesses to the Bombing of Fort Stevens*

**Vernon Grieg, a soldier:** He was in the 249th Coast Artillery stationed at Fort Stevens, and he was concerned over the readiness of the Coastal Defenses on the coasts of America. "I mean, it was stuff that went back to the Spanish-American War. I think it was a case where the government had failed. We just came out of the Great Depression, the defenses of this country were very low, and we just didn't have anything. I heard this explosion down on the beach, and so I thought I better get up and see what it might have been. By that time, another explosion happened. I ran up the stairs to the Command Post, and everyone up there was excited. I asked Major Houston what we had going out there, and he says, 'I'm sure we got ourself a Japanese submarine firing at us.'

You gotta remember, it was the times when the Japanese, everything was going their way, and they were defeating everything in their path. And people out here on the Coast were scared. They really expected, maybe it sounds foolish now, but they expected to have an actual attack along our Coast. We were plotting them on the board at the time, and Major Houston was always checking with me. He says, 'We got anything? They got in close to us yet?' I said, 'No, anything we show here, they're about 2,000 yards out of our range.' And it certainly didn't make any sense to fire at something you couldn't reach and give your position away. We all wanted to go and engage. I mean, we had been in intensive training here for a year, year and a half, and here was our chance."

**Joseph Burdic, soldier:** "About three or four days after the Pearl Harbor attack, there was a rumor that there was a Japanese Fleet off the Coast. And suppose they'd had an aircraft carrier with the group? My first thought was that the men were returning from pass and probably had a little too much to drink and were just being noisy. Then somebody said, 'The Japanese are shelling us.'"

**Don Sheldon, soldier:** "I had returned back to my job in the switchboard room, time for me to go on shift. And I was sitting there, and all of a sudden, I am telling you that switchboard just lit up, and I soon found out that we were under attack by a Japanese submarine, which was firing offshore."

**William Wilson, soldier:** "There was a group of loggers, fishermen, and farmers, and they were all organized primarily to defend the Coast in case of an invasion by the Japanese. As we went down to different areas of [the county] to tell them what they were supposed to be shooting at, they knew probably more about firing weapons than most of the people in the military."

The fears of the soldiers and civilians were not imaginary. Following Pearl Harbor, nine Japanese submarines were sent to attack the major cities of the American West Coast. The order was eventually rescinded. However, enemy submarines still stalked the dark waters of the Pacific. Among the nine submarines sent to the West Coast, was the Japanese submarine, *I-25*, commanded by Meiji Tagami. On June 21, 1942, the *I-25* was ordered to attack Fort Stevens. Under the cover of darkness, the submarine surfaced and fired its five-and-a-half-inch guns at the fort.

**Lester Madison, soldier:** "Everybody is running around trying to get out, and I stopped them at the head of the stairs to get them to go back, get their rifles, get their packs on, and get their clothes on before they went outside. If I hadn't done that, I'm sure they'd have gone outside without their clothes on."

**Alden Addie, soldier:** "I was running the switchboard for the searchlight battery, which was Battery G of the 249th Coast Artillery. The officers down there said, 'Don't turn the lights on because they'll see where we're at.' In other words, don't give our positions away."

The close proximity of Fort Stevens to the surrounding communities of Astoria, Warrenton, and Hammond, exposed thousands of civilians to the attack. While the soldiers were preparing to fire back, the officers of the Fort were facing a difficult decision. Controversial to this day, the decision not to return fire angered many of the soldiers.

**Edwin Jolley, soldier:** "Battery Russell called in a few minutes, and said, 'Battery Russell, loaded and ready to fire.' I repeated that to the Colonel, and he discussed it with the other officers, and he turned back to me and said, 'Tell them that I order them not to fire. I repeat: you will not fire.' I gave this message to the operator, and he, in turn, turned to his officer and told him. And I heard over the phone, 'Who in the hell gave that order?' Colonel Doney was standing close enough to me that he could hear this message, and he told me, 'Give me the phone,' and I did. And he said, 'This is Colonel Doney. I told you, "You will not fire. If you fire one round, I'll court-martial the whole 249th."'"

**Richard Emery, soldier:** "Naturally, we were quite frustrated. There was a lot of anger. We felt that we should have been able to fire back, and we never got what we considered a satisfactory answer about getting the order not to fire."

**Hoxie, soldier:** "Well, the next day I went out towards the beach until I could find a shell hole and started walking around it. [One piece] I picked up quite a way from it, but it stayed on top of the ground. Dug [two] out of the shell hole."

**Richard Emery, soldier:** "Before the attack, I think we all were just a little bit complacent. And then after the attack happened, we realized we were vulnerable. If nothing else, it made us much more alert and much more aware of the fact that we were in a war. We were on instant alert. The guys slept with their guns, slept with the machine guns. Everybody slept with their rifles."

**Glenn Weybright, soldier:** "I guess there's a lot of American soldiers that'd like to get back at the Japanese. That was one of the reasons that I joined the Air Corps because I thought I could go over and drop a few bombs on them."

**Richard Emery, soldier:** "When I got off duty that morning, I went right down to Personnel and put my application in for pilot training."

**Margaret Swindler, civilian:** "I started getting ready for bed when I heard the first shell. I knew right away that it wasn't target practice of the guns at Fort Stevens because the sound was altogether different. I think the attack affected me mostly in making me realize there really was an enemy lurking off our shoulders who might be ready to attack the mainland of the United States at any time. In the morning, the first thing I did was turn the radio on and hear that the Japanese had shelled Fort Stevens, so my worst fears were confirmed"

**Victoria Lamb, civilian:** "The first thing I remember was hearing a swinging sound right over the Columbia Beach Road out here, and that's what brought my husband and I to our feet because it was an unusual sound, and we were worried about it."

**Norma Sheldon, civilian:** "When the first shell hit, we figured that it was an invasion. That was our first thought, in our household."

**Helen Healy, civilian:** "I could see the firing going on at the Fort, and that was frightening, and I wasn't sure what it was, but there was a blackout in Astoria when I got there, and I had to walk home in the dark. The next morning, my feelings about the war had changed because I heard on the radio that was indeed a Japanese attack."

*ABOAVE: Entrance to the US Forest Service trail near Brookings, Oregon that traces the three bombings by Japanese Master Pilot Fujita. It is today a public hiking trail.*

The bombings were Japanese Master Pilot Fujita's own idea and the plan was approved by the Japanese Imperial Navy. Fujita also wrote a bestselling book after the war about his bombing of the US mainland.

For the third time, the Japanese submarine *I-25* was set to attack the United States. The *I-25* was the only Japanese submarine to provide a plane to bomb the USA. Emperor Hirohito's younger brother, Japanese Prince Takamatsu, served as its commander who brought Fujita and the infamous "Glenn" plane to the United States. The Emperor Hirohito was regarded as a god, vastly more powerful than mortals. It was seen as a tremendous honor to die for him. Master Pilot Fujita's scheme fascinated Prince Takamatsu. Since it was his strategy, historians coined the term "Fujita Plan."

Fujita flew reconnaissance missions over the Western Pacific, the Western US, Australia, New Zealand, New Caledonia, and the Fiji Islands after serving as a warrant officer in occupied China, where the genocide of innocent civilians was a daily occurrence. He pondered his plan to bomb the United States and Australia directly as he flew around the beaches on recon.

He persuaded the Japanese Imperial Army (JIA) brass, and just before his third deployment to the US mainland, he was shown a map of the Western United States.

The Oregon forest is about 75 miles above the California state line. He was told "the woodlands in this area have been ordered to be destroyed. You'll be the first person to bomb the mainland of the United States! Bombing the trees will put the adversary in a lot of trouble. The Americans will panic when they know we can demolish their homes from thousands of kilometers away. The US Navy will be forced to recall its battleships, giving us a considerable advantage against the Japanese at Guadalcanal. Morale in the US would plummet and perhaps the victims would persuade Roosevelt to pull out of the Pacific. Their land is ours to inherit."

The Fujita Plan was a blueprint for decreasing morale among the American people and spreading dread along the Pacific Coast. American historians did not discover this until after the war.

At that time, Americans didn't think it was possible to fly from Japan to the US. However, the Yokosuka E14Y "Glen" type-plane was hurled from the Japanese submarine. A system of nicknames for Japanese planes, like "Glen" in this case, was developed by the US and UK during the war. Once the submarine arrived off the Pacific Coast by an air hanger sub, the plane was assembled together and launched.

In 1983, Fujita remarked in his own version of the Fujita Plan: "I was totally certain that submarine could execute this sort of task. The submarine's operational range was unusually long, encompassing the whole West Coast of the United States. Target cities included Seattle, Portland, San Francisco, Los Angeles, and San Diego."

On September 9, 1943, the plane's pieces were moved from the submarine's hangar and put on a catapult. Fujita and his co-pilot Okuda sat in their seats with bated breath. Two bombs, each having 520 firing elements and a diameter of over 300 feet with a temperature of 1500 degrees, were carried.

"On a southeastern route, I flew toward the Blanco Lighthouse on Oregon's coast, then inland for about 50 miles. 'The bombs will be dropped here,' I said to Okuda, with my left hand grabbing for the bomb-release knob. I also yanked on the doorknob." Another dreadful bomb was launched.

Early one morning, Howard Gardner, a US Forest Ranger stationed at Mt. Emily, was frying eggs when he heard a strange clang. He looked out over the early sea of fog in the Siskiyuo National Forest. As he wrenched his arm up, Howard called to his colleague Bob Larson. "Come here now!! Take a peek at what's going on here!! What is the purpose of this pontoon plane?" The Japanese pilots fixed their eyes on the forest which was ablaze with fire and smoke. Despite the fact that it wasn't a military base, Fajita claimed he felt good about causing some damage.

Over at the Mt Emily Ranger Station, a peculiar cloud developed. Howard and Keith Johnson battled their way to the bomb site late that day through eight miles of dense brush. Keith would later serve in the Navy and would write home about this Japanese attack. Other support arrived later to prevent the blaze did not become a roaring disaster.

Fujita's strategy was successful. Brookings was a crazy whirlwind of activity. The Army Western Defense leapt into action as P-38s surveyed the skies. Cars with US government license plates came and went. The "G" Company of the 174th Infantry, 44th Division, was quickly ordered to defend Oregon's southern coast from invasion. Commander Eddy Waldrop would recall, "We would have one hell of a time if the enemy had been serious about any landing. Each man was limited to five to ten rounds of ball ammunition. We had mostly Springfield rifles and a few Garand M-1's. Bandon's American Legion Building was our company headquarters. We only had our own telephone lines to the several outposts and a teletype for communication with higher headquarters."

Rumors, on the other hand, were significantly more ferocious and spread much faster than the raging forest fire. As if that wasn't enough, the Japanese submarine *I-25* came off the coast of Oregon again on September 29th and catapulted the "Glen" plane into the air a second time. Fujita was the one who wanted to come back to repeat the success. Japanese built ten distinct submarines that could carry floatplanes; several could carry two planes and one type could even carry three.

Eighteen years later in 1962

The Junior Chamber of Commerce and the Jaycees of Brookings invited Pilot Nobuo Fujita to their Annual Azalea Festival. This invitation caused quite a bit of controversy. He was the only person who had ever bombed the United States. Many Americans who had lost a parent, sibling, husband, or son in the Pacific War, as well as many more who had served in the Pacific, did not feel it was appropriate. The majority of people, particularly those who were old enough, recalled the Japanese Government's treachery that occurred only 21 years before at Pearl Harbor. Although many Americans realized that not all the Japanese public may have wanted that horrific war, the average citizen fell in line quickly supporting their government's aggression toward the US.

At the same time as the Japanese Fleet was preparing to destroy Pearl Harbor and the surrounding area, the United

States, in good faith, were negotiating with the Japanese Empire. To divert the US's attention away from the problem, Japan pretended to negotiate. As a result of this, there were still a lot of bitter feelings toward Japanese World War II veterans.

When Fujita visited Brookings for the Azalea Festival in 1962, he gave to the town the same sword he had with him when bombing Brookings in 1942. The sword is currently on exhibit in the Brookings Library. The "surrendering" of one's sword to the victor is symbolic of disarmament and appreciation of the triumph, according to Samurai custom. In general, the festival went well. Fujita had been back several times since.

*ABOVE: A "GLEN" type Japanese bomber takes off from I-25, just as Fujita's plane did when it bombed the USA.*

I-25, a participant tin the Pearl Harbor attack, also fired and hit the SS Connecticut 10 mi off the US West Coast. The damaged tanker managed to escape but ran aground at the mouth of the Columbia River.

# WASHINGTON STATE

On Sunday, June 7, 1942, the American Merchant Vessel SS *Coast Trader* was torpedoed and sunk by the Japanese submarine *I-26*, thirty-five miles southwest of Cape Flattery near the Straits of Juan de Fuca. Fifty-six survivors from the 3,286-ton freighter were eventually rescued by the fishing vessel *Virginia I* and the Canadian Corvette HMCS *Edmunston* (K-106).

The Japanese vessel *I-26* was a 356-foot Junsen Type-B Class submarine built in Kobe, Japan, in 1941. With a crew of 101 officers and men, they were the Japanese Navy's largest and most successful class of underwater boats. The submarines, called "I-boats," were fast, had long range, and even carried a small collapsible floatplane (a Yokosuka E14Y1 "Glen") which could be launched by compressed-air catapult from the foredeck. The *I-26* was one of nine Japanese B-class submarines prowling the West Coast from the Aleutian Islands to San Diego during 1941 and 1942.

The *I-26* was also responsible for sinking the SS *Cynthia Olson*, the first American Merchant vessel to be sunk by a Japanese submarine in World War II. The SS *Cynthia Olson*, enroute from Tacoma, Washington, to Honolulu, Hawaii, was torpedoed on December 7, 1941, some 1,000 miles northeast of Honolulu. All thirty-five crewmembers were lost.

### USS Camden and USS Larry Doheny

In addition to these accounts, there are two fairly unknown stories involving two US tankers that were torpedoed off the south Oregon coast by the infamous Japanese submarine *I-25*. The first story was the USS *Camden* on October 4, 1942, which was hit hard and nearly sunk near Coos Bay. The second incident occurred on October 6, 1942, when the *I-25* torpedoed and sank the USS *Larry Doheny* off Gold Beach.

### SS John A. Johnson out in the Pacific

Harold L. Clark recalls the Japanese machine-gunned unarmed American sailors in the lifeboats and killed ten of them.

Although this sinking occurred out further in the Pacific; it is included due to its compelling story of execution at sea. Harold L. Clark was a typical member of the crew of the SS *John A. Johnson*. He was young (many of the crew were just 17 or 18 years old), and he manned one of the guns protecting the ship. He is one of the crew questioned by the Captain of the *Argus* the day following the sinking.

"I was on watch on the starboard wing of the bridge. At about 9:10 (pm), I spotted wake in the water, about four hundred to four hundred and fifty yards away from the ship. I reported the wake to the bridge over phone. Missing man (Cloyd) was on the phone at bridge. Torpedo hit ship, knocking me some fifteen feet away and water and oil came down all over me. General Quarters was sounded.

**A lifeboat approaches the *Argus***   "Lieutenant Yates came up and told me to help man the number #6 gun. I proceeded to the number #6 gun, and there, I sighted an explosion on the stern of the ship. It looked like was another torpedo. The ship began to break in two. The abandon-ship signal sounded on the whistle. I proceeded to boat deck, port side, where a raft had been tripped. I jumped over and got on to the raft.

"We drifted around the stern of the ship. The ship was now in two separate sections. We paddled away from the bow of the ship. We saw an object about three hundred feet away from us. We signaled about the object, thinking it was another raft, and it returned the signal. It came to the surface and turned out to be a submarine, and it started coming toward us.

"About one hundred and fifty feet from us, the submarine machine-gunned us. I could see tracers going over our heads. We jumped into the water. The submarine passed by about one hundred and fifty feet. We swam back and got on the raft. The submarine circled and came back at us again.

"We dove into the water again. This time, the submarine hit the raft, and as it passed by, they fired again with a machine gun, tracers hitting water near me. The submarine was from three hundred to four hundred feet long, with a stepped-up conning tower and clipper-type bow. Five American flags were painted on port side of the bow. Men on the submarine were yelling 'Bonsai' and cursing at us.

"The submarine had two guns with one forward and one aft. The first shot fired after ramming was a single shot by pistol. I saw one machine gun aft coning tower on bridge, and I saw man at gun. There were approximately fifteen men on the bridge.

"The submarine passed on and made a circle about one-half mile from us. It came at us again and passed about two hundred feet, but it did not bother us. After the submarine left, we saw one boat. We tried to get to it, but we didn't make it.

"About one-half hour later, the submarine shelled both portions of ship. Both sections caught fire.

**Lifeboat #3, with the raft in tow, approaches the *Argus***

"Two or three hours after the ship caught fire, the forward portion of ship blew up. About fifteen minutes before the explosion occurred, we sighted the first American plane. After the explosion, there were two planes. We signaled one of the planes, and the plane answered. More planes came over occasionally. At dawn, we could still see the glow of the burning ship."

# BALLOON BOMBS  OPERATION FU-GO

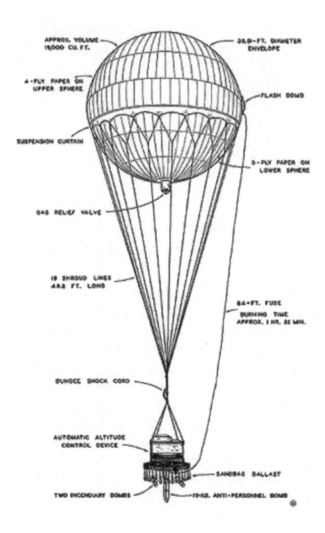

APPROX. VOLUME
19,000 CU. FT.

4-PLY PAPER ON
UPPER SPHERE

SUSPENSION CURTAIN

GAS RELIEF VALVE

19 SHROUD LINES
49.2 FT. LONG

BUNGEE SHOCK CORD

AUTOMATIC ALTITUDE
CONTROL DEVICE

TWO INCENDIARY BOMBS

32.0-FT. DIAMETER
ENVELOPE

FLASH BOMB

3-PLY PAPER ON
LOWER SPHERE

64-FT. FUSE
BURNING TIME
APPROX. 1 HR. 22 MIN.

SANDBAG BALLAST

15-KG. ANTI-PERSONNEL BOMB

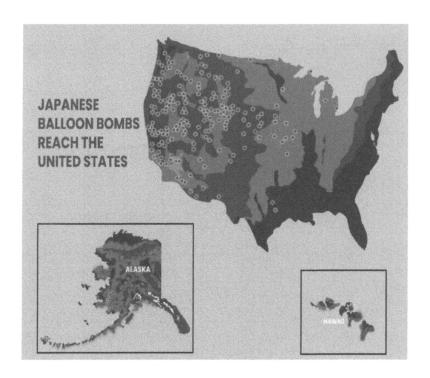

JAPANESE BALLOON BOMBS REACH THE UNITED STATES

Operation Fu-Go A Fu-Go (ふ号[兵器], fugō [heiki], "Code Fu [Weapon]"), or fire balloon (風船爆弾, fūsen bakudan, "balloon bomb")

A hydrogen balloon, with a load varying from a 33 lb. (15 kg) anti-personnel bomb intended to kill people and four 11-lb (5.0 kg) incendiary devices to start fires. It was designed as a weapon intended to make use of the jet stream over the Pacific Ocean and drop bombs on American cities, forests, and farmland. The airstreams, some 30,000 feet in the upper stratosphere, enabled easy passage for the lethal explosives. It only took three days to reach America. The balloon bomb was, in fact, the world's first interconnectional ballistic missile, and it was delivered by an ingenious method. These balloon attacks were the longest ranged assaults in the history of warfare until that time. Since then, the only time that range was exceeded was when the British Black Buck Vulcan

XM607 flew 8,000 miles from Ascension Island to the Falkland Islands to sortie Argentina. Regardless, the 1982 flight cannot adequately be compared to the 1942 Balloon Bomb. The advanced jet was designed for the nuclear age. The Balloon Bomb was invented utilizing low-cost materials and low-level technology and it still posed a real threat at the time. That was its genius. It was Japanese ingenuity.

It was one of the biggest secrets of World War II until decades after the war. As a result, many eyewitness accounts have been lost to history. The fear of the balloon bomb was not unfounded since we can see how deadly the bombs were in Oregon. Some were frightening to people due to their remarkably large size, up to 33 feet in diameter. The unfamiliar appearance shocked and dumbfounded American civilians. Some of the detonations were witnessed in the American West and even in the Mid-West. There were many close calls and near misses. Many people assumed it was impossible for the origin of these balloon bombs to have been from Japan or Germany. Both countries were approximately 5000 miles away. That distance from the Axis countries made the bombs even more terrifying. The location of their origin was assumed to be within the US, indicating the enemy was present in our own country.

Between 1944 and 1945, the Japanese military launched more than 9,000 bomb-set balloons across the Pacific. Years later, as many as 300 of them were found. It is estimated today there could be as many as 1000 that landed in the US and Canada. But the real figure after 75 years is still unknown. The balloon bombs landed in Alaska, Hawaii, California, Oregon, Washington, Idaho, Wyoming Montana, Utah, Nevada, Arizona, Texas, Idaho, North Dakota, South Dakota, Kansas, Nebraska and as far east as Iowa and Michigan. Canada, and Mexico also reported balloon bomb sightings. British Columbia (57) and Alberta (20) had quite a few. The states the with greatest numbers were Alaska (36), Oregon (45), Washington (28), California (23), Idaho (12) Wyoming (11) and Montana (35). Although some of these sightings made their way into the newspapers, their existence was labeled classified by the US and Canadian governments until many years after the war.

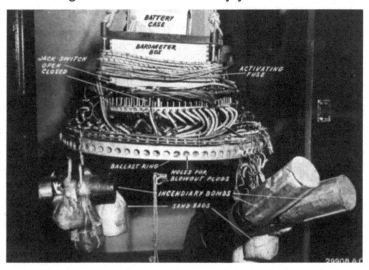

*The barometer was key to the operation of the balloon bomb. If the pressure increased to near standard pressure at sea level (approximately 14.7 psi or 101.35 kPa), the sand bags would be released in order to allow the device to ascend, keeping it afloat. Photo: Wikimedia Commons*

But how many times could the balloon bomb drop a sandbag and ascend again? Assumptions were made, and various numbers of sandbags were tried. The unpredictability of air pressure changes was the biggest factor in the loss of a bomb before reaching the US. These balloons had the capability of lifting heavy weight, 265 pounds for the sandbags alone. Its biggest drawback is that there was no control available to release the bombs over specific targets.

*"Japan's World War II Balloon Bomb Attacks on North America"* by Robert C. Mikesh is still the most comprehensive description of the weapon and how it worked to date. It also contains the lists with data of where balloon bombs were found. The book is an unparallel historical record on the Japanese weapon. The diagrams are outstanding (page 56 and page 57), illustrating at least 48 components and how they work together.

I would recommend this book for anyone who wants to understand the entire balloon bomb operation, how it actually worked. There have been other books since this book published that have given more detailed accounts of particular sightings. Robert C. Mikesh's book was done early enough before information would have been otherwise lost. The lists available are the best starting point for future research of lesser-known sightings. The list is also available in *"FU GO The Curious History of Japan's Balloon Bomb Attack on America"* by Ross Coen. Oregen, Washington and British Columba appear to have the largest number found so far.

I met several people the Western US in the 1980s that vividly recalled seeing a balloon bombs. One huge explosion in Utah has recollected. It appears that only a handful of accounts have ever been recorded. More research should be done to find the children and grandchildren of these witnesses, and perhaps gather more detail. Alaska had 36 balloon bombs found or sighted. This is more than any state outside Oregon, yet the recorded histories are few. I'm sure at least a few good stories could be recovered in Alaska. The same applies to British Columbia, with 57 located. Research has been done at the University of British Columbia; the link is in my References Section.

## Biological weapons

A justified concern was the threat that Japan may have included biological agents in the balloon bombs to infect the American population. This fear was not unfounded because the Japanese conducted the largest inhumane biological development of weapons in history during the war. Unit 731, one of Japan's biological warfare research centers, killed as many as 12,000 people. The number of people killed not only included Chinese, but also Americans, British, Dutch, Australians, Russians, Mongolians, and Koreans who died from the experiments performed by Unit 731 between 1939 and 1945. No prisoner came out alive from Unit 731's gates. Unit 731 and Unit 100, two of Japan's biological warfare research centers, were set up in spite of the Geneva Protocol of 1925 banning biological and chemical warfare.

Led by Lieutenant-General Ishii Shiro, three-thousand Japanese researchers worked at Unit 731's headquarters in Harbin, infecting thousands of human beings in China with diseases such as the plague and anthrax, and then eviscerated them without anesthesia to see how the diseases infected human organs. Testimonies from participants shed some light about parts of the experiments. American POWs are said to have had diseases from these experiments after the war.

During the war, the Japanese Imperial Army used biological weapons, killing or injuring an estimated 580,000 people throughout China. This number is based on conclusions from objective evidence at the International Conference of Bacteriological Warfare, held in December 2002, in Chnangde, Hunan Provance, China. These diseases continued after the war. The exact death toll will never be known.

In the US, the balloon bombs that were found were handled by trained experts. The Army often wore gas masks when defusing the bombs in the event they contained bioagents. Sections of the balloon bombs were sent to American and Canadian labs for analysis. The list of these possible bioweapon agents that were known to have been developed by the Japanese for warfare were: melioidosis, Japanese B encephalitis, Rift Valley Fever, Aoki's disease (acute tularemia), anthrax, typhus, dysentery, psittacosis, variolla, and others. Livestock infections designed to be employed against food supplies were foot and mouth disease, and pleural pneumonia.

*"Operation Cherry Blossoms at Night" in San Diego, California*

Japanese military commanders considered biological attacks on Dutch Harbor, Alaska; Calcutta, India; and parts of Australia, but they didn't carry them out like they did on a mass scale in China. Other schemes the Japanese proposed included infecting US cattle and grain crops, and using balloon bombs as a means to disperse plague agents in North America.

By 1944, Japan's military fortunes had turned for the worse when US Forces launched an amphibious invasion of Saipan Island in the Marianas. Separately, a Japanese submarine was dispatched to the island of Turk with twenty biowarfare specialists onboard, including two medical officers and deadly pathogens. However, it was sunk enroute by another American submarine, the USS *Swordfish*. During the Battle *of Iwo Jima*, Unit 731 planned to deploy bioweapons via two German-made gliders, according to Japanese pilot Shoichi Matsumoto. However, the two gliders broke down in flight while being transferred from Japan to Unit 731's base in China.

As the likely possibility of total defeat loomed larger over the Japanese military, General Ishii conceived Operation PX in December of 1944 as a last-ditch suicide mission on the continental United States. The target was San Diego, California. The delivery mechanism would be new I-400 class of submarine aircraft carriers nearing completion—the largest type of submarine to enter service during World War II. These massive vessels measured well over 122 meters, displaced 6,670 tons, and carried a 140-millimeter gun and three Aichi M6A Seiran floatplanes. Aircraft could be stowed in the sub's hangar due to their folding wings and removable floats.

By using similar methods to the plague attack in China on a more densely populated urban area, it was hoped that plague-flea bombs would start an epidemic that would kill tens of thousands of Californians. Commando teams aboard the submarines would land on US soil and further disseminate cholera and plague.

The attack, code-named *Operation Cherry Blossoms at Night*, was scheduled for September 22, 1945—five weeks after the Japanese surrender on August 15. While some sources characterize the war's ending as aborting the attack, others state the bioweapon bombing was cancelled considerably earlier in March of 1945 by General Yoshijiro Umezu. An account by flight instructor Toshimi Mizobuchi implies that personnel were being assembled as late as July, 1945 to carry out the attack. Even if a biological attack on the US was carried out, it would have been illogical to believe that success could reverse Japan's defeat.

# OREGON

## *Six Americans were killed by a Japanese balloon bomb in Bly, Oregon*

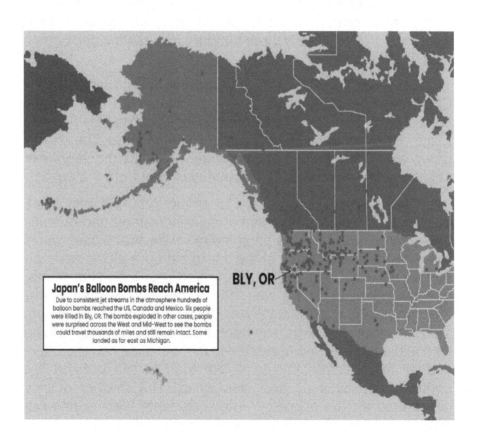

BLY, OR

**Japan's Balloon Bombs Reach America**

Due to consistent jet streams in the atmosphere hundreds of balloon bombs reached the US, Canada and Mexico. Six people were killed in Bly, OR. The bombs exploded in other cases, people were surprised across the West and Mid-West to see the bombs could travel thousands of miles and still remain intact. Some landed as far east as Michigan.

Six persons were killed on Gearhart Mountain, Oregon, by a Japanese balloon bomb. It was the only state in the continental US to have civilians killed by an Axis Force on land during World War II.

The United States adopted strict censorship to keep the Japanese from learning about the arrival of the balloon bombs. The government wanted to deny any knowledge the Japanese would find useful regarding the landing of the weapons in the US. Any information could enable them to make more successful launchings in the future. The news of these incidents was not permitted to be broadcast on radio or in publications. Many balloon bombs had been discovered by May 1945, although the general public was unaware of their existence. In total, nearly three hundred of these balloon bombs have been found.

Pastor Archie Mitchell of the Christian Missionary Alliance Church in Bly and his wife, Elsye, accompanied five Sunday School children to Gearhart Mountain for lunch on May 5, 1945. Elsye was pregnant with their first child at the time. The church group was fully oblivious of the danger posed by the Japanese balloon bombs since their existence was kept from the public.

They traveled a road to the picnic grounds that were extremely muddy with ruts since major snowmelt had recently been. While driving up the unpaved road, Pastor Mitchell let his wife and the five kids out of the car to set up a picnic while he parked the car. Nearby on the ground was a balloon bomb, and not knowing what it was, one of the kids unintentionally touched it, and it immediately exploded. After the explosion, the Pastor ran to the gruesome scene, but there was nothing he could do. It was inconceivable to him because his wife Elsye and all five children lay dead. He tried to put out the fire engulfed her body as she was dying. The military quickly descended on the scene. Worried residents tried to find out what was going on. Still, due to the immediate military status keeping the event secret, it would be hours before even family members were notified.

The victims were of Elsye Mitchell, age 26, Eddie Engen, 12, Jay Gifford age 13, Sherman Shoemaker, 11, Dick Patzke, 14, and his sister Joan Patzke "Sis," 13. Several of the families of those killed were interviewed in Ilana Sol's documentary, "*On Paper Wings*". We appreciate the permission from Ilana to print some of the interviews here.

**Betty Patzke:**

**Sister of Dick and Joan Patzke (both killed by the balloon bomb)**

"Dick always liked to go out with the weathermen—the forestry—and they'd send up these weather balloons. Now I can't tell what he was thinking in his mind, but I wonder if maybe he thought that was some kind of a weather balloon that had somehow come down and that's why they ran up to see it."

"Well, I think Bly was a nice, little town. Because there were ten of us in the family—the children—we always had a good time together, and kids would come to our house 'cause they always had someone there their age to play with. I was really close to Sis. I just wonder what she would be like if she was living today. Sometimes I think about that . . . and Dick too. What would have happened? But God took 'em. So, we have to know that He knows better."

"Years later, Dottie [sister of Dick and Sis Patzke] had invited me over for a meal, and she had invited Archie [the Pastor] too. And I can remember him sitting in that little breakfast nook, and we were all talking. Never thought that I'd ever be Archie's second wife [they later married], but we were just talking about everything and it just seemed like we were drawn together because we both experienced some sadness that had happened. When you talk about something like that, as bad as it seems you know when that happened and everything, I look at my four children. They never would have been, and you know I'm so thankful for all of four of my children and my ten grandchildren. That they wouldn't have been if this—that tragedy hadn't had happened. Maybe that's a strange way to look at it, but I've thought about that a lot of times."

### Diane Jordan:

### Sister of Sherman Shoemaker (killed by the balloon bomb)

"We were close. It was a close community, and there were so few people—I don't think there were more than 750-800 people in that entire community. There was no rhyme or reason as far as my parents were concerned. They didn't understand. They'd had no advanced knowledge of anything special. We knew we were at war, but the thought of war coming right to our front door never entered any of our minds. My parents did not feel that it would be good for me to have graphic description of this, so the only information I could get when they came to get me on Sunday was that my brother was dead and that I wouldn't even be able to see him again. I didn't believe it, and I kept saying, 'Did you look? Did they look everywhere?' In my childish mind, I kept thinking they had made a mistake. So, I locked myself in our family car when we got home and got into the backseat—it was one of the large old-fashioned cars—and I sobbed my eyes out. I don't know how long. After the shock of the emotion was replaced with anger, just a feeling of such rage that only you can imagine that a child would feel."

### Eva Fowler:

### Elsye Mitchell's sister (Elsye was pregnant and killed in the attack).

"Elsye was very active in church, and that's where she met Archie Mitchell. Somebody called them and told them they were to go to the Christian Missionary Alliance Church in Bly for Archie to take over the pastorate there. Elsye had found out that she was pregnant, and she was very ill, and she had planned *not* to go on this picnic with Archie and the Sunday

School class kids. But she had made this chocolate cake, and that morning just before they left, she said she was feeling good enough that she would go with them."

"They drove up to the mountain, and Archie found a place that he thought would be a good place for a picnic, so he stopped his car and Elsye and the kids got out. And he saw the kids, and Archie said that it was really hard on him because he was told not to even tell the parents of these children what really had happened. And he said, 'No, I've got to tell them.' And that was when we were all told. I was still—I was in high school. And we were all told not to talk about this over the phone. It was not to be put in the newspapers or the radio or anything."

"Archie said the kids hollered, 'Look what we found!' And he told us, 'I hollered, 'Don't touch anything. Get back!' Archie said that Elsye had been killed in an accident. And he said, 'I can't tell you anymore.' We just presumed that it was a car accident, until the next morning on the radio, we heard then that there was an unidentified object that exploded in the woods in Bly. And it didn't give the names or anything, but it mentioned that a pastor's wife and children were killed at that time. Archie came to our house within just a day or two and told us the details and his hands were all yellow because of the petric acid from the bomb. And he was, with his hands, trying to put out the fire on the children's and Elsye's clothes."

"Some of the people in the Bly church felt that Archie might want to leave Bly, but he said, 'No.' He said this is where he belonged and he was getting attached to the people there, and he knew that because of this incident, he felt that the people there in Bly needed him. And so, he stayed there, and then it was after that, two years later, that he married the older Patzke sister, Betty. But I do feel that if they had told the Americans— or allowed them to broadcast this—that there would have been more bombs sent on the balloons."

**Dottie McGinnis:**

**Sister of Dick and Sis Patzke (both killed by the balloon bomb)**

"We went to [a friend] Desiree Mahoney's home because we knew the Mahoney girls. And while we were there, Mrs. Mahoney got a phone call from her husband. And she told us, 'You better get back to Bly—something terrible has happened there.' And she wouldn't tell us what it was. We didn't know what had happened for sure until that evening about 6:30, when the Colonel and his staff came over to my mom's, and told us that it was a Japanese balloon bomb that had exploded.

While the balloon bombs were originally designed to self-destruct, many malfunctioned and did not do so. As more and more were found, the government needed a plan. We all thought if anything happened, my brother Dick would be involved because he was such a curious young man, and I said, 'Is Dick dead?' and they said, 'Yes.' I said, 'What about Sis?' And they said, 'Yes.' And then they named all the others, and it was 'yes' for all of them except for Archie, the pastor who had taken the children up there.

Immediately I went home to where my mom was, and I went in the bedroom where she was, and I put my arms around her. And she said, 'It's going to be all right, Dottie. It's going to be all right.' And she just patted me, and I was the one that cried, not her. It was the same day it was in the paper about the war ending in Europe and also about this balloon bomb—it didn't say that; it just said a blast."

**Cora Conner:**

**Switchboard operator**

"It was a small town: lumber mills, cowboys. After we moved to town from the mill, the war of course had broken out, and everybody that could work in the mill they put to work 'cause it was real hard to get people, you know. There just weren't enough people. I worked in the switchboard; we took in the telegrams, and there was several—[sigh] quite of few—death messages that came over, and it was very sad because you were close to everybody. And it was just like the family really when you had to deliver one. The phone rang, and this man came charging through the door. He says, 'I've gotta have an outside line. I've gotta have an outside line now!' And he called Lakeview and said there had been an explosion with people involved and he needed help right away. And I don't know what all they told him, but he told me that that was not to leave that office and that the lines were to be kept open.

"I couldn't even talk to my mother about it. So, I just clammed up and it froze right in my heart. And it was nearly 40 years before I could talk even to my family. My husband knew something had happened, but he didn't know the story."

"In Bly, military communication about the balloon bomb explosion was kept top-secret. This made things difficult for Cora Conner, whose switchboard was at the center of communication that day."

"I was told not to leave the room, not to talk to anybody. Not to let anybody in, not to pull the lines up, and all that. So, there I sat, and along late in the afternoon with all the confusion and stuff going on with the military cars, people started gathering out front of the telephone office. And it was quite a crowd, and they were yelling, shaking their fists, 'We know that you know what's happening. You better tell us; it's our kids.' And the fact that they didn't know anything—and I couldn't tell 'em anything—it made them very furious at me."

Obituaries in local papers simply attributed the deaths to a mysterious blast. Two weeks after the explosion in Bly, the government lifted the censorship policy so that the public could be warned about the balloon bombs and further tragedies could be prevented, but by that time, a much bigger story had already hit the papers. Cora continues, "I've been so traumatized by this thing. It was all bottled up, and I wouldn't go drop by the monument after it was put in place. I just couldn't do it. So, it has taken a long time, and John was the one really started the healing process of all this."

One of the great ironies of the Bly Balloon Bomb tragedy was that school aged children were killed in America; the balloon itself was made in Japan by school aged children.

*ABOVE: Rev. Archie Mitchel runs to his wife after the explosion that killed Elsye Mitchell, age 26, Eddie Engen, 12, Jay Gifford age 13, Sherman Shoemaker, 11, Dick Patzke, 14, and his sister Joan Patzke "Sis", 13.*

*Walter Morris*
*2nd Lt., 555th Parachute Battalion*
*"Operation Firefly"*

*Daring African American "smokejumpers" parachuted into forest fires to fight and disarm the Japanese balloon bombs.*

Major commanders in Europe were cautious about the possibility of having highly-trained black paratroopers being captured by the Nazis. The Japanese were floating balloon bombs across the Pacific Ocean, taking advantage of the jet stream's easterly flow, in an attempt to start forest fires in the northwestern United States. The Forest Service asked the military for help, and the 555th Battalion (also known as the "Triple Nickle") was ready. This African American battalion, the "Triple Nickle", answered some 36 fire calls with more than 1,200 individual jumps during the summer of 1945, operating in Pendleton and Chico, California. The operation covered all of the northwestern states.

During fire operations, the battalion suffered numerous injuries and one fatality. Malvin L. Brown, a medic assigned to the battalion's headquarters company, died on August 6, 1945, after falling during a let-down from a tree in the Siskiyou

National Forest near Roseburg, Oregon. His death is the first-recorded smokejumper fatality during a fire jump.

Walter Morris discusses the balloon Bomb and his service to help mitigate the attacks.

"The Forest Service asked for help in fighting the many fires that were spreading throughout the West Coast. The fires were due in part to incendiary bombs carried by balloons on the trade winds from Japan to the US coast - from Washington to Oregon to California and even Montana. These fire bombs landed and started fires on impact. "

"These balloons were made of a special laminated mulberry paper which was shellacked with a persimmon-juice sealant, thus, the balloons could survive the 7,500-mile crossing against high altitude winds. The Japanese launched balloons that rose to an altitude that carried them across the Pacific Ocean, allowing them to land in the northeastern part of the United States and a few in Canada. These 30-foot-wide balloons had bombs attached to them, which were either highly explosive or incendiary in nature."

"The trigger mechanism was simple, but not always effective: a small barometer was set to trigger the release of a few sand bags at a time which kept the balloons rising and descending as they were cruising across the Pacific at altitudes between 20,000 to 40,000 feet. When all 32 sand bags were released, the altitude control mechanism took over in releasing the bombs, and simultaneously ignited the slow-burning fuses that set off the self- destruct devices. The balloons were launched by the thousands. Many of them reached the United States, but did not cause the damage which was anticipated. The United States learned from this attack that the Japanese balloons used the air currents. Later, the US Air Force Strategic Air Command bombers used this knowledge of air currents on flights to plan attacks on the Russian mainland. The fires started by the balloons, and with the added problem of careless campers and lightning, became too much for forest firefighters. What to do?

Call the Army, with its 400 well-trained paratroopers ready and able to perform "Operation Firefly".

"The 555th Battalion was ordered westward to Camp Pendleton, Oregon, to begin two weeks of training in the proper method of fighting forest fires. Firefighting, of course, was an entirely new experience for them. But it was in this field that our new training program began on May 22. Wills [Chief of Training Operations] set up one of his brilliant, loaded-training schedules. It was a three-week program, which included demolitions training, tree climbing and techniques for descent if we landed in a tree, handling firefighting equipment, jumping into pocket-sized drop zones studded with rocks and tree stumps, survival in wooded areas, and extensive first-aid training for injuries, particularly broken bones. We learned to do the opposite of many things we learned and used in normal jumps, like deliberately landing in trees instead of avoiding them. "

"We would jump with full gear, including fifty feet of nylon rope for use in lowering ourselves when we landed in a tree. Our steel helmets were replaced with football helmets with wire mesh face protectors. Covering our jumpsuits and/or standard army fatigues was Air Corps fleece-lined flying jacket and trousers. Gloves were standard equipment, but not worn when jumping because bare hands manipulated shroud lines better. Naturally, our physical training program was intensified, because missions often found us miles from civilization and in heavily wooded and mountainous terrain. It paid off handsomely, because few injuries occurred and only one death."

"On most of our missions, we would work with forest rangers. They were a fine group of men. They could walk up the hills like a cat on a snake walk. They taught us how to climb, use an axe, and what vegetation to eat. At the same time, we underwent an orientation program with Forest Service maps. "And, above all, our morale and spirit of adventure never sagged in the face of this unusual mission. On June 8, we began working with bomb disposal experts of the Ninth Army Service Command, learning the touchy business of handling unexploded bombs, as well as how to isolate areas in which a bomb, or suspected bomb, was located. Some of us with infantry bomb training, and graduates from the Parachute Demolition School at Benning, served as assistant instructors. Then came the new parachute. The parachute training was under a civilian, Frank Derry, who had designed the special chute for jumping in heavily forested areas. A special feature of the so-called "Derry Chute" was its ability to maneuver. By pulling the white shroud line, the chutist could turn himself into a 360-degree circling movement. This, in turn, gave him a wider choice of landing areas which is a vital factor when trying to avoid tangles with the highest trees in the thickly-timbered areas. By mid-July, the entire battalion had qualified as "smokejumpers" which was the Army's first and only airborne firefighters. Soon, our operations would range over at least seven western states, and in a few instances, southern Canada. And there would be two home bases - one in Pendleton, Oregon, and one in northern California at the Chico Air Base. The roar of the propellers brought me back to the job at hand. I looked up and saw the red light turn green. The Jump Master gave the order to jump. We arrived at our fire. All thirty-four enlisted men and two officers jumped and assembled on the ground about five hundred feet from the burning trees. We at once established camp and began to work on a fire line. Several enlisted men were injured during the operation. I sent one officer and some men to carry the wounded down the mountain to a waiting truck. One soldier had a broken leg above the knee and one soldier had a crushed chest. They went by PBY plane to a Tacoma, Washington, hospital."

# CALIFORNIA

In Hayfork, a small community in northern California, about 40 miles west of Redding, involved one of the earliest balloon bomb sightings:

"On February 1, 1945, a Japanese balloon bomb was spotted by several local residents drifting over the Trinity National Forest area and slowly descending. No one knew what it was, but an alert forest ranger called the military authorities at the Presidio of San Francisco and reported it. Meanwhile, the balloon came to rest on top of a 6-foot dead fir tree in the forest near a local road. In the next few hours, several people gathered in the area to gaze up at the strange object."

"Shortly after dark, there was a tremendous blast. The balloon's gas bag disappeared in a fireball and the balloon's undercarriage came crashing to the ground. No one was hurt. Forest rangers kept the curious onlookers well back from the fallen debris until Army personnel arrived. Upon examination, it was found to be a Japanese balloon bomb with four incendiary bombs, and one highly explosive bomb still aboard with the bomb releasing mechanism still very much intact. It later proved to be one of the most intact balloon bombs yet to fall into American hands. As was usual in instances like this, the local people were told what it was, but were asked to keep secret what they had seen."

Alturas was another location in California where the weapon was found floating on its way, and was shot down by a P-38. This bomb was one of only a few ever shot down.

*ABOVE: Manhattan Project Site in Hanford, Washington shut down by a Japanese balloon bomb. Photo from Manhattan Project National Park*

# WASHINGTON

## *Manhattan Project in Hanford*

Creating a bomb based on the power of the atom was considered impossible by many scientists during World War II. The Manhattan Project did just that, building a bomb that would detonate an unprecedented large radius. It was discovered that incredible amounts of energy could be released when splitting atoms apart, particularly using Uranium and Plutonium. This was considered only theoretical until Albert Einstein wrote a letter to President Roosevelt about the process. Three critical Manhattan Project sites worked on developing the atom bomb: Los Alamos, New Mexico; Oak Ridge, Tennessee; and the Hanford Site in Washington state.

Los Alamos, New Mexico, was the center of the program for designing and testing the bomb. Two types of atomic bombs were constructed from the element of uranium U-235 and plutonium Pu-239. The Oak Ridge, Tennessee Center extracted the isotope U235 from raw uranium for use in the bomb. Isotope U235 was the component that was used to create the atomic explosion. The Hanford Site in Washington state developed plutonium from a new type of nuclear reactor. This process was discovered in 1940 by scientists studying how to split atoms. Plutonium is created in a reactor when uranium atoms absorb neutrons.

The Los Alamos and Oak Ridge Sites may have had their share of Soviet and German spies, but the Hanford Site had the strangest attack, that of a Japanese balloon bomb. One of the thousands of balloon bombs was sent by the Japanese to America. However, this particular balloon bomb hit the power lines to the Hanford Atomic Bomb Development Site and shut it down for half a day. It had always been considered a wild coincidence that the event happened just as Hanford was producing the plutonium used for the atomic bomb that would be dropped on Nagasaki in Japan.

The Hanford Site sits on 586-square-miles of desert in southeastern Washington state. In 1943, the Site was used to produce plutonium for the bomb that ended World War II. Nuclear Physicist Charles Clark had become well-versed in the science and the history of the Manhattan Project. "What happened at Hanford was a fluke," Clark said. "One of the balloons draped over the main electric transmission line from the Grand Coulee Dam and the Bonneville Dam on the Columbia River, causing a short circuit and shutting down the Hanford Cooling Plant. The Japanese had no idea what was going on at the plant, or if they even knew it existed," according to Clark.

"The engineers who built the plant, and the DuPont Company running the facility, had constructed several backups, including a coal-fired generator that kicked in as soon as the power went down, and the processing continued uninterrupted. The power was off for one-fifth of a second," according to Col. Franklin Matthias, the engineer in charge of the facility. "The operators had also set up the emergency system designed to drop emergency rods into the reactor to shut it down, but the balloon attack did not trigger it."

"We never had the guts enough to test that," Matthias said in an interview published on the Atomic Heritage Foundation website. The scientists had warned that even the slightest interruption in the cooling system could lead to an explosion of radioactive material, but they weren't sure. The balloon bomb at Hanford never exploded; it just shorted out the power.

"Had the backup not been there, it would have been 'fire city' at the reactor site," Clark said. It could have been a meltdown similar to the Russians' incident at Chernobyl in 1986. The backup systems worked as planned, even though they were not regularly tested.

# MONTANA

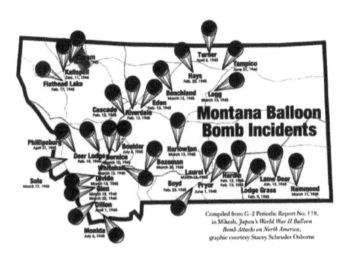

Montana Balloon Bomb Incidents

Compiled from G-2 Periodic Report No. 118, in Mikesh, *Japan's World War II Balloon Bomb Attacks on North America*, graphic courtesy Stacey Schneider Osborne

H istorian Jon Axline told a story about Oscar Hill and his

son, who, in 1944, were cutting firewood seventeen-miles southwest of Kalispell, Montana. They found a strange parachute-like object with Japanese writing and a Rising Sun symbol. Sheriff Duncan McCarthy took the object to a Kalispell garage. Rumors flew, and soon five-hundred people crowded into the garage in Kalispell to take a look. It turned out to be a Japanese balloon rigged to carry a bomb.

As the war wound down, it was the beginning of an aerial attack on the United States by Imperial Japan. The Japanese also intended the balloon bombs as psychological weapons designed to cause confusion and spread panic. The Japanese called them *Fu-Go.* They were the first intercontinental weapons in history, a low-tech predecessor to the ballistic missiles of the twentieth century.

## WYOMING

*Japanese balloon bomb was found in Thermopolis, Wyoming. One of the first balloon bombs found during the war. The size of the balloon indicates a heavy bomb was attached. Per the technology at the time, the heavier the bomb, the more deadly it was. Photo from the University of Wyoming Archives.*

There were eight confirmed *Fu-Go* balloon bombs found in Wyoming: near Thermopolis, Basin, Manderson, Kirby, Powell, Glendo, Newcastle, and Gillette.

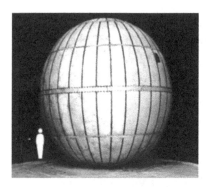

*This type of 30-foot diameter balloon inflated in Japan in 1944. Photo provided by the Japanese government after the war. US Navy National Museum.*

# MICHIGAN

One of the biggest surprises of the balloon bomb attacks and the war itself was the arrival of two of the missiles in faraway Michigan. To have made it to the West Coast 5000 miles away was considered impossible. To go another 2500 miles for a total of 7500 miles goes beyond the imagination.

Nine-year-old Lawrence "Buzz" Bailey and two neighbor kids ran excitedly toward a large balloon floating to Earth on farmland in North Dorr, a rural community in Allegan County south of Grand Rapids. It was Feb. 23, 1945, and they didn't realize they were discovering the remnants of a Japanese attack on the US. Bailey went on to serve in the US Army in Germany in the early 1950s. "I tell the guys in the VFW post that I was in the Second World War at age 9," says Bailey, "I was a balloon expert."

A family member volunteered to transport the kids to the landing spot. When they discovered it, the platform had been completely consumed by fire. They carried it across a field before loading it into their truck. After that, they transported it to their home and hid it in the basement. It was large enough to sprawl completely over the basement floor. Their mother quickly called the sheriff. The deputies first believed it was a weather balloon, but a call to the Weather Bureau showed there weren't any weather balloons in the air that day. The sheriff immediately contacted the FBI. The next day, the government sent agents to seize the balloon. They instructed the family not to talk about it again and pretend it never occurred when they seized the balloon.

After declassifying information regarding the Japanese balloon, the families realized what they had uncovered fifteen years later. They were relieved the bomb had exploded beforehand because they may not have survived had they begun carrying it across a field with the bomb intact.

Nearly three-hundred balloons or their components were later found in North America, and the two most easterly were discovered in Michigan at North Dorr. Another was found near 8 Mile and Gill roads in Farmington, Michigan, the following month.

# NEBRASKA

The year was 1945, and Omaha, Nebraska, appeared relatively safe until one night in April when a Japanese bomb fell in Dundee. The war in Europe was not over yet, but Germany's hopes for a Nazified Europe were nearly finished. The War would be over in Europe soon, and the war in the Pacific raged on. The *Battle of Okinawa* held the hearts of Americans, with more Americans killed in that two-month battle than in any other military campaign in our history. While Omaha residents were listening to the radio's news of the war, a Japanese bomb dropped on their town. The government asked Americans not to talk about the balloon bombings. If the word got back to the Japanese, their military experts could track the operation of their balloon bomb and use the data to improve future bombings. Lannie McNichols, Art Haney, and Al Capps remembered it clearly. Lannie McNichols grew raised in Omaha, Nebraska, near the location of the balloon attack. Dundee is the name of this well-known section of town. She was a tiny girl when the bomb burst across the street in the middle of the night.

"They had no idea how anything would travel from Japan to Omaha, but it did!". "I believe they were taken aback, but we simply stood there like, 'Well, that's something I've always known,'" McNichols added. "In terms of the battle, this was a minor episode. It is, nonetheless, critical in the history of

Omaha," Haney stated. Today, the only remnant of the balloon blast is a plaque between 50th and Underwood streets. Nobody was hurt in Omaha, but three weeks later, a lady and five children were murdered by one of the balloon bombs in Oregon.

As Lannie noted, the psychological toll was severe, and the breadth of Japan's or any country's technological capacity to strike America's heartland was genuinely frightening. Located in the country's center, Dundee, an Omaha suburb, was not prepared for an enemy bomb to drop on them. Many people immediately thought of fireworks when a loud boom and a flash of light were seen in the sky above 50th and Underwood Streets in Dundee on April 18. A select few weary residents emerged with their robes on. Some returned to their beds after seeing nothing worrisome.

But the surrounding neighborhood was quickly alerted that the explosion was caused by an incendiary device carried by a Japanese balloon. Hal Capps was ten years old when the bomb blew up. "Something occurred in the neighborhood that night, but no one is talking about it," he remembers his father telling him upon returning from work at the Buffett grocery store in Dundee. Residents were welcomed by name at Sidney Buffett's grocery business. Warren Buffett's great-grandfather started it in 1869. In 1915, Ernest Buffett, Warren's grandfather, relocated the business to 5015 Underwood, precisely where the Balloon bomb would explode the night of April 18, 1945. Warren Buffett is, of course, very well-known. He is one of the most successful entrepreneurs and investors in the United States today. Currently, he serves as Berkshire Hathaway's chairman and CEO. A notable self-made magnate, he had more than $109.5 billion as of January 2022, making him the world's ninth richest person. According to the Forbes Global Ranking, Berkshire Hathaway is now the eighth biggest public business globally, the tenth-largest conglomerate in terms of revenue, and the largest financial services firm. Omaha is still the company's home base.

*The historical plaque in the Dundee area of Omaha commemorates the balloon bomb explosion at 50th and Underwood streets. Nearby is the location of Warren Buffett's great-grandfather's store, the beginning of the family's business ventures.*

# TEXAS

Three separate Texan counties experienced explosions from a balloon bomb nearly simultaneously.

Texas is the only state to have sinkings from German U-boats off its coast and airdrops of Japanese balloon bombs. These occurred in three counties. Many more were assumed to have landed but never witnessed.

Inez Heeter, an Eastland County Civilian Air Corps Spotter, took note. As part of the US Government's Ground Observer Corps, she spent the years during the war watching the skies of Texas for enemy planes.

Mrs. Heeter, despite her vigilance, had never seen anything unusual until March 23, 1945, when she noticed a huge balloon floating above the Magnolia Oil Refinery and across the town of Desdemona, descending slightly to reveal the Imperial Japanese Rising Sun emblem on top of the balloon. Mrs. Heeter took up the phone and phoned the necessary numbers. After waiting years to contact the number the military provided her in case of a sighting, she was only to be met with suspicion on the other end of the line. However, she wasn't the only one who saw the balloon that day.

The guys at the Magnolia Refinery also saw it and wondered aloud, "What the heck is that?" Pug Guthery, a 14-year-old boy from Desdemona, got off a school bus when a balloon passed above and landed in a field approximately two kilometers away. Pug dashed off to investigate what he'd just witnessed. By the time he arrived near the balloon, it had flattened out and was ordinary, but for the large Rising Sun emblem on top. Other students getting off a different school bus saw the same balloon and ran across the field to investigate. Pug Guthery got a breath of something that smelled like creosote and backed away. Pug remembered, "It looked like leather. It was a tough substance."

The other youngsters, on the other hand, were not so careful. They ripped the balloons apart with pocket knives, removing portions of the balloon and a section of the grass rope that ringed it to take home as souvenirs. Fortunately, this balloon had already detonated its explosives. The following day, military personnel arrived at the Desdemona school, lined up the pupils, and told each one, "Give it back, kid," without reason.

A second Japanese balloon landed in Comanche County's little town of Comyn. According to Wade Cowan, a member of Company D of the Texas State Guard at the time, "When fully stretched, it was approximately 30 feet tall and contained five metal canisters. Four of the explosives were incendiaries, while the fifth was a fragmentation or anti-personnel weapon."

A third balloon was discovered the following day by Ivan Miller, a rancher on the Barney Davis property near Woodson in Throckmorton County. In1992, his widow, Florence Miller, told Mike Kingston of the Texas Almanac that her husband stated the balloon was "as large around as a house" and had numerous smaller replicas of the Rising Sun around the bottom. Schoolchildren had spotted this balloon, and it, like the Desdemona balloon, was missing innumerable sections. Miller called the local postmaster, who in turn told other government authorities, who showed up at school the following day and demanded that the students return their souvenirs from the balloon bomb.

# KANSAS

*ABOVE: Balloon bomb photographed by a local resident Edwin North, the man who discovered it near Bigelow, Kansas.*

# UTAH

Box Elder County hugs the western periphery of the Great Salt Lake. In February 1945, Sheriff Hyde received a phone call. This was a call the Sheriff knew could show up at any moment, but he hoped he'd never receive it. A hysterical woman shouted, "An unexplained flying object and close to the ground!" Shirreff Hyde did not hesitate; he jumped into his car and flew at a high speed. Astonishingly, when he arrived at the house, there it was; a floating object of some kind as clear as the morning was bright. He followed the anomaly in his car through the pasture as far as possible but then pursued it on foot. The Balloon bomb was moving at a fairly good clip; he suspected it was the Japanese Balloon weapon he had heard about.

When he finally caught up to it, he saw the bomb dangling below the balloon and knew he would have to be exceedingly careful. If he touched it, or if it touched the ground, it would likely detonate.

Taking a tremendous risk, Hyde grabbed one of the shroud lines. The wind intensified; the balloon was carried into the air. In a surreal fashion, it took Sheriff Hyde high up in the air along with it! He abruptly flew through the air on a 30-foot-high ride, hanging on to the lethal weapon. Hyde knew what he was doing; he was trying to secure a Japanese Balloon Bomb for analysis by the Federal Government. A contribution to the war effort yet attained.

He was eventually able to secure it when it landed on the ground. FBI agents and military showed up soon enough, thanked the Sheriff and took all the components ways. As far as the Sheriff knew, as typical with the federal government, the device was never to be seen again.

Thanks to Sheriff Hyde, the recovered weapon was one of the only Balloon Bombs ever retrieved, completely intact at that time. His bravery at great risk to himself resulted in findings the military would not otherwise have obtained. He was honored later that year at a ceremony in Salt Lake City, attended by the Utah Governor and the Army and Navy "brass."

## Where you can see Japanese balloon bombs today

Today, Japan displays its wartime invention at the Museum of the Japanese Imperial Army's Noborito Laboratory in Kawasaki, a suburb of Tokyo near Japan's Meiji University. Exhibits include a one-tenth-sized Japanese Imperial Army paper balloon bomb model. There is also an extensive display with the history of the balloon bombs posted at the Kitakyushu Municipal Center and other government buildings throughout Japan that includes a US map similar to the one above.

The remains of balloon bombs continue to be discovered after the war. Eight were found in the 1940s, three in the 1950s, and two in the 1960s. In 1978, a ballast ring, fuses, and barometers were found near Agness, Oregon, and these bomb parts are now part of the collection of the Coos Historical & Maritime Museum. In 1972, a Japanese balloon discovered in Oregon was displayed at the Smithsonian in Washington, DC. After being transferred to the Air and Space Museum, the Institute says it's either on loan or in storage. Now you can see the device nearly intact at the International Balloon Museum in Albuquerque, New Mexico. The South Dakota Cultural Heritage Center in Pierre, South Dakota, has a balloon bomb recovered nearby on display.

The remains of a Balloon Bomb were also found in Lumby, British Columbia, in October 2014. This bomb was detonated by the Royal Canadian Navy Ordnance Disposal team. The size of the explosion was indicative of not only Canadian munitions. Based on the size of the blast, it was clear that Japanese explosives were still lethal seventy years later.

The remains of another balloon bomb were found near McBride, British Columbia, in October 2019. It was found by a hunter looking for mountain goats in the British Columbia wilderness. There was evidence of a small fire nearby, suggesting that the bomb may have started the fire during the war. In Ottawa, Ontario, the Canadian War Museum also has a full intact balloon on display. Klamath Falls, Oregon, has a museum with balloon bomb parts and an informative presentation.

A documentary that extensively covers the history: *On a Wind and a Prayer*, directed and produced by Michael White, 2005. An action-packed documentary was released in December 2021. In this film, *Great Balloon Bomb Invasion*, historian Martin Morgan leads a first-of-its-kind hunt to find the bombs still lying undetected on North American soil.

# ATTACKS ON THE EAST COAST OF THE UNITED STATES FROM 1942 THROUGH 1945

*The US Army's Logo for the Eastern Defense Command.*

*Since the East Coast was the Command's area of operation, the sea is shown with the mythological sign "Neptune's Trident". It represents the three-fold essences of nature: Becoming, Being, and Dying.*

# East Coast Memorial

## American Battle Monuments Commission

""The losses by submarines of our Atlantic seaboard and in the Caribbean now threaten our entire war effort..."

GENERAL GEORGE MARSHALL, US ARMY CHIEF OF STAFF WORLD WAR II

"The only thing that ever really frightened me during the war was the U-boat peril."

SIR WINSTON CHURCHILL

"The United States Navy was woefully unprepared materially and mentally for the U-boat Blitz. On the Atlantic Coast...it had no plans for a reasonable protection to shipping...and were unable to improvise them..."

SAMUEL ELLIOT MORRISON, SENIOR OFFICER AND US NAVY HISTORIAN DURING WORLD WAR II

"It was the worst defeat ever suffered by the US Navy, because unlike Pearl Harbor, it was not a surprise attack."

NATHAN MILLER, *WAR AT SEA*

"Some experts think that if Hitler had 50 more U-boats in 1939, Germany would have won the war."

WOLFGANG FRANK, THE SEA WOLVES

Since September 11, 2001, lower Manhattan has been overshadowed by Ground Zero, with the new Freedom Tower and the World Trade Center Memorial (WTC). This area is one of the three sites of America's worst terrorist attacks. Within walking distance of the WTC site, another profound memorial commemorates another attack on our country that killed thousands of people nearly 60 years earlier.

Many are surprised to learn the parallel of this other memorial to 9/11 in that Germany killed nearly 5000 people in American waters, some so close that the carnage was seen from coastal beach towns. Almost all the dead were civilians or Merchant Marines. They were killed along the entire Eastern

Coast from Maine all the way down to Florida, and across the Gulf of Mexico, down to the coast of the Caribbean.

Three hundred and eleven ships were torpedoed, and of that number, two hundred and fifty-five ships were sunk, and fifty-six ships were damaged. Three hundred and three hundred and sixty-three ships were also sunk in the Caribbean. In determining the number of vessels sunk or damaged, the accounting can vary due to where the boundary between America and the Caribbean is considered to be.

The German submarine campaign along our East Coast sunk the largest number of American ships during any campaign in World War II. This exceeds the number killed in the attack on Pearl Harbor. I wish I could tell the story of those three hundred and eleven ships. However, the space limitations in this book do not permit me to do so. Unfortunately, personal accounts cannot be located for every attack and sinking. With that in mind, I will describe one or two notable histories off the coast of each state's shoreline. It should be kept in mind that many more ships were attacked and sunk off these states than are described here. Some of that additional history is covered in books listed in the Citations Section. Many vessels were American, yet many were from the Caribbean, South America, Canada, the UK and other countries.

*ABOVE: Located in lower Manhattan, the East Coast Memorial is dedicated to those thousands of Americans who gave their lives in World War II on our eastern coastline.*

Conceived in the days after the Pearl Harbor attack, Operation Paukenschlag (*Operation Drumbeat*) was a long-range assault on Allied shipping in American coastal waters. The Germans believed that the United States would be unprepared for a direct attack, and unfortunately, they were right. The U-boats pushed the limits of their operational range by striking the US coast.

The German effort paid off, and it defeated the American war efforts early. When the German submarines arrived off American shores in mid-January, they found a country that made few preparations for war. Most American Merchant ships traveled without escorts, lights remained ablaze in cities and towns along the shore, and there were few bombers and destroyers that harassed them. There were many easy targets; U-boat commanders called this "The Second Happy Time."

"The First Happy Time" was in 1940 after the fall of France, when Britain was alone to defend its shipping. This was unlike conventional warfare, when one opponent seeks to invade and conquer.

The strategy of *Operation Drumbeat* was to destroy as many tankers and freighters before they could arrive in the United Kingdom, thereby starving England into losing the war. *Operation Drumbeat* prepared a very realistic design. All manner of supplies, including food, medics, military hardware, ammunition, planes, and much else, were being delivered to the United Kingdom, and these supplies were crucial for its survival. The UK was the last of the dominos left to fall in Europe, and it was enduring an air invasion for many months, waiting for the sea invasion to come. The UK government prepared to evacuate to Canada. Europe belonged to the Nazis, and as a result, the only imports to the UK were from the US, Canada, and some South American countries.

The Germans decided to use some of their submarines to plant mines off the entrances of New York Harbor, Delaware Bay, and the Chesapeake Bay. Three German submarines planted mines on or about June 12, 1942, with Boston being substituted for New York at the last moment. Only the Chesapeake operation proved profitable for the Germans, with three American ships sunk and two damaged before the mines could be swept. The German submarines also planted mines near Boston, and a similar operation was done at the mouth of the Mississippi on July 25. This operation went undetected until the opening of German records after the war, when these actions were disclosed. Five more German mine-laying operations along the East Coast during 1942 brought halts to American shipping until the US Navy swept and disposed of them.


Conceived in the days after the Pearl Harbor attack, Operation Paukenschlag (*Operation Drumbeat*) was a long-range assault on Allied shipping in American coastal waters. The Germans believed that the United States would be unprepared for a direct attack, and unfortunately, they were right. The U-boats pushed the limits of their operational range by striking the US coast.

The German effort paid off and it defeated the American war efforts early. When the German submarines arrived off American shores in mid-January, they found a country that made few preparations for war. Most American Merchant ships traveled without escorts, lights remained ablaze in cities and towns along the shore, and there were few bombers and destroyers that harrassed them. There were so many easy targets, U-boat commanders called this "The Second Happy Time".

"The First Happy Time" was in 1940 after the fall of France, when Britain was alone to defend its shipping. This was unlike conventional warfare when one opponent seeks to invade and conquer.

The strategy of *Operation Drumbeat* was to destroy as many tankers and freighters before they could arrive in the United Kingdom, thereby, starving England into losing the war. *Operation Drumbeat* prepared a very realistic design. All manner of supplies including food, medics, military hardware, ammunition, planes, and much else were being delivered to the United Kingdom, and these supplies were crucial for its survival. The UK was the last of the dominos left to fall in Europe, and it was enduring an air invasion for many months, waiting for the sea invasion to come. The UK government prepared to evacuate to Canada. Europe belonged to the Nazis, and as a result, the only imports to the UK were from the US, Canada, and some South American countries.

The Germans decided to use some of their submarines to plant mines off the entrances of New York Harbor, Delaware Bay, and the Chesapeake Bay. Three German submarines planted mines on or about June 12, 1942, with Boston being substituted for New York at the last moment. Only the Chesapeake operation proved profitable for the Germans with three American ships sunk and two damaged before the mines could be swept. The German submarines also planted mines near Boston, and a similar operation was done at the mouth of the Mississippi on July 25. This operation went undetected until the opening of German records after the war when these actions were disclosed. Five more German mine-laying operations along the East Coast during 1942 brought halts to American shipping until the US Navy swept and disposed them.

## Hitler's Plan to Attack the United States

*"The United States kept up the tall talk and left her coast unguarded. Now I dare say she is quite surprised."*

Adolph Hitler, June 1942

Dr. Gerhard Weinberg is one of the most celebrated and renowned World War II historians known worldwide. His volumes are used as textbooks in many countries. He was a refuge from Europe during the war, and he joined the US Army, serving in the occupation of Japan just after the surrender. In 1959, Dr. Weinberg discovered the manuscript of Hitler's second book in the Army's treasure trove of Nazi Party material captured 14 years earlier in Berlin. The book reveals in writing more specific intentions of Hitler and the Nazi Party with regard to America.

In Weinberg's book, *Germany, Hitler and World War Two*, the author emphasizes that Hitler assumed he would have to fight the US at some point. In *Hitler's Second Book*, edited by Gerhard Weinberg, Hitler asserted that the predation for war with the United States was one of the efforts of the Nazi Party.

Since the goal was ultimately global expansion, the US would likely stand in Hitler's way. The size of the US itself gave some indication of its capabilities, including a potentially large military. Dr. Weinberg presents the problem that the US was too far away from Germany. While the purpose of the U-boats attacks in North America was to keep war materials from reaching the UK, the eventual problem was how to attack America itself. A German bomber called *"Amerika Bomber"* was developed, and it included a sizable payload of bombs that could be flown over the Atlantic Ocean and back. This bomber would have been completed in 1946 if it weren't for the presence of the Allied Armies in Europe.

Dr. Weinberg also calls our attention to how fast Hitler declared war on America after the Japanese attacked Pearl Harbor. Being the only other Axis Power strong enough to go up against America, Hitler presumed his odds increased. Secretary of State Cordell Hull urged President Roosevelt to ask Congress to declare war on Germany at the same time as declaring war on Japan since there was intelligence that indicated that Hitler was committed to declaring war on the US if Japan attacked America. FDR disagreed and chose to focus on Japan instead. Hitler made good on his promise several days after the Pearl Harbor attack, declaring war on the United States on December 11.

Dr. Weinberg further explains, "It had been an assumption of Hitler's since the 1920s that Germany would, at some point, fight the United States. As early as the summer of 1928, he asserted in his second book (not published until I did it for him in 1961) that strengthening and preparing Germany for war with the United States was one of the tasks of the National Socialist Movement."

Dr. Winberg continues, "Because Hitler's aims for Germany's future entailed an unlimited expansionism of global proportions and because he thought the United States as a country which with its population and size might at some time constitute a challenge to German domination of the globe, a war with the United States had long been part of the future he envisioned for Germany, either during his own rule of it or thereafter.

"To overcome these practical obstacles, Hitler built up the German Navy and began work on a long-range bomber -- the notorious "Amerika Bomber" -- which would be capable of flying to New York and back without refueling. Although the bomber proved difficult to construct, Hitler embarked on a crash-building program of super battleships promptly after the defeat of France. In addition, he began accumulating air and sea bases on the Atlantic coast to facilitate attacks on the United States. In April 1941, Hitler secretly pledged that he would join Japan in a war on the United States. This was critical. Only if Japan declared war would Germany follow.

"Hitler was caught out of town at the time of Pearl Harbor and had to get back to Berlin and summon the Reichstag to acclaim war. His great worry, and that of his foreign minister, was that the Americans might get their declaration of war in ahead of his own. As Joachim von Ribbentrop explained it, 'A great power does not allow itself to be declared war upon; it declares war on others.' He did not need to lose much sleep; the Roosevelt Administration was quite willing to let the Germans take the lead. Just to make sure, however, that hostilities started immediately, Hitler had already issued orders to his Navy, straining at the leash since October 1939, to begin sinking American ships forthwith, even before the formalities of declaring war. Now that Germany had a big Navy on its side (Japan's), there was no need to wait even an hour."

## Nazis Attack America's East Coast

### Operation Paukenschlag (Operation Drumbeat)

Germany killed nearly five thousand people on the US East Coast, with 311 American ships hit, 255 American ships sunk (1,425,996 GRT), and 56 American ships damaged (397,444 GRT). These figures do not include the Caribbean, with an estimated 363 ships sunk there and more off the coast of South America. Thirty-six ships were sunk off Brazil alone. Forty U-boats in total came to the United States to wage war. Most Americans who survived the sinkings ended up in lifeboats, rafts, or hanging onto debris, sometimes wishing they had gone down with the ship. Once they were in the sea, that was just the beginning. Most were never found or died in the lifeboats and thrown over. Starvation and dehydration were the norms, accompanied by the intense sun and freezing temperatures. The human body can only survive a short time without food and even less without water. The *Battle of the Atlantic* was the longest battle of World War II, beginning in September 1939 through May 1945. Germany would build over eleven hundred U-boats during the war. There were nine types, with one type completely using electric power. There were four mini-U-boats and several experimental single units.

Admiral Carl Donitz was Supreme Commander of the Kriegsmarine's U-boat Command (*Befehlshaber der Unterseeboote* (BdU). In 1935, Admiral Erich Raeder chose Donitz to reconstitute Germany's Submarine Force in defiance of the Treaty of Versailles. He was promoted to Grand Admiral of the German Navy in 1943, and he was Hitler's appointed successor. Donitz would be convicted of Wars Crimes and Crimes Against Peace at the Nuremberg War Crimes trials. He would serve a prison sentence instead of facing execution. On April 30, 1945, after the death of Adolf Hitler and by Hitler's Last Will and Testament, Donitz was named Hitler's successor as Head of State. It is quite clear from Hitler's will that Donitz was his most trusted advisor and that he would continue Hitler's Nazi agenda.

In January 1943, Donitz achieved the rank of *Großadmiral* (Grand Admiral), and he was considered the main enemy of Allied Naval Forces in the *Battle of the Atlantic*. Although Donitz attempted to portray himself as a purely military man dedicated to the Fatherland after the war, the truth was far from it.

By his admission, Donitz was a dedicated Nazi and supporter of Hitler. He held anti-Semitic beliefs and insisted that *Kriegsmarine* (Nazi German Navy) officers adhere to his political views. Following the war, Donitz was indicted as a major war criminal at the Nuremberg Trials on three counts: (1) Conspiracy to commit crimes against peace, war crimes, and crimes against humanity; (2) Planning, initiating and waging wars of aggression; and (3) Crimes against the Laws of War. He was found not guilty of committing crimes against humanity but guilty of committing crimes against peace and war crimes against the Laws of War. He was sentenced, but he only served 14 years.

Nevertheless, the U-boat commanders would not always follow the directive to the letter, allowing some American crew members to board their lifeboats before the Germans fired a final torpedo. About lifeboat survivors, the Germans U-boat sailors did not have the same negative reputation as the Japanese did with regard to their ruthless firing on lifeboats. However, the Germans were known to do so in certain cases. However, the British and the US sunk German and Japanese Merchant ships. But there was not a moral equivalency between the Axis and the Allies. Japan and Germany dragged the US and UK into the war.

Donitz's standing Order was: "No attempt of any kind must be made at rescuing members of ships sunk, and this includes picking up persons in the water and putting them in lifeboats, righting capsized lifeboats, and handing over food and water. Rescue runs counter to the most primitive demands of warfare for the destruction of enemy ships and crews. Be hard...."

What about the German U-boats made them unique from other countries' submarines? The U-boat was designed as a smaller, more agile sub capable of "hit and run." Its wake was smaller, and in general, a U-boat was harder to detect by sonar or radar due to its size. The U-boats were built primarily to sink merchant ships, although they certainly sunk their fair share of naval vessels. They were not used to transport war materials, as were the Japanese, British, and large American submarines.

U-boats were very effective due to a combination of factors: there was a competition between U-boat captains to sink the greatest tonnage in a month. The competition got fierce and personal, with U-boat captains often pushing their crews very hard for their own glory. The U-boat commander had a special relationship with the Fuhrer. The tactical advantage was, of course, that they were to be all but invisible to the American fighters and tankers. The success of the U-boats was in part due to the American's inability to find the "fish" and then ensure their demise. At that time, the American Navy didn't have a large enough presence on the East Coast. The American convoys had not started until later in 1942, which protected many of their ships from the disastrous effects of the U-boat torpedoes.

Beginning in 1939, the strategy as planned by Donitz was to sink as many merchant ships as possible headed for Britain. The UK would have only a 2-week supply of heating fuel at times. Their society could easily have collapsed. In 1940 along with the bombings of England, surrender to Germany looked like a real possibility.

The Americans and British called them "Greywolves." "Wolfpack" was a common description since their tactic at times was that of a real wolf pack, meaning a group encirclement. The Merchant Marine and Navy Armed Guard called the torpedoes "eels."

Radar could be used to detect U-boats only when they were on the surface, which was not the majority of the time. Radar was used to detect distant aircraft and ships. Radar would give a great advantage because the enemy would be detected without knowing it. To disrupt radars, enemies would use *radar jammers.* The *radar jammers* would interrupt the waves coming out of the radar. After this happens, the radar wouldn't be able to get signals that the enemies were near. The greatest advantage to using radar is that the enemies will lose the element of surprise. The Germans would sometimes use *radar detectors.* By utilizing these *radar detectors*, the Germans could learn where the radars were positioned so it would be easier to bypass them.

. Sonar devices were used to detect distant objects such as submarine boats or mines. They would send out soundwaves and then wait for echoes of the sounds to come back. Sonar is an acronym for **SO**und **N**avigation **A**nd **R**anging. Navy bombers would use high-definition sonar to find U-boats during the day when they submerged. But unfortunately, sonar devices were not installed to a greater extent until later in the year. America was unprepared. The U-boats did not utilize radar or sonar. However, they did use hydrophone (sound-seeking) technology. The implementation of radar and sonar became one factor that gave the Allied Navies an advantage. But these technologies were only a tool; the human skill was still the greatest factor in determining the success of finding and sinking U-boats.

In Germany, U-boat sailors were celebrities. They were an elite military group, even though a U-boat Commander only needed to be a lieutenant. Women would shower U-boat sailors with flowers against a backdrop of live music in their honor upon their arrival. German children even collected U-boat commander cards, like American kids collected baseball cards. The number of volunteers for U-boat assignments was so overwhelming that men had to be turned away. U-boats would ultimately sink over 2200 Allied Merchant ships and 175 Naval vessels. These are staggering numbers considering how small the U-boat was and how limited the number of torpedoes (about 4-6 torpedoes) they contained. Because of the small number of torpedoes on each U-boat, they couldn't afford to miss a target.

*ABOVE: Merchant Marines and US Navy Armed Guard were amazed at how fast a U-boat would appear with no indication they were nearby just moments earlier.*

The list corresponding to these maps of ships and U-boats sunk is located in Appendix V.

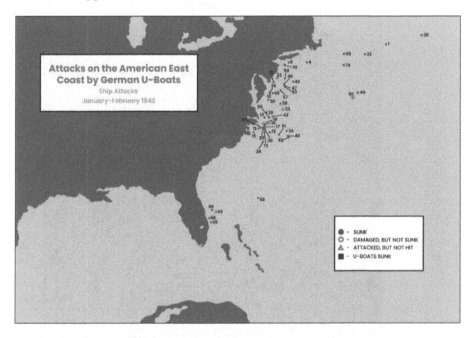

After Hitler's Declaration of War on the US on December 11, 1941, it didn't take long before the first U-boat **was launched** against America. After that point, many U-boats followed.

Able to read radio traffic, the British warned Canada and the US Commander-in-Chief of the Atlantic Fleet (CINCLANT) in January 1942 that U-boats were on their way to their shores. Since Naval assets were defending the West Coast and fighting the Japanese in the Pacific, the US Navy could not locate the original five U-boats. The Eastern Sea Frontier was the Navy's defense in 1942. In addition to providing escorts for convoys, the Frontier was responsible for the sea-air rescue, harbor defense, shipping lane patrol, minesweeping, and air operations.

The designated Commander of the Eastern Sea Frontier (COMEASTSEAFRON) was Admiral Adolphus Andrews, who suffered from a lack of destroyers, minesweepers, and air support to combat the U-boat threat. He was in the worst of all possible situations, and that is, under attack with little defense.

The *U-125* (Captain Folkers) was the first to sail to our country in World War II. Throughout December 1941, many other U-boats sailed to the US, including *U-123* (Captain Hardegen) on the 23rd, *U-66* (Captain Zapp) on the 24th, and finally, the last two Paukenschlag boats with *U-130* (Captain Kals) and *U-109* (Captain Bleichrodt), sailing on the 27th. With virtually no US Navy defending the East Coast, the attacks were devastating for America. In these 60 days alone, U-boat German captains managed to attack seventy-four ships, six of which were torpedoed but not sunk, with several attacks off the coasts of Canada and Newfoundland. This resulted in the total number of deaths of approximately 1000 people, with at least that many who were injured. In addition, over 1,000,000 tons and millions of dollars worth of supplies and war materials were lost. At that point, the Allies were that much closer to losing the war. The sinkings by the U-boats were supposed to be kept secret from the American public to prevent the Germans from achieving their goal of terrorizing the American people. Although they started with five U-boats, eventually, there would be forty in total coming to the United States to attack.

On December 23, 1941, *U-123,* the deadliest U-boats on the Eastern Coast, left for its first phase of *Operation Drumbeat*. Admiral Donitz ordered the U-boats to sink the maximum number of vessels even though these vessels were known to have no means of self-defense.

After sinking the *Cyclops* and *Norness*, the German Captain Hardegen decided to bottom his U-boat (i.e., place it on the ocean bottom) and wait for nightfall before proceeding into the New York Harbor itself. He sunk several American ships and a British civilian ship during the night. The highest death toll from a ship sunk by U-boats off the East Coast was on January 19, when he torpedoed the Canadian civilian passenger ship *HMS Lady Hawkins* killing 250 people. Anyone could easily recognize the ship as a civilian passenger ship, and no doubt Hardegan did, but he had no qualms about killing innocent unarmed civilians with no military objective. It was not carrying supplies for the Allies.

Hardegen then proceeded south along the coast, submerging and surfacing at night during the day. Apart from one air attack on January 16, Hardegen did not experience any resistance from the United States Navy or United States Army Air Forces. Hardegen also sank three freighters off Cape Hatteras, NC, in shallow waters close to shore. A couple of hours later, he happened upon five more merchant ships traveling in a group and attacked them with his last two torpedoes and his 105 mm deck gun, sinking a freighter and claiming the tanker *Malay* (8,207 Gross Registered Tons-GRT) as well. Although badly damaged, *Malay*, traveling empty, had enough buoyancy to stay afloat and made its way to New York under her power five days later. Werner Winter, Captain of the *U-103*, would sink five ships from February 2 through February 5.

On January 23, Hardegen received another signal, confirming he had been awarded the Knight's Cross of the Iron Cross personally by Adolph Hitler himself for sinking over 100,000 GRT of Allied shipping. He returned home to Lorient, France, on February 9 and received a hero's welcome. He then left for Berlin to see the Fuhrer. Hardegan, Captain of the *U-123*, was not the most successful U-boat commander, but he sunk the most tonnage in the American Theater of War.

## MARCH-APRIL 1942

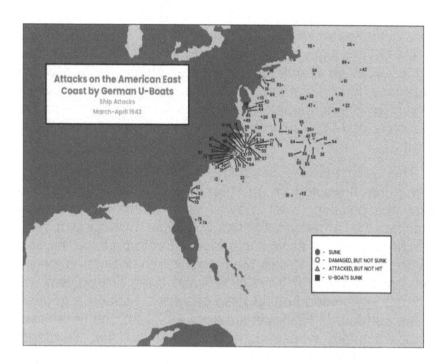

Attacks on the American East Coast by German U-Boats
Ship Attacks
March-April 1942

● - SUNK
O - DAMAGED, BUT NOT SUNK
△ - ATTACKED, BUT NOT HIT
■ - U-BOATS SUNK

March 1942 through April 1942 was the most deadly period of attacks by German U-boats near the coasts of the US. Ninety-eight ships were attacked, with thirteen damaged but stayed afloat. Forty-eight American ships were attacked in March and fifty American ships in April, most of them occurring near North Carolina's coast.

When the Paukenschlag U-boats returned to their French bases in February, the next wave of U-boats had already hit America's coastline. The following U-boat waves included many of Germany's most experienced commanders like Topp (*U-552*), Hardegen in *U-123* again, Witt (*U-129*), Degen *(U-701)*, Schnee (*U-201*), Mohr (*U-124*) and Lassen (*U-160*) to name a few. An additional dozen new U-boats were also assigned to attack the United States.

On March 2, 1942, Hardegen left for his final patrol, his second attack in American waters. Hardegen's first successes were achieved when he sank the American tanker *Muskogee* (7,034 GRT) on March 22 and the British tanker *Empire Steel* (8,150 GRT) on March 24. The latter attack expended four torpedoes, and since the tanker carried gasoline, it burned fiercely for five hours before sinking, with no survivors spotted. The crew of *U-123* nicknamed that night the "*Tanker Torch Night.*"

The Q-Ship was a camouflaged freighter that had hidden deck guns. It would lure a U-boat to attack, and then when it went into position, blast it away. On March 26, Hardegen attacked the American Q-ship USS *Atik*, mistaking it for a Merchant freighter, as was intended. After torpedoing the ship, Hardegen surfaced to sink the freighter with deck guns, only to find the *Atik* trying to ram *U-123* and open fire on him with cannons concealed behind false bulwarks. Making a getaway on the surface, *U-123* received eight hits, with one of the crew members fatally wounded. Approaching the *Atik*, Hardegen sank it with another torpedo.

Hardegen's second patrol was along the Florida coast. In late March, he reached the target area, attacking the American tanker *Liebre* (7,057 GRT) on April 1 with his deck gun. Although the tanker was badly damaged, an approaching patrol craft forced Hardegen to submerge and leave the area. *Liebre* was towed to port and was ready to sail again by mid-July.

Georgia and Florida were now targeted, with ships being lost and people killed. In March 1942, large numbers of U-boats operated off North Carolina's Outer Banks, sinking or damaging twenty-five ships (the *U-124* alone wrecked five of them). U-boat attacks, which previously concentrated north and east of Cape Hatteras, were now occurring further south off Cape Lookout and Cape Fear. The strikes were close to shore because the shipping lanes had been tightened as a defensive measure due to a shallow sea bottom. Cape Hatteras on the Outer Banks was so dangerous that merchant ships were ordered to pass it only in daylight to lessen the likelihood of attack.

The U-boats would only surface at night, and they were much faster on the surface due to less sea friction to overcome when in motion. The U-boats were powered by hybrid systems, diesel engines and a matrix of batteries. But it had to surface to recharge its batteries since the diesel exhaust had to discharge above the surface. Therefore, the U-boat had to come out of the water to recharge its batteries.

During the last twenty days of March 1942, U-boats claimed twenty-three ships off the North Carolina coast. On March 18, the single worst night for shipping of the war in the Atlantic, U-boats destroyed five ships. In April, attacks from as many as seventeen different U-boats peaked, with twenty-seven Allied ships sunk or damaged within the 200-mile zone off North Carolina. Two hundred miles out was American territory. The first four months of 1942 saw nearly seventy ships torpedoed and sent to the ocean bottom. More than 90 percent of the ships lost at Torpedo Junction during the four years of submarine attacks went down between January and July 1942.

The British Royal Admiralty sent a commander to Washington to plead with American Naval officials to start a system of convoys. The British had learned from experience that the most effective tactic against U-boat attacks was to escort groups of Merchant ships with warships. Any attempt to sink a Merchant ship by a U-boat would bring nearby armed Navy ships to counter them. But the British were not the only ones decrypting enemy codes. The German Beobachtungs-Dienst (B-Dienst) radio monitoring service was able to read some convoy codes, giving the Germans an advantage in the early years of hunting down British Merchant ships. The British ships usually sailed along with American ones in the North Atlantic.

Finally, on March 26, the US Navy responded to a U-boat attack. *U-71* torpedoed the tanker *Dixie Arrow* and stayed around to watch it burn. The *USS Tarbell* dropped depth charges, but the *U-71* escaped, and the *Tarbell* picked up the survivors. It wasn't until the night of April 13-14 that the first U-boat was sunk. The destroyer USS *Roper* used its new radar technology to detect *U-85* off the North Carolina coast. The *Roper* sunk the submarine and then dropped depth charges for good measure.

By April, the US finally had a plan utilizing a fleet of sixty-five anti-submarine vessels. No tankers hauled oil around the Atlantic Ocean unless they had escorts. From then on, most Merchant ships traveled in escorted convoys, known as *bucket brigades*, along the coast. At night, Merchant ships were put into sheltered harbors. However, these safety measures were not enough to thwart the U-boats from attacking American ships.

As a solution to the Allied convoys, Karl Donitz popularized the Wolf Pack, or "*Rudeltaktik*," which was to have a catastrophic effect on the Allied ships. Some convoys contained hundreds of ships, and many escorts and anti-submarine warships were many miles long. With the Allied safety-in-numbers under the convoy system, U-boats lost their ability to select isolated, easy targets distributed around the country. The few U-boats that discovered a convoy had difficulties striking it since anti-submarine warships were guarding them.

U-boats operated in packs and preyed indiscriminately on cargo ships across the Atlantic. To counter the convoy system, a wolf-pack approach was designed. While the British/American convoys had organized commerce shipping and established a protective perimeter around the ships, the U-boats continued to operate independently. The plan was to arrange a pack of U-boats and postpone an assault until all boats were in position to launch a coordinated massed attack. This would overwhelm the escorts since the assault boats' sheer numbers and the surprise element would confuse the defense.

The first boat to establish contact was designated as the "*shadower,*" which was tasked with maintaining contact and informing the *BdU* (U-Boat Headquarters in Berlin) of the convoy's whereabouts. The "*shadower*" would stay out of the convoy's visual range, often sinking during the day and traveling on the surface at night. When a sufficient number of boats closed on the convoy, the *BdU* would signal to attack, which was normally around nightfall when the modest silhouette of the U-boat made detection difficult.

Once the assault signal was issued, each commander was free to use a variety of tactics. Some shot at great range, generally with a spread of many torpedoes, beyond the perimeter of the escorts. Whichever methods were used, the overall goal was to assault at night and retreat during the day, with continual attacks lasting several days as more boats arrived.

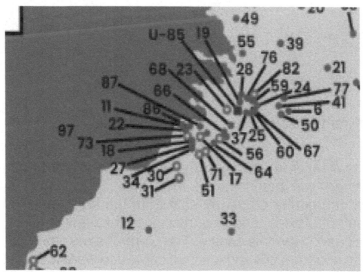

*North Carolina and Virginia coasts March-April, 1942*

**The list corresponding to these maps of ships and U-boats sunk is located in Appendix V.**

## MAY-JUNE, 1942

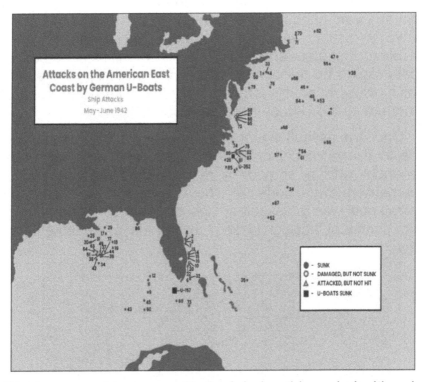

Eighty-seven ships were attacked during this period with only ten staying afloat.

It is clear from this map that compared to the March-April timeframe, the beginning of America's new convoy system shifted the center of gravity shift from the northeastern US to the Gulf of Mexico, and in particular to the New Orleans area, as well as to Florida's coasts. The Germans assumed correctly that the southern US and the Gulf of Mexico were less prepared than the East Coast. The *"milkcow"* (a larger U-boat) would supply and enable the smaller U-boats to travel farther to the

Gulf. The oil coming from Texas as well as Louisiana were heavily targeted by the U-boats in the Gulf.

The larger U-boat, dubbed the *"milkcow"* by the Germans, could carry 2500 tons of supplies and torpedoes to restock the smaller U-boats, usually near Bermuda. The oil tankers originating from Texas, Louisiana, and South America were knocked off by the U-boats in rapid secession. The record of the number of U-boat attacks in one day was seven American ships.

German engineers based their design on the existing much larger *Type IXD*, but they shortened and gave it a much wider upper deck. The hull was also deeper and constructed of thicker pressure hull, giving it deeper diving capabilities than *Type VII* and *Type IX*. To maximize storage capacity, it didn't have any torpedo attack capability, but it was fitted with anti-aircraft weapons for self-defense. Two 37mm cannons were fitted, one forward and one aft of the bridge, and a single 20mm on a platform aft. The *Type XIV* shared many components with the *Type VIIC,* and the bridge was identical to the *Type IX*.

*ABOVE: Because of their role as supply U-boats, the Type XIV was nicknamed "milk-cows" (milchkuh).*

They acted as force multipliers, wherein a network of supply U-boats would replenish operational boats with the much-needed torpedoes, food, fuel, and other provisions. They also carried a doctor onboard and a bakery which provided freshly baked bread. In effect, *Type XIV* enabled operational boats to remain much longer in their patrol zones, significantly increasing their presence.

During this 60-day period, the first two U-boats (*U-352* and *U-158*) were destroyed and sunk off the US Coast by American bombers.

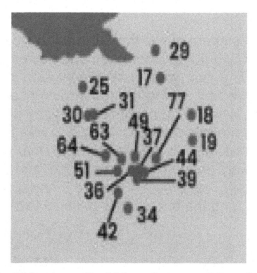

*The Gulf of Mexico off of New Orleans May-June, 1942*

**The list corresponding to these maps of ships and U-boats sunk is located in Appendix V.**

# JULY-AUGUST, 1942

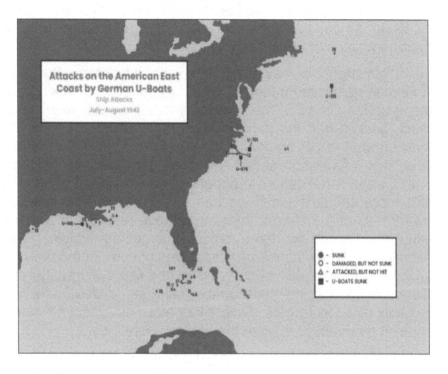

**The list corresponding to these maps of ships and U-boats sunk is located in Appendix V.**

Due to the Navy's convoy system and lessons learned, the threat subsided. Still, twenty-six American ships were sunk by German U-boats from July 1942 through August 1942. In addition, three American ships were attacked but not sunk. The Caribbean Sea was still convenient for the U-boats to attack ships. This period was a peak for U-boats in the Caribbean, with seventy-four sinkings of American, British, and Dutch ships. U-boats came back to America's East Coast in 1943, 1944, and 1945, sinking US ships up to, and even after, they had orders to stand down and surrender.

Unfortunately, this was not the last time America would suffer attacks from the U-boats. Germany continued to wreak havoc in the north, and south Atlantic Ocean, Europe, Greenland, Iceland, Russia, the Mediterranean, Africa, and even in the Pacific up until the end of the war; from the Arctic Circle to Africa, the subs continued their campaign to sink merchant ships of Allied Nations.

In hindsight, it may have been an advantage that the American government tried to cover up the U-boat sinkings to the American public. The blow to morale would have been much greater had the public known the extent of Germany's threat upon the US territory. Although the government tried to keep this information secret, at times, the news of sinkings ended up in American newspapers. The other point of view is that more should have been told to the public. The greater awareness of the U-boat threat may have resulted in a more extensive search for them before they could attack. The expression "*Loose Lips Sink Ships*" was popular at the time as a warning not to talk about ship schedules. In reality, the Germans needed little intelligence-gathering to determine the location of good targets since silhouettes of American ships showed themselves against the lighted shorelines.

By late 1942, technology had improved and was installed in aircraft. The Leigh lights were powerful searchlights. Magnetic Anomaly Detection (MAD) refers to magnetometers to detect submarines. A mass of ferromagnetic material created a detectable disturbance in an electromagnetic field. This disturbance could be sensed by instrumentation.

The development of the Fido homing torpedo turned the aircraft into a more effective submarine liquidator. The Fido was a small anti-submarine homing torpedo, also known as the "Mark 24" Mine. The homing device contained four crystal hydrophones arranged around the body of the torpedo along with a simple guidance system that steered toward the loudest noise that could find the U-boat. Shore and ship-based technologies such as high-frequency direction finding and magnetic loops could now help aircraft find enemy U-boats with varying degrees of success.

Throughout the world in World War II, the UK lost 1660 ships (some with Americans onboard) by German U-boats, while the United States lost 549 ships and the Soviet Union lost 106 ships.

By late 1942 as the War focused on the Mediterranean and North Africa, Hitler ordered more U-boats into Europe rather than on the American Coast. Donitz disagreed with Hitler because he knew he could defeat England by adding more wolfpacks to the strategy in the North Atlantic. This was one of Hitler's big blunders of World War II, from which the Allies were blessed. This was the second time Donitz was prevented from going full force. The first time was in 1939, when Hitler started the war in Europe instead of waiting a year to build up more naval assets, as Donitz strongly advised.

By May 1943, the operational capability of the U-boat was in serious jeopardy. The number of sinkings reversed; now, it was the Germans who were being defeated at sea. The Germans named May 1943 "Black May." The secret enigma machine codes were broken by the British at Bletchley Park. Most, but not all U-boat locations, would then be determined. Given the time to build more destroyers and develop sonar technology, the US Navy would forge ahead out in the Atlantic, well-prepared to find and destroy U-boats. Once a U-boat was detected, the Navy would pursue it for as long as it took, and then they would sink it. Most U-boats were destroyed by the end of the war.

A few of the well-known classic books on the U-boat war in the United States are *Operation Drumbeat* by Michael Gannon, *Torpedo Junction* by Homer Hickam and *The Fuhrer's U-boats in American Waters* by Gary Gentile. Clay Blair's two-volume set *Hitler's U-boat War, The Hunters* and *The Hunted* are also very good resources on this subject. Rear Admiral Historian Samuel Eliot Morrison's *The Battle of the Atlantic* focuses well on the U-boat war. Hundreds of books on the U-boats have been published.

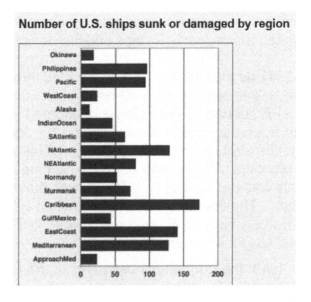

**Number of U.S. ships sunk or damaged by region**

*ABOVE: The greatest number of American Merchant ships were sunk off the Caribbean, the East Coast, and the North Atlantic in World War II. US Merchant Marine Website. USMM.ORG*

*ABOVE: This photo has been enhanced at the horizon; the original showed ships slightly smaller. The scene demonstrates*

*in the beginning of the U-boat war and the ease at which the U-boats could operate without fear of reprisal.*

# MAINE

The mystery of the USS *Eagle 56* was finally solved nearly seventy years after it sunk. The discovery and investigation of the wreck site resulted in a US Navy Board of Inquiry reversing its erroneous findings from decades earlier. The Navy acknowledged it made a blunder. The US Navy Board of Inquiry insisted that a boiler explosion caused the explosion that sank it during the war. This reversal was unprecedented.

The striking story of the USS *Eagle 56* is one of mystery and intrigue. The Germans would continue to travel thousands of miles to the American East Coast to sink American ships up to their surrender. By doing so, Germany was arbitrarily killing with no apparent military advantage. It was common knowledge among Germans that the war was all but lost at this time. These American ships were not invading Germany or Nazi-occupied territories.

On February 23, 1945, as the American flag was being raised over Iwo Jima by US Marines, Germany sent *U-853* on a third war patrol to attack US Coastal shipping. Under the command of Helmut Frömsdorf, the crossing of the Atlantic was slow because he used a method called *Schnorchel* (snorkel) to remain submerged to avoid being spotted by aircraft. A submarine snorkel is a device that allows a submerged submarine to operate its diesel engines while still taking in air from above the surface. The snorkel was simply a pipe with a valve on one end which extended above sea level while the boat was submerged. The tube consisted of an intake and exhaust pipe, where outside air was drawn into the U-boat and exhaust gases expelled from the exhaust pipe. The shut-off valve prevented seawater from entering the intake if the mouth of the tube dipped below the surface. It was widely used on German U-boats during the last year of World War II.

*Hunt for Eagle 56: Lost to History*, a Smithsonian Channel documentary, revealed the untold tale of forty-nine sailors who perished off the Maine coast. Only thirteen of the sixty-two crew members of the USS *Eagle 56* survived. For decades, survivors and their families have been tormented by questions and doubts about the disaster. Finally, a civilian-led diving expedition aimed to locate the missing debris and ascertain what occurred. The group unearthed new evidence underwater and interviewed eyewitnesses.

The ship's wreckage was discovered in June 2018, and a civilian crew dived and explored it. According to a video taken by the divers, the boilers of the USS Eagle 56 were still intact. It was proven that *Eagle 56* was sunk by the German U-boat *U-853* off the coast of Maine on April 23, 1945, while towing targets for US Navy bomber training.

The USS *Eagle 56* was the second-to-last US Navy battleship sunk by Nazi Germany. Ordered to the Gulf of Maine, *U-853* sank the USS *Eagle Boat 56* near Portland on April 23. The USS *Frederick C. Davis* (*DE-136*) was the last warship sunk by a German U-boat when U-546 torpedoed it on April 24, 1945.

On the same day as the USS Eagle 56 sinking, the USS *Selfridge* (*DD-357*) launched nine depth charges against an "unknown" U-boat nearby. The next day, the USS *Muskegon* made sonar contact with *U-853* and attacked it, but it was not destroyed. On the 6th of May, *U-853* was pursued and sunk by Navy and Coast Guard ships during the *Battle of Point Judith* off Rhode Island are still intact today. The ship's steel plating is beginning to rust, but the location has been declared a war grave, with all its safeguards.

In 2001, after the wreck was dived and new evidence extrapolated by civilians, the Navy changed its mind. The Navy admitted that the ship was sunk by hostile fire, and they awarded Purple Hearts to the survivors and relatives of the dead.

### Reclassification

In 2001, the Naval Historical Center reviewed the case after much deliberation and reclassified the sinking as a combat loss. In June 2001, Purple Heart medals were awarded to three survivors and the next of kin of those killed. Today, this was the only time in US Navy history that its own Court of Inquiry's findings was reversed.

A commemorative plaque was erected on the grounds of Fort Williams Park near Portland Head Light. In Maine, not only did the enemy sink ships, but it also landed spies. The *U-1230* landed two intelligence agents at Hancock Point near Bar Harbor, Maine, on November 29, 1944. The saboteurs were arrested the next month, but the *U-1230* torpedoed and sank the Canadian ship, *Cornwallis,* off the Maine coast, killing forty-four of its crew members.

# NEW HAMPSHIRE

## Portsmouth Naval Base

*ABOVE: German "Mini-Subs" entered Portsmouth Harbor during World War II. For many years, the "Molch Salamander" was on display at the Portsmouth Naval Base.*

Germany developed the one-person "*Molch Salamander*" class U-boat, which carried two external torpedoes. One pilot operated it and was brought across the Atlantic by a larger U-boat. The Germans deployed five distinct types of "Mini-Subs," with one being a two-man *Unterseeboot*. Hundreds of these "Mini-Subs" were used in short-range operations with varying degrees of success in Europe. The entrance to Portsmouth Harbor involved one of the subs. The "*Molch Salamander*" could have easily torpedoed anchored Navy vessels. Fortunately, the US Navy's underwater magnetic loop that extended to Appledore Island at the Isles of Shoals detected its presence.

The sub was located and taken to Portsmouth Naval Shipyard, where it was displayed for a time after the war. Sea mines, planted by a full-sized U-boat, were discovered in Portsmouth Harbor and were safely detonated after the war. These Mini-Subs (the *Molch*, *Birber*, *Neger*, *Marder,* and *Seehund)* can be seen today at museums throughout Europe, the US, and Canada.

*Above: On May 18, 1945, the 245-foot U-805 was the first to arrive. It had surrendered in the North Atlantic and was towed into Portsmouth Harbor. Green dye was released by the Coast Guard, marking the spot in the Harbor for the U-boat to rendezvous with a tugboat carrying Navy officials and news reporters.*

The *U-805* surrendered at the mouth of the Port. Subsequently, the U-boat was transferred to a shipyard for publicity. The inmates were transported to Portsmouth Naval Prison by bus, also known as *The Castle*. The *Kriegsmarine* German sailors were interrogated by interpreters from the Office of Naval Intelligence (ONI). The ONI looked for technical information on jet aircraft, ballistic missiles, guided bombs, and nuclear weapons. Scientists in Nazi Germany had a good understanding of nuclear science. Atomic physics and nuclear weapons had its roots in that country in the 1920s. Germans were the first to split the atom. In 1932, Nazi scientist Werner Heisenberg was awarded the Noble Prize for the creation of quantum mechanics.

A reporter interviewed a captain of one of the U-boats at WHEB-AM. The journalist spoke with U-boat sailor Lt. Albert Finster, and he said Finster was a classic Nazi in that he blamed England for the war, without a basis for his statement. Two more German U-boats arrived the next day: *U-873* was pulled into the Harbor at 2:00 pm, followed by *U-1228*. A wire service report later that night added to the excitement.

## U-234 A Unique Surrender

Near Newfoundland, the USS *Sutton* seized *U-234* carrying three high-ranking German officials and two dead Japanese scientists.

The *U-234* was going to Japan, still fighting the Allies in the ongoing Pacific War. It was rumored to be carrying men and supplies to aid the Japanese war effort. On Saturday, May 19, at 7:30 am, *U-234* arrived in Portsmouth and was met by a swarm of journalists.

The high-ranking German officers on board made it a massive news story as *U-234* was the most valuable prize of all the Nazi U-boats. A disassembled *Messerschmitt ME 262* jet fighter, prototypes, technical specifications of new armaments, and numerous senior weapons technicians were aboard the U-boat.

The two Japanese scientists refused to board the USS *Sutton.* They committed suicide, and the Germans buried them at sea. It was believed the Japanese scientists were working with the Nazis to deliver atomic bomb technology and other weapons to be used against the Allies. A major part of *U-234*'s cargo, 1,232 pounds of uranium oxide, was kept a secret by the US government.

# RHODE ISLAND

*ABOVE: A depth charge seeking out U-853 raises a geyser off the stern of the Coast Guard frigate USS Moberly off Point Judith, Rhode Island, on the morning of May 6, 1945. (National Archives, NARA II)*

The Battle of Point Judith

Just as Nazi Germany was surrendering to the Allied Powers, sixty-seven men died in the *Battle of Point Judith* off the Rhode Island coast. Those killed included 55 German submariners and 12 American Merchant Mariners. U-853 killed the American Merchant Marines on the SS Black Point. At that time, all U-boats were ordered to cease all hostilities against the Allies. The Germans disregarded the order and wanted to seek final revenge. On May 6, 1945, the war had all but ended.

The Nazi submarine, *U-853,* was harassing US ships off the New England coast in May 1945. Previous US efforts to hunt the sub down were so ineffective that it was nicknamed the *"Moby Dick."* *U-853* was on its third patrol, and it had already sunk a US Navy vessel, the *USS Eagle Boat 56*.

The *Battle of Point Judith* began on May 5 when it torpedoed the *SS Black Point*, a ship carrying coal to Boston at Point Judith, located on the western side of Narragansett Bay. SS *Black Point* capsized within 15 minutes. Twelve men died, while thirty-four men made it into lifeboats and were rescued by the *SS Kamen*, a Yugoslavian freighter. It was the last ship sunk by a German U-boat in US waters. News of the attack was relayed to Naval Headquarters on the East Coast.

At first, the U-boat tried to flee, hiding by lying still in eighteen fathoms of water. Sonar detected the submarine's bearings, and the crews of the *USS Atherton* and the *USS Moberly* dropped depth charges and hedgehogs over the spot where they thought they'd find the *U-853*. The hedgehog could fire up to twenty-four mortars ahead or the ship's side when attacking a U-boat. They hit their target around midnight, and fifty-five German sailors perished with the vessel.

The U-boat still lies at the bottom of the Atlantic. It has continued to claim lives, as it is a popular but dangerous site for divers. In 2018, the National Oceanic and Atmospheric Administration and a robotics company took photos of the German U-boat sunk in the *Battle of Point Judith*.

# MASSACHUSETTS

## U-boats and German Mines in Boston Harbor

*ABOVE: The US Navy extensively mined the Boston Harbor. It is believed a German U-Boat hit this mine in Boston Harbor. One night in 1942, a disturbance was detected in the Harbor, causing the alarm system to be activated and alerted the harbor defense system. The U-boat got away, but examination revealed that it had a large gash, most likely due to the sub's propeller hitting the explosive device. It never detonated, a close call for the unidentified U-boat. This mine can be seen today on Georges Island in Boston Harbor.*

Yet Germany also mined the Boston Harbor. On June 12, 1942, *U-87* snuck into Boston Harbor and mined the entrance.

Thankfully, no ships were sunk as a result of the location. U-boats mined the seas around New York, the Chesapeake Bay, Charleston Harbor, and Florida. New England and the rest of the country were taken off guard by the initial U-boat assaults. New England lost nine ships in the early months of the battle. There was no anti-submarine defense to prevent the ships' destruction with deadly torpedoes.

Boston enforced blackouts in August 1942, and radio transmission was restricted. The Harbor became a critical ammunition supply for the Navy's Atlantic Fleet. The Ammunition Depot worked shifts around the clock to meet the needs of the war. Many Navy installations were here.

An employee recalled seeing one submarine searching the seas near Brant Rock in 1943. As soon as the alarm was sounded, it vanished. Coast Guard boats and watchmen were looking for any security breaches in Boston Harbor and the Depot's perimeter. The fear was great since an attack on the Depot would have been tremendous devastation. The detonation of manufactured ammunition itself would have destroyed the Depot. It would not have taken a very large bomb to do such devastating destruction—the Ammunition Depot comprised approximately 2,000 civilians and 1,100 sailors and marines.

*ABOVE: The Angelus' only existing photo from an old newspaper. Even an old historic schooner carrying only molasses was not safe from the U-boats.*

At 11.30 hours on 19 May 1943, the Angelus (Master Edward Jensen) was stopped by U-161 north of Bermuda and sunk by gunfire after the crew of ten men abandoned the ship in a lifeboat. When the boat was found after five days by USS Turner (DD 648), only two were still alive; the others, including the master, had died from exposure. The two survivors landed in Portland, Maine, on 27 May 1943. The ship was too small to be carrying any war material or fuel. The sinking is another example of the German's attempts to terrorize by sinking ships, with no military advantage to them.

Attack on the SS *Atlantic States* saved by the crew.

At 22.40 hours on April 5, 1945, the unaccompanied SS *Atlantic States* was about two hours out of port near Cape Cod when it was struck on the starboard side of the stern by a torpedo from *U-879*. The explosion destroyed the screw and rudder and destroyed the steering engines. The ship quickly settled at the stern, and the watch below secured the engines as water began to enter the engine room. Without the ability to maneuver the ship, the Master directed the majority of the four lifeboats ten minutes later.

The Master, Chief Mate, Radio Operator, Armed Guard Officer, and one Able Seaman remained on board and trimmed the vessel by opening valves in the pump room. This courageous undertaking saved the tanker from sinking. The Armed Guards departed at 23 hours as the waters started to breach over the well deck. The well deck is the midship deck that is lower than the bow or stern decks. It was towed and repaired later that summer.

## SS Port Nicholson and SS Cherokee

U-87 sank the SS Port Nicholson troopship and the SS Cherokee. The Port Nicholson (Master Harold Charles Jeffery) was struck in the engine room, killing two crew members on watch below. A second torpedo struck aft, causing the ship to drop in the stern. A corvette, the Canadian HMCS Nanaimo, rescued the Master, eighty crew members, and four gunners. The ship was still floating at sunrise.

The Master decided to reboard the ship to examine the damage and possibly save it. The Master, the Chief Engineer, one officer, and three others from the corvette comprised the boarding party. After the group boarded the vessel, strong waves destroyed its damaged bulkheads, causing it to sink immediately.

The men managed to board a lifeboat they launched. Still, the sinking ship's suction flipped it, killing the Master, the Chief Engineer, a Canadian officer from the HMCS Nanaimo (Lt John Molson Walkley, RCNVR), and one other mariner. The group from the Port Nicholson and the Canadian Officer would have never been killed if they did not attempt to save it. This was a unique case.

The corvette picked up the remaining two men from the boarding party and transported them to Boston. But the story doesn't end there. The Port Nicholson was unusual in another capacity. Over the years, it has been believed that the Port Nicholson was carrying the world's most valuable cargo: 1,707,000 oz. of platinum in 400 oz. bars. The story was that this platinum was a partial payment from the Soviet Union to the United States for the millions of dollars of military hardware and aircraft. However, I have not located any documentation to substantiate this claim.

On the same day, June 16, 1942, *U-87* launched one torpedo at the SS *Cherokee*, the leading ship of Convoy *XB-25,* located northeast of Cape Cod. The Master witnessed the attack on the *Port Nicholson.* He believed the first torpedo struck and assumed the second one missed. But both torpedoes struck the *Port Nicholson.*

The *Cherokee* was damaged under the bridge by one torpedo on the port side. The explosion raised the vessel completely out of the water, a rare and even more shocking experience for the crew than typical Merchant shipping attacks.

Ninety seconds later, a second torpedo impacted the port bow, sinking the ship by the bow with a 60-degree list to port within six minutes. The waves and extreme list prohibited lifeboats from being launched. Only seven rafts could be thrown into the ocean.

The ship carried nine officers, 103 crew members, 11 Navy Armed

Guards, 46 passengers from the US Army, three officers, sixty-two crew members, one Armed Guard, and twenty passengers perished. The American steam freighter *Norlago* rescued forty-four survivors and landed them at Provincetown, Massachusetts, the same day. The USCGC *Escanaba* picked up thirty-nine others and transported them to Boston.

# NEW YORK

## *Panic in New York City*

*ABOVE: An Air Warden (with CDC insignia on his arm) directs New Yorkers in the crisis with sirens blaring. The subway was considered one of the safest places during a bombing in New York City. Basements and air raid shelters were not always safe since buildings could collapse.*

In December 9, 1941, two days after the attack on Pearl Harbor, the first air raid warning of the war blew its ominous blare over New York City. It was hard to believe the blast could be heard city-wide, from the Battery to Midtown to

Harlem. Immediately in the thick of the panic, air raid wardens volunteered or were assigned for duty. The Army revealed to the public that hostile planes targeting New York City were only two hours distant at midday. Then all hell broke loose.

Many squadrons of Army Air Corps fighter planes took to the skies from Mitchel Field on Long Island to take out the assailants. City radio stations went off the air to prevent the enemy access to a homing station. However, this made it impossible for New Yorkers to know the facts or how to protect themselves. Since radio broadcasts weren't allowed at this time, the police were put on high alert to notify the public what the sirens meant. No one knew if the sirens were part of an exercise or an indication of a real attack.

Schoolchildren were immediately sent home as a precaution. However, many enemy plane spotters were teenagers and knew what to look for throughout the city. Fortunately, an enemy plane looked distinctly different compared to American aircraft. The spotters had photos of German, Japanese, and American planes to help identify oncoming aircraft.

"One hundred thousand air raid wardens rushed to the rooftops of buildings to protect the city. Wardens volunteered to convince residents to turn out their lights. The main purpose of wardens was to patrol the streets and rooftops during blackouts and ensure that no light was visible. Throughout the country, these wardens were all volunteers. If a light was spotted, the warden would alert the person responsible by shouting, "Put that light out!" or "Cover that window! Don't you know there's a war on?"

Manned by the Army, anti-aircraft guns were deployed around the city that night. The rooftops were full of them. Cranes could be seen hoisting the big guns as high as twenty stories. Police moved large quantities of firearms and ammunition from storage vaults to stations across the city. Everyone was urged to prepare for an invasion from both land

and sea. Guards were posted throughout the hectic chaos in tunnels, docks, airports, and train stations. Crowds stormed grocery stores buying out the contents. There was real danger just by being trampled upon in the crazy food markets.

On Wall Street, a wave of selling on the New York and American Stock Exchanges caused losses of hundreds of millions of dollars. It was the worst stock market crash since May 1940, when the Nazis conquered Western Europe. A million students were sent home from school. Office workers flooded out into the streets. All tunnels and bridges were blocked by traffic.

The Japanese Consulate on Fifth Avenue was certainly acting strange. The police detected the distinct odor of burning papers. Like what happened at the Japanese Embassy in Washington, DC, the Nippon secrets were going up in smoke.

Mayor Fiorello LaGuardia created even further panic by broadcasting from his City Hall desk. He warned the Metropolis area that it was a target for an army of hostile agents and squads of enemy planes. LaGuardia announced to New Yorkers not to feel completely safe just because you're on the Atlantic Coast. That isn't reassuring." He stated he wouldn't be surprised if the city was attacked at any time." City Council President Morris exclaimed, "Everyone's a soldier now!" Seven hundred men had enlisted at the United States Navy's local recruiting station on Church Street that day.

As thousands of people looked up at the sky, they saw two hundred and eighty American planes surging above at Mitchel Field. This was the largest air group in American history to go into flight for a defensive engagement to protect the American Homeland. Occupants of houses near the Air Base were evacuated, and all commercial flights were canceled. Every fighter plane on Mitchel Field took to the air that day. "Information received that a squadron of warplanes is heading toward Long Island, identity unknown at this time," police patrol cars radioed at 12:45 pm. Police radio cars received this news just minutes later that the planes were "anticipated in the New York City region within 10 minutes."

The US Government told the city they had very limited time before the warplanes would arrive, and then that afternoon, the New York Police announced through bullhorns, "Ten minutes until the bombing starts!" People were frantically running to find secure basements. The anticipation was unbearable, and they were told there would be no further warning. To say the afternoon was getting tense for New Yorkers would be an understatement. New Yorkers are a tough breed, but the distress from an impending enemy air bombing was too much under these dire circumstances.

"Enemy Planes Near NY From Atlantic!" was announced on the front page of the afternoon newspapers. The papers would sell out in minutes. A small fire broke out when the fighters assigned to combat the danger returned to Mitchel Field. This fire was interpreted as an attack, resulting in more rumors being spread. By 1:45 pm, the "all clear" signal was given by radio, and people returned to work while their children had an early day off. It had been nearly three days since the country had been at war, and New Yorkers wondered what would happen to them next.

*The coming enemy air attack was considered common knowledge. New Yorkers would never forget that day.*

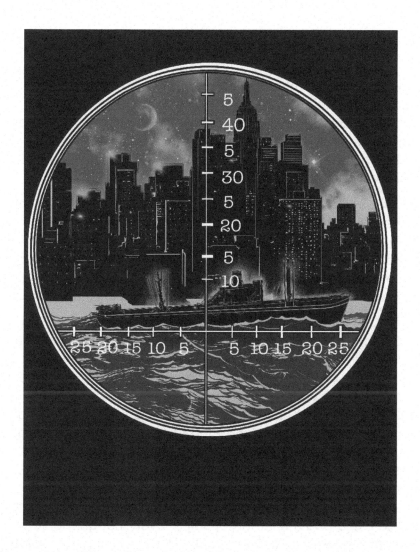

*Above: view from Captain Hardegen's periscope. The Nazi U-boat commander who attacked ships in the New York City area was elated to be the first invader. "I would have given away a kingdom for this moment...."*

Captain Hardegen commanded *U-123*, one of the five original German U-boats assigned to *Operation Drumbeat*. *Operation Drumbeat* was a long-range strike on Allied ships in American coastal waters. Unfortunately for the United States, the German planners were correct in their premise that the US would be caught off guard if attacked directly.

When the German U-boats arrived in mid-January off the coast of the United States, they discovered a country that had made only basic war preparations. Most trade ships traveled without escorts, city and town lights remained on along the coast, and the bombers and destroyers that targeted the U-boats were scarce.

The well-defined goal of *U-123* was to reach New York Harbor. It was a very symbolic event for the Nazis. For navigation purposes, Hardegen was given a large-scale chart of the Eastern shoreline from 1870, a simple tourist map, and a reference to the 1939 World's Fair. This last reference would be the most useful to him because it included a detailed map of New York Harbor.

On April 12, 1942, the *U-123* sunk the *Cyclops* (killing 88 of the 181 sized crew) on its way to Nova Scotia. On January 14, the *U-123* sunk the *Norness* off Long Island, with 39 of the 41 crew barely surviving. The U-boat almost ran aground off the Rockaways, but then it was able to regain its navigational system. The view was clear for the *U-123* because all the lights showed brightly from Coney Island and the headlights of passing cars. The *U-123* sank the tanker *Coimbra* just outside Harbor on the night of January 15, aided by the silhouettes produced by the bright shore lights. The shore lights typically helped the U-boats spot target ships, even though the vessels themselves kept their lights out. Thirty-six men out of the *Coimbra*'s forty-six crew were killed that night by the *U-123*.

Captain Hardegan did not appear to have an aversion to attacking defenseless Americans sailing in merchant ships. He was quite pleased to be the first of his conquering nation. The German perspective is a stark contrast compared to the American attitude, which hated the idea of conquering. The Allies' temporary occupation during the war was only necessary to end the war and the Nazi's reign. Americans didn't take any pleasure in invading or dominating another country, unlike Hardegan and his peers.

The long-awaited event became real on the night of January 15: Captain Hardegan's German U-boat *U-123* entered the New York Harbor. The *U-123* crew knew the significance of their presence in New York to Americans. New York City seemed to be the symbolic center of America, with the Statue of Liberty standing proudly in the New York Harbor. Understanding this significance, the crew of *U-123* was elated when they came within sight of the city itself. With all the lights burning brightly, it was quite a sight and a major accomplishment for the Germans. To be in New York as an enemy, free to travel at will, was euphoric for them. They were proud to be the first Germans to invade America since Hitler's Declaration of War.

Years later, in a New York Times interview, Hardigan stated, "I cannot describe the feeling with words, but it was unbelievably beautiful and great." He later wrote of approaching close enough to see Manhattan's bright lights from his U-boat. He continued in the interview, "I would have given away a kingdom for this moment if I had one. We were the first to be here, and for the first time in this war, a German soldier looked upon the coast of the USA."

Hardegan became a celebrity of sorts in the United States, going on a book tour with author Michael Gannon, discussing his role in Germany's Operation Drumbeat. After sinking many oil tankers during the war, Hardegan was rewarded by the American oil industry by doing big business as a petroleum entrepreneur in Germany. He became very wealthy, and he was elected to the Bremen Legislator. Hardegan even drove an expensive Mercedes with the stylish license plate "U-123". He lived until he was 105 years old, passing away in 2015.

*SS Muskogee: A Merchant Marine ship's saga.*

*ABOVE: The famous photo that was taken by a German on the U-123. The Merchant Marines were struggling to survive. These American sailors and the entire crew died at sea. But the photo would be discovered by an American POW, and their legacy would live on.*

On March 22, the German U-Boat *U-123* came across an American tanker, the SS *Muskogee*, 425 miles northeast of Bermuda. The *U-123* followed the SS *Muskogee* for two hours to get a good shooting angle before launching a single torpedo that sunk the ship. When the U-boat surfaced, seven men on the crew were on a raft. Hardegan, the captain of the *U-123*, questioned the crew about their ship, which was a 7,034-ton tanker that delivered oil from Venezuela to Halifax. Hardegan then abandoned them in the dangerous seas; The survivors had no idea where they were located. None of these men were ever seen again, nor were any of the other thirty-four crew members of the SS *Muskogee*.

Rudolph Meisinger, a German war correspondent on board the *U-123*, took several photos of the sinking ship and the survivors. A photo of Meisinger's ended up in a German newspaper. Fate would play its hand in that an American POW would see this newspaper while on a German prisoner ship. He held onto it until after the war. In the 1960s, this former American POW published the photo in the Merchant Marine newsletter, asking if someone could identify the fallen. Finally, he was notified by one of the families that one of the victims was their relative. News of this series of events was widely published.

The photo and news inspired sculpturer Marisol Escobar to design America's only Merchant Marine Memorial. It is considered one of the unique statues in America today. This Memorial incorporates the tide of the Hudson River into its presentation. The New York Harbor tide covers a mariner being pulled up from the water twice a day, an ingenious design.

Commissioned by the American Merchant Mariners Memorial, Inc., it was conceived in 1976. In 1988 after an extensive competition, the artist Marisol Escobar was chosen to develop her design. Situated off-shore from the north end of Battery Park and just south of Pier A, the monument stands on a rebuilt stone breakwater in the harbor. The bronze-figure group and boat are based on the actual historical event, represented by the famous photo of the American victims. Marisol developed a series of studio sketches from this photograph, then fashioned a clay maquette as her winning design proposal for the monument.

*ABOVE: National Merchant Marine Memorial, New York Harbor, New York City*

# NEW JERSEY

*ABOVE: U-578 sank the RP Resor near Barnegat Inlet, Long Beach Island, New Jersey. The US Navy sent the destroyer, the USS Jacob Jones (DD-130) to find and sink U-578. Instead, the U-578 sank the USS Jacob Jones. Nearly all the USS Jacob Jones crew were killed. This was a Navy ship.*

Merchant Marine traffic was always heavy during the war. As a result, the local Lakehurst Air Station provided blimps to look for U-boats and drop depth charges if spotted. Merchants of the ships were routinely torpedoed off New Jersey's shoreline within a few miles of the beach. When American ships were torpedoed, heavy black smoke would billow into the sky, and fires would light up the night. The brightness of the flames could be seen from the shore. Beaches were covered with oil, wreckage, and even at times, dead bodies of American sailors. The wrecks were reported in local newspapers with descriptions of the glow seen in the distance.

When the German U-boat *U-578* sank the American tanker RP *Resor* near Manasquan, New Jersey, on February 28,

1942, it was carrying a full supply of crude oil. A local newspaper hired a boat to go out to the burning victims. A reporter and a photographer were in awe of the spectacle. The flames could be seen up to Belmar, 30 miles away. Forty-eight men died, nearly the entire crew. Seaman John Forsdal and Coxswain Daniel Hey were the only ones to survive.

Residents at Barnegat Inlet, where the famous lighthouse shines, weren't concerned about tar washing up on the beaches; they got oil instead. There was a lot of oil coming from the sinking tanker. Larger quantities of oil decimated these beaches during World War II than in any other tanker accident in the Post-War Era.

The RP *Resor* did not sink immediately. It was towed to its current location, some 30 miles east of Barnegat Lighthouse. *U-578*, the same U-boat that sank the RP *Resor* off the coast of Northern Jersey on February 28, was still on the lookout. At sunrise, the *U-578* sighted the Navy's USS *Jacob Jones*, a destroyer sent out to find this very same U-boat that sunk the *Resor*. The irony is striking.

The USS *Jacob Jones* (DD-130) and the *U-578* were about 25 miles off the coast of Cape May when the Germans launched several torpedoes to decimate the destroyer. Two torpedoes hit the Jacob Jones from the *U-578*. The first torpedo struck on the portside and ignited the ship′s magazine. We know what happened to the USS *Arizona* in Pearl Harbor and how devastating an explosion can be when a torpedo strikes the ship's magazine (ammunition). The blast destroyed immeasurably more of this US Navy destroyer. The second torpedo struck on the portside and carried away a large section of the ship. Thirty survivors abandoned ship on four or five rafts. When it couldn't get any worse, the *Jacob Jones's* own depth charges exploded, killing survivors on a raft. A US Army observation plane sighted the rafts and called their position to USS *PE-56*. Due to rough seas, the ship was forced to abandon the search-and-rescue operation after three hours. The USS

*PE-56* rescued only twelve survivors, and one of them died en route to Cape May.

Only 11 sailors out of the 145 crew members of the USS *Jacob Jones* made it to shore alive, making that a 93% kill rate. This rate would be quite high for a U-boat going against a US Navy destroyer in World War II. This happened right off the populated New Jersey coastline while the American destroyer was attempting to sink the very U-boat that destroyed it and killed nearly its entire crew.

Many surviving U-boats returned to Germany after the war ended in 1945, but some U-boats, like the *U-858*, surrendered to America. The *U-858* surfaced and signaled its intentions of surrendering off the coast of New Jersey. A surrender ceremony was to be held over the wreck of the USS *Jacob Jones (DD-130)*, and the *U-858* was directed to those coordinates. This formal ceremony was a big international news story because it was the first time a U-boat surrendered. Photographers on blimps and helicopters circled the perimeter as the ceremony took place. The German crew of the *U-858* was taken as Prisoners of War on May 14, 1945, while an American team transported the submarine to Lewes, Delaware. U-boat battles in New Jersey came to an end at that time.

There was an earlier USS *Jacob Jones*, also a US Navy destroyer. By coincidence, the first USS *Jacob Jones* (DD-61) was also sunk by a German U-Boat off the Sicily Islands, England, in World War I on December 6, 1917. It was torpedoed by *U-53* with the loss of 66 Navy personnel, becoming the first United States destroyer ever sunk by enemy action.

# DELAWARE

ABOVE: Watchtowers left from the War still stand on Delaware's beaches. They can still be climbed today. You can look out at the same view the volunteer spotters had eighty years ago, watching the sea and the skies for the enemy U-boats or planes.

Delaware Beach watchtowers are a sight locals and beachcombers take for granted. These watchtowers remain an enduring symbol of the American public's perseverance and diligence in defending our shorelines. The watchtower above was one of fifteen watchtowers in Delaware and New Jersey used as observation posts to detect enemy vessels and direct the artillery fire from nearby coastal batteries. An observer could see miles out to sea. Cape Henlopen State Park, Delaware Seashore State Park, and Fenwick Island State Park are home to eleven concrete watchtowers built before or during World War II to observe the shoreline, the Delaware Bay, and Delaware River.

To determine the location of a hostile vessel, the coordinates of the lines of sight between two different towers were noted and given to the battery commander. The angle between each building and the U-boat could then be determined using direct measurement. The angles were then plotted in relation to the known distance between the two towers to form a triangle (triangulation). This chose the angle and the direction of the battery's artillery fire.

Construction of these watchtowers took place from 1939 to 1942, with the intention of the buildings having a 20-year lifespan. Quite a few of these buildings remain over 60 years later. Currently, eleven watchtowers stand on the Delaware shore, and two remain near Cape May, New Jersey. Fort Miles can also be visited today at Cape Henlopen State Park in Delaware. There were two additional watchtowers on the New Jersey shoreline in North Wildwood and Wildwood Crest. Unfortunately, these New Jersey watchtowers have been torn down.

The German Navy launched its final attack codename "*Operation Seawolf*" on the East Coast in the closing days of World War II. A few months before Hitler committed suicide and the war ended on May 8, 1945, the German Navy sent six boats from its bases in Norway to attack the East Coast. The Germans hoped to repeat the successes of *Operation Drumbeat*. The German U-boats, *U-853* and *U-858,* were part of that attack. The *U-853* sank one of the last ships destroyed in World War II, the collier USS *Black Point*, near the entrance to Long Island Sound. *U-853* was sunk on May 6, 1945, by four American sub-chasers, and it became the last U-boat destroyed in US waters. On May 14, 1945, its sister U-boat, *U-858*, surrendered at Fort Miles, Delaware. The *John R. Williams* was sunk in Delaware Bay on June 24, 1942, by a mine assumed to be left by one of the U-boats that entered the Bay earlier that year.

*ABOVE: After the crew surrendered at the end of World War II, U-858 was towed to Cape Henlopen, Delaware. (National Archives, NARA II)*

# MARYLAND

*German mine laying occurred in the Chesapeake Bay, only hours from Washington, DC.*

E ven though Maryland area shipyards and other facilities contributed to fighting the war, the Chesapeake Bay itself was threatened by the German Navy. U-boats posed a very real risk. At least two U-boats carried out successful attacks on Allied shipping at the entrance of the Chesapeake Bay. In June 1942, *U-701* arrived at the Bay on a top-secret mission to lay mines in the Chesapeake Bay's shipping channels. On June 15-16, the *H.E. Blum* and Santore were sunk, and these mines damaged another vessel. *U-701* torpedoed, but it failed to sink a British tanker not far from the Chesapeake Lightship.

On July 28, 1943, *U-230* laid twenty-four mines near a US Navy Base. The Germans hoped for success like they had with sea mines a year earlier. Fortunately, there is no record of Allied ships striking these German sea mines. Courageous crews of US minesweepers swept American waters, and those German sea mines were disarmed.

Today, another U-boat, *U-1105*, Type VII-C/41, lies at the bottom of Chesapeake Bay. It was not a war casualty, and it never got close to the US shores during World War II. This U-boat, nicknamed the *"Black Panther,"* was launched in 1944, and it stalked Allied convoys off the coast of Ireland. But *U-1105* had advanced technology that later caught the attention of US Army and Navy engineers. The *U-1105* was one of less than ten U-boats covered in sound-absorbent rubber tiles to evade sonar detection. This concept was later utilized on the American *"Stealth"* Bomber in the 1990s. *U-1105* was also fitted with a *Balkongerät* (literally 'Balcony equipment'). This was an improved version of *Gruppenhorchgerät* (group listening device). The *Balkongerät* had forty-eight hydrophones and enhanced electronics, which enabled more accurate readings to be taken for detecting nearby ships.

After the war, the *U-1105,* also known as the *"Black Panther,"* was brought to the United States for study. When the research was complete, the U-boat was used for target practice in the Patuxent River until it went down in 1949. For nearly four decades, it remained forgotten on the bottom of the Chesapeake Bay. In 1985, the broken hull was re-discovered by recreational divers off Piney Point. Today, the *U-1105* site is an official Maryland State Historic Shipwreck Site. It is a popular site for sports divers.

These accounts only scratch the surface of the important role of Chesapeake Bay in World War II. To learn more about US Navy in World War II, see the great resources of the US Naval Academy Museum and the nine other Navy museums.

# VIRGINIA

*War in America. On June 16, 1942, the local Daily Press stated that "an enemy submarine sank two large American cargo ships yesterday in front of thousands of people at the Virginia Beach Resort."*

The most effective German mining operation occurring during World War II in the United States happened at Virginia Beach.

*ABOVE: Fifteen German mines destroyed two ships and caused damage to three more, in front of thousands of people of all ages near Virginia Beach.*

Virginia holds a special place in the foundation of American history. Much of the Constitution and Bill of Rights originated in Virginia when it was a colony. In 1607. The first British landed on Virginia's beaches and established the British Empire's first colony, Jamestown. Our nation was born out of the British surrender at Yorktown, all within boating distance of Virginia Beach. Ft. Monroe was built due to the events of the War of 1812. It is where the mighty "Ironclads of the Civil War," the *Mariner* and *Monitor*, came to blows in 1864. Many historical events transformed America within the Chesapeake Bay surroundings of Virginia, known as the Tidewater area. We don't hear about the history of German attacks and the sinking of American ships right off the Virginia Coast. U-boat attacks resulted in the killing of American civilians in the Virginia Beach area.

On June 15, 1942, at 5:02 pm, hundreds of witnesses from the Virginia Beach shoreline to Ft. Monroe, some 30 miles, witnessed the *Battle of the Atlantic* with explosions on the beach. Sunbathers who walked onto the sunny sand that day never expected to end up in the middle of a battle zone of World War II.

Fifteen mines were floating just under the waterline across the Chesapeake Bay's entrance, destroying three ships and causing damage to more. It was the most successful German U-boat mine-laying operation in America.

The large tanker SS *Robert C. Tuttle* was streaming near the entrance of the Chesapeake Bay with Convoy *KN-109* when it unexpectedly exploded. The blast was so powerful that people felt the force from the ground on the beach and even on the nearby boardwalks. The multi-story plume of smoke became so black and high up in the sky; it could be seen from the Hotel Chamberlin in far-off Hampton, ten miles away.

A half-hour later, a second blast damaged the tanker *Esso Augusta* to such an extent it could not run its engines. Three more explosions occurred that evening and over the next two days due to fifteen mines planted across the waterway entrance. The *Santore* was another ship sunk. For miles, people were shaken on the Virginia Beach Promenade, as were the terrified sailors on commercial ships. Crews of the Navy patrol vessels and aircraft raced to the horrific scene.

According to the war journal written for the Commander of the Navy's Eastern Sea Frontier, Adolphus Andrews, "As bomber planes, a Navy blimp, and a half-dozen Navy ships flew over the area in search of the daring submarine raider, dumping bombs and depth charges that blasted great geysers of water upward, the sunbathers stared seaward transfixed. No one needed to urge the vacationers to get off the beach. German U-Boat Captain Degen and his *U-701* were far gone from Virginia waters when the mines began exploding due to contact with the ships. This area caused the interruption of shoreline shipping, the employment of many ships and men in sweeping actions, and the sinking of three vessels with severe damage to a fourth."

"A great huge plume of water sprang up over the tanker," said resident Anne Henry, describing what she saw from her counter at Jard's Drugstore at 25th and Atlantic. "It was deafeningly loud," she remembers. "However, we all ran out to the boardwalk to take a look. "The explosions resonated beneath the feet of spectators standing in the water. A great huge plume of water sprang up over the tanker," recalled Anne Henry, describing what she saw from her counter at Jard's Drugstore at 25th and Atlantic. "It was deafeningly loud," she remembers. "We all ran out to the boardwalk to take a look."

Navy planes and a blimp began circling overhead within minutes, staring down into the seas between the zigzagging ships. According to the Daily Press, police began clearing the beach at the 24th Street Coast Guard Station, where crowds watched as boats landed, carrying survivors and a dead crewman's body. The racing patrol craft was so near the coastline that Anne Henry could see their depth charges roll into the water.

"Can you imagine a calm, tranquil Virginia Beach, with tourist season just getting started and these huge explosions exploding on your doorstep?" Anne Henry reminisces. "There were explosives in the sea."

A depth charge triggered another mine around 6:30 pm, rocking but not seriously injuring the warship USS *Bainbridge* while the frantic search for the culprit continued. An hour later, the British anti-submarine trawler HMS *Kingston Ceylonite* hit another mine, causing a secondary explosion in its magazine that caused it to sink in two minutes, killing eighteen sailors right in front of the beach! The seashore rocked the next morning again, despite the arrival of minesweepers from Little Creek and Yorktown, who discovered and detonated nine more mines on June 16.

*ABOVE: Freighter sunk by U-boat off of Virginia coast, 1942 (National Archives, NARA II)*

## SS David H. Atwater

Nearly everyone on board was intentionally killed by German gunfire before sinking. Twenty-four out of a crew of twenty-seven were dead. They were never permitted to get onto lifeboats.

On April 3, 1942, it was clear to the gunner on the U-boat *U-552* (German Captain Erich Topp) that the Americans on the deck of the SS *David H. Atwater* (Master William Keith Webster), located about ten miles east of Chincoteague Island, Virginia, were unescorted and unarmed. Captain Topp had followed the USS *David H. Atwater* underwater, then he surfaced and began to shell the vessel without warning. Ninety-three shots were fired from 600 yards, hitting the ship with about 50 shots and setting it on fire.

**USCGC** *Legare* **(WPC 144)** observed the gunfire and headed for the ship, and upon arrival at the scene forty-five minutes after the attack, saw the vessel sinking, leaving two feet of mast above water. The crew of eight officers and nineteen men had been unable to leave the ship in lifeboats, and most jumped overboard and drowned. All the officers died, and only three men who dove overboard and swam to an empty lifeboat survived the attack. The survivors and three bodies were picked up by the US Coast Guard vessel **USCGC** *CG-218* and taken to Chincoteague Inlet. Today, Chincoteague Island is the gateway to the Virginia portion of Assateague Island and the Chincoteague National Wildlife Refuge, home of the famous swimming Chincoteague wild ponies and "Sea Cowboys," who guide them through the bay.

# FIRST U-BOAT SUNK

*ABOVE: A SB2U "Vindicator" anti-sub scout and bomber attacking to hit the submerged U-boat.*

*ABOVE: U-boat is under attack by a US Army bomber.*

Underwater Archeologist Tane Casserley, with the National Oceanographic and Atmospheric Administration, is currently heading up a program to locate all sunken U-boats and the ships sunk by these stealthy German subs.

Casserley explains that the *U-701* proceeded to assault off Cape Hatteras, destroying a patrol boat on June 19, damaging two Merchant ships on June 26 and 27, and finally sinking the 14,504-ton *William Rockefeller*, one of the world's largest tankers at the time, on June 28. On July 7, however, its luck ran out when Army bomber *A-29, a* sub-hunter from Cherry Point, NC, appeared out of nowhere and grabbed it on the surface.

A U-boat can typically see an aircraft before the plane sees it, in which it would then submerge in 30 seconds. Casserley describes the scene: "The aircraft just happens to see the U-boat on the horizon through a break in the clouds at the opportune time. They were barely below the surface when the depth charges burst, and it was too late for them to escape away." Though sixteen members of the crew of the *U-701* were able to escape the damaged hull, the majority of them arrived on the surface without life jackets. As a result, Lt. Harry Kane and his four airmen tore off their own vests and tossed them to the struggling swimmers in six- to eight-foot waves. They also launched their own life raft and used smoke floats to indicate the location.

The *A-29*, however, lost sight of the survivors after circling out in a vain attempt to locate assistance, and it was still leading a large number of other aircraft in the hunt when it was obliged to return home. They arrived with barely five minutes of gasoline remaining and found that no one believed them. Casserly claims that "no Army Air Force plane had ever destroyed a U-boat before."

After two days, a Navy blimp discovered the disoriented and extremely sunburned German U-Boat Captain Degen and the few surviving members of his *U-701* crew. They were all flown to a Norfolk Navy hospital by seaplane. When Kane and his airmen arrived two days later, Degan was still there. "After all those days in the sea, Degen was badly burnt and weary — and when they walked in, he was sitting in a chair in pajamas and a medical robe, Ed Offley wrote in The Burning Shore. However, Degan climbed to his feet and gave a military salute. Afterward, Kane bent down to hear a few words from Degan and whispered in his ear: "'Congratulations. Nice assault.'"

# THE MIRICLE BABY

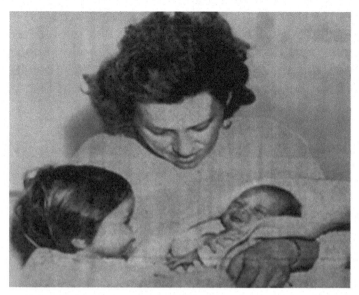

*ABOVE: Desanka Mohorovicic with daughter Vesna and her newborn Jesse Roper. (Associated Press)*

The SS *City of New York* was a cargo and passenger ship that sailed between New York and Cape Town, South Africa. The American-South African Line owned it. The *City of New York* neared Hatteras in the afternoon on March 26. The ship contained eighty-eight officers and crew, nine Navy Armed Guards, and forty-seven passengers, including Desanka Mohorovicic, a 28-year-old Yugoslav woman who was eight months pregnant, and her two-year-old daughter Vesna.

Desanka Mohorovicic embodied Europe's plight at the hands of the Nazis. She and her husband, Joseph, a diplomat from a well-known Yugoslav family, had fled Europe for the protection of British-controlled Cape Town. Joseph was hired at Yugoslavia's government-in-exile in New York to begin shortly after they arrived. Because Desanka was too far advanced in her pregnancy, authorities in Cape Town refused to allow her to sail. As a result, they agreed that Joseph would go to New York alone, while Desanka would accompany Vesna and the new baby as soon as possible.

Desanka was informed that she would be allowed to sail only a few weeks after Joseph left. She reserved a spot on the next passenger ship, the SS *City of New York*, departing Cape Town for herself and Vesna. She stated, "1 did not have to think long about it; I chose to go. I wanted to be at my husband's side as a wife and mother. It's difficult to live in a world divided by continents and uncertainty. I set out on my journey with immense trust and confidence, and I had no fear."

On March 29, the USS *City of New York* was barely a day out of New York when it arrived at Cape Hatteras just before 1 pm. A storm darkened the southeastern sky.

When the first torpedo from the *U-160* struck, Desanka and Vesna slept in their bunks. Desanka heard people rushing. She looked for life vests but couldn't find them since they were buried by fallen furniture. The cabin door was jammed shut. Although eight months pregnant, Desanka had a strong sense of survival. She slammed herself against the door, forcing it open. She and Vesna ascended a staircase to the main deck, where they discovered the crew preparing to launch the lifeboats. They passed a sailor who saw they were without life vests and offered them his. Desanka never found out his name or if he lived or died that day.

Mother and daughter slid down a rope ladder into a lifeboat. The crew attempted to lower the boat, but the chain caught on something. The boat swung in mid-air, still connected to the sinking ship. A second torpedo rocked the City of New York like a miracle, jarring the lifeboat loose. It fell straight into the water and did not capsize. Desanka was shocked at how rough the sea appeared from the low-riding lifeboat than from the main deck. The SS *City of New York* sunk under the lifeboats. A mast nearly grabbed Desanka's lifeboat on the way down. The U-boat disappeared.

The castaways were drenched in hard-hitting rain when the storm eventually broke. Desanka and Vesna gathered on the lifeboat's port-side bench. The boat was also occupied by fifteen other individuals, including the ship's doctor, Dr. Leonard H. Conly, a physician from New York City. Conly had fractured two ribs, and he was in agony after losing his grasp on a rope and plunging forcefully into the lifeboat.

Charles Van Gordon commanded Desanka's lifeboat. He kept the boat pointed towards the wind. The water was very rough, with waves hitting the boat from all sides. Because the boat was in the Gulf Stream, where water temperatures may exceed 70 degrees in March. Regardless, the survivors didn't experience good luck despite the water's temperature. At Cape Hatteras, the Gulf Stream went in a northeast direction. If the lifeboat didn't go in the right direction at that point, it would bring them into the center of the Atlantic.

The survivors were pummeled with chilly rain after nightfall. They didn't have enough warm clothing. Desanka subsequently wrote about "bitter, bitter cold and bitter rain" and "black water mountains." Vesna sat on her mom's lap, falling in and out of sleep.

"Doctor, the baby is here!" Desanka screamed out at about 2:30 am the next day. Despite his damaged ribs, Conly was taking his turn at the oars. He had to crawl awkwardly across other castaways to get to her side. Captain Van Gordon tried to hold the boat steady as others tried to cover Desanka. "She was really brave," said Able Sailor Leroy Tate. "She never cried out in pain or wept the entire time. Her feet were always submerged in water. She was drenched from head to toe."

While Dr. Conly worked, the waves furiously rocked the boat. He told *The New York Times* that "it seemed like he was on a picturesque railway. On these 15-to-20-foot waves, we were swooping up and down." He delivered a healthy baby boy and let the ocean clean him up. The infant cried out.

"How could you believe you would die when a newborn baby was crying?" the infant's sister, Vesna, pondered many years later. Some of Desanka's lifeboat mates were "superstitious," she claimed and regarded the baby as a positive sign. Others in the lifeboat were too terrified and distracted to notice. "I felt bad for the mother," one remembered, 'but there was simply so much going on that I didn't think about it."

Concerned about the cold wind, the doctor asked a fellow woman on the lifeboat whether he could cover the infant in her turban. The doctor pulled the turban from the woman's head and swaddled the infant in it, and handed the baby to Desanka as Desanka slipped the swaddled baby under her blue wool dress beneath her life jacket. Naturally, Desanka was completely exhausted.

Captain Van Gordon comforted Vesna. Van Gordon took on a grandfatherly manner as he pointed out the constellations in the night sky to the lifeboat child. By the next day, the storm had passed, but the Gulf Stream had already pushed the lifeboat 75 miles out to sea.

Admiral Andrews' lone destroyer, the USS *Roper*, had already discovered another of the *City of New York*'s lifeboats and two of its rafts, rescuing forty-eight people. The USS *Roper* found the lifeboat Desanka and other passengers were on just before daybreak on March 31, roughly forty hours after the disaster. As long as a football field, the destroyer approached the lifeboat and lowered a cargo net. The doctor handed the newborn baby to a young sailor on board the destroyer, who was taken aback when he realized he was holding a baby instead of a sack of personal items.

The *Roper*'s crew erupted with applause. Desanka will never forget the image of the sailors handing her son to safety. "Divine, courageous sailors," she called them in Croatian, "*Divini hrabni mornari.*" In honor of the destroyer, she named her son Jesse Roper Mohorovicic; The USS *Roper* was named after a Navy gunboat commander who died trying to save a crew member from a fire.

.As the *Roper* got closer to the dock, Dr. Conly and Captain Van Gordon created a birth certificate. The City of New York's logbook indicates that the baby was born at sea.

The Navy notified the next of kin of the *City of New York*'s crew and passengers. Joseph Mohorovicic had no idea his wife had departed Cape Town. Joseph, too, had endured a difficult journey to America. His ship, which had sailed from Cape Town, had barely made it as far as the Windward Islands and then was torpedoed at Port Castries St. Lucia. Joseph had been in the hospital for three days, recovering from injuries and a ruptured eardrum. He then took a Coast Guard ship to New York City.

Joseph's functions at the Yugoslav Embassy in New York included transcribing teletyped communications into English. On April 1, he was startled by a Navy dispatch informing him that a Yugoslav lady had given birth in a lifeboat. He received a telegram from the American-South African Line's general manager: "MRS MOHOROVICIC AND HER DAUGHTER WERE ON THIS VESSEL. LANDING IN THE UNITED STATES. IS A WAR CASUALTY STOP, AND WE WERE LANDED AT ST. VINCENTS HOSPITAL IN NORFOLK, VIRGINIA. MRS MOHOROVICIC HAD A BABY IN A LIFEBOAT AT SEA, AND IT IS ALSO IN THE SAME LIFEBOAT. FROM HOSPITAL, OUR REPRESENTATIVES FROM PRESENTING AND ASSISTING THEM WHERE THE DOCTORS REPORT THEY ARE IN GOOD CONDITION."

Joseph made it to Norfolk on the first train. He was reunited with his family the next morning and was surrounded by media. Desanka thanked her saviors and downplayed her trauma. "I (had) hoped to have my kid here, in free America," she added, her English a bit broken. "We're fine now that he's arrived. God's grace."

The 'Lifeboat Baby' story was featured on the top page of *The New York Times* and hundreds of other publications. "Great in its eternal symbolism, great in its simple, almost accidental statement of the deep mysteries of death and life with which we are all surrounded," declared an editorial in the *International Herald Tribune.* Desanka's tale was transmitted to European resistance fighters through shortwave radio. Jesse was dubbed "the baby Hitler couldn't get" by ladies after the family relocated to a largely Jewish area in New York.

The end of the story of the *City of New York*'s tale was mostly ignored by the media. The ship's last lifeboat was discovered two weeks after it was launched off the shore of Delaware, more than 300 miles northeast of Hatteras. Only two individuals remained alive out of the twenty, including a seaman and a three-year-old child. Like Desanka, the girl's mother had sailed from Cape Town with her daughter to join her husband in New York. One hour before an aircraft discovered the lifeboat, the mother had died of hunger and exposure. The child pleaded with the seaman not to throw her mother overboard like the other bodies, and he consented. The final lifeboat of the *City of New York* was never recovered.

.

*ABOVE: Survivors are amazed to see a baby born on their survival vessel, an overcrowded life boat.*

# NORTH CAROLINA

The Outer Banks of North Carolina, now a popular summer vacation area packed with beach houses, was remote and isolated during World War II. The next island south, Ocracoke Island, was even more isolated, with no contact with the mainland except a weekly mail boat. The residents were very happy that way, but World War II directly came to their homes. These barrier islands include the Outer Banks from Virginia, south to Cape Hatteras, Ocracoke Island, Portsmouth Island (uninhabited today) and Cape Lookout National Seashore. The islands lie parallel to the mainland.

The Outer Banks is the area where the cold waters of the Labrador Current, which originates around the coast of Norway, collide with the warm waters of the Gulf Stream. These conditions make for some rough waters.

Moreover, there are very shallow areas called the Dimond Shoals. These are dangerous seas and have sunken over two thousand ships over the centuries. The shoals necessitate an extremely narrow sea lane. The lane is the only safe shipping channel along the coast of North Carolina. As a result, it was easy for the U-boats to find tankers and freighters to sink. German U-boats continuously attacked Allied ships in this area. From December 1941 until August 1942 to Americans, it was known as "*Torpedo Alley.*" Seventy ships were sunk off North Carolina, from January to April 1942.

On the 18th of March, U-boats sank five ships in the single deadliest night for shipping in the war. Attacks by as many as seventeen distinct U-boats peaked in April, with twenty-seven Allied ships destroyed or damaged on the coast of North Carolina. Nearly one ship sunk per day in April. A Navy installation was built on Ocracoke Island, supplemented with the Picket Patrol.

*Recalling the U-boat Attacks: A Merchant Marine,*
*Coastal Picket Patrol, US Coast Guard, and a*
*Resident Eyewitness in the Outer Banks*

Francis "Biff" Bowker,
Merchant Marines Seaman

**Few precautions at first:** "Until [we] got convoys, [the ships] just went straight along. Lots of ships were still shining their lights. They were coming up with their lights on, and the submarines just sat out there, and—pow, pow—two or three torpedoes out there, and sunk them with their lights, especially some of the foreign ships."

**A close call:** "On the way up, we ran into thick, thick fog. We saw smoke from ships sinking in the distance, but we were pretty well out. At night, I heard this thrum-thrum-thrum-thrum. I had the eight to twelve watch that night. I knew what it was, because I had heard submarines before, up around Long Island Sound, where they build them. I heard them on the surface. I knew what they sounded like, so I told them, 'That's a submarine—not very far off.' The captain wouldn't pay any attention; he just went down below, and he said, 'Oh, that's just a Norwegian motor ship going through.' I said, 'If you were that Norwegian motor ship, you'd be going like the devil. You wouldn't be charging your batteries.' Anyhow, he just got mad and went down below. We knew what was going on, and that submarine out there didn't make us feel any better. We had rigged up a lifeboat. We didn't have too many good preservers. We just didn't know what to do. We were worried."

**Picking up survivors:** "We had strict orders to not pick up any [survivors from U-boat sinking] because those submarines are probably just waiting for you to come. Later on, I was in a troopship. I saw a lifeboat right ahead. They took the men aboard quickly. They had plenty of ropes over the side. It was just a shortstop. They took off—not knowing if they were going to get torpedoed."

**A very close call:** "That old tanker I was in was an old World War I tanker, and all of a sudden, there was a tanker coming out the other way, and he just burst in one great big sheet of flame. The radio operator came up to see the captain— I was on the bridge at the time—and he said, 'I've just heard from that submarine. He just called us and said we're next.' That's when we put her full speed ahead."

## Mack Womac, Coastal Picket Patrol "The Hooligan Navy"

**Rumors about the Germans:** "We thought they might try to land somebody here. There were all kinds of rumors going around."

**Beachcombing:** The ship *Harry F. Sinclair Jr.* was burning off the Cape Lookout, and we went down there two or three different times."

**In the Hooligan Navy:** "[I was on a wooden sailboat for the so-called Hooligan Navy.] The one I was on was 70 feet long. It was equipped with six or eight depth charges on the stern, but this one was equipped with a sonar that we dropped over the side. This was just a big brown thing, and the guy listened on the earphone to see if he could pick up a ping. All we had on board was six rifles and one pistol. We couldn't do much, but they had us out there—we had to go. We were lucky—we didn't find [a submarine]."

**Sent out to wrecks:** "Whenever we got called out, we knew we were going out to a ship that had been torpedoed. That's all we were told. The guy that was in charge of the boat—they took the boat out—he knew more about it than we did, and he never said no more than 'We got to go. You all are the ones that are picked to go.' It seemed like it took us forever to get there [to the wreck]. We could see the orange glow in the sky a long time before we got to it. Then all we could do was go around and around, picking up someone that was alive. It's a terrible feeling. They were sitting ducks, that's what they were. Just waiting to be shot. And that's a terrible death, burning to death."

*ABOVE: The ship Harry F. Sinclair Jr. was torpedoed by U-203, burning off the Cape Lookout, NC, just south of Ocracoke Island. It was witnessed by Mack Womac of the Coastal Picket Patrol. The Outer Banks Patrol used civilian fishing boats.*

## Arnold Tolson
## Ocracoke Island, North Carolina
## U.S. Coast Guard Cutter 8367

**Pulling in bodies from the shore:** "That night, [an explosion] shook the whole island. It was an awful explosion off Ocracoke Island. The next morning, as we got to the beach and started riding north, I saw this man in the surf. We pulled down and stopped; I got him by the arm and pulled him on the beach. We put him in the truck and headed back over to the Coast Guard station. [Then] I saw Elwood Austin come running. He said, 'There's a man in the water, about to wash up on the beach.' I said, 'Why didn't you pull him out?' He said, 'I was down there fishing, and when he come in, I left.' I said, 'Where was he at?' He said, 'I'll go show you,' so we got on the truck and he showed me about he saw him, and we pulled him in too."

**Digging graves:** "[Aycock Brown, the man identifying the bodies] said, 'I know this man. I was down aboard his ship. He got an English flag to put on a grave of another British sailor.' We had to bury him, so I went to see a fellow by the name of Charlie Mack, and I told him I'd found a couple of battery boxes that I'd like to use for coffins. He said, 'Take them.' We got the battery boxes, we wrapped the bodies in blankets, and the Williams family donated the ground for us to bury them. I got some sailors, and we went up there and dug the graves. Everyone's emotion was very high."

# Gibb Gray,
## Eyewitness to World War II in the Outer Banks
## Avon, NC

**Chaos became routine:** "We sort of got used to it. It would be mostly in the distance away—the explosions. We weren't too scared. It just become a regular routine."

**Oil in the ocean:** "[The ocean] would probably be five or six inches deep of oil, and then what we'd have to do is come right back over to the village, to my dad's store over there, and we'd get rags and clean our feet off, because that oil is hard to get off. And then we'd go back and continue swimming, those hot summer days."

**Finding a washed-up lifeboat:** "My friend and I went over to the beach one morning, and the first thing we saw was a lifeboat that had washed up during the night. On the side of it was the name S.S. *Alexandria*. It had shrapnel holes in it. We had no way to get the thing open, so we went into the village, got a hammer and screwdriver to go in there and get the rations. Unfortunately, there was a Coast Guard truck—they were taking rations out. We said, 'We found this boat a short while ago.' We thought they would give us some candy, but they didn't."

**Reusing tires from the sea:** "[Tires washed ashore,] and tires and tubes were rationed in those days. They would use [washed-ashore tires], but they had a long stem on them to pump the iron in them, and you could see a car going down the road with that stem flopping, hitting the sand. You knew where it came from."

**Watching *The City of Atlanta* burn:** "We went to bed around ten o'clock and were woken up around two o'clock by a violent explosion. It shook our house all over. We all got up to the windows, and it was all a bright red glow—*The City of Atlanta*."

**On the sinking of the *Dixie Arrow*:** "I was on my way to school, and the whole ground shook. We looked out toward the ocean, and when we looked down to the lighthouse, it was south of the lighthouse, but a little bit to the east. It was the *Dixie Arrow*. We skipped school then to watch the lifeboats."

*Above: The sinking of the SS Dixie Arrow was sunk on March 26, 1942, by U-71 and only miles from the shoreline. It was witnessed by residents of the Outer Banks from land, including Gibb Gray.*

# Remembering Jim Gaskill and the SS Caribsea

*Above: The SS Caribsea. Jim Gaskill, along with twenty-seven of his shipmates, would die. Only seven of the crew would survive. It appears remarkable that Jim's ship would go down with him, only miles from his home.*

The SS *Caribsea* had passed through Cape Lookout three days before, going to Norfolk, Virginia, from Santiago, Cuba, with 3,600 tons of highly flammable manganese ore. The Navy requested that the *Caribsea*'s Master restrict its speed to four knots so the freighter would not approach Cape Hatteras until after daybreak; the Navy believed the biggest threat from the U-boats was at Hatteras, sixty miles ahead.

Third Mate Jim Baughm Gaskill's shift had ended, and the officer who relieved him asked whether he wanted to stay in the wheelhouse until the Ocracoke lighthouse was sighted off the freighter's port bow. Gaskill said that he had seen the lighthouse enough and needed to sleep. His father's hotel was almost next door to the lighthouse. It is unknown whether Jim would have lived had he stayed on deck. We can only speculate.

Two torpedoes struck the ship a short time later, the first striking the number two hold and the second torpedo bursting the ship's boilers. Only the seven men who were on deck made it out alive. The ship went down bow in less than three minutes, killing twenty-one men, including Gaskill. Gaskill might have lived if he had only one more chance to see the cherished Ocracoke lighthouse. His remains were never discovered.

An oar off the SS *Caribsea* took four days on heavy seas to go forty-three miles into Ocracoke Inlet, where it bumped up against the pilings of the Pamlico Inn, which was Merchant Marine Captain Jim Baughm Gaskill's birthplace.

Chris Gaskill just happened to be walking along the beach on the south end of Ocracoke Island on March 14, 1942, when he noticed a rectangular item washing up in the surf.

He decided to examine what he found, and he noticed a large frame containing a certificate that appeared to be official. "Other documents appeared to have formerly been inside the frame, but there was only one in the frame now," according to Gaskill.

The paper was a certificate from the United States Department of Commerce certifying the qualifications of a Third Mate on a Merchant Marine ocean steam vessel.

Chris Gaskill was astounded about his discovery of the certificate. He became gravely concerned when he read the individual's name to whom the license was granted.

The license amazingly belonged to his cousin, Jim Gaskill, the Ocracoke native killed on the SS *Caribsea*. Chris Gaskill had been unaware of his cousin's location since the beginning of the war, so seeing the license was an extremely shocking moment for him. Gaskill returned to the village immediately, alerting his family and the US Coast Guard.

*ABOVE: Jim Gaskill's Parents' Pamlico Inn*

The Pamlico Inn, a popular Ocracoke Island hotel on the border of the Pamlico Sound and Teaches Hole Channel south of Silver Lake, was owned and managed by Jim Gaskill's father. Someone at the Inn observed a floating piece of wreckage that appeared to be an oar beating against the pilings of the Inn's pier just one day after Chris Gaskill discovered Jim's Third Mate certificate. The piece of wood was picked up out of the bay, and an etched ship's name, "SS *Caribsea*," was discovered on the other side of it. Aware of Jim's horrible demise, it gave the family the chills. What were the chances, coming from Cuba, for Jim's ship to get sunk by a U-boat close to his parents' hotel, both the oar from his ship and his license being washed up on a nearby beach!

Gaskill's Third Mate license and the "SS *Caribsea*" oar were among the wreckage floating in the sea after the ship rapidly burst apart. Despite huge odds, severe storms, and a strong current, these two remarkable items made it to Ocracoke Island in three days, more than forty-three miles away.

The license and the oar were the only *Caribsea* relics discovered.

The oar's journey was especially extraordinary as it made a turn into and traveled through Ocracoke Inlet, against the daily tidal discharge of Teaches Hole Channel, avoiding sandbars and shallow bays, to dock at Jim Baughm Gaskill's birthplace, his father's Pamlico Inn.

In a 1997 interview, Jim's cousin, 82-year-old Owen Gaskill, observed, "It was extraordinary for something like that to happen. My first cousin discovered his license among the countless individuals who comb the beach. All of the licenses were gone save Jim's when my cousin discovered the huge frame. His was the only license remained in the enormous frame, and it hadn't been harmed by the water during the storm."

The oar was donated to Ocracoke resident Homer Howard so that he could make a cross out of it. The cross has remained on the altar of Ocracoke's Methodist Church ever since. From afar, the basic wooden cross appears inconspicuous to the average visitor. Only under close examination of the base reveals two small plates with the following inscriptions: "Captain James B. Gaskill was born on July 2, 1919, and died on March 11, 1942. This crucifix was made from the wreckage of the ship on which Capt. Gaskill perished."

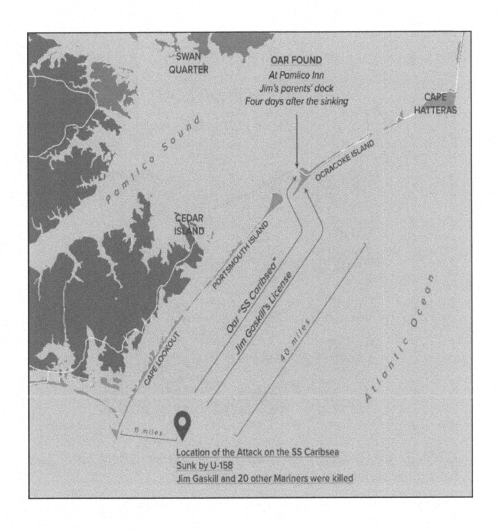

*ABOVE: This map shows the location of the SS Caribsea sinking on 11 March 1942. Note the distance Jim Gaskill's license and the ship's oar traveled. The oar and license would arrive exactly where his parents and cousin could find them four days later.*

# CAROL DILLON
## BUXTON, NC

ABOVE: Carol Dillon, in front of the house where she was raised, experienced America under attack.

Interview with Carol Dillion, born and raised on the Outer Banks, NC

### The Germans demanded food from terrified fishermen:

"Submarines [were] coming up and the Germans asking if we had fresh fruit or fresh food. Stuff like that, but they never harmed our fisherman. They [the U-boats] would surface up alongside the fisherman! They were shooting at our ships to intimidate them! They would surface—well, of course, this was daylight. It got to where people wouldn't go out and fish anymore after that happened. They had it good. They gave it to them. It got to a point where they didn't fish out there much.

They were afraid of what they would do if they didn't get it [food]."

## Germans that came on the shore. They weren't American lifeboats:

"I've heard some stories, but I don't know. We knew they were coming ashore because they found lifeboats in the dunes, and that's when they started to foot patrol. Well, they knew that they were not ours. They weren't American lifeboats. That's what they said, anyway. Our mother used to take in boarders, and she had a woman who was married to the captain of the Coast Guard station out here. She would find things out from him. Course if it was really juicy, she would tell it."

## Dead bodies washed up on the beach:

"Some of them, you know, were not whole bodies, so they really tried to keep the kids away from seeing things like that. I saw a lot of lifeboats that were washed ashore, and the beach was full of tar. Everybody had to wipe the tar off their feet and their shoes. It got worse, and I finally had to quit going to the beach because he [my horse] did not like for me to wash his hooves with kerosene. I got off the beach with my horse. Life wasn't that different for us because we were pretty isolated anyway. We didn't have a highway, and it took forever to get to the little ferry that they called a ferry. It was an old wooden thing."

## Shaking our house, almost blowing windows out:

"I was 13. I had just turned 13 in December. Pearl Harbor was the 7th, and I was 13 on the 17th. The worst of the war we had was the spring of '42. That's when we lost most of our ships. And they would get a lot of em', and they would get two at a time. The worst time I remember we were in school—I was in the 8th grade—and a German U-boat explosion almost blew a window out. It was a good mile from the coastline. I was a pretty big girl for 13, it almost knocked me—but it didn't knock me out of my bed. The mattress shook so bad that it lifted me up. I'll say that. They've always told me that it almost knocked me out of bed, which is really true."

"I was 13, and it looked the worst when I was in the 8th grade in the schoolhouse. They must have got two or three ships at the same time. Attacking convoys, you know, with multiple ships at one time. It blew people's windows out near the shore. The teacher told us to run, course she didn't have to tell us. The hall didn't have any windows so we ran into the hall."

"Yeah, it was—I don't know if it was morning or afternoon. We were in school. We were in school hours. So, they didn't get them just at night. They got them during the daytime too."

**We had enough sense to be scared:**

"People were very jumpy for the first time in, well centuries really. Because of our unique location on the coast, our history goes back hundreds of years. We were involved with pirates, the War of 1812, the Revolutionary War, the Civil War, and WWI. But you know, this was so different; the U-boats were surfacing at night, and people could actually hear the Germans talking over the short-wave radio. I wasn't allowed on the beach at night, except the one time that I almost got killed.

"I don't know how they [the Coast Guard foot patrolling the beach] got to us so quick cause we didn't see them. My cousin and I will never forget what I said to him, "Stop you fool. They're going to shoot you.' We turned around; we pulled two frozen looks. It was the Coast Guard."

"It was the beginning of the war. They [the Coast Guard] didn't have any vehicles. They were all walking between Coast Guard stations then, so they only had about a four- or five-mile walk from one station to the other."

**German visits and demands many years after the war:**

"I used to work at the Coast Guard station every Wednesday in the summer. Oh, it was maybe five years ago now. I spent three or four years up there every Wednesday. New people took over, so they quit the program. And I would just talk, like I'm talking to you about the war."

"The Germans were said to have a German here to hear my talk. I was talking about the German bodies that would come ashore. I said to him, 'Now look, I am the only one living that was left during the war and I can tell you where they are.' He took it as a good sign. I mean, I didn't say I know exactly where they were, but I know they were back by the old Coast Guard station. I said, 'I know where they are, but I'm not going to tell you. I did not know exactly where they were.' They wanted to honor them like giving a service. I'm not going to do that. I'm not going to tell you where they are. And I don't know of anyone else living who can tell you. His name was Hans just like the Hans that was here. He didn't listen to what I was saying. Actually, later, I found out later the German government had sent them here to find out."

**How I became the central figure of the novel "Taffy of Torpedo Junction" after the war:**

"One of my teachers was Nell Wise Wechter who remembered the things I would tell her during the war. Years later in the 1950s, she wrote the book based on me at 13 years old, the U- boats, and the German spies at Hatteras, NC. She wanted kids to know the history of the war here. "*Taffy of Torpedo Junction*" became a best seller and standard reading in North Carolina, especially among kids. The novel has been attributed to bringing awareness of the U-boat war around the "Tar Heel State" and even nationally. Nell Wise Wechter went on to publish a number of other novels."

*ABOVE: On the Outer Banks and Ocracoke Island, residents would find bodies of dead Merchant Marine and US Navy Armed Guard washed up on the beach after a U-boats had sunk ships.*

# JIM AND CAROLL GRAY
## BUXTON, NC

*ABOVE: Jim and Carroll Gray were a few of the last remaining witnesses on the Outer Banks of North Carolina who remember the U-boat attacks.*

When I arrived at the home of Jim Gray in August 2016, the bayside house struck me as just what a visitor would envision. The home of an independent seafaring person was nestled behind low-hanging trees with boats tied to the dock in the back. Brothers Jim and Carroll Gray were very hospitable and spent a lot of time, which I sincerely appreciated. It was one of my most memorable interviews. They described the war years on the islands so well you could feel them rather than imagine them. The old relics they collected from local shipwrecks were fascinating.

Jim Gray:

"The shoreline was known as "*Torpedo Junction*," and it was one of the Germans' easiest targets. During the war years, we could hear the explosions, particularly tankers, when they were torpedoed. You could hear them clearly. The thunder sometimes cut right through you. You made no mistake in knowing what it was. It was like a wave of pressure in the air that hit you. You could feel it."

"We'd go over to the beach. And one Sunday, we saw clearly from the beach, three tankers burning at one time! I couldn't believe what I was seeing, all within sight of the beach. In some cases, flames, in other cases, completely dense black smoke rising up. Huge clouds. I think that was one thing that really surprised us; the unbelievable size of those clouds! We had never seen anything so big, never seen the skyscrapers in cities yet, we were only ten, but that's about how high they were. This happened not in European waters, not in international seas, but off an American beach, just where I grew up. The worst of it was they were unarmed civilians, minding their own business, and the next minute, boom! They're gone. It stays with you, something you will never forget as long as you live."

We would climb on the roof of the house and see the ships burning. You could see the glow of the ships; the people would hear em'. The windows would rattle. They'd see the light of the fires and they would actually start to have small prayer meetings to ask God for protection. It was a real close community being out here, they'd have other get-togethers just to talk about the attacks and prepare for the worst like a German landing on the shore or bad injuries from U-boat gunfire. And even the people that were retired Coast Guard were going out to save those poor people stranded. Anyone with a fishin' rig would go."

In 1942, the British Royal Navy sent twenty-four armed trawlers to assist the US Navy in defending America's coastline. On May 11 of that year, German *U-558* torpedoed one of those trawlers, the HMT *Bedfordshire*, killing all thirty-seven members of the British and Canadian Royal Navies aboard. Only four bodies were ever recovered as they washed ashore on Ocracoke Island.

Though far from home, these British sailors were given a proper burial in a small plot of land donated by the people of Ocracoke, with a national flag of the United Kingdom that is recognized as being "Forever England." Their fate was confirmed the following year after *U-558* was sunk, resulting in the capture of Kapitänleutnant Krech and his ship's diaries. The month prior, a British sailor from the sunken Merchant ship, *San Delfino,* had been buried in Buxton.

Carroll Gray:

"We went to the funeral of the British sailors. That was a big deal for me. I was ten years old and we weren't supposed to go by ourselves. We had to take the small ferry, well more like a big raft across the Inlet, sometimes the water was rough there. There had been stories over the years of people lost in the Inlet due to all the rough weather. So, we didn't tell our parents we were going. It was out of great respect for those that died for us. That was the reason, so we all didn't feel like we weren't doing anything wrong. I'll always remember it."

The Royal Navy flag, draped over Captain Cunningham's coffin, was one of several that he himself had requisitioned for the burial of other British sailors, one he provided just a month earlier.

In May of every year, a ceremony and reception are held here, commemorating the sinking of the HMT *Bedfordshire* and honoring the four sailors interred here. All representatives from the US Coast Guard, US Navy, British Royal Navy, and Canadian Royal Navy participate in the ceremony, which includes a reading of the crew list, the playing of bagpipes, and a 21-gun salute.

Caroll Gray explains, "The war was a constant presence in our lives. My mother witnessed the battle firsthand. Our father was missing in action when Jim and I were at the burial.

"During the war, my father, Cyrus Rufman Gray, served in the Coast Guard and was tasked with landing troops in Guadalcanal. We believed he was gone for good after being absent for a time. Thank God he was discovered alive later."

"We didn't have access to power or indoor plumbing. But we didn't realize how fortunate we were. It was a delight to be away from the stress of contemporary life. But suddenly, we find ourselves in the middle of a major war before anyone notices! The effects of World War II were felt more strongly in Buxton and Ocracoke than almost any place else in the United States."

After the war, Jim worked for NASA for many years, and Caroll spent many years in the Coast Guard. As I was leaving Jim, he handed me a notebook that he had been putting together over the years, containing newspapers regarding the HMS *Bedfordshire* and his life during the war. He said, "I've been saving it all these years, and I would like you to have it." I felt truly honored he would entrust me with it being very meaningful to him, even though I had only met him just hours before. He said, "When the time comes, you will know what to do with it." Information contained in that binder is published here. I am honored to have known these men.

### SS *Byron D. Benson*

On April 5, 1942, German U-Boat *U-522* fired one torpedo from a distance of 1000 yards, seven and a half miles off Kitty Hawk, North Carolina. It hit the SS *Byron D. Benson* between the large #7 and #8 oil tanks. The explosion sent burning oil hundreds of feet in the air and all over the tanker.

The crew of eight officers and twenty-nine men were in a state of panic, abandoning ship into two lifeboats without orders, resulting in the engines not being secured, with the vessel still moving at six knots. Ten men in the lifeboat of the Master were seen drifting into flaming water, and unfortunately, they were not seen again. The USS Hamilton picked up four officers and twenty-one men in the other lifeboat.

*ABOVE: On April 5, 1942, German U-boat U-522 fired one torpedo from 1000 yards into the Byron D. Benson. The ship sunk seven and a half miles from Kitty Hawk, NC.*

On 11 June 1942, the *F.W. Abrams* was sunk by a mine left behind. In July 1942, other ships sank by mines off the NC Coast were the *Chilore* and *Keshena,* while the *Mowinckel* was only damaged.

The Museum of the Atlantic at Cape Hatteras, Ocracoke Island Museum, and the National Park Service on Ocracoke Island are great resources on the U-boat war off North Carolina's Outer Banks.

## Did a German U-Boat attack the Bromide Factory in Kure Beach near Wilmington, NC?

Wilmington's Navy Veteran, well-established World War II Historian and prolific writer Wilbur Jones is an achiever well recognized in the World War II history community. He was single-handedly responsible for moving the US Government to have Wilmington, NC designated the first World War II Heritage City. That's quite a feat. Wilmington has an honored tradition with regard to World War II History. The Battleship North Carolina sat proudly on the 75th Anniversary of V-J Day when President Trump formally declared Wilmington a World War II City and literally saluted Wilbur Jones for all his efforts.

Two hundred and thirty-four ships were built in Wilmington during the war. More soldiers and sailors trained in North Carolina than in any other state, nearly 2 million. The USS North Carolina was awarded more battle stars in World War II than any American battleship. So, Cpt. Wilbur Jones (Ret.) has a lot to be proud of when giving his Wilmington World War II Tours. One of the sites he stopped at to speak to his tour was kept quiet until after the war. Perhaps a secret history. It is believed a Type IX type long-range U-boat fired several shells at the Kure Beach Ethyl-Dow chemical plant on July 25, 1943.

The company is so named since it formed ethylene from bromide extracted from the sea. This was an important ingredient for military aircraft fuel, so naturally, the plant was important for the war effort. How would the Germans know about it? Between the wars, an effort was made by Germany to establish locations of important war industries in the US.

Along with his sister, John Gregory III now owns a shorefront cottage built by his grandparents in the late 1930s. John commented, "It wasn't just because my grandparents saw it, but lots of other people at the time, too."

Gregory's grandmother told him, "The next morning, neighbors spoke of seeing the light or hearing the firing.

Gregory's grandfather told an Army officer about their experience. His reaction was, 'Nothing happened. You didn't see anything.' But they knew what they and their neighbors saw – a German submarine."

Could the U-66 have been in the vicinity? According to *www.uboat.net*, U-66 sunk the SS Bloody Marsh on July 2, 1943, and did not return to Lorent, France, until Sept 1, 1943. There appear to be many witnesses, including the plant manager. Ralph Horton who was on plant duty that night stated, "We were blacked out on the ocean side. Their aim wasn't that good; we heard the whistling sound. We were on the fourth floor and could see the shells exploding at the water's edge." Army Lt. Carlton Sprague, 558th Anti-Aircraft Artillery Battalion training at nearby Fort Fisher that night, remembered the attack. The commander of the local Coast Guard Auxiliary confirmed it as well.

Richard MacMichael, a historian with the Museum of the Atlantic in Halifax, Nova Scotia, concurs. "U-Boats sank ships just outside Halifax and New York Harbors," he said. "So, it's not outside the realm of possibility that a submarine might be looking at targeting places along the East Coast, even later in the war." And the fact that the story of the Kure Beach incident didn't emerge until after the war isn't all that surprising, he says. "I'm not surprised if someone said, 'We don't want this released," says McMichael. "You can imagine the panic. It would have been something they would have wanted hushed up." A U-boat did fire shells and hit a land target on Bell Island, Newfoundland.

Forty U-boats came to America and more to South America. The Japanese only sent nine, with three separate shelling of land locations on the West Coast.

After the war, the concept of firing on a land-based site did not always fit in with memories. Moreover, during the war, the government hid that these attacks had happened.

A great deal came out after the war, and hence the shelling of the Ethly-Dow Plant, although not proven, was possibly another secret history of World War II. Wilbur Jones's book *A Sentimental Journey: Memoirs of a Wartime Boomtown* covers the event and the witnesses' statements. Today, a historical sign in front of the Gergory's cottage tells of the event.

## SOUTH CAROLINA

*ABOVE: An eerie feeling overcame sailors on the submarine chaser USS SC-1048. Empty lifeboats from the SS Boody Marsh seemed to find their way to USS SC-1048. Running into unoccupied lifeboats were unheard of in the maritime world.*

*Moreover, sailors were always superstitious about ships' names, especially on the ship's first voyage, and it was the first. The name "SS Boody Marsh" made the crew uneasy since from the beginning of their voyage. Four Navy Armed Guards went missing.*

The unescorted tanker, SS *Bloody Marsh,* was on a maiden voyage (the first time it ever sailed) when its torpedo indicator (a sonar device) sounded after detecting the approach of a torpedo from the German U-boat *U-66*. The Master of the SS *Bloody Marsh* ordered a course change to the hard left. Still, thirty seconds later, the torpedo struck the port side of the engine room, destroying the room completely, flooding the compartment, and killing one officer and two men on watch below. The hull was ruptured from midship to the engine room on the port side. As the tanker settled slowly by the stern, gradually losing headway, the after-gun crew reported that the conning tower would not open fire because the explosion had jammed the gun. The forward gun did not get into action because it could not be brought to bear.

Most of the ten officers, forty men, and twenty-seven Armed Guards (the ship was armed with one 5in, one 3in, and eight 20mm guns) left the ship in four lifeboats and three rafts, except the Armed Guard Commander and three of his men. Twenty minutes after the attack, a second torpedo struck the port side amidships, broke the ship in two, and immediately sank the tanker about 75 miles east of Savannah, Georgia. The four-Armed Guards jumped overboard as the water reached the after-gun platform. At 06:00 hours, a Navy blimp sighted the survivors and signaled that help was on the way. *USS SC-1048* picked them up at 09:00 hours and landed them at Charleston, South Carolina.

*On 11 Sep 1943, the USS Rapidan (AO 18) was damaged by a mine laid on 27 August by U-107 off Charleston, SC.*

*The mine detonated about 100 yards off the starboard quarter, and the ship went to Charleston to be repaired. She returned to service on 25 September. The German U-boats were supposedly gone on the South Carolina coast. Typically, these beaches are quiet and serene, but that changed on July 2, 1943. Imagine months of explosions from one small minefield!*

# GEORGIA

## April 8, 1942
## U-boat attack off St. Simons Island, Georgia

*ABOVE: The oil tanker, SS Oklahoma, sunk off St. Simon's Island on April 8, 1942.*

*ABOVE: Lieutenant Reinhard Hardegen, Commander of U-123, sunk SS Esso Baton Rouge off St. Simon's Island on April 8, 1942.*

There was torpedo damage to the hull of the SS *Esso Baton Rouge*. Dockyard workers had the gruesome task of removing the bodies of several dead sailors before repairs could be made to refloat the ship.

In a torpedo attack off St. Simons Island, Georgia, the German U-boat U-123 sank two oil tankers, the SS Oklahoma and the SS Baton Rouge. A total of twenty-two Merchant Seamen were killed in the attack.

Lt. Olaf H. Olsen, Sr., a member of the Georgia State Guard, went out on his boat to rescue survivors, and he captured a photo of one of the sunken tankers. After being raised, the two ships were carried to Brunswick for repairs. After resuming combat service, both ships were finally sunk in the Atlantic Ocean.

On April 8, 1942, the German U-boat *U-123* sank two US cargo ships off the coast of St. Simons Island. The blasts shattered glass windows in Brunswick, and early the next morning, it caused a near-panic that lasted until the following day, when the same U-boat sank the SS *Esparta* off the coast of Cumberland Island, plunging the ship to the seafloor and splashing her cargo of oranges and foil-wrapped turkeys ashore. In total, twenty-three crew members were killed.

The attacks boosted the military and industrial capabilities of the region. Fifty thousand men and women flocked to Brunswick to help build the Liberty Shipyard. Later, the ships transformed the town from a struggling Depression-era village of fifteen thousand people to a flourishing metropolis of bars, restaurants, and stores.

From a vast wooden hanger north of town, the War Department erected Glynco Naval Air Station, from which a squadron of blimps surveyed the Atlantic for German U-boats. To accommodate the military's growing presence, the government confiscated the King and Prince Hotel on St. Simons for bachelor officers' rooms and a radar training facility.

During World War II, when American Air and Naval Forces attacked prowling German U-boats off Georgia's Atlantic Coast, it was the state's closest encounter with actual combat activities. During the war, five Allied commercial ships were sunk off the coast of Georgia. However, by late 1943, Georgia's coastal defenses had improved to the point in which German U-boats no longer dared to strike the country.

Georgia was well out of range of any potential enemy aircraft, and hostile U-boat attacks on Georgia's seas were considered unlikely. To begin with, the state's coastline is quite short, stretching only about 100 miles between the South Carolina and Florida borders. The continental shelf off Georgia's coast is shallow, with only a few feet of water concealing enemy U-boats' conning towers, making them vulnerable to surveillance and attack.

Georgia was pretty well-defended except for not having a natural barrier to the open sea. Due to its economic and industrial importance to the American war effort, the state quickly became home to several key military outposts.

The anti-submarine effort relied heavily on Chatham Army Airfield and Hunter Army Airfield, located near Savannah. With fixed-wing and lighter-than-air anti-submarine aircraft, the Glynco Naval Air Station near Brunswick was one of the most effective military stations in the U-boat war. Several small coastal patrol and anti-submarine vessels were stationed in Savannah's harbor. War was encroaching on their shores.

Despite extensive pre-war planning for securing Georgia's coastline, when the United States entered World War II on December 8, 1941, the area remained vulnerable to attack.

Anti-submarine patrols were chaotic and sporadic at first, and American admirals initially refused to force commerce ships to travel in uncomfortable convoy formation. Worse, numerous Georgia coastal villages openly disobeyed orders for midnight blackouts due to the impact on the tourism business.

The defenders were jolted out of their complacency when the U-boat threat finally hit home in the spring of 1942.

The commander of the German submarine *U-123*, Reinhard Hardegen, sank the cargo *City of Atlanta* in January 1942, Georgian namesake. The 5,200-ton commercial ship was stationed in Savannah, and most of the forty-three seamen slain in the attack were locals.

Hardegen led his U-boat into America two months later on his second combat mission. As it cruised south along the Eastern shore, the *U-123* sank four ships before entering Georgia waters. Off St. Simon's Island coast, the *U-123* crept into a shallow-water ambush position.

On April 8, 1942, the German U-boat ace noticed a large ship silhouetted against the brightly lighted coastline. A torpedo launched by Hardegen sank the 9,200-ton oil tanker *Oklahoma*. Less than an hour later, he located and smashed another tanker, the 8,000-ton *Esso Baton Rouge.*

The next morning, the *U-123* sank a third ship, the steamer SS *Esparta*, fourteen miles south of Brunswick. Hardegen then went south to the Florida seas, sinking four more ships before returning to base.

Twenty-three crew members died as a result of the Georgia assaults. Survivors were rescued and carried to land by several Coast Guard ships and a private boat owned by Coca-Cola executive Charles Candler. The two tankers were finally retrieved and refloated since they sank in shallow water and were located near the coast. After extensive repairs, both ships were able to rejoin the combat effort. Later in the war, the same two ships were sunk by U-boats a second time, but this time it was permanent.

The massacre near Georgia's coast enraged the entire state.

The huge blasts from the exploding tankers shattered windows in Brunswick, and heavy oil contaminated the area's beaches for weeks. Rumors of German saboteurs landing on the beach circulated across the coastal villages. The Roosevelt Administration felt compelled to act rapidly to eliminate the threat of U-boats off the coast of the United States. The Navy finally adopted the British convoy ship idea, which resulted in a major increase in Air and Naval Patrols.

Airship *Squadron 15*'s submarine-hunting blimps were stationed at Glynco Naval Air Station, providing 24-hour protection against U-boats, critical for Georgia's security. In the summer of 1943, two more American tankers were lost about 150 miles east of Brunswick.

This account of the *Gulfamerica* sinking was recently published in the New Georgia Encyclopedia, an online resource for Georgia public school and university students. John Vanzo, an avid World War II militaria collector, also gave several U-boat relics to the Coastal Georgia Historical Society's Maritime Center Museum on St. Simon's Island, where the story was set. *Steel Boat, Iron Hearts, Hans Gobbler*, Vanzo's book about the wartime exploits of the German U-boat *U-505*, was published in 2005.

# FLORIDA

*Florida, "The Sunshine State," had at least twenty-four ships sunk by German U-boats off their coast in 1942 alone. From Jacksonville to Miami, Palm Beach to Key West, Panama City to Port St. Lucie, and Dry Tortugas to Cocoa Beach to Jupiter Inlet, the clandestine executioners (i.e., the German U-boats) were lying in wait. Oil tankers from Texas and New Orleans and freighters from South America would become its prey. The subs would leave behind deadly sea mines. Only one ship, the Edward Luckenbach, was sunk in Florida from a German mine off of Key West in July 1942. Florida also has the distinction of being one of three states to have German spies landing ashore by a U-boat.*

### Battle of Jacksonville:

On the night of April 10, *U-123* torpedoed and sank the SS *Gulfamerica* off the coast of Jacksonville, Florida. Remarkably, the SS *Gulfamerica* was on its maiden voyage from Philadelphia to Port Arthur, Texas, with 90,000 barrels of fuel oil. After hitting the ship with a torpedo, Commander of the U-boat *U-123*, Reinhard Hardegen, closed in for the kill with his deck gun.

Possibly thousands of people witnessed the sinking of the SS *Gulfamerica* because, just by chance, there happened to be a dance letting out at that time. The U-boat captain could see the faces of the Friday night fun-seekers on the boardwalk. He gazed with amazement at the people on the roller coaster as he sent Americans to their death. Shallow waters compelled Hardegen to take up station barely 820 feet from the tanker. The sinking of the SS *Gulfamerica* is best known as the most witnessed sinking by a U-boat off American shores in World War II.

A total of two officers, two Armed Guards, and fifteen crewmen were killed in the sinking, while kids on boardwalk rides and playing games were close by. Soon the roadways leading to Jacksonville Beach were clogged with hundreds of private cars attempting to reach the shore to witness the excitement. Even the U-boat Captain could see the backed-up traffic. The tanker was blazing after a period of firing with their deck gun, so Hardegen decided to leave the scene.

Subsequently, planes flew overhead, using parachute flares to identify the U-boat, while a destroyer and several smaller patrol boats closed in. After the war, Hardegan would claim he acted humanely by avoiding firing into the boardwalk. In the Post-War Era, many Americans were sometimes regarding the Germans' claims of humanity. Someone who was there, Martin Willaims Jr. from Jacksonville, clearly saw along with others that the tracers were from the deck guns were aimed at the crew and lifeboats.

*Martin G. Williams, Jr.*

*At 14 years old, Martin witnessed the sinking of the SS Gulfamerica by U-123.*

On April 10, 1942, Martin G. Williams, Jr, a young 14-year-old, witnessed an astonishing event:

"Between approximately 9:00-10:00 pm while I was at my father's bingo parlor on the boardwalk in Jacksonville Beach, Florida, I heard a strange thudding noise. I looked out in the ocean and noticed a red glow to the southeast, far out in the ocean. Shortly thereafter, another noise occurred and a bright yellow flame appeared to rise upward. Then people gathered on the boardwalk.

In front of the bingo, parlor was the Jacksonville Beach Pier. On the Pier, there was a dance going on, the Fireman's Ball, which was held annually. People attending the dance ran to the railings and out on the fishing pier to get a better look.

After much shouting and confusion, the word was passed around that a German U-boat had torpedoed a freighter off the coast. In the glow, you could see the U-boat had surfaced and was shooting from its deck gun. It fired approximately 12 to 13 shells before it began to shoot tracer bullets from its machine gun. *These tracers were aimed at the crew and lifeboats as they abandoned ship. With binoculars, some people could see the flaming ship and water and the poor crew struggling with the lifeboats.*

Shortly, the city officials cut off all electric power in order to quench all light sources. The U-boat had already used the light to its advantage by putting the ship in between it and the lighted coast, which created a fine silhouette target. Of course, thedamage was already done. Within the hour, you could see ships, assumed to be Patrol Craft or Coast Guard vessels from Mayport Naval Station, heading toward the disaster. They were blinkingtheir code lights between the various vessels.

Military personnel were ordered back to their bases, especially Naval personnel stationed at Mayport Naval Station, ten miles away at the mouth of the St. Johns River.

Special buses and taxis were offering free rides to the Base. The city was in the dark and there was general chaos with people trying to drive home in the dark.

The next morning, more details were in the newspaper, and there were many rumors. It was learned that the Coast Guard or Navy vessels were able to rescue a few of the survivors, but many were dead and missing. Over the next few days, a few of the bodies washed ashore, and along with some of my young friends, we began to see what happens when you are at war. After that night, there was a complete blackout at Jacksonville Beach, and we knew the war had come to our coast. For the next three years, there were many more sinkings. It was a night that I never forgot."

*ABOVE: Near Dry Tortugas National Park at 07.49 hours on July 15, 1942, the unescorted Pennsylvania Sun (Master Frederick Lyall) was hit by one torpedo from U-571, about 125 miles west of Key West, while steaming on a zigzag course at 14 knots.*

*Near Coast of Florida U- 134 shot down K-74: The only US Navy blimp to be destroyed by enemy action in World War II.*

*ABOVE: A typical Navy blip was used to patrol the coasts and drop depth charges on U-boats sighted.*

US Navy's widely deployed airships, generally in winter, were not an issue. The K class was the primary type deployed in the Atlantic, with one hundred and thirty-four of them constructed before and during World War II. While blimps were effective at locating and holding down U-boats until more assistance came, they were not authorized to attack surfaced U-boats. Instead of doing that, instruction directed them to strike just as the U-boat dived.

What occurred to Blimp Squadron ZP-21's *K-74* on patrol east of the Florida Straits in the Bahamas demonstrates why this rule was implemented. *K-74* established visual contact with the German U-boat *U-134* as it surfaced and headed toward a nearby tanker and ship. To safeguard these ships, Lieutenant Nelson G. Grills, Captain of the *K-74*, opted to strike *U-134*. As a result, *K-74* suffered a humiliating defeat in the contest.

On July 18, 1943, just before midnight, *K-74* attacked at a range of 250 yards with its 50-caliber machine gun. The bombardier launched two depth charges straight above, but unfortunately, this maneuver failed to sink the U-boat. A further pass would be required. Meanwhile, *U-134*'s anti-aircraft battery returned *K-74*'s fire, successfully striking it. The starboard engine of the blimp was destroyed, the cells containing the airship's helium were repeatedly punctured, and it started to deflate. The out-of-control balloon quickly settled in the ocean.

Upon reaching the ocean's surface, the *K-74* crew abandoned their ship. The balloon took an extended period to sink. Lieutenant Grills, Captain of the *K-74*, re-entered the gondola to ensure no secret documents were thrown overboard. He was inadvertently separated from the others upon exiting and chose to swim to shore.

Lieutenant Grills was picked up the next morning by *SC-657,* located six miles from *K-74.*

Meanwhile, the remaining eight crew members remained in contact and were discovered by a Grumman J4F amphibian the next morning. Unfortunately, the amphibian could not land due to the strong seas, but it located the destroyer *Dahlgren,* which rescued seven of the remaining eight crew members. Minutes before the *Dahlgren* arrived, the eighth crew member was attacked and killed by a shark.

# THE GULF OF MEXICO

*"The Americans apparently had not anticipated the appearance of U-boats in such far distant parts of the Caribbean as the Gulf of Mexico. Once again, we had struck them in a soft spot."*

*Admiral Donitz, April 1942*

When, the second group of U-boats, left their German bases in Europe for the United States; several had orders to enter the Caribbean and Gulf of Mexico. Most of the U-boats sent to the Gulf of Mexico were type IX-C U-boats, large ocean-going submarines designed for sustained operations far from any support facilities. They had a range of more than 13,000 nautical miles and could easily operate in the Caribbean, Gulf of Mexico, and the South Atlantic without needing to refuel. Type IX-C U-boats were armed with a 105mm deck gun, a 37mm anti-aircraft gun, a 20mm anti-aircraft gun, and had six torpedo tubes; four at the bow and two at the stern. They carried six extra torpedoes internally and had five external torpedo containers (three at the stern and two at the bow), which stored ten additional torpedoes. A total of twenty-two torpedoes allowed type IX-C U-boat captains to follow a convoy and strike night after night.

One of the IX-C U-boats to enter the Gulf of Mexico was *Unterseeboot 171 (U-171)*. The *U-171* was sent to the Gulf of Mexico under the command of Günther Pfeffer. *U-171* sank three ships in the Gulf of Mexico: the oil tanker *Amatlan* near the Texas-Mexico border, the oil tanker *R.M. Parker Jr.* off Louisiana, and the freighter *Oaxaca* off Port O'Connor.

The *Oaxaca* was a freighter that had previously been a German-owned ship, but when World War II broke out, the

Mexican government took possession of the ship and changed the name. The *Oaxaca* was a 6,000-ton freighter that normally carried dry cargo and no oil. The captain of the *Oaxaca* was Francisco Rodríguez Reybell.

On July 26, 1942, the *Oaxaca* left the port of Corpus Christi with a load of rubber, caustic soda, and other miscellaneous cargo. The crew of the *Oaxaca* mistakenly thought that by keeping close to shore, they would be safe from any U-boat attack. That night, the *U-171* sighted the *Oaxaca* sailing up the Gulf Coast, eleven miles from Port O'Connor. The *U-171* fired two torpedoes, one of which hit the *Oaxaca* and detonated it with a loud explosion. The *Oaxaca* broke in half and sank within three or four minutes of being hit.

Six of the thirty-six crewmen were killed. The Air Force Base on Matagorda Island was being built, and workers who were asleep in temporary housing on the island were awakened by the torpedo exploding. They assisted many of the survivors as they were brought to shore.

On Oct. 9, 1942, while returning to base, *U-171* hit a mine and sank in the Bay of Biscay off the western coast of France. Twenty-three other German U-boats were also sent to the Gulf of Mexico during World War II to sink ships and cause havoc; some of these include:

**U-507**, under the command of *Kapitänleutnant* Harro Schacht, sank the cargo ship *Alcoa Puritan* with its deck gun about 45 miles south of the New Orleans on May 6, 1942, and then shocked authorities by torpedoing and sinking the gasoline tanker *Virginia* in the mouth of the Mississippi River on May 12, with the loss of twenty-six sailors.

**U-506**, commanded by Knight's Cross winner Erich Würdemann, attacked eight ships in the Gulf of Mexico from May 10 to May 20, 1942. Four of these ships were badly damaged. The other four ships sunk, including the tanker *Gulfpenn, transporting 4 million gallons of gasoline from Port Arthur to Philadelphia, Pennsylvania, when a torpedo hit it from* *the U-506 off* Louisiana. The *Gulfpenn* exploded and sank quickly after torpedoing; thirteen crew members perished.

*U-166*, commanded by Hans-Günther Kuhlmann, sank four ships off Louisiana from July 11 to July 30, 1942. One of the ships that sank was the passenger ship, *Robert E. Lee*, carrying 407 passengers and crew, with twenty-five people losing their lives in the sinking.

*U-126*, commanded by Knight's Cross winner Ernst Bauer, sank several ships off Cuba, including the Merchant ship *Kahuku*. A sailor from the *Kahuku*, Archie Gibbs of Roscoe, Texas, was held captive on the *U-126* for four days before being released in an inflatable rubber boat within sight of land.

*U-156* was sent to the Caribbean on a secret mission to attack the oil refinery and tank farm on the island of Aruba. The attack failed when the first shot from the 105mm deck gun prematurely exploded in the barrel, damaging it. This happened because the protective cap at the end of the barrel was not removed before the gun was fired, causing the end of the barrel to burst. Working at top speed, Captain Werner Hartenstein and his crew cut off the barrel's damaged part, but the alarm sounded in Aruba, and the attack was called off. This freak accident saved what was then the world's largest oil refinery from a surprise attack. Hartenstein later sank two cargo ships off Cuba with his sawed-off deck gun.

After U-boats sank an alarming number of ships off the Gulf Coast, a panic set in and rumors rampant, the most famous of these rumors concerned U-boat crewmen coming ashore to watch movies in New Orleans or going shopping in Houston.

By the end of World War II, fifty-six ships were sunk, with fourteen ships damaged by German U-boats in the Gulf of Mexico. Twenty-four U-boats were used in these operations, with the *U-166* being the only U-boat lost. For many years, *U-166* was thought to have been sunk by a US Coast Guard aircraft on August 1, 1942, but it was sunk two days earlier by depth charges from the US Navy sub-chaser, *PC-556*. The

Coast Guard aircraft may have spotted and attacked the *U-171* instead, inflicting no damage. The mystery of the *U-166* was solved in 2001 when it was found off of Louisiana in 5,000 feet of water, one mile from the shipwreck of its last victim, the passenger ship *Robert E. Lee.*

Of the 54 type IX-C U-boats built, only the *U-505* survived World War II. *The US Navy captured U-505* in 1944, and it is now on display in Chicago, Illinois, at the Museum of Science and Industry. It is the only enemy vessel still in existence that was captured by the US and not returned. Fitted with six torpedo tubes below the waterline (4 at the bow and two at the stern), they carried 22 torpedoes with one periscope in the control room (deleted from types IXC onwards) and two in the tower. Type IX had five external torpedo containers (3 at the stern and two at the bow), which stored ten additional torpedoes. As mine-layers, they could carry 44 TMA (contact type, floating and moored) or 66 TMB mines (magnetic, sensed ships and stayed on the seafloor)

*ABOVE: An all too familiar scene off the US East Coast and in the Gulf of Mexico in 1942. Survivors hang onto life as they watch other people go down with their ship. Thousands would lose their lives.*

# LOUSIANA

One American family who narrowly escaped death were Ray and Ina Downs. They were on board the freighter *Heredia* with their two children, Sonny, 8, and Lucille, 11, en route from Central America to the United States.

In the 1940s, civilians were routinely transported aboard tankers. There weren't many passenger liners at the time, so civilians bought tickets on freighters. Ray was returning home to San Antonio, Texas, after the attack on Pearl Harbor to voluntarily join the Army. He and his family decided to leave Central America and go home, taking the ship, *Heredia.*

Before reaching their destination of New Orleans, the *Heredia* stopped at a port in Corpus Christie. Even With the worry of the possibility of encountering U-boats, the Downs family was not permitted to disembark even though they had all the necessary paperwork to do so, including their American passports. The family was ordered to get back on the freighter and go to the New Orleans Port.

They were not given any explanation for this, except that it was "wartime regulations." That phrase didn't make any sense to the Downs or anyone else. The traffic from ships in Corpus Christi was relatively light compared to how busy the New Orleans Port was during the war. There was a mistake or misjudgment on the part of the federal officials. Attacks by U-boats were a big source of concern, as there had been an influx of them in the area recently.

Because of this U-boat concern, Master Erwin F. Colburn (Merchant Marine equivalent of Captain) of the *Heredia* kept a large number of his crew on watch all night. The ship came to a standstill early in the morning, and the Downs family huddled around and put on their lifejackets.

Meanwhile, the German U-boats *U-506* and *U-507* competed for the largest tonnage sunk across the Gulf. On May 19, 1942, at 08:56 hours, *U-506* fired three torpedoes upon the *Heredia*. The first and second torpedoes slammed through the ship. The ship sank in three minutes after the third torpedo hit Heredia's amidships on the starboard side. The Downs family ran through the corridors, trying to find an escape route. The family nearly drowned as the ocean water came gushing down the stairs to the lower deck.

The blasts destroyed two lifeboats and two rafts, blew up the decks, and stopped the engines. The Merchant Marine's eleven commanders, 37 crew members, eight passengers, and six US Navy Armed Guards ran out of time to launch the lifeboats, and only two rafts made it to safety. Ina and Lucille Downs both made it out by clinging to huge debris.

Along with his father, another passenger, and the ship's captain, Sonny Downs clung to a balsa wood raft covered in canvas. They fought off sharks, hypothermia, starvation, and thirst in the blazing sun. After a rescue plane spotted them, they were rescued by a shrimp boat eighteen hours later. Sonny's mother, Ina, was found on the same ship.

Ina was alone, floating in the ocean, surrounded and covered by oil from the sunken ship. She claimed it was her prayers that saved her life. The ship's second mate saved Sonny's sister, Lucille. She kept her spirits up while floating in the Gulf by singing her mother's favorite hymn, "Nearer My God to Thee." Of the 62 people on the ship, 35 died. The Downs family lost everything they owned, but they were fortunate to make it home alive.

ABOVE: The Downs Family after surviving separately at sea. Although Ray and Sonny were together, they all braved extreme temperatures of cold heat, thirst, hunger, anxiety and sharks.

# ALABAMA

**ALABAMA and MISSISSIPPI were on constant alert. Orange Beach, Alabama, was affected because German U-boats were actively sinking ships in the Gulf.**

The Gulf of Mexico was swarming with German U-boats, and numerous American ships were sunk, with many lives lost. Orange Beach, Alabama, residents were required to keep blackout curtains and turn out all exterior lights during curfew. This was done to prevent German U-boats from identifying the coast and bombers from detecting the shoreline in the event of an attack. Some may have thought these preparations were overdone, but it turned out that fears of German assaults were justified.

The passenger ship SS *Robert E. Lee* carried two hundred and eighty-three people, most of them being survivors of other sunk ships. The ship was on its way to New Orleans from Trinidad. On July 30, 1942, about twenty-five miles from the Mississippi River's mouth, the ship was hit by a torpedo launched from the German U-boat *U-166*. The ship sank in fifteen minutes. While the bulk of the passengers could make it safely to lifeboats, the attack claimed the lives of twenty-five people.

Remarkably, the passengers aboard the *Robert E. Lee* were mostly survivors of previously torpedoed ships on their way to the US. Thus, this was their second time being sunk and surviving! Among the rescued were all 39 men from the *Andrea Brøvig*, 32 men from the *Høegh Giant,* and 44 men from the *Stanvac Palembang*, while one man from the latter died in the sinking.

Captain Herman H. Callaway of Orange Beach Charter Fishing reported that his father was fishing in the Gulf in 1942; he discovered pieces of the SS *Robert E. Lee*: the name of the ship, the SS *Robert E. Lee*, was written on two lifeboat oars floating in the Gulf.

*ABOVE: Mexican ship, the Oaxaca, burns from the U-boat attack. Mexico declares war on Germany.*

# TEXAS

Texas is the only state to have both sinkings from German U-boats off its coast as well as being hit by Japanese balloon bombs. Three separate balloon bombs descended on three different Texan counties during the same week of March 23, 1945. Quite remarkable considering Texas is in the center of the country.

The *Oaxaca* (formerly known as the German *Hameln*) was a Mexican freighter, sunk on July 26, 1942, just a few hours after leaving the port of Corpus Christi, Texas, by the German Type IX submarine *U-171*. One torpedo hit the ship, causing it to split in half and sink in three or four minutes. Six members of the crew perished.

The shipwreck is about eleven nautical miles from the coast of Port O'Connor, Texas, and it was submerged in 60-64 feet of water. The ship lies upright on the seafloor in two sections according to side-scan sonar and sub-bottom profiler data. The sinking inspired Mexico to declare war on Germany. Mexico created an air force that fought alongside the Allies in Europe with the US.

The German U-boat *U-166* sank in the Gulf of Mexico on July 30, 1942; the *Robert E. Lee*'s security boat, the USS *PC-566*, discharged a depth charge at the U-boat.

Several German U-boats were patrolling the area off the southeast Texas coast. Sunken warships like the *U-166* have been discovered over time, and they serve as a stark reminder of how close our adversary was.

"Research implies there were more than twenty different U-boats active in the Gulf in 1942 and 1943," according to the Texas Historical Commission. A U-boat fleet posed such a significant threat to the US Coast that Texas communities such as Beaumont, Port Arthur, Sabine Pass, and Galveston were alleged to have implemented blackouts to successfully limit their visibility to the submarines. Today, *U-166* is laying on the bottom of the Gulf, only a few miles off the Texas beach.

*TOP PHOTO: Typical depth charge dropped to destroy the U-boat.*

*BOTTOM PHOTO: "Hedgehogs" could be launched up to 850 feet.*

*Neither weapon needed to hit a U-boat to damage it.*

*ABOVE: A hedgehog explodes after being fired toward a U-boat in the Atlantic.*

# APPENDIXES

## CANADA

*Torpedo was discovered just after the battle on Bell Island, Newfoundland.*

Canada is an integral component when viewing the

*American Theater*. America shares the St. Lawrence River, and it borders New York State. The security of both the United States and Canada was at stake. Canada had naval attacks on both its coasts. The *Battle of the St. Lawrence*, like the attacks off the US East Coast, was a subset of the larger *Battle of the Atlantic*. The German Campaign was to disrupt transportation from North America to the United Kingdom. The ports of Halifax and Sydney in Nova Scotia became important staging areas for supply convoys moving overseas.

German U-boat attacks continued across the Atlantic from the US, picking off ships from and to Canada. The route was the shortest, beginning from North America to Greenland, Iceland, and Europe. This route gave the German U-boats plenty of opportunities to hunt and attack ships, both in Canada and America.

German U-boats repeatedly invaded the waters of the St. Lawrence River and Gulf between 1942 and 1944, sinking twenty-three ships and killing hundreds of people. The Navy in the Great Lakes and the Central Defense Command were tasked with supporting Canada. The *Battle of the St. Lawrence* involved marine and anti-submarine actions throughout the lower St. Lawrence River and the Gulf of Saint Lawrence, Strait of Belle Isle, Anticosti Island and Cabot Strait from May through October 1942, September 1943, and again in October through November 1944.

Two events in the battle took place in 1942 when German U-boats attacked four Allied ore carriers at Bell Island, Newfoundland. The carriers SS *Saganaga* and *SS Lord Strathcona* were sunk by *U-513* on September 5, 1942, while U-518 sank the SS Rosecastle and PLM 27 on November 2 with the loss of sixty-nine lives. The U-boat launched a torpedo at the loading pier at Bell Island.

POW camp prisoners riot and break out attempts across the St. Lawrence River from New York State.

### Battle of Bowmanville:

In October 1942, between 1,500 and 4,000 prisoners revolted against the POW guards at Bowmanville Prisoner of War Camp. U-boats were captured off of Canada earlier that year. Commandeers and sailors were taken as prisoners.

U-boat Commanders Horst Elfe, Kretschmer, and others barricaded themselves in the mess hall, arming themselves with sticks, iron bars, and makeshift weapons. Approximately one hundred Canadian soldiers from another base in Kingston arrived, and they stormed the mess hall using only ice hockey sticks. After several hours of fighting, the Canadians brought high-pressure water hoses and soaked the cabin thoroughly until the prisoners agreed to come out peacefully. During later incidents in the battle which spanned several days, a Canadian soldier suffered a skull fracture.

### Operation Kiebitz

*Operation Kiebitz* was a failed German operation intended to organize the escape of four skilled U-boat commanders from a Canadian Prisoner of War camp in Bowmanville, Ontario. The subsequent counteroperation by the Royal Canadian Navy, *Operation Pointe Maisonnette*, became a key engagement in the *Battle of the St. Lawrence. It* was also successful in thwarting the Germans' plan.

### Prisoner escape plan

The Kriegsmarine developed the plan in 1942, and it was to be carried out in September 1943. The escape plan was that Horst Elfe (Captain of *U-93*), Hans Ey (Captain of *U-433)*, Otto Kretschmer (Captain of *U-99)*, and Hans Joachim Knebel-Döberitz (Executive Officer of *U-99)* would escape from Camp

30 in Bowmanville and make their way 1,400 kilometers (870 mi) through eastern Canada to northern New Brunswick, where they would rendezvous with a U-boat off Pointe de Maisonnette on Chaleur Bay. Executive Officer Knebel-Döberitz was the former adjutant of Admiral Karl Dönitz and, along with Captain Kretschmer, was thought to be the primary reason behind this risky operation.

Coded messages were sent through the International Committee of the Red Cross to the German prisoners at Camp 30 in Bowmanville, east of Toronto. These messages were intercepted by Canadian military intelligence and Canadian police, who were screening all prisoner communications. The Canadian authorities did not tell the prisoners that their plans were detected. The Royal Canadian Navy hoped to get a rare chance to seize a German U-boat in Canadian waters. The Germans arrived at the location at the appointed time, only to be arrested by Mounties and Naval personnel, who were waiting to coordinate a surface task force that would attempt to attack and seize the U-boat.

### Operation Pointe Maisonnette

To capture the U-boat, the Royal Canadian Navy and the Canadian Army established a portable surface radar array onshore at the Pointe de Maisonnette (New Brunswick) lighthouse, which would be used to locate the submarine by a task force of several warships centered on HMCS *Rimouski*. *Rimouski* was outfitted with an experimental diffuse lighting system that was considered revolutionary. Under the command of Desmond Piers, the ship and the rest of the task group were hidden nearby to wait for the German submarine.

*U-536*, which had been tasked with picking up the escaping Naval officers, arrived off Pointe de Maisonnette at the appointed time on the night of September 26, 1943. The Royal Canadian Navy and Canadian Army personnel onshore signaled with a light that the escapees used. However, the U-boat commander was suspicious, particularly after his hydrophones picked up the sound of the Canadian task group nearby. He opted to remain submerged and began to evade the Canadian warships, which searched throughout the night and attempted unsuccessfully to attack *U-536* with depth charges.

Despite evading the Canadians' trap in Chaleur Bay that September, *U-536* was sunk the following month northeast of the Azores by one British and two Canadian warships, claiming 38 lives.

Estevan Point Lighthouse on Vancouver Island, BC

The Japanese submarine *I-26* shelled the Estevan Point Lighthouse on Vancouver Island's Western Coast on June 20, 1942, just miles from Washington State's San Juan Islands. On the night of the attack, lightkeeper Robert M. Lally, a World War I veteran who had worked at Estevan Point since 1926, saw a ship of some kind on the horizon firing several dozen rounds at him. None of the rounds reached the lighthouse.

The first shell landed right in front of the light. Lally shut it off immediately. The other rounds landed behind him, where he couldn't observe. Why would the Japanese conduct an attack on a Canadian lighthouse? It was a radio-direction-finding station, one of the most important ones in the North Pacific, and this was located at the lighthouse. It had the most coverage on any Canadian broadcasting location on the West Coast. Commercial shipping from Japan would have been familiar with the station running up to the war over the years. The lighthouse was a relatively straightforward target to hit. The lighthouse keeper's son, fishing in a boat, said he saw the Japanese I-26 submarine, and his daughter reported she saw it.

The next night, *I-26* assaulted Fort Stevens in Oregon, which defended the Columbia River's mouth. As a result of the strike, most of the lights and navigation aids on the West Coast were turned off for the duration of the war.

# APPENDIX II

# CARRIBEAN AND SOUTH AMERICA

Ligia Domench, PhD. *Imprisoned in the Caribbean,* pages 165

167, shows that three hundred and sixty-three ships were sunk

in the Caribbean in World War II.

Aruba was attacked on February 16, 1942. Aruba in the Lesser Antilles, situated 27 kilometers north of Venezuela in the southern Caribbean Sea, was home to two massive oil refineries.

On February 13, the German submarine U-156, commanded by Fregattenkapitän Werner Hartenstein, arrived in the seas around Aruba to perform surveillance for a wolfpack consisting of five German submarines (U-67, U-502, U-129, U-156, and U-161) and two Italian subs.

At 0131 hours on February 16, U-156 surfaced 1.5 kilometers off the Lago refinery in Saint Nicolas Harbor, hitting the British tanker Pedernales with one torpedo, killing eight of the ship's twenty-six-man crew. Ornamented, a British tanker, rose its anchor and tried to depart but was struck by a torpedo from U-156, killing fifteen of its twenty-two crew members. In

0313 hours, U-156 surfaced at Oranjestad Port, firing a torpedo at the American tanker Arkansas (owned by the Texas Company, more often referred to as Texaco), resulting in fatalities.

The smaller-caliber 37-millimeter cannon fired sixteen rounds and struck two targets, denting an oil storage tank and tearing a hole in a structure. The mission ended when the Axis submarines landed at the French colony of Martinique, also in the Lesser Antilles part of France. Vichy, France, was a Nazi ally. They suffered just two fatalities during this expedition, which resulted in the loss of six tankers (with a combined weight of 14,149 tons), but caused no damage to shore infrastructure.

Mona, Puerto Rico, suffered an assault. In March 1942, a German submarine bombed the Island's southern shore. On June 4, 1942, the German submarine U-68 sank the oil tanker, MV C.O. Stillman, 41 nautical miles (76 kilometers) southwest of Isla de Mona.

Attack on Curaçao, April 19, 1942. These strikes are only examples but, combined with the sinking of South American freighters, caused some Latin American countries to declare war on Germany and join the Allies in 1943.

Battle of the River Plate off of Argentina: The first Naval battle of WWII was in the Western Hemisphere. The British hunted for the Nazi battleship *Admiral Graf Spee* throughout the war after having many British sunk by this advanced Nazi battleship.

Although not an attack on America, the first naval battle fought during World War II was between Germany and the UK on December 13, 1939. It ended off the Atlantic coast of South America. The German battleship *Admiral Graf Spee* was busy sinking British ships early in the war against Britain. The *Graf Spee* encountered one of the British Naval units, composed of three Royal Navy cruisers (HMS *Exeter*, *Ajax*, and *Achilles*), while the unit was patrolling off the River Plate estuary of Argentina and Uruguay.

In a bloody engagement, *Admiral Graf Spee* successfully repulsed the British attacks. Captain Hans Langsdorff then brought his damaged ship to shelter in neutral Uruguay for repairs. However, British intelligence successfully deceived Langsdorff into believing that a much superior British force had now gathered to wait for him. He scuttled his ship at Montevideo to save his crew's lives before committing suicide. German combat losses were 96 killed or wounded against 72 British sailors killed and 28 wounded. Two Royal Navy cruisers had been severely damaged.

## Brazil

German Navy U-boats sank thirteen Brazilian Merchant ships, causing severe damage to Brazilian shipping. In total, twenty-one German U-boats and two Italian submarines caused the sinking of thirty-six Brazilian merchant ships, causing 1,691 drownings and 1,079 other casualties. The sinkings were the main reason that led the Brazilian government to declare war against the Axis.

Finally, President Vargas declared war on Germany and Italy on August 22, 1942. It is known that nine U-boats were sunk off the Brazilian Coast throughout the war.

# APPENDIX III

# HOW CLOSE WAS AN AXIS VICTORY?

Historical changes of the military strategies, including intelligence gathering, are typically the foundation of determining an alternate history. A revision of even minor events would change the outcome of the war. Due to the scope of World War II, several opportunities abound for an alternate history. Nothing illustrates the likelihood of defeat of the Allies more than the Axis' development of *Weapons of Mass Destruction*.

By 1945, a Japanese atomic bomb (*"genzai bakudan"*) described in Robert K. Wilcox's book *Japan's Secret War* disclosed declassified information regarding the Japanese atomic bomb. This book tells the development, including the names, dates, locations of facilities, cyclotrons, methods, tests, and more. Before the war, Japanese nuclear scientists studied under the world's top atomic scientists, including Nobel Laureates Niels Bohr, Ernest Lawrence, Enrico Fermi, and others. An alternate process unknown to the Allies was said to have been used to separate U-235 from U-238, one of the most difficult challenges in building the bomb.

The Japanese Navy was said to have successfully detonated a test atomic bomb at Hunhnam, Korea (in North Korea today) on August 10, 1945. In mid-1946, Captain Snell of the twenty-fourth Criminal Investigation Detachment in Korea reported the summary of his interview with a Japanese officer up his chain-of-command. The officer was in charge of security for the *Genzai Bkudan Test.*

The Japanese did not prevent Korean boats from anchoring in the area, and they did not warn Korean civilians. The bomb exploded near an inlet of the Sea of Japan with Japanese official observers twenty miles away donning eye protection. The detonation took place at sunrise. The fireball was at least 3000 feet in diameter, and it formed a mushroom cloud in the stratosphere. Ships are said to have vaporized in the harbor. The Japanese officer said the test explosion to be the size of those in Hiroshima or Nagasaki.

A bomber need not have been necessary to deploy the weapon. Delivery methods by Kamikaze planes to the invading US forces were considered. Another approach would have been sending a disguised ship into San Francisco or Los Angeles and detonating the atomic bomb before American forces could prevent the explosion. After the war, Japanese nuclear scientists accepted positions and a comfortable existence in Huntsville, Alabama, working for the Government.

The Japanese Army exposed the Chinese population to deadly viruses during the war, killing 540,000 civilians. This bio-weapon killed over four times the number who died in the atomic bombings of Hiroshima and Nagasaki.

The German atomic bomb was never developed; however, the use of "dirty bombs" was considered by the Wehrmacht. Nuclear science has its roots in pre-war Germany before and during the Third Reich. Before the war, American and British atomic scientists had to study in Germany, including the Director of the American Manhattan Project, Dr. Robert J. Oppenheimer. The Germans universities were far ahead of any Allied country in nuclear science and technology. It was Nazi Germany that first understood the process of splitting the atom, showing how the power could be released.

The radiation that Nazi Germany developed could be used against Allied troops without warning. The Allies were so concerned that this type of weapon could be used that Giger counters were employed on the sands of Normandy on D-Day to check for radiation. The German Military Industrial Complex had already established an advanced deployment of chemical weapons in WWI. How could Germany have delivered such weapons to attack the United States? In *Target America: Hitler's Plan to attack the United States* by World War II, historian James P. Duffy reports on several German delivery methods of bombing the US, including using the advanced Messerschmitt 242 jets that could easily make the round-trip from Germany to the US and back again to Germany. An intercontinental ballistic missile was under development. It was completed in the US by German scientists after the war. Another important work on the subject is Manfred Griehl's book, *Luftwaffe Over America: The Secret Plans to Bomb the United States in World War II*.

By late 1944, the main thrust of the U-boat was assumed to be over. But in November 1944, a new and even deadlier threat was to be launched on the US from Germany. The Eastern Sea Frontier, the Navy command responsible for protecting the United States' East Coast from Canada to Florida, was instructed to commence intense anti-U-boat patrols up to 250 miles from New York City, with good reason. In January 1945, US intelligence confirmed that U-boats were spotted with rocket launchers in Nazi-occupied Norway. German Armaments Minister Albert Speer announced that U-boats with long-range rockets V-1 and V-2 would be attacking New York City in February. By March, US Intelligence discovered evidence that nine U-boats with missiles were on their way to the northeast coast of the US. The Germans named their offensive Grupp Seewolf (Group Seawolf), and America's counteroffensive was Operation Teardrop.

In December 1944, German spies William Colepaugh and Erich Gimpel, who had landed in Maine by *U-1230* and then captured in New York, told U.S. interrogators that a group of rocket-equipped submarines was being readied for attacking the New York City.

Operation Teardrop was the largest single American naval deployment in the Atlantic, with two aircraft carriers and twenty destroyers on a mission to find and destroy the rocket-carrying U-boats. The *U-1235* and *U-880* were sunk and were reported to have created a much larger explosion than before in U-boats sinkings during the war. The Navy believed that these U-boats contained more powerful weapons than just torpedoes. Although never confirmed by underwater archaeology, the US government thought it was likely the V-1 or V-2 rockets were on board these U-boats, ready to fire. Regardless, it was an available technology the Germans could have easily used at the time.

# APPENDIX IV


# THE STATISTICS OF KIAS AND CIVILIANS KILLED IN WORLD WAR II


What was the total number of deaths in World War II? We rarely hear of the enormous numbers of those killed in World War II. An estimated 25 million civilians were killed by the Japanese Military, with most of the genocide in China, Korea, Burma, the Philippines, and other South Pacific locations. Genocide committed by Germany in World War II is said to be larger (includes mostly the Soviet Union and Europe), but the exact numbers will never be known. The chart below appears to be relatively accurate.

Looking at the chart below, it is clear that 4% of all those killed were civilians in Axis countries, mostly Japan and Germany. Germany had twice the number of military personnel and twice the number of civilians who died compared to Japan.

In extreme contrast to the Germans and Japanese, 58% of all those killed in World War II were civilians of Allied countries, mostly in China, the Soviet Union and Poland; Indonesia and India's losses were largely, but not completely, from famine as a result from the war.

Axis Military lost only half of the number of Allied Military, 13% vs. 25% of total deaths. Poland, Lithuania, and Latvia had the greatest percentages. The Soviet Union, with the highest losses, had nearly 12 million military and 12 to 19 million civilians killed as a result of the German invasion, and its subsequent defense. Due to Japan's invasion of its country,

China lost nearly 16 million civilians and almost 4 million military personnel killed.

Relative to those killed in Allied countries, it is not surprising to expect the number of Germans and Japanese killed since they were the aggressors. The Soviet Union was an aggressor nation aligned with Germany for the first two years of the war in Europe, but they did not suffer many casualties. Nearly all of its fallen are a result of Germany's invasion of the Soviet Union.

The total numbers are killed in the War are staggering, with possibly 70 to 80 million dead. It is unclear whether or not the American public or the international community understands the depth of the horrendous cataclysm mankind survived.

Yet, to those familiar with this history, it is nearly inconceivable to them as well.

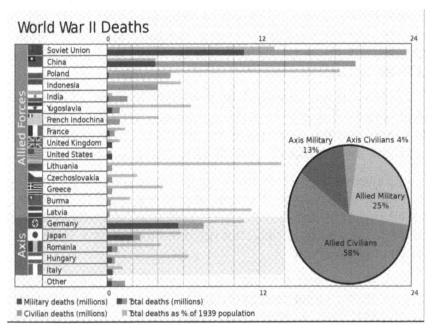

https://en.wikipedia.org/wiki/World_War_II_casualties, *The Soviet Union, had the highest losses. China was a close second.*

# APPENDIX V SHIPS AND U-BOATS SUNK OR DAMAGED OFF THE EAST COAST

## U-BOAT ATTACKS ON AMERICAN/CANADIAN COASTS
### DATE/U-BOAT/SHIP'S NAME:

### January-February1942

1. 01/11/42   U-123 Cyclops

2. 01/12/42   U-130 Frisco

3. 01/13/42   U-130 Friar Rock

4. 01/14/42   U-123 Norness

5. 01/14/42   U-552 Dayrose

6. 01/15/42   U-123 Coimbra

7. 01/15/42   U-203 Catalina

8. 01/16/42   U-86  Toorak #

9.  01/17/42  U-203 Octavian

10. 01/17/42 U-123 Sanjose

11. 01/18/42 U-552 Frances Salman

12. 01/18/42 U-66  Allan Jackson

13. 01/18/42 U-123 Brazos

14.  01/19/42 U-109 Empire Kingfisher

15. 01/19/42 U-66  Lady Hawkins

16. 01/19/42 U-123 City of Atlanta

17. 01/19/42 U-123 Ciltvaira

18. 01/19/42 U-123 Malay #

19. 01/21/42 U-203 North Gaspe #

20. 01/21/42 U-754 Belize

21. 01/21/42 U-754 William Hansen

22. 01/21/42 U-130 Alexandra Hoegh

23. 01/21/42 U-203 Rosemonde

24. 01/22/42 U-66  Norvana

25. 01/22/42 U-553 Inneroy

26. 01/22/42 U-130 Olympic

27. 01/23/42 U-109 Thirlby

28. 01/23/42 U-82  Leiesten

29. 01/23/42 U-66  Empire Gem

30. 01/23/42 U-66  Venore

31. 01/24/42 U-754 Mount Kitheron

32. 01/25/42 U-130 Varanger

33. 01/25/42 U-125 Olney *

34. 01/26/42 U-125 West Ivis

35. 01/26/42 U-754 Jcarion

36. 01/27/42 U-130 Francis E. Powell

37. 01/27/42 U-130 Halo #

38. 01/30/42 U-106 Rochester

39. 01/31/42 U-82  Belmont

40. 01/31/42 U-109 Tacoma Star

41. 02/01/42 U-751 Corilla #

42. 02/02/42 U-103 W.L. Steed

43. 02/02/42 U-106 Amerikaland

44. 02/03/42 U-751 Silveray

45. 02/04/42 U-103 San Gil

46. 02/04/42 U-103 India Arrow
47. 02/05/42 U-103 China Arrow
48. 02/06/42 U-t07 Major Wheeler
49. 02/06/42 U-751 Empire Sun
50. 02/08/42 U-108 Ocean Venture
51. 02/09/42 U-108 Tolosa
52. 02/11/42 U-t08 Blink
53. 02/13/42 U-5Z6 Empire Spring
54. 02/14/42 U-566 Meropi
55. 02/14/42 U-432 Buarque
56. 02/16/42 U-564 Opalia #
57. 02/18/42 U-432 Olinda
58. 02/18/42 U-432 Miraflores
59. 02/18/42 U-108 Flat ves.w/bridge
60. 02/19/42 U-128 Pan Massachusetts
61. 02/19/42 U-96 Empire Seal
62. 02/19/42 U-96 Lake Osweya
63. 02/20/42 U-432 Azalea City
64. 02/21/42 U-96 Torungen
65. 02/21/42 U-504 Republic
66. 02122/42 U-128 Cities Svc. Empire
67. 02/22/42 U-96 Kars
68. 02/22/42 U-504 W. D. Anderson
69. 02/26/42 U-504 Mamura
70. 02/27/42 U-578 R. P. Resor
71. 02/27/42 U-432 Marore

72. 02/28/42  U-653 Leif

73. 02/28/42  U-578 Jacob Jones

74. 02/28142 U-588 Carperby

## U-boat Attacks off American/Canadian Coasts Date/U-boat/Ship's Name:

## March -April 1942

1. 03/02/42   U-587 Unident. subchaser

2. 03/04/42   U-587 St. Johns Docks

3..03/05/42   U-404 Collamer

4. 03/06/42   U-587 Hans Egede

5. 03/06/42   U-94   APC Nort. Princess

6. 03/07/42   U-155 Arabutan

7. 03/08/42   U-94   Cayru

8. 03/09/42   U-96   Tyr

9. 03/10/42   U-588 Gulftrade

10. 03/10/42 U-94   Hvosleff

11. 03/11/42 U-158 Caribsea

12.' 03/13/42 U-158 John D. Gill

13. 03/13/42 U-404 Tolten

14. 03/13/42 U-332 Albert F. Paul

15. 03/13/42 U-332 Trepca

16. 03/14/42 U-404 Lemuel Burrows

17. 03/14/42 U-158 Olean #

18. 03/15/42 U-158 Ario

19. 03/16/42 U-332 Australia

20. 03/16/42 U-404 San Demetria

21. 03/16/42 U-124 Ceiba

22. 03/17/42 U-71  Ranja

23. 03/17/42 U-124 Acme#

24. 03/17/42 U-124 Kassandra Louloudi

25. 03/18/42 U-124 E.M. Clark

26. 03/18/42 U-124 Papoose

27. 03/18/42 U-124 W. E. Hutton

28. 03/19/42 U-332 Liberator

29. 03/20/42 U-71  Oakmar

30. 03/21/42 U-124 Esso Nashville#

31. 03/21/42 U-124 Atlantic Sun #

32. 03/21/42 U-373 Thursobank

33. 03/23/42 U-124 Naeco

34. 03/23/42 U-754 British Prudence

35. 03/24/42 U-552 Ocana

36. 03/25/42 U-105 Narragansett

37. 03/26/42 U-71  Dixie Arrow

38. 03/26/42 U-123 Atik (Carolyn)

39. 03/26/42 U-160 Equipoise

40. 03/27/42 U-105 Svenor

41. 03/29/42 U-160 City of New York

42. 03/29/42 U-571 Hertford

43. 03/31/42 U-754 Menominee

44. 03/31/42 U-754 Ontario #

45. 03/31/42 U-754 Barnegat

46. 03/31/42 U-754 Allegheny

47. 03/31/42 U-71  San Gerardo
48. 03/31/42 U-71  Eastmoor
49. 04/01/42 U-754 Tiger
50. 04/01/42 U-160 Rio Blanco
51. 04/02/42 U-123 Liebre #
52. 04/02/42 U-552 David H Atwater
53. 04/03/42 U-754 Otho
54. 04/03/42 U-572 Ensis #
55. 04/04/42 U-552 Byron T. Benson
56. 04/06/42 U-160 Bidwell
57. 04/06/42 U-571 Koll
58. 04/06/42 U-754 Kollskegg
59. 04/06/42 U-552 British Splendour
60. 04/07/42 U-552 Lancing
61. 04/07/42 U-84  Nemanja
62. 04/08/42 U-123 Oklahoma #
63. 04/08/42 U-123 Esso Baton Rouge #
64. 04/09/42  U-552 Atlas
65. 04/09/42 U-123 Esparta
66. 04/09/42 U-160 Malchace
67. 04/09/42 U-203 San Delfino
68. 04/10/42 U-552 Tamaulipas
69. 04/10/42 U-85  Chr. Knudsen
70. 04/10/42 U-123 Gulfamerica
71. 04/11/42 U-203 Harry F. Sinclair #
72. 04/11/42 U-160 Ulysses

73. 04/12/42 U-203 Stanvac Melbourne #

74. 04/12/42 U-123 Leslie

75. 04/13/42 U-123 Korsholm

76. 04/14/42 U-203 Empire Thrush

77. 04/14/42 U-571 Margaret

78. 04/15142 U-575 Robin Hood

79·. 04/16142 U-572 Desert Light

80. 04/16142 U-123 Alcoa Guide

81. 04/17142 U-201 Victoria #

82. 04/18/42 U-136 Axtell J. Byles #

83. 04/19/42 U-572 Empire Dryden

84. 04/19/42 U-654 Steelmaker

85. 04/19/42 U-109 Harpagon

86. 04/20/42 U-654 Agra

87. 04/20/42 U-84 Chenango

88. 04/20/42 U-201 Eris

89. 04/20/42 U-752 West Imboden

90. 04/21/42 U-576 Pipestone County

91. 04/21/42 U-201 San Jacinto

92. 04/22/42 U-201 Derryheen

93. 04/23/42 U-752 Reinholt

94. 04/24/42 U-576 Tropic Star #

95. 04/24/42 U-136 Empire Drum

96. 04/28/42 U-136 Arundo

97. 04/29/42 U-402 Ashkabad

98. 04/30/42 U-576 Taborfjell

# U-boat Attacks off American/Canadian Coasts Date/U-boat/Ship's Name:

## May-June 1942

1. 05/01/42   U-752 Bidevind
2. 05/01/42   U-109 La Paz #
3. 05/01/42   U-109 Worden
4. 05/01/42   U-136 Alcoa Leader
5. 05/02/42   U-402 Cythera
6. 05/03/42   U-506 Sama
7. 05/03/42   U-564 Ocean Venus
8. 05/03/42   U-109 Laertes
9. 05/04/42   U-507 Norlindo
10. 05/04/42 U-564 Eclipse #
11. 05/04/42 U-507 Munger T. Ball
12. 05/04/42 U-507 Joseph M. Cudahy
13. 05/04/42 U-564 Delisle #
14. 05/05/42 U-333 ]ava Arrow #
15. 05/06/42 U-333 Amazone
16. 05/06/42 U-333 Halsey
17. 05/06/42 U-507 Alcoa Puritan
18. 05/07/42 U-507 Ontario
19. 05/08/42 U-507 Torny
20. 05/08/42 U-564 Ohioan
21. 05/08/42 U-588 Greylock #
22. 05/09/42 U-564 Lubrafol
23. 05/09/42 U-588 Kitty's Brock

24. 05/10/42 U-333 Clan Skene
25. 05/10/42 U-506 Aurora
26. 05/11/42 U-558 Bedfordshire
27. 05/11/42 U-553 Nicoya
28. 05/12/42 U-553 Leto
29. 05/12/42 U-507 Virginia
30. 05/13/42 U-506 Gulfpenn
31. 05/13/42 U-506 David McKelvy
32. 05/13/42 U-564 Potrero del Llano
33. 05/14/42 U-593 Stavros
34. 05/15/42 U-507 Amapala
35. 05/15/42 U-751 Nicarao
36. 05/16/42 U-506 Wm. C. McTarnahan
37. 05/16/42 U-506 Sun
38. 05/16/42 U-135 Fort Qu'Appelle
39. 05/16/42 U-506 Gulf Oil
40. 05/17/42 U-432 Foam
41. 05/17/42 U-653 Peisander
42. 05/19/42 U-506 Heredia
43. 05/19/42 U-103 Ogontz
44. 05/20/42 U-506 Halo
45. 05/20/42 U-106 Faja de Oro
46. 05/21/42 U-588 Plow City
47. 05/22/42 U-432 Zurichmoor
48. 05/23/42 U-588 Margot
49. 05/24/42·U-753 Haakon Hauan

50. 05125/42 U-593 Persephone

51. 05/27/42 U-753 Hamlet

52. 05/28/42 U-506 Yorkmoor

53. 05/30/42 U-404 Alcoa Shipper

54. 06/01/42 U-404 West Notus

55. 06/02/42 U-553 Mattawin

56. 06/02/42 U-578 Berganger

57. 06/03/42 U-404 Anna

58. 06/??/42 U- Poseidon

59. 06/07/42 U-653 Gannet

60. 06/07/42 U-158 Hermis

61. 06/07/42 U-135 Pleasantville

62. 06/09/42 U-432 Kronprinsen

63. 06/11/42 U-158 Sheherazade

64. 06/12/42 U-158 Cities Svc. Toledo

65. 06/15/42 U-701 Robert C. Tuttle      (German mine)

66. 06/15/42 U-701 Esso Augusta #

67. 06/15/42 U-701 Kingston Ceylonite  (German mine)

68. 06/15/42 U 701 Bainbridge           (German Mine)

69.  06/15/42 U-67  Managua

70. 06/15/42 U-87  Port Nicholson

71. 06/15/42 U-87  Cherokee

72. 06/17/42 U-701 Santore #

73. 06/18/42 U-129 Millinocket

74. 06/19/42 U-701 YP 389

75. 06/20/42 U-67  Nortind

76. 06/22/42 U-202 Rio Tercero

77. 06/23/42 U-67   Rawleigh Warner

78. 06/24/42 U-404 Ljubica Matkovic

79. 06/24/42 U-373 John R. Williams

80. 06/24/42 U-404 Manuela

81. 06/24/42 U-404 Nordal

82. 06125/42 U-701 Tamesis #

83. 06/27/42 U-701 British Freedom #

84. 06/27/42 U-404 Mo/danger

85. 06/28/42 U-701 William Rockefeller·

86. 06/29/42 U-67   Empire Mica

87. 06/29/42 U-158 Everalda

**U-boat Attacks off American/Canadian Coasts Date/U-boat/Ship's Name:**

**July-Aug 1942**

1. 07/01/42   U-202 City of Birmingham

2. 07/06/42   U-67   Bayard

3. 07/07/42   U-571 Umtata

4. 07/07/42   U-67   Paul H. Harwood #

5. 07/08/42   U-571  J A. Moffett, Jr

6. 07/08/42   U-571  Nicholas Cuneo

7. 07/10/42   U-67   Benjamin Brewster

8. 07/12/42   U-84   Andrew Jackson

9. 07/13/42   U-67   R. W. Gallagher

10. 07/15/42   U-571 Pennsylvania Sun #

11. 07/15/42   U-576   J A. Mowinckel #

12. 07/15/42  U-576  Chilore

13. 07/15/42  U-576  Bluefields

14. 07/19/42  U-84  Baja California

15. 07/19/42 U-129  Port Antonio

16. 07/20/42  U-132 Frederika Lensen

17. 07/21/42  U-84  Wm. Cullen Bryant

18. 07/25/42  U-89  Lucille M.

19. 07/26/42 U-171 Oaxaca

20. 07/28/42  U-754  Ebb

21. 07/29/42 U-132 Pacific Pioneer

22. 07/30/42 U-166 Robert E. Lee

23. 08/05/42 U-458 Draco

24. 08/12/42  U-508 Santiago de Cuba

25. 08/12/42  U-508 Manzanillo

26. 08/13/42 U-171 R.M. Parker

**U-boats sunk off American Coast and Attacking Ship**
**January-August 1942**

1. 04/14/42  U-85  USS Roper

2. 05/09/42  U-352 USCGC Icarus

3. 06/13/42  U-157 USCGC Thetis

4. 07/03/42  U-215 HMS Le Tigre

5. 07/07/42  U-701 Aircraft

6. 07/17/42  U-576 Aircraft/ Unicoi

7. 08/01/42  U-166 Aircraft

# Damaged but not Sunk  * Attacked but not Hit

# CITATIONS

*Title Page: The American Flag recovered on D-Day Returned to the US 75 years later.*

*https://taskandpurpose.com/news/normandy-beach-d-day-american-flag/*

## PROLOGUE

Guarding the United States and its Outposts. Stetson Conn, Rose, Englemann and Byron Fairchild. p.16-79

http://www.armed-guard.com/

http://www.usmm.org/faq.html

The Mathews Men: Seven Brothers and the War Against Hitler's U-Boats, William Geroux.    p.100

https://www.encyclopedia.com/.../military-affairs-nonnaval/civil-defense

https://www.coastguardmodeling.com/index.php/cg-history/world-war-ii/battle-of-the-north-atlantic/the-hooligan-navy/

The Hemingway Patrols, Terry Mort. p.17

Hemingway at War, Terry Mort, pages 97-103, 176-177

https://www.gocivilairpatrol.com/about/history-of-civil-air-patrol#

http://redcross.org

https://livinghistoryfarm.org/farminginthe40s/money_03.html

https://en.wikipedia.org/wiki/War_bond

https://www.nps.gov/articles/rationing-in-wwii.htm

Army Air Defense of the Western Hemisphere World War II, https://www.ibiblio.org/hyperwar/AAF/I/AAF-I-8.html


Western Union Telegram:  Wicki Commons

**Authors' interviews**

Bee Haydu, March 28, 2018

Rosie Anderson April 7 2015

James Rubin, Nov 11 2013


Washington DC:

American Treasures, Steven Puleo p. 180

**PART ONE WEST COAST**

**Hawaii**

Joe McDonald *https://*www.uh.edu*/engines/*mcdonald.*htm*
Lt Kermit Tyler *https://*pearlharbor.*org/*kermit-tyler-mistake
George Elliot   https://pearlharbor.org/the-opana-radar-station/

Presentation on the Pearl Harbor Attack, given December 7, 2011. Louella Large, past President of the Sons and Daughters of Pearl Harbor Survivors.

https://www.history.com/news/the-midget-subs-that-beat-the-planes-to-pearl-harbor

https://pearl-harbor.com/georgeelliott/

https://ibiblio.org/pha/myths/radar/mcdonald_2.html

https://historynewsnetwork.org/article/123754

## Author's interviews

Joe Lockard, May 12, 2011

Frank Schimmel June 27, 2020

The Nihau Incident: The True Story of the Japanese Fighter Pilot, who, after the Pearl Harbor attack, crash-landed on the Hawaiian Island of Niihau and Terrorized the Residents, Allen Beekman. P. 30-63

## Alaska

https://www.nps.gov/aleu/index.html,

interviews: Charlie House.

https://alaskahistoricalsociety.org/muktuk-marstons-five-point-plan/

Center of the Storm: The Bombing of Dutch Harbor and the Experience of Patrol Wing Four in the Aleutians, Summer 1942, Jeff Dickrell. p.31-65

Staff Sergeant Ed Walker and "Castner's Cutthroats" 1941-1943: Fighting WW2 in the Aleutian Islands, Alaska. Ed Walker  p. 28-101

Men of the Tundra, Maj. Muktuk Marston p 37-63, p 56-89

Attu Boy: A Young Alaskan's WWII Memoir, Nick Golodoff. p .13-29

Last Letters from Attu, Mary Breu. p.148-175

http://dev.hlswilliwaw.com/attu/attu_jones.htm

Attu Boy: A Young Alaskan's World War II, Nick Golodoff. (autobiography)

https://www.alaskannature.com/aleut.htm 08/25/21

Last Letters from Attu, Mary Breu.

Castner's Cutthroats : http://fortressdefense.com/attu

https://www.nps.gov/articles/000/battle-of-attu-60-years.htm

https://ww2-history.fandom.com/wiki/Banzai_Charge

Alaska-Siberia Connection: The World War II Air Route, Otis Hays, Jr.

Buidr Island: https://www.upi.com/Archives/1988

**California**

https://www.historynet.com/phantom-japanese-raid-on-los-angeles-during-world-war-ii/

Panic on the Pacific: How America Prepared for a West Coast Invasion, Bill Yenne. p.111.159

https://carriagemuseum.org/articles/the-japanese-bombardment-of-ellwood/

Letter from George Goman to Mr.Tompkins August 23rd, 1965, Santa Barbara Library/ Archives

Residents' accounts: https://www.santabarbaraca.gov/gov/depts/lib/collections/local_history_resources.asp


**Author's Interview:** Putty Mills, July 2020

Los Angeles Times Feb 25,1942, Evening Vanguard, 26 Feb 1942, quoted in The Battle of Los Angeles 1942: "The Mystery Air Raid" Terrenz Sword P.75-79

Moe Surofsky Collection

(AFC/2001/001/24754), Veterans History Project, Library of Congress

Daily Breeze, Redondo Beach, Dec. 8, 1991.

https://en.wikipedia.org/wiki/SS_Emidio#cite_note-21

SS Absaroka, January 26, 1942, issue of LIFE magazine,


SS John A Johnson

http://www.eyewitnesstohistory.com/sunk.htm

At night on 19 February 1942, I-17 covertly landed on Point Loma, San Diego  San Diego's Navy, Bruce Linder. p. 120

**Washington**

https://dev.historylink.org/File/7166

**Oregon**

Fujita Flying Samurai: His Aerial Bombing of the Continental United States in World War II – Documentary Bert and Margie Webber

The Fujita Plan: Japanese Attacks on the United States & Australia During the Second World War, Mark Felton

Silent Siege –I and II: Japanese Attacks on North America in World War II, Bert Webber

Bombs Over Brookings: The World II Bombings of Curry County, Oregon and the Postwar Friendship Between Brookings and the Japanese Pilot, Nobuo Fujita and William McCash

Friends of Old Ft. Stevens:  visitftstevens.com


**BALLOON BOMBS**

Walter Morris, 2nd Lt., 555th Parachute Battalion
http://triplenickle.com/history.htm

FuGo: The Curious History of Japan's Balloon Bomb Attack on America, Ross Coen. List of Locations p.216-245

Japan's WWII Balloon Bomb Attacks on North America, Robert C. Mikesh. List of Locations p. 61-89 technical data and illustrations p.40-69.

Plan for Defense of Bacteriologic Warfare in connection with Japanese Balloon Bombs. 20 July 1945, Box 10 RG 160. NARA II.

## Oregon

https://www.usni.org/magazines/proceedings/1961/june/i-bombed-usa

Silent Siege – III: Japanese Attacks on North America in World War II – Ships Sunk Air Raid Bombs Dropped Civilians Killed Bert Webber

https://www.smithsonianmag.com/history/1945-japanese-balloon-bomb-killed-six-americansfive-them-children-oregon-180972259/

## California

Japanese Balloon Bombs exploded at Hayfork, California 2-1-45. FBI report 65-3734, 2 March 1945, Box 41, RG 499, NARA II.

https://www.warhistoryonline.com/world-war-ii/operation-cherry-blossoms-night.html?firefox=1

https://lostcoastoutpost.com/2015/mar/11/70-years-later-remembering-japanese-attack-hayfork/

## Wyoming

University of Wyoming Archives

## Kansas

Silent Siege III, Bert Webber p.275

**Utah**

Silent Siege III, Bert Webber p.204

**Nebraska**

https://www.omahamagazine.com/2014/09/15/303748/bombs-bursting-in-air

**Michigan**

https://www.freep.com/in-depth/news/local/michigan/2019/11/14/japanese-bombed-michigan-world-war-ii-balloons/4111349002/

**Texas**

https://www.texasalmanac.com/articles/the-bombing-of-texas

**PART TWO EAST COAST**

www.u-boat.net

https://german-navy.de/kriegsmarine/ships/uboats/index.html

**Maine**

https://www.smithsonianchannel.com/shows/hunt-for-eagle-56

**New Hampshire**

https://www.newenglandhistoricalsociety.com/the-sensational-surrender-of-four-nazi-u-boats-at-the-portsmouth-naval-shipyard

Germany's Last Mission: The Failed Voyage of U-234 to Japan, Joesph Mark Scalia. p.177 -197

## Massachusetts

http://www.bostonharborbeacon.com/2012/07/28/u-boats-made-it-a-tough-summer-for-boating-in-1942/

German Mines

https://www.patriotledger.com/story/news/2008/06/12/66-years-ago-today-world/40150770007/

## Rhode Island

https://www.newenglandhistoricalsociety.com/flashback-photo-battle-point-judith/

https://www.smallstaebighistory.com

## New York

Operation Drumbeat: The Dramatic True Story of Germany's First U-Boat Attacks Along the American Coast in World War II, Michael Gannon. 214-241

New York City Panic: https://www.nydailynews.com/new-york/panic-pearl-harbor-nyc-cusp-wwii-article-1.789858

## New Jersey

https://en.wikipedia.org/wiki/R.P._Resor_(ship)

Photo: https://www.aukevisser.nl/inter/id157.htm

## Delaware

World War II and the Delaware Coast, Michael Morgan.p.122-175

Delaware's Ghost Towers: The Coast Artillery's Last Stand During the Darkest Days of World War II, Willaim C. Grayson. p. 2-25

**Maryland**

https://outlookbythebay.com/2014/06/25/when-the-war-came-to-the-bay/

**Virginia**

The Burning Shore: How Hitler's U-Boats Brought World War II to America, Ed Offley p. 184-193

The Approaching Storm: U-Boats off the Virginia Coast During WWII, Alpheus J. Chewning, p. 71,131

Miracle Baby:

https://coastalreview.org/2021/03/mother-gives-birth-during-u-boat-attack/

Daily Press, Virginia Tidewater Area

**North Carolina**

Operation Drumbeat, Michael Gannon, p-64-101, 149-191

Torpedo Junction, Homer H. Hickam Jr. p. 7-157

The Burning Shore: How Hitler's U-Boats Brought World War II to America, Ed Offley. It covers the U-boat attacks as well as the post war friendship between Kane and Degan and their effort to establish the historical record.

*Operation Drumbeat*: The Dramatic True Story of Germany's First U-Boat Attacks along the American Coast in World War II Michael Gannon, *varies*

Torpedo Junction: U-Boat War Off America's East Coast, 1942 Homer H. Hickam, Jr

A Sentimental Journey: Memoirs of a Wartime Boomtown. Wilbur D Jones, Jr. p.51-54

War Zone, World War II off the North Carolina Coast, Kevin P. Duffus. P 131-133

Interviews: Ocracoke Island Historical Society

Jim Gaskill:

https://www.carolinacountry.com/departments/departments/feature-story/torpedoed

**Author's interviews:**

Carol Dillion, Feb 2018

Carroll and Jim Gray, August 2016

IMAGES wickicommons.com

**South Carolina**

SS Bloody Marsh

https://oceanexplorer.noaa.gov/okeanos/explorations

**Georgia**

Vanzo, John. "U-boat Attacks during World War II." New Georgia Encyclopedia, last modified May 9, 2019. https://www.georgiaencyclopedia.org/articles/history-archaeology/u-boat-attacks-during-world-war-ii/

**Florida**

Interview, Martin G. Williams. Florida Beaches Museum. Jacksonville FL

IMAGES wickicommons.com

U-boat.net

Blimp sinking: The Battle of the Atlantic 1942–45. Mark Lardas. P.47

## Alabama

www.orangebeachal.gov/facilities/indian-sea-museum/about.


## Louisiana


So Close to Home: A True Story of an American Family's Fight for Survival During World War II Michael J. Tougias and Alison O'Leary. P. 58-138

https://www.victoriaadvocate.com/news/education/the-night-world-war-ii-came-to-the-texas-coast

## Texas

https://en.wikipedia.org/wiki/Oaxaca_(ship)

## APPENDIX

### Canada:

The Battle of the St. Lawrence: The Second World War in Canada Nathan M. Greenfield

Enemy Offshore! Japan's Secret War on North America's West Coast, Brendan Coyle and Melanie Arnis

### Caribbean

Imprisoned in the Caribbean, Ligia T. Domenech, Phd. p.165-167, Shipping Losses

Night of the Long Tankers: Hitler's War Against Caribbean Oil, David Bercuson and Holger H. Herwig

### South America

https://nationalinterest.org/blog/reboot/how-hitler%E2%80%99s-atlantic-assault-brought-south-american-world-war-ii-184747

## How Close Was An Axis Victory?

U-boat Rockets: https://en.wikipedia.org/wiki/Rocket_U-boat

Japan's Secret War: Japan's Race Against Time to Build its Own Atomic Bomb Robert K. Wilcox.p.15-18

https://www.historyonthenet.com/japan-developed-atomic-bomb-ww2-laid-groundwork-north-koreas-nuclear-program

The History Channel Producer: Cafe Productions, 2010.

https://en.wikipedia.org/wiki/Japanese_nuclear_weapons_program

Atlanta Constitution, David Snell, October 2, 1946

Nazi Science: Myth, Truth, and the German Atomic Bomb Mark Walker. p. 5-41, 181,194,199.

*The Statistics of KIAs and Civilians Killed in World War II: https://en.wikipedia.org/wiki/World_War_II_casualties*

# FURTHER RECOMMENDED REFERENCES

## HAWAII -PEARL HARBOR

Dec. 7 1941: The Day the Japanese Attacked Pearl Harbor Gordon W. Prange with Donald M. Goldstein and Katherine V. Dillon

Day of Infamy, Walter Lord

At Dawn We Slept: The Untold Story of Pearl Harbor, Gordon W. Prange

Secret Missions: The Story of an Intelligence Officer, Ellis M. Zacharias

## ALASKA

The Capture of Attu: A World War II Battle as Told by the Men Who Fought There Lt. Robert J. Mitchell with Sewell T. Tying and Capt. Nelson L. Drummond Jr.

The Forgotten War: A Pictorial History of World War II in Alaska and Northwestern Canada Stan Cohen

Bering Sea Escort: Life Aboard a Coast Guard Cutter in World War II Robert Erwin Johnson

U-Boats against Canada: German Submarines in Canadian Waters Michael L. Hadley

War on Our Doorstep: The Unknown Campaign on North America's West Coast Brendan Coyle

Enemy Offshore! Japan's Secret War on North America's West Coast, Brendan Coyle and Melanie Arnis

The Storm on Our Shores: One Island, Two Soldiers, and the Forgotten Battle of World War II. Mark Obmascik

The Aleutians 1942-43: Struggle for the North Pacific Brian Lane Herder

The Aleutians Campaign: June 1942-August 1943 Naval Historical Center Department of the Navy

War Comes to Alaska: The Dutch Harbor Attack. June 3-4, 1942 Norman Edward Rourke

The Capture of Attu: As told by the Men who Fought There, Robert Mitchell Sewell Tyng Nelson Drummond

The Thousand-Mile War: World War II in Alaska and the Aleutians, Brian Garfield

Ghosts in the Fog: The Untold Story of Alaska's WWII Invasion, Samantha Seiple


## WEST COAST

The American Magic: As gripping as any fiction-the true story of American code breakers and the defeat of Japan in WWII, Ronald Lewin

Aleutian Headache: Deadly World War II Battles on American Soil, Bert Webber

Silent Siege –I and II: Japanese Attacks on North America in World War II Bert Webber

Silent Siege – III: Japanese Attacks on North America in World War II – Ships Sunk Air Rais Bombs Dropped Civilians Killed Bert Webber

Operation Storm: Japan's Top Secret Submarines and Its Plan to Change the Course of World War II, John J. Geoghegan

Japan at War: An Oral History, Haruko Taya Cook and Theodore F. Cook

Retaliation: Japanese Attacks and Allied Countermeasures on the Pacific Coast in World War II, Bert Webber

https://ojs.library.ubc.ca/index.php/bcstudies/article/download/191006/188950/   Balloon Bombs in British Columbia


## EAST COAST

Washington Goes to War: The Extraordinary Story of the Transformation of a City and Nation, David Brinkley

Rosie the Riveter: Women Working on the Home Front in World War II, Penny Colman

Torpedoes in the Gulf: Galveston and the U-Boats, 1942-1943 Melanie Wiggans

I Was There: To Face the Night of the U-Boats: When Hitler's Submarines Ruled in World War II, Paul Lund and Harry Ludlam

Target America: Hitler's Plan to Attack the United States James P. Duffy

Sailing on Friday: The Perilous Voyage of America's Merchant Marine, John A Butler

Steel Boat Iron Hearts: A U-boat Crewman's Life Aboard U-505, Hans Goebeler and John Vanzo

The Atlantic Campaign, Dan Van Der Vat

Letters Home 1944-1945: Women Airforce Service Pilots, Bernice "Bee" Falk Haydu

Americans Remember the Home Front: An Oral Narrative of the World War II Years in American, Roy Hoopes

A Measureless Peril: America in the Fight for the Atlantic, the Longest Battle of World War II, Richard Snow

Black May: The Epic Story of the Allies Defeat of the German U-Boats in May 1943, Michael Gannon

Bloodstained Sea: The U.S. Coast Guard in the Battle of the Atlantic, 1941-1944 Michael G. Walling

Unsung Sailors: The Naval Armed Guard in World War II, Justin F. Gleichauf

U-Boats Offshore: The Never-Before-Told Story of Hitler's Strike Against America, Edwin P. Hoyt

The Battle of the Atlantic: Hitler's Gray Wolves of the Sea and the Allies' Desperate Struggle to Defeat Them, Andrew Williams

Merchant Mariners at War: An Oral History of World War II, George J. Billy and Christine M. Billy

The Air-Raid Warden Was a Spy: And other Tales from Home-Front America in World War II, William B. Breuer

Secret War at Home: The Pine Grove Furnace Prisoner of War Interrogation Camp, John Paul Bland

Top Secret Tales of World War II, William B. Breuer

U-Boats Offshore: When Hitler Struck America, Edwin P. Hoyt

The Fuhrer's U-Boats in American Waters, Gary Gentile

Lost in the Victory: Reflections of American War Orphans of World War II, Susan Johnson Hadler and Ann Bennett Mix

Germany's Last Mission to Japan: The Failed Voyage of U-234, Joseph Mark Scalia

No Surrender: True Stores of the U.S. Navy Armed Guard in World War II, Gerald Reminick

Germany Hitler & World War II, Gerhard L. Weinberg

Long Night of the Tankers: Hitler's War Against Caribbean Oil, David J. Bercuson and Holger H. Herwig

*All That Jesus Commanded*

# Books by John Piper

*Battling Unbelief*

*Bloodlines*

*Brothers, We Are Not Professionals*

*Come, Lord Jesus*

*The Dangerous Duty of Delight*

*Desiring God*

*Don't Waste Your Life*

*Expository Exultation*

*Fifty Reasons Why Jesus Came to Die*

*Finally Alive*

*Five Points*

*Future Grace*

*God Is the Gospel*

*God's Passion for His Glory*

*A Godward Life*

*A Hunger for God*

*Let the Nations Be Glad!*

*A Peculiar Glory*

*The Pleasures of God*

*Providence*

*Reading the Bible Supernaturally*

*The Satisfied Soul*

*Seeing and Savoring Jesus Christ*

*Sex, Race, and the Sovereignty of God*

*Spectacular Sins*

*Taste and See*

*Think*

*This Momentary Marriage*

*What Is Saving Faith?*

*When I Don't Desire God*

*Why I Love the Apostle Paul*

# All That Jesus Commanded

*The Christian Life according to the Gospels*

John Piper

WHEATON, ILLINOIS

ISBN-13: 978-1-4335-8505-0

ePub ISBN: 978-1-4335-8508-1

PDF ISBN: 978-1-4335-8506-7

**Library of Congress Cataloging-in-Publication Data**

Names: Piper, John, 1946- author.
Title: All that Jesus commanded : the Christian life according to the Gospels / John Piper.
Other titles: What Jesus demands from the world
Description: Wheaton, Illinois : Crossway, 2023. | Formerly published: What Jesus Demands from the World. Wheaton, Ill. : Crossway Books, 2006. | Includes bibliographical references and index.
Identifiers: LCCN 2022048211 (print) | LCCN 2022048212 (ebook) | ISBN 9781433585050 | ISBN 9781433585081 (epub) | ISBN 9781433585067 (pdf)
Subjects: LCSH: Jesus Christ—Teachings. | Bible. Gospels—Criticism, interpretation, etc.
Classification: LCC BS2415 .P49 2023 (print) | LCC BS2415 (ebook) | DDC 232.9/54—dc23/eng/20230110
LC record available at https://lccn.loc.gov/2022048211
LC ebook record available at https://lccn.loc.gov/2022048212

Crossway is a publishing ministry of Good News Publishers.

| RRD | | | 32 | 31 | 30 | 29 | 28 | 27 | 26 | 25 | 24 | 23 |
|-----|-----|-----|-----|-----|-----|-----|-----|-----|-----|-----|-----|-----|
| 13 | 12 | 11 | 10 | 9 | 8 | 7 | 6 | 5 | 4 | 3 | 2 | 1 |

# Contents

*All authority in heaven and on earth*
*has been given to me.*

JESUS

# Acknowledgments

THIS BOOK WAS POSSIBLE because generosity has flowed to me from more streams than I can mention here, indeed more streams than I know. But I gladly mention several. When I was a pastor of Bethlehem Baptist Church, the elders and congregation gave me a five-month leave from preaching in 2006. This was part of their kindness on the twenty-fifth anniversary of our ministry together at the church. Without this extended time away, this book would not have been written.

The happy combination of solitude and fellowship at Tyndale House in Cambridge, England, with its abundant resources, provided the ideal setting for this kind of research and writing. Bruce Winter, whose long and faithful tenure as Warden was coming to an end while I was there, was gracious and stimulating in his welcome and friendship. The staff and readers of Tyndale House made our stay a glad and fruitful season. God knows the anonymous hands that opened to make this stay possible.

David Mathis, Justin Taylor, and Ted Griffin read the manuscript for the first edition with care and helped me make hundreds of improvements. Lane Dennis and his team at Crossway encouraged and supported this project from conception to reality. That is just as true of the Crossway team today, under the leadership of Josh Dennis, as it was then. David Mathis is still lending his careful eye to the editing, joined this time by Scott Hubbard. My wife, Noël, set up house in a new place, set me free to write, and read every word with the eyes that only a gifted wife can bring. Everything I do hangs on her support.

When someone asks, "How long did it take you to write this book?" I often answer, "Sixty years." I know it's not a satisfactory answer. But it does tell the truth that the streams of generosity that have come together to create this book have been flowing into my life from the start. I do not doubt that experiences I had from Summit Drive Grade School in Greenville, South Carolina, in the 1950s to the University of Munich in the early 1970s and the ministry of the Word for twenty-five years at Bethlehem shaped what is in this book. There is no separating life and the labor of writing.

For all the countless streams of generosity—known and unknown—that have flowed into my life, I thank Jesus, who created me and called me and governs all my days, as he does the governments of the world and the galaxies of the universe. I pray that he will use this book to make himself known and treasured and obeyed as the only Savior from our sin and the only Sovereign over the world.

# Suggestions for How
# to Read This Book

LONG BOOKS SEEM DAUNTING because we think we should start at the front and read to the back and not skip anything. I don't expect most people to read this book that way. I hope some will. I did structure the book so that matters at the front may help the reader understand matters further on. And there is a kind of foundation, progression, and climax. But the chapters have enough independence that most of them can be read without the others. It will be obvious when one chapter depends on another.

Therefore, I invite you to step in anywhere. You don't have to read the Introduction first. I hope that the way Jesus's commands are interwoven will draw you further in, from one issue to another.

I have tried to keep the chapters relatively short so that in general they can be read at one sitting for those who only have limited time from day to day. This is why some of the chapters deal with the same command from different angles. I thought it better to handle the matter in several chapters rather than in one long one.

Since the focus is on the commands of Jesus in this book, much about his life and death is not here. If you want to see how I have tried to portray these more fully, you can look at two other (shorter!) books where I deal with Jesus and his death: *Seeing and Savoring Jesus Christ*

(Crossway, 2004) and *Fifty Reasons Why Jesus Came to Die* (Crossway, 2006). And, of course, there are important books by others that I will be referring to along the way.

Most of all I hope you will pray as you read. Even if you are not accustomed to praying, ask God to protect you from any mistakes I may have made and to confirm to you what is true. In the end, what matters is the effect that God produces in our lives through his written word by his Spirit. That's what makes prayer so crucial. In prayer we ask God to transform us in that way.

Finally, may the living Jesus fulfill the purpose of his word as you read: "These things I have spoken to you, that my joy may be in you, and that your joy may be full" (John 15:11).

# The Aim of the Book

THIS BOOK WAS ORIGINALLY PUBLISHED in 2006 under the title *What Jesus Demands from the World*. This new edition with a new title is substantially the same with minor revisions and rearrangements. The new title, *All That Jesus Commanded: The Christian Life according to the Gospels*, is intended to make more clear the relevance of this book for every Christian. It deals with every command Jesus gave and how it relates to Christian living today. It draws out the meaning of these commands from the four Gospels themselves not the rest of the New Testament.

The aim of this book is God-glorifying obedience to Jesus. To that end I am seeking to obey Jesus's last command: "Make disciples of all nations . . . *teaching them to observe all that I have commanded you*" (Matt. 28:19–20). Jesus's final command was to teach all nations to keep his commandments.

## The Impossible Final Command

Actually, the final command was more precise than that. He did *not* say, "Teach them all my commandments." He said, "Teach them *to observe* all my commandments." You can teach a parrot all of Jesus's commandments. But you cannot teach a parrot to *observe* them. Parrots will not repent, and worship Jesus, and lay up treasures in heaven, and love their enemies, and go out like sheep in the midst of wolves to herald the kingdom of God.

Teaching people to parrot all that Jesus commanded is easy. Teaching them to *observe* all that Jesus commanded is *impossible*. Jesus used that word. When a rich man could not bring himself to let go of his riches and follow him, Jesus said, "It is easier for a camel to go through the eye of a needle than for a rich person to enter the kingdom of God. . . . With man it is *impossible*, but not with God. For all things are possible with God" (Mark 10:25–27).

Therefore, the person who sets himself to obey Jesus's final commission—for example, to teach a rich man to *observe* the command to "renounce all that he has" (Luke 14:33)—attempts the impossible. But Jesus said it was *not* impossible. "All things are possible with God." So the greatest challenge in writing this book has been to discern God's way of making impossible obedience possible.

Jesus said that this impossible goal happens through *teaching*. "Make disciples . . . *teaching* them to observe all that I have commanded you." There is, of course, more to it than that—like the atoning death of Jesus (Mark 10:45) and the work of the Holy Spirit (John 14:26) and prayer (Matt. 6:13). But in the end Jesus focused on teaching. I take this to mean that God has chosen to do the impossible through the teaching of all that Jesus commanded. That's what I pray this book will prove to be—a kind of teaching that God will use to bring about impossible obedience to Jesus. And all of that for the glory of God.

### Teaching and Obedience That Glorify God

The reason I emphasize the glory of God is because Jesus did. He said, "Let your light shine before others, so that they may see your good works and *give glory to your Father who is in heaven*" (Matt. 5:16). The ultimate goal of Jesus's commandments is not that we observe them by doing good works. The *ultimate* goal is that God be glorified. The obedience of good works is penultimate. But what is ultimate is that in our obedient lives God be displayed as the most beautiful reality in the world. That is Jesus's ultimate goal[1] and mine.

This helps me answer the question: What kind of teaching of Jesus's commandments might God be willing to use to bring about such impossible obedience? If the aim of obedience is ultimately the glory of God, then it is probable that the teaching God will use is the kind that keeps his glory at the center. Therefore, my aim has been to keep the supremely valuable beauty of God in proper focus throughout the book.

### Keeping the Commandments Connected to Jesus and His Work

How then do we keep the beauty of God in proper focus in relation to Jesus's commandments? By treating the meaning and motivation of the commands in connection with the person and work of Jesus. The person and work of Jesus are the primary means by which God has glorified himself in the world. No revelation of God's glory is greater. Jesus said, "Whoever has seen me has seen the Father" (John 14:9). Therefore, his *person* is the manifestation of the glory of God. To see him as he really is means seeing the infinitely valuable beauty of God. Jesus also said, as he was praying, "I glorified you on earth, having accomplished the work that you gave me to do" (John 17:4). Therefore, his *work* is a manifestation of the glory of God. When we see what he achieved and how he did it, we see the majesty and greatness of God.

Therefore, my aim has been *to probe the meaning and the motivation of Jesus's commands in connection with his person and work.* What emerges again and again is that what he is commanding is a life that displays the worth of his person and the effect of his work. His intention is that we not disconnect what he commands from who he is and what he has done.

---

1    See especially *Command #47.*

We should not be surprised, then, that Jesus's final, climactic command is that we teach all nations to observe all that he commanded. This leads to his ultimate purpose. When obedience to his commands happens, what the world sees is the fruit of Jesus's glorious work and the worth of his glorious person. In other words, they see the glory of God. This is why Jesus came and why his mission remains until he comes.

### A Sketch of the Person and Work of Jesus

Anticipating what we will see later in the book, the briefest sketch of Jesus's person and work should be given here, so that from the start the commands rest on their proper foundation. Jesus came into the world, sent by God, as the long-awaited Jewish Messiah. When Jesus asked his disciples who they thought he was, Peter answered, "You are the Christ [that is, Messiah], the Son of the living God." To this Jesus responded, "Blessed are you, Simon Bar-Jonah! For flesh and blood has not revealed this to you, but my Father who is in heaven" (Matt. 16:16–17).

When Jesus was on trial for his life, the charge was blasphemy, and eventually treason against Caesar, because of his apparent claims to be the Messiah, the King of Israel, the Son of God. The Jewish high priest asked him, "Are you the Christ, the Son of the Blessed?" And Jesus said, "I am, and you will see the Son of Man seated at the right hand of Power, and coming with the clouds of heaven" (Mark 14:61–62).

### Why Jesus Favored the Title "Son of Man"

Even though Jesus acknowledged that he was the Messiah, the Son of God, his favorite designation for himself was "Son of Man." At one level this title carries the obvious meaning that Jesus was truly human. But because of its use by the prophet Daniel, it probably is a very exalted claim of universal authority.

Behold, with the clouds of heaven there came one like a son of man, and he came to the Ancient of Days and was presented before him. And to him was given dominion and glory and a kingdom, that all peoples, nations, and languages should serve him; his dominion is an everlasting dominion, which shall not pass away, and his kingdom one that shall not be destroyed. (Dan. 7:13–14)

The reason Jesus favored the title "Son of Man" for himself was that the terms *Messiah* and *Son of God* were loaded with popular political pretensions. They would give the wrong impression about the nature of his messiahship. They could easily imply that he fit in with the conceptions of the day that the Messiah would conquer Rome and liberate Israel and set up his earthly kingdom. But Jesus had to navigate these political waters by presenting himself as truly the Messiah, even the divine Son of God with universal authority, but also reject the popular notion that the Messiah would not suffer but immediately rule.

The term *Son of Man* proved most useful in this regard because though it did carry exalted claims for those who had ears to hear, on the face of it he was not making explicit claims to political power. Under this favorite title (while not rejecting the others), Jesus was able to make his claims that the long-awaited messianic kingdom of God had come in his ministry.[2]

## The Kingdom of God Had Come into History

The Jewish people longed for the day when the Messiah would come and bring the kingdom of God. The kingdom would mean that the enemies of Israel are defeated, sins are wiped away, diseases are healed, the dead are raised, and righteousness, joy, and peace hold sway on the earth with the Messiah on the throne. Jesus arrived and said, "The time is fulfilled, and the kingdom of God is at hand;

---

2    For a helpful overview of the titles of Jesus in the Gospels in the space of eight pages see Craig L. Blomberg, *Jesus and the Gospels*, 2nd ed. (Nashville: Broadman & Holman, 2009), 470–478.

repent and believe in the gospel" (Mark 1:15). What he meant was that in his own ministry the liberating, saving reign of God had arrived. "If it is by the finger of God that I cast out demons, then *the kingdom of God has come upon you. . . .* The kingdom of God is *in the midst of you*" (Luke 11:20; 17:21).

But there was a mystery. Jesus called it "the secret of the kingdom of God" (Mark 4:11). The mystery was that the kingdom of God had come in history *before* its final, triumphant manifestation. Fulfillment was here, but consummation was not here.[3] The kingdom would arrive in two stages. In the first stage the Messiah would come and suffer, and in the second stage the Messiah would come in glory (Luke 24:46; Mark 14:62).

### He Came to Serve and Die for Sins and Rise Again

Therefore, the primary work of Jesus on the earth during his first coming was to suffer and die for the forgiveness of sins. He said, "Even the Son of Man came not to be served but to serve, and to give his life as a ransom for many" (Mark 10:45). And at the Last Supper with his disciples, he took the cup and said, "This is my blood of the covenant, which is poured out for many for the forgiveness of sins" (Matt. 26:28).

Dying was not his only mission. But it was central. In shedding his blood he purchased the new-covenant promises. The new covenant was God's promise that all who enter the coming kingdom will have their sins forgiven, will have the law written on their hearts, and will know God personally (Jer. 31:31–34). The blessings of this covenant are crucial in enabling us to obey Jesus's commandments. Which makes Jesus's death of supreme importance in bringing about the impossible obedience that he commands.

But there was more to his mission. When John the Baptist was perplexed about whether Jesus was really the Messiah, he sent word to

---

3    For an excellent book-length treatment of the kingdom of God in the ministry of Jesus see George Ladd, *The Presence of the Future* (Grand Rapids, Mich.: Eerdmans, 1974).

him from prison: "Are you the one who is to come, or shall we look for another?" Jesus answered, "Go and tell John what you hear and see: the blind receive their sight and the lame walk, lepers are cleansed and the deaf hear, and the dead are raised up, and the poor have good news preached to them. And blessed is the one who is not offended by me" (Matt. 11:3–6). In other words, "All my healing and preaching are a demonstration of my messiahship, but don't take offense that I am not fulfilling the political expectation of earthly rule. I *am* the one who is to come, but my central mission (in this first coming) is suffering—to give my life as a ransom for many."

When his mission was accomplished, after three days in the grave, Jesus rose from the dead. This was God's plan. It was an act of supreme authority over death. "No one takes [my life] from me, but I lay it down of my own accord. I have authority to lay it down, and I have authority to take it up again. This charge I have received from my Father" (John 10:18). When he was raised, he appeared to his disciples on many occasions and gave them proof that he was physically alive (Luke 24:39–43). He opened the Scriptures to them so they could see more fully how he fulfilled God's promises (Luke 24:32, 45). Then he commissioned them to be his witnesses, instructed them to wait for the promised Holy Spirit, and ascended into heaven (Luke 24:46–51).

### Obedience Is the Fruit of His Work and the Display of His Glory

On the basis of who he was and what he accomplished, Jesus gave his commands. The commands cannot be separated from his person and work. The obedience he commands is the fruit of his *redeeming work* and the display of his *personal glory.* That is why he came—to create a people who glorify his gracious reign by bearing the fruit of his kingdom (Matt. 21:43).

When he said, "The Son of Man came to seek and to save the lost" (Luke 19:10), he was speaking about Zacchaeus who had just been so transformed that he gave half his possessions to the poor (Luke 19:8). In other words, the Son of Man came to save people from their suicidal love affair with possessions and to lead them into a kind of impossible obedience that displays the infinite worth of Jesus. Therefore, my effort in this book has been to hold together the meaning and motivation of Jesus's commands, the greatness of his work, and the glory of his person.

## A Word about Method

I will give more detail about my method in the Appendix, "A Word to Biblical Scholars" (which I invite everyone to read!), but it seems good to include at this point some crucial guiding choices that I have made. My method is to reflect on the meaning and motivation of Jesus's demands *as they appear in the New Testament Gospels* in the context of his person and work. I do not cite the rest of the New Testament for my understanding of Jesus in the Gospels. Citing the whole New Testament is a perfectly legitimate thing to do, and in my preaching I do not hesitate to bring Scriptures from anywhere to help make any text plain, provided I don't change the meaning of either text. But in this book I have given my rendering of Jesus almost entirely through the lens of his own words as recorded in the Gospels. One of my subordinate aims in this approach is to encourage confidence in the unity of the New Testament, because the upshot of this portrayal is so compatible with what the other New Testament writers taught.

## A Word about "Commanding"

Jesus's last word to his disciples in Matthew 28:20 was that they should teach the nations "to observe all that I have *commanded* you." "Command" is a tough word. We should be sobered and humbled by it. But Jesus is not only tough. He is also tender.

These two ways of relating to us come together in what Jesus says on either side of his final command to make disciples. On one side he says, "All authority in heaven and on earth has been given to me" (Matt. 28:18). And on the other side he says, "Behold, I am with you always, to the end of the age" (Matt. 28:20). The one says, "I give commands because I have the right. All authority in the universe is mine." The other says, "I give commands because I will help you. I will be with you forever."

I have tried to structure the chapters of the book to draw the reader from shorter chapters and gentler commands toward the more difficult, but no less precious, commands of Jesus.[4] This is not merely stylistic or tactical. It is theologically fitting. Most of the first nineteen chapters do not command any external action. They are essentially about what happens in the mind and heart. These come first because the kind of obedience Jesus commands moves from the inside (where the value of Jesus is savored) to the outside (where the value of Jesus is shown).

Of these chapters, the first seven are "You Must Be Born Again," "Repent," "Come to Me," "Believe in Me," "Love Me," "Listen to Me," and "Abide in Me." When these commands are seen for what they really are, they turn the absolute authority of Jesus into a treasure chest of holy joy. When the most glorious person in the universe pays all my debts (Matt. 20:28), and then commands that I come to live with him and enter into his joy (Matt. 25:21), there can be no more desirable command imaginable. To such a one I say, with Augustine, "Command what you wish, but give what you command."[5]

## Dare Jesus Claim to Command the Whole World?

Jesus's final instruction to his disciples not only tells them to teach all he "commanded," but that they should do this to all the nations—to the whole world. "Go therefore and make disciples of all nations . . . teaching them to observe all that I have commanded you" (Matt. 28:19–20).

---

4 For how I chose which commands to include in the book see page 417.

5 Augustine, *Confessions*, trans. R. S. Pine-Coffin (New York: Penguin Books, 1961), 40 (X, xxix).

Two objections arise. One is: *Did* he give his commands to the whole world? The other is: *Dare* he give commands to the whole world?

One may ask: Did Jesus give all these commands to the world, or did he give them to his disciples? Is this an ethic for the world or for the followers of Jesus? The answer is: The commands he gave only to his disciples are also meant for the world because he demands all people everywhere to become his disciples. That is the point of his final command: "Go therefore and make disciples of *all nations*, baptizing them in the name of the Father and of the Son and of the Holy Spirit, teaching them to observe all that I have commanded you" (Matt. 28:19–20). Jesus dares to lay claim to "all nations"—all ethnic groups on the planet.[6] No exceptions. Jesus is not a tribal deity. All authority in the universe is his, and all creation owes its allegiance to him.

### Advancing with All Authority but No Sword

He does not send his people to make disciples with a sword. His kingdom does not come by force, but by truth and love and sacrifice and the power of God. "My kingdom is not of this world. If my kingdom were of this world, my servants would have been fighting" (John 18:36). Jesus's followers do not kill to extend his kingdom. They die. "If anyone would come after me, let him deny himself and take up his cross and follow me" (Mark 8:34). "Some of you they will put to death" (Luke 21:16). Not only will they put the followers of Jesus to death, but they will do it in the name of their religion. "The hour is coming," Jesus says, "when whoever kills you will think he is offering service to God" (John 16:2).

Jesus has all authority in heaven and on earth, but for now he restrains his power. He does not always use it to prevent his people's pain, even though he could and sometimes does. He is with us to the end of the age but not always to rescue us from harm. He calls us to walk the same

---

6 In the final two chapters of this book, I draw out the implications of this verse for the world and explain the meaning of "all nations" more fully.

road he walked. "If they persecuted me, they will also persecute you" (John 15:20). "If they have called the master of the house Beelzebul, how much more will they malign those of his household" (Matt. 10:25).

The universal authority of Jesus produces a mission of *teaching*, not a mission of terror. His aim is God-glorifying obedience to all that he commanded. The kind of obedience that glorifies God is free and joyful, not constrained and cowering. Even when the cost is supreme, the joy is triumphant because the cause of Jesus cannot fail. "Blessed are you when others revile you and persecute you and utter all kinds of evil against you falsely on my account. Rejoice and be glad, for your reward is great in heaven" (Matt. 5:11–12). It is a costly mission, but a joyful one.

My prayer for this book is that it will serve that global mission—to "make disciples of all nations . . . *teaching them to observe all that I have commanded you.*" I pray I am a faithful echo of Jesus when he said, "He who sent me is true, and I declare *to the world* what I have heard from him" (John 8:26).

*Jesus answered . . . "Do not marvel that I said*
*to you, 'You must be born again.'"*

JOHN 3:5, 7


*Jesus answered him, "Truly, truly, I say to you, unless one*
*is born again, he cannot see the kingdom of God."*

JOHN 3:3

# You Must Be Born Again

IN THE THIRD CHAPTER OF JOHN'S GOSPEL, Jesus is speaking to "a man of the Pharisees named Nicodemus, a ruler of the Jews" (John 3:1). Pharisees were the experts in the Jewish Scriptures. This is why Jesus was astonished that Nicodemus was baffled about what Jesus meant by "You must be born again." Nicodemus asks, "How can a man be born when he is old? Can he enter a second time into his mother's womb and be born?" (John 3:4). Jesus responds, "Are you the teacher of Israel and yet you do not understand these things?" (John 3:10).

### A New Spirit I Will Put within You

In other words, an expert in the Jewish Scriptures should not be baffled by Jesus's command, "You must be born again." Why not? Because there are so many clues in the Jewish Scriptures that Jesus and Nicodemus had in common. God had promised a day when he would cause his people to be born again. One of God's clearest promises is in the book of Ezekiel. Jesus echoed Ezekiel's words when he said, "Unless one is born of water and the Spirit, he cannot enter the kingdom of God" (John 3:5). Being "born again" is described as a birth from water and Spirit. Those two terms, "water" and "Spirit," are linked in Ezekiel 36:25–27. God says:

> I will sprinkle clean water on you, and you shall be clean from all
> your uncleannesses, and from all your idols I will cleanse you. And
> I will give you a new heart, and a new spirit I will put within you.
> And I will remove the heart of stone from your flesh and give you a
> heart of flesh. And I will put my Spirit within you, and cause you to
> walk in my statutes and be careful to obey my rules.

God promises cleansing from sin and the gift of a new human spirit by the presence of his own divine Spirit. Jesus thinks Nicodemus should make the connection between his command to be born again and Ezekiel's promise of a new spirit and the gift of God's Spirit. But he doesn't. So Jesus explains further by describing the role of God's Spirit in bringing about this new spirit: "That which is born of the flesh is flesh, and that which is born of the Spirit is spirit" (John 3:6).

### The Dead Cannot See

Flesh is what we are by nature. It refers to ordinary humanity. By our first birth we are only flesh. This natural human condition, as we experience it, is spiritually lifeless. We are not born spiritually alive with a heart that loves God. We are born spiritually dead.

That's what Jesus implied when he said to a would-be disciple who wanted to go home to a funeral, "Leave the *dead* to bury their own dead" (Luke 9:60). In other words, some are physically dead and need burying. Some are spiritually dead and can bury them. He implied it again when, in his parable of the prodigal son, the father says, "This my son was *dead*, and is alive again" (Luke 15:24). That's why "unless one is born again he cannot see the kingdom of God" (John 3:3). The dead can't see. That is, they can't see God's kingdom as supremely desirable. It looks foolish or mythical or boring. So they "cannot enter the kingdom of God" (John 3:5). They cannot because it is foolishness to them.

Jesus sees all of humanity divided into two parts: those who are merely born once—"born of the flesh," "the (spiritually) dead"—and those who are "born again" by the Spirit of God—those who are alive to God and see his kingdom as true and supremely desirable.

## The Wind Blows Where It Will

Nicodemus is not entirely wrong to be baffled. There is a mystery. Jesus says so in John 3:8, "The wind blows where it wishes, and you hear its sound, but you do not know where it comes from or where it goes. So it is with everyone who is born of the Spirit." In other words, "Nicodemus, you need new spiritual life—a second birth."

And what Jesus requires from Nicodemus, he requires from all. He is speaking to everyone in the world. No one is excluded. No ethnic group has a greater bent toward life. Dead is dead—whatever our color, ethnicity, culture, or class. We need spiritual eyes. Our first birth will not get us into the kingdom of God. But we do not cause ourselves to be born again. The Spirit does that. And the Spirit is free and blows in ways we do not comprehend. We must be born again. But this is a gift of God.

Look away from yourself. Seek from God what he alone can do for you. Moral improvement of the old you is not what you need. New life is what the whole world needs. It is radical and supernatural. It is outside our control. The dead do not give themselves new life. We must be born again—"not . . . of the will of the flesh nor of the will of man, but of God" (John 1:13). That is what Jesus commands of us and from all the nations of the world.

*From that time Jesus began to preach, saying,*
*"Repent, for the kingdom of heaven is at hand."*

MATTHEW 4:17


*I have not come to call the righteous*
*but sinners to repentance.*

LUKE 5:32


*The men of Nineveh will rise up at the judgment with this*
*generation and condemn it, for they repented at the preaching*
*of Jonah, and behold, something greater than Jonah is here.*

MATTHEW 12:41


*Unless you repent, you*
*will all likewise perish.*

LUKE 13:3, 5

# Repent

THE FIRST COMMAND OF JESUS'S public ministry was, "Repent." He spoke this command indiscriminately to all who would listen. It was a call for radical inward change toward God and man.

## What Is Repentance?

Two things show us that repentance is an internal change of mind and heart rather than mere sorrow for sin or mere improvement of behavior. First, the meaning of the Greek word behind the English "repent" (μετανοέω, *metanoeō*) points in this direction. It has two parts: *meta* and *noeō*. The second part (*noeō*) refers to the mind and its thoughts and perceptions and dispositions and purposes. The first part (*meta*) is a prefix that regularly means movement or change. In view of the way this prefix regularly functions,[1] we may infer that the basic meaning of *repent* is to experience a change of the mind's perceptions and dispositions and purposes.

---

1  For example, *meta* is used as a prefix in the words *metabainō* (transfer or change from one place to another), *metaballō* (change one's way of thinking), *metagō* (lead or move from one place to another), *metatithēmi* (convey from one place to another, put in another place, transfer), *metamorphoō* (change in a manner visible to others, be transfigured), *metastrephō* (cause a change in state or condition, change, alter), and *metaschematizō* (change the form of something, transform, change), etc.

The other factor that points to this meaning of "repent" is the way Luke 3:8 describes the relationship between repentance and new behavior. It says, "Bear fruits *in keeping with* repentance." Then it gives examples of the fruits: "Whoever has two tunics is to share with him who has none, and whoever has food is to do likewise" (Luke 3:11). This means that repenting is what happens inside of us. Then this change leads to the fruits of new behavior. Repentance is not the new deeds but the inward change that bears the fruit of new deeds. Jesus is commanding that we experience this inward change.

### Sin: An Assault on God

Why? His answer is that we are sinners. "I have not come to call the righteous but *sinners* to repentance" (Luke 5:32). What was Jesus's view of sin? In the parable of the prodigal son, Jesus describes the son's sin like this: "He squandered his property in reckless living . . . [and] devoured [it] with prostitutes" (Luke 15:13, 30). But when the prodigal repents he says, "Father, I have sinned *against heaven* and before you. I am no longer worthy to be called your son" (Luke 15:21). Therefore, throwing your life away on reckless living and prostitutes is not just humanly hurtful; it is an offense against heaven—that is, against God. That's the essential nature of sin. It's an assault on God.

We see this again in the way Jesus taught his disciples to pray. He said that they should pray, "Forgive us our *sins,* for we ourselves forgive everyone who is *indebted* to us" (Luke 11:4). In other words, sins that God forgives are compared to the ones people commit against us, and those are called *debts.* Therefore, Jesus's view of sin is that it dishonors God and puts us in *debt* to restore the divine honor we had defamed by our God-belittling behavior or attitudes. Later we will see how that debt gets paid by Jesus himself (Mark 10:45). But for us to enjoy that gift he says we must repent.

Repenting means experiencing a change of mind so that we can see God as true and beautiful and worthy of all our praise and all our obedience. This change of mind also embraces Jesus in the same way. We know this because Jesus said, "If God were your Father, you would love *me*, for I came from God" (John 8:42). Seeing God with a new mind includes seeing Jesus with a new mind.

## The Universal Need for Repentance

No one is excluded from Jesus's command to repent. He made this clear when a group of people came to him with news of two calamities. Innocent people had been killed by Pilate's massacre and by the fall of the tower of Siloam (Luke 13:1–4). Jesus took the occasion to warn even the bearers of the news: "Unless you repent, you will all likewise perish" (Luke 13:5). In other words, don't think calamities mean that some people are sinners in need of repentance and others aren't. *All* need repentance. Just as all need to be born again (John 3:7), so all must repent because all are sinners.

When Jesus said, "I have not come to call the righteous but sinners to repentance" (Luke 5:32), he did not mean that some persons are good enough not to need repentance. He meant some *think* they are (Luke 18:9), and others have already repented and have been set right with God. For example, the rich young ruler desired "to justify himself" (Luke 10:29), while "the tax collector . . . beat his breast, saying, 'God, be merciful to me, a sinner!' [and he] went down to his house justified [by God!]" (Luke 18:13–14). (For more on Luke 18:9–15, see *Command #20*.)

## There Is an Urgency to This Command
## Because Judgment Is Coming

Therefore, none is excluded. All need repentance. And the need is urgent. Jesus said, "Unless you repent, you will all likewise *perish*." What did he mean by *perish*? He meant that the final judgment of God will fall on those who don't repent. "The men of Nineveh will rise up at the judgment with this generation and condemn it, for they repented at the preaching of Jonah, and behold, something greater than Jonah is here" (Matt. 12:41). Jesus, the Son of God, is warning people of the judgment to come and is offering escape if we will repent. If we will not repent, Jesus has one message for us: "Woe to you" (Matt. 11:21).

This is why his command for repentance is part of his central message concerning the kingdom of God. He preached that the long-awaited kingdom of God is present in his ministry. "The time is fulfilled, and the kingdom of God is at hand; repent and believe in the gospel" (Mark 1:15). The gospel—the good news—is that the rule of God has arrived in Jesus to save sinners before the kingdom arrives at his second coming in judgment. So the command to repent is based on the gracious *offer* that is present to forgive and on the gracious *warning* that someday those who refuse the offer will perish in God's judgment.

## To All Nations Beginning from Jerusalem

After he had risen from the dead, Jesus made sure that his apostles would continue the call for repentance throughout the world. He said, "Thus it is written, that the Christ should suffer and on the third day rise from the dead, and that *repentance* and forgiveness of sins should be proclaimed in his name to all nations, beginning from Jerusalem" (Luke 24:46–47). So the command of Jesus to repent goes to all the nations. It comes to us, whoever we are and wherever we are, and lays claim on us. This is the command of Jesus to every soul: Repent. Be changed deep within. Replace all God-dishonoring, Christ-belittling perceptions and dispositions and purposes with God-treasuring, Christ-exalting ones.

*Come to me, all who labor and are heavy*
*laden, and I will give you rest.*

MATTHEW 11:28

*Jesus stood up and cried out, "If anyone thirsts,*
*let him come to me and drink."*

JOHN 7:37

*Jesus said to them, "I am the bread of life;*
*whoever comes to me shall not hunger."*

JOHN 6:35

*You refuse to come to me that you may have life.*

JOHN 5:40

*When he had said these things, he cried out with a loud voice,*
*"Lazarus, come out." The man who had died came out.*

JOHN 11:43–44

# Come to Me

WHEN A PERSON IS BORN ANEW and experiences repentance, his attitude about Jesus changes. Jesus himself becomes the central focus and supreme value of life. Before the new birth happens and repentance occurs, a hundred other things seem more important and more attractive: health, family, job, friends, sports, music, food, sex, hobbies, retirement. But when God gives the radical change of new birth and repentance, Jesus himself becomes our supreme treasure.

### His Yoke Is Easy, and His Burden Is Light

Therefore, his command that we come to him is not burdensome. It means coming to the one who has become everything to us. Jesus did not come into the world mainly to bring a new religion or a new law. He came to offer himself for our eternal enjoyment and to do whatever he had to do—including death—to remove every obstacle to this everlasting joy in him. "These things I have spoken to you, that my joy may be in you, and that your joy may be full" (John 15:11). When Jesus commands that we do things—like "Come to me"—the essence of these commands is that we experience the life that most fully savors and spreads his supreme worth.

As Jesus looks out over the religions of the world—including the Judaism of his day—he sees people who are laboring under heavy loads to earn the favor of whatever deity they believe in. He did not come to replace that God-appeasing load with another one. He came to carry that load and call us to himself for rest. "Come to me, all who labor and are heavy laden, and I will give you rest. Take my yoke upon you, and learn from me, for I am gentle and lowly in heart, and you will find rest for your souls. For my yoke is easy, and my burden is light" (Matt. 11:28–30). Make no mistake, there *is* a yoke and a burden when we come to Jesus (there would be no commands if this were not true), but the yoke is easy, and the burden is light.

### There Is a Burden, but It's Not Jesus

But perhaps it's not easy and light the way we think it is. Jesus also said, "The gate is narrow and the way is *hard* that leads to life" (Matt. 7:14). The reason it is hard is not because Jesus is a hard taskmaster. It's hard because the world is a hard place to enjoy Jesus above all. Our own suicidal tendency to enjoy other things more must be crushed (Matt. 5:29–30). And besides our own sin, many people are angered that we do not love what they love. So Jesus warned, "Some of you they will put to death. You will be hated by all for my name's sake" (Luke 21:16–17).

But Jesus is not the burden. When we come to him, he is the burden-lifter, the soul-satisfier, and the life-giver. "Jesus stood up and cried out, 'If anyone thirsts, let him come to me and drink'" (John 7:37). Coming to Jesus means coming to drink. And the water we drink in fellowship with Jesus gives everlasting life. "Whoever drinks of the water that I will give him will never be thirsty forever. The water that I will give him will become in him a spring of water welling up to eternal life" (John 4:14). The command that we come to Jesus is the command to come to the fountain of life and drink.

Jesus is not satisfied to lure us into obedience with images of life-giving water. He will also draw us with promises of life-sustaining bread.

"I am the bread of life; he who comes to me shall not hunger" (John 6:35). Jesus himself is the bread of heaven—the source and essence of everlasting life. He will draw us with promises of deliverance from perishing (John 3:16). The command that we come to him is therefore like the command of a father to his child in a burning window, "Jump to me!" Or like the command of a rich, strong, tender, handsome husband to an unfaithful wife, "Come home!" Or like the command of a rescue squad that finds you on the point of death, dehydrated after days in the desert, "Drink this!"

### "You Refuse to Come to Me That You May Have Life"

But the personal tragedy of sin and spiritual blindness is that people do not come. Jesus grieved over his people. "O Jerusalem, Jerusalem, the city that kills the prophets and stones those who are sent to it! How often would I have gathered your children together as a hen gathers her brood under her wings, and you would not!" (Matt. 23:37). "You search the Scriptures because you think that in them you have eternal life; and it is they that bear witness about me, yet you refuse to come to me that you may have life" (John 5:39–40).

Why don't people come to Jesus? At one level the answer is because they "*refuse* to come." In other words, people do not want to come. Some call this the choice of free will. Jesus would probably say it is the choice of a will enslaved to sin. "Truly, truly, I say to you, everyone who commits sin is a slave to sin" (John 8:34). Jesus would say that people do not come to him because they are enslaved to their supreme preference for other things. "The light has come into the world, and people loved the darkness rather than the light . . . everyone who does wicked things hates the light and does not come to the light" (John 3:19–20).

How then has anyone ever come, since we are all enslaved to sin and spiritually dead (see *Command #1*)? Jesus's answer was that God, in his great mercy, overcomes our resistance and draws us: "No one can come to me unless the Father who sent me draws him" (John 6:44).

"No one can come to me unless it is granted him by the Father" (John 6:65). God grants the gift of new birth and repentance, which opens the eyes of the spiritually blind to the truth and beauty of Jesus. When this happens, all suicidal objections fall. We are finally free. And, finally free from slavery, we come.

### "Lazarus, Come Out!"

Jesus came into the world to gather his flock from all the world (John 11:52). He lays down his life for them and commands that they come to him. Though he weeps over those who do not come, he will not be frustrated in his design. He will succeed in gathering a people for himself. He speaks with absolute sovereignty when he says, "I have other sheep that are not of this fold. I must bring them also, and they will listen to my voice. So there will be one flock, one shepherd" (John 10:16). He *must* bring them. They *will* heed his voice. They *will* come.

When you hear the voice of Jesus saying, "Come to me," pray that God would give you eyes to see Jesus as irresistibly true and beautiful. Pray that you would hear this command the way Lazarus did when he was dead. "[Jesus] cried out with a loud voice, 'Lazarus, come out.' The man who had died came [out of his grave]" (John 11:43–44). When you come to Jesus like this, you will never cease to praise and thank him for his sovereign grace.

*Let not your hearts be troubled. Believe*
*in God; believe also in me.*

JOHN 14:1

*Believe me that I am in the Father and the Father is in*
*me, or else believe on account of the works themselves.*

JOHN 14:11

*While you have the light, believe in the light,*
*that you may become sons of light.*

JOHN 12:36

*[Jesus] said to Thomas, "Put your finger here, and*
*see my hands; and put out your hand, and place it*
*in my side. Do not disbelieve, but believe."*

JOHN 20:27

# Believe in Me

WHY DOES JESUS COMMAND that we believe in him? And what does believing in him really mean? The reason Jesus commands that we believe in him is that all human beings are in a desperate situation, and only Jesus can rescue us. He commands belief in himself because we cannot rescue ourselves but must look entirely to him for help. Jesus is the only one who can save us from this danger. For our own sake he commands that we trust him. It is as though a fireman finds you almost unconscious in a burning building that is about to collapse, throws his insulated tarp over you, picks you up, and says, "Hold still as I carry you. Don't move. Don't try to help me. I will get you out. You must let me do it. Trust me."

## The Desperate Situation We Are In

Of course, most people don't feel the need for a divine fireman to rescue them. So what is this desperate situation that only Jesus can rescue us from? Jesus put it like this. Notice the words "perish," "condemned," and "wrath of God."

> For God so loved the world, that he gave his only Son, that whoever believes in him should not perish but have eternal life. For God did

not send the Son into the world to condemn the world, but in order that the world might be saved through him. Whoever believes in him is not condemned; but whoever does not believe is condemned already, because he has not believed in the name of the only Son of God. . . . Whoever believes in the Son has eternal life; whoever does not obey the Son shall not see life, but the wrath of God remains on him. (John 3:16–18, 36)

The desperate situation we are in, Jesus says, is that we are under the wrath of God. This is owing to our sin (see *Command #2*). God is just, and his anger is rightly kindled against human attitudes and behaviors that belittle his worth and treat him as insignificant. All of us have done this. In fact, we do it every day.

### God Sent Jesus to Die in Our Place

But the amazing truth is that God has sent his Son Jesus into the world not to add to this condemnation, but to rescue us from it. And the way Jesus rescues us is by taking the condemnation on himself, dying in our place, and then commanding not heroic acts of penance but that we trust him. Jesus said, "I am the good shepherd. The good shepherd lays down his life for the sheep" (John 10:11). In other words, Jesus's death was purposeful. He intentionally laid it down in our place.

Jesus saw himself as the fulfillment of the astonishing prophecy of Isaiah 53 (cf. Luke 22:37; Isa. 53:12). Seven hundred years before Jesus came, Isaiah prophesied that a Servant of the Lord would come to die for his people.

We esteemed him stricken, smitten by God, and afflicted. But he was wounded for our transgressions; he was crushed for our iniquities; upon him was the chastisement that brought us peace, and with his stripes we are healed. All we like sheep have gone astray; we have turned every one to his own way; and the LORD has laid on him the iniquity of us all. (Isa. 53:4–6)

The reason Jesus commands that we believe on him is that there is nothing we can add to this rescue from the wrath of God. Jesus became our substitute. The sins that should have brought condemnation on us, God laid on Jesus. God's love planned an amazing exchange: Jesus endured what we deserved so that we might enjoy what he deserved— eternal life. And the way we come to enjoy this life is by believing in Jesus. That's what he said: "Truly, truly, I say to you, whoever *believes* has eternal life" (John 6:47; cf. Luke 8:12).

### What Does Believing in Jesus Mean?

Therefore, not many questions are more important than this: What does believing in him really mean? First, it means believing certain historical facts to be true. When Jesus's disciple Thomas doubted that Jesus was raised physically from the dead, Jesus came to him and said, "Put your finger here, and see my hands; and put out your hand, and place it in my side. Do not disbelieve, but believe" (John 20:27). Belief is not a leap in the dark. It has foundations and content. It is based on what really happened in history.

But believing in Jesus means more than knowing true things about Jesus. It means trusting him as a living person for who he really is. This is why Jesus spoke of simply believing *in him*. "Believe in God; believe also *in me*" (John 14:1; cf. Matt. 18:6). Believing *in* Jesus is more than believing *about* Jesus. We trust *him*.

### Being Satisfied with All That God Is for Us in Jesus

Notice that Jesus offers himself to us not merely as a rescuer to be trusted but as living water to be drunk—not to mention offering himself to us as Shepherd (Matt. 26:31), Bridegroom (Matt. 9:15), Treasure (Matt. 13:44), King (John 18:36), etc. What does it mean to "believe in" Jesus as life-giving water?

Jesus said, "If anyone thirsts, let him come to me and drink" (John 7:37). "Whoever drinks of the water that I will give him will never be thirsty forever. The water that I will give him will become in him a spring of water welling up to eternal life" (John 4:14). In another place, Jesus connected this drinking with believing in him and coming to him: "I am the bread of life; whoever *comes* to me shall not hunger, and whoever *believes* in me shall never thirst" (John 6:35). In other words, believing in Jesus and drinking the water that wells up to eternal life are the same.

Believing in Jesus when he offers himself to us as life-giving water does not mean merely believing *that* this water gives life. Water gives life when we drink it. Jesus gives life by being trusted. Trusting Jesus as water, therefore, means drinking the water. That is, it means "receiving" Jesus and all the life-giving grace of God that comes to us in him. "Whoever *receives* me receives him who sent me" (Matt. 10:40; cf. John 13:20). Believing in Jesus includes drinking Jesus as the soul-thirst-quenching water of life. That is, it means savoring and being satisfied with all that God is for us in Jesus.

### The Fireman Illustration Was Inadequate

So the illustration I used above of trusting the fireman is insufficient. It's true as far as it goes. Jesus is a rescuer. We must hold still, not move, and let him carry us to safety out of the burning wrath of God. But it is possible to trust a fireman that you do not admire. He may be an adulterer and drunk in his time off. He doesn't ask you to believe in him for all that he is, or to receive him, or to savor his life. But Jesus does. He is so much more than a rescuer. Therefore, believing in him is more than trusting in his rescue skills.

Jesus came not only to rescue us from condemnation but also that we might enjoy everlasting life, which means that we might experience all that God is for us in him. "This is eternal life," he said, "that they know you the only true God, and Jesus Christ whom you have sent"

(John 17:3). He knows what we need far better than we do. We need rescue from the wrath of God, and we need a soul-satisfying relationship with God. This is what Jesus came to give. It comes to us in one way alone—by believing in him. Therefore, he gives his command to the world: "Believe in me."

*Whoever loves father or mother more than me
is not worthy of me, and whoever loves son or
daughter more than me is not worthy of me.*

MATTHEW 10:37

*Jesus said to them, "If God were your Father, you would
love me, for I proceeded and came forth from God."*

JOHN 8:42, RSV

# Love Me

## Jesus Commands the Emotions

I recall reading a book in college that argued: love cannot be a feeling because it is commanded, and you can't command the feelings. In other words, love must simply be an act of the will or a deed of the body without involving the emotions or affections. But the problem with this argument is that the premise is false: Jesus *does* command the feelings. He commands that our emotions be one way and not another.[1]

He commands, for example, that we *rejoice* in certain circumstances (Matt. 5:12), and that we *fear* the right person (Luke 12:5), and that

[1] The most thorough study on emotions in the New Testament is now Matthew Elliott's *Faithful Feelings: Emotion in the New Testament* (Leicester, England: Inter-Varsity Press, 2005). He writes, "Part of the essence of the Christian is how he or she feels. We must recover some of the insight of Jonathan Edwards, Calvin, Augustine and others as they rightly emphasize the role of emotion in the believer's life. With a little work we can come up with a clear idea of the emotional characteristics of the members of the kingdom of God. They love God and each other, they take joy in what Jesus has done in the past and what he will do in the future. They have secure hope that God will triumph. They become angry at sin and injustice and are jealous for God. They embrace the sorrow of the suffering as their own and grieve over sin. But this emotional life is rarely glimpsed in our theologies where emotion is not emphasized as a sign of true faith. Not only do Christians live the ethics of the kingdom, they also feel the attitudes and emotions of the kingdom. This is part of the picture that is very clear in the New Testament. These feelings are a result of good theology and are a necessary component of faith" (263–64).

we not *feel shame* over him (Luke 9:26), and that we forgive *from the heart* (Matt. 18:35), and so on. If a feeling is proper to have, Jesus can command it. The fact that I may be too corrupt to experience the emotions that I ought to have does not change my duty to have them. If Jesus commands it, I should have it. My moral inability to produce it does not remove my guilt; it reveals my corruption. It makes me desperate for a new heart—which Jesus came to give (see *Command #1*).

## Love for Jesus Is Not Less Than Deep Affection

Jesus's command that we love him may involve *more* than deep feelings of admiration for his attributes and enjoyment of his fellowship and attraction to his presence and affection for his kinship, but it does not involve *less*. At least two things that he said show this. He said, for example, that our love for him must exceed the love we have for mother and father and son and daughter. "Whoever loves father or mother more than me is not worthy of me, and whoever loves son or daughter more than me is not worthy of me" (Matt. 10:37). The love that binds us to these relationships is not mere willpower. It is deep with affection. Jesus says that the love we must have for him is not less than that, but more.

The other evidence that Jesus requires our love to be more than good deeds is in John 14:15. Jesus said, "If you love me, you will keep my commandments." Sometimes people use these words to say: loving Jesus *is* keeping his commandments. That's not what it says. It says that keeping Jesus's commandments comes *from* our love for him. It does not *separate* deeds from love, but it does *distinguish* them. First we love him. Then because of this—overflowing from this—we do what he says. Love is not synonymous with commandment-keeping; it is the root of it. So the love that Jesus commands is something very deep and strong—like the closest family bonds of affection that we have but greater than that and more than that.

## Love for Jesus Springs from a New Nature

Jesus's command to be loved like this implies that we must have a new nature—a new heart. How else can we love someone we have never seen more affectionately than we love our dear children? Loving like this is not in our fallen human nature. Jesus made this plain when he said to those who did not love him, "If God were your Father, you would love me" (John 8:42). In other words, "The reason you do not love me is that you are not in the family of God. You don't have the family nature—the family spirit, the family heart, preferences, tendencies, inclinations. God is not your Father."

Jesus came as God's unique, divine Son (Matt. 11:27) so that fallen sinners like us could become non-divine sons of God with hearts and ways like his. "To all who did receive him, who believed in his name, [Jesus] gave the right to become children of God" (John 1:12). That's why Jesus could say, "Love your enemies . . . and you will be sons of the Most High" (Luke 6:35). Through the new birth (*Command #1*) and faith (*Command #4*), Jesus gives us the rights and the inclinations of the children of God. At the center of those inclinations is love for Jesus, God's Son.

## He Who Is Forgiven Little, Loves Little

How God enables us to love Jesus more than we love our closest friends and relatives is not a total mystery. The gift of the new birth and repentance—the new nature of a child of God—is brought about through seeing the glory of Jesus's love *for us*. Jesus taught this provocatively at a dinner party. A strict Pharisee, who had little love for Jesus, invited Jesus to dinner. While they were reclining at the low Middle-Eastern table, a prostitute entered and poured ointment—mingled with her tears—on Jesus's bare feet and wiped his feet with her hair. The Pharisee was indignant that Jesus would allow this.

So Jesus asked a question of the Pharisee: If a moneylender forgave two debtors, one who owed him five thousand dollars and the other fifty, which would love him more? He answered, "The one, I suppose, for whom he cancelled the larger debt." Jesus agreed, then said, "Do you see this woman? I entered your house; you gave me no water for my feet, but she has wet my feet with her tears and wiped them with her hair. You gave me no kiss, but from the time I came in she has not ceased to kiss my feet. You did not anoint my head with oil, but she has anointed my feet with ointment." Then Jesus concluded: "She loved much. But he who is forgiven little, loves little" (Luke 7:36–48).

This is a story about the way great love for Jesus comes into being. It comes into being when we are given eyes to see the beauty of Jesus in the way he loved us first. We did not love him first. He loved us first (John 15:16). Our love for Jesus is awakened when our hearts are broken because of our sin (unlike the judgmental Pharisee) and when we taste the sweetness of Jesus's forgiving love preceding and awakening our love for him.

### The Command That We Love Him Is an Act of Love

There is no doubt that this love will produce the fruit of obedience to Jesus's other commandments (John 14:15), and that it will incline us to fulfill the ministry he gives us to do (John 21:15–22), and that it will produce a longing that Jesus be honored and blessed (John 14:28; 5:23). But beneath all this fruit is the fundamental reality of heartfelt love for Jesus—strong feelings of admiration for his attributes, abiding enjoyment of his fellowship, undying attraction to his presence, warm affection for his kinship, and strong gratitude for loving us before we loved him.

These emotions and this fruit are what Jesus meant when he referred to our being "worthy" of him: "Whoever loves father or mother more than me is not *worthy* of me" (Matt. 10:37). Loving Jesus with these affections and with this fruit makes us "worthy" of Jesus. This does not mean that we deserve Jesus, as in the phrase "the laborer is *worthy* of his wages" (Luke 10:7, NASB). It means that Jesus deserves this kind of love. Our worthiness means that he has produced in us affections and behaviors that are suitable and fit for his worth. They correspond properly to his value. (Compare the use of the word "worthy" in the phrase, "Bear fruits worthy of [that is, suitable to] repentance," Luke 3:8, NKJV.)

Jesus commands that he be loved by the world because he is infinitely worthy to be loved. And since our love for him is the enjoyment of his glory and presence and care, therefore Jesus's command that we love him is one more way that his love overflows on us.

*He called the people to him again and said to them, "Hear me, all of you, and understand."*

MARK 7:14

*As he said these things, he called out, "He who has ears to hear, let him hear."*

LUKE 8:8

*Take care then how you hear.*

LUKE 8:18

*And a woman named Martha welcomed him into her house. And she had a sister called Mary, who sat at the Lord's feet and listened to his teaching. But Martha was distracted with much serving. And she went up to him and said, "Lord, do you not care that my sister has left me to serve alone? Tell her then to help me." But the Lord answered her, "Martha, Martha, you are anxious and troubled about many things, but one thing is necessary. Mary has chosen the good portion, which will not be taken away from her."*

LUKE 10:38–42

# Listen to Me

THE ENTIRE LIFE AND WORK OF JESUS is one great argument why we should listen to his word. Page after page of the New Testament Gospels pile up reasons to turn off the television and listen to Jesus. Here are some of those reasons—and why so many don't listen.

### No One Ever Spoke like This Man

Jesus's ministry was so astonishing and so threatening that his adversaries wanted him out of the way. So the Pharisees "sent officers to arrest him" (John 7:32). But to their dismay the officers came back empty-handed, not because Jesus had good bodyguards, but because his teaching was so stunning. "The officers . . . came to the chief priests and Pharisees, who said to them, 'Why did you not bring him?' The officers answered, 'No one ever spoke like this man!'" (John 7:45–46). When they listened to Jesus, they could not follow through with their mission to arrest him.

### Jesus Speaks the Very Words of God

When Jesus finished his famous Sermon on the Mount, "the crowds were astonished at his teaching, for he was teaching them as one who had authority, and not as their scribes" (Matt. 7:28–29). This authority was not because of a personality trait or a pedagogical technique. The reason is much deeper. His words have authority and power, Jesus says, because they are the words of God. "I have not spoken on my own authority, but the Father who sent me has himself given me a commandment—what to say and what to speak" (John 12:49). "What I say, therefore, I say as the Father has told me" (John 12:50; cf. 8:28). "The word that you hear is not mine but the Father's who sent me" (John 14:24). Jesus's words have authority because when he speaks, God speaks. Jesus speaks *from* God the Father and *as* God the Son.

### Jesus's Words Silence Supernatural Powers

But the authority of Jesus's words is not only the compelling power of God-revealed truth. There is another dimension. It also carries the force to defeat supernatural powers. Once when Jesus met a demon-possessed man he rebuked him and said, "Be silent, and come out of him!" (Mark 1:25). When the demon convulsed the man and came out, the crowd was amazed and said, "What is this? A new teaching with authority! He commands even the unclean spirits, and they obey him" (Mark 1:27). This same power of Jesus's word healed leprosy (Matt. 8:3), deafness (Mark 7:34–35), and blindness (Matt. 9:28–30). And most remarkable of all, with a simple word three times Jesus raised the dead. "Little girl, I say to you, arise" (Mark 5:41–42). "Young man, I say to you, arise" (Luke 7:14–15). "Lazarus, come out" (John 11:43–44).

### Jesus Has the Words of Eternal Life

Therefore, Jesus's words were *life* in more ways than one. They could sustain physical life and restore physical life. But more important than that, they were the indispensable way to *eternal* life. It is a wonderful thing to be raised from the dead—but not if you are simply going to perish later in hell. The most precious thing about the words of Jesus, and the most important reason to listen to him, is that his words lead to eternal life.

Once when Jesus had finished teaching some hard things, "many of his disciples turned back and no longer walked with him." So Jesus said to the twelve apostles whom he had chosen, "Do you want to go away as well?" To which Peter responded, "Lord, to whom shall we go? You have the words of eternal life" (John 6:66–68). This was not mere enthusiasm for a charismatic teacher. Jesus confirmed Peter's judgment: "It is the Spirit who gives life; the flesh is of no avail. The words that I have spoken to you are spirit and life" (John 6:63). Jesus agrees. He speaks the words of eternal life. Everyone who wants eternal life should listen to the words of Jesus.

How do Jesus's words give eternal life? We have already seen that eternal life comes through believing in Jesus: "This is the will of my Father, that everyone who looks on the Son and believes in him should have eternal life" (John 6:40; see *Command #4*). The reason the words of Jesus lead to eternal life is that they awaken this faith. Belief in Jesus does not come by the waving of a magic wand. It comes by hearing the word of God through Jesus.

### Jesus's Words Awaken Faith

One of Jesus's most important parables was about sowing seed on four kinds of soil. The seed represents the word. One kind of soil is the trampled path where the seed falls and the birds snatch it away. Jesus explains it like this: "The ones along the path are those who have heard; then the devil comes and takes away the word from their hearts, so that they may *not believe and be saved*" (Luke 8:12). What this shows is that Jesus sees his word as the key to believing and being saved. If the word is taken away, there will be no faith in Jesus. And if there is no faith in Jesus, there will be no salvation—no eternal life. First comes hearing the word of Jesus, then comes belief in Jesus, then comes eternal life. "Whoever *hears* my word and *believes* him who sent me has eternal *life*" (John 5:24).

The reason Jesus's words awaken faith in him is that they reveal who he really is and what he does to obtain eternal life for us. We see the glory of Jesus and the all-sufficiency of his work through his word. But not everybody does. Some hear his words but do not hear them as true and compelling. They see what he is talking about but do not see it as beautiful and convincing. So Jesus said, "This is why I speak to them in parables, because seeing they do not see, and hearing they do not hear, nor do they understand" (Matt. 13:13).

### Why Do They Not Hear and Believe?

Why do so many people not hear what Jesus is saying? Jesus said to his most bitter adversaries, "You seek to kill me because my word finds no place in you" (John 8:37). That is a striking phrase: "my word finds no place in you." Their minds and hearts are shaped (or stuffed) in such a way that when he speaks, what he says won't fit in their hearts. This seems to imply that there is a certain readiness for Jesus's word that goes before his word and enables us to hear him. That is in fact what Jesus teaches.

When Jesus was on trial at the end of his life, Pilate pressed him to confess that he claimed to be the king of the Jews. Jesus responded by saying, "For this purpose I was born and for this purpose I have come into the world—to bear witness to the truth" (John 18:37). Jesus came to speak the truth. His words are truth. Pilate responded cynically, "What is truth?" (v. 38). In other words, there was "no place" in Pilate for Jesus's words. But that did not take Jesus off guard. Nor did it mean that Pilate had hindered God's plan. Jesus had the final and decisive word about Pilate: "Everyone who is *of the truth* listens to my voice" (John 18:37).

So now we have another striking phrase—not only, "My word finds no place in you," but also the even more remarkable phrase, "Everyone who is *of the truth* listens to my voice." On the one hand, there are people whose hearts and minds have *no room* for the voice of Jesus. And on the other hand, there are people who are "*of the truth.*" They listen to Jesus. They do have room for his word. There is, you might say, a truth-shaped readiness to hear the voice of Jesus.

## Whoever Is of God Hears the Words of God

Jesus describes these two kinds of listeners with two other phrases: If they do not hear they are not "of God," and if they hear they are his "sheep." The non-listeners he describes like this: "Whoever is *of God* hears the words of God. The reason why you do not hear them is that you are not *of God*" (John 8:47). Now we have three descriptions of the non-listeners: they have "no place" for Jesus's word, they are not "of the truth," and they are not "of God." This is a sobering revelation. It means that our condition as fallen sinners unfits us for hearing the truth—especially as it comes from Jesus.

We are not neutral like a metronome wand poised straight up between truth and error—waiting dispassionately to be inclined to one side or the other. No, we are heavily tilted toward selfishness and all the errors that support it. When Jesus speaks, unless God acts to give us ears to hear and eyes to see, there will be no place in us for the words of Jesus.

This explains why Jesus said:

I thank you, Father, Lord of heaven and earth, that you have hidden these things from the wise and understanding and revealed them to little children; yes, Father, for such was your gracious will. All things have been handed over to me by my Father, and no one knows who the Son is except the Father, or who the Father is except the Son and anyone to whom the Son chooses to reveal him. (Luke 10:21–22)

When he had said this, he turned to his disciples and said, "Blessed are the eyes that see what you see!" (Luke 10:23). Blessed indeed! Blessed *by God*. This seeing is the work of God. Only God can give us eyes to see and ears to hear. That's why Jesus says that those who do not listen to his words are not "of God" (John 8:47). This is the *blessing* we desperately need—the blessing that God would make in our hearts a place for the truth.

### "My Sheep Hear My Voice"

Finally, Jesus calls those who do have a place for truth his *sheep*: "My sheep hear my voice, and I know them, and they follow me" (John 10:27). Therefore, we can know we are his sheep if we listen to his voice. We know we are his sheep if there is a truth-shaped place for his word in our hearts, and we welcome what he says.

Therefore, I urge you on behalf of Jesus, listen to his word. Be like Mary and sit at his feet (Luke 10:39, 42). Don't turn away from the command of his Father given on the Mount of Transfiguration: "This is my beloved Son, with whom I am well pleased; *listen to him*" (Matt. 17:5). Don't miss the merciful attraction in the words, "Heaven and earth will pass away, but my words will not pass away" (Mark 13:31). Don't hate yourself by rejecting the one who said, "These things I have spoken to you . . . that your joy may be full" (John 15:11; cf. 17:13). Listen to Jesus.

*Abide in me, and I in you. As the branch cannot
bear fruit by itself, unless it abides in the vine,
neither can you, unless you abide in me.*

JOHN 15:4

*As the Father has loved me, so have I
loved you. Abide in my love.*

JOHN 15:9

*If you abide in my word, you are truly my disciples, and
you will know the truth, and the truth will set you free.*

JOHN 8:31–32

# Abide in Me

JESUS'S COMMANDS ARE FOR A LIFETIME. He does not command a *once-for-all* decision to repent or come or believe or love or listen. Rather he commands that we go on repenting, coming, believing, loving, and listening. The transformation of repentance continues. Coming to Jesus again and again continues. Believing in him hour by hour continues. Listening to his word as the daily source of spiritual life continues. Jesus commands the engagement of our minds and hearts every day of our lives.

A transaction with Jesus in the past that has no ongoing expression in our lives was a false transaction. When Jesus said, "If you abide in my word, you are truly my disciples" (John 8:31), he meant that if we *don't* abide, we are *not* truly his disciples. And the opposite of *true* disciples is *false* disciples. That's what we are if we count on past experiences without ongoing devotion to Jesus.

## A Lifelong Extension of Encountering Jesus

One way that Jesus taught the necessity of an ongoing devotion was to command, "Abide in me." There is nothing uniquely religious about the word *abide*. In the language of the New Testament, it is the ordinary word for "stay" or "continue" or sometimes "dwell." Jesus meant: "Stay in me. Continue in me. Keep me for your dwelling." It is the lifelong extension of encountering Jesus.

The context of this command is the analogy of a vine and its branches. Jesus compares himself to the vine and us to branches:

> Abide in me, and I in you. As the branch cannot bear fruit by itself, unless it abides in the vine, neither can you, unless you abide in me. I am the vine; you are the branches. Whoever abides in me and I in him, he it is that bears much fruit, for apart from me you can do nothing. (John 15:4–5)

This picture helps us understand what Jesus meant by abiding in him. The main point of the analogy is that power to bear fruit—that is, power to live a fruitful life of Christ-like love (John 15:12)—flows from Jesus if we stay vitally connected to him. Then we are like a branch connected to the vine so that all the life-sustaining, fruit-producing sap can flow into it. Jesus is explicit in claiming to be the power that we need to live fruitful lives. He says, "Apart from me you can do nothing." Abiding in Jesus means staying vitally connected to the life-giving, power-giving, fruit-producing branch, namely, Jesus.

## The Moment-by-Moment Cause of Every Good Thing

In other words, Jesus commands that he be the moment-by-moment cause of every good thing in our lives. "Apart from me you can do *nothing*." Nothing! Really? Well, we could sin and stop bearing fruit and perish without him. But that's not what he promises to produce. He means: "Without me you can do nothing truly good, truly God-honoring and Christ-exalting and self-abasing and eternally helpful for others." Abiding in Jesus means staying vitally connected, hour by hour, to the one who alone produces in our lives everything he commands.

## If You Abide, You Bear Fruit

But practically, what does this mean in our experience? What is this "staying vitally connected"? How do we do this? One important part of the answer is to make clear that abiding in Jesus is *not* the same as bearing fruit or keeping his commandments. Fruit-bearing and commandment-keeping are the *result* of abiding. *If* we abide, we bear fruit.

Jesus does not contradict this when he says, "If you keep my commandments, you will abide in my love" (John 15:10). This does not mean keeping his commandments *is* abiding in his love. That would be like saying: fruit *is* being connected to the vine. No. Fruit is the *result* of our being connected to the vine. They are not the same thing. What Jesus means is that if you don't keep the commandments, that is, if you don't bear the fruit of love (for love is the sum of his commandments, John 15:12), you have ceased to abide in him. For the truth stands: "Whoever abides in me . . . bears much fruit" (John 15:5).

So the answer to our question, "How do we abide in Jesus?" is *not* "by bearing fruit" or "by keeping the commandments." That misses the whole point. The point is to discover *how* to bear fruit. The answer is, by abiding in Jesus. And so the question becomes: How do we abide in Jesus? What does it mean in actual experience?

## Practically, How Do We Abide in Jesus?

Jesus uses two other similar phrases that point to the answer. He refers to abiding in his *love*. And he refers to abiding in his *word*. Both of these point toward abiding as continual *trust* in the truth of Jesus's words and in the certainty of his love.

## Abiding Means Trusting in Jesus's Love

Not to abide in Jesus's love would mean that we stop believing that we are loved by Jesus. We look at our circumstances—perhaps persecution or disease or abandonment—and we conclude that we are not loved by Jesus anymore. That's the opposite of abiding in the love of Jesus. So abiding in his love means continuing to believe, moment by moment, that we are loved.

Everything that comes into our lives under Jesus's sovereign authority (Matt. 8:8) is part of his love for us. If it is pleasant, he says, "That's how my Father cares for the birds of the air and the lilies of the field; how much more you!" (cf. Matt. 6:26–30). And if it is painful, he says, "Fear not, the worst that can happen is death, and I have overcome death. I will be with you to the end. And you will be repaid at the resurrection of the just" (cf. Matt. 10:28; 28:20; John 11:25–26; Luke 14:14). Abiding in Jesus means trusting that this is true—and true *for you*. That is, it means living on this truth moment by moment. It flows to us like sap flows to a branch. We receive it and get our life from it every day.

### Abiding Means Trusting in Jesus's Word

Similarly, this is true with the phrase, "Abide in my *word*" (John 8:31). This cannot mean merely, "Keep my commandments." Rather it means, "Keep on trusting my word. Keep on trusting what I have revealed to you about myself and my Father and my work." The context of John 8:31–32 confirms this: "Jesus said to the Jews who had believed in him, 'If you abide in my word, you are truly my disciples, and you will know the truth, and the truth will set you free.'" The result of abiding in Jesus's word is being set free. From what? From sin. That's the slavery Jesus has in mind, as John 8:34 shows: "Everyone who commits sin is a *slave to sin*" (RSV). So freedom from sin is the fruit of abiding in the word. "If you abide in my word . . . the truth will set you free." Not sinning is the *fruit*, not the *definition*, of abiding in the word. So keeping the commandments of Jesus, which is another way of describing liberation from sin, is not the meaning of abiding in his word but the fruit of it.

So we conclude that abiding in Jesus—in his love and in his word—is trusting that he really is loving us at every moment and that everything he has revealed about himself and his work for us and our future with him is true. We are taken back to what we saw in the chapter on believing in Jesus (*Command #4*). Believing in Jesus as our living water means *drinking* the water—savoring it and being satisfied with it. So it is with the sap that flows from the vine to the branch. We receive it, drink it, savor it, and satisfy our souls with it. This daily ever-renewed satisfaction in Jesus is the key to bearing fruit.[1] This is what it means to abide in Jesus.

## Jesus Keeps Us Abiding

As easy as it seems to abide, to stay implanted, to drink, to rest in Jesus, the truth is that we are often tempted to find our life-giving sap from another plant. And besides our own sinful tendencies, the devil himself wants to snatch us out of the vine, and we must pray daily, Jesus said, that God would "deliver us from evil" (Matt. 6:13). Therefore, we need to remind ourselves that Jesus does not leave us to ourselves. Even though he commands us to abide in him—and we are responsible to abide there, and guilty if we don't abide—nevertheless he himself keeps us there. And we would not abide there without his crucial keeping.

Jesus showed us this in at least three ways. He said that no one can snatch his own sheep (that is, his own true branches) out of his hand.

My sheep hear my voice, and I know them, and they follow me. I give them eternal life, and they will never perish, and no one will snatch them out of my hand. My Father, who has given them to me, is greater than all, and no one is able to snatch them out of the Father's hand. (John 10:27–29)

Then he prayed to his Father that God would cause us to keep on abiding in his name (that is, in Jesus). "Holy Father, keep them in your name, which you have given me. . . . While I was with them, I kept them in your name . . . and not one of them has been lost except the son

---

1  I have tried to explain this and give many practical examples of how this works in real life in the book *Future Grace* (Sisters, Ore.: Multnomah, 1995).

of destruction, that the Scripture might be fulfilled" (John 17:11–12). So it is *God* who does the decisive work in keeping us in the vine.

Then Jesus himself illustrated how he prays for his own disciples and preserves them from falling away. He predicted Simon Peter's three denials on the night before his death. But then he spoke with sovereign authority to Simon in words that should encourage all of us. "Simon, Simon, behold, Satan demanded to have you, that he might sift you like wheat, but I have prayed for you that your faith may not fail. And when you have turned again, strengthen your brothers" (Luke 22:31–32). Jesus prayed for Simon's keeping and knew it would happen. He said, "*When* you have turned" not "*If* you turn." God's answer to Jesus's prayer was sovereignly decisive. Yes, Simon's faith faltered, and he sinned by denying Jesus. But his faith did not fail utterly. He was not cut off from the vine. Jesus prayed for him. And there is no reason to think Jesus has ceased praying for us this way today.[2]

We are not idle in the battle to abide in Jesus. But in the end the battle is assured because it does not depend finally on us. Jesus wins. No one can snatch us out of his hand. He and his Father are greater than all. Therefore, his command that we abide in him is that we keep trusting the one who keeps us trusting.

---

2   Some commentators on the Bible disagree that Jesus keeps his own by making sure that they keep abiding in him. They point, understandably, to John 15:1–2, 6: "I am the true vine, and my Father is the vinedresser. Every branch of mine that does not bear fruit he takes away, and every branch that does bear fruit he prunes, that it may bear more fruit. . . . If anyone does not abide in me he is thrown away like a branch and withers; and the branches are gathered, thrown into the fire, and burned." Does this mean that we can be truly attached to the life-giving vine and then later be "taken away" and "thrown into the fire"? I don't think that is what Jesus is saying, mainly because of the three reasons given above. Rather, I think Jesus means that there are those who appear to be truly in the vine but are not. They have a kind of attachment, but it is not real and life-giving. Judas is the clearest example in Jesus's ministry. He was "attached" to Jesus for three years: there was a kind of influence flowing into him, and he received many blessings from Jesus. But he was not truly attached in a life-giving way. So eventually he was "taken away"—not away from true life, but away from the artificial attachment that looked real for a season but was not.

*If anyone would come after me, let him deny himself and take up his cross and follow me. For whoever would save his life will lose it, but whoever loses his life for my sake will find it.*

MATTHEW 16:24–25

*Follow me, and I will make you become fishers of men.*

MARK 1:17

*I am the light of the world; he who follows me will not walk in darkness, but will have the light of life.*

JOHN 8:12, RSV

*Follow me, and leave the dead to bury their own dead.*

MATTHEW 8:22

*If you would be perfect, go, sell what you possess and give to the poor, and you will have treasure in heaven; and come, follow me.*

MATTHEW 19:21

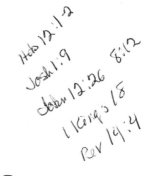

COMMAND #8

# Take Up Your Cross
# and Follow Me

JESUS WAS FULLY HUMAN AND FULLY GOD (John 1:1, 14). He was not God with a human veneer—like a costume. He was a real, flesh-and-blood man, a carpenter's son (Mark 6:3). So when he said to fishermen or tax collectors, "Follow me," their obedience was a concrete, physical act of putting their feet on the ground and walking behind Jesus and being part of his traveling team.

## Following Jesus When He Is Not Here

But Jesus knew that he would not always be on earth to have followers in this physical sense. "I am going to him who sent me. . . . I tell you the truth: it is to your advantage that I go away, for if I do not go away, the Helper will not come to you. But if I go, I will send him to you" (John 16:5, 7). Jesus was fully aware that the movement he began would continue after he had gone back to his Father in heaven. This was his plan (see *Command #45*).

Therefore, the command that we follow him was relevant not only for his physical days on earth but for all time. He made this clear at the end of his earthly ministry. He had risen from the dead and was about to ascend to the Father. He told Peter that he would suffer martyrdom someday after Jesus was gone. Peter wondered if he was the only one, and asked Jesus what would happen to his fellow apostle, John. Jesus answered, "If it is my will that he remain until I come, what is that to you? You follow me!" (John 21:22).

What this implies about "following Jesus" is that it happens after he is gone. Until Jesus comes again, he expects his disciples on earth to follow him. So following Jesus is not limited to physically walking around Palestine behind him. Jesus commands it from every person in every country in every age.

### Following Jesus Means Joining Him in What He Was Sent to Do

When Jesus said to Peter and Andrew, who were fishermen by trade, "Follow me, and *I will make you become fishers of men*" (Mark 1:17), he was using imagery relevant to them for something that applies to everyone who follows Jesus. The command to follow Jesus means that everyone should join him in what he came to do. And he tells us repeatedly what that was. "The Son of Man came . . . to give his life as a ransom for many" (Mark 10:45). "The Son of Man came to seek and to save the lost" (Luke 19:10). "I have not come to call the righteous but sinners to repentance" (Luke 5:32). "I came that they may have life and have it abundantly" (John 10:10). "What shall I say? 'Father, save me from this hour'? But for this purpose I have come to this hour. Father, glorify your name" (John 12:27–28).

In summary, then, he came to "die for the nation [of Israel], and not for the nation only, but also to gather into one the children of God who are scattered abroad" (John 11:51–52). He came to *gather* a people—specifically, to gather a people in allegiance to himself for the glory of his Father—by dying to save them from their sins and to give them eternal life and a new ethic of love like his (John 13:34–35). Therefore, when he commands that we follow him, he means that we join him in that task of gathering: "Whoever does not *gather* with me scatters" (Luke 11:23). There are no neutral followers; we either scatter or gather. Following Jesus means continuing the work he came to do—gathering a people in allegiance to him for the glory of his Father.

## Following Jesus into Suffering

Continuing the work he came to do even includes the suffering he came to do. Following Jesus means that we share in his suffering. When Jesus calls us to follow him, this is where he puts the emphasis. He knows he is heading to the cross, and he commands that we do the same. He designs his entire life and ministry to go to Jerusalem and be killed. "I must go on my way today and tomorrow and the day following, for it cannot be that a prophet should perish away from Jerusalem" (Luke 13:33).

So he "set his face to go to Jerusalem" (Luke 9:51). And he knew exactly what would happen there. It was all planned by his Father when he sent him into the world.

> See, we are going up to Jerusalem, and the Son of Man will be delivered over to the chief priests and the scribes, and they will condemn him to death and deliver him over to the Gentiles. And they will mock him and spit on him, and flog him and kill him. And after three days he will rise. (Mark 10:33–34)

That's the plan—down to the details of being spit on.

That was the design of his life. And he knew that his own pain would also fall on those who followed him. "If they persecuted me, they will also persecute you" (John 15:20). So the unflinching focus of his command was that we follow him in suffering. "If anyone would come after me, let him deny himself and take up his cross and follow me" (Matt. 16:24). Jesus put the emphasis on self-denial and cross-bearing.

**Suffering for Jesus with Joy Shows His Supreme Value**

He did not die to make this life easy for us or prosperous. He died to remove every obstacle to our everlasting joy in making much of him. And he calls us to follow him in his sufferings because this life of joyful suffering for Jesus's sake (Matt. 5:12) shows that he is more valuable than all the earthly rewards that the world lives for (Matt. 13:44; 6:19–20). If you follow Jesus only because he makes life easy now, it will look to the world as though you really love what they love, and Jesus just happens to provide it for you. But if you suffer with Jesus in the pathway of love because he is your supreme treasure, then it will be apparent to the world that your heart is set on a fortune different from theirs. This is why Jesus commands us to deny ourselves and take up our cross and follow him.

**Suffering for Jesus Is Temporary; Pleasure in Jesus Is Eternal**

Of course, the pain is temporary. He does not call us to eternal suffering. That's what he rescues us from. "Whoever loves his life loses it, and whoever hates his life *in this world* will keep it for *eternal life*" (John 12:25). "Whoever loses his life for my sake and the gospel's will *save* it" (Mark 8:35). Suffering for Jesus is temporary. Pleasure in Jesus is eternal. When Peter said (perhaps with a tinge of self-pity), "See, we have left everything and followed you," Jesus responded, without coddling Peter's self-pity, "Everyone who has left houses or brothers or sisters or father or mother or children or lands, for my name's sake, will receive a hundredfold and will inherit eternal life" (Matt. 19:27, 29). In other words, there is no ultimate sacrifice in following Jesus. "You will be repaid at the resurrection of the just" (Luke 14:14). "Your reward is great in heaven" (Matt. 5:12).

Even before heaven, joy abounds along the hard road that leads through death to resurrection. Nothing can compare with the joy of walking in the light with Jesus as opposed to walking in the darkness without him. Jesus said, "I am the light of the world. Whoever follows me will not walk in darkness, but will have the light of life" (John 8:12). Following Jesus does indeed lead through suffering and death. But the path is luminous with life and truth. Jesus promised, "I am with you always, to the end of the age" (Matt. 28:20). And where Jesus is present there is joy—joy in sorrow for now but joy nevertheless. "These things I have spoken to you, that my joy may be in you, and that your joy may be full" (John 15:11).

## Ruptures in Relationships with People

This is why the ruptures caused by following Jesus are not devastating. There are ruptures in relationships with people, relationships with possessions, and relationships with our vocation. Jesus has jolting ways of describing the cost of following him in relation to people. "Follow me, and leave the dead to bury their own dead" (Matt. 8:22). "If anyone comes to me and does not hate his own father and mother and wife and children and brothers and sisters, yes, and even his own life, he cannot be my disciple" (Luke 14:26 ). In other words, following Jesus is so supremely important that it calls for behaviors that are sometimes going to look like *hate* to the world. I have seen this lived out in agonizing choices that missionaries make to take their little children to risky places and leave aging parents behind, well cared for, but perhaps never to be seen on earth again. Some call it loveless. But Jesus has his eyes on the nations and what love requires in their case.

## Ruptures in Relationships with Possessions

Following Jesus also ruptures our relationship with possessions. There once was a rich young man who loved his possessions too much. So Jesus cut to the heart of his idolatry with the command, "If you would be perfect, go, sell what you possess and give to the poor, and you will have treasure in heaven; and come, follow me" (Matt. 19:21, see

*Command #20*). If something gets in the way of following Jesus, we must get rid of it.

And this is not unique to that rich man but applies to all of us: "*Any one* of you who does not renounce all that he has cannot be my disciple" (Luke 14:33). Renouncing what you have may not always mean selling it all. Jesus commended Zacchaeus for giving *half* of his goods to the poor (Luke 19:8–9). But renouncing *all* does mean that everything we have is totally at Jesus's disposal for purposes that please him and that it must never get in the way of radical obedience to his command of love.

### Ruptures in Relationships with Vocation

Then there is the rupture that following Jesus brings to our vocation. When Jesus called the twelve to follow him, none of them was a professional Jesus-follower. They were fishermen and tax collectors and the like. They had jobs. Incredibly, it went something like this: "As [Jesus] passed by, he saw Levi the son of Alphaeus sitting at the tax booth, and he said to him, 'Follow me.' And he rose and followed him" (Mark 2:14). Just like that! (As far as we know.) For most of us it was not that simple. But it does happen.

And it may happen to you. Not everyone should leave his vocation to follow Jesus. When one man wanted to leave his homeland and follow Jesus, Jesus said, "Go home to your friends and tell them how much the Lord has done for you, and how he has had mercy on you" (Mark 5:19). Most of us should stay where we are and follow Jesus in all the radical ways of love demanded by our present position and relationships.[1] But not everyone. For some—perhaps you (even as you read this)—following Jesus will mean a risky rupture in your vocation. Do not be afraid to follow him away from the familiar.

---

1   For more on what obedience to Jesus looks like in the secular workplace, see the chapter "Making Much of Christ from 8 to 5," in John Piper, *Don't Waste Your Life* (Wheaton, IL: Crossway, 2003), 131–54.

## Following Jesus Is Costly and Worth It

Jesus has no desire to trick you into following him with a kind of bait and switch. He is utterly upfront about the cost. In fact, he urges you to count the cost. "For which of you, desiring to build a tower, does not first sit down and count the cost, whether he has enough to complete it? . . . Or what king, going out to encounter another king in war, will not sit down first and deliberate whether he is able with ten thousand to meet him who comes against him with twenty thousand?" (Luke 14:28, 31). Let the call to follow Jesus be clear and honest. "In the world you will have tribulation. But take heart; I have overcome the world" (John 16:33). It is costly, and it is worth it.

*Jesus answered, "The most important [commandment] is, 'Hear, O Israel: The Lord our God, the Lord is one. And you shall love the Lord your God with all your heart and with all your soul and with all your mind and with all your strength.'"*

MARK 12:29–30

*Woe to you Pharisees! For you tithe mint and rue and every herb, and neglect justice and the love of God. These you ought to have done, without neglecting the others.*

LUKE 11:42

*But I know that you do not have the love of God within you. I have come in my Father's name, and you do not receive me. If another comes in his own name, you will receive him.*

JOHN 5:42–43

# Love God with All Your Heart, Soul, Mind, and Strength

JESUS CAME TO RESTORE HUMAN BEINGS to the kind of relationship with God and each other that we were created for. The most important thing he has to say about that restored relationship with God is that we were meant to love God with all our heart and soul and mind and strength. Jesus assumes that loving God means loving him for who he really is, and so his vision of who God is permeates all that he says.

### Know God, and Love Him for All That He Is

God is the Creator. He created human beings (Matt. 19:4) and all the universe (Mark 13:19). He sustains all he made, governing its smallest details of birds and lilies. "Are not two sparrows sold for a penny? And not one of them will fall to the ground apart from your Father" (Matt. 10:29; cf. 6:30). He is a God of wisdom (Luke 11:49) and righteousness (Matt. 6:33) and power (Matt. 22:29) and wrath (John 3:36) and compassion (Luke 15:20) and love (John 3:16). He is a person, not a mere force, and can be known as a Father who loves us as his children

(John 1:12; 16:27). Jesus commands us to love this God with all that we are for all that he is.

To love God we must know him. God would not be honored by groundless love. In fact, there is no such thing. If we do not know anything about God, there is nothing in our mind to awaken love. If love does not come from knowing God, there is no point in calling it love *for God*. There may be some vague attraction in our heart or some unfocused gratitude in our souls, but if they do not arise from knowing God, they are not love for God.

### Jesus: Revelation of God, Litmus Test of Our Love for God

Therefore, Jesus came into the world to make God known, that he might be truly loved. Jesus said to his disciples:

> "If you had known me, you would have known my Father also. From now on you do know him and have seen him." Philip said to him, "Lord, show us the Father, and it is enough for us." Jesus said to him, "Have I been with you so long, and you still do not know me, Philip? Whoever has seen me has seen the Father. How can you say, 'Show us the Father'?" (John 14:7–9)

Jesus so deeply reveals God that receiving Jesus becomes the test of loving God and having him as our Father. "If God were your Father, you would love me" (John 8:42). If we won't have Jesus, we don't have God. He made himself the measure of our knowing and loving God. "I know that you do not have the love of God within you. I have come in my Father's name, and you do not receive me. If another comes in his own name, you will receive him. How can you believe, when you receive glory from one another and do not seek the glory that comes from the only God?" (John 5:42–44).

In other words, Jesus is so fully God-reflecting and God-exalting that denying him means denying God. Jesus knows that his adversaries "do not have the love of God within [them]" because they do not receive him. "The one who rejects me rejects him who sent me" (Luke 10:16). If they loved God, they would love him. He makes God known more clearly and more fully than any other revelation. Therefore, it cannot be that one has love for God but rejects Jesus.

### "I Made Known to Them Your Name"

Therefore, if we are to love God, we must know him as he is revealed in Jesus. Before Jesus came, God awakened love by the revelation of himself in his word—which always pointed toward Jesus. "You search the Scriptures," Jesus said, "because you think that in them you have eternal life; and it is they that bear witness about me" (John 5:39). But now that Jesus has come, it is the revelation of Jesus himself that awakens love to God. "No one knows the Father except the Son and anyone to whom the Son chooses to reveal him" (Matt. 11:27).

This is what Jesus did for his disciples. He made God known. In Jesus's prayer in John 17, he says, "I made known to them your name, and I will continue to make it known" (v. 26). This is the long-awaited fulfillment of the prophecy in the Law of Moses: "The Lord your God will circumcise your heart and the heart of your offspring, so that you will love the Lord your God with all your heart and with all your soul, that you may live" (Deut. 30:6). Jesus is the fulfillment of that prophecy. Therefore, we cannot love God apart from the revelation of Jesus who changes our hearts to know God so that we see him as compellingly beautiful.

### Seeing and Savoring God as Compellingly Beautiful

The reason I use the phrase "compellingly beautiful" is to stress two things. One is that loving God is not a mere decision. You cannot merely decide to love classical music or country western music, much less God. The music must become compelling. If you don't love it, something must change inside you. That change makes it possible for the mind to experience the music with a compelling sense of its attractiveness. So it is with God. You do not merely decide to love him. Something changes inside you, and as a result, he becomes compellingly attractive. His glory—his beauty—compels your admiration and delight.

The other thing I am emphasizing in the phrase "compellingly beautiful" is that love for God is not essentially behavior but affection—not deeds but delight. God's glory becomes our supreme pleasure. We begin to prefer above all else to know him and see him and be with him and be like him. There are several important reasons for believing that love for God is most essentially an experience of the affections not behavior.

**Loving God Is First, Loving Our Neighbor Is Second**

First, Jesus distinguished the first and second commandment. He said, "You shall love the Lord your God with all your heart and with all your soul and with all your mind. This is the great and first commandment. And a second is like it: You shall love your neighbor as yourself" (Matt. 22:37–39). Therefore, loving God cannot be defined as loving our neighbor. They are different. Loving God is first. Loving our neighbor is second. The first is primary and depends on no greater obedience. The second is secondary and depends on loving God. They are not separated, for true love for God will always bring about love for people. But they are different. This means that the behaviors of love toward others are not the essential meaning of loving God. They are the overflow or fruit of loving God. Loving God is not the way we treat others. It is a compelling admiration and delight in God.

**"Their Heart Is Far from Me"**

Second, Jesus said to the Pharisees when they criticized the freedom of his disciples, "Well did Isaiah prophesy of you hypocrites, as it is written, 'This people honors me with their lips, but their heart is far from me; in vain do they worship me'" (Mark 7:6–7). Jesus says that external actions—even religious ones directed toward him—are not the essence of worship. They are not the essence of love. What happens in the heart is essential. The external behaviors will be pleasing to God when they flow from a heart that freely admires and delights in God—that is, when they flow from love for God.

## The Opposite of Loving God Is Hating and Despising

Third, Jesus said, "No one can serve two masters, for either he will hate the one and love the other, or he will be devoted to the one and despise the other. You cannot serve God and money" (Matt. 6:24). The opposite of loving God is "hating" and "despising." These are strong emotional words. They imply that the positive counterpart is also a strong emotion. So loving God is a strong inward emotion, not a mere outward action. But someone might say that "serve" is the key word here and implies that love for God is serving God. But that is not what it says. It says that the reason you cannot serve two masters (God and money) is that behind the behaviors of serving are two diametrically opposed passions: hate versus love, devotion versus despising. Jesus does not equate loving God with serving God. He roots serving God in loving God.

## An Adulterous Generation Seeks for a Sign

Fourth, when the Pharisees, who had no love for Jesus (or God, John 5:42), said to him, "Teacher, we wish to see a sign from you," Jesus replied in a way that shed light on the nature of loving God. He said, "An evil and adulterous generation seeks for a sign, but no sign will be given to it except the sign of the prophet Jonah" (Matt. 12:39). Why does he call them "adulterous" for seeking a sign? Because God was Israel's husband (Ezek. 16:8), and Jesus was God coming to reclaim his unfaithful wife. That's why he alludes to himself as the "bridegroom" (Matt. 25:1–13).

Why would a wife (Israel represented by her leaders) stand before her husband (Jesus) and demand a sign that he was her husband? Jesus says it is not owing to innocent ignorance. It's owing to an *adulterous* heart. In other words, Israel does not love her husband. She loves other suitors—like the praise of men (Matt. 23:6) and money (Luke 16:14). What this teaches us about the love Jesus commands us to have for God is that it is like a faithful wife's love for her husband—not mere external behavior but heartfelt affection and admiration and delight. It should be modeled not on the service of a slave but on the Song of Solomon. "We will exult and rejoice in you; we will extol your love more than wine; rightly do they love you" (Song 1:4).

### With Heart, Soul, Mind, and Strength

When Jesus commands that we love God with all of our heart, soul, mind, and strength, he means that every faculty and every capacity of our being should express the fullness of our affection for God—the fullness of all the ways that we treasure him. These four faculties and capacities overlap in meaning:[1] heart, soul, mind, and strength. But they are not identical. "Heart" highlights the center of our volitional and emotional life without excluding thought (Luke 1:51). "Soul" highlights our life as a whole, though sometimes distinguished from the body (Matt. 10:28). "Mind" highlights our thinking capacity. And "strength" highlights the capacity to make vigorous efforts both bodily and mentally (Mark 5:4; Luke 21:36).

The function of these faculties and capacities in relation to loving God is to demonstrate that love.[2] It may be that "heart" is mentioned

---

1   Concerning "heart" and "mind," consider that the one other place in the four Gospels where "mind" (διάνοια) occurs other than in the command to love God "with all your mind" (ἐν ὅλῃ τῇ διανοίᾳ σου) is Luke 1:51, where it is translated "thoughts" and happens in the "heart": "He has shown strength with his arm; he has scattered the proud in the *thoughts* [διανοίᾳ] of their hearts." So "mind" and "heart" are not always distinct. Concerning "heart" and "soul," consider that Jesus said, "Do not fear those who kill the body but cannot kill the *soul*. Rather fear him who can destroy both *soul* and body in hell" (Matt. 10:28). This implies that "soul" is the fullness of life or personhood apart from the body. Therefore, it would include the "heart," even though it is more.

2   In the command to love God "*with* all your heart and *with* all your soul and *with* all your mind and *with* all your strength" the Greek prepositions behind the English translation "with" are not the same each time this command is used in the Gospels. All three Gospels are quoting Deuteronomy

first because it is seen most especially as the *source* of love that is expressed through the soul (life), mind (thought), and strength (effort). Luke especially seems to take it that way, because he uses a different Greek preposition in the phrase "*with* all your heart" from what he uses in translating the other three phrases (see note 2). In any case, the point is that every faculty and capacity that we have should display at every moment that God is our supreme treasure.

### Every Capacity Treasures God above All Things

Loving God is most essentially treasuring God. And loving him with *all* the heart and *all* the soul and *all* the mind and *all* the strength means that every faculty and every capacity treasures God above all things and in such a way that our treasuring of any other thing is also a treasuring of God. In other words, there may be other good things that we may rightly treasure in some measure. But we may not treasure them in the place of God. We may only treasure them as expressions of treasuring God. If one of our human capacities finds pleasure in anyone or anything in such a way that this pleasure is not also a delight in God, then we have not loved God with all that capacity.

---

6:5 where the Hebrew preposition used is בְּ (בְּכָל־לְבָבְךָ וּבְכָל־נַפְשְׁךָ וּבְכָל־מְאֹדֶךָ). But Matthew 22:37 translates the preposition with ἐν every time (ἀγαπήσεις κύριον τὸν θεόν σου ἐν ὅλῃ τῇ καρδίᾳ σου καὶ ἐν ὅλῃ τῇ ψυχῇ σου καὶ ἐν ὅλῃ τῇ διανοίᾳ σου). Mark 12:30 translates it with ἐξ every time (ἀγαπήσεις κύριον τὸν θεόν σου ἐξ ὅλης τῆς καρδίας σου καὶ ἐξ ὅλης τῆς ψυχῆς σου καὶ ἐξ ὅλης τῆς διανοίας σου καὶ ἐξ ὅλης τῆς ἰσχύος σου). Because of this, I am inclined to see ἐν and ἐξ as two ways of expressing the same instrumental meaning of the Hebrew word בְּ. In other words, both more or less mean "by." The heart and soul and mind and strength are the instruments *by* which we demonstrate love for God. A slight variation to this interpretation is suggested by Luke's peculiar way of translating Deuteronomy 6:5. He uses the preposition ἐξ in relation to "heart" but ἐν in relation to "soul," "strength," and "mind (ἀγαπήσεις κύριον τὸν θεόν σου ἐξ ὅλης [τῆς] καρδίας σου καὶ ἐν ὅλῃ τῇ ψυχῇ σου καὶ ἐν ὅλῃ τῇ ἰσχύϊ σου καὶ ἐν ὅλῃ τῇ διανοίᾳ σου, καὶ τὸν πλησίον σου ὡς σεαυτόν, Luke 10:27). One wonders if Luke intended to say that the heart is the "source" (hence ἐξ), while the soul, mind, and strength are the spheres in which this love is demonstrated (hence ἐν). That would fit what I am stressing, namely, that love for God is a matter most essentially of the affections (of the heart) and secondarily demonstrated in the action of the life of mental and physical effort.

This way of seeing love for God is confirmed by the way God was loved in the Psalms. Jesus saw himself as the goal and focus and fulfillment of the Old Testament Scriptures, including the Psalms (Matt. 5:17; Luke 24:27; John 5:39). We would expect him to command us to have a love that extends and fulfills what the psalmists experienced. In the Psalms we read of love to God that is absolutely exclusive: "Whom have I in heaven but you? And there is nothing on earth that I desire besides you" (Ps. 73:25). "I say to the Lord, 'You are my Lord; I have no good apart from you'" (Ps. 16:2). What can this exclusivity possibly mean, since the psalmists also speak, for example, of loving other people (Ps. 16:3)?

We get a clue in Psalm 43:4 where the psalmist says, "Then I will go to the altar of God, to *God my exceeding joy.*" This last phrase ("my exceeding joy") is literally, "the gladness of my rejoicing" or "the joy of my exultation."[3] This points to God as the joy of all our joys. In all my rejoicing over all the good things that God has made, God himself is the heart of my joy, the gladness of my joy. In all my rejoicing in everything, there is a central rejoicing in God. Every joy that does not have God as the central gladness of the joy is a hollow joy and in the end will burst like a bubble. This is what led Augustine to pray, "He loves Thee too little who loves anything together with Thee, which he loves not for Thy sake."[4]

### Let Not Your Love Grow Cold

Therefore, I conclude that Jesus's command to love God with all our heart and soul and mind and strength means that every impulse and every act of every faculty and every capacity should be an expression of treasuring God above all things. Jesus warned that this most important of all commands would be widely forsaken in the last days.

---

3  The Hebrew phrase is two words for joy or rejoicing (שִׂמְחַת גִּילִי).

4  Augustine, *Confessions*, trans. R. S. Pine-Coffin (New York: Penguin, 1961), Book 10, Chapter XXIX.

"Because lawlessness is increased, most people's love will grow cold" (Matt. 24:12, NASB).

Beware lest your love for God grow cold in these days. Remember, we will love him to the degree that we know him. And remember that only Jesus can make him known in truth and fullness (Matt. 11:27). Therefore, look steadily at Jesus and pray that he would reveal God as compellingly beautiful. "Whoever has seen me has seen the Father" (John 14:9).

*Blessed are you when people hate you and when they
exclude you and revile you and spurn your name as
evil, on account of the Son of Man! Rejoice in that
day, and leap for joy, for behold, your reward is great
in heaven; for so their fathers did to the prophets.*

LUKE 6:22–23

*Behold, I have given you authority to tread on serpents
and scorpions, and over all the power of the enemy,
and nothing shall hurt you. Nevertheless, do not
rejoice in this, that the spirits are subject to you, but
rejoice that your names are written in heaven.*

LUKE 10:19–20

*The kingdom of heaven is like treasure hidden in a field,
which a man found and covered up. Then in his joy he
goes and sells all that he has and buys that field.*

MATTHEW 13:44

*These things I have spoken to you, that my joy may
be in you, and that your joy may be full.*

JOHN 15:11

# Rejoice and Leap
# for Joy

## Surprised by Joy

Jesus's command that we "rejoice . . . and leap for joy" (Luke 6:23; cf.
Matt. 5:12) is astonishing for so many reasons that it would take whole
books to unfold all of its surprising implications.[1] Half a century ago
C. S. Lewis responded to this surprise by looking at the inescapable
evidence in the Gospels. He wrote:

> If we consider the unblushing promises of reward and the staggering
> nature of the rewards promised in the Gospels, it would seem that our
> Lord finds our desires not too strong, but too weak. We are half-hearted
> creatures, fooling about with drink and sex and ambition when infinite
> joy is offered us, like an ignorant child who wants to go on making
> mud pies in a slum because he cannot imagine what is meant by the
> offer of a holiday at the sea. We are far too easily pleased.[2]

---

1   I wrote a little book to get people started on this path, *The Dangerous Duty of Delight* (Sisters,
    Ore.: Multnomah, 2001), and a bigger book to go deeper, *Desiring God: Meditations of a Christian
    Hedonist* (Sisters, Ore.: Multnomah, 2003).
2   C. S. Lewis, *The Weight of Glory, and Other Addresses* (Grand Rapids, Mich.: Eerdmans, 1965), 2.

In other words, the command that we be happy is not marginal or superfluous. It is a shocking wake-up call to people who are finding their happiness in all the wrong places. Jesus's solution to our love affair with sin is not merely that we tear out our sin-loving eyes (Matt. 5:29) but that we be mastered by joy in a new reality, namely, God.

### In His Joy He Goes and Sells All That He Has

Central to his preaching was the announcement that the kingdom of heaven had come near. Jesus meant that he was the King and that his work was the arrival of the saving rule of God (Luke 11:20; 17:20–21). So he told a very short parable to show how people come into the kingdom. He said, "The kingdom of heaven is like treasure hidden in a field, which a man found and covered up. Then *in his joy* he goes and sells all that he has and buys that field" (Matt. 13:44).

The parable means that God's saving presence and sovereign reign are so valuable that when people see them for what they really are—treasure hidden in the field—they count everything as nothing compared to the vast fortune of being part of that reign. And Jesus leaves no doubt about the internal experience of that "conversion." It is joy-driven. He says, "*In his joy* he goes and sells all that he has and buys that field."

It cannot be otherwise. Jesus came into the world with *good* news, not bad news. He does not call us to a willpower religion that feels only duty and no delight. He calls us to himself and to his Father. Therefore, he calls us to joy. Of course, it is not joy in things. Jesus is not preaching a health, wealth, and prosperity gospel—one of America's most lamentable exports to the world. It is joy in *God* and in his *Son*.

This is why the parable describes coming to the kingdom as "selling all." The command that we have joy does not encourage us to retreat one millimeter from the radical demand of Luke 14:33, "Any one of you who does not renounce all that he has cannot be my disciple." We renounce all those joy-giving things because we have found the treasure hidden in the field and we have been given eyes to see that this treasure—this glorious God—is infinitely more valuable than everything we possess or could possess in this world. This is why we renounce it all with joy.

## Self-Denial and the Quest for Joy

This is the meaning of self-denial. Renounce everything on earth in order that you might have Jesus. Sell all, so that you might have the kingdom. C. S. Lewis captures the spirit of Jesus's demand for self-denial when he says:

> The New Testament has lots to say about self-denial, but not about self-denial as an end in itself. We are told to deny ourselves and to take up our crosses in order that we may follow Christ; and nearly every description of what we shall ultimately find if we do so contains an appeal to desire.[3]

In other words, we deny ourselves because beyond self-denial is great reward. Jonathan Edwards goes even deeper in his analysis of how Jesus's demand for self-denial relates to his demand for joy.

> Self-denial will also be reckoned amongst the troubles of the godly. . . . But whoever has tried self-denial can give in his testimony that they never experience greater pleasure and joys than after great acts of self-denial. Self-denial destroys the very root and foundation of sorrow, and is nothing else but the lancing of a grievous and painful sore that effects a cure and brings abundance of health as a recompense for the pain of the operation.[4]

3  Ibid., 1.

4  Jonathan Edwards, "The Pleasantness of Religion," in *The Sermons of Jonathan Edwards: A Reader*, ed. Wilson H. Kimnach, Kenneth P. Minkema, and Douglas A. Sweeney (New Haven, Conn: Yale University Press, 1999), 23–24.

If this is true, then Jesus's demand for self-denial is another way of calling us to radically pursue our deepest and most lasting joy. They are not competing commands. They are like the command to be cancer-free and the command to have surgery.

### Our Joy Is Not Mainly in Prosperity but in Obedience and Pain

What astonishes us most immediately when Jesus says, "Rejoice . . . and leap for joy" is that he is saying it precisely in the context of pain. "Blessed are you when people hate you and when they exclude you and revile you and spurn your name as evil, on account of the Son of Man! Rejoice in that day, and leap for joy" (Luke 6:22–23). When Jesus commands that we rejoice, he has not forgotten the kind of world we live in. It is filled with suffering. And he promises that some of that suffering will fall on us as his disciples. "They will lay their hands on you and persecute you, delivering you up to the synagogues and prisons . . . and some of you they will put to death. You will be hated by all for my name's sake" (Luke 21:12, 16–17). "If they have called the master of the house Beelzebul, how much more will they malign those of his household" (Matt. 10:25). "If they persecuted me, they will also persecute you" (John 15:20).

Jesus has not forgotten that. In fact, he commands that we follow him in that painful path of love (see *Command #8*). Therefore, the joy he commands now ("in that day," Luke 6:23) is not chipper. It is not joy-lite. It is not superficial or marked with levity. This is the mistake of too many people and too many churches. They think that Jesus's demand for joy is a demand to tell jokes or weave slapstick into Christian corporate life. I don't smell the Jerusalem-bound Jesus in that atmosphere. Something has gone wrong.

What's wrong is that the aroma of suffering is missing. For Jesus the demand for joy is a way to live with suffering and to outlast suffering. Therefore, this joy is serious. It's the kind you fight for by cutting off your hand (Matt. 5:30) and selling your possessions (Matt. 13:44) and carrying a cross with Jesus to Calvary (Matt. 10:38–39). It has scars. It sings happy songs with tears. It remembers the dark hours and knows that more are coming. The road to heaven is a hard road, but it is not joyless.

## The Root of Holiness

Jesus's command that we rejoice is the key that unlocks his demand for holiness. What chokes the purifying power of spiritual life and destroys Jesus's would-be disciples are the "cares and riches and pleasures of life" (Luke 8:14). And what severs these strangling vines most decisively is the power of a superior pleasure. Jesus said that it is "in his joy" that the believer sells everything. In other words, it is his joy that cuts the stranglehold of sin.

Many Christians think stoicism is a good antidote to sensuality. It isn't. It is hopelessly weak and ineffective. Willpower religion usually fails, and even when it succeeds, it gets glory for the will, not for God. It produces legalists, not lovers. Jonathan Edwards saw the powerlessness of this approach and said:

We come with double forces against the wicked, to persuade them to a godly life. . . . The common argument is the profitableness of religion, but alas, the wicked man is not in pursuit of [moral] profit; 'tis pleasure he seeks. Now, then, we will fight with them with their own weapons.[5]

In other words, the pursuit of pleasure in God is not a compromise with the sensual world but is in fact the only power that can defeat the lusts of the age while producing lovers of God.

---

5   Ibid. The preceding and following paragraphs are adapted from John Piper, "A God-Entranced Vision of All Things: Why We Need Jonathan Edwards 300 Years Later," in *A God-Entranced Vision of All Things: The Legacy of Jonathan Edwards*, ed. John Piper and Justin Taylor (Wheaton, Ill.: Crossway, 2004), 29.

### The Root of Joy in Suffering Is Great Reward: Jesus

Jesus bases our present joy explicitly on the hope for great reward. "Rejoice in that day, and leap for joy, for behold, *your reward is great in heaven*" (Luke 6:23). He does not define the reward. But in the whole context of his life and message, the essential reward is fellowship with Jesus himself and with God the Father through him (John 17:3, 24).

There are several pointers to this understanding. For example, Jesus says to his disciples just before his death, "You have sorrow now, but *I will see you again* and your hearts will rejoice, and no one will take your joy from you" (John 16:22). The indomitable joy that Jesus promises is based on his own presence: "I will see you again."

Similarly Jesus says, "These things I have spoken to you, that my joy may be in you, and that your joy may be full" (John 15:11). This fullness of joy is mentioned by John the Baptist, and he bases it on the presence of Jesus, comparing Jesus to a bridegroom and himself to his friend: "The friend of the bridegroom, who stands and hears him, *rejoices greatly at the bridegroom's voice*. Therefore this joy of mine is now complete" (John 3:29).[6] John's "complete" joy is based on the presence of Jesus.

Therefore, I conclude that the essence of the reward that we count on to complete our joy is the fullness of the presence of Jesus experienced in the age to come. The reason that we can rejoice *now* is not only that we taste that future fellowship in hope but also that Jesus is with us now by his Spirit. He promised us, as he left to return to the Father, "I will not leave you as orphans; I will come to you" (John 14:18). "I am with you always, to the end of the age" (Matt. 28:20). He said that the Spirit of truth would come and make Jesus gloriously real to us even though he is physically absent. "When the Spirit of truth comes, he will . . .

---

6  The word "complete" (πεπλήρωται) translates the same Greek word (πληρόω) that is used in John 15:11 (πληρωθῇ), 16:24 (πεπληρωμένη), and 17:13 (πεπληρωμένην). Each refers to the joy of the disciples being full. Since John 3:29 and 16:24 base that joy on the presence of Jesus, we may assume the other two very likely refer to that as well.

glorify me, for he will take what is mine and declare it to you" (John 16:13–14). Therefore, even though we can't see Jesus now, we hope in him with great joy, and he sustains that joy by his continual presence.

### Jesus Purchases and Provides Our Joy

How then shall we obey this command of Jesus to "rejoice . . . and leap for joy"? We will take heart from the fact that Jesus offered himself to die for the forgiveness of our sins—the forgiveness of our failures to rejoice in him as we ought. At the Last Supper, he took the cup of wine and said, "This is my blood of the covenant, which is poured out for many *for the forgiveness of sins*" (Matt. 26:28). This is why he came in the first place: "The Son of Man came . . . to give his life as a ransom for many" (Mark 10:45). So our joy has this solid foundation: Jesus shed his blood so that our failures to rejoice in him might be forgiven.

Then we take heart that he promised to work for us in such a way that the very love that the Father has for the Son would be the experience of our own hearts. He prayed, "I made known to them your name, and I will continue to make it known, that the love with which you have loved me may be in them, and I in them" (John 17:26). Consider carefully that the love the Father has for the Son is not a merciful, forgiving love. The Son has no sin and no flaw. He needs no mercy. The love the Father has for the Son is nothing but infinitely joyful admiration and fellowship. This is what Jesus says will be in us. Therefore, I take this to be a promise to work in us to make sure that our joy will be the very joy that the Father has in the Son. We are not left to ourselves to rejoice in Jesus as we ought. Jesus is committed to making it happen.

### The Command to Rejoice in Jesus as a Means to Glorify Jesus

Finally, I conclude from Jesus's commitment to glorify the Father and the Son (John 17:1) that his intention to sustain our joy in him is part of what it means for us to glorify the Father and the Son. In other words, I conclude that rejoicing in the Father and the Son is essential to glorifying God. If this is true, we have a powerful confirmation of the duty to pursue our joy—namely, because it displays the glory of God. This truth should make us tremble at the horror of not rejoicing in God. We should quake at the fearful lukewarmness of our hearts. We should waken to the truth that it is a treacherous sin not to pursue our fullest satisfaction in God. There is one final word for finding delight in the creation more than in the Creator: *treason*. What a motivation this should be to obey the command of Jesus, "Rejoice . . . and leap for joy."

## There Is No Limit to the Intensity of Joy in Jesus

It is true that a passion for happiness can be misdirected to wrong objects, but it cannot be too strong. Jonathan Edwards argued for this in a sermon that he preached on Song of Solomon 5:1. The text reads, "Eat, friends, drink, and be drunk with love!" Edwards drew out of the text the following doctrine: "Persons need not and ought not to set any bounds to their spiritual and gracious appetites." Instead, he says, they ought

> to be endeavoring by all possible ways to inflame their desires and to obtain more spiritual pleasures. . . . Our hungerings and thirstings after God and Jesus Christ and after holiness can't be too great for the value of these things, for they are things of infinite value. . . . [Therefore] endeavor to promote spiritual appetites by laying yourself in the way of allurement. . . .[7] There is no such thing as excess in our taking of this spiritual food. There is no such virtue as temperance in spiritual feasting.[8]

7  Quoted from an unpublished sermon, "Sacrament Sermon on Canticles 5:1" (circa 1729), edited version by Kenneth Minkema in association with *The Works of Jonathan Edwards*, Yale University.

8  Jonathan Edwards, "The Spiritual Blessings of the Gospel Represented by a Feast," in *Sermons and Discourses, 1723–1729*, ed. Kenneth Minkema, in *The Works of Jonathan Edwards*, Vol. 14 (New Haven, Conn.: Yale University Press, 1997), 286. The preceding two paragraphs are adapted from "A God-Entranced Vision of All Things," 27–28.

Therefore, be encouraged that God made you to rejoice in him. Do not settle for any lesser joy. Lay yourself in the way of allurement. That is, fix your eyes on the all-satisfying treasure of Jesus Christ who loved us and gave his life as a ransom for our everlasting joy.

*And do not fear those who kill the body but cannot kill the soul.*
*Rather fear him who can destroy both soul and body in hell.*

MATTHEW 10:28

*But as for these enemies of mine, who did not want me to reign*
*over them, bring them here and slaughter them before me.*

LUKE 19:27

*Then he will say to those on his left, "Depart from me,*
*you cursed, into the eternal fire prepared for the devil*
*and his angels." . . . And these will go away into eternal*
*punishment, but the righteous into eternal life.*

MATTHEW 25:41, 46

# Fear Him Who Can Destroy
# Both Soul and Body in Hell

## The Descriptions Jesus Uses for Hell

Jesus spoke of hell more than anyone else in the Bible. He referred to it as a place of "outer darkness" where "there will be weeping and gnashing of teeth" (Matt. 8:12). In other words, all the joys that we associate with light will be withdrawn, and all the fears that we associate with darkness will be multiplied. And the result will be an intensity of misery that makes a person grind his teeth in order to bear it.

Jesus also refers to hell as a "fiery furnace" where law-breakers will be thrown at the end of the age when he returns. "The Son of Man will send his angels, and they will gather out of his kingdom all causes of sin and all law-breakers, and throw them into the fiery furnace. In that place there will be weeping and gnashing of teeth" (Matt. 13:41–42). He calls it "the hell of fire" (Matt. 5:22), "eternal fire prepared for the devil and his angels" (Matt. 25:41), "unquenchable fire" (Mark 9:43), "eternal punishment" (Matt. 25:46).

This last description—"eternal punishment"—is especially heart-rending and fearful because it is contrasted with "eternal life." "These will go away into eternal punishment, but the righteous into eternal life." In this contrast we hear the tragedy of loss as well as suffering and endlessness. Just as "eternal life" will be a never-ending experience of pleasure in God's presence, so "eternal punishment" will be a never-ending experience of misery under God's wrath (John 3:36; 5:24).

### Hell Is Not a Mere Natural Consequence of Bad Choices

The word *wrath* is important for understanding what Jesus meant by hell. Hell is not simply the natural consequence of rejecting God. Some people say this in order to reject the thought that God sends people there. They say that people send themselves there. That is true. People make choices that lead to hell. But it is not the whole truth. Jesus says these choices are really deserving of hell. "Whoever says, 'You fool!' will be liable to [that is, guilty of, or deserving of] the hell of fire" (Matt. 5:22). That is why he calls hell "punishment" (Matt. 25:46). It is not a mere self-imposed natural consequence (like cigarette smoking leading to lung cancer); it is the penalty of God's wrath (like a judge sentencing a criminal to hard labor).

The images Jesus uses of how people come to be in hell do not suggest natural consequence but the exercise of just wrath. For example, he pictures the servant of a master who has gone on a journey. The servant says, "My master is delayed," and he "begins to beat his fellow servants and eats and drinks with drunkards." Then Jesus says (referring to his own sudden second coming), "The master of that servant will come on a day when he does not expect him and at an hour he does not know and will cut him in pieces and put him with the hypocrites. In that place there will be weeping and gnashing of teeth" (Matt. 24:48–51). This picture represents legitimate and holy rage followed by punishment. Jesus will "put" (θήσει) him with the hypocrites.

Jesus told another story to illustrate his departure from the earth and his return in judgment. He said, "A nobleman went into a far country to receive for himself a kingdom and then return. . . . But his citizens hated him and sent a delegation after him, saying, 'We do not want this man to reign over us'" (Luke 19:12, 14). When the nobleman returned in his kingly power to reward those who had trusted and honored him with their lives, he punished those who rejected his kingship: "As for these enemies of mine, who did not want me to reign over them, bring them here and slaughter them before me" (Luke 19:27). Again the picture is not one of hell as a disease resulting from bad habits but of a king expressing holy wrath against those who rebuff his gracious rule.

## Fear Him Who Can Destroy Both Soul and Body in Hell

This is why Jesus said, "Fear him who can destroy both soul and body in hell" (Matt. 10:28). The fear he commands is not fear of hell as a natural consequence of bad habits, but of God as a holy judge who sentences guilty sinners to hell. This command to fear God as a holy judge seems discouraging at first. It seems as though following Jesus means leading a life of anxiety that God is angry with us and is ready to punish us at the slightest misstep. But that is not what Jesus calls us to experience as we follow him.

It seems amazing to us, perhaps, that immediately following his warning to "fear him who can destroy both soul and body in hell," Jesus says something designed to give us deep peace and full confidence under God's fatherly care. The very next sentence goes like this: "Are not two sparrows sold for a penny? And not one of them will fall to the ground apart from your Father. But even the hairs of your head are all numbered. *Fear not*, therefore; you are of more value than many sparrows" (Matt. 10:29–31).

In the same breath Jesus says, "Fear God who casts into hell" and "Do not fear because God is your Father who values you more than the sparrows and knows your smallest need." In fact, the all-providing fatherly care of God is one of Jesus's sweetest and most pervasive teachings:

> Look at the birds of the air: they neither sow nor reap nor gather into barns, and yet your heavenly Father feeds them. Are you not

of more value than they? . . . Therefore do not be anxious, saying, "What shall we eat?" or "What shall we drink?" or "What shall we wear?" For the Gentiles seek after all these things, and your heavenly Father knows that you need them all. (Matt. 6:26, 31–32)

### God Is to Be Feared, and God Is to Be Trusted

How does Jesus mean for us to experience these two truths about God—he is to be feared, and he is to be trusted? It won't do to simply say that "fear of God" means "reverence for God" rather than "being afraid of him." That does not fit with the words, "Fear him who, after he has killed, has authority to cast into hell. Yes, I tell you, fear him!" (Luke 12:5). Of course, it is true that we should reverence God, that is, stand in awe of his holiness and power and wisdom. But there is also a real fear of him that can coexist with sweet peace and trust in him.

The key is that God himself is the one who removes his wrath from us. Our peace does not come from our removing the God of wrath from our thinking, but from his removing his wrath from us. He has done that by sending Jesus to die in our place so that, for everyone who believes in Jesus, God's wrath is taken away. "As Moses lifted up the serpent in the wilderness," Jesus said, "so must the Son of Man be lifted up [on the cross to die], that whoever believes in him may have eternal life [not wrath]. . . . Whoever does not obey the Son shall not see life, but the *wrath* of God remains on him" (John 3:14–15, 36). When Jesus cried out on the cross, "My God, my God, why have you forsaken me?" (Mark 15:34), he was experiencing the wrath of God's abandonment in our place—for he had never done anything to deserve being forsaken by God. And when he said finally from the cross, "It is finished" (John 19:30), he meant that the price of our salvation—our deliverance from God's wrath and into all God's blessings—had been paid in full.

Jesus had said that he came "to give his life as a ransom for many" (Matt. 20:28), and now the full ransom was paid, and the work of absorbing and removing the wrath of God was finished. Now, he says, everyone who believes has everlasting fellowship with God and is fully assured that the wrath of the Judge is gone. "He does not come into judgment, but has passed from death to life" (John 5:24).

## Fearing Unbelief

What then is left to fear? The answer is *unbelief*. For those who follow Jesus, fearing God means fearing the terrible prospect of not trusting the one who paid such a price for our peace. In other words, one of the means that God uses to keep us peacefully trusting in Jesus is the fear of what God would do to us if we did not believe. The reason we do not live in the discomfort of constant fear is because we believe. That is, we rest in the all-sufficient work of Jesus and in our Father's sovereign care. But at those moments when unbelief tempts us, a holy fear rises and warns us what a foolish thing it would be to distrust the one who loved us and gave his Son to die for our anxiety-free joy.

## Hugging God's Neck Takes Away Fear

One illustration has helped me see how this experience works. When my oldest son Karsten was about eight years old, we went to visit a man who owned a huge dog. When we opened the door, the dog looked at my son almost eye to eye. That's a fearful prospect for a little boy. But we were assured the dog was harmless and that he really liked children. After a while we sent Karsten to the car to get something we forgot. As he ran across the yard, the dog gave a deep growl and loped up behind him. The owner leaned out of the door and called to Karsten, "You better just walk; he doesn't like it when people run away from him."

A huge dog that loves children but does not like people to run away from him is what God is like. If we will trust him and enjoy him and throw our arms around his strong neck, he will be everything we ever hoped for in a friend. But if we decide that there are other things we want more than him and turn to run away, he will get very angry. Jesus said this as clearly as we could wish in Luke 19:27, "But as for these enemies of mine, who did not want me to reign over them, bring them here and slaughter them before me." Fearing God means fearing the terrible prospect of running away from the merciful, all-providing, all-satisfying reign of King Jesus.

## Hell Means That Sin Is Unfathomably Serious

Jesus's command that we fear the one who can destroy both soul and body in hell teaches us to see sin as more serious than we ever dreamed. The reason so many people feel that eternal hell is an unjust punishment for our sin is that they do not see sin as it really is. This is because they do not see God as he really is. When Jesus tells us what he will say to those who are going to hell he says, "Then will I declare to them, 'I never knew you; depart from me, you workers of *lawlessness*'" (Matt. 7:23). They are workers of "lawlessness." That is, they break God's law. Sin is against God first, then man.

Therefore, the seriousness of sin arises from what it says about God. God is infinitely worthy and honorable. But sin says the opposite. Sin says that other things are more desirable and more worthy. How serious is this? The seriousness of a crime is determined, in part, by the dignity of the person and the office being dishonored. If the person is infinitely worthy and infinitely honorable and infinitely desirable and holds an office of infinite dignity and authority, then rebuffing him is an infinitely outrageous crime. Therefore, it deserves an infinite punishment. The intensity of Jesus's words about hell is not an overreaction to small offenses. It is a witness to the infinite worth of God and to the outrageous dishonor of human sin.

## The Precious Gift of Fear

Therefore, give heed to Jesus's clear command to fear the one who can destroy both soul and body in hell. Hear it as a great mercy. What a wonderful thing it is that Jesus warns us. He does not leave us ignorant of the wrath to come. He not only warns. He rescues. This is the best effect of fear: it wakens us to our need for help and points us to the all-sufficient Redeemer, Jesus. Let it have this effect on you. Let it lead you to Jesus who says to everyone who believes in him, "Fear not, little flock, for it is your Father's good pleasure to give you the kingdom" (Luke 12:32).

*fear of god*

*II TIM 1:7*

*Ps 27:1*

*Prov 19:23*

*II Thes 1:2*

*hearing aide*

*The hour is coming, and is now here, when the true worshipers*
*will worship the Father in spirit and truth, for the Father*
*is seeking such people to worship him. God is spirit, and*
*those who worship him must worship in spirit and truth.*

JOHN 4:23–24

*Then Jesus said to him, "Be gone, Satan! For it is written,*
*'You shall worship the Lord your God*
*and him only shall you serve.'"*

MATTHEW 4:10

*This people honors me with their lips,*
*but their heart is far from me;*
*in vain do they worship me,*
*teaching as doctrines the commandments of men.*

MATTHEW 15:8–9

*No one can serve two masters, for either he will hate the*
*one and love the other, or he will be devoted to the one*
*and despise the other. You cannot serve God and money.*

MATTHEW 6:24

COMMAND #12

# Worship God in Spirit and Truth

*Handwritten margin notes:*
*Calvin & Hobbes*
*Col 3:16*
*Rom I*
*Eph 2:8-10*
*Prov 3:5·6*

EVERYONE IN THE WORLD WORSHIPS SOMETHING. From the most religious to the most secular, all people value something high enough to build their lives around it. It may be God, or it may be money. But what makes it worship is the driving power of some cherished treasure that shapes our emotions and will and thought and behavior. Into this universal experience of worship Jesus commanded, "Worship [God] in *spirit* and *truth*" (John 4:24). In other words, bring your experience of worship into conformity with what is *true* about God, and let your *spirit* be authentically awakened and moved by that truth.

## The Hour Is Coming and Is Now Here

When he said this, he was talking to a Samaritan woman near her hometown. She had challenged him about the difference between places where Samaritans and Jews worship. She said, "Our fathers worshiped on this mountain, but you say that in Jerusalem is the place where people ought to worship" (John 4:20). Jesus responded by turning her attention away from geography to something astonishing that was happening in her very presence. He said, "Woman, believe me, the

81

hour is coming when neither on this mountain nor in Jerusalem will you worship the Father. . . . The hour is coming, *and is now here*, when the true worshipers will worship the Father in spirit and truth" (John 4:21, 23). This is a radical statement—to say that the hour *is now here* when worship in Jerusalem would cease! What did he mean?

Jesus made the breathtaking claim to be the long-awaited Jewish Messiah. The woman said to him, "I know that Messiah is coming (he who is called Christ). When he comes, he will tell us all things." Jesus responded, "I who speak to you am he" (John 4:25–26). So when Jesus says that the time "is now here" when we will no longer worship in Jerusalem, he meant that the kingdom of the Messiah has dawned and there is going to be a radical break in the way people worship.

### "Destroy This Temple, and in Three Days I Will Raise It Up"

The reason is that Jesus intended to take the place of the temple himself. In other words, the "place" where worship would happen—the "place" where people would meet God from now on—would be Jesus, not the temple in Jerusalem. He communicated this in several ways. For example, he stood in the temple and said, "Destroy this temple, and in three days I will raise it up" (John 2:19). The people were astonished and said, "It has taken forty-six years to build this temple, and will you raise it up in three days?" But the Gospel writer explained, "He was speaking about the temple of his body" (John 2:21). In other words, Jesus meant that when he was raised from the dead, he would be the new "temple"—the new meeting place with God.

Jesus said something almost as startling when he was criticized for letting his disciples pick grain and eat it on the Sabbath. Jesus's response to this criticism was to point out that David, the king of Israel, had fed his band of men with the bread of God's house that was only designed for the priests to eat. He made the connection with himself and his band of men by saying, "I tell you, something greater than the temple is here" (Matt. 12:6). In other words, "The

Messiah, the son of David, is here, and he himself is going to take the place of the temple."

### Not in This Mountain or in Jerusalem, but in Spirit and in Truth

So when Jesus said to the Samaritan woman, "The hour is coming, and *is now here*, when the true worshipers will worship the Father in spirit and truth," he meant that a whole new approach to God in worship had come with the coming of the Messiah himself. No longer would geography be relevant: "Neither on this mountain nor in Jerusalem will you worship the Father." Instead, what takes the place of external geographic concerns are internal spiritual concerns: "Those who worship him must worship in spirit and truth." The external places of Samaria and Jerusalem are replaced with the spiritual realities of "spirit and truth." What matters now is not where you worship but whether you worship God in accordance with the truth and whether your spirit is authentically awakened and moved by that truth.

### All Worship Should Be through Jesus and of Jesus

The key new truth is that worship now happens through Jesus. He is the temple where we encounter God. This is true first because he poured out his blood "for the forgiveness of sins" (Matt. 26:28) and "gave his life as a ransom for many" (Mark 10:45) and opened the way through his own crucified and risen body for us to be reconciled with God (John 3:16, 36). There is no way that sinners could offer acceptable worship to God without having Jesus's blood as a go-between with God.

It's true that worship now happens through Jesus because he himself is God. He is not simply the mediator of worship between us and the Father; he is also the one to *be* worshiped. He made this claim indirectly and directly. He forgave sins, which only God can do (Mark 2:5–11). He accepted worship from his disciples (Matt. 14:33; 28:9). He claimed eternal preexistence with God: "Truly, truly, I say to you, before Abraham was, I am" (John 8:58). He said he was one with the

Father: "Whoever has seen me has seen the Father" (John 14:9). "I and the Father are one" (John 10:30). So all should "honor the Son, just as they honor the Father" (John 5:23). Therefore, all worship "in truth" will be worship of Jesus *and* through Jesus. For "whoever does not honor the Son does not honor the Father who sent him" (John 5:23).

### Worship in Spirit

What about the phrase "in spirit"? "The hour is coming, and is now here, when the true worshipers will worship the Father *in spirit*" (John 4:23). Some interpreters take this to refer to God's Holy Spirit. I have taken it to refer to *our* spirit. But probably these two interpretations are not far apart in Jesus's mind. In John 3:6 Jesus connects God's Spirit and our spirit in a remarkable way. He says, "That which is born of the Spirit is spirit." In other words, until the Holy Spirit quickens our spirit with the birth of new life, our spirit is so dead and unresponsive, it does not even qualify as spirit. Only that which is born of the Spirit is (a living) spirit. So when Jesus says that true worshipers worship the Father "in spirit," he means that true worship comes only from spirits made alive and sensitive by the quickening of the Spirit of God.[1]

This "spirit" is essential in worship. Otherwise worship is dead. Or to use Jesus's phrase, it is "in vain." "This people honors me with their lips, but their heart is far from me; *in vain* do they worship me" (Matt. 15:8–9). A heart (and spirit) alive and engaged with God is essential. Jesus is contrasting authentic worship in spirit and truth with external worship that focuses on Samaria and Jerusalem. What makes it authentic is not only that the worshiping *mind* grasps the truth of Jesus, but also that the worshiping *spirit* experiences awakening and is moved by the truth that the mind knows. A person who has no affections for God awakened by the truth of Jesus is not worshiping "in spirit and

---

1  This paragraph is adapted from John Piper, *Desiring God: Meditations of a Christian Hedonist*, revised and expanded edition (Sisters, Ore.: Multnomah, 2003), 82.

truth."[2] And a person with great affections built on false views of God is not worshiping "in spirit and truth." Jesus commands both: worship in spirit and in truth. *The highest form of worship is obedience to God* (handwritten annotation)

## All of Life Is Worship

One implication of this vision of worship is that it applies to all of life as well as to services of corporate worship. The essence of worship lies in our mind's true vision of God and our spirit's authentic affections for God. This means that whenever we display the worth of God by words or actions that flow from a spirit that treasures him as he really is, we are worshiping in spirit and in truth. We may be at work or at home or at church. It doesn't matter. What matters is that we see the glory of God in Jesus (truth), and we treasure him above all else (spirit), and then we overflow by treating others with self-sacrificing love for their good. Few things display the beauty of God more. For followers of Jesus, therefore, all of life should be this kind of worship.

This is powerfully illustrated by the connection Jesus makes between worshiping God and serving God. When Satan tempted Jesus to worship him, Jesus responded, "Be gone, Satan! For it is written, 'You shall *worship* the Lord your God and him only shall you *serve*'" (Matt. 4:10). Serving was often attached to worshiping as an outward expression of religious ministry in the temple. But now the temple is Jesus. How is the "service" of worship transformed?

## You Cannot Serve God and Money

We get a surprising glimpse of what service[3] to God means for Jesus in Matthew 6:24. He said, "No one can serve two masters, for either he will hate the one and love the other, or he will be devoted to the one

---

2  See chapter 3, "Worship: The Feast of Christian Hedonism" in *Desiring God* for a fuller defense of this statement and how it fits with the reality that our feelings are unstable, sometimes high and sometimes low.

3  The word for "serve" in Matthew 6:24 (δουλεύω) is not the same as the word for "serve" in Matthew 4:10 (λατρεύω). The latter usually refers to the religious activity in the temple. The former

and despise the other. You cannot serve God and money." The surprising thing here is that serving God is compared to serving money. But how do you serve money? Not by helping money or meeting money's needs. You serve money by treasuring it so much that you shape your whole life to benefit from what money can do for you.

So it is with God in the way Jesus sees the service of worship. We do not help God or meet God's needs ("The Son of Man came *not* to be served," Mark 10:45). Rather we serve God by treasuring him so much that we shape our whole life so as to benefit from what he can do for us. And, unlike money, what God can do for us above all other treasures is *be* for us everything we have ever longed for.

### The Infinite Worth of God in Jesus

Therefore, all of life is service to God. That is, all of life is shaped by our passion to maximize our experience of the supreme worth of God in Jesus. So we end where we began. All the world worships something. From the most religious to the most secular, all people value something high enough to build their lives around it—even if unconsciously. Jesus commands that every person in the world build his life around the infinite worth of God in Jesus. Consider what you are worshiping. Then ask Jesus to open your eyes to the *truth* of God's supreme worth and to awaken your *spirit* to treasure him above all.

---

usually refers to what a slave does for a master. My point is that it is precisely the newness of Jesus's situation that makes plain how even the "slave" kind of service is worship in a new way.

*And he told them a parable to the effect that they ought always to pray and not lose heart.*

LUKE 18:1

*Pray for those who persecute you.*

MATTHEW 5:44

*But when you pray, go into your room and shut the door and pray to your Father who is in secret.*

MATTHEW 6:6

*And when you pray, do not heap up empty phrases as the Gentiles do.*

MATTHEW 6:7

*Pray then like this: "Our Father in heaven, hallowed be your name."*

MATTHEW 6:9

*Pray earnestly to the Lord of the harvest to send out laborers into his harvest.*

MATTHEW 9:38

*How much more will the heavenly Father give the Holy Spirit to those who ask him!*

LUKE 11:13

*Ask, and you will receive, that your joy may be full.*

JOHN 16:24

*Whatever you ask in my name, this I will do, that the Father may be glorified in the Son.*

JOHN 14:13

COMMAND #13

# Always Pray and
# Do Not Lose Heart

JESUS INTENDS TO CREATE A PRAYING PEOPLE. His command is clear, and the issue is so important that he tells us *why, how, for whom,* and *what* we are to pray. And though we might think that the Son of God would be above the need to pray, he sets the example for us, as a perfect human being, by rising early in the morning to pray (Mark 1:35) and seeking times alone to pray (Matt. 14:23) and sometimes spending the whole night in prayer (Luke 6:12) and, in the end, preparing for his suffering by prayer (Luke 22:41–42).

## Why? For the Glory of God

*Why* did Jesus think prayer was so important for his followers? The reason is that prayer corresponds with two great purposes of God that Jesus came to accomplish: God's glory and our joy. Jesus said, "Whatever you *ask* in my name, this I will do, that the Father may be *glorified* in the Son" (John 14:13). Prayer is designed by God to display his fullness Psalms and our need. Prayer glorifies God because it puts us in the position of the thirsty and God in the position of the all-supplying fountain.[1]

---

1  I do not mean to imply that prayer is only asking and not also thanking and praising and confessing. But this chapter simply focuses on prayer as petition, which is the main way Jesus talks about it.

Jesus knew the Psalms and read Psalm 50:15 where God, like Jesus, commands that we pray for help and shows that this gives glory to God: "Call upon me in the day of trouble; I will deliver you, and you shall glorify me." Prayer is designed as a way of relating to God, so that it is clear *we* get the help and *he* gets the glory. Jesus said that he had come to glorify his Father. "I glorified you on earth, having accomplished the work that you gave me to do" (John 17:4). Part of what God had given him to do was to teach his disciples to pray, because when we pray in Jesus's name, "the Father [is] glorified in the Son" (John 14:13).

### Why? For Our Joy

The other purpose Jesus came to accomplish was our joy. Everything he taught was aimed to free us from eternal joy-killers and fill us with the only joy that lasts—joy in God. "These things I speak in the world, that they may have my joy fulfilled in themselves" (John 17:13). One of his most pervasive teachings for our joy was the teaching on prayer, and he made his motive explicit: our joy. "Ask, and you will receive, that your joy may be full" (John 16:24). The most wonderful thing about prayer, as Jesus commands it, is that it is perfectly suited to secure God's glory and our joy.

These are great incentives for us to obey Jesus's command that we "always . . . pray and not lose heart" (Luke 18:1). To these he adds other incentives, because he is so eager for us to feel hopeful in our praying. He says, for example, "Your Father knows what you need before you ask him" (Matt. 6:8). The point is that we don't need to multiply pious phrases in prayer hoping that we might awaken God's attention or inclination. He is our caring Father, and he is all-knowing. He will answer. Then Jesus underlines God's readiness to answer by comparing him to a human father, but pointing out that God is far more eager to answer than human fathers.

> Ask, and it will be given to you; seek, and you will find; knock, and it will be opened to you. . . . Which one of you, if his son asks him

for bread, will give him a stone? Or if he asks for a fish, will give him a serpent? If you then, who are evil, know how to give good gifts to your children, how much more will your Father who is in heaven give good things to those who ask him! (Matt. 7:7–11)

So in answer to the question *why* we should pray, Jesus says: because God is very inclined to hear and answer our prayers—which is not surprising, since prayer is designed to magnify God's glory while sustaining our joy in him.

## How? Simplicity

*no hail marys + our fathers*

*How* then are we to pray? The readiness of God to answer and his perfect knowledge of what we need before we ask means that we should be simple in our wording and reject anything like a repetitive mantra that would imply God is aroused by our monotonous incantations. "When you pray, do not heap up empty phrases as the Gentiles do, for they think that they will be heard for their many words. Do not be like them, for your Father knows what you need before you ask him" (Matt. 6:7–8).

## How? With Perseverance

This does not mean there is no place for perseverance in prayer. In fact, Jesus is explicit in telling us to be persistent in prayer over a long period of time, if necessary, as we seek some crucial breakthrough in the cause of righteousness for his glory (Luke 11:5–8; 18:1–8). The point is not to finally break God's resistance but to discover, by patient prayer, God's wisdom as to the way and time the prayer should be answered. He is not disinclined to help his children and glorify his name. He simply knows better than we do when and how the answer should come. Therefore, our persistence in prayer shows both our confidence that God is our only hope and that he will act in the best way and the best time in response to our persistent pleas.

## How? Through His Death and in His Name

The confidence that we have in prayer is owing to Jesus. He did not just teach us to pray—he died for us and rose again to remove insuperable obstacles to prayer. Without the death of Jesus, our sins would not be forgiven (Matt. 26:28) and the wrath of God would still be against us (John 3:36). In that condition, we could expect no answers to prayer from God. Therefore, Jesus is the ground of all our prayers. This is why he taught us to pray in his name. "Whatever you ask *in my name*, this I will do, that the Father may be glorified in the Son" (John 14:13; cf. 16:23–24). Ending our prayers "in Jesus's name, amen" is not a mere tradition; it is an affirmation of faith in Jesus as the only hope of access to God.

## How? With Faith

This implies that Jesus does indeed want us to pray *with faith*. "Whatever you ask in prayer, you will receive, *if you have faith*" (Matt. 21:22; cf. Mark 11:24). Some have taken verses like this and turned them into the power of positive thinking. They believe that if we can be confident that something will happen, it will indeed happen. But that would be faith in our faith. When Jesus teaches us how to "move mountains" by faith, he says explicitly, "Have faith *in God*" (Mark 11:22). There seem to be times when God makes clear to us that his will is to do a particular thing. In that case we may be perfectly confident that very thing will be done. In that sense Jesus says to us, "Whatever you ask in prayer, believe that you have received it, and it will be yours" (Mark 11:24). It is God who does it, and our belief rests on him and his revealed will. Otherwise, we would be God, and he would run the universe according to our will, not his.

Jesus makes it clear that there is a kind of filter that our prayers must pass through in order to be sure that they are according to God's will. "If you abide in me, and my words abide in you, ask whatever you wish, and it will be done for you" (John 15:7). Here Jesus's promise is more clearly qualified than in Mark 11:24.[2] Are we trusting in him as our all-supplying vine? And are his words shaping our minds and hearts so that we discern how to pray according to his wisdom?

Praying in faith does not always mean being sure that the very thing we ask will happen. But it does always mean that because of Jesus we trust God to hear us and help us in the way that seems best to him. It may mean that he gives us just what we ask, or that he gives us something better. Will a father give a son a stone if he asks him for bread? No. But neither will he give him bread if it is moldy. He may give him cake. Sometimes God's answers will overwhelm us with their excess. Other times they taste more like medicine than food and will test our faith that this medicine is really what we need.

### How? Not for the Praise of Others

In view of all this, it should be clear that the reward of prayer comes from God, not man. But Jesus shows us that the human heart is capable of turning the most beautifully Godward act in a manward direction and ruining it. He warns us:

> When you pray, you must not be like the hypocrites. For they love to stand and pray in the synagogues and at the street corners, that they may be seen by others. Truly, I say to you, they have received their reward. But when you pray, go into your room and shut the

---

2    Even in the context of Mark 11:24, there is an implied qualification of the promise, "Whatever you ask in prayer, believe that you have received it, and it will be yours." The very next verse says, "And whenever you stand praying, forgive, if you have anything against anyone, so that your Father also who is in heaven may forgive you your trespasses" (Mark 11:25). This means that even if you ask for forgiveness and believe that you have it, you will *not* have it unless you forgive the one who has something against you. This makes it clear that the promise is not as sweeping as it sounds at first. There are limits. You cannot simply manipulate God by the power of being confident in what you ask. There are moral guidelines. This is what Jesus is saying with the condition, "If . . . my words abide in you, ask whatever you wish, and it will be done for you" (John 15:7). The words of Jesus shape the attitude and content of our prayers.

door and pray to your Father who is in secret. And your Father who
sees in secret will reward you. (Matt. 6:5–6)

Jesus hates hypocrisy—like appearing to love God when what you really
love is the praise of man. His most disparaging language was reserved
for "hypocrites." He called them children of hell, "blind guides," "full
of greed and self-indulgence," "whitewashed tombs" (Matt. 23:15, 24,
25, 27). The command is unmistakable: "Beware of the leaven of the
Pharisees, which is hypocrisy" (Luke 12:1). The implication for prayer
(and fasting and almsgiving, Matt. 6:1–4, 16–18) is: Treasure God, and
all that he will be for you, in prayer, but do not treasure the praise of
man. And, most of all, do not turn a God-treasuring act of prayer into
a man-treasuring act of hypocrisy.

**For Whom?**

*For whom* does Jesus command that we pray? Clearly ourselves. Not
because we are deserving. Prayer has nothing to do with deserving.
It's all mercy. We pray for ourselves because we are weak. We are so
prone to sin and utterly dependent on preserving grace to sustain our
flawed obedience. "Pray then like this," Jesus said, "lead us not into
temptation, but deliver us from evil" (Matt. 6:9, 13). That is a prayer
for ourselves first, since we know our own frailty and vulnerability
better than anyone. Then it is a prayer for the other followers of Jesus
and the world.

No one is to be excluded from our prayers. When Jesus tells us to
pray, "Hallowed be your name" (Matt. 6:9), he means that we should
pray this for anyone who does not yet hallow God's name. And if our
selfish hearts should think of some adversary that we do not like, Jesus
is unsparing—these too must be blessed in our prayers. "Love your enemies and pray for those who persecute you" (Matt. 5:44); "bless those
who curse you, pray for those who abuse you" (Luke 6:28). None must
be excluded from our love, and none may be excluded from our prayers.

**What?**

Finally, *what* does Jesus command that we pray? What are we to ask the Father to do? Jesus's summary answer is called the Lord's Prayer (Matt. 6:9–13).

Our Father in heaven,
1. hallowed be your name.
2. Your kingdom come,
3. your will be done, on earth as it is in heaven.
4. Give us this day our daily bread,
5. and forgive us our debts, as we also have forgiven our debtors.
6. And lead us not into temptation, but deliver us from evil.

We pray for ourselves and for other followers of Jesus and for the world (1) that we would reverence and cherish the name of God above things. This is the first function of prayer—to pray that people would pursue the glory of God. (2) We pray that God's saving, purifying, Jesus-exalting rule would hold sway in our lives and would finally come in universal manifestation and extent. (3) We pray that we would do the will of God the way the angels do it in heaven—namely, without hesitation and full of zeal and thoroughness. (4) We pray for the practical provisions of body and mind that make an earthly life of obedience possible. (5) We pray for forgiveness for our daily failures to honor God as we ought. That is, we ask God to apply to us each day the perfect redemption that Jesus obtained once for all when he died on the cross. (6) We pray that God would protect us from the evil one and from the temptations that would bring us to ruin and weaken our witness for him.

The Lord's Prayer shows us the astonishing nature of prayer. It puts in the position of greatest importance the prayer for God's name to be glorified, God's kingdom to advance and triumph, and God's will to be accomplished on the earth the way it's happening in heaven. This means that God intends to use human prayers to accomplish his most ultimate and universal purposes. For example, Jesus tells us to pray for the workers that will be required to spread the gospel to all the nations. "Pray earnestly to the Lord of the harvest to send out laborers into his harvest" (Matt. 9:38). Yet nothing is more certain than that the kingdom of God will triumph. Jesus said, "I will build my church, and the gates of hell shall not prevail against it. . . . This gospel of the kingdom will be proclaimed throughout the whole world as a testimony to all nations, and then the end will come" (Matt. 16:18; 24:14). There is no uncertainty about the triumph of God. Nevertheless, in God's providence, it depends on human prayer.

This implies that prayer is not only a duty of man but a gift of God. Jesus will awaken in his people the spirit of prayer that asks for everything it will take to accomplish God's purposes in the world. The prayers of Jesus's followers and the purposes of God will not fail.

*Do not be anxious about your life, what you will eat or what you will drink, nor about your body, what you will put on. Is not life more than food, and the body more than clothing?*

MATTHEW 6:25

*Therefore do not be anxious about tomorrow, for tomorrow will be anxious for itself. Sufficient for the day is its own trouble.*

MATTHEW 6:34

*Fear not, little flock, for it is your Father's good pleasure to give you the kingdom.*

LUKE 12:32

*Do not fear for I am with you*
*Do not be afraid for I am your God* 41:10,13

# Do Not Be Anxious about the Necessities of Daily Life

*what about contentment.*

THERE HAVE BEEN KINGS who find it very effective to keep their subjects in constant anxiety. If the people are anxious about their life and worry about where their next meal is coming from, then perhaps they will be more willing to do the king's bidding in order to get the food they need from the king's storehouse. Anxiety keeps them in their place. Fear makes the monarchy firm.

## Jesus Does Not Secure His Kingship by Cultivating Anxiety

But one of the greatest things about Jesus is that he does not want his people to be anxious. He does not secure his kingship by cultivating anxiety. On the contrary, the aim of Jesus's kingship[1] is to free us from anxiety. He doesn't need to keep us anxious in order to establish his power and superiority. They are untouchable and invincible. Instead, he exalts his power and superiority by working to take away our anxiety.

---

1  Jesus claims to be a king, though not the kind people expected. He says in John 18:36, "My kingdom is not of this world. If my kingdom were of this world, my servants would have been fighting, that I might not be delivered over to the Jews. But my kingdom is not from the world." See also Matthew 25:31, 34; John 12:14–15.

When Jesus says, "Do not be anxious about tomorrow," he is commanding the kind of life that everybody would want—no anxiety. No fear of man or menacing circumstances. But how does Jesus expect this command to come true when we see things all around us that make us anxious? Jesus gives us help in two extended treatments about anxiety and fear, one having to do with anxiety over the basics of life, like food, drink, clothing (Matt. 6:25–34), the other having to do with anxiety over the hurt that men can do to us (Matt. 10:24–31). In the first passage Jesus sustains our ability to press on joyfully when we can't see how all our needs will be met. In the second passage, which I deal with in the next chapter, Jesus motivates us to press on boldly in the cause of truth when people threaten us.

### The Anxieties of Daily Life

Everyone can see plainly Jesus's main point in Matthew 6:25–34: "Do not be anxious." Verse 25: "Do not be anxious about your life." Verse 31: "Do not be anxious, saying, 'What shall we eat?'" Verse 34: "Do not be anxious about tomorrow." But that is the negative way of stating the main point of this passage. There is a positive way found in verse 33—namely, instead of being anxious, "Seek first the kingdom of God." In other words, when you think about your life or your food or your clothes—or your spouse or your job or your mission—don't fret about them. Instead, make God the King in that affair and in that moment. That is, hand over the situation to his kingly power, and do his righteous will with the confidence that he will work for you and meet all your needs. If we believe in the kingship of our heavenly Father, we do not need to be anxious about anything. Virtually everything else in this text is support for Jesus's command.

### Life Is More Than Food, and the Body Is More Than Clothing

I see at least eight reasons Jesus gives for his disciples not to be anxious. The *first* is given in verse 25. "Do not be anxious about your life, what you shall eat or what you shall drink, nor about your body, what you shall put on." Why? "Because life is more than food, and the body is more than clothing." What does this mean?  *Laras dad*

Why do we tend to get anxious about food and clothing? Because there are three things that we would lose if we didn't have food and clothing. First, we would lose some pleasures. After all, food tastes good. Second, we would lose some human praise and admiring glances if we didn't have nice clothes. Third, we would possibly lose our life if we had no food at all or weren't protected from the cold. So the reason we get anxious about food and clothing is because we don't want to lose physical pleasures or human praise or life.

To this fear Jesus responds: if you are gripped by anxiety over these things, you have lost sight of the greatness of life. Life was not given primarily for physical pleasures, but for something greater—the enjoyment of God (Luke 12:21). Life was not given primarily for the approval of man but for something greater—the approval of God (John 5:44). Life was not even given primarily for extension on this earth, but for something greater—eternal life with God in the age to come (John 3:16).

We ought not to be anxious about food and clothing because food and clothing cannot provide the *great* things of life—the enjoyment of God, the pursuit of his gracious favor, the hope of eternity in his presence. We get anxious about food and clothing to the same degree that we lose sight of the great purposes of a God-centered life.

## Look at the Birds of the Air

The *second* reason Jesus gives for not being anxious is in Matthew 6:26: "Look at the birds of the air: they neither sow nor reap nor gather into barns, and yet your heavenly Father feeds them. Are you not of more value than they?" What we see when we look at the birds is not a lesson in laziness. They dig their worms and snatch their bugs and pad their nests with strings and leaves. But Jesus says it is *God* who feeds them. Birds don't anxiously hoard things as though God will not do the same tomorrow. They go about their work—and we should go about our work—as though, when the sun comes up tomorrow, God will still be God.

### You Cannot Add One Cubit to Your Span of Life

The *third* reason not to be anxious is that it's fruitless. "And which of you by being anxious can add a single hour to his span of life?" (Matt. 6:27). The argument is very pragmatic: Anxiety doesn't get you anywhere. It doesn't do you any good. Whatever problem is causing you to feel anxious, you can be sure your anxiety will not reduce the problem. It will only make you miserable while you try to deal with it. So don't be anxious. It's useless.

### Consider the Lilies of the Field

The *fourth* reason Jesus gives for not being anxious is based on the lilies. "And why are you anxious about clothing? Consider the lilies of the field, how they grow; they neither toil nor spin; yet I tell you, even Solomon in all his glory was not arrayed like one of these. But if God so clothes the grass of the field, which today is alive and tomorrow is thrown into the oven, will he not much more clothe you, O you of little faith?" (Matt. 6:28–30).

When you look at a lily, which has no will or instinct of its own to labor and spin, yet is adorned with beautiful form and color, Jesus says you should draw at least this one conclusion: God delights to adorn things. But if his delight finds expression in adorning grass that's here today and gone tomorrow, then surely his delight in adornment will express itself in how he clothes his children!

But someone may protest, "God has not adorned me!" Or: "God has not adorned the poor Christians in many destitute situations around the world." That's true. Very few followers of Jesus are dressed like Solomon. But we couldn't do our work if we were. That's the way Jesus spoke about John the Baptist: "Behold, those who are dressed in splendid clothing and live in luxury are in kings' courts"—but not John the Baptist! He had prophetic work to do and wore "a garment of camel's hair and a leather belt around his waist, and his food was locusts and wild honey" (Luke 7:25; Matt. 3:4). "Among those born of women there has arisen no one greater than John the Baptist" (Matt. 11:11). The adornment Jesus promised does not mean that we will have exorbitant clothes, but that we will have the clothes we need. Where have you ever seen a disciple of Jesus who did not have the adornment he needed to do what God had called him to do?

But let's be careful. We must not measure the perfection of God's provision by some standard below his calling. He does not call us to live in palaces, but to take up our crosses and love people no matter the cost. And when we have finished carrying our crosses—on torn shoulders, if God wills—there will be kingly robes for us all. The promise to meet all our needs does not mean he will make us rich. It does not even mean he will keep us alive ("Some of you they will put to death," Luke 21:16). It means he will give us all that we need to do the will of God (see below on Matt. 6:33).

### Your Heavenly Father Knows That You Need Them All

The *fifth* and *sixth* reasons why a follower of Jesus shouldn't be anxious are given in Matthew 6:32. We shouldn't be anxious about what we eat or drink or wear because "[fifth reason] the Gentiles seek after all these things; and [sixth reason] your heavenly Father knows that you need them all." Anxiety about the things of this world puts us on the same level with the world of unbelievers. It shows that we are really very much like the world in what makes us happy. And Jesus assumes that we will not want to be like that. It also shows that we don't think our Father in heaven knows our needs. Or perhaps we don't think he has the heart of a loving Father. Anxiety shows that we are too close to the world and too far from God. So don't be anxious—the world has nothing eternal to offer, and your loving heavenly Father knows your needs now and forever.

## All These Things Will Be Added to You

The *seventh* reason not to be anxious is that when you seek the kingdom of God first, he works for you and provides all your needs. "Seek first the kingdom of God and his righteousness, and all these things will be added to you" (Matt. 6:33). "All these things" does not mean everything we *think* we need, but everything we really need. And real needs are determined by what God calls us to do, not what we feel like doing. God will give us "all these things" that we need to fulfill his calling on our lives.

## Tomorrow Will Be Anxious for Itself

The *last* argument is, "Do not be anxious about tomorrow, for tomorrow will be anxious for itself. Let the day's own trouble be sufficient for the day" (Matt. 6:34, RSV). In other words, God has appointed to each day its portion of pleasure and pain, as the old Swedish hymn says, especially in the last two lines of this verse.

> Day by day, and with each passing moment,
> Strength I find, to meet my trials here;
> Trusting in my Father's wise bestowment,
> I've no cause for worry or for fear.
> He whose heart is kind beyond all measure
> Gives unto each day what He deems best—
> Lovingly, its part of pain and pleasure,
> Mingling toil with peace and rest.[2]

So don't misappropriate God's allotted troubles for tomorrow. That is, don't bring them forward into today in the form of anxiety. Believe that God will be God tomorrow. Tomorrow there will be grace for tomorrow's troubles. That grace is not given today.

---

2  Karolina Wilhelmina Sandell-Berg, "Day by Day" (1855).

The main point of all this is clear and unmistakable: Jesus does not want his followers to be anxious. He does not secure his kingdom by keeping his subjects in a state of worry. On the contrary, according to Matthew 6:33, the more primary and central his kingship becomes in our lives, the less anxiety we will have.

Since Jesus believes that reasons delivered in words (we have seen eight of them) help to overcome anxiety, it would make sense that we keep these reasons before our minds and seek to make them part of our mental and emotional life. I think this implies that it would be wise to memorize Matthew 6:25–34. I know of no way to weave these eight counter-anxiety realities into the fabric of our minds and hearts that omits remembering them.

Cory ten boom on plane

Just as lou said - we all fear death
1) life is more than food
2) God feeds us
3) It is fruitless
4. based on the lilies
5+6 we are too close to the world
7 seek His kingdom - he provides your needs
8 todays troubles are enough

*You will be dragged before governors and kings for my*
*sake, to bear witness before them and the Gentiles.*
*When they deliver you over, do not be anxious how*
*you are to speak or what you are to say, for what you*
*are to say will be given to you in that hour.*

MATTHEW 10:18–19

*A disciple is not above his teacher, nor a servant above*
*his master. It is enough for the disciple to be like his*
*teacher, and the servant like his master. If they have*
*called the master of the house Beelzebul, how much*
*more will they malign those of his household.*

*So have no fear of them, for nothing is covered that will not*
*be revealed, or hidden that will not be known. What I tell you*
*in the dark, say in the light, and what you hear whispered,*
*proclaim on the housetops. And do not fear those who kill the*
*body but cannot kill the soul. Rather fear him who can destroy*
*both soul and body in hell. Are not two sparrows sold for a*
*penny? And not one of them will fall to the ground apart from*
*your Father. But even the hairs of your head are all numbered.*
*Fear not, therefore; you are of more value than many sparrows.*

MATTHEW 10:24–31

# Do Not Be Anxious about the Threats of Man

EVEN IF WE GAIN A MEASURE of victory over the fear that all our needs will not be met (dealt with in the previous chapter), there remains the gut-wrenching fear of speaking the truth when it may cost us our lives. That's what Jesus deals with in Matthew 10:24–31. It is especially relevant in our day as the likelihood increases that tolerance will hold sway for everyone except the person who claims that everyone must give absolute allegiance to Jesus.

The aim of Jesus in Matthew 10:24–31 is to give us the courage to speak his truth with clarity and openness no matter what the cost. As with Matthew 6:25–34, the main point of this text is plain from the three repetitions of the command not to fear. Verse 26: "So have no fear of them." Verse 28: "Do not fear those who kill the body." Verse 31: "Fear not therefore; you are of much more value than many sparrows." Jesus's aim is clear: be fearlessly courageous. But courageous to do what?

### What You Hear Whispered, Proclaim upon the Housetops

Jesus has something very specific in mind that is threatened by fear and advanced by courage. He says in Matthew 10:27–28, "What I tell you in the dark, say in the light; and what you hear whispered, proclaim upon the housetops. And do not fear . . ." In other words, the fear Jesus focuses on in this passage is the fear of speaking clearly (in the light) and openly (on the housetops) when that speaking might get you in trouble.

So here's the command: "Don't be afraid to speak clearly and openly what I have taught you, even if it costs you your life." The rest of Jesus's words here are motivation—five reasons why we should have courage in the cause of truth.

### They Will Malign You like They Did Jesus

First, notice the word "so" or "therefore" at the beginning of Matthew 10:26: "*So* [therefore] have no fear of them." In other words, fearlessness flows from what Jesus just said—namely, "If they have called the master of the house Beelzebul, how much more will they malign those of his household." How does that help make us fearless?

Jesus's reasoning seems to go like this: "Your mistreatment for speaking the truth is not some unexpected, random, meaningless experience; instead it's the same way they treated me, and so it's a sign that you belong to me. So don't be afraid of the names they call you when you speak out plainly. Those very names bind you and me together."

### Nothing Is Covered That Will Not Be Revealed

Second, notice the word "for" in the middle of that same verse 26.[1] "So have no fear of them; *for* [here comes the second reason not to be afraid] nothing is covered that will not be revealed, or hidden that will not be known." How does that help us overcome fear and be courageous in the cause of truth?

It helps us by assuring us that the truth we are speaking will triumph. It will be vindicated in the end. People may reject it now. They may call it demonic. They may cast it out. They may try to bury it and hide it

---

1   Some English Bible translations drop these important words because they think it helps the flow of thought. For example, the 1984 *New International Version* drops this crucial word "for" (γάρ). It is there in the Greek original, and it is important.

from the world and pretend that it does not exist. But Jesus says, "Take heart in the cause of truth, because in the end all truth will be revealed. All reality will be uncovered. And those who spoke it with clarity and openness will be vindicated."

### Fear Not; You Can Only Be Killed!

Third, Jesus says, fear not; you can only be killed! "And do not fear those who kill the body but cannot kill the soul" (Matt. 10:28). In other words, the worst thing your opponents can do to you when you speak the truth is kill your body. And that leaves the soul untouched and happy in God forever. But if you keep silent, if you forsake the path of truth and fall in love with the praise of men, you could lose your very soul. If you want to fear something, fear that (see *Command #11*). But don't fear what man can do to you. All he can do is dispatch your soul to paradise. Fear not.

### Even the Hairs of Your Head Are All Numbered *getting to be fewer*

Fourth, don't fear to speak the truth, but be courageous and speak clearly and openly because God is giving close and intimate attention to all you do. Matthew 10:30 means at least that much. Jesus says, "Even the hairs of your head are all numbered." In other words, the suffering you may undergo in speaking the truth is *not* because God is disinterested in you or unfamiliar with your plight. He is close enough to separate one hair from another and give each one a number. Fear not; he is close. He is interested; he cares. Be of good courage, and speak the truth whatever the cost.

### Not One of Them Will Fall to the Ground without Your Father's Will

Finally, fear not because God will not let anything happen to you apart from his gracious will. "You are of more value than many sparrows" (Matt. 10:31). "Not one of them will fall to the ground without your

Father's will" (Matt. 10:29, RSV). Jesus's point is: God governs the world right down to the smallest events like birds falling to the ground. Therefore, no harm can befall you but what God wills. This confidence has given great courage to the followers of Jesus for centuries. Many have spoken in the words of missionary Henry Martyn, "If [God] has work for me to do, I cannot die."[2] We are immortal until the work God has for us is done.

## So Do Not Fear the Face of Any Man

Therefore, the command of Jesus stands, and there is sufficient reason to obey it with joy and courage. Don't be anxious about the ordinary needs of life, and don't fear the threats of man. Don't yield to the spirit of the age that woos us into peaceful silence when the truth is being trampled. "Do not think that I have come to bring peace to the earth," Jesus said. "I have not come to bring peace, but a sword" (Matt. 10:34). Not the sword of steel, but the sword of truth that gives life to all who believe. Love the truth, therefore, and what you learn from Jesus in the solitude speak from the housetop. And do not fear the face of any man.

---

2  *Journal and Letters of Henry Martyn* (New York: Protestant Episcopal Society for the Promotion of Evangelical Knowledge, 1851), 460. The original English edition of 1837 was published in London and edited by the Rev. S. Wilberforce, M. A., Rector of Brighstone.

*Whoever exalts himself will be humbled, and
whoever humbles himself will be exalted.*

MATTHEW 23:12

*The tax collector, standing far off, would not even lift up his eyes
to heaven, but beat his breast, saying, "God, be merciful to me,
a sinner!" I tell you, this man went down to his house justified.*

LUKE 18:13

*Blessed are the poor in spirit, for theirs
is the kingdom of heaven.*

MATTHEW 5:3

*Beware of the scribes, who like to walk around in long
robes, and love greetings in the marketplaces and the
best seats in the synagogues and the places of honor at
feasts. . . . They will receive the greater condemnation.*

LUKE 20:46–47

*So you also, when you have done all that you were
commanded, say, "We are unworthy servants;
we have only done what was our duty."*

LUKE 17:10

# Humble Yourself by Making War on Pride

ONE OF THE REASONS JESUS RESERVED his most disparaging descriptions for hypocrites (see *Command #13*) was that the root of hypocrisy is pride. And Jesus's abomination of pride is evident in the frequency and variety of his calls for humility.

## Pride: Defiance, Desert, Delight

Pride is difficult to define because its manifestations are subtle and often do not look like arrogance. We can see this if we compare boasting and self-pity as two forms of pride.

Boasting is the response of pride to success. Self-pity is the response of pride to suffering. Boasting says, "I deserve admiration because I have achieved so much." Self-pity says, "I deserve admiration because I have sacrificed so much." Boasting is the voice of pride in the heart of the strong. Self-pity is the voice of pride in the heart of the weak. Boasting sounds self-sufficient. Self-pity sounds self-sacrificing. The reason self-pity does not look like pride is that it appears to be needy. But the need arises from a wounded ego, and the desire is not really for others to see us as helpless but as heroes. The need that self-pity feels does not come from a sense of unworthiness but from a sense of unrecognized worthiness. It is the response of unapplauded pride.[1]

Jesus dissects the depths of pride. He exposes its multiple layers and manifestations. At the bottom of it is a complex disposition of self-rule, merit, and pleasure in feeling superior to others. Or, to be alliterative, there is a combination of *defiance* (against God as rightful ruler), *desert* (of better treatment than we get), and *delight* (in feeling above others). None of these may be obvious.

A person can be passively defiant while avoiding blatant rebellion, and yet deeply committed to ultimate self-determination. Or a person can seem to feel unworthy by constantly deprecating himself in public, but all the while feel angry that others do not recognize this as a virtue. Or a person can express delight in feeling superior to others by boasting or by craving that others would praise him for not boasting.

## Pride: A Sense of Merit   *We are all beggars*

Jesus focuses on the visible expressions of pride that he can point to. Luke tells us why he told the parable of the boasting Pharisee and the broken tax collector (see *Command #20*). "He told this parable to some who trusted in themselves that they were righteous, and treated others with contempt" (Luke 18:9). This is what I meant by the disposition of merit—the sense that one deserves something good from God.

This sense of merit goes hand in hand with boasting that we are superior to others. So the merit-conscious Pharisee says in Luke 18:11–12, "God, I thank you that I am not like other men, extortioners, unjust, adulterers, or even like this tax collector. I fast twice a week; I give tithes of all that I get." The fact that he says he thanks God does not obscure the pleasure that he gets in feeling superior. There is a difference between a humble delight in becoming a better person by God's grace and a proud delight in being able to see yourself as superior to others.

---

1   This paragraph comes from John Piper, *Desiring God: Meditations of a Christian Hedonist* (Sisters, Ore.: Multnomah, 2003), 302.

Pride does not delight in the growth of holiness, but in the increasing ability to feel superior.

### Craving the Praise of Men

Even if we do not have a strong sense of merit, we may crave the same result, namely, the praise of men. Jesus warns us not to give to charity or pray or fast in order to be seen by others. "Beware of practicing your righteousness before other people in order to be seen by them" (Matt. 6:1). "When you pray, you must not be like the hypocrites. For they love to stand and pray in the synagogues and at the street corners, that they may be seen by others" (Matt. 6:5). "And when you fast, do not look gloomy like the hypocrites, for they disfigure their faces that their fasting may be seen by others" (Matt. 6:16). Jesus calls them "hypocrites" because in their praying and fasting they want to appear as if they treasure God, but in fact they treasure the praise of men. That is one dimension of pride.

Praise for piety is not the only kind of praise that pride craves. It also craves praise for power and wealth. So Jesus says to his disciples, "The kings of the Gentiles exercise lordship over them, and those in authority over them are called benefactors. But not so with you" (Luke 22:25–26). In other words, do not delight in having superior power or superior wealth. The pleasures of being "over" or "above" others does not come from humble trust in the grace of God. It comes from a heart of pride. *Frau doktor*

There are a hundred ways pride positions itself to get the praise of man. It may involve where you sit at a meeting or how you carry yourself in a market or what title you put in front of your name. "[The scribes and Pharisees] love the place of honor at feasts and the best seats in the synagogues and greetings in the marketplaces and being called rabbi by others" (Matt. 23:6–7). The issue here is not that being called rabbi is always wrong or that sitting in a place of honor is always wrong. The issue here is what you love—what you need and crave and treasure. Pride is driven by the desire to be honored by men with places and titles.

## Pride Is Loveless

Then Jesus shows how loveless pride is. Just before saying, "They do all their deeds to be seen by others" (Matt. 23:5), Jesus says, "They tie up heavy burdens, hard to bear, and lay them on people's shoulders, but they themselves are not willing to move them with their finger" (Matt. 23:4). In other words, they teach high moral standards but do not have the mercy or the spiritual wisdom to help people carry the load. They are loveless.

That's no surprise for two reasons: One is that the proud do not really want others to advance beyond them. That would mean losing one of their reasons for feeling superior. The other reason is that the proud do not understand the way that God's grace really works to help sinners make progress in holiness without getting proud. They don't lift a finger to show the repentant sinner how Jesus's yoke is easy and his burden is light (Matt. 11:30) because they do not experience it as easy and light. The moral duty that they strive to fulfill is kept heavy so that there can be a sense of merit and boasting in the achievement. If it were light and easy, where would be the boasting?

## We Are Unworthy Servants

So in Jesus's teaching there is a very close connection between humility and servanthood. To be humble is to be a servant. They are not the same. But humility leads to joyful readiness to do lowly service. The disciple moves from poverty of spirit to childlike trust in God's grace to a heart of servanthood and acts of service.

In Jesus's famous Beatitudes the very first one is, "Blessed are the poor in spirit" (Matt. 5:3). That is, blessed are the people who do not find a basis for merit or desert when they look within themselves. They are the opposite of those "who trusted in themselves that they were righteous" (Luke 18:9). They know that they have nothing in themselves to commend them to God.

They happily assume the place of unworthy servants whom Jesus describes in Luke 17:10—"When you have done all that you were commanded, say, 'We are unworthy servants; we have only done what was our duty.'" This is a profound statement—and utterly devastating to the last vestige of pride. Jesus says, no degree of obedience, from the worst to the best, merits any absolute claim on God. A perfectly obedient human should say—it would be part of his obedience—"I am an unworthy servant." That is, "I do not put you in any absolute sense in debt to reward me." This conviction is the root of humility—that we deserve nothing good from God.

Or to put it positively like the brokenhearted tax collector, everything good that we get from God is mercy. It is undeserved. "God, be merciful to me, a sinner!" (Luke 18:13). "This man went down to his house justified," Jesus said (Luke 18:14). The joy of the humble does not reside in being deserving, but in receiving mercy.

define good

*Truly, I say to you, unless you turn and become like children,*
*you will never enter the kingdom of heaven. Whoever humbles*
*himself like this child is the greatest in the kingdom of heaven.*

MATTHEW 18:3–4

*Let the greatest among you become as the*
*youngest, and the leader as one who serves.*

LUKE 22:26

*A disciple is not above his teacher, nor a servant above*
*his master. . . . If they have called the master of the*
*house Beelzebul, how much more will they malign*
*those of his household. So have no fear of them.*

MATTHEW 10:24–26

# Humble Yourself in Childlikeness, Servanthood, and Brokenhearted Boldness

THE KEY TO HUMILITY is not merely feeling the absence of merit (as we saw in the last chapter), but feeling the presence of free grace. Humility is not only like the servant who says, "I am an unworthy servant"; humility is also like a child at rest in his father's arms. Jesus said, "Truly, I say to you, unless you turn and become like children, you will never enter the kingdom of heaven. Whoever *humbles himself* like this *child* is the greatest in the kingdom of heaven" (Matt. 18:3–4). We must humble ourselves in both ways: like an unworthy servant and like a trusting child.

What is the point of the comparison with a child? If we stay close to the original context, the focus would fall mainly on three terms: *humility* (or lowliness), *little ones*, and *belief*.

## Humility

In Matthew 18:4 Jesus says, "Whoever *humbles* himself like this child is the greatest in the kingdom of heaven." The Greek verb for "humble" did not generally describe a positive virtue in Jesus's day. It meant generally to crush, bring down, afflict, humiliate, and degrade.[1] The word was chosen because Jesus's command was not a romantic one, as though childlikeness were sweet and easy. For a strong, self-confident, self-sufficient, intelligent, resourceful, controlling person, Jesus's command was devastating. Jesus knew that children were not models for imitation in his day. The reason he chose them is because of "their powerlessness and their low social standing."[2] His command is that we end our love affair with power and status and self-sufficiency and rights and control.

## Little Ones

This is confirmed by the term "little ones" that Jesus uses to describe childlike disciples. He says, "Whoever causes one of *these little ones* who believe in me to sin, it would be better for him to have a great millstone fastened around his neck and to be drowned in the depth of the sea" (Matt. 18:6). He describes believers as "little ones," and he describes little ones as those who "believe." Both terms are important. "Little ones" emphasizes that they are not great in the eyes of the world. They are not strong. They are not self-sufficient. Instead, what marks them is that they "believe in me." That is, they trust not in themselves but in Jesus.

## Trust

This is probably the main focus in Jesus's comparison between his disciples and children. Children may have all kinds of faults, but in a normal, healthy family they trust their daddy to take care of them. They do not lie awake wondering where the next meal is coming

---

1  See the article on ταπεινός *(tapeinos)* in *Theological Dictionary of the New Testament*, ed. Gerhard Kittel and Gerhard Friedrich, Vol. VIII (Grand Rapids, Mich.: Eerdmans, 1972), 4–9. "[In the Greek and Hellenistic world] men 'exploit,' 'oppress,' . . . 'humble,' 'put down' . . . 'humiliate others by breaking their spirit.'. . . That man should humble himself is rejected" (4).

2  Ulrich Luz, *Matthew 8–20: A Commentary*, trans. James E. Crouch, ed. Helmut Koester, Hermenia (Minneapolis: Augsburg Fortress, 2001), 428.

from. They do not fret in the stroller that the sky is turning gray. "The child is, by its very position, lowly . . . and lives by instinctive confidence."[3] They are both lowly and non-great by the standards of worldly acclaim. And they are happy, anxiety-free, and confident that everything they need will be provided. The world does not give honorary degrees to children. It does not write books about their accomplishments. We do not put children in charge of anything. But children are not the least bothered by any of that. They are content to be cared for by their parents.

Of course, Jesus is not calling us to be as unproductive or as immature as children. That's not the point of the comparison. The point is that we not love being stronger or more intelligent or richer than others—that our joy does not reside in a feeling of superiority. The point is that we not begrudge the absence of recognition if the world does not value what Jesus calls us to do. We must not fret over being thought lowly and even foolish by worldly standards. Instead we must "believe" in Jesus the way a child believes. We must find our security and meaning and joy in Jesus and all that our heavenly Father is for us in him (see *Command #4*).

## Lowliness Leads to a Spirit of Servanthood

Jesus emphasizes that this poverty of spirit and this childlike lowliness and trust lead to a spirit and life of servanthood. More than once Jesus's disciples were found to be arguing with each other about which of them was the greatest, or would be the greatest, in the kingdom of heaven. Jesus responded each time with more or less the same command: "If anyone would be first, he must be last of all and servant of all" (Mark 9:35). Sometimes he illustrated his point by putting a child in their midst and saying, "Whoever receives one such child in my name receives me, and whoever receives me, receives not me but

3   Alexander McClaren, *The Gospel According to Matthew: Chapters XVII to XXVII* (London: Hodder and Stoughton, n.d.), 3.

him who sent me" (Mark 9:37). In other words, if you are willing to work in the nursery and happily take the children onto your lap, you will be "first."

Even at the Last Supper, when he was preparing to give his life in the ultimate demonstration of servant-love, the disciples were arguing about who was the greatest—so deeply engrained in us is this craving. He said, "The kings of the Gentiles exercise lordship over them, and those in authority over them are called benefactors. But not so with you. Rather, let the greatest among you become as the youngest, and the leader as one who serves. For who is the greater, one who reclines at table or one who serves? Is it not the one who reclines at table? But I am among you as the one who serves" (Luke 22:25–27). Jesus cut straight from the desire to be great among men to the alternative lifestyle, namely, lowly (youth-like) service.

### How Jesus Served and Will Serve

What does service mean? In Matthew 20:26–28, Jesus connects his command that we serve others with his own service of us and shows us the kind of thing he has in mind. "Whoever would be great among you must be your servant, and whoever would be first among you must be your slave, even as the Son of Man came not to be served but to serve, and to give his life as a ransom for many." Service means doing things out of love that are costly to ourselves but aim to bring temporal and eternal benefit to others.

Astonishingly, the servant role of Jesus does not end with his earthly life. He portrays his second coming not only as a demonstration of great power and glory (Mark 13:26), but also as a time when he will again take the lowly (but beautiful) role of servant: "Blessed are those servants whom the master finds awake when he comes. Truly, I say to you, he will dress himself for service and have them recline at table, and he will come and serve them" (Luke 12:37). Jesus will never stop serving us. Does this not incline your heart to serve others as you follow the one who loved you and gave himself for you and never stops serving you? The heart of a saved sinner who seeks to follow Jesus does not ask, "How can I have maximum prestige or applause?" It asks, "How can I do the greatest good for people who need my help, no matter what it costs me?"

When Jesus said (repeatedly), "Whoever exalts himself will be humbled, and whoever humbles himself will be exalted" (Matt. 23:12; Luke 14:11; 18:14), he was warning against the great service-killer (self-exalting pride) and calling for the great service-maker (Christ-dependent humility).

## Brokenhearted Boldness in the Cause of Truth

One of the crucial roles of servanthood needed in our day is brokenhearted boldness in the proclamation of God's truth. I mention this because the spirit of relativism in our day has created an atmosphere in which speaking the truth with conviction and calling others to believe it is not considered humble. The typical condemnation of Jesus's claim to be the only way to heaven (John 5:23; 14:6) is that it is arrogant.

G. K. Chesterton saw this coming in 1908 when he wrote,

What we suffer from today is humility in the wrong place. Modesty has moved from the organ of ambition. Modesty has settled upon the organ of conviction; where it was never meant to be. A man was meant to be doubtful about himself, but undoubting about the truth; this has been exactly reversed. Nowadays the part of a man that a man does assert is exactly the part he ought not to assert—himself. The part he doubts is exactly the part he ought not to doubt—the Divine Reason. . . . The new skeptic is so humble that he doubts if he can even learn. . . . There is a real humility typical of our time; but it so happens that it's practically a more poisonous humility than the wildest prostrations of the ascetic. . . . The old humility made a man doubtful about his efforts, which might make him work harder. But the new humility makes a man doubtful about his aims, which makes him stop working altogether. . . . We are on the road to producing a race of man too mentally modest to believe in the multiplication table.[4]

If humility is not compliance with the relativism of our day, then what is it? I hope what we have seen in this chapter sheds light on this question and helps us see how, for the sake of Jesus and in the service of others, we should boldly speak what Jesus taught us. Here are at least five implications of what we have said in the last two chapters.

### Humility: Five Implications for Bold Truth-Telling

First, humility begins with a sense of subordination to God in Jesus. "A disciple is not above his teacher, nor a slave above his master" (Matt. 10:24). Our conviction does not come from exalting ourselves but from submitting ourselves to the one who reveals himself to us in his word and commands us to speak it.

Second, humility does not feel a right to better treatment than Jesus got. "If they have called the head of the house Beelzebul, how much more will they malign the members of his household" (Matt. 10:25). Therefore, humility does not return evil for evil. It is not a life based on perceived rights. It is a life of sacrifice.

Third, humility asserts truth not to bolster ego with control or with triumphs in debate. It speaks truth as a service to Christ and as love to the adversary. "What I [Jesus] tell you in the dark, say in the light. . . . Do not fear" (Matt. 10:27–28).

Fourth, humility knows it is dependent on grace for all  knowing and believing and speaking. "Apart from me you can do nothing" (John 15:5). This will create a demeanor that is neither cocky nor timid.

---

4  G. K. Chesterton, *Orthodoxy* (Garden City, NY: Doubleday and Co., 1957), 31–32.

Fifth, humility knows it is fallible, and so considers criticism and learns from it, but also knows that God has made provision for human conviction and that he calls us to persuade others. Jesus told us that the church should stand ready to correct the wayward member (Matt. 18:15–17). And he told us that even though we are fallible and may need correction, we should unashamedly go and make disciples of all nations, telling them to do everything Jesus commanded (Matt. 28:19–20).

## Humility: The Gift to Receive All Things as a Gift

When I contemplate closing this chapter with a section on *how* we obey the command to humble ourselves, I see that the answer lies not in a new technique but in the previous chapters on repenting (*Command #2*) and coming to Jesus (*Command #3*) and believing in Jesus (*Command #4*) and loving Jesus (*Command #5*) and abiding in Jesus (*Command #7*) and taking up our cross with Jesus (*Command #8*). In all of this, the answer emerges: Humility does not flow directly from the performance of a self-renouncing will. The reason is that as soon as we renounce our will, we are aware of the accomplishment and are caught in the temptation to feel proud of this very act of renouncing. How can we escape this trap?

At the bottom, true humility senses that humility is a gift beyond our reach. If humility is the product of reaching, then we will instinctively feel proud of it. Humility is the gift to receive all things as a gift thankfully and unself-consciously. Perhaps I can end on a personal note about how I (imperfectly) fight this battle. On December 6, 1988, I made the following entry in my journal. It's my own confession of need and my answer to the question of how we humble ourselves.

Is not the most effective way of bridling my delight in being made much of, to focus on making much of God? Self-denial and crucifixion of the flesh are essential, but O how easy it is to be made much of even for my self-denial! How shall this insidious motive of pleasure in being made much of be broken except through bending all my faculties to delight in the pleasure of making much of God! Christian Hedonism[5] is the final solution. It is deeper than death to self. You have to go down deeper into the grave of the flesh to find the truly freeing stream of miracle water that ravishes you with the taste of God's glory. Only in that speechless, all-satisfying admiration is the end of self.

---

5   For what this term refers to more fully see John Piper, *Desiring God: Meditations of a Christian Hedonist* (Sisters, Ore.: Multnomah, 2003). The summary sentence of Christian Hedonism is: God is most glorified in us when we are most satisfied in him. And so a Christian Hedonist is one who makes delighting in Jesus Christ the great pursuit of his life because he believes this pursuit is the best way to show that Jesus is the most glorious Reality in the universe.

God our father.
and creater of all

Help us to humble ourselves before you
and see the vanity of honor as a
conceit of men's minds that may
stand between you and us.

Pray especially for those who mourn
that as you comfort them that
they may draw nearer to Jesus

*You have heard that it was said to those of old, "You shall not murder; and whoever murders will be liable to judgment." But I say to you that everyone who is angry with his brother will be liable to judgment; whoever insults his brother will be liable to the council; and whoever says, "You fool!" will be liable to the hell of fire.*

MATTHEW 5:21–22

# Do Not Be Angry—Trust God's Providence

AGAIN AND AGAIN we have seen that Jesus commands what we, by ourselves, cannot do. Sometimes, as with the command to love or to believe, we try to make his commands doable by defining them as mere external acts or mere decisions of the will. We think these are more in our control than our emotions are. Perhaps. But when it comes to anger, Jesus explicitly does the opposite of what we try to do in making his commands more external and more doable. He is saying that the external act of murder is wrong and, more radically, that the internal experience of anger behind it is wrong. So he commands (along with the Law of Moses) that we not *do* the external act of murder, but goes further and commands that we not *feel* the internal emotion of anger that lies behind the act.

### No One Decides to Get Angry

We can feel how radical this is if we stop to ponder that no one *decides* to get angry. We don't see an outrageous act of heartless cruelty and injustice and then ponder whether anger would be a good response and then, after consideration, choose to start feeling the proper level of anger. Nobody lives that way. Anger happens. It's spontaneous. It is not a rational choice. It is an unpremeditated experience.[1] Something happens, and anger rises in our heart. What makes it rise when it does, and with the strength and duration it rises, is a combination of the evil we observe and the condition of our mind and heart. Jesus's command, therefore, is not that we master the expressions of our anger with self-control, though that is often what duty requires. His demand is that there be a change in our condition. He is calling for a deep inward transformation of mind and heart that does not give rise to the anger we should not have. He described this change in different ways: for example, new birth (*Command #1*) and repentance (*Command #2*) and faith (*Command #4*).

Therefore, what we say in this chapter about the command not to be angry is rooted in the other teachings of Jesus. He is not interested in mere psychological and emotional changes. He is interested in newborn disciples who live by faith in his saving work and present help. *He* shed his blood; *we* experience forgiveness (Matt. 26:28). *He* paid the ransom; *we* are freed from the condemnation and bondage of sin (Mark 10:45; John 8:32). *He* brought the kingdom of God; *we* experience God's transforming rule (Luke 11:20). *He* is the vine; *we* are the branches. Without him we can do nothing (John 15:5). That includes obeying the command not to be angry.

### What Is Anger?

As with all emotions, which exist before words and independently of words, anger is hard to define with words. But we should try because evidently there are different experiences called anger, some of which are sinful and some of which are not. For example, in Mark 3:5 Jesus

---

1  I don't mean to imply that what we do with our wills has no effect on our anger. You can decide to dwell on an offense and so intensify your anger. You can choose to focus your attention on the mercy of Christ toward you and reduce your anger. But my point is that the actual experience is not controlled immediately by the will the way raising your right hand is.

himself is angered by religious leaders who do not want him to heal a man on the Sabbath. "He looked around at them *with anger*, grieved at their hardness of heart." And Jesus repeatedly referred to *God's* anger either directly as the wrath of God in judgment (John 3:36; Luke 21:23) or indirectly in parables (Matt. 18:34; 22:7; Luke 14:21).

A standard English dictionary defines anger as "a strong feeling of displeasure and usually antagonism." The reason the phrase "a strong feeling of displeasure" can't stand by itself is that we don't think of really bad tasting food as awakening anger, even though there may be strong displeasure. That displeasure needs another component before it is experienced as anger. If someone keeps feeding us terrible food, and we sense that they are doing it intentionally, then we may get angry. Anger seems to be a more or less strong displeasure about something that is happening willfully and, we feel, should not be happening.

Of course, we do sometimes get angry when that is not the case. If we trip over a root, we may turn around and kick the root in anger. If we bump our head on the kitchen cabinet, we may smack the cabinet door in anger. But in our best moments we look at those reactions as foolish. We intuitively sense that we are imputing willfulness to the root and the cabinet, as if they did something to us on purpose.

This is why the young Jonathan Edwards resolved not to get angry at inanimate objects. His Resolution #15 said, "*Resolved,* Never to suffer the least motions of anger towards irrational beings."[2] Therefore, the difference between anger and other emotions of displeasure is that anger involves strong displeasure with something that is happening intentionally that we think should not be happening.

### Jesus's Anger and Ours

If Jesus, as the ideal human being, could feel and express anger, we are compelled to ask what he is prohibiting in Matthew 5:22 when he said,

2  Jonathan Edwards, *Memoirs of Jonathan Edwards, A. M.,* in *The Works of Jonathan Edwards,* ed. Edward Hickman, 2 vols. (Edinburgh: Banner of Truth, 1974), I:xxi.

"Everyone who is angry with his brother will be liable to judgment." In his human perfection he wove a whip and turned over the tables of the money-changers in the temple (John 2:15; Matt. 21:12). He felt anger and grief in the synagogue (Mark 3:5). He called the scribes and Pharisees children of hell (Matt. 23:15) and "blind fools" (Matt. 23:17) and "whitewashed tombs" (Matt. 23:27).

I do not assume that Jesus alone is permitted to experience anger because he is the Son of God and that no other humans may. The Bible that he read and affirmed (John 10:35; Matt. 5:18) described the anger of holy men of old (Exod. 32:19; Num. 16:15; Neh. 5:6; Ps. 4:4). I think the solution is found rather in trying to define what makes anger good and what makes it bad. He helps us do this both in the context of Matthew 5:22 and in the other things that he said. Let's look first at the other things he said, then come back to the context of Matthew 5:22.

I see at least five factors in Jesus's teaching that govern whether an experience of anger is legitimate or not. They can be described with five key words. In this chapter, we will deal with three of them: *love*, *proportion*, and *providence*. In the next chapter we will deal with *mercy* and *servanthood* as they relate to anger.

## Love and Anger

For human anger to be good, it must be governed by love for those who make us angry. Jesus said, "Love your enemies and pray for those who persecute you. . . . Do good to those who hate you, bless those who curse you" (Matt. 5:44; Luke 6:27–28). These commands exert a controlling effect on the nature of our anger. They tell us that legitimate anger may not delight in or desire the damnation of the ones who make us angry. If our anger is going to be good, it must be governed by our obedience to the command to bless and pray for and do good to those who make us angry.

This shapes the very definition of anger. If we assume that anger *always* involves feelings of vindictiveness and vengeance and hostility, then by definition good anger is impossible. But that is not the only way godly people have experienced anger. Jesus's own experience of anger tells us that good anger does exist. Therefore, we should define it so that it may be governed by love. In other words, we should assume that with Jesus's help we can be angry with someone and at the same time pray for him, bless him, and do good to him. This anger would be a strong displeasure with what they have done—and even with the corrupt heart from which the deed came—but at the same time we would desire their good and pray for it and work for it. Such anger would not have to be evil.

## Proportion and Anger

Jesus teaches that a holy response to evil should be proportionate to its degrees of moral flagrancy. For example, he illustrates God's purpose to punish some people worse than others with this parable:

> That servant who knew his master's will but did not get ready or act according to his will, will receive a severe beating. But the one who did not know, and did what deserved a beating, will receive a light beating. Everyone to whom much was given, of him much will be required, and from him to whom they entrusted much, they will demand the more. (Luke 12:47–48)

One implication from these words is that if punishment should vary because of different degrees of evil, then so should the degrees of anger in response to evil.

In other words, our anger should be governed not only by our love for the one who makes us angry, but also by the seriousness of his offense. If our anger is out of proportion to the offense, it is not good anger. This is more obvious when we think of not being angrier than the offense deserves. We have all experienced an anger that is more intense than the offense calls for. A father raging against a three-year-old son and hitting him uncontrollably would be a clear example of anger that is out of proportion.

It is less obvious that too little anger might be a fault as well. The absence of anger in the presence of evil is not necessarily a fault. Jesus clearly tells us not to be angry with our brother (at least in some circumstances), which implies that there must be situations in which anger would seem to be natural, but we should not have it. How that is possible we will see in a moment. But for now we must also say that there are *bad* reasons for not getting angry as well as good ones. A person may be undiscerning or insensible about the seriousness of sin, the offense that it is to God, and the damage it can do to people. The absence of anger in such a case is disproportionate to the seriousness of evil and is not good.

### Providence and Anger

One of the greatest truths that Jesus taught to help us be free from sinful anger is the truth of God's all-encompassing providence—that is, his wise and sovereign control over all things for the good of his children. The rise and strength of our anger should be governed by our trust in God's providence—that he is ruling over the evil that makes us angry and will not let anything befall us that is not ultimately good for us.

The rage that could rise in our hearts when we are treated unjustly and when we watch loved ones treated cruelly would be natural and strong. When dealing with these threats, Jesus spoke directly to our fear, not our anger. But the implications for anger are plain. He said, "Do not fear those who kill the body but cannot kill the soul. Rather fear him who can destroy both soul and body in hell. Are not two sparrows sold for a penny? And not one of them will fall to the ground apart from your Father. But even the hairs of your head are all numbered. Fear not, therefore; you are of more value than many sparrows" (Matt. 10:28–31).

The point is, first, that the smallest details of life on earth are governed by God—not a bird falls to the ground apart from him. And the second point is that God is near, and his acquaintance with our situation is total—even the hairs of your head are all numbered. Conclusion: Nothing will befall you apart from his wise and loving providence over your circumstances. Don't fear. And, by implication, don't be angry in a way that contradicts your confidence in God's care over your life. God's providence should change the way we experience circumstances that would otherwise be totally infuriating.

When he was predicting what would befall his disciples in the future Jesus said, "You will be delivered up even by parents and brothers and relatives and friends, and some of you they will put to death. You will be hated by all for my name's sake. But not a hair of your head will perish" (Luke 21:16–18). Here again we are assured in a shocking way that even if we are killed for Christ ("some of you they will put to death"), nevertheless we will be totally safe—"not a hair of your head will perish." God's providence will govern all the evil that comes against us so that his good purposes are fulfilled. This will have an effect on the way we experience anger. Evil is being done, but it does not have the last say, and in the end even serves God's hidden designs. There may be anger, but the bitterness and sting and hostility of it will be removed by this confidence.

### Rejoice in Persecution

One of the clearest illustrations of how God's providence overcomes the controlling effect of anger is Jesus's command that we rejoice when we are persecuted unjustly. He says, "Blessed are you when others revile you and persecute you and utter all kinds of evil against you falsely on my account. Rejoice and be glad, for your reward is great in heaven, for so they persecuted the prophets who were before you" (Matt. 5:11–12). Few things would ordinarily make us angrier than such unjust treatment. Not only are we being hurt by this reviling and persecution, but Jesus emphasizes that it is "evil" and it is "false." These factors tend to infuriate us.

But Jesus utterly transforms that ordinary, understandable emotional experience of anger. Instead of saying, "Be legitimately angry," or "Try to control your anger," he says the most incredible thing imaginable: "Rejoice and be glad." The language in Luke 6:23 is even more extraordinary. He says, "Rejoice in that day, and *leap* for joy." Anger at being persecuted unjustly cannot be unaffected by this command. Our rage at unjust treatment cannot remain untransformed if we rejoice over the same treatment.

Rejoicing does not mean that we approve of the treatment. It does not mean that we stop thinking it is unjust. It probably does not mean there is *no* anger whatsoever. Some kind of holy anger—strong emotional disapproval—may be emotionally compatible with joy. The human soul in the image of God is that complex. And we know, from all that Jesus taught us about God, that God experiences anger and joy simultaneously because he sees and responds perfectly to all evil and all good at the same time.[3]

Our joy in the presence of persecution is possible because of God's providence. Not a hair of your head will perish (when they kill you). Not a bird (or a hateful blow to your head) falls without the will of your Father. Providence governs your suffering. And in the end, "Your reward is great in heaven." This is Jesus's argument why joy and not anger can dominate our experience of persecution: "Rejoice and be glad, *for your reward is great in heaven*" (Matt. 5:12). Therefore, good anger is governed by faith in the all-wise, all-powerful, merciful providence of God.

---

3  Jesus, for example, taught us that God feeds all the birds and clothes all the lilies in the world (Matt. 6:26–30), and that no bird falls to the ground apart from his attention (Matt. 10:29), and that every hair of our head is known and numbered (Matt. 10:30), and that in all the hostilities of life not a hair of our head perishes (Luke 21:18). In other words, God is perfectly aware of every micro-detail of what happens in the world, and his wrath (John 3:36) and joy (Luke 15:7) happen in perfect proportion to what he sees. Since there is unbelief and repentance happening simultaneously all the time, he is able to respond to both with different emotions simultaneously all the time.

*"Lord, how often will my brother sin against me, and I forgive him? As many as seven times?" Jesus said to him, "I do not say to you seven times, but seventy times seven."*

MATTHEW 18:21–22, RSV

*First take the log out of your own eye, and then you will see clearly to take the speck out of your brother's eye.*

MATTHEW 7:5

# Do Not Be Angry—Embrace
# Mercy and Forgiveness

## Mercy and Anger

Anger is not only influenced by God's providence assuring us of his present care and future reward (as we saw in the previous chapter), it is also governed by the heartfelt memory that the forgiveness of our sins is owing to mammoth mercy. Jesus teaches that living with the awareness that we are forgiven felons (because of assaults on God's honor) will break the power of unrighteous anger in our lives. He illustrates this when his disciples ask about how often they should forgive people.

Jesus's disciples are aware of how maddening it can be when someone sins against us not just once but over and over. Few things make us angrier. So Jesus's disciple, Peter, said to him, "Lord, how often will my brother sin against me, and I forgive him? As many as seven times?" Jesus said to him, "I do not say to you seven times, but seventy-seven times" (Matt. 18:21–22). The question cries out to be asked, how in the world is that possible when someone has hurt us for the seventieth time?

Jesus answers with a parable about the kingdom of heaven that shows how closely the kingdom is tied to the power to forgive. He says to Peter and the others who can hear, "Therefore the kingdom of heaven may be compared to a king who wished to settle accounts with his servants" (Matt. 18:23). It is significant that he calls this parable a comparison to the kingdom of heaven. That means that the triumph over anger through forgiveness is a part of God's rule (kingdom) in the lives of his people. Forgiveness is not simply a psychological technique for managing human relationships—it is the work of God and the fruit of the forgiveness that Jesus said he would obtain with his own blood (Matt. 26:28).

### How We Forgive Seventy-Seven Times

The parable says that a king had a servant who owed him the staggering amount of ten thousand talents (Matt. 18:24). "The giant size of this amount is illuminated by the fact that King Herod had a yearly income of about 900 talents, and that Galilee and Peraea [the 'land beyond the Jordan'], in the year 4 BC brought in 200 talents in taxes."[1] So it appears that either this amount is an intentional exaggeration (as when we say "zillions" of dollars), or this servant was a high-ranking official who had the connections to embezzle huge amounts from the king's treasury over many years. In any case, Jesus describes his debt as virtually incalculable.

The king threatened to sell him and his family. But "the servant fell on his knees, imploring him, 'Have patience with me, and I will pay you everything' [an impossibility, it seems, in view of the amount]. And out of pity for him, the master of that servant released him and forgave him the debt" (Matt. 18:26–27). This forgiveness is as spectacular as the size of the debt. That is the point. Jesus wants us to realize that sin is an incalculable debt to God. We could never pay it back. We can never settle accounts with God. No amount of penance or good works or apologies can pay the debt of dishonor we have heaped upon God by our sins.

---

1   Walter Grundman, *Das Evangelium Nach Matthäus* (Berlin: Evangelische Verlagsanstalt, 1968), 423.

But this servant did not receive this forgiveness for what it was—stunning, undeserved, heart-humbling, mercy-awakening. Jesus reports no word of gratitude and no word of amazement from this servant. Incredible! He simply tells the incomprehensible events that happened next: "When that same servant went out, he found one of his fellow servants who owed him a hundred denarii [one denarius was a day's wage for a laborer], and seizing him, he began to choke him, saying, 'Pay what you owe.' So his fellow servant fell down and pleaded with him, 'Have patience with me, and I will pay you.' He refused and went and put him in prison until he should pay the debt" (Matt. 18:28–30). In other words, this man's experience of "forgiveness" from the king did not change his anger. He seized and choked his fellow servant.

The king heard of it and was (legitimately!) angry (Matt. 18:34). He said to him, "You wicked servant! I forgave you all that debt because you pleaded with me. And should not you have had mercy on your fellow servant, as I had mercy on you?" The king "delivered him to the jailers, until he should pay all his debt" (Matt. 18:32–34). The conclusion to the parable goes straight to the heart of the issue of anger and forgiveness. Jesus says, "So also my heavenly Father will do to every one of you, if you do not forgive your brother from your heart" (Matt. 18:35).

The point of this parable is that God has no obligation to save a person who claims to be his disciple if that professing disciple has not received the gift of forgiveness for what it really is—infinitely precious, amazing, undeserved, heart-humbling, mercy-awakening. If we claim to be forgiven by Jesus, but there is no sweetness of forgiveness in our hearts for other people, God's forgiveness is not there (cf. Matt. 6:14–15; Mark 11:25).[2]

---

2  The point of Jesus's parable is not to address the larger issue of whether we can truly experience the forgiveness of God and then lose that forgiveness. We have seen in *Command #7* that Jesus teaches that he will not let any of his true disciples fall away. The point of this parable is that divinely offered forgiveness that does not transform our lives into forgiving people will not save us.

Remember, this parable was told to help Peter deal with Jesus's command to forgive seventy-seven times (Matt. 18:22). That is, it was told to help us deal with the anger that naturally arises in our hearts when someone hurts us for the seventieth time. The solution, Jesus says, is to live in the overwhelmingly amazed awareness that we have been forgiven a debt larger than all the wrongs ever done against us. Or to put it another way: we should live in the astonished awareness that God's anger against us has been removed, though we have sinned against him far more than seventy-seven times. The effect of this awareness is a broken, contrite, tenderhearted joy. And this brokenhearted joy governs our anger. The only good anger is the kind that is shaped by this humble heart.

### "First Take the Log out of Your Own Eye"

One other saying of Jesus confirms how he designs mercy as a way of governing our experience of anger. One of the ways that anger expresses itself is in judging others. Jesus gave us a command in this regard:

> Judge not, that you be not judged. For with the judgment you pronounce you will be judged, and with the measure you use it will be measured to you. Why do you see the speck that is in your brother's eye, but do not notice the log that is in your own eye? Or how can you say to your brother, "Let me take the speck out of your eye," when there is the log in your own eye? You hypocrite, first take the log out of your own eye, and then you will see clearly to take the speck out of your brother's eye. (Matt. 7:1–5)

The command not to judge sounds as absolute as the command not to be angry. "Judge not, that you be not judged." But what follows the command shows us that there is a kind of judging that is bad and a kind of judging that is necessary and good—just like there is good and bad anger. When Jesus says, "First take the log out of your own eye, and then you will see clearly to take the speck out of your brother's eye," he shows that it is necessary to make judgments about the speck in a brother's eye. What turns this kind, caring, healing judgment into the judgmentalism that Jesus forbids is the failure to see the log in our own eye.

It is the same as the unforgiving servant failing to live in the awareness of the "log-debt" that he had been forgiven (ten thousand talents), so that he could gladly forgive the "speck-debt" of his brother (one hundred denarii). Jesus assumes that when we see the log in our own eye, we know how to remove it—that is, we know how to find forgiveness and help from Jesus. Otherwise the delicate procedure of removing the speck from the eye of our brother would not be possible. You can't do delicate, loving eye surgery with a log hanging out of your eye.

So the point of Jesus's words about judging are to show us how the anger of judgmentalism can be broken. It is broken by a broken heart. We live in the consciousness of our own great sinfulness and in the awareness that only the mercy of Jesus can take the log out of our eye with forgiveness and healing. This awareness turns angry judgment into patient and loving forbearance and delicate correction. Legitimate anger may remain because we are displeased that eye-specks bedevil people we love. But that anger is not the anger of judgmentalism. Good anger is governed by the experience of mercy.

## Servanthood and Anger

We are tempted to be angry not only when we are repeatedly hurt, but when we are told what to do by others—especially if we don't want to do it. This anger is often rooted in the kind of pride that does not feel any duty or joy in servanthood. But everything Jesus teaches about serving others leads us to experience servanthood another way (cf. *Command #17*). Central to being a disciple of Jesus is the willingness to embrace self-denial and cross-bearing: "If anyone would come after me, let him deny himself and take up his cross and follow me" (Matt. 16:24).

Jesus goes to the cross to die for others. He calls us to go with him and, if necessary, die for others. This readiness to suffer as a part of following Jesus gives rise to a spirit of servanthood that does not get angry when demands are put upon us. Jesus used an amazing phrase to express this: "slave of all." He said, "Whoever would be first among you must be *slave of all*. For even the Son of Man came not to be served but to serve, and to give his life as a ransom for many" (Mark 10:44–45).

Jesus does not mean that following him is a begrudging, joyless affair. "These things I have spoken to you, that my *joy* may be in you, and that your joy may be full" (John 15:11). Martin Luther captured the joyful spirit of Christian "slavery" when he said in 1520, "A Christian man is the most free lord of all, and subject to none;[3] a Christian man is the most dutiful servant of all, and subject to every one."[4] We are not our own. We belong to Jesus. What he bids us do, we do—lest we hear him say, "Why do you call me 'Lord, Lord,' and not do what I tell you?" (Luke 6:46).

This spirit of submission transforms the experience of anger. As "slaves of all," the emotional experience of being required to do things we didn't plan to do is not the same as it would be if we were *lords of all*. For Jesus's sake the slave rejoices to serve the good of others. He says with his Master, "My food is to do the will of him who sent me and to accomplish his work" (John 4:34). What we were sent to do is serve. Good anger is governed by the contentment Jesus gives in serving others, even those who do not deserve it.

**What Kind of Anger Is Jesus Prohibiting?**

We return now to Jesus's prohibition of anger. "You have heard that it was said to those of old, 'You shall not murder; and whoever murders will be liable to judgment.' But I say to you that everyone who is angry

---

3   This is what Jesus meant when he said to Simon Peter, "'What do you think, Simon? From whom do kings of the earth take toll or tax? From their sons or from others?' And when he said, 'From others,' Jesus said to him, 'Then the sons are free'" (Matt. 17:25–26). Then to show that the free sons (disciples) are also servants, he told Peter to pay anyway (Matt. 17:27).

4   Martin Luther, "The Freedom of a Christian," in *Three Treatises* (Philadelphia: Fortress, 1960), 277.

with his brother will be liable to judgment" (Matt. 5:21–22). In view of all we have seen, I would make the observation here that the anger Jesus is forbidding is the anger behind murder. In other words, he is intensifying the command not to murder. He is pointing out that it is not only the act of murder but the feeling behind it that is worthy of condemnation. In other words, he is not prohibiting all anger but the kind that leads toward murder.

This focus of his prohibition is confirmed by the two illustrations he gives next: "Whoever insults his brother will be liable to the council; and whoever says, 'You fool!' will be liable to the hell of fire" (Matt. 5:22). These refer to *external* actions, not just internal anger. Therefore, they reveal the kind of anger Jesus has in mind. In his mind, as he condemns anger, anger is a strong feeling of displeasure *including* feelings of contempt and hostility that seek expression in murder or pejorative name-calling. All *such* anger he forbids. But I do not assume from this that Jesus would condemn *all* anger, especially his own (Mark 3:5). All of his other teachings guide us in discerning whether our anger is justified, especially the teachings we dealt with under the headings of love, proportion, providence, mercy, and servanthood.

## The Vine Is the Source for Stilling the Force of Anger

Nevertheless, the demand not to be angry is radical and devastating. It puts us face to face with the impossibility of saving ourselves. Jesus's demand is not something we can do in our own power. Becoming angry is not a choice we make. It is a fruit on the branch of our lives. The question is: What vine are we a part of? And whose fruit will we bear? The demand of Jesus not to be angry is, therefore, also a demand that we abide in him as our vine. "Whoever abides in me and I in him, he it is that bears much fruit, for apart from me you can do nothing" (John 15:5).

*Not everyone who says to me, "Lord, Lord," will
enter the kingdom of heaven, but the one who
does the will of my Father who is in heaven.*

MATTHEW 7:21

*If you would enter life, keep the commandments.*

MATTHEW 19:17

*The tax collector, standing far off, would not even lift up his eyes
to heaven, but beat his breast, saying, "God, be merciful to me,
a sinner!" I tell you, this man went down to his house justified,
rather than the other. For everyone who exalts himself will be
humbled, but the one who humbles himself will be exalted.*

LUKE 18:13–14

# Do the Will of My Father Who Is in Heaven—Be Justified by Trusting Jesus

## External Conformity to Laws Is Not Enough

A wealthy man asked Jesus, "Good Teacher, what must I do to inherit eternal life?" (Mark 10:17). Jesus answered his question in two steps. First, he said, "You know the commandments: 'Do not murder, Do not commit adultery, Do not steal, Do not bear false witness, Do not defraud, Honor your father and mother'" (Mark 10:19). In other words, he connected eternal life with keeping God's law. "If you would enter life, keep the commandments" (Matt. 19:17).

The man responded, "Teacher, all these I have kept from my youth" (Mark 10:20). Was this true? Maybe at one level it was. Perhaps there were no external behaviors that contradicted God's laws. But what about his heart? Jesus had said in another place, "Unless your righteousness exceeds that of the scribes and Pharisees, you will never enter the kingdom of heaven" (Matt. 5:20; see *Commands #25–27*). The problem with these rigorous law-keepers was that they focused on externals alone: "Woe to you, scribes and Pharisees, hypocrites! For you clean the outside of the cup and the plate, but inside they are full of greed and self-indulgence" (Matt. 23:25). Was that true of this wealthy man?

The second step in Jesus's answer to the man's question reveals a serious problem in his heart. Jesus said, "You lack one thing: go, sell all that you have and give to the poor, and you will have treasure in heaven; and come, follow me" (Mark 10:21). This is amazing. He says he only lacks "one thing." Presumably if he had that one thing, then he would be perfect. In fact, that's the way Matthew records Jesus words, "If you would *be perfect*, go, sell what you possess and give to the poor, and you will have treasure in heaven; and come, follow me" (Matt. 19:21). So he is *not* perfect. He has not kept God's law perfectly. And therefore he will not inherit eternal life unless this "one thing" happens that he is missing.

### "You Lack One Thing"

What is this "one thing"? It sounds like three things: Sell what you possess, give it to the poor, follow me. How are these three demands really one? These demands may be summed up like this: "Your attachment to your possessions needs to be replaced by an attachment to me." It is as though the man stood there with his hands full of money and Jesus said, "You lack one thing; reach out and take my hands." To do this the man must open his fingers and let the money fall. The "one thing" is not what falls out of his hands, but what he takes into his hands.

When a person treasures Jesus above money, the poor are always the beneficiaries. That's why Jesus mentions the poor. But the main point concerns what is happening between this man and Jesus. "You lack one thing. You lack me. Stop treasuring money, and start treasuring me. You want to inherit eternal life. You want to enter the kingdom of heaven. I am the treasure of heaven. If you would have treasure in heaven, you must have me. If you prefer money over me now, you will not enter heaven where I am the treasure. But if you treasure me now above your money, 'you will have treasure in heaven.' I will be there. Only by your attachment to me will you inherit eternal life.

If you would be perfect—which is the only way into God's king-dom—follow me."

## Perfection through Jesus

This is a critical lesson for us. Jesus does not scorn the law of God. He does not say that keeping the commandments is unimportant. He says, "If you depend on keeping the commandments alone, you will not inherit eternal life. There will always be something lacking." The standards of the law are perfection. "You therefore must be perfect," Jesus said, "as your heavenly Father is perfect" (Matt. 5:48). He does not lower that standard. Instead, he demands it from the whole world. And then he offers it through attachment with himself. "If you would be perfect . . . come, follow me." Jesus is the only path to perfect obedi-ence. And perfect obedience is required for eternal life.

The crucial question is: *How* is Jesus the path to perfection? One historic answer is that Jesus himself is our perfection. That is, when we are connected with him by faith, God counts us to be perfect because of Jesus, even though in ourselves we are not. Another historic answer is that Jesus, by his presence and power within us, transforms us so that we really begin to love as he does and move toward perfection, which we finally obtain in heaven. It seems to me that Jesus gives us good reason to believe that both of these answers are true.

Jesus said that he came "to give his life as a ransom for many" (Mark 10:45) and that his blood would be "poured out for many for the forgiveness of sins" (Matt. 26:28) and that believing in him as he was lifted up on the cross would give eternal life to undeserving sinners (John 3:14–15). All of this implies that Jesus's life and death are our only hope of escaping wrath (John 3:36) and obtaining heaven. Jesus said concerning the most intentional law-keepers in Israel, "None of you keeps the law" (John 7:19). And he very bluntly called even his disciples "evil." "If you then, *who are evil*, know how to give good gifts to your children, how much more will your Father who is in heaven give good things to those who ask him!" (Matt. 7:11). In other words, all humans are sinners under God's holy wrath with no hope of eternal life based on their own obedience. Jesus came to solve that problem.

Jesus solves it by removing the wrath of God. He removes it by enduring the punishment we deserved and paying the debt we could never pay (see *Command #11*). Therefore, because of Jesus's shed blood, all our sins are canceled and God does not see us as sinful or imperfect anymore. This is owing to our attachment to Jesus by faith.

### "This Man Went Down to His House Justified"

But Jesus teaches that there is more to our perfection than the absence of guilt. He tells a parable of a Pharisee and a tax collector who went up to the temple to pray. These two men represent the groups that were popularly viewed as most righteous (the Pharisees) and most sinful (the Jewish tax collectors, who compromised themselves by working for the Romans and fleeced their own people to line their pockets).

The Pharisee highlighted his obedience to the law: "I am not like other men, extortioners, unjust, adulterers, or even like this tax collector. I fast twice a week; I give tithes of all that I get" (Luke 18:11–12). But the tax collector, Jesus says, "standing far off, would not even lift up his eyes to heaven, but beat his breast, saying, 'God, be merciful to me, a sinner!' I tell you, this man went down to his house *justified*, rather than the other" (Luke 18:13–14).

The word "justified" is crucial. It captures the very purpose of the parable. Luke introduced this parable by saying: "He also told this parable to some *who trusted in themselves that they were righteous*, and treated others with contempt" (Luke 18:9). Therefore, the parable is dealing with the question of how to be "righteous" before God.

The word "justified" and the word "righteous" are built on the same word in the original Greek. The verb means to "declare righteous" the way a judge does in a courtroom. He does not *make* a defendant righteous. He *recognizes and declares* him as righteous. This is the way the verb is used in Luke 7:29. "When all the people heard this . . . they *declared God just* [literally, they justified God]." Justifying God cannot mean *making* God just or righteous. It means declaring him to be righteous. That is what God does to the tax collector in Luke 18:14: "This man went down to his house *justified*"—that is, this man was declared by God to be righteous.

So the parable dramatically contrasts those who "trusted in themselves that they were righteous" (because of their extensive law-keeping) with those who despaired of their own righteousness and looked away from themselves to the mercy of God to declare them righteous even though they were not. Note carefully that in this parable those "who trusted in themselves that they were righteous" were even willing to give God the credit for the ability to produce this righteousness: "God, *I thank you* that I am not like other men" (Luke 18:11). But that was to no avail. Our own righteousness, even if produced by God's grace, is not a sufficient foundation for vindication in God's holy presence.

### The Rich Man Needs Jesus for His Righteousness

Jesus does not go into detail about how his own obedience and death provide the foundation for justification, but we have good reason to think God's declaration of righteousness is given to sinners who look to Jesus as their only hope of acceptance with God. Jesus said to the wealthy man, "Your law-keeping will not get you into the kingdom. You are not perfect. You lack one thing. Come to *me*." Jesus was what he lacked. If being declared righteous, though he was not, was the man's only hope (as the parable of the tax collector shows[1]), then Jesus is the foundation of that declaration. That is why the man must let go of his money and come to Jesus.

---

1   It is significant that Luke weaves together first the parable of the Pharisee and the tax collector (Luke 18:9–14), with a word about needing to receive the kingdom like a child (Luke 18:15–17), with the story of the rich ruler who lacks one thing, namely, Jesus, to complete his obedience (Luke 18:18–23). It is as though the truth of the justification of the ungodly by faith is being illustrated in the following stories.

So in one sense, the perfection that the rich man lacked is found in Jesus. God will count the man as perfect if he stops depending on his money and starts depending on Jesus. That is the first historic answer to the question, how is Jesus the path to perfection? In relationship to him we are counted as perfect, even though we are still sinners. This is what it means to be justified. We will deal with the second answer in the next chapter, namely, that Jesus, by his presence and power within us, transforms us so that we really begin to love as he does and move toward perfection.

*Whoever does the will of God, he is my*
*brother and sister and mother.*

MARK 3:35

*Blessed rather are those who hear the word of God and keep it!*

LUKE 11:28

*Not everyone who says to me, "Lord, Lord," will*
*enter the kingdom of heaven, but the one who*
*does the will of my Father who is in heaven.*

MATTHEW 7:21

# Do the Will of My Father Who Is in Heaven—Be Transformed by Trusting Jesus

WE SAW IN THE PREVIOUS CHAPTER that the rich man who was seeking eternal life "lacked one thing." If he "would be perfect," he needed Jesus (Matt. 19:21). Jesus is the path to perfection. But *how* is he the path to perfection? The last chapter answered: by being the basis of our perfection before God as we trust him. Now we turn to another answer, which is also true: Jesus, by his presence and power within us, transforms us so that we really begin to love as he does and move toward perfection.

### Some Measure of Real, Lived-Out Obedience Is Required

The answer of the last chapter by itself does not account fully for Jesus speaking the way he does about doing the will of God. Jesus says that doing the will of God really is necessary for our final entrance into the kingdom of heaven. "Not everyone who says to me, 'Lord, Lord,' will enter the kingdom of heaven, but the one who does the will of my Father who is in heaven" (Matt. 7:21). He says that on the day of judgment he really will reject people because they are "workers of lawlessness." "Then will I declare to them, 'I never knew you; depart from me, you workers of lawlessness'" (Matt. 7:23). He says people will "go away into eternal punishment" because they really failed to love their fellow believers: "As you did not do it to one of the least of these, you did not do it to me" (Matt. 25:45).

There is no doubt that Jesus saw some measure of real, lived-out obedience to the will of God as necessary for final salvation. "Whoever does the will of God, he is my brother and sister and mother" (Mark 3:35). So the second historic answer to the question, how is Jesus the path to perfection? has been that he enables us to change. He transforms us so that we really begin to love as he does and thus move toward perfection that we finally obtain in heaven.

I say it that way because Jesus does not give us any indication that we can be perfected in this present age. He teaches us to pray the Lord's Prayer, and he puts right beside the petition "Give us this day our daily bread," the petition "Forgive us our debts, as we also have forgiven our debtors" (Matt. 6:11–12). In other words, just as we pray daily for bread, we should pray daily for forgiveness. Therefore, Jesus does not anticipate a time in this age when we will not need daily forgiveness.

That is why I say Jesus transforms us so that we really *begin* to love as he does so that we move *toward* perfection that we *finally obtain in heaven*. But though our lived-out perfection only comes in heaven, Jesus really does transform us now, and this transformation is really necessary for final salvation. But the *way* our new behavior is necessary is different from the way trusting Jesus for our perfection is necessary. Trusting Jesus connects us with him. Then, because of Jesus's work alone, God counts us righteous, even before our behavior is transformed. The tax collector who cried out, "God, be merciful to me, a sinner!" (Luke 18:13) would not dare point to any righteous behavior in himself as the basis of his justification. He looked away from what he was and pled for mercy. God declared him righteous before his behavior changed. Therefore, trusting Jesus is necessary in order to be connected to Jesus who is the foundation of our justification. But new, transformed behavior is necessary as the *fruit* and *evidence* of this connection with Jesus.

## Every Healthy Tree Bears Good Fruit

We saw in *Command #7* that being connected with Jesus by faith results in a new life of love. That's the fruit Jesus produces as he works within us: "I am the vine; you are the branches. Whoever abides in me and I in him, he it is that bears much fruit, for apart from me you can do nothing" (John 15:5). In another place he makes it clear that being a "healthy tree"—that is, being a person who truly believes in him—will bear good fruit: "Every healthy tree bears good fruit, but the diseased tree bears bad fruit" (Matt. 7:17).

The fruit does not make the tree good. The tree makes the fruit good. Good deeds do not attach us to Jesus. They are not the ground of our being declared righteous. Trusting Jesus connects us with Jesus. This connection results in God's declaration that we are perfect, and this same connection releases the power that produces fruit. The reason Jesus can say, "Every tree that does not bear good fruit is cut down and thrown into the fire" (Matt. 7:19) is not because the fruit is the basis of our acceptance with God—the tax collector had no fruit to offer—but because the absence of fruit shows we are not connected to Jesus.[1]

Therefore, when Jesus commands that we do the will of his Father who is in heaven, he means two things. First, he means, "Believe in me as your only hope for a perfect righteousness that is not your own.

---

1   Though it may cause confusion, it is possible to use the word "justify" to describe how the fruit of good behavior works in the day of judgment. The fruits can "justify" us in the sense of proving that we are believers and belong to Jesus and have a right standing with God in him. That is how I understand Matthew 12:37: "By your words you will be *justified*, and by your words you will be condemned." It is as though the Judge said, "The evidence is compelling: your words warrant the judgment that you are a true believer in my Son and have rested your case with him and banked on his righteousness for acceptance in this court." Or: "Your words justify [warrant, validate] the conclusion of this court that you have trusted in the righteousness of Jesus Christ for your justification in this court."

This perfection is the foundation of your acceptance with God and your inheritance of eternal life." This is why, when people asked him, "What must we do, to be doing the works of God?" he could simply answer, "This is the work of God, that you *believe* in him whom he has sent" (John 6:28–29). Believing in Jesus is the first and most essential aspect of God's will for us. Second, he means, "This same faith that attaches you to me for justification also attaches you to me the way a branch relies on a vine, and in this way you bear the fruit of love that fulfills the law of God in real, lived-out behavior."

### Is God's Will Today Expressed in the Old Testament Law?

Looking back now to the wealthy man who came to Jesus and asked, "Good Teacher, what must I do to inherit eternal life?" (Mark 10:17), how does the keeping of the law fit into Jesus's answer? Jesus's first answer to the man was, "If you would enter life, keep the commandments" (Matt. 19:17). We have seen that even though commandment-keeping will never provide a righteousness good enough to gain acceptance with God, nevertheless, the effort to do God's will is essential. The question now is, is God's will today expressed in the Old Testament law? A simple yes would be misleading. And a simple no would be misleading. Rather we must say something like: yes, provided the law is filtered through the sieve of all the changes brought about by Jesus, who is the goal and fulfillment of the law.

Jesus said, "Everything written about me in the Law of Moses and the Prophets and the Psalms must be fulfilled" (Luke 24: 44). The Law and the Prophets were all aiming toward Jesus. Not surprisingly, when he came they would be fulfilled and changed. Jesus spoke about this change carefully and respectfully: "Do not think that I have come to abolish the Law or the Prophets; I have not come to abolish them but to fulfill them. For truly, I say to you, until heaven and earth pass away, not an iota, not a dot, will pass from the Law until all is accomplished" (Matt. 5:17–18).

Abolition is not Jesus's purpose. Fulfillment is. And when the law is fulfilled in Jesus, its original use changes dramatically. A new era has dawned, and Jesus's followers will relate to the law differently from how Israel did. That's why Jesus said, "The Law and the Prophets were until John [the Baptist]; since then the good news of the kingdom of God is preached, and everyone forces his way into it" (Luke 16:16).

**How Our Experience of the Law Changes with the Coming of Jesus**

Here is a simple sketch of the changes that have happened in our experience of the law since Jesus has come.

First, when Jesus taught that "whatever goes into a person from outside cannot defile him" (Mark 7:18), he virtually nullified the Old Testament ceremonial laws. Mark makes this simple comment, "Thus he declared all foods clean" (Mark 7:19). "On his own authority alone, Jesus set aside the principle of ceremonial purity embodied in much of the Mosaic legislation."[2] From now on "the sons are free" (Matt. 17:26), and we may eat or not eat according to what love demands.

Second, I mention love as the central criterion of our behavior because this is a second thing Jesus did in regard to changing how we experience the law: he said that it was all summed up in love. "So whatever you wish that others would do to you, do also to them, for this is the Law and the Prophets" (Matt. 7:12). In saying this, Jesus directed us away from a focus on the commandments per se and toward a relationship with himself that bears the law-fulfilling fruit of love (see *Command #32*).

Third, Jesus told a parable about the owner of a vineyard whose tenants would not give him his produce. He repeatedly sent them servants whom the tenants beat. Finally, he sent his son whom they killed. All this represented God's relation to Israel as a people. The great majority of them did not render the fruit of worship and obedience, and finally

---

2  George Ladd, *The Presence of the Future* (Grand Rapids, Mich.: Eerdmans, 1974), 285.

they killed the Son of God (Matt. 21:33–41). Jesus asked his listeners what the owner should do. They said, "He will put those wretches to a miserable death and let out the vineyard to other tenants who will give him the fruits in their seasons" (Matt. 21:41). Jesus applied this correct answer to his Jewish listeners in a cataclysmic way, signifying a huge change in the law.

He said, "Therefore I tell you, the kingdom of God will be taken away from you [Israel] and given to a people producing its fruits" (Matt. 21:43). In other words, God is turning his primary redemptive focus from Israel to the Gentile nations (see *Command #50*). The people of God would no longer be defined by ethnicity or by participation in the theocratic system of kings and priests and judges and all the ceremonial and civic laws that held that system together. The people would be defined by faith in Jesus and the fruit of love.

The implications of this change were huge. No longer is it God's will that his people take vengeance in his name on the wicked, as in the case of the conquest of Canaan (Deut. 9:3–6). No longer do God's people (the followers of Jesus) govern themselves by putting to death blasphemers (Lev. 24:14) or adulterers (Lev. 20:10) or fornicators (Deut. 22:21) or Sabbath-breakers (Exod. 31:14) or sorceresses (Exod. 22:18) or false witnesses (Deut. 19:16, 19) or those who disobey their parents (Exod. 21:15, 17). Such commands of the law were woven together with the theocratic, civic government of an ethnic people that no longer applies to a people of God with no ethnic or political identity but rather is scattered through all the ethnic and political groups of the world (Matt. 28:19).

Fourth, the entire religious system involving priests and temple and sacrifices reached its goal and end in Jesus. We saw in *Command #12* that Jesus himself, by his death and resurrection, took the place of the temple and the sacrifices for sin. Therefore, the laws governing how one was reconciled with God through that system are fulfilled and ended with the death and resurrection of Jesus.

### Believe on His Son, and Bear the Fruit of Love

I conclude therefore that Jesus's demand that we do the will of his Father and that we keep the commandments is a demand that we do what Jesus required of the wealthy man who asked how to inherit eternal life. Jesus's most urgent demand is that we stop treasuring money and start treasuring himself as our only hope of having the "one thing" that we lack—perfect righteousness. Yes, we should keep the commandments, but only as they come through the filter of their fulfillment in Jesus. Practically, this means we should look to Jesus himself, revealed in his life and death and teaching, for the guidance we need. We must depend on Jesus's power to do that the way a branch depends on a vine. In this way Christ, not Moses, gets all the glory for the purchase and the performance of the new covenant.

But even with this divinely enabled transformation (Mark 10:27), our righteousness is not perfect in this life, and it will not suffice for our right standing before God. Therefore, Jesus's demand that we do the will of his Father and that we keep his commandments is also a demand that we despair of making our obedience the ground of God's acceptance. Our transformation is the fruit of our union with Jesus. That union is where the ground of our acceptance lies. And that union is established by believing in Jesus. The fruit demonstrates the reality of the union and the authenticity of faith. This is God's will—that we believe on his Son, that we enjoy our union with him, that we rest in God's merciful declaration of our perfection and acceptance, and that we bear the fruit of love.

*And someone said to him, "Lord, will those who are saved be few?" And he said to them, "Strive to enter through the narrow door. For many, I tell you, will seek to enter and will not be able."*

LUKE 13:23–24

*In Harm's Way*

1 Tim 1:9
Ecc 11:7
1 Pet 5:8
John 12:9
Ps 16:7
Mat 7:13-14

COMMAND #22

# Strive to Enter through the Narrow Door, for All of Life Is War

*Pilgrim's Progress*

*Grail Hist Am Heritage*

JESUS TAUGHT US THAT LIFE IS WAR. When he said, "*Strive* to enter through the narrow door" (Luke 13:24), the Greek word behind the English *strive* is recognizable in English transliteration: *agōnizesthe* (ἀγωνίζεσθε). You can see the word *agonize* in that Greek word. The implication is that we must struggle, wrestle, and exert ourselves. But the most important fact about the word "strive" is that the one other place where we find it on Jesus's lips is John 18:36, where he says his disciples would be "fighting" if his kingdom were of this world. "My kingdom is not of this world. If my kingdom were of this world, my servants *would have been fighting* [*ēgōnizonto*, ἠγωνίζοντο], that I might not be delivered over to the Jews." So here the phrase "strive to enter" means that entering is a battle.

**Strive to Enter What?**

Entering what? The kingdom of God. This is plain from the following context. After saying that we should "strive to enter through the narrow door," he refers to a master of a house who rises and shuts the door so

163

that no one else can enter (Luke 13:25). Those outside knock and say, "Lord, open to us," but the master says, "I do not know where you come from." Then they say, "We ate and drank in your presence, and you taught in our streets." But he responds, "Depart from me, all you workers of evil!" (Luke 13:25–27).

Then Jesus applies this picture to the real situation of some who will be excluded from the kingdom of God while Gentiles from all over the world will "recline at table in the kingdom of God." "In that place there will be weeping and gnashing of teeth, when you see Abraham and Isaac and Jacob and all the prophets *in the kingdom of God* but you yourselves cast out. And people will come from east and west, and from north and south, and recline at table *in the kingdom of God*" (Luke 13:28–29).

So the "narrow door" through which we must "strive" to enter is the door to the kingdom of God. Outside there is "weeping and gnashing of teeth" (Luke 13:28). This is one of the ways Jesus refers to hell: "Throw them into the fiery furnace. In that place there will be weeping and gnashing of teeth" (Matt. 13:50). The alternative to entering by the narrow gate is destruction. "Enter by the narrow gate. For the gate is wide and the way is easy that leads to *destruction*" (Matt. 7:13). In other words, what is at stake when Jesus commands that we "strive to enter" is heaven and hell. It is an ultimate issue.

### The Greatest Threat Is Our Own Sin Every Day

But what does Jesus want us to strive against so that we can enter through the narrow door? What are the obstacles? If life is war, who is the enemy? In our striving, the aim is not to hurt anyone. Jesus is clear that we are to love our enemies and do good to those who hate us (Luke 6:27). Saying that life is war does not mean that we make war on people, but on sin, especially our own. In fact, it is only our own sin that can keep us from entering the kingdom, not anyone else's. The sin of others can hurt us, even kill us. But that does not keep us from entering the kingdom of God. Our own sin is the greatest threat to entering the kingdom of God. But temptation to sin comes from an amazing variety of sources.

Jesus is demanding serious personal vigilance. The command to "watch" is one of his most frequent commands. The idea is that we must be awake and alert and ready, lest the temptations of life take us off guard and we be overcome and ruined. Jesus said to his disciples in the Garden of Gethsemane, "Watch and pray that you may not enter into temptation. The spirit indeed is willing, but the flesh is weak" (Mark 14:38). This command is relevant to all of life. Temptations abound, and Jesus does not take them lightly. The watchword of all of life is, watch, be alert.

I say *all of life* because Jesus warned that the days just before his second coming would be in many ways very normal. It will be, Jesus says, like the days of Noah before the flood came and swept people away who were utterly unsuspecting. They were not watchful. Life seemed too normal, so they were not vigilant. "As in those days before the flood they were eating and drinking, marrying and giving in marriage, until the day when Noah entered the ark . . . so will be the coming of the Son of Man. . . . Therefore, *stay awake*, for you do not know on what day your Lord is coming" (Matt. 24:38–39, 42). Nothing is more normal than eating and drinking and marrying. The point is that we must be vigilant all the time, not just when the times feel perilous. They are always perilous. Soul-destroying temptations to unbelief and sin are present in everyday, normal life. Striving to enter through the narrow door is a lifelong, all-day, every-day calling.

## Pain and Pleasure Can Keep Us from Entering through the Narrow Door

Jesus's demand for vigilance is all-embracing. Both the pleasant parts of life and the painful parts of life present dangers to the soul. In the parable of the four soils he warns about both. The painful and the pleasant threaten to destroy the faith-sustaining work of the word in our lives. When the word falls on rocky ground it sprouts, then dies. This represents those who hear the word, but then "tribulation or persecution arises on account of the word" (Matt. 13:21), and they fall away. They do not enter through the narrow door.

When the word falls on thorny ground it sprouts, then dies. This represents those who hear the word, but then "they are choked by the cares and riches and pleasures of life" (Luke 8:14). They do not enter through the narrow door. One person falls away because of pain (tribulation or persecution); the other person falls away because of pleasure (riches and pleasures of life). The call for vigilance is all-embracing. There is no unembattled place in this life.

Surprising to us perhaps, Jesus's demand for vigilance is directed more often at the pleasures of life than the pain. Some people are driven away from God by their pain, but more are lured away by their pleasures. Pleasures seldom awaken people to their need for God; pain often does. So Jesus is more concerned to warn us about the dangers of prosperity than the dangers of poverty.

## The Perils of Praise and Physical Indulgence

One powerful lure away from the kingdom of God is the praise of man. Therefore, Jesus said, "Beware of the scribes, who like to walk around in long robes, and love greetings in the marketplaces and the best seats in the synagogues and the places of honor at feasts" (Luke 20:46). "Beware" means be alert, take care, pay close attention to. This is a call for vigilance against the lure of following those who live for the praises of man. "Beware of practicing your righteousness before other people in order to be seen by them" (Matt. 6:1). We feel good when people speak well of us. It may not be wrong. But it is dangerous. It is a time for vigilance. "Woe to you," Jesus says, "when all people speak well of you, for so their fathers did to the false prophets" (Luke 6:26).

Less subtle is the lure of physical indulgence. Jesus focuses on alcohol and the dissipating effects it has on our minds and bodies. He says, "But watch yourselves lest your hearts be weighed down with dissipation and drunkenness and cares of this life, and that day come upon you suddenly like a trap" (Luke 21:34). There are drugs and foods and practices that "weigh down" the heart. They make the heart sluggish. This is the opposite of vigilance. We will not "strive to enter through the narrow door" if we are self-indulgent and use drugs or food or drink in a way that dulls our spiritual alertness and vigilance.

### Money Is a Mortal Threat to Entering through the Narrow Door

The danger Jesus warns against most often is the danger of money. It is a mortal danger. Heaven and hell hang in the balance in our vigilance against the lure of money. Jesus made this as clear as possible with the words, "It is easier for a camel to go through the eye of a needle than for a rich person to enter the kingdom of God" (Mark 10:25). The issue is entering the kingdom. Striving for wealth is not the striving that leads to the narrow door.

Over and over Jesus warns us to be vigilant against the lure of riches. "Do not lay up for yourselves treasures on earth" (Matt. 6:19). "You cannot serve God and money" (Matt. 6:24). "Do not be anxious, saying, 'What shall we eat?' or 'What shall we drink?' or 'What shall we wear?'" (Matt. 6:31). "The deceitfulness of riches and the desires for other things enter in and choke the word" (Mark 4:19). "Sell your possessions, and give to the needy" (Luke 12:33). "Where your treasure is, there your heart will be also" (Matt. 6:21). "Any one of you who does not renounce all that he has cannot be my disciple" (Luke 14:33). "But woe to you who are rich, for you have received your consolation" (Luke 6:24). "Blessed are you who are poor, for yours is the kingdom of God" (Luke 6:20).[1] "Take care, and be on your guard against all

---

1   Even though he pronounces a woe on the rich (Luke 6:24) and pronounces blessedness on the poor (Luke 6:20), he does not mean that mere finances make one blessed or damnable. We know

covetousness, for one's life does not consist in the abundance of his possessions" (Luke 12:15).

### The "Healthy Eye" Will Help Us Strive to Enter the Narrow Door

It appears, then, that striving to enter the kingdom of God through the narrow door is largely a battle about how we relate to money. We should linger here since Jesus did. He is jealous that we "guard against all covetousness." He is deeply concerned with our "eyes" when it comes to the treasure of our lives. We see this in a puzzling statement he made in Matthew 6:22–23: "The eye is the lamp of the body. So, if your eye is healthy, your whole body will be full of light, but if your eye is bad, your whole body will be full of darkness. If then the light in you is darkness, how great is the darkness!" In other words, if the eye is good (literally, "single"), the whole body will be full of light. But if the eye is bad, the body will be full of darkness. In other words, how you see reality determines whether you are in the dark or not.

You will naturally ask, what does that have to do with money? First of all, notice that these words of Jesus are sandwiched between the command to lay up treasures in heaven (6:19–21) and the warning that you can't serve God and money (6:24). Why is this saying about the good and bad eye sandwiched between two teachings on money? I think it's because what makes the eye good is how it sees God in relation to money. That's the issue on either side of this saying. In Matthew 6:19–21 the issue is: You should desire heaven-reward, not earth-reward.

---

this, first, because he also says, "Woe to you who laugh now" (Luke 6:25) and "Blessed are you who weep now" (Luke 6:21), and we know from this very context that disciples are to rejoice now (Luke 6:23). So Jesus assumes that we are going to qualify his seemingly absolute statements here. The rich and the poor who are blessed are those for whom Jesus is their supreme treasure and therefore seek to use their wealth or poverty to magnify the worth of Jesus above money and what it can buy. We also know Jesus did not pronounce damnation and blessedness on mere financial condition because he told the rich young ruler to sell all that he had (Mark 10:21) but commended Zacchaeus for giving half of his money away (Luke 19:8–9). However, having said all that, it is significant that Jesus considers wealth so dangerous and poverty so auspicious; he simply says woe to the one and blessed be the other.

Which, in short, means: desire God, not money. In Matthew 6:24, the question is whether you can serve two masters. Answer: you cannot serve God and money.

This is a double description of light! If you are laying up treasures in heaven, not earth, you are walking in the light. If you are serving God, not money, you are walking in the light. Between these two descriptions of the light, Jesus says that the eye is the lamp of the body and that a good eye produces a fullness of this light. So, what is the good eye that gives so much light and the bad eye that leaves us in the dark?

**What Is the Good Eye?**

One clue is found in Matthew 20:15. Jesus has just said that men who worked one hour will be paid the same as those who worked all day, because the master is merciful and generous. And besides, they all agreed to their wage before they worked. Those who worked all day grumbled that the men who worked one hour were paid too much. Jesus responded, "Is your eye bad because I am good?" (Matt. 20:15 AT), using the same words for your "bad eye" found in Matthew 6:23.

What is bad about their eye? What's bad is that their eye does not see the mercy of the master as beautiful. They see it as ugly. They don't see reality for what it is. They do not have an eye that can see mercy as more precious than money.

Now bring that understanding of the "bad eye" back to Matthew 6:23 and let it help us discern the meaning of the "good eye." What would the good eye be that fills us with light? It would be an eye that sees the Master's generosity as more precious than money. Which means that the good eye sees God and his ways as the great Treasure in life, not money. The good eye sees things as they really are. God is really more valuable than all that money can buy.

You have a good eye if you look to God and love to maximize the reward of his fellowship—that is, lay up treasure in heaven. You have a good eye if you look at Master-money and Master-God and see

Master-God as infinitely more valuable. In other words, a "good eye" is a wisely valuing eye, a discerning eye, an astutely treasuring eye. It doesn't just see facts about money and God. It doesn't just perceive what is true and false. It sees beauty and ugliness; it senses value and worthlessness; it discerns what is really desirable and what is undesirable. The seeing of the good eye is not neutral. When it sees God, it sees God-as-beautiful. It sees God-as-desirable.

That is why the good eye leads to the way of light: laying up treasures in heaven and serving God, not money. The good eye is a *single* eye. It has *one* Treasure: God. When that happens in your life, you are full of light. And this is so important that Jesus adds in Luke 11:35, "Therefore *be careful* lest the light in you be darkness." In other words, be vigilant. Don't be casual or slack or careless about this matter. Strive, wrestle, fight to keep your eye good. That is, do what you must to see God, not money, as supremely valuable and desirable.

In the next chapter we will continue to unfold the implications of Jesus's command to strive to enter by the narrow door. We will see how he calls for vigilance and watchfulness in regard to false prophets and false christs and the suddenness of his second coming. And then we will turn to the question, how does the demand for vigilance fit with his command that we rest in him? How does the seriousness of watchfulness fit with the sweetness of Jesus's care?

*Enter by the narrow gate. For the gate is wide and the way is easy that leads to destruction, and those who enter by it are many. For the gate is narrow and the way is hard that leads to life, and those who find it are few.*

MATTHEW 7:13–14

*This cup that is poured out for you is the new covenant in my blood.*

LUKE 22:20

# Strive to Enter through the Narrow Door, for Jesus Fulfills the New Covenant

JESUS'S DEMAND FOR VIGILANCE—"strive to enter through the narrow door"—is owing to the many dangers that threaten our souls. One of the most frequent imperatives on Jesus's lips is, "Look out!" "Watch!" "Be alert!" We have seen in the previous chapter the need for striving against the perils of pain and pleasure: the deceit of money, the praise of man, the lure of physical indulgence. We turn now to the perils of false prophets and false christs and the danger of nostalgia for the days when the cost of discipleship was not so high. Then we turn to the crucial question: Is all this vigilance and all this striving to enter through the narrow door consistent with the sweet invitations of Jesus to come to him and find rest?

## The Perils of False Prophets and False Christs

Jesus warns us that false prophets and even false christs will abound. In fact, the first warning he gives us after saying, "The gate is narrow and the way is hard that leads to life" is this: "Beware of false prophets, who come to you in sheep's clothing but inwardly are ravenous wolves.

You will recognize them by their fruits" (Matt. 7:15–16). This is not a casual remark. It is a life-and-death warning: "False christs and false prophets will arise and perform signs and wonders, to lead astray, if possible, the elect. *But be on guard*; I have told you all things beforehand" (Mark 13:22–23). Be on guard! Keep your eyes open! Watch! Be vigilant! Strive to enter by the narrow door.

Jesus underscores that the door is *narrow* that leads to life. Not every claim will fit through the narrow door of the kingdom of God. There are many false christs. In this context *Christ* means Jewish Messiah—the one who fulfills all God's promises and brings in the kingdom and sits on the throne of David ruling over all the world. There is only one Christ, and the rest are "false christs." Jesus is the only Messiah. Therefore, the door is as narrow as faith in Jesus, the only true Messiah and King of kings.

I have sat in my office with followers of another "christ" and pleaded with them to turn to the true and only Christ, Jesus. They said that the Christ had come in our day and that he was gathering a people now for himself. I read to them Luke 17:24 to show them that Jesus said when he comes it would be globally unmistakable and that anyone who says it has already happened is a pretender: "For as the lightning flashes and lights up the sky from one side to the other, so will the Son of Man be in his day." They said that in order to understand the secret meaning of this verse I would need to read a book written by their leader, the "christ" they believed in. As they left I stood at my window watching them walk across the parking lot and prayed for them. I gave thanks that God had helped me "be on guard." Jesus said this would happen and helped me watch as I sat there in my office. This vigilance is part of what it means to "strive to enter through the narrow door."

### You Do Not Know When Your Lord Is Coming

What gives Jesus's demand for vigilance and striving its unusual urgency is the warning that the time of his second coming is unknown to any of us. "*Stay awake*, for you do not know on what day your Lord is coming. . . . Watch therefore, for you know neither the day nor the hour" (Matt. 24:42; 25:13). When Jesus tells us to "watch" or "stay awake" because we do not know the time of his second coming, he does not mean that we skip sleep and look out our windows. We know this because the command to "watch" is the climax of the parable of the ten virgins, five of whom were wise and five of whom were foolish, but all of whom slept. The wise made sure they had oil in their lamps so that when the bridegroom came they might go out with their lamps to greet him. That was their job. Jesus says that all ten of them "became drowsy and slept" (Matt. 25:5). He did not criticize the wise virgins for sleeping.

When the bridegroom came at midnight (representing the second coming of Jesus to earth at an unexpected hour), Jesus said, "Those who were ready [the five wise virgins] went in with him to the marriage feast, and the door was shut" (Matt. 25:10). The foolish virgins had to go get oil because they were unprepared. When they returned they cried out, "Lord, lord, open to us" (Matt. 25:11). But the bridegroom (representing Jesus) answered, "Truly, I say to you, I do not know you" (Matt. 25:12). The lesson Jesus draws out of this parable is, "*Watch* therefore, for you know neither the day nor the hour" (Matt. 25:13). But all ten of the virgins were asleep, including the five wise virgins. That's how we know that when Jesus says, "Watch!" he does not mean skipping sleep and looking out our window.

He means, be watchful over your life. Be watchful over what the Bridegroom has called you to do. The wise virgins had done the will of the Master: their lamps were fully prepared. Sleeping was just fine because they had done their jobs. Therefore, one way to describe "striving to enter through the narrow door" is: Fulfill your calling. Be vigilant to do what God has called you to do. You will be happy if Jesus comes and finds you heartily engaged in your earthly calling for his glory. "Who then is the faithful and wise manager, whom his master will set over his household, to give them their portion of food at the proper time? Blessed is that servant whom his master will find so doing when he comes" (Luke 12:42–43). Striving to enter the kingdom by the narrow door includes vigilant faithfulness in the work Jesus has left us to do. As he said in one of his parables, "Engage in business until I come" (Luke 19:13)—do with all your might what he has given you to do.

## Perseverance and the Peril of Nostalgia

One of the great temptations to keep us from fulfilling what Jesus calls us to do is that we grow weary in the battle and look back on how easy life was before we started to follow him. Strive to enter through the narrow door means, fight for perseverance. The zeal of many would-be followers of Jesus grows cold, and they drift away. Jesus said, "Because lawlessness will be increased, the love of many will grow cold. But the one who endures to the end will be saved" (Matt. 24:12–13). In other words, one of the factors that makes the door to the kingdom of God narrow is that striving to enter must last to the end.

Therefore, Jesus warns us against nostalgia for the former days of worldliness. He says that the stress of the last days of this age will tempt people to look back. So with stark simplicity he warns, "Remember Lot's wife" (Luke 17:32). This was a reference to a woman in the Old Testament who was leaving her hometown of Sodom because God was about to destroy the city for its sin. Tragically, like so many would-be followers of Jesus who begin to leave the old way of sin, she looked back. "Lot's wife . . . looked back, and she became a pillar of salt" (Gen. 19:26). God saw an idolatrous heart in her backward glance toward Sodom. This was her true love, not God. Striving to enter through the narrow door means taking heed to the warning of Jesus: "No one who puts his hand to the plow and looks back is fit for the kingdom of God" (Luke 9:62).

## How Does Striving to Enter by the Narrow
## Door Relate to Resting in Jesus?

The question must now be asked: Is all this vigilance and all this striving to enter through the narrow door consistent with the sweet invitations of Jesus to come to him and find rest? If this striving and vigilance sounds like a miserable and burdened way to live, keep in mind that Jesus rebuked the lawyers who burdened people with impossible laws without giving any help: "Woe to you lawyers also! For you load people with burdens hard to bear, and you yourselves do not touch the burdens with one of your fingers" (Luke 11:46). And most of all, keep in mind how Jesus invited people into his fellowship: "Come to me, all who labor and are heavy laden, and I will give you rest. Take my yoke upon you, and learn from me, for I am gentle and lowly in heart, and you will find rest for your souls. For my yoke is easy, and my burden is light" (Matt. 11:28–30).

What makes the commands of Jesus to strive and to be vigilant seem burdensome is the assumption that we are left to ourselves. Our natural tendency is to think that if Jesus tells us to do something and makes this a condition for entering the kingdom of God and having eternal life, he will then stand back and merely watch to see if we will do it. We do not naturally think that if he commands something, he will enable us to do it.

## Jesus Came to Fulfill the New Covenant in His Blood

But Jesus knew that he had come to fulfill the "new covenant" promised by the prophet Jeremiah. At the end of his life at the Last Supper, he took the cup that represented his blood and said, "This cup that is poured out for you is the *new covenant* in my blood" (Luke 22:20).

What was new about the "new covenant" was that the commands of God would not merely be written on stone (Exod. 24:12), as in the covenant with Moses, but would now be written on the hearts of God's people. God promised through Jeremiah, "Behold, the days are coming, declares the Lord, when I will make a new covenant with the house of Israel and the house of Judah, not like the covenant that I made with their fathers on the day when I took them by the hand to bring them out of the land of Egypt. . . . But this is the covenant that I will make with the house of Israel after those days, declares the Lord: *I will put my law within them, and I will write it on their hearts*" (Jer. 31:31–33).

Jesus came to inaugurate this new covenant through his life and death and resurrection and by the sending of the Holy Spirit. The prophet Ezekiel wrote that the way the new covenant would secure the obedience of God's people (the striving to enter through the narrow door) was by God's Spirit being given to them and by their own spirit being made new. God said through Ezekiel, "I will put my Spirit within you, and cause you to walk in my statutes. . . . A new spirit I will put within them. I will remove the heart of stone from their flesh and give them a heart of flesh, that they may walk in my statutes and keep my rules and obey them" (Ezek. 36:27; 11:19–20). God's intention was to give his commands *and* the ability to do them. That is the new covenant.

By his shed blood Jesus purchased this new covenant for all who trust him. Then, on the basis of the forgiveness of sins that he obtained for his people (Matt. 26:28), he gave them the promise of the Holy Spirit. He said:

> I will ask the Father, and he will give you another Helper, to be with you forever, even the Spirit of truth . . . he dwells with you and will be in you. . . . When the Helper comes, whom I will send to you from the Father, the Spirit of truth, who proceeds from the Father, he will bear witness about me. . . . He will glorify me, for he will take what is mine and declare it to you. (John 14:16–17; 15:26; 16:14)

## Without Christ Our Striving Would Be Losing

Therefore, by his death and by the sending of the Spirit, Jesus obtains the new-covenant promises for those who trust him. And the heart of that covenant is that our sins are forgiven, and the Spirit of God is given to help us do what Jesus commands, namely, strive to enter by the narrow door. In other words, Jesus's command that we "strive to enter" does not mean he stands aloof and watches. As Martin Luther wrote in his famous hymn:

> Did we in our own strength confide, our striving would be
> losing;
> Were not the right Man on our side, the Man of God's own
> choosing:
> Dost ask who that may be? Christ Jesus, it is He;
> Lord Sabaoth, His Name, from age to age the same,
> And He must win the battle.[1]

We are not left to ourselves in our striving. The command to strive is the command to experience the powerful striving of God on our behalf in fulfillment of his new-covenant promise to cause us to walk in his statutes (Ezek. 36:27). We will see this all the more clearly and forcefully in the next chapter, which deals with the presence of the kingdom of God and the presence of eternal life and the way to maintain hope and joy and peace as we strive to enter through the narrow door.

---

1   Martin Luther, "A Mighty Fortress Is Our God" (1529).

*Truly, I say to you, whoever does not receive the*
*kingdom of God like a child shall not enter it.*

MARK 10:15

Lord just save us from
ourselves. Keep us stead fast
in your word - + in faith toward you

Esther

# Strive to Enter through the Narrow Door, for You Are Already in the Kingdom's Power

THE COMMAND TO STRIVE TO ENTER the kingdom of God through the narrow door should be heard in connection with the truth that God has already done something to make that striving full of hope and confidence. We strive not with fretting that we will not enter but with assurance that not only *will* we enter, but that in a decisive sense we have already entered. This may sound paradoxical: strive to enter, for you have entered. But it is profoundly true for all who trust in Jesus.

## The Secret of the Kingdom of God: It Is Here

At the center of Jesus's message is the claim that both the kingdom of God and eternal life are *present* experiences as well as *future* promises. In other words, when Jesus commands that we strive to enter the kingdom through the narrow door, he is focusing on the future experience of final joy and perfect fellowship with God when the kingdom comes in fullest measure in the future. Strive to enter that. But the "secret of the kingdom" (Mark 4:11) that Jesus revealed to his disciples was that the kingdom had *already* arrived in his ministry and that his followers enter it *now* and experience its power even before its final consummation.[1] For example, Jesus said, "If it is by the finger of God that I cast out demons, then *the kingdom of God has come upon you*. . . . Behold, the kingdom of God *is in the midst of you*" (Luke 11:20; 17:21). In his ministry the kingdom of God, which will be consummated in the future, has come near, and its power is in delivering people from bondage to Satan and sin.

Which means, for the followers of Jesus, that our striving to "enter through the narrow door" is done in the power of the kingdom that we have received as a free gift. Recall how Jesus put it: "Truly, I say to you, whoever does not *receive* the kingdom of God like a child shall not *enter* it" (Mark 10:15). We now receive it as a gift by faith and experience its power. By this power of the kingdom we will walk the "hard way" and enter the "narrow door." Paradoxically, we strive to *enter* the kingdom from *inside* the kingdom. The present power of the kingdom is here, and we have entered into that power by faith. The consummation of the kingdom, with its victory over death and disease and all sin, is still future, and we are not yet there.

### Eternal Life Is Ours Now

The same interconnection between the future and the present is true of *eternal life*, not just of the kingdom of God. On the one hand, Jesus speaks of eternal life as a future inheritance: "Everyone who has left houses or brothers or sisters or father or mother or children or lands,

---

1  "The mystery of the Kingdom is the coming of the Kingdom into history in advance of its apocalyptic manifestation. It is, in short, 'fulfillment without consummation.' . . . The new truth, now given by revelation in the person and mission of Jesus, is that *the Kingdom which is to come finally in apocalyptic power, as foreseen in Daniel, has in fact entered into the world in advance in a hidden form to work secretly within and among men*." George Ladd, *The Presence of the Future* (Grand Rapids, Mich.: Eerdmans, 1974), 222. Emphasis added.

for my name's sake, will receive a hundredfold and *will inherit eternal life*" (Matt. 19:29; cf. 25:46). But on the other hand, he teaches that believing on him means having eternal life now: "Truly, truly, I say to you, whoever hears my word and believes him who sent me *has* eternal life. He does not come into judgment, but *has passed from death to life*" (John 5:24; cf. 3:36). By trusting Jesus we have eternal life now, but we will come into the fullest experience of it in the future.

### The Presence of Life and Kingdom Does Not Produce Presumption but Joy

Jesus's teaching about this truth—that entering the kingdom of God and entering eternal life are both present experience and future hope—does not express itself in presumption and carelessness. It does not produce the attitude that says, "I'm already saved; it does not matter how I live. I do not need to be vigilant. I do not need to strive to enter through the narrow door." That is not the way a person talks who has entered eternal life and has been grasped by the power of God's kingdom. Instead this truth expresses itself in joyful striving.

To some people striving does not sound like a joyful way to live. It sounds burdensome. But that is not the way followers of Jesus experience it. Of course, taking up our cross and denying ourselves and becoming the "slave of all" (Mark 10:44) is often painful. But it is not oppressive. There is joy at every turn. This was the point of *Command #10*, "Rejoice and Leap for Joy" (Luke 6:23). In fact, it is the joy of having eternal life now and being in the kingdom of God now and knowing our sins are forgiven now and enjoying the fellowship of Jesus now that sustains our ability to strive toward that future entrance through the narrow door into the consummation of God's kingdom. That is the point of the little parable in Matthew 13:44: "The kingdom of heaven is like treasure hidden in a field, which a man found and covered up. Then in his joy he goes and sells all that he has and buys that field." Joy is the sustaining motive for selling all—for striving to enter through the narrow door.

This is an illustration of how doing something difficult and seemingly oppressive—selling all you have—is carried by joy. "*In his joy* he goes and sells all that he has." That is the banner flying over all our striving as we follow Jesus: *In our joy* we fight off every temptation that would destroy our soul with deceptive pleasures or deceptive pain. We fight as those who *must* fight and *will* win. The striving is essential, and its outcome for Christ's sheep is certain. "My sheep hear my voice, and I know them, and they follow me. I give them eternal life, and they will never perish, and no one will snatch them out of my hand" (John 10:27–28).

### Help for the Fainthearted

The command of Jesus that we "strive to enter through the narrow door" is overarching. It gives a sense of urgency to all his commands. It does not refer to a class of commandments but to all of them. It is a command that we take all his word seriously. It calls for lifelong, everyday, hour-by-hour vigilance over our thoughts and feelings and actions. Therefore, it troubles some followers of Jesus who are fainthearted. I have tried to help us all take heart. It may be practically useful to close this chapter with a summary list of ways to maintain hope and joy as we strive together to enter through the narrow door.

### The Fight Is to Cherish What We Have, Not to Earn What We Don't

First, remember that the main battle is the battle to keep seeing Jesus as the supreme treasure of your life. He does not call us to fight for plastic jewels. Following Jesus is the result of finding a treasure hidden in a field—an infinitely valuable treasure. Then in our joy we gladly "let goods and kindred go, this mortal life also"[2] to enjoy that treasure to the full. Striving to enter through the narrow door is only as hard as treasuring Jesus above all things.

---

2  Martin Luther, "A Mighty Fortress Is Our God" (1529).

The battle is not to do what we don't want, but to want what is infinitely worthy of wanting. The fight is not the oppressive struggle to earn God's final rest, but the satisfying struggle to rest in the peace that Jesus freely gives. "Come to me, all who labor and are heavy laden, and I will give you rest. Take my yoke upon you, and learn from me, for I am gentle and lowly in heart, and you will find rest for your souls. For my yoke is easy, and my burden is light" (Matt. 11:28–30). The commands of Jesus are only as hard to obey as his promises are hard to treasure and his presence is hard to enjoy.

**Jesus Promises to Help Us Do the Impossible**

Second, remember that Jesus promises to help us obey his command. "I am the vine; you are the branches. Whoever abides in me and I in him, he it is that bears much fruit, for apart from me you can do nothing" (John 15:5; cf. *Command #7*, "Abide in Me"). He promised to be with us to the end of the age (Matt. 28:20). He promised not to leave us like orphans when he returned to heaven, but to come to us and help us (John 14:16–18). He acknowledges that what he commands is impossible, but then promises omnipotent help: "With man it is impossible, but not with God. For all things are possible with God" (Mark 10:27). Don't think of striving to get his favor. Think of striving with the favor of his help.

**Forgiveness and Justification Are at the Bottom of Our Striving**

Third, remember that forgiveness of sins and justification by faith are at the bottom of our striving (see *Command #20*). We do not strive for them. We strive because we have them. Jesus offers forgiveness in Matthew 26:28 ("This is my blood of the covenant, which is poured out for many for the forgiveness of sins"), and he offers justification in Luke 18:13–14 ("The tax collector, standing far off, would not even lift up his eyes to heaven, but beat his breast, saying, 'God, be merciful to me, a sinner!' I tell you, this man went down to his house justified"). Our standing with God as forgiven and righteous is the ground of our striving, not the goal of our striving. We must strive to enter because that is the mark of the one who belongs to Christ. If we do not strive, we do not bear the mark of belonging to Jesus. But the striving does not create the relationship. The secure relationship produces the joyful striving.

### Perfection Awaits the Age to Come

Fourth, keep in mind that perfection awaits the age to come. We do wish that we could be free from all sinful feelings and thoughts and actions now. That longing and that labor are part of our striving. But we would despair if perfection in this life were a prerequisite for entering through the narrow door. There *is* a perfection required. We saw it in our treatment of *Command #20* ("If you would be perfect, go, sell what you possess," Matt. 19:21), but no human can achieve it. Only Jesus fulfills all righteousness (Matt. 3:15). This is why he teaches us to pray, not once, but every day, "Forgive us our debts" (Matt. 6:12). Very bluntly Jesus calls his disciples (not would-be disciples, but committed disciples) "evil"—"If you then, *who are evil,* know how to give good gifts to your children . . ." (Matt. 7:11). Let us then take heart that the mark of a true follower of Jesus is not yet perfection but rather unrelenting battle against sin. We fail, but we do not fall away.[3] We stumble, but we do not fall headlong into apostasy.

### Jesus Prays for Us That We Not Fail

Fifth, remember that the reason we do not fall away is that Jesus is not only helping us by his presence and Spirit, but is also praying for us. Jesus said to Peter who was about to deny him three times, "I have

---

3  The term "fall away" can refer to a temporary departure from Christ in fear followed by repentance and restoration. For example, in Matthew 26:31, Jesus said to his disciples, "You will all fall away because of me this night. For it is written, 'I will strike the shepherd, and the sheep of the flock will be scattered.'" But I am using the term here in its more absolute sense. True followers of Jesus will not fall away utterly and finally.

prayed for you that your faith may not fail. And when you have turned again, strengthen your brothers" (Luke 22:32). Jesus knew Peter would sin, and he knew he would turn back from his sinful denial. He said, "*When* you have turned," not "*If* you turn." He did not use his sovereign power to prevent Peter's sin, but he did use it to prevent Peter's falling away. There is no reason to think Jesus has stopped praying like that for his loved ones. God will answer his Son when he prays, "Holy Father, keep them in your name, which you have given me, that they may be one, even as we are one" (John 17:11).

### We Are Striving to Enter Our Father's House

Sixth, remember your position as a true *child* of God. Jesus taught his disciples to know and trust God as their personal *Father* in heaven. Before Jesus came, Israel as a people thought of God as the Father of the nation, but relating to God *individually* as Father was unusual. But Jesus made it central and referred to it again and again. The implication was: God loves you personally as his child and will take care of you. Bank on it.

This did not apply to everyone. For example, he said to some, "If God were your Father, you would love me, for I came from God and I am here. . . . You are of your father the devil, and your will is to do your father's desires" (John 8:42, 44). This is very important for Jesus's followers: If God is our Father, we love Jesus. This means that being a child of God involves having a new nature. The mark of this new nature is a love for Jesus. Therefore, loving Jesus is a sure sign that we are the children of God.

And if we are already children, we may have deep confidence that our striving to enter the narrow door of our Father's house will succeed. He will see to it. He is our Father now. He is not watching to see if we will strive hard enough to become his children. He is actively helping us get home. For example, when we are tested publicly to see if we will testify of Jesus as we ought, Jesus says not to worry: "It is not you who speak, but the Spirit of *your Father* speaking through you" (Matt. 10:20). Not a single sparrow falls to the ground apart from "your Father," Jesus says. "Fear not, therefore; you are of more value than many sparrows" (Matt. 10:29, 31). That's the spirit of confidence that comes from being a child of God.

### Your Name Is Written in Heaven

Seventh, remember, as you strive to enter through the narrow door, that your name is written in heaven. Jesus said, "Do not rejoice in this, that the spirits are subject to you, but rejoice that your names are written in heaven" (Luke 10:20). If everybody's name is written in heaven, there is no reason to rejoice, but many are on the way to destruction, not the narrow door: "The way is easy that leads to destruction, and those who enter by it are many" (Matt. 7:13). Not all names are written there. Having your name written in heaven means that God will deliver you from evil and bring you to his kingdom. Jesus had read about this book in a prophet he knew well, Daniel 12:1: "There shall be a time of trouble, such as never has been since there was a nation till that time. But at that time your people shall be delivered, *everyone whose name shall be found written in the book*."

### You Were Chosen by God and Given to Jesus

Eighth, remember that Jesus is not collecting disciples whom God has not known. God knew his own first and wrote them in his book. Now the Father is drawing them to his Son for salvation. "All that the Father gives me will come to me, and whoever comes to me I will never cast out" (John 6:37). The followers of Jesus belonged to God first and then were given to Jesus (John 17:9). If someone comes to Jesus, it is because the Father knew him and gave him to the Son. That's why Jesus said, "No one can come to me unless it is granted him by the Father" (John 6:65). When they come, Jesus reveals the Father to them, and the Father keeps them from falling away: "I have manifested your name to the people whom you gave me out of the world. Yours they were, and you gave them to me" (John 17:6). "My Father, who has given them to me, is greater than all, and no one is able to snatch them out of the Father's hand" (John 10:29). When you remember and rejoice that you are a chosen child of God, your striving will not be oppressive or slavish.

## Jesus Sustains Our Striving by His Joy

Ninth, remember that joy in God is the key way that Jesus enables us to strive to enter through the narrow door. First, Jesus says, "I am the vine; you are the branches . . . apart from me you can do nothing" (John 15:5). Then he says, "These things I have spoken to you, that my joy may be in you, and that your joy may be full" (John 15:11). In other words, the way Jesus enables us to strive successfully to enter through the narrow door is by imparting to us his joy. Then later he adds, "No one will take your joy from you" (John 16:22). This joy in Jesus and all that God is for us in him sustains lifelong striving to enter though the narrow door.

## Our Striving Will Not Be in Vain

Vigilance is the mark of the followers of Jesus. They know that "the gate is wide and the way is easy that leads to destruction" (Matt. 7:13). They are serious about life. Heaven and hell are at stake. Therefore, they are seriously joyful. The Son of God has rescued them from the guilt and power of sin. They are children of God. Their names are written in heaven. They have received the Helper, the Spirit of truth. They have the promise of Jesus to be with them to the end of the age. They know that he is praying for them. They rejoice that they stand righteous before God because of Jesus. They have received the kingdom. They have eternal life as a present possession. And they marvel that no one can snatch them out of God's hand. In this joy they are energized to strive to enter by the narrow door. And they are confident their striving will not be in vain.

*For I tell you, unless your righteousness exceeds that of the scribes and Pharisees, you will never enter the kingdom of heaven.*

MATTHEW 5:20

*Woe to you, scribes and Pharisees, hypocrites! For you are like whitewashed tombs, which outwardly appear beautiful, but within are full of dead people's bones and all uncleanness. So you also outwardly appear righteous to others, but within you are full of hypocrisy and lawlessness.*

MATTHEW 23:27–28

*For from within, out of the heart of man, come evil thoughts, sexual immorality, theft, murder, adultery, coveting, wickedness, deceit, sensuality, envy, slander, pride, foolishness. All these evil things come from within, and they defile a person.*

MARK 7:21–23

*Blessed are the pure in heart, for they shall see God.*

MATTHEW 5:8

# Your Righteousness Must Exceed That of the Pharisees, for It Was Hypocritical and Ugly

JESUS SAID THAT WE CANNOT enter the kingdom of heaven if our righteousness does not exceed that of the scribes and Pharisees (Matt. 5:20). Someone might take this to mean that we must out-Pharisee the Pharisees. They were the most meticulous Jewish students of the Mosaic law and the most rigorous enforcers of its details. The tradition had grown up that there were 246 positive commandments in the Law (the first five books of the Bible) and 365 prohibitions.[1] Getting these right and keeping them meticulously was the vocation of the

---

1   Maimonides (1135–1204) was a Spanish-born Jewish philosopher and physician, probably the greatest medieval Jewish scholar. He published a definitive list of the laws of the Pentateuch (the first five books of the Bible). He put the number at 613, two more than the traditional number because he treated, "I am the LORD your God" (Exod. 20:1) and "Hear, O Israel: The LORD our God, the LORD is one" (Deut. 6:4) as positive commandments. "He reckoned that since there were 248 distinct parts of the human body, one was to remember to obey God's positive commands with 'all one's self,' and since there were 365 days of the year, one was to remember not to disobey God's commands each day of the year. Since the time of Maimonides, his count of 613 laws has been accepted as the traditional number." John Sailhamer, *The Pentateuch as Narrative* (Grand Rapids, Mich.: Zondervan, 1992), 481; all 613 commandments are listed on pages 482–516.

Pharisees. So does Jesus mean that we are to be even more meticulous in tallying up the laws and shaping our behavior around them?

John Stott answers:

> It is not so much, shall we say, that Christians succeed in keeping some 240 commandments when the best Pharisees may only have scored 230. No. Christian righteousness is greater than pharisaic righteousness because it is deeper, being a righteousness of the heart. . . . The righteousness which is pleasing to [God] is an inward righteousness of mind and motive. For "the Lord looks on the heart."[2]

This is the right answer. But to see it clearly we need to take a look at what Jesus saw when he looked at the righteousness of the scribes and Pharisees. It is not a pretty picture.

### Jesus and the Pharisees: Anger and Entreaty

No group awakened anger and aching in the heart of Jesus like the Pharisees. Matthew 23 is the most severe chapter in all four Gospels. It is unremitting criticism of the Pharisees. Yet it ends with an echo of the aching in Jesus's heart: "O Jerusalem, Jerusalem, the city that kills the prophets and stones those who are sent to it! How often would I have gathered your children together as a hen gathers her brood under her wings, and you were not willing!" (Matt. 23:37). And this longing for the Pharisees is also expressed in the parable of the prodigal son and the attitude of the elder brother of the prodigal. He represents the Pharisees and scribes who criticized Jesus for eating with sinners. "The Pharisees and the scribes grumbled, saying, 'This man receives sinners and eats with them'" (Luke 15:2).

Jesus told the parable of the prodigal son in answer to this criticism. The point of the parable was that Jesus's eating with sinners was not

---

2   John R. W. Stott, *The Message of the Sermon on the Mount* (Leicester, England: Inter-Varsity, 1978), 75. The reference to God looking on the heart is from 1 Samuel 16:7; see also Luke 16:15.

God's complicity with sin but God's pursuit of sinners. But at the end of the parable Jesus reaches out to the Pharisees. He describes the father (who represents God) as coming out and entreating the pharisaic older son to join the celebration of his lost brother's being back home. In other words, the parable is a merciful offer to the Pharisees to join the celebration of grace in Jesus's life and ministry.

But the elder son will not leave his angry position of self-righteous *servant* to join the joyful position of being a son: "Look, these many years I have *served* you, and I never disobeyed your command, yet you never gave me a young goat, that I might celebrate with my friends" (Luke 15:29). He sees himself as a deserving servant, not a freely loved son. The father's last words to this elder brother are full of the ache Jesus felt for the Pharisees: "Son, you are always with me, and all that is mine is yours.[3] It was fitting to celebrate and be glad, for this your brother was dead, and is alive; he was lost, and is found" (Luke 15:31–32). The brother, it seems, will not do what is fitting. He will not love mercy. He wants to be treated for his own merit, not his father's mercy. The parable is open-ended. The Pharisees who are listening should hear an invitation to them. Jesus will welcome them into the celebration of grace and salvation if they will lay down their judgmental self-righteousness and delight in mercy.

3   This does not mean that the Pharisees are saved. We know that Jesus expects that they will be cast out of the kingdom if they do not repent. He said in Matthew 8:11–12, "I tell you, many will come from east and west [that is, Gentiles] and recline at table with Abraham, Isaac, and Jacob in the kingdom of heaven, while the sons of the kingdom will be thrown into the outer darkness. In that place there will be weeping and gnashing of teeth." What Jesus means is that his kinsmen, the Jewish people (represented in their leaders by the Pharisees and the elder brother), were in a position of extraordinary privilege. God had given them the law and the covenant and the promises and had come in the flesh as the Jewish Messiah. The kingdom of God belonged to the Jewish people, so to speak, as a natural inheritance. But the ministry of Jesus revealed that many in Israel did not love the God of Israel and were proving themselves unsuited to receive the inheritance. As long as the elder brother insists on being not a joyful son but an angry servant, he will not be able to receive the blessing of what is happening in the house. This is the meaning of the ominous words of Jesus in Matthew 21:43, "Therefore I tell you, the kingdom of God will be taken away from you [the Jewish leaders who oppose Jesus] and given to a people producing its fruits [Jews and Gentiles who have faith in Jesus and follow him on the Calvary road of love]."

But very few of the Pharisees, as far as we know, made that move. Apparently Nicodemus did. He was the Pharisee who came to Jesus with questions at night and heard Jesus say, "Unless one is born again he cannot see the kingdom of God" (John 3:3). We find Nicodemus after the death of Jesus making an extremely risky move for "a ruler of the Jews" (John 3:1). He brought seventy-five pounds of spices to honor Jesus's dead body (John 19:39) and joined with Joseph of Arimathea to give Jesus a proper burial. The Bible does not say he had become a disciple, though it calls Joseph one (Matt. 27:57). But it is hard to imagine a Pharisee taking such a risk if he had not come to faith in Jesus. But that was rare. For the most part, the Pharisees were entrenched in enmity toward Jesus to the end.

**What the Pharisees Loved: Praise, Money, Sex**

The picture Jesus paints of them is tragic and ugly. The root problem is that their hearts are far from God. He said to them in Matthew 15:7–8, "Well did Isaiah prophesy of you, when he said: 'This people honors me with their lips, but their heart is far from me.'" Their hearts do not treasure God; they treasure money, praise, and sex.

After Jesus told a parable about the right use of money in Luke 16:1–9, the Pharisees ridiculed him. Luke says that the reason was that they "were lovers of money" (Luke 16:14). Later Jesus said, "Beware of the scribes . . . who devour widows' houses" (Luke 20:46–47). That is, they create rules and preserve traditions that make temple-giving a substitute for caring for the poor, even your own parents (Mark 7:9–13). And when Jesus described what was in the heart of the Pharisees he said they were "full of greed and self-indulgence" (Matt. 23:25). In all their thoroughgoing religiosity, they did not love God; they loved money.

And they loved the praise of man. The reward they sought for what they did was not the enjoyment of God's fellowship, but the admiration of others. Jesus said, "They do all their deeds to be seen by others. For they make their phylacteries broad and their fringes long, and they love the place of honor at feasts and the best seats in the synagogues and greetings in the marketplaces and being called rabbi by others" (Matt. 23:5–7). This love affair with the praise of man made genuine faith in the self-sacrificing Christ impossible. So Jesus said to them,[4] "How can you believe, when you receive glory from one another and do not seek the glory that comes from the only God?" (John 5:44). Their hearts were not drawn to God as their reward, but to the praise of man.

And as is usually the case with those who are driven by the love of money and human praise, the Pharisees were also, it seems, often involved in illicit sex. Jesus calls them a "wicked and *adulterous* generation." "Then some of the scribes and Pharisees answered him, saying, 'Teacher, we wish to see a sign from you.' But he answered them, 'An evil and *adulterous* generation seeks for a sign'" (Matt. 12:38–39). I argued in *Command #9* that this refers at least in part to the *spiritual* adultery of Israel's not wanting to have Jesus as their true husband. But it is natural to assume that the word "adulterous" implies that the alternative "husbands" include not just money and human praise but also illicit sex. When the heart is not deeply entranced by the glory of God, it is usually driven along by the pitiful powers of money and the praise of man.

### Hypocrisy: The Cloak of Law-Keeping Exactitude

What made this idolatry so ugly to Jesus was that it all came in clean religious clothing. This was the essence of what he called hypocrisy. "Woe to you, scribes and Pharisees, hypocrites! For you clean the outside of the cup and the plate, but inside they are full of greed and self-indulgence" (Matt. 23:25). Cleaning the outside of the cup refers to using the law of God to conceal the rejection of God. This made Jesus more angry than anything else. "Woe to you, scribes and Pharisees,

---

4   The Pharisees are not explicitly mentioned in John 5, but "the Jews" mentioned in John 5:10, 15, 16, 18 are probably the spokesmen for the people, namely, the scribes and Pharisees. The role they play is identical to what the Pharisees play elsewhere.

hypocrites! For you are like whitewashed tombs, which outwardly appear beautiful, but within are full of dead people's bones and all uncleanness. So you also outwardly appear righteous to others, but within you are full of hypocrisy and lawlessness" (Matt. 23:27–28). These are strong words to describe the hearts of the Pharisees: greed, self-indulgence, dead bones, unclean, hypocrisy, and lawlessness. All of that cloaked with law-keeping exactitude.

But it gets worse. In the next chapter we will see some of the love-less behaviors this inner corruption produces. It should be clear at this point that the righteousness of the Pharisees will not avail with God. We must have a righteousness that exceeds what we see in the Pharisees.

*Watch and beware of the leaven of the Pharisees and Sadducees.*

MATTHEW 16:6


*You blind guides, straining out a gnat and swallowing a camel!*

MATTHEW 23:24


*Woe to you, scribes and Pharisees, hypocrites! For you clean the outside of the cup and the plate, but inside they are full of greed and self-indulgence. You blind Pharisee! First clean the inside of the cup and the plate, that the outside also may be clean.*

MATTHEW 23:25–26


*They tie up heavy burdens, hard to bear, and lay them on people's shoulders, but they themselves are not willing to move them with their finger.*

MATTHEW 23:4

# Your Righteousness Must Exceed That of the Pharisees— Clean the Inside of the Cup

JESUS'S DESCRIPTION OF the heart of the Pharisees, which we saw in the previous chapter, is devastating: greed, self-indulgence, dead bones, uncleanness, hypocrisy, lawlessness. Not surprisingly, when this kind of heart protects and provides for itself by looking "righteous" on the outside, it necessarily majors on the minors of righteousness.

### Blind to Spiritual Proportion

It is easier to tithe than to love justice, mercy, and faithfulness. "Woe to you, scribes and Pharisees, hypocrites! For you tithe mint and dill and cumin,[1] and have neglected the weightier matters of the law: justice and mercy and faithfulness" (Matt. 23:23). They were blind to any sense of spiritual proportion: "You blind guides, straining out a gnat and swallowing a camel!" (Matt. 23:24). And what makes matters worse, when the blind become guides, other people are hurt, even destroyed.

---

1 Mint, dill, and cumin are spices and represent the minutiae of their external obedience in contrast to the magnitude of their internal corruption.

"They are blind guides," Jesus said, "and if the blind lead the blind, both will fall into a pit" (Matt. 15:14).

Which means their spiritual blindness and deadness was both suicidal and murderous. They were destroying themselves and others. "Woe to you Pharisees!" Jesus warned. "For you are like unmarked graves, and people walk over them without knowing it" (Luke 11:44). Coming in contact with the dead was viewed as defiling. Ironically, in all their effort to remain ceremonially clean, they proved to be not only dead themselves but hurtful to others by their deadness.

## The Hellish Condition of Being Mercilessly Demanding

Nor did they care. As is regularly the case with self-righteous hypocrites, their attitude toward others is mercilessly demanding. "They tie up heavy burdens, hard to bear, and lay them on people's shoulders, but they themselves are not willing to move them with their finger" (Matt. 23:4). In other words, their use of the law is merciless. Unlike Jesus, whose yoke is easy and burden is light (Matt. 11:28–30) because he grants what he commands,[2] they only command and do not lift a finger to help. In this way they not only perish themselves but drag people down with them. "Woe to you, scribes and Pharisees, hypocrites! For you shut the kingdom of heaven in people's faces. For you neither enter yourselves nor allow those who would enter to go in" (Matt. 23:13).

Strictly speaking, this is hellish. Hell-bound hypocrites labor to take others with them. With profound love for lost and vulnerable people, Jesus unleashed his fury against the agents of hell: "Woe to you, scribes and Pharisees, hypocrites! For you travel across sea and land to make a single proselyte, and when he becomes a proselyte, you make him twice as much a child of hell as yourselves" (Matt. 23:15). Jesus is not speaking in vague metaphors here. They are children of hell because the devil is their father, not God. Jesus said to them, "If God were your Father, you

---

2   See *Demands #7, 21, 23, 24.*

would love me, for I came from God and . . . he sent me. . . . You are of your father the devil, and your will is to do your father's desires" (John 8:42–44). In other words, their heart is shaped in its affections and choices by the will of Satan. Their disposition is formed by the fashions of hell.

The Pharisees try to deflect this assessment of themselves by turning the tables and accusing Jesus of working for Satan. They say, "It is only by Beelzebul, the prince of demons, that this man casts out demons" (Matt. 12:24). But Jesus points out that his Satan-defeating ministry cannot be explained by complicity with Satan: "If Satan casts out Satan, he is divided against himself. How then will his kingdom stand?" (Matt. 12:26). No, the fact remains: it is the Pharisees who are the "brood of vipers" who cannot speak good because they *are* evil. "How can you speak good, when you are evil? For out of the abundance of the heart the mouth speaks" (Matt. 12:34).

### Clean the Inside So That the Outside Also May Be Clean

This is the essence of their problem: their heart is evil and "hard" (Mark 3:5; 10:5). All their religious and moral effort is spent cleaning the outside and guarding what goes into their mouths, not what comes out of their heart. It was absolutely crucial for his disciples that Jesus make plain to them that the Pharisees have this backwards. So he explains to them in private, "Do you not see that whatever goes into the mouth passes into the stomach and is expelled? But what comes out of the mouth proceeds from the heart, and this defiles a person. . . . But to eat with unwashed hands does not defile anyone" (Matt. 15:17–20).

The Pharisees were acting like fools—as though the God who made the outside did not care about the inside even more. "You fools!" Jesus cried out, "Did not he who made the outside make the inside also?" (Luke 11:40). Then he told them as plainly and as straightforwardly as possible what they needed to do: "You blind Pharisee! First clean the inside of the cup and the plate, that the outside also may be clean" (Matt. 23:26). Or in another place he expressed it more indirectly and provocatively. He said, "But give as alms those things that are within, and behold, everything is clean for you" (Luke 11:41).

Contrary to this counsel, the Pharisees gave alms to be seen by men (Matt. 23:5). In other words, their heart was not in it. When they gave to the poor, they did not give their heart. That is, they did not give love. They did not care whether the poor became children of hell or children of heaven. They simply wanted to be admired for their deed. Jesus's remedy for this is: "Clean the inside of the cup and the plate, that the outside also may be clean." First comes the transformation of the inside. Then, as a result ("so that," ἵνα), the outside will be clean. Jesus cares about behavior, but not by itself.

This is why a merely social gospel will never find an advocate in Jesus. "Do good things" is not Jesus's main message. Absolutely indispensable to any God-pleasing, Jesus-obeying deeds is, "First clean the inside of the cup." And the "so that" shows that the only external behavior that counts with Jesus is what grows out of a transformed heart. "First clean the inside of the cup and the plate, *that* [ἵνα] the outside also may be clean." The outside matters, but only as the fruit of the inside.

### Stott Was Right

Now we are in a position to see how right John Stott was in the quote at the beginning of the previous chapter. What does Jesus mean when he says, "Unless your righteousness exceeds that of the scribes and Pharisees, you will never enter the kingdom of heaven" (Matt. 5:20)? Stott answered, "Christian righteousness is greater than pharisaic righteousness because it is deeper, being a righteousness of the heart. . . . The righteousness which is pleasing to [God] is an inward righteousness of mind and motive. For 'the Lord looks on the heart.'"[3] Of course, Stott believes that this true righteousness will have external, visible expression in life. But the decisive thing is the righteousness of the heart.

3    John R. W. Scott, *The Message of the Sermon on the Mount* (Leicester: Inter-Varsity Press, 1978), 75. Cf. 1 Sam. 16:7; Luke 16:15.

## An Ugly "Righteousness" Is Easy to Exceed—and Hard

In view of what we have seen, this is exactly what Jesus meant. Jesus's portrayal of the Pharisees' "righteousness" is so ugly, our response may be, that it is easy to exceed. That would be true in one sense and false in another. The true part is that Jesus said, "My yoke is easy, and my burden is light" (Matt. 11:30). He does not want to be in the category of those who "load people with burdens hard to bear" but do "not touch the burdens with one of [their] fingers" (Luke 11:46). Therefore, it is right to think that in one sense the righteousness that Jesus commands is "easy" and his burden is "light."

But in another sense, as we saw in *Command #18*, it is hard. In fact, it is not just hard but impossible. When the rich man turned away from Jesus and went the way of the Pharisees, in love with his money, Jesus commented about how hard it is to "cleanse the inside of the cup" and stop loving money: "With man it is impossible, but not with God. For all things are possible with God" (Mark 10:27). He meant that, left to himself, this man cannot change his heart. He treasures money more than he treasures Jesus. That is what must be changed. That is the righteousness that the Pharisees do not have.

The righteousness that exceeds the Pharisees' righteousness is the new heart that trusts Jesus and treasures him above money, praise, sex, and everything else in the world. Treasuring what is infinitely valuable is, in one sense, the easiest thing in the world—like being commanded to enjoy your favorite food. But when our hearts do not treasure Jesus in this way, changing on our own is beyond us.

## Six Antitheses Show the Righteousness That Exceeds That of the Pharisees

After saying in Matthew 5:20 that our righteousness must exceed that of the scribes and Pharisees, Jesus goes on in the rest of that chapter of the Sermon on the Mount to show that while true righteousness includes loving deeds, it is decisively and essentially internal. *Decisively* because what is on the inside decides whether the external behavior has value before God.

And *essentially* because the essence of the behavior's goodness is its inward motive, not the movements of muscles or the effects on externals. All that Jesus said about the hypocrisy of the Pharisees leads us to this conclusion.

Jesus confirms this in the rest of Matthew 5. He gives six examples of how an external reading of the law must be driven inwardly until the demand of God penetrates the heart and lays claim on the heart's deepest affections. Sometimes these six commands are called *antitheses* because Jesus puts his command in contrast (antithesis) to what the Pharisees were making of the Old Testament law and the temporary accommodations of the law itself.[4]

### From No Murder to No Anger

First, Jesus refers to the commandment not to murder. Over against the mere external application of it, he gives the commandment not to be angry and says that anger, even without the external act, is like murder (Matt. 5:21–26). So we see that the righteousness that exceeds that of the Pharisees is essentially the internal change that does not get angry when wronged (see *Commands #18–19*).

### From No Adultery to No Lust

Second, Jesus refers to the command not to commit adultery, and over against its merely external application, he puts the command not

---

4   Jesus so strongly affirmed the Mosaic law in Matthew 5:17–18 and elsewhere that it is hard to imagine that his commands in Matthew 5:21–48 should be understood as antithetical to the *true* meaning of the law itself. "Do not think that I have come to abolish the Law or the Prophets; I have not come to abolish them but to fulfill them. For truly, I say to you, until heaven and earth pass away, not an iota, not a dot, will pass from the Law until all is accomplished" (Matt. 5:17–18). This is why I say that Jesus puts his command in antithesis to what the Pharisees were making of the Old Testament law. They were treating the law narrowly and as mainly external. Jesus shows that something far deeper is called for, and far more extensive. I do not mean to imply that Jesus did not ever raise some of the standards that were in the Mosaic law. There were parts of the law that were temporary accommodations to the hardness of man's heart. For example, Jesus said, "Because of your hardness of heart Moses allowed you to divorce your wives, but from the beginning it was not so" (Matt. 19:8). With the appearing of the Messiah and the arrival of the power of God's kingdom and the inauguration of the new covenant (see *Command #23*) and the giving of the Holy Spirit, Jesus commanded his disciples to pursue a higher standard than Moses did in permitting actions because of the hardness of the human heart.

to lust: "But I say to you that everyone who looks at a woman with lustful intent has already committed adultery with her in his heart" (Matt. 5:28). So he shows that the righteousness that exceeds that of the Pharisees is essentially the inner change that overcomes the heart's bondage to illicit sexual desire. The righteousness Jesus demands is not just the act, but the purity of heart behind the external chastity.

### From Divorce to Faithfulness

Third, he refers to the provision for divorce in the Old Testament and puts over against it the higher ideal of not divorcing our wives. "But I say to you that everyone who divorces his wife, except on the ground of sexual immorality, makes her commit adultery. And whoever marries a divorced woman commits adultery" (Matt. 5:32). The righteousness that exceeds that of the scribes and Pharisees is the new ability to find an answer to marriage problems not in the external solution of divorce but in the transformation of the heart.[5]

### From Oath-Keeping to Simple Honesty

Fourth, Jesus refers to the commandment that we "perform to the Lord what you have sworn" (Matt. 5:33). Over against it he calls for something more radical and more inward. He demands that our heart be so transparently honest that there is no need for external confirmations (like oaths) to buttress our simple yes and no. The righteousness that exceeds that of the scribes and Pharisees is the inward commitment to total truthfulness that makes "I swear" superfluous.

### From Retaliation to Loving Contentment

Fifth, Jesus quotes the law, "An eye for an eye and a tooth for a tooth." Then in contrast, he gives six commands: "But I say to you, [1] Do not resist the one who is evil. [2] But if anyone slaps you on the right

---

5   For more on Jesus's view of divorce and remarriage see *Commands #40, 41, 42.*

cheek, turn to him the other also. [3] And if anyone would sue you and take your tunic, let him have your cloak as well. [4] And if anyone forces you to go one mile, go with him two miles. [5] Give to the one who begs from you, and [6] do not refuse the one who would borrow from you" (Matt. 5:39–42). All of these are behaviors, not just inward dispositions.

Therefore, we should not say that the righteousness that exceeds that of the scribes and Pharisees is merely internal. It clearly involves acts of remarkable patience and self-denial and love. But neither can we miss the fact that these six commands are so radically contrary to natural, human (pharisaic!) selfishness that they are impossible to do without an inner change that puts our contentment and security in something other than what this world offers, namely, in Jesus.

### From Limited Love to Loving Our Enemies

Finally, Jesus quotes the distortion of the Old Testament law (Lev. 19:18): "You have heard that it was said, 'You shall love your neighbor and hate your enemy'" (Matt. 5:43). Then he contradicts the distortion: "But I say to you, Love your enemies and pray for those who persecute you" (Matt. 5:44). Love becomes visible in sacrificial deeds of service. But love is not first visible. It is first a change in the heart.

This is plain from the command that we "*pray* for those who persecute" us. Prayer means that we really do wish them well.[6] We are praying for their salvation and their everlasting joy and that God's merciful saving will be done in their lives. This will not happen if there is only a raw commitment to act with external courtesy toward our enemies. If we are going to pray for them truly, our hearts will have to be dramatically changed from selfishness to security in Jesus. This change, together with the deeds that flow from it, is the righteousness that exceeds that of the scribes and Pharisees.

---

6   For reflections on the imprecatory psalms that express a will for the enemy's destruction, see "Excursus on Hating the Wicked" in *Command #29*.

In the next chapter we turn to the battle for this inner purity and love that the Pharisees lacked. It is as radical as cutting off your hand and tearing out your eye. But we will also see that the security we enjoy rests not merely on the *demonstration* of a different heart from what the Pharisees had, but also on our *location* in the forgiveness, acceptance, love, and eternal life of God.

*Blessed are the pure in heart, for they shall see God.*

MATTHEW 5:8

*But I say to you that everyone who looks at a woman with lustful intent has already committed adultery with her in his heart. If your right eye causes you to sin, tear it out and throw it away. For it is better that you lose one of your members than that your whole body be thrown into hell. And if your right hand causes you to sin, cut it off and throw it away. For it is better that you lose one of your members than that your whole body go into hell.*

MATTHEW 5:28–30

*Every healthy tree bears good fruit, but the diseased tree bears bad fruit.*

MATTHEW 7:17

# Your Righteousness Must Exceed That of the Pharisees, for Every Healthy Tree Bears Good Fruit

THE FAILURE OF THE PHARISEES was that they focused their moral efforts on cleaning the "outside of the cup" and neglected the purity of the heart. In this chapter we focus on the battle for that purity that goes beyond the Pharisees. As with all battles, the question of triumph looms. Will we win this battle? Therefore, at the end we will turn our attention to the ground of our assurance in God's forgiveness, acceptance, love, and life.

**Purity of Heart: To Treasure One Thing**

When Jesus says in Matthew 5:8, "Blessed are the pure [καθαροὶ] in heart, for they shall see God," he is describing the righteousness that exceeds that of the scribes and Pharisees. He uses the same word "pure" (καθαρός) in describing what the Pharisees need: "You blind Pharisee! First clean [καθάρισον] the inside of the cup and the plate, that the outside also may be clean [καθαρόν]" (Matt. 23:26). The impurity that Jesus cares about most is our failure to trust and love God. The heart is made for God—to trust him and love him. The meaning of *impure* is anything that takes God's place or lessens the degree of our faith in and our love for God.

Søren Kierkegaard wrote a book entitled *Purity of Heart Is to Will One Thing*.[1] That title comes close to the essence of purity. I would only change the word "will" to "treasure." *Willing* can be taken too easily to mean an act of the soul against our true desires. But willing to have God that way would not be purity of heart. Purity rises to the degree that God is *treasured* supremely in Jesus. This is what the Pharisees failed to do, and what the superior righteousness does.

The change of heart that creates a new treasuring of Jesus is a gift of God that we experience when the eyes of our hearts are opened to see Jesus as more to be desired than any other reality. Jesus refers to that change as new birth (see *Command #1*) or repentance (see *Command #2*). It is the assumed summons of Jesus behind all his other comands. Get a new heart. Be born again. That is what we are seeing implicitly here in the demand for a righteousness or a purity that exceeds that of the scribes and the Pharisees. This demand is a call most deeply for the new birth.

This internal change is a gift. God comands it, and God gives it. Jesus says, "You must be born again" (John 3:7), but also says, "The wind blows where it wishes, and you hear its sound, but you do not know where it comes from or where it goes. So it is with everyone who is born of the Spirit" (John 3:8). Jesus gives the command. The free and unpredictable Spirit gives the gift. *Our* responsibility is to see the Jesus who is really there and trust him for all that he is.

### The Life-and-Death Battle for Purity of Heart

What is clear from Jesus's teaching is that keeping and growing the gift of purity and the righteousness that surpasses that of the Pharisees is a life-and-death battle. We are not passive. *Jesus* gives the decisive

---

1  Søren Kierkegaard, *Purity of Heart Is to Will One Thing* (San Francisco: Harper Perennial, 1956).

power, as John 15:5 says, "Apart from me you can do nothing." But *we* experience that power in the willingness to engage in radical and persistent attacks on our own sinfulness. Jesus pronounced a blessing on "those who hunger and thirst for righteousness." They are the ones who "shall be satisfied" (Matt. 5:6). Hunger and thirst are relentless. They never stop. They are signs of life. We will do almost anything in our power to satisfy hunger and thirst. That is how Jesus teaches us to pursue purity.

For example, when dealing with the impurity of inward sexual lust, Jesus commands that we do whatever it takes because our souls are at stake.

> If your right eye causes you to sin, tear it out and throw it away. For it is better that you lose one of your members than that your whole body be thrown into hell. And if your right hand causes you to sin, cut it off and throw it away. For it is better that you lose one of your members than that your whole body go into hell. (Matt. 5:29–30)

This may be what Jesus is referring to when he says, "From the days of John the Baptist until now the kingdom of heaven has suffered violence, and the violent take it by force" (Matt. 11:12).[2] Taking the kingdom by force may be a way of repeating what Jesus says about the fight against lust: tear out your eye or cut off your hand—do whatever it takes—to inherit the kingdom and not go to hell. Take the kingdom by force—force against your sin, not force against God. The battle for righteousness in our hearts is fierce.

## The Radical Point of Tearing Out the Right Eye

Notice three things about this battle. One is that the eye is the first organ to be attacked. "If your right eye causes you to sin, tear it out."

2   See George Ladd, *The Presence of the Future* (Grand Rapids, Mich.: Eerdmans, 1974), 163–64.

Even though the issue is sexual sin, he does not say, "Cut off your sexual organ to avoid the deed." He says, "Tear out your eye to avoid the desire." The battle is for purity of heart before the purity of the bed. Without the purity of heart, everything in the bed is impure.

Second, notice that he says to tear out your *right* eye. The significance of this is that it leaves the left one intact to awaken just as much lust as before. Therefore, Jesus's point is not that literally tearing out the right eye is going to solve anything. The point is not that inward desires can be controlled by external maiming. The point is how enormous the stakes are. They are so great, we must do what we have to do to defeat the bondage of sinful desire. It is astonishing how many people deal with their sin casually. Jesus commands otherwise. Fight for a pure heart with the same urgency as tearing out an eye and cutting off a hand.

Third, notice what is at stake: hell. "It is better that you lose one of your members than that your whole body be thrown into hell." Many Christians who love the truth of justification by grace alone through faith alone—which I love, and which I believe Jesus teaches (see *Command #20*)—find it difficult to take these threats of Jesus at face value. But there is no way to avoid them. They are strewn throughout the Gospels, and they clearly imply that if we forsake the battle for purity, we will perish.

## The Experience of Assurance Rests on Our Location and Demonstration

If we do not have a righteousness that exceeds that of the scribes and Pharisees, Jesus says, we will not enter the kingdom of heaven (Matt. 5:20). Everything we have seen in this chapter shows that Jesus is not thinking here mainly of his own righteousness that is imputed to us.[3] He is thinking of the kind of internal transformation and external application revealed in the following six antitheses of Matthew 5:21–48.

---

3 For Jesus's understanding of justification by faith and the imputation of righteousness, see *Command #20*.

How then do we enjoy security in Jesus when what he requires is real change of heart and real righteous behavior? I tried to answer this question especially in *Command #24*. Indeed I am trying to give an answer to it throughout the book. So I close this chapter with another summary statement. Think of our sense of security—our assurance that we are going to enter the final manifestation of the kingdom of God at the end of the age—resting most decisively on our *location* in God's invincible favor, but also on our behavioral *demonstration* that we are truly in that location.

What I mean by *location* in God's invincible favor is at least six glorious truths about those who have trusted in Jesus. (1) We belonged to God before we belonged to Jesus (John 17:6), that is, we were in God's favor before we ever had any righteousness at all. (2) Our names are written in heaven among the citizens whom God intends to bring there (Luke 10:20). (3) We are justified—declared righteous—by faith in God's free mercy because of Christ (Luke 18:14). Jesus assured us that we need not, and dare not, trust in any righteousness of our own as the basis for our location in his favor. Luke tells us that Jesus's parable of the Pharisee and the tax collector was addressed "to some who trusted in themselves that they were righteous, and treated others with contempt" (Luke 18:9). (4) We are ransomed from every enemy that would destroy our souls (Mark 10:45). (5) We are forgiven all our sins through the blood of Christ (Matt. 26:28). (6) We possess now the new life of the Spirit which is eternal (John 5:24).

That is our location. It is complete and perfect: we cannot be any more chosen, written, justified, ransomed, forgiven, or eternal than we are. That is the decisive rock of our security and assurance. It is objective, outside of us, and unchanging.

## The Demonstration of Our Location

What I mean by the *demonstration* is that the way we live shows our location. It does not create the location. God establishes our location through faith alone. But he has ordained that it be fitting for the location to have a demonstration in the world. This is the righteousness that exceeds that of the scribes and Pharisees. It is necessary, not optional. That is, Jesus assumes that if there is no demonstration of our location in God's favor, then the location does not exist. Jesus says this demonstration is necessary for final salvation (as we say, going to heaven), because God wills to be glorified both for the grace of establishing our *location* in his eternal favor once for all *and* for the grace of supplying the help we need to *demonstrate* this location by our conduct. None who is located by faith in God's invincible favor will fail to have all that is necessary to demonstrate this in life.

The assurance that our demonstration will be infallibly enabled by God rests on numerous realities. For example, (1) Jesus promises that nothing can snatch us out of his hand (John 10:28–29). (2) He promises that a Helper will come and not leave us to ourselves in this battle (John 14:16, 26; 15:26). (3) Jesus himself promises to be with us to the end of the age (Matt. 28:20). (4) Jesus prays that our faith will not fail and that the Father will keep us (Luke 22:32; John 17:11, 15). (5) Jesus assumes imperfection and makes provision for it (Matt. 6:12). (6) Jesus taught that what is required of us, even when it is impossible from our side, is not impossible with God (Matt. 19:26). (7) What is required in our demonstration is that there be evidence of God-given life, not flawlessness. These and other truths give us assurance that God's work in our lives will bring about the grace-exalting demonstration required in the last day.

### Every Healthy Tree Bears Good Fruit

The picture Jesus used to illustrate the necessity of demonstration is the picture of a tree and its fruit. "Every healthy tree bears good fruit, but the diseased tree bears bad fruit. A healthy tree cannot bear bad fruit, nor can a diseased tree bear good fruit. Every tree that does not bear good fruit is cut down and thrown into the fire" (Matt. 7:17–19).

When he says that "a healthy tree cannot bear bad fruit," he does not mean that no follower of his ever sins. The natural way of thinking about the present tense of a Greek verb like "bear" is "go on bearing." So Jesus would be saying, "A healthy tree cannot *go on bearing* bad fruit." In other words, a tree is cut down not for bad fruit here and there. It is cut down for producing so much bad fruit that there is no evidence that the tree is good. What God will require at the judgment is not our perfection, but sufficient fruit to show that the tree had life—in our case, divine life.

"I tell you, unless your righteousness exceeds that of the scribes and Pharisees, you will never enter the kingdom of heaven" (Matt. 5:20). May God grant us to trust Christ alone for the security of our location in God's invincible favor and for the help that he promises to change our hearts and lead us in demonstrable acts of love.

*But I say to you, Love your enemies and*
*pray for those who persecute you.*

MATTHEW 5:44


*Love your enemies, do good to those who hate you, bless*
*those who curse you, pray for those who abuse you.*

LUKE 6:27–28


*If you love those who love you, what benefit is that to you?*
*For even sinners love those who love them. And if you do*
*good to those who do good to you, what benefit is that to*
*you? For even sinners do the same. And if you lend to those*
*from whom you expect to receive, what credit is that to you?*
*Even sinners lend to sinners, to get back the same amount.*

LUKE 6:32–34


*Sanctify them in the truth; your word is truth.*

JOHN 17:17

# Love Your Enemies—
# Lead Them to
# the Truth

JESUS'S COMMAND THAT WE love our enemies, be merciful, make peace, and forgive assumes that there are people who are hard to love. The command is expressed in different ways because people are hard to love in different ways. Jesus calls some people our "enemies," which means they are against us. They want to see us fail. Love them, Jesus says (Matt. 5:44; Luke 6:27, 35). Others may not be our personal enemies in this way, but simply people whose character or personality or condition makes them unattractive or even repulsive. Be merciful to them, Jesus says (Matt. 5:7; 18:33; Luke 10:37). Don't base your treatment of them on what they attract or deserve but on mercy. Others may be our relatives or friends who have taken offense at something we have done—rightly or wrongly—and the relationship is cold or non-existent. Strive to be reconciled to them, Jesus says (Matt. 5:23–26). Others may or may not have anything against you, but you do against them. Forgive them, Jesus says (Matt. 6:14–15). Don't let laziness or pride or anger keep you from the humble work of forgiving, peacemaking, and reconciliation.

### Having Enemies May Mean You Are in Step with Jesus

Jesus's command also assumes that we *will* have enemies and that not all will be reconciled to us, no matter what we do. He shows us that having enemies is not necessarily a bad thing but may mean we are keeping in step with him. For example, he pronounced a blessing on those who are persecuted on account of their allegiance to him. "Blessed are you when others revile you and persecute you and utter all kinds of evil against you falsely *on my account*" (Matt. 5:11). In other words, having enemies is to be expected: "If they have called the master of the house Beelzebul, how much more will they malign those of his household. . . . If they persecuted me, they will also persecute you" (Matt. 10:25; John 15:20).

In fact, Jesus warned that if there were no persecution, it may be a sign of being more like a false prophet than like Jesus: "Woe to you, when all people speak well of you, for so their fathers did to the false prophets" (Luke 6:26). Enmity between the world and the followers of Jesus is rooted in the truth that the world rejects him (John 18:37) and in the deep difference Jesus makes when he changes a person: "If you were of the world, the world would love you as its own; but because you are not of the world, but I chose you out of the world, *therefore the world hates you*" (John 15:19; cf. 17:14). Therefore, we should not assume that if we have enemies we must have done something wrong. That may be true, and we should search our hearts for unnecessary offenses and repent, but Jesus said very plainly that *faithful* disciples will have enemies. Expect it.

### Love Those Who Kill and Those Who Snub

It is remarkable that Jesus draws attention to both severe persecution and mere snubbing as the kinds of enmity we must deal with. We might think that he would deal only with the worst kind of enmity and assume the other would take care of itself. But evidently he thinks we need to be told not only to love when our life is threatened, but also to love when our ego is threatened by a mere slight. Consider the range of enmity he mentions.

We are to love those who persecute us (Matt. 5:44), hate us (Luke 6:27), curse us, abuse us (Luke 6:28), strike us on the cheek, take our cloak (Luke 6:29). Those are all behaviors that would typically hurt us deeply, either physically or emotionally or both, and might kill us (Matt. 10:21; Luke 11:49). To all this we are to respond with love. But besides these very painful kinds of enmity, little things can bother us as well. Jesus said, for example, "If you greet only your brothers, what more are you doing than others? Do not even the Gentiles do the same? . . . And if you do good to those who do good to you, what benefit is that to you?" (Matt. 5:47; Luke 6:33). Here Jesus is dealing with simple acts like greeting and doing acts of kindness, and the issue is: How readily do we greet someone or do a kindness to someone who is a mere stranger or who has done nothing for us? They have not hurt us. They show us no enmity. They are just going about their business showing us no attention. We may feel it as a snub. Or we may not feel anything. Jesus says, love them. Don't love just the ones who recognize you and do good things for you. Love the persecutor, and love the person who simply acts as if you are not alive.

All this raises two basic questions. First, what is this love? What does it look like? How much of us does it involve? Second, where does it come from? How does it arise in our hearts, and how is it sustained over time and drawn out of us when all that is natural would seem to say, "No love is required here, or even possible"? Let's take first the question about what this love is.

### Love Preserves the Truth of the Bible

The first answer to the question of what this love involves is so obvious we may not see it. In commanding us to love our enemies, Jesus is confronting and correcting a bad use of the Bible. "You have heard that it was said, 'You shall love your neighbor and hate your enemy.'

But I say to you, Love your enemies and pray for those who persecute you" (Matt. 5:43–44). In the very act of commanding love, he loves us by correcting a false and harmful interpretation of Scripture.

The Jewish Scriptures that Jesus shared with his contemporaries did not say, "You shall hate your enemy." They said, "You shall not take vengeance or bear a grudge against the sons of your own people, but you shall love your neighbor as yourself" (Lev. 19:18). Some had taken these references to "your own people" and to "neighbor" and concluded that the command to love applies only to neighbors—our own kind. The first act of love Jesus calls for in his command is by his own example of how he gives the command: he shows us that love rejects the bad interpretation of God's word and sets forth the truth.

### Truth Is the Root of Love

I mention Jesus's example of love first not only because it is the first and most immediately present act of love in Jesus's words, but also because in our time in history, love is often contrasted with the defense of truth. That is not what Jesus demonstrates. Not here or anywhere. If someone had said to Jesus the words, "Love unites; doctrine divides," I think Jesus would have looked deep into that person's soul and said, "True doctrine is the root of love. Therefore, whoever opposes it, destroys the root of unity."

Jesus never opposed truth to love. He did the opposite. He said that he himself is the embodiment and sum of truth: "I am the way, and the *truth*, and the life" (John 14:6). Referring to himself he said, "The one who seeks the glory of him who sent him is *true*, and in him there is no falsehood" (John 7:18). At the end of his life, what prompted Pilate's cynical question, "What is truth?" (John 18:38) was Jesus's comprehensive assertion about why he had come into the world: "For this purpose I was born and for this purpose I have come into the world—to bear witness to the *truth*" (John 18:37). Even his adversaries saw how indifferent Jesus was to people's opinions and how devoted he seemed to be to truth. "Teacher, we know that you are *true* and do not care about anyone's opinion" (Mark 12:14). And when Jesus left the world and returned to the Father in heaven, the Spirit he sent in his place was called "the Spirit of truth." "But when the Helper comes, whom I will send to you from the Father, *the Spirit of truth*, who proceeds from the Father, he will bear witness about me" (John 15:26).

Therefore, unlike so many who compromise the truth to win a following, Jesus did the opposite. Unbelief in his hearers confirmed that a deep change was needed in *them*, not in the truth. "Everyone who is of the truth listens to my voice" (John 18:37). "Whoever is of God hears the words of God. The reason why you do not hear them is that you are not of God" (John 8:47). "Because I tell the truth, you do not believe me" (John 8:45). In other words, when the truth does not produce the response you want—when it does not "work"—you don't abandon the truth. Jesus is not a pragmatist when it comes to loving people with the truth. You speak it, and if it does not win belief, you do not consider changing the truth. You pray that your hearers will be awakened and changed by the truth. "You will know the truth, and the truth will set you free (John 8:32). "Sanctify them in the truth," Jesus prayed; "your word is truth" (John 17:17).

When Jesus prays that people be "sanctified in the truth," he reveals the roots of love. Sanctification, or holiness, as Jesus understands it, includes being a loving person. He is praying that we would become loving people and would be merciful and peaceable and forgiving. That is all included in the prayer, "Sanctify them." And all this happens in and by the truth, not separate from the truth. The effort to pit love against truth is like pitting fruit against root. Or like pitting kindling against fire. Or like pitting the foundation of a house against the second-floor bedroom. The house will fall down, and the marriage bed with it, if the foundation crumbles. Love lives by truth and burns by truth and stands on truth. This is why Jesus's first act of love in commanding love is to correct a false interpretation of Scripture.

### The Unloving Use of Truth

Of course, it is possible to use truth unlovingly. For example, when a village of Samaria would not receive Jesus "because his face was set toward Jerusalem" (Luke 9:53), James and John knew this was a truth-insulting response. It was an assault on the truth of Jesus. So they said to Jesus, in defense of the truth, "Lord, do you want us to tell fire to come down from heaven and consume them?" (Luke 9:54). The answer was swift and blunt: "He turned and rebuked them" (Luke 9:55).

But the solution to that unloving response was not to stay in the village and alter the truth to get a better response. He did not say to the Samaritans, "Doctrine divides, love unites, so let's put our doctrinal differences aside and have relational unity." No, the solution was, "And they went on to another village" (Luke 9:56). There are many people yet to be loved with our truth. We will keep offering the saving truth in love wherever we can, and we will not be violent with those who reject us. But the truth will not be changed. It is the root of love's life, and the kindling of love's fire, and the foundation of love's strength. When Jesus commanded that we love our enemies by contrasting this with the interpretation that said, "Love your neighbor and hate your enemy," he was lovingly showing us that correcting false interpretations of the Bible is one crucial way to love our enemy.

### Challenging the Absoluteness of the Beloved

The next obvious implication of Jesus's words for the meaning of love is that it is not unloving to call someone an enemy. We live in an emotionally fragile age. People are easily offended and describe their response to being criticized as being hurt. In fact, we live in a time when emotional offense, or woundedness, often becomes a criterion for deciding if love has been shown. If a person can claim to have been hurt by what you say, it is assumed by many that you did not act in love. In other words, love is not defined by the quality of the act and its motives, but by the subjective response of others. In this way of relating, the wounded one has absolute authority. If he says you hurt him, then you *cannot* have acted lovingly. You are guilty. Jesus will not allow this way of relating to go unchallenged.

Love is not defined by the response of the loved. A person can be genuinely loved and feel hurt or offended or angered or retaliatory or numb without in any way diminishing the beauty and value of the act of love that hurt him. We know this most clearly from the death of Jesus, the greatest act of love ever performed, because the responses to it covered the range from affection (John 19:27) to fury (Matt. 27:41–42). That people were broken, wounded, angered, enraged, and cynical in response to Jesus's death did not alter the fact that what he did was a great act of love.

This truth is shown by the way Jesus lived his life. He loved in a way that was often not felt as love. No one I have ever known in person or in history was as blunt as Jesus in the way he dealt with people. Evidently his love was so authentic it needed a few cushions. It is owing to my living with the Jesus of the Gospels for fifty years that makes me so aware of how emotionally fragile and brittle we are today. If Jesus were to speak to us the way he typically spoke in his own day, we would be continually offended and hurt. This is true of the way he spoke to his disciples and the way he spoke to his adversaries.[1] People were offended

---

1   To his own disciples he spoke bluntly calling them "evil" (Matt. 7:11) and "of little faith" (Matt. 6:30; 8:26; 14:31; 16:8; 17:20) and a "faithless . . . generation" (Matt. 17:17) and telling a would-be disciple who wanted to go to a funeral to let the dead bury their dead (Luke 9:60). He was blunt with his hosts who invited him to dinner: "You gave me no kiss, but from the time I came in she has not ceased to kiss my feet. You did not anoint my head with oil, but she has anointed my feet with ointment" (Luke 7:45–46). "He said also to the man who had invited him, 'When you give a dinner or a banquet, do not invite your friends or your brothers or your relatives or rich neighbors, lest they also invite you in return and you be repaid. But when you give a feast, invite the poor, the crippled, the lame, the blind'" (Luke 14:12–13). He said he was glad that God had hidden truth from the "wise and understanding": "I thank you, Father, Lord of heaven and earth, that you have hidden these things from the wise and understanding and revealed them to little children" (Matt. 11:25). He would not answer those who played word games with the crowds (Matt. 21:23–27). He called Herod a "fox" (Luke 13:32) and excoriated the Pharisees with "brood of vipers" (Matt. 23:33) and "whitewashed tombs" (Matt. 23:27) and "blind guides" (Matt. 23:16) and "hypocrites" (Matt. 23:13) and

in his day as well. "Do you know," his disciples asked him, "that the Pharisees were *offended* when they heard this saying?" (Matt. 15:12). His response to that information was brief and pointed: "Every plant that my heavenly Father has not planted will be rooted up.[2] Let them alone; they are blind guides" (Matt. 15:13–14). In other words, "They are plants that do not produce the fruit of faith because God has not planted them. They don't see my behavior as love because they are blind, not because I am unloving." These and dozens of other things he said to both friend and foe in ways that would rock us back on our emotional heels and make many of us retreat in self-pity.

The point of this is that the genuineness of an act of love is not determined by the subjective feelings of the one being loved. Jesus uses the word "enemies." That would be offensive to some, especially since he goes on to unpack his point with words like, "And if you greet only your *brothers*, what more are you doing than others?" (Matt. 5:47). He does not fret over the possible criticism that he is not being careful enough to distinguish real enemies from annoying brothers. Jesus seems to expect us to handle tough words like "enemy" mingled with tender family words like "brother."

**Love Is Not Oblivious or Uncaring about Its Effects**

I do not mean to say that love is oblivious to the words it uses or the effects they may have on others. Love does care about blessing the

---

"fools" (Matt. 23:17). And of course, he made a whip and drove out the money-changers from the temple (Matt. 21:12). All this, and so much more, would simply put Jesus so far outside the range of emotional tolerance in our day that his behavior would simply not feel loving. All of which goes to show that the criterion of what love is does not reside in the subjective response of the one being loved.

2   "Those plants his Father had planted were those who had received the revelation of Jesus's character from the Father—a revelation he had concealed from the 'wise and prudent' (Matt. 11:25–27; 13:11–17; 16:16–17; cf. 14:33)." Craig S. Keener, *A Commentary on the Gospel of Matthew* (Grand Rapids, Mich.: Eerdmans, 1999), 413. The saying is parallel with John 10:26, "You do not believe because you are not part of my flock" (at). Or John 18:37, "Everyone who is of the truth listens to my voice." Or John 8:47, "Whoever is of God hears the words of God. The reason why you do not hear them is that you are not of God."

loved one. It desires to bring the loved one out of pain and sorrow and into a deeper experience of joy in God—now and forever. But I am stressing another side of the problem that seems unusually prevalent in our psychologized world. I am simply drawing attention to the fact that *feeling* unloved is not the same as *being* unloved. Jesus is modeling for us in his life the objectivity of love. It has real motives and real actions. And when they are loving, the response of the loved one does not change that fact.

This is good news for the lover, because it means that *God* is God and the loved one is *not* God. The judgment of the wounded loved one is not absolute: It may be right, or it may be wrong. But it is not absolute. God is absolute. We give an account to him. And he alone knows our hearts. The decisive thing about our love when we stand before God is not what others thought of it, but whether it was real. That some people may not like the way we love is not decisive. Most people did not recognize Jesus's love in the end—and still do not today. What matters is not that we are justified before men, but that God knows our hearts as truly (though not perfectly) loving. And he alone can make that final judgment (Luke 16:15).

*Love your enemies and pray for those who persecute you.*

MATTHEW 5:44

*Pray for those who abuse you.*

LUKE 6:28

*Father, forgive them, for they know not what they do.*

LUKE 23:34

# Love Your Enemies—Pray for Those Who Abuse You

BEFORE TURNING TO THE COMMAND that we pray for those who persecute us and abuse us, we need to draw out one more clarification of Jesus's command, namely, that love hates the evil that destroys the ones we love.

## Love Hates the Evil That Destroys Persons

We cannot claim to desire the good of the beloved and be indifferent to what destroys him. Jesus's command to love our enemy implies that love must hate the evil that destroys the beloved. If there were a universe in which there was no evil that hurt people or dishonored Jesus, there would be only love and no hate. There would be nothing to hate. But in a world like ours it is necessary not only that we love and hate, but that our love include hate.

### Excursus on Hating the Wicked

This is perhaps the best place to insert some thoughts on the kind of hatred that Jesus read about in the Psalms that are sometimes called the imprecatory psalms— that is, psalms that express hatred for God's enemies and call down divine curses on them. These would include Psalm 5:10; 10:15; 28:4; 31:17–18; 35:4–6; 40:14–15; 58:6–11; 69:22–28; 109:6–15; 139:19–22; 140:9–10. Psalm 139:19–22 says, "Oh that you would slay the wicked, O God! O men of blood, depart from me! They speak against you with malicious intent; your enemies take your name in vain! Do I not hate those who hate you, O LORD? And do I not loathe those who rise up against you? I hate them with complete hatred; I count them my enemies."

We know that Jesus was aware of these psalms and that he did not criticize them but quoted them as authoritative Scripture. At least one of the most severe of them (Psalm 69) seems to have been a favorite from which Jesus, in his human nature, drew guidance and encouragement and self-understanding (John 15:25=Psalm 69:4, "They hated me without a cause." John 2:17=Psalm 69:9, "Zeal for your house will consume me." Matt. 27:34=Psalm 69:21, "They offered him wine to drink, mixed with gall"). This psalm prays, "Pour out your indignation on them, and let your burning anger overtake them" (69:24).

Consider in some of these psalms that *love* for the enemy has been pursued for a long time. "They repay me evil for good . . . when they were sick—I wore sackcloth" (35:12–13). "In return for my love they accuse me, but I give myself to prayer. So they reward me evil for good, and hatred for my love" (109:4–5). Though unexpressed, this may be the case for all the psalms. The wickedness in view has resisted love.

Consider also that hatred may refer at times (not always) to moral repugnance, not personal vengeance. This is not the same as saying, "Hate the sin and love the sinner" (which can be good counsel, but not all there is to say). There is a kind of hate for the sinner (viewed as morally corrupt and hostile to God) that may coexist with pity and even a desire for his salvation. The hate is moral repugnance, not desire for destruction. The analogy with food may help. You may hate spinach (because of its taste) while affirming its worth and desiring that it have its beneficial effect. So it is possible to hate a person in the sense of finding his character loathsome (say, a cannibalistic murderer and child-abuser) while being willing to lay down your life for his salvation. The hate that Jesus forbids to us is the hate that wills a person's destruction.

However, there may come a point when wickedness is so persistent and high-handed and God-despising that the time of redemption is past and there only remain irremediable wickedness and judgment. For example, Jesus speaks of unforgivable sin (Matt. 12:32). He says of the Pharisees who have evidently crossed the line of no return, "Let them alone; they are blind guides. And if the blind lead the blind, both will fall into a pit" (Matt. 15:14). That is an ominous "Let them alone." Craig Keener compares it to Matthew 7:6, "Do not waste your pearls on swine."[1] It seems that Jesus continues what the Psalms affirm, namely, that there comes a point of such extended, hardened, high-handed lovelessness toward God that it may be appropriate to give a person up to destruction and call down anathema on him. Jesus makes it plain that this will happen at the end of the age. He says that the King "will say to those on his left, 'Depart from me, you *cursed*, into the eternal fire prepared for the devil and his angels'" (Matt. 25:41).

From all this, and from the fact that Jesus affirms the divine inspiration of the Psalms (Matt. 22:43; John 10:35), I conclude that he saw the psalmist speaking under the guidance of the Holy Spirit and foreshadowing the Messiah and Judge, who has the ultimate right to call down judgment on the enemies of God. This is not personal

---

1   Craig Keener, *A Commentary on the Gospel of Matthew* (Grand Rapids, Mich.: Eerdmans, 1999), p. 413.

vindictiveness. It is a prophetic execution of what will happen at the last day when God casts all his unrepentant enemies into hell (Luke 12:5; Matt. 22:13; 25:30). We would do well to leave such final assessments to God and realize our own corrupt inability to hate as we ought. While there is unforgivable sin, we are told to love our enemies and pray for those who persecute us and return good for evil (as David did in Psalm 35:12–13; 109:4–5). This is our vocation by faith. Let us tremble and trust God, lest we fail, and find ourselves on the other side of the curse.

To illustrate the truth that in a world like ours it is necessary that our love include hate, consider what Jesus says in John 5:29 that in the last day when the dead are raised, all people will rise, "those who have done good to the resurrection of life, and those who have done *evil* to the resurrection of judgment." This means that there is *evil* in the world that leads to the final destruction of people we love. How does love feel about that evil? My point is that love hates that evil. We do not hate God's judgment. That is just and wise. But we do hate the evil that leads a person to oppose God and incur his judgment.

## There Is No Evil That Hurts Only You

One might be tempted to say at this point that the evil I must hate is only the evil that hurts another person but not the evil that hurts me. In other words, it would not be unloving to *you* if I engage in evil behavior that only involves me. Jesus would say, there is no such behavior. Why not? Because everything I do affects my delight in Jesus and my ability to display him as valuable. That is what we were made for (Matt. 5:16; 10:32). We were made to display the worth of Jesus to others, that they might increasingly awaken to it and enjoy it and reflect it forever. That is the greatest good we can do for them. That is what it means to love them. But if we do things to ourselves that damage our delight in Jesus and damage our display of his worth to others (and that is the very essence of evil—it damages our delight in Jesus and our ability to display his worth), then we rob them of what God made us to give them—a display of his worth. That is the opposite of love. Therefore, love must hate evil, whether it is evil the loved one is doing to his own peril, or the evil I am doing to my own *and his* peril.

I point out the relationship between love and hate simply to waken us from the sentimental slumbers of much love-talk. There are people, especially in our day, whose worldview is so relativistic and whose personality so morally flaccid that they do not even have a category for evil, lest they find themselves offending the demand for tolerance of all views. Jesus would say: Tolerance of all views is the opposite of love. It condones what destroys. We cannot read the words of Jesus with an honest heart and conclude that he denies the existence of evil that destroys and good that leads to everlasting joy. Therefore, to minimize or deny the existence of evil, rather than hating it, makes one partner to the destruction of human persons. This is not the love that Jesus commands.

**"Pray for Those Who Persecute You"**

Jesus gives numerous examples of the kinds of behaviors involved in loving our enemies. The first mentioned in the Sermon on the Mount after the command to love is prayer. "Love your enemies and *pray* for those who persecute you" (Matt. 5:44). And *"Pray* for those who abuse you" (Luke 6:28). This is enormously important in telling us how Jesus thinks about what love is. First, it tells us that love *really wants* the good of the enemy. This is confirmed by the supplementary command, *"Bless* those who curse you" (Luke 6:28). To bless is to desire someone's well-being and turn it into an expressed longing directed to God. For example, Jesus knew the famous blessing from Numbers 6:24–26, "The LORD bless you and keep you; the LORD make his face to shine upon you and be gracious to you; the LORD lift up his countenance upon you and give you peace." Do this, he says, for your enemy. Your enemy needs the light of God's countenance to shine on him and melt his heart.

Therefore, it is clear from this specific command that love is not merely behavior. To be sure, it *is* doing good for the enemy, but not merely that. It is also a heart desire. I base this on the assumption that when we pray for our enemies, we ask for God's blessing *from our heart.* Jesus is not commending hypocritical prayer. He is not calling for show-prayer. He is calling for real prayer, that is, real Godward desire for the good of our enemy. Love really wants the enemy to experience God's best. Doing good things is not enough. The heart must aim at the best we can hope for the enemy.

**What to Pray for Our Enemies**

Not only that, the command to pray for our enemy tells us what that best is that we should want for our enemy. Fourteen verses after this command in the Sermon on the Mount Jesus tells us what he expects us to pray. He tells us to pray like this:

> Our Father in heaven,
> hallowed be your name.
> Your kingdom come,
> your will be done,
>     on earth as it is in heaven.
> Give us this day our daily bread,
> and forgive us our debts,
>     as we also have forgiven our debtors.
> And lead us not into temptation,
>     but deliver us from evil. (Matt. 6:9–13)

It would be unwarranted to think that the loving prayer for our enemy should ask for less important things than we are told to pray for ourselves. So I assume this prayer is what we should pray for our enemies.

- This means that we should ask God that our enemy first and foremost come to hallow God's name, that he value God above all and reverence him and admire him in proportion to God's worth.
- We should pray that our enemy come under the saving sway of God's kingly rule and that God would exert his kingly power to make our enemy his own loyal subject.
- We should pray that our enemy would love to do the will of God the way the angels do it in heaven with all their might and without reservation and with purest motives and supreme joy.
- We should pray that God would supply our enemy with all the physical resources of food and clothing and shelter and education and health care and transportation, etc. that he needs to fulfill God's calling on his life. We should want this for him the way we want it for ourselves.
- We should pray that his sins would be forgiven and that he would be a forgiving person.
- And finally we should pray that God protect him from temptation and from the destructive powers of the devil.

This is what love prays.

It is pathetic to see love stripped of God. Even some Christians are misled into thinking you can love someone without longing for and praying for and aiming at the exaltation of God in the heart of their enemy. What is so sad about this is that it not only betrays the diminished place of God in the heart of the Christian, but also implies that there can be real love where we don't care if someone perishes eternally, as long as they prospered here on earth. It is true that our love and prayer may not succeed in wakening our enemy to faith in Jesus and to the hallowing of God's name. Love is the *aim* of our sacrifice, not its success. We may or may not succeed in the Jesus-exalting, God-hallowing transformation we aim at. But a heart that does not aim at our enemy's eternal joy in Jesus is not the full-orbed, robust love that Jesus commands. It is a narrow and pathetic substitute, no matter how creative and sacrificial and media-admired the labor is for our enemy's earthly welfare. Love prays for our enemy with all the aims and longings of the Lord's Prayer.

### "Father, Forgive Them, for They Know Not What They Do"

The most compelling example of praying for one's enemy was the prayer of Jesus on the cross. After the simple, understated fact in Luke 23:33, "There they crucified him," Jesus prayed, "Father, forgive them, for they know not what they do" (Luke 23:34). This prayer draws together three acts of the heart involved in loving our enemies: prayer, forgiveness, and mercy. Jesus is unremitting in commanding that his disciples be forgiving people.

When Peter asked him, "Lord, how often will my brother sin against me, and I forgive him? As many as seven times?" Jesus answered, "I do not say to you seven times, but seventy-seven times" (Matt. 18:21–22). In other words, "Don't set limits, Peter. Let the mercy in your heart be as bottomless as mine toward you." "Be merciful, even as your Father is merciful" (Luke 6:36). Mercy and forgiveness are needed when there is real guilt, real offense. The "enemy" has really wronged you, and you "deserve" suitable recompense. That is when mercy and forgiveness become relevant and urgent. Mercy says, "I will treat you better than you deserve." And forgiveness says, "I am willing not to count your offense against you. I want the relationship to be restored."

### Why Do They Need Forgiveness If They Don't Know What They're Doing?

Jesus's prayer illustrates this, even though at first it seems not to. He says, "Father, forgive them, for they know not what they do." "Forgive those who murder me because they don't know what they are doing." This raises the question: Why forgive a person for what he does not know he is doing? Wouldn't we say: "Father, since they don't know what they are doing, they are not guilty and don't need to be forgiven"?

Isn't it either-or? Either you know what you are doing and need to be forgiven, or you don't know what you are doing and you don't need to be forgiven? Why does Jesus draw attention to their ignorance of what they are doing *and* ask God to forgive them?

The answer is that they are guilty for not knowing what they are doing. Forgiveness is only needed for the guilty. Nobody can forgive an innocent person. So when Jesus says, "Father, forgive them," he means they are guilty. Then when he says, "For they don't know what they are doing," he must mean, "And they *should* know what they are doing. And they are guilty for not knowing what they are doing." In other words, they have so much evidence of the truth that the only explanation for their ignorance is they don't want to see it. They are hard and resistant and have a guilty blindness. That is why they need to be forgiven.

So here are Gentiles and Jews killing the Son of God, the Messiah of Israel, the most innocent and loving man who ever existed. But they did not know who they were killing. For this ignorance they were guilty and in need of forgiveness. And amazingly, Jesus is praying for them that his Father would open their eyes and help them to see their sin, repent, and be forgiven. That is the beautiful thing about this prayer of Jesus: It declares guilt and offers forgiveness at the same time. It helps us love our enemies by reminding us that our enemies are really guilty and that this must not stop our love and mercy and forgiveness. Most of all it helps us because we know that Jesus was suffering for *us* and praying for *us*. We are called to love and forgive our enemies because we have been loved and forgiven when we were the enemies of God.

*Peter came up and said to him, "Lord, how often*
*will my brother sin against me, and I forgive him?*
*As many as seven times?" Jesus said to him, "I do not*
*say to you seven times, but seventy-seven times."*

MATTHEW 18:21–22

*But I say to you who hear, Love your enemies,*
*do good to those who hate you.*

LUKE 6:27

*And if you greet only your brothers, what more are you*
*doing than others? Do not even the Gentiles do the same?*

MATTHEW 5:47

# Love Your Enemies—Do Good
# to Those Who Hate You, Give
# to the One Who Asks

WE CLOSED THE PREVIOUS CHAPTER by dealing with prayer as a form of love for our enemies. That was clear from Jesus's command to "Love your enemies and *pray* for those who persecute you" (Matt. 5:44). We took Jesus's prayer for his enemies as one example. His focus was forgiveness: "Father, forgive them" (Luke 23:34). Forgiveness and reconciliation are clearly near the heart of Jesus's life and message. Hence we need to dig into these commands more deeply here, then turn to several other forms of enemy love (greeting those outside our group, doing good to those who hate us, turning the other cheek, and giving to the one who asks). Finally, we will wrestle with the question whether all of these commands, like giving to the one who asks, are absolutely the only way that love responds.

## The Opposite of Forgiveness Is Not Alienation

Forgiveness from the heart—not just the mouth—is demanded by Jesus from his disciples: "So also my heavenly Father will do to every one of you [referring to God's punishment in the parable of the unforgiving servant], if you do not *forgive your brother from your heart*" (Matt. 18:35). The opposite of forgiveness is not alienation. The opposite is holding a grudge. The reason for this clarification is that you may have a forgiving heart and be ready to let a painful wrong go, but the one who wronged you may not be willing to repent or even recognize that a wrong was done. Therefore, even though you offer forgiveness, the relationship may not be healed. We know this because Jesus offered forgiveness continually, but not all were reconciled to him. So the opposite of forgiveness is holding a grudge, not removing alienation. We are responsible for what we do, not for what others do. We are responsible for our hearts, not theirs.

But Jesus makes clear that the *effort* to be reconciled is crucial. We should make all reasonable efforts to be reconciled to those who have taken offense at our words or actions. I say all *reasonable* efforts because not every offense people take is warranted. Jesus would have done nothing else with his life if he had to seek out every individual scribe and Pharisee personally who was angry with him. We must keep this in mind when we read Jesus's demand for reconciliation. He said, "If you are offering your gift at the altar and there remember that your brother has something against you, leave your gift there before the altar and go. First be reconciled to your brother, and then come and offer your gift" (Matt. 5:23–24). I take the words, "If . . . your brother has something against you" to mean: "If . . . your brother has something *legitimate* against you."

Someone always had something against Jesus. There was never a moment of his public ministry when someone was not offended at him. If he had not been allowed to worship before approaching all these people individually to be reconciled, he never would have worshiped. So it is with most of his representatives throughout history. They have always had irreconcilable adversaries. In fact, Jesus warned us that we are probably not being his faithful followers if "all people speak well of you" (Luke 6:26). Rather, "Blessed are you when people hate you and when they exclude you and revile you and spurn your name as evil, on account of the Son of Man!" (Luke 6:22).

### Resisting Reconciliation Imperils the Soul

So the point of Matthew 5:23–24 is that if a brother has a true reason to be hurt or offended by something we did, we should move quickly to be reconciled. We can see how crucial this is from the use of the word "so" or "therefore" (οὖν) at the beginning of verse 23: "*So* if you are offering your gift at the altar and there remember that your brother has something against you . . ." This connecting word means that Jesus had just said something that makes the command of verses 23–24 urgent. Here's what he had said: "Everyone who is angry with his brother will be liable to judgment . . . and whoever says, 'You fool!' will be liable to the hell of fire" (Matt. 5:22). In a word, this means: despising your brother imperils your soul.

"*Therefore* . . ." verses 23 and 24 follow. If contempt for a brother or sister imperils our soul—if it threatens to cut us off from God forever, as verse 22 says (by referring to hell)—then we can't go happily on our way to worship with something like that in our heart. It must be dealt with, Jesus said, and quickly! Since despising a brother brings us into peril with God, it is unlikely that God would receive our worship while we are despising a brother in our heart.

But that is *not quite* what Jesus says in verses 23–24. He does not explicitly focus on our anger, but on the relationship that has been damaged by our sin. The focus of Matthew 5:21–22 was indeed on our anger and contempt. And the word "so" at the beginning of verse 23 shows that this anger is still behind what Jesus is about to say. But what he, in fact, does say moves away from our subjective feelings of anger or contempt to the relationship that has been wrecked by our anger. The command is, "Leave your gift there before the altar and go. First be reconciled to your brother, and then come and offer your gift" (Matt. 5:24). Jesus assumes that this will involve putting your anger aside. But the focus is on the concrete steps you should take to talk to the offended brother. This will involve confessing your sin and asking for forgiveness. It is one of the hardest things that a proud, fallen human being can do. But when it happens, the doors of heaven are open for the sweetest experience of worship.

## Love Greets People outside Our Group

Loving our enemy includes those who are hard to love, whether a hostile stranger or a bad-tempered spouse. And therefore the ways of love that Jesus commands are as varied as self-sacrifice at the one end of the spectrum and a simple greeting at the other end. It is remarkable that in the context of enemy-love Jesus says something as ordinary as, "If you greet only your brothers, what more are you doing than others? Do not even the Gentiles do the same?" (Matt. 5:47). People concerned with global suffering and international injustices might think this is ridiculously individualistic and insignificant. Greetings? Does it really matter in a world like ours whom we say hello to on the street? Jesus knows that the true condition of our heart is revealed not just by the global causes we espouse, but by the daily acts of courtesy we show. Relentlessly he pursues the transformation of our hearts, not just the alteration of our social agendas.

## "Do Good to Those Who Hate You"

But the change of our hearts will result in radically altered social agendas. One of the examples of loving our enemies that Jesus gives is God's daily mercy on this rebellious world: "He makes his sun rise on the evil and on the good, and sends rain on the just and on the unjust" (Matt. 5:45). Sun and rain are two essential things beyond our human control that are needed for crops to grow. So Jesus is saying that God reaches down to his enemies and helps meet their needs for food and water. He does not wait for them to repent. He shows mercy. Therefore, loving our enemy means practical acts of helpfulness in the ordinary things of life. God gives his enemies sunshine and rain. You give your enemies food and water. This and many other practical things are included in the simple little phrase "do good." "Do good to those who hate you" (Luke 6:27, cf. vv. 33, 35).

## Doing Good through Healing

One of the commands to do good to others that was prominent in the ministry of the twelve apostles during Jesus's ministry was the command to heal. Behind this command was Jesus's own authority to heal. The ministry of healing was a large and essential part of Jesus's ministry. It was a manifestation of the arrival of the kingdom of God. So preaching the kingdom and healing went hand in hand: "He went throughout all Galilee, teaching in their synagogues and *proclaiming the gospel of the kingdom* and *healing every disease* and every affliction among the people" (Matt. 4:23).

The ministry of healing was also one of the primary attestations of Jesus's messiahship. When John the Baptist, sitting in Herod's prison, began to doubt that Jesus was the Messiah, he sent word to Jesus and asked, "Are you the one who is to come, or shall we look for another?" Jesus answered by pointing to his healing ministry: "Go and tell John what you hear and see: the blind receive their sight and the lame walk, lepers are cleansed and the deaf hear, and the dead are raised up, and the poor have good news preached to them. And blessed is the one who is not offended by me" (Matt. 11:3–6; see also Matt. 9:6).

The miracles of healing that Jesus did were meant to be a witness to his unique role as the Messiah and Son of God. "The works that I do in my Father's name bear witness about me" (John 10:25). Therefore, Jesus called people to believe in him because of his works: "Believe the works, that you may know and understand that the Father is in me and I am in the Father. . . . Believe me that I am in the Father and the Father is in me, or else believe on account of the works themselves" (John 10:38; 14:11).

## The Authority of Jesus and the Command to Heal

Nevertheless, though the miracles of Jesus bore special witness to his unique relation to God and his unique authority, he bestowed a measure of this authority on his disciples. This became the foundation of his command to heal. "He called to him his twelve disciples and *gave them authority* over unclean spirits, to cast them out, and *to heal* every disease and every affliction" (Matt. 10:1). Having given them this authority, he commanded them to extend his own pattern of ministry: "Proclaim as you go, saying, 'The kingdom of heaven is at hand.' Heal the sick, raise the dead, cleanse lepers, cast out demons" (Matt. 10:7–8).

This was true not only of the Twelve but also of a wider group of seventy-two. "After this the Lord appointed seventy-two others and sent them on ahead of him" (Luke 10:1). His command to them was, "Heal the sick . . . and say to them, 'The kingdom of God has come near to you'" (Luke 10:9).

## How Shall We Obey the Command to Heal?

From this, the question rises about our responsibility today to continue the healing ministry of Jesus as a witness to the arrival of the kingdom in his life and work. There are those who say that we should indeed continue the ministry of Jesus today, preaching and performing miraculous healings in the same way he did. Others argue that such miraculous gifts and authority ceased with the disappearance of the apostles and the first generation of believers.

My own view lies between these two positions. I think the first group needs to come to terms with the role that miraculous healings had in bearing witness to the unique person and work of Jesus. In other words, it does seem that the astonishing ministry of miraculous healing that Jesus and some of his first followers had was part of the extraordinary events surrounding the incarnation of God's Son. The consistency and completeness with which Jesus healed was unparalleled in human history. Every ministry of miraculous healing after the events of those first days falls far short of what Jesus actually did. I don't think this is owing to unbelief but to the intended uniqueness of Jesus and those foundational days. What Jesus did in healing and raising the dead was to reveal and anticipate the kind of thing that would happen fully in the age to come.

On the other hand, I do not see any reason to deny that some measure of miraculous healing should accompany the ministry of the gospel today. I suspect there will always be differing judgments as to how prominent that ministry should be. The best way forward, it seems to me, is to have an appreciation *both* for the reality of miraculous healing as a witness to God's compassion and power *and* for the centrality of the word of God in saving sinners and the sovereignty of God in healing as he pleases. Therefore, obedience to Jesus today will for some groups mean a return to the centrality of the word, and for other groups a discovery of the freedom and merciful power of God in healing.

## Doing Good When Hated

The miracles of Jesus did not always result in saving faith. Some were more impressed with his power than his person. At one point Jesus's own brothers were more enamored by the public acclaim Jesus was getting than by the spiritual beauty revealed through his miracles. They tried to get him to be more public with his miracles in Jerusalem: "No one works in secret if he seeks to be known openly. If you do these things, show yourself to the world." To which John adds, "For not even his brothers believed in him" (John 7:4–5). And one must ponder with grief the stunning fact that Judas probably did miracles of healing along with the other apostles, but in the end he betrayed Jesus.

Therefore, even the ministry of healing can fall within the command, "Do good to those who hate you." We should pause and let this sink in. *Hate* is a very strong word. Think of what it might look like and feel like to be hated. And then ponder the marvel of doing good for the one who hates you. Jesus certainly knew what it was like to be hated

(Luke 19:14; John 7:7; 15:18, 24–25), and he laid his life down for all of his enemies who would receive his love. When Jesus said, "Greater love has no one than this, that someone lay down his life for his *friends*" (John 15:13), he was not measuring the greatness of his love by the fact that he was dying for his *friends*, but by the fact that he was *dying*—and doing it *freely*. By referring to his *friends* he meant that the purpose of his death to remove the wrath of God (John 3:14–15, 36) and forgive sins (Matt. 26:28) would only be experienced by those who are now enemies but lay down their enmity and become his friends.

And Jesus made it clear that just as he was hated, we certainly will be hated if we follow him. "You will be hated by all for my name's sake" (Matt. 10:22). And this will be all the more painful because the hate will sometimes come from former friends: "Many will fall away and betray one another and hate one another" (Matt. 24:10). Think of the kinds of emotions that naturally rise in your heart when someone really hates you and lies about you and wants to hurt you. Most of us have such a strong sense of rights that we feel immediately justified in getting even. Jesus demands that our hearts change. There may be legitimate indignation over the evil, but the heart must want the hater's good and "do good." Our love may bring contrition to the hater's heart, or it may be trampled in the dirt (like the love of Jesus). But that is not our business. Jesus says, "Do good to those who hate you."

### Turn the Other Cheek, and Give to the One Who Asks

Jesus becomes graphic in his illustrations of this command to return good for evil. "To one who strikes you on the cheek, offer the other also, and from one who takes away your cloak do not withhold your tunic either. Give to everyone who begs from you, and from one who takes away your goods do not demand them back" (Luke 6:29–30). The challenge I feel as I face these radical commands is how to let them have their full impact on my heart and life and yet not take them more absolutely than Jesus intended. My fear is that if I make any qualification I will minimize their intended force. On the other hand, they will also lose their force if they seem so unrealistic that people just pass over them as irrelevant to real life. So I will try to find the middle way of showing that Jesus does not absolutize these illustrations of love, but does not water them down to the irrelevance of mere middle-class morality either.

### "The Laborer Deserves His Wages"

There are several overlapping reasons why I believe Jesus means for us to take these commands as illustrative of the kind of thing love *often* does, rather than the exact thing love *always* does. First, the requirement that we always comply with someone's demand, and even give more than what is demanded, would undermine, it seems, the principle of justice in the economic order that Jesus himself approves. On the one hand, Jesus says, "Give to everyone who *asks* from you [the word is general rather than a technical term for "beg"], and from one who takes away your goods do not demand them back" (Luke 6:30). But on the other hand, Jesus approved of giving laborers what was a fair wage, not simply what they wanted their employer to give them (Matt. 20:9–14).

Jesus embraced the economic principle, "The laborer deserves his wages" (Luke 10:7), which seems to imply that the laborer is not bound to give labor without wages, and the employer is not bound to give wages without labor. The economic order, which Jesus supports, would collapse if either labor or management used Jesus's command, "Give to him who asks" as a warrant to demand that the other (in obedience to Jesus!) give without any recompense. Nevertheless, Jesus says to his disciples that in their ministry, "You received without paying; give without pay" (Matt. 10:8). So on the one hand we have the statements that call for radical freedom from the need for recompense ("Give to everyone who asks from you"), and on the other hand we have the statements that affirm the economic order that is built on the principle of a just recompense—even in ministry: "The laborer deserves his wages" (Luke 10:7). It seems to me, therefore, that Jesus's command to "give to everyone who asks from you" is not a universal or absolute command for all circumstances, but is one frequent way that love acts.[1]

## When Doing Good Does Not Give

Another pointer that these commands are not absolute for every situation is that the two commands—"do good" to those who hate us and "give to everyone who asks"—may not always lead us to the same behavior. We may have a very good plan for what would "do good" for a person that would involve *not* giving him what he asks for. And giving him what he asks for may not do him good. This is easily seen in recovery programs where the plan involves no alcohol during the time of residency. If the patient demands money for a drink, we will say to him in love that this is not the way we can "do good" to him right now.

Jesus did not always give to the one who asked from him. One example is when the chief priests and the elders asked Jesus, "By what authority are you doing these things, and who gave you this authority?" Jesus tested their authenticity. They failed the test, and he said, "Neither will I tell you by what authority I do these things" (Matt. 21:23, 27). What this means is that "doing good" is not always identical with giving to those who ask.

## When Candidates for Love Compete

A third pointer that these commands are not absolute for every situation is that we almost always have competing candidates for our

---

1   We could pose the same question about three other aspects of the social order besides the economic order: the family, education, and government. In the family, would Jesus support discipline that turns the other cheek to the child who strikes his parent? Would Jesus support education in which the teacher gives grades according to what the students demand? Would Jesus oppose a state use of police force in subduing criminals rather than telling the police to turn the other cheek? I suspect we would find that the principle holds: Jesus endorses the legitimate use of the law of recompense in these spheres of the social order. This would mean that the radical commands we are looking at are not meant to be the only way love acts. Rather, they are valid for believers as one frequent way of loving radically within the generally supported economic order as a witness to the truth that the order of this world is not absolute or ultimate; Jesus is.

love. In other words, what love seems to demand for one person is a behavior that will not be loving to another person. Very simply, what if two people demand from you the same thing at the same time? Or what if the money you have set aside to pay the rent for a poor person is demanded by a beggar? Or what if a thief demands to have the keys to your car when your child is in the backseat? Most of the time, any choice to give our time or money to one person means it cannot go to another person. Therefore, we have no choice but to apply principles *other* than simply the command to give, in order to decide the most loving way to give. So I conclude that Jesus's commands to give to those who ask and lend expecting nothing in return are not ultimate or absolute for every situation. The very command of love that he is illustrating functions to guide how they are applied.[2]

Typically commentators will say that these commands are *hyperbole*— rhetorical overstatements.[3] I would ask them to clarify whether they mean: hyperbole in the *kind* of action that Jesus calls for, or hyperbole in the *frequency* it is required. My own sense is that the latter is correct.

2    This point about competing claimants to our love is part of the foundation for why followers of Jesus may at times support very tough measures against people who are hurting or about to hurt others. The use of force by police and by the military is defended on these grounds in part. If force is not used against one person or group of persons, then they will hurt or kill or enslave others. So, even though using force does not look like "turning the other cheek" (Matt. 5:39; Luke 6:29), it is in fact an effort to love one person or group better than if we simply let aggressive people run over them. In such situations Jesus's demand is that we seek extraordinary wisdom—"Behold, I am sending you out as sheep in the midst of wolves, so be *wise* as serpents and innocent as doves" (Matt. 10:16; cf. Luke 12:42). And besides wisdom, he is calling for a radical freedom from the need for earthly riches and security and honor. See more on this below.

3    Craig Keener, in his *Commentary on the Gospel of Matthew* (Grand Rapids, Mich.: Eerdmans, 1999), gives wise and measured comments in regard to most of these commandments in Matthew 5:38–48. For example, he recognizes that Matthew 5:40 ("And if anyone would sue you and take your tunic, let him have your cloak as well") "if followed literally, would leave most disciples stark naked. . . . To deny that Jesus here literally advocates nudity (an offense to Jewish culture that would surely have called for comment in the other sources!) and living on the street—that is to affirm that Jesus is speaking the language of rhetorical overstatement (5:18–19, 29–32; 6:3)—is not to tone down the seriousness of his demand. Jesus produced hyperbole precisely to challenge his hearers, to force them to think about what they valued. Jesus' words in this case strike at the very core of human selfishness, summoning his disciples to value others above themselves in concrete and consistent ways" (195).

In other words, I don't want to deny that any of these commands should be fulfilled literally at times. Rather, I think what is hyperbolic is the impression that these behaviors are the *only* way love acts in response to the situations described. I think Jesus himself gives us ample indications that he does not mean that. There are times when "doing good" for someone will not include giving whatever he asks.

What then do these radical commands mean? What shall we do in response to them? If they are not absolutely the way to act in every situation, what are they? To that we turn in the next chapter, as well as to the question, how is it possible to love like this?

*To one who strikes you on the cheek, offer the other also, and from one who takes away your cloak do not withhold your tunic either. Give to everyone who begs from you, and from one who takes away your goods do not demand them back.*

LUKE 6:29–30

*Love your enemies and pray for those who persecute you, so that you may be sons of your Father who is in heaven.*

MATTHEW 5:44–45

*Be merciful, even as your Father is merciful.*

LUKE 6:36

*Love your enemies, and do good, and lend, expecting nothing in return, and your reward will be great.*

LUKE 6:35

# Love Your Enemies to Show That You Are Children of God

AT THE END OF THE PREVIOUS CHAPTER we were wrestling with Jesus's radical command, "To one who strikes you on the cheek, offer the other also, and from one who takes away your cloak do not withhold your tunic either. Give to everyone who begs from you, and from one who takes away your goods do not demand them back" (Luke 6:29–30). We argued that Jesus does not mean that these responses are the only way love acts. In this chapter we turn to a more positive statement of what is required of us, and then to the question, how are we able to love like this?

### Jesus Is Our Treasure, Our Security, and Our Honor

What then is Jesus demanding in the radical commands like those of Luke 6:29–30? I cannot escape the implication that behind and within these commands is the demand to be radically free from the love of money and from the need for earthly security and honor. Turning the other cheek even though the backhanded slap is an infuriating public dishonor, and lending without expecting repayment, and taking the time out of your schedule to carry a soldier's burden twice as far as he demanded[1]—all of these things imply that your treasure and your security and your honor are in heaven and not on the earth. Jesus has become for you radically satisfying. If this were not the case one can only imagine that the heart would be seething with rage while doing good and suffering the indignity. Therefore, I infer that in all these commands, Jesus is calling for a change of heart that looks to Jesus and his reward rather than what this world can give.

But it would be a mistake to stress only that Jesus is calling for a change of heart that treasures Jesus more than money and security and honor. He is also calling for real good to be done for our enemy and that we should really want this good to be done. We have seen this most clearly in the command that we bless and pray for our enemies (Matt. 5:44; Luke 6:28). The real good that we must aim at, if we love our enemies, is that all the petitions of the Lord's Prayer come true for them. To desire these things from our heart for our enemies, and to lay down our lives to bring them about, that is love.

## Dealing with a Skilled Liar

I would add one more description of what this love looks like. It seems to me that in all the complexity of life that can easily help us rationalize disobedience to these commands, we should default to literal obedience when we are unsure of what love calls for. For example, should I give to those who ask for money on the street in my context in urban America? How do I "do good" to those who ask? Jesus did not seem to be as concerned about being taken advantage of as I am (Matt. 5:40, 42). I am often angered by the lies I am being told. This anger makes me feel justified in giving nothing. But I do not think this is the spirit of Jesus.

---

1   Matthew 5:41, "And if anyone forces you to go one mile, go with him two miles." "Because tax revenues did not cover all the Roman army's needs, soldiers could requisition what they required . . . and legally demand local inhabitants to provide forced labor (Matt. 27:32)." Craig S. Keener, *Commentary on the Gospel of Matthew* (Grand Rapids, Mich.: Eerdmans, 1999), 199.

I think the spirit of Jesus would first feel compassion even for a skilled liar. Then it would desire to move into the life of that liar with the good news that Jesus came into the world to save liars. Then it would try, if the other demands of love allow, to engage the person more deeply and, if possible, take him somewhere to eat together and talk. If that is not possible, then love may give freely even knowing the person is probably a con artist. And at times love may say no—for example, if the person has been back many times and has proven to be a liar and consistently refused a relationship of love. But my point is, when these things are less clear, the spirit of Jesus seems to me to call for freehanded giving.

### How Can We Love Like This?

The final question I ask now about Jesus's command to love our enemies is: *How* can we do this? Where does power to love like this come from? Think how astonishing this is when it appears in the real world! It is an amazing thing when a person loves like this. To see it in a high degree in anyone is rare. This should make us sober and strip us of all presumption and set us seeking the power to be like this. If we limit our answer to what we see in the immediate contexts of Matthew 5:38–48 and Luke 6:27–36, there are three interwoven answers.

### In the Security and Help of Our Heavenly Father

The first is found in the promise that if we love our enemies we will be sons of God: "Love your enemies and pray for those who persecute you, *so that you may be sons of your Father who is in heaven*" (Matt. 5:44–45). Someone may take this to mean that you must first become a person who loves his enemies *before* you can be a child of God. But it may also mean—as I think it does—love your enemies and so *prove yourself to be what you are—a child of God*. That is, show that you are a child of God by acting the way your Father acts. If you are his, then his character is in you, and you will be inclined to do what he does.

God loves his enemies—the evil and the unjust—in sending rain and sunshine on them instead of immediate judgment (Matt. 5:45).

There are several reasons for thinking that Jesus is not saying, You are not a child of God until you prove you can love your enemy, but rather is saying, You *show* you are a child of God by loving your enemy. The first comes from the immediate paragraph and its parallel in Luke. In Matthew 5:48 Jesus says, "You therefore must be perfect, as your heavenly Father is perfect." And in Luke 6:36 he says, "Be merciful, even as your Father is merciful." Both these statements assume that the disciples are being called to love (perfectly) because they *are* children of God, not in order to *become* children of God.

Confirming this understanding of Matthew 5:45 ("so that you may be sons of your Father" = "so that you may prove to be sons of your Father"), there are other parallels that use similar words. For example, in John 15:8 Jesus says, "By this my Father is glorified, that you bear much fruit and so *prove to be my disciples*." The words "prove to be" translate the same verb (γένησθε) that is used in Matthew 5:45. Jesus says fruit-bearing is possible because they are *already* disciples—that is, they are branches in the vine who is Jesus (John 15:5)—and now they will prove themselves to be so by doing what branches do, namely, bear fruit (see also John 8:31).

Another argument that our sonship is proved rather than created by loving our enemies is from the earlier part of Matthew 5, where Jesus says, "Let your light shine before others, so that they may see your good works and give glory to your *Father* who is in heaven" (5:16). Notice two things: one is that Jesus speaks to his disciples and calls God their Father. He does not say, "He may *become* your Father." He says, "He *is* your Father." Second, notice that when people see the good works of the disciples (like loving their enemies), they give glory *to their Father*. Why? Because their Father is in them helping them and enabling them to do the good works. If they did the good works on their own, so that they could then become children of their Father, the world would see their good works and give *them* the glory. So Jesus not only says that God is *already* the Father of the disciples before they do the good works, but also, by implication, that this is the very reason they can do the loving works they do. The light that shines through them *is* the light of their Father's love within them.

So when Jesus says, "Love your enemies, and pray for those who persecute you, *in order that you may be sons of your Father who is in heaven*," he does not mean that loving our enemies earns us the right to be children of God. You can't earn the status of a child. You can be born into it. You can be adopted into it. You can't work your way into it. Jesus means that loving our enemies shows that God has already become our Father, and that the only reason we are able to love our enemies is because he loves us and has met our needs first.

Therefore, the first answer to *how* we can love our enemies is that being children of God has set us free from anxiety. We do not fear that our treasure or security or honor can be lost by the ill-treatment of our enemy or by the loss of earthly possessions. This is the point of Matthew 6:31–32, "Do not be anxious, saying, 'What shall we eat?' or 'What shall we drink?' or 'What shall we wear?' For the Gentiles seek after all these things, and *your heavenly Father knows that you need them all.*" Similarly, that's the point of Matthew 10:29–31, "Are not two sparrows sold for a penny? And not one of them will fall to the ground apart from *your Father.* . . . Fear not, therefore; you are of more value than many sparrows." The intimate knowledge and tender, sovereign care of our omnipotent, all-wise, heavenly Father frees us for the radical kind of risks and losses that enemy-love demands.

## "Your Reward Will Be Great"

Interwoven with this empowerment is another one in the immediate context of the commands. Jesus promises "great reward"—not in this life, but in heaven, if we love our enemies. "Love your enemies, and do good, and lend, expecting nothing in return, *and your reward will be great,* and you will be sons of the Most High" (Luke 6:35). I say the two sources of power are *interwoven* because the "great reward" is connected to "you will be sons of the Most High." In other words, when you prove yourselves to be sons of God by loving your enemy, your inheritance as sons is secured. Sons are heirs, and heirs of God are heirs of everything. "Blessed are the meek, for they shall inherit *the earth*" (Matt. 5:5).

The reason I say that the reward is *in heaven* and not on the earth is, first, that loving our enemy may cost us our lives (Luke 21:16). Jesus said our joy in the midst of persecution is based on our reward in heaven: "Blessed are you when others revile you and persecute you and utter all kinds of evil against you falsely on my account. Rejoice and be glad, *for your reward is great in heaven*" (Matt. 5:11–12). The joy that sustains us in the midst of persecution, as we endeavor to love our enemies, is not based mainly on what this world can offer, but on what God will be for us as our Father, and what Jesus will be for us as our King, in the age to come (see Luke 14:14).

### As You Have Freely Received Mercy, Freely Give It

A third truth that enables us to love our enemy is interwoven with the other two in Luke 6:36, "Be merciful, even as your Father is merciful." The implication here is not only that God is already our Father, and that his inheritance is our joy-sustaining reward in suffering, but also that the mercy of God has already been shown to us through his Son Jesus. This means that the mercy we are called to show is not just modeled on God's mercy but is rooted in the saving experience of God's mercy. Jesus put it like this, "You received without paying; give without pay" (Matt. 10:8).

In other words, God has forgiven our sins freely because of Jesus. "Your sins are forgiven . . . your faith has saved you; go in peace" (Luke 7:48, 50). This forgiveness, Jesus says, is purchased for us by his own blood (Matt. 26:28). We did not deserve it or earn it. We received it by faith. He came "to give his life as a ransom for many" (Mark 10:45). He did not come to call the righteous but sinners (Luke 5:32). Therefore, the stunning news is: tax collectors and the prostitutes go into the kingdom of God before scribes and elders (Matt. 21:31). Which means that we came into the position of a forgiven disciple of Jesus, a citizen of his kingdom, and a child of God by faith, not by loving our enemy first.

Now that we have received all this "without pay"—without buying it or earning it or deserving it—now we are called: freely you received love when you were enemies of God; now freely give love to your enemies.

*"Teacher, which is the great commandment in the Law?" And he said to him, "You shall love the Lord your God with all your heart and with all your soul and with all your mind. This is the great and first commandment. And a second is like it: You shall love your neighbor as yourself. On these two commandments depend all the Law and the Prophets."*

MATTHEW 22:36–40

*So whatever you wish that others would do to you, do also to them, for this is the Law and the Prophets.*

MATTHEW 7:12

# Love Your Neighbor as Yourself, for This Is the Law and the Prophets

THE FOCUS OF THE "SECOND" COMMANDMENT—"You shall love your neighbor as yourself" (Matt. 22:39)—is not on whether the receiver of love is an enemy or a friend but on whether the one who loves desires the neighbor's good as he desires his own. Its importance is seen by the two stupendous things that lie on either side of it. On one side is the greatest commandment in the Word of God—"You shall love the Lord your God with all your heart and with all your soul and with all your mind." On the other side is the assertion that everything[1] written in the Law and the Prophets hangs on these two commandments. We are in the company of incomparable superlatives—the two greatest commandments in the entire Word of God, and all of that Word hanging on them. We should take off our shoes in reverence here. There are few texts of Scripture greater than this.

## An Overwhelming and Staggering Command

The second commandment seems to me to be an overwhelming commandment. It seems to demand that I tear the skin off my body and

---

1 Matthew 22:40, "On these two commandments depend all the Law and the Prophets."

wrap it around another person so that I feel that I am that other person; and all the longings that I have for my own safety and health and success and happiness I now feel for that other person as though he were me. It is an absolutely staggering commandment. If this is what it means, then something unbelievably powerful and earthshaking and reconstructing and overturning and upending will have to happen in our souls. Something supernatural. Something well beyond what self-preserving, self-enhancing, self-exalting, self-esteeming, self-advancing, fallen human beings like me can do on their own.

Underlining the greatness of this commandment is the fact that it is surpassed only by the command to love God with our whole being. I have devoted a chapter to that commandment (*Command #9*). But also underlining the importance of the second commandment is the sweeping statement that all the Law and the Prophets hang on it when it is linked with the first commandment. "On these two commandments depend all the Law and the Prophets" (Matt. 22:40). This phrase, "Law and Prophets" refers to the whole Old Testament, as we can see in Luke 24:27, "Beginning with Moses and all the Prophets, he interpreted to them in *all the Scriptures* the things concerning himself."

This is an amazing statement. Here we have the authority of the Son of God telling us something utterly crucial about the origin and design of the entire plan and Word of God. First, consider the sheer fact that *Jesus said this.* He didn't have to say it. The lawyer who drew him into this discussion didn't ask about this. Jesus went beyond what he asked ("Which is the great commandment in the Law?" Matt. 22:36) and said more. He seems to want to push the importance and centrality of these commandments as much as he can. He said that the commandment to love God is the great and foremost commandment. He said the commandment to love your neighbor as you love yourself is "like it" (Matt. 22:39). That's enough to raise the stakes here almost as high as they can be raised. We have the greatest commandment in all of God's revelation to humanity (love God), and we have the second greatest, which is like the greatest (love your neighbor as yourself).

But Jesus doesn't stop there. He wants us to be stunned at how important these two commandments are. He wants us to stop and wonder. So he adds, "On these two commandments depend all the Law and the Prophets." They are also the two commandments from which everything else in the Scriptures flows.

## On These Two Commandments Hang the Whole Law and the Prophets

What does this mean? Answering this question opens a window into heaven. We will see this if we start by contrasting what Jesus says here in Matthew 22:40 with what he says in Matthew 7:12. This verse is better known as the Golden Rule. One way to see it is as a good commentary on "Love your neighbor as you love yourself." In that context, Jesus has just said that God will give us good things if we ask and seek and knock, because he is a loving Father. Then in Matthew 7:12 he says, "So whatever you wish that others would do to you, do also to them, for this is the Law and the Prophets."

Notice that Jesus refers to the Law and the Prophets as he did in Matthew 22:40. He says, if you do to others what you would have them do to you, then "this is the Law and the Prophets." In Matthew 22:40 he said, "On these two commandments hang the whole Law and the Prophets." Note that the first commandment—loving God with all your being—is not mentioned in Matthew 7:12. Instead, Jesus simply says that treating others the way we would like to be treated "is the Law and the Prophets."

## Does Jesus Sum Up the Old Testament without God?

We must be careful here. Some people over the centuries have tried to take sentences like the Golden Rule and say that Jesus was mainly a profound teacher of human ethics and that what he taught is not dependent on God or any relationship with God. They say, "See, he can sum up the whole Old Testament, the Law and the Prophets, in practical human relationships that don't even mention God."

I say we must be careful here, because thinking like that not only ignores the great things Jesus said about God elsewhere and the amazing things he said about himself coming from God to give his life as a ransom for many (Mark 10:45), it also ignores the immediate context. Matthew 7:12 begins with the word "so," or in some versions, "therefore." "*So* whatever you wish that others would do to you, do also to them." What this shows is that the Golden Rule depends on what went before—on our relationship to God as our Father who loves us and answers our prayers and gives us good things when we ask him (Matt. 7:7–11).

The immediately preceding verse (Matt. 7:11) says, "If you then, who are evil, know how to give good gifts to your children, how much more will *your Father* who is in heaven give good things to those who ask him! *Therefore* . . . [keep the Golden Rule]." This logical connection means God is upholding the Golden Rule by his fatherly provision. His love for us—and our trusting, prayerful love back to him—is the source of power for living the Golden Rule. So you can't turn Jesus into a mere teacher of ethics. He is here and always God-saturated.

**Loving God Becomes Visible in Loving Others**

But still, Jesus does say that treating others as you want to be treated "is the Law and the Prophets." He does not say here that two commandments are the Law and the Prophets, but only one. This seems significantly different from Matthew 22:40 where the Law and the Prophets depend on both commandments.

Why does he say it in this way? I think what he means is that when you see people love like that (fulfill the Golden Rule), what you are seeing is the visible expression of the aim of the Law and the Prophets. This behavior among people manifests openly and publicly and practically what the Old Testament is about. It fulfills the Law and the Prophets by making the aim visible. Loving God, however, is *invisible*. It is an internal passion of the soul. But it comes to expression when you love others. So loving others is the outward manifestation, the visible expression, the practical demonstration, and therefore the fulfillment of loving God and therefore of what the Old Testament is about.

So there is a sense in which the second commandment (to love your neighbor) is the visible goal of the whole Word of God. It's not as though loving God is not here, or that loving God is less important; rather, loving God is made visible and manifest and full in our visibly, practically, sacrificially loving others. I think that is why the second commandment stands by itself here as an expression of what the Law and the Prophets are—". . . for this *is* the Law and the Prophets." Loving our neighbor is not the Law and the Prophets independently of loving God. Rather, loving our neighbor is based on our love for God and, as the overflow of it, is what the Law and the Prophets were aiming at.

**How Do the Law and Prophets Hang on Love?**

Now let's return to Matthew 22:37–40. Here Jesus *does* mention both love for God and love for neighbor, and he explicitly says in verse 40, "On these two commandments depend all the Law and the Prophets." Why? I want to suggest that he is saying something different from, but not contradictory to, Matthew 7:12. Here he does not say that these two commandments "are" the Law and the Prophets. He says that the Law and the Prophets *depend* on these two commandments. "On these two commandments depend all the Law and the Prophets."

Here we are facing the window into heaven that I mentioned earlier. Jesus says here that the Law and the Prophets literally *hang* like a stone around the neck (Matt. 18:6) or a man on a cross (Luke 23:39). What do they hang on? They hang on love. This is the reverse of what Matthew 7:12 says. There Jesus said that the Law and Prophets lead to and find expression in love. But here in Matthew 22:40 Jesus is saying the reverse: love leads to and finds expression in the Law and the Prophets. The Law and the Prophets are hanging on—depending on—something before them, namely, God's passion that this world, this history of humankind, be a world of love to God and radical, other-oriented love to each other.

Let me try to put this in a picture, so we can see it more plainly. Picture the God-inspired history of redemption from creation to consummation as a scroll. This is the Law and the Prophets (and the New Testament). The story of God's acts and purposes in history are told in this scroll, along with God's commandments and promises. Matthew 7:12 tells us that when the people of God love their neighbor as they love themselves, the purpose of this scroll is being fulfilled. Its aim is being expressed visibly and manifested practically so "that [people] may see your good works and give glory to your Father who is in heaven" (Matt. 5:16). So the scroll is leading to love. Love is flowing from the scroll.

## The Window into Heaven

But then Jesus gives us an incomparable perspective. He opens a window into heaven, so to speak. He lifts us out of history and out of the world for a moment and shows us the scroll from a distance. Now we can see it whole—the Law and the Prophets, the Old Testament, the story of redemption, the purposes and acts of God in history. And what we see is that the scroll is *hanging* by two golden chains, one fastened to each end of the scroll handles. Then Jesus lifts our eyes to heaven, and we see the chains run up and disappear into heaven. Then he takes us into heaven, and he shows us the upper ends of the chains. They are fastened to the throne of God. One chain is fastened to the right arm of the throne where the words are inscribed: "You shall love the Lord your God with all your heart and with all your soul and with all your mind." And the other chain is fastened to the left arm of the throne where the words are inscribed, "You shall love your neighbor as yourself."

Jesus turns to us and says, "The whole scroll, the whole Law and the Prophets, the whole history of redemption and all my Father's plans and acts, hang on these two great sovereign purposes of God: that he be loved by his creation, and that they love each other as they love themselves." I believe it would not be too much to say that all of creation and all the work of redemption, including the work of Christ as our suffering, dying, and rising Redeemer, and all of history, hang on these two great purposes: that humans love God with all their heart, and that from the overflow of that love we love each other.

Which means that love is the origin (Matt. 22:40) and the goal (Matt. 7:12) of the Law and the Prophets. It is the beginning and the end of why God inspired the Bible. It is the fountainhead and spring at the one end and the shoreless ocean at the other end of the river of redemptive history—remembered and promised in the Word of God. Surely God's purpose is that we take this commandment with tremendous seriousness. It would be wise in this majestic context that we not assume we yet have seen the fullness of what love is or that it already has the centrality in our lives that it should. Jesus is saying: All of Scripture, all of his plans for history, *hang* on these two great purposes: that he be loved with all our heart, and that we love each other as we love ourselves.[2]

---

2   Though I have not handled in detail a closely related command of Jesus that he gave in the context of controversy over the law, it should at least be mentioned in this chapter: "Go and learn what this means, 'I desire mercy, and not sacrifice'" (Matt. 9:13; cf. 12:7). In sum, it seems that Jesus is saying that there are clues in the Old Testament, like this quote from Hosea 6:6, that, if we truly understood them, would enable us to see that all the law was pointing beyond the ceremonial and the external to the heartfelt love commanded by Jesus.

*. . . as yourself.*

MATTHEW 22:39

# Love Your Neighbor with the Same Commitment You Have to Your Own Well-Being

IN THIS CHAPTER WE TURN to look more closely into the command itself, especially the devastating phrase "as yourself." "Love your neighbor[1] *as yourself*" (Matt. 23:39) is a very radical command. What I mean by "radical" is that it cuts to the *root* of our sinfulness and exposes it and by God's grace severs it.

### The Root of Sin: The Desire to Be Happy Apart from God

The root of our sinfulness is the desire for our own happiness *apart from God* and *apart from the happiness of others in God*. I mean that to be read carefully. Let me say it again: The root of our sinfulness is the desire to be happy *apart from God* and *apart from whether others find their eternal happiness in God*. All sin comes from a desire to be happy cut off from the glory of God and cut off from the good of others. The command of Jesus cuts to this root, exposes it, and severs it.

---

1  We will see in the following chapter how Jesus defines the scope of the word *neighbor*, but suffice it to say here that any attempt to narrow it along ethnic or family or associational lines would fly into the face of Jesus's intention. The one in need along your path, the one you can help, is your neighbor.

Another name for this root of sinfulness is *pride*. Pride is the presumption that we can be happy without depending on God as the
source of our happiness and without caring if others find their happiness
in God. Pride is the contaminated and corrupted passion to be happy.
It is corrupted by two things: (1) the unwillingness to see God as the
only fountain of true and lasting joy, and (2) the unwillingness to see
other people as designed by God to share our joy in him. If you take
the desire to be happy and strip away from it God as the fountain of
your happiness and strip from it people as the ones you hope will share
your happiness in God, what you have left is the engine of pride. Pride
is the pursuit of happiness anywhere but in the glory of God and the
good of other people for God's sake. This is the root of all sin.

**What Does "as Yourself" Mean?**

Now Jesus says, "Love your neighbor as yourself." And with that commandment he cuts to the root of our sinfulness. How so? Jesus says
in effect: "I start with your inborn, deep, defining human trait—your
love for yourself. My command is, 'You shall love your neighbor *as
yourself.*' You love yourselves. This is a given. I don't command it;
I assume it.[2] All of you have a powerful instinct of self-preservation
and self-fulfillment. You all want to be happy. You all want to live,
and to live with satisfaction. You want food for yourself. You want
clothes for yourself. You want a place to live for yourself. You want
protection from violence against yourself. You want meaningful or
pleasant activity to fill your days. You want some friends to like you
and spend some time with you. You want your life to count in some
way. All this is self-love. Self-love is the deep longing to diminish
pain and to increase happiness." That's what Jesus starts with when
he says "as yourself."

2   I think the modern effort to see "self-love" here as "positive self-image" and to see a command
    that we seek this positive image so that we can then love others is profoundly mistaken. See John
    Piper, "Is Self-Love Biblical?" *Christianity Today* 21 (August 12, 1977): 6–9.

Everyone, without exception, has this human trait. This is what moves us to do this or that. Even suicide is pursued out of this principle of self-love.[3] In the midst of a feeling of utter meaningless and hopelessness and numbness of depression, the soul says, "It can't get any worse than this. So even if I don't know what I will gain through death, I do know what I will escape." And so suicide is an attempt to escape the intolerable. It is a misguided act of self-love.

## Jesus Starts with the Given and the Goodness of Self-Love

Now Jesus says, "I start with this self-love. This is what I know about you. This is common to all people. You don't have to learn it. It comes with your humanity. My Father created it. In and of itself it is good." To hunger for food is not evil. To want to be warm in the winter is not evil. To want to be safe in a crisis is not evil. To want to be healthy during a plague is not evil. To want to be liked by others is not evil. To want your life to count in some significant way is not evil. This was a defining human trait before the fall of man into sin, and it is not evil in itself.

Whether it has become evil in your life will be exposed as you hear and respond to Jesus's commandment. He commands, "*As you love yourself, so love your neighbor.*" Which means: As you long for food when you are hungry, so long to feed your neighbor when he is hungry. As you long for nice clothes for yourself, so long for nice clothes for your neighbor. As you work for a comfortable place to live, so desire a comfortable place to live for your neighbor. As you seek to be safe and secure from calamity and violence, so seek comfort and security for your neighbor. As you seek friends for yourself, so be a friend to your neighbor. As you want your

3  Blaise Pascal, the French mathematician and philosopher, wrote, "All men seek happiness. This is without exception. Whatever different means they employ, they all tend to this end. The cause of some going to war, and of others avoiding it, is the same desire in both, attended with different views. The will never takes the least step but to this object. This is the motive of every action of every man, even of those who hang themselves." *Pensées* (New York: E. P. Dutton, 1958), 113, Thought #425.

life to count and be significant, so desire that same significance for your neighbor. As you work to make good grades yourself, so work to help your neighbor be able to make good grades. As you like to feel welcome in a new company of people, so seek to make others feel welcome. As you would that men would do to you, do so to them.

## Your Self-Seeking Becomes the Measure of Your Self-Giving

In other words, make your *self-seeking* the measure of your *self-giving*. When Jesus says, "Love your neighbor as yourself," the word "as" is very radical: "Love your neighbor *as* yourself." That's a *big* word: "as"! It means: If you are *energetic* in pursing your own happiness, be energetic in pursuing the happiness of your neighbor. If you are *creative* in pursuing your own happiness, be creative in pursuing the happiness of your neighbor. If you are *persevering* in pursuing your own happiness, then persevere in pursuing the happiness of your neighbor.

In other words, Jesus is not just saying, seek for your neighbor the *same things* you seek for yourself but also seek them in the *same way—* with the same zeal and energy and creativity and perseverance. And with the same life-and-death commitment when you are in danger. Make your own self-seeking the measure of your self-giving. Measure your pursuit of the happiness of others, and what it should be, by the pursuit of your own. How do you pursue your own well-being? Pursue your neighbor's well-being that way too.

Now this is very threatening and almost overwhelming, because we feel immediately that if we take Jesus seriously, we will not just have to love others "as we love ourselves," but we will have to love them *instead* of loving ourselves. That's what it seems like. We fear that if we follow Jesus in this and really devote ourselves to pursuing the happiness of others, then our own desire for happiness will always be preempted. The neighbor's claim on my time and energy and creativity will always take priority. So the command to love my neighbor as I love myself really feels like a threat to my own self-love. How is this even possible?

If there is born in us a natural desire for our own happiness, and if this is not in itself evil but good, how can we give it up and begin only to seek the happiness of others at the expense of our own?

## How the First Commandment Sustains the Second

I think that is exactly the threat that Jesus wants us to feel, until we realize that this—exactly this—is why the first commandment is the first commandment. It's the first commandment that makes the second commandment doable and takes away the threat that the second commandment is really the suicide of our own happiness. The first commandment is, "Love the Lord your God with all your heart and with all your soul and with all your mind" (Matt. 22:37). The first commandment is the basis of the second commandment. The second commandment is a visible expression of the first. Which means this: Before you make your own self-seeking the measure of your self-giving, make God the focus of your self-seeking. This is the point of the first commandment.

"Love God with all your heart" means: find in God a satisfaction so profound that it fills up all your heart. "Love God with all your soul" means: find in God a meaning so rich and so deep that it fills up all the aching corners of your soul. "Love God with all your mind" means: find in God the riches of knowledge and insight and wisdom that guide and satisfy all that the human mind was meant to be.

In other words, take all your self-love—all your longing for joy and hope and love and security and fulfillment and significance—and focus it on God, until he satisfies your heart and soul and mind. You will find that this is not a canceling out of self-love. This is a fulfillment and transformation of self-love. Self-love is the desire for life and satisfaction rather than frustration and death. God says, "Come to me, and I will give you fullness of joy. I will satisfy your heart and soul and mind with my glory." This is the first and great commandment.

And with that great discovery—that God is the never-ending fountain of our joy—the way we love others is forever changed.

When Jesus says, "Love your neighbor *as yourself*," we don't respond by saying, "Oh, this is threatening. This means my love for myself is made impossible by all the claims of my neighbor. I could never do this." Instead we say, "Oh, yes, I love myself. I have longings for joy and satisfaction and fulfillment and significance and security. But God has called me—indeed he has commanded me—to come to him first for all these things. He commands that my love for him be the form of my love for me." That's not a misprint. My love for him is the form of my self-love. That is, all the longings that would satisfy me (self-love) I direct to him and find satisfied in him. That is what my self-love now *is*. It is my love for God. They have become one. My quest for happiness is now nothing other than a quest for God. And he has been found in Jesus.

### Self-Love, Fulfilled in God-Love, Becomes the Measure of Neighbor-Love

So what then is Jesus commanding in the second commandment (that we love our neighbor as ourselves)? He is commanding that our self-love, which has now discovered its fulfillment in God-love, be the measure and the content of our neighbor-love. Or to put it another way, he is commanding that our inborn self-seeking, which has now been transposed into God-seeking, overflow and extend itself to our neighbor. So, for example:

- If you are longing to see more of God's bounty and liberality through the supply of food and rent and clothing, then seek to show others the greatness of this divine bounty by the generosity you have found in him. Let the fulfillment of your own self-love in God-love overflow into neighbor-love. Or better: seek that God, who is the fulfillment of your self-love, will overflow through your neighbor-love and become the fulfillment of your neighbor's self-love.

- If you want to enjoy more of God's compassion through the consolations he gives you in sorrow, then seek to show others more of God's compassion through the consolations you extend to them in sorrow.
- If you long to savor more of God's wisdom through the counsel he gives in stressful relationships, then seek to extend more of God's wisdom to others in their stressful relationships.
- If you delight in seeing God's goodness in relaxed times of leisure, then extend that goodness to others by helping them have relaxed, healthy times of leisure.
- If you want to see more of God's saving grace powerfully manifested in your life, then stretch out that grace into the lives of others who need that saving grace.
- If you want to enjoy more of the riches of God's personal friendship through thick and thin, then extend that friendship to the lonely through thick and thin.

In all these ways neighbor-love does not threaten self-love because self-love has become God-love, and God-love is not threatened, diminished, or exhausted by being poured into the lives of others.

*But he, desiring to justify himself, said to
Jesus, "And who is my neighbor?"*

LUKE 10:29

*Whatever you wish that others would do to you, do
also to them, for this is the Law and the Prophets.*

MATTHEW 7:12

*A new commandment I give to you, that you love one
another: just as I have loved you, you also are to love
one another. By this all people will know that you are
my disciples, if you have love for one another.*

JOHN 13:34–35

# Love Your Neighbor as Yourself and as Jesus Loved Us

I DON'T PRESUME in the previous chapters to have solved all perplexities in the life of love. There are competing claims on our limited time and resources. There are hard choices about what to give up and what to keep. There are different interpretations of what is good for another person. I don't mean that all of that becomes simple.

### Radical Command and Radical Provision

What I do mean is this: loving God sustains us through all the joy and pain and perplexity and uncertainty of what loving our neighbor should be. When the sacrifice is great, we remember that God's grace is sufficient. When the fork in the road of love is unmarked, we remember with joy and love that his grace is sufficient. When we are distracted by the world and our hearts give way temporarily to selfishness and we are off the path, we remember that God alone can satisfy, and we repent and love his mercy and patience all the more.

It is a very radical command. It cuts to the root of sin called pride—the passion to be happy (self-love) contaminated and corrupted by two things: (1) the unwillingness to see God as the only fountain of true and lasting joy, and (2) the unwillingness to see other people as designed by God to receive our joy in him. But that is exactly the corruption of self-love that Jesus counteracts in these two commandments. In the first commandment, he focuses the passion to be happy firmly on God and God alone. In the second commandment, he opens a whole world of expanding joy in God and says, human beings—everywhere you find them—are designed to receive and enlarge your joy in God. Love them the way you love yourself. Give them—through every practical means available—what you have found for yourself in God.

### Warning: Don't Narrow the Meaning of "Neighbor"

Before we leave the commandment to love our neighbor as ourselves, we need to hear a warning that Jesus sounded. He warned us that when we hear the command, "Love your neighbor as yourself" we should not try to justify our lovelessness by narrowing down who the neighbor is. He sounded this warning with the parable of the Good Samaritan.

Once "a lawyer stood up to put him to the test, saying, 'Teacher, what shall I do to inherit eternal life?'" Jesus answered him, "What is written in the Law? How do you read it?" The lawyer responded with the two great commandments: "You shall love the Lord your God with all your heart and with all your soul and with all your strength and with all your mind, and your neighbor as yourself." Jesus said, "You have answered correctly; do this, and you will live."[1] Then the lawyer said something that Jesus did not like. Luke describes the motive behind the man's next words: "But he, desiring to justify himself, said to Jesus, 'And who is my neighbor?'" (Luke 10:25–29).

Of all the many issues that could be taken up from the parable of the Good Samaritan, I focus only on one. Jesus responds to the lawyer's self-justifying question with a parable that does not answer his question but changes it. He changes the question from *What kind of person*

---

1   See *Command #20* for reflections on how this relates to Jesus's understanding of justification by faith alone.

*is my neighbor?* to *What kind of person am I?* He changes the question from *What status of people are worthy of my love?* to *How can I become the kind of person whose compassion disregards status?*

Jesus exposes the lawyer's duplicity by showing him that he already knew the answer to his question and was only trying to trap Jesus (Luke 10:25). Now the lawyer knows that his motives have been exposed and that he needs to confess or cover his hypocrisy. He chooses to cover it—or to give it another name; he chooses to "justify himself" (Luke 10:29). He does so by saying something like, "Well, you know, Jesus, it's not so easy to figure out who our neighbor is. Life is complicated. Which kind of people do we have to love? Who qualifies for being a neighbor in this command, 'Love your neighbor'? Every race? Every class? Both sexes? All ages? Outcasts? Sinners?"

### A Question Jesus Will Not Answer

How does Jesus answer? He does not like this question—carving humanity up into groups, some of whom are worthy of our love and others of whom are not. Jesus does not answer the question, "Who is my neighbor?" He tells a parable that changes the question. Between Jerusalem and Jericho a man falls among robbers. Luke 10:30 says they "stripped him and beat him and departed, leaving him half dead." The first two people to pass by are a priest and a Levite[2]—the most religious folks—and they both pass by on the other side of the road (Luke 10:31, 32). Then came a Samaritan, not even a Jew, and the key phrase about this man is at the end of Luke 10:33, "He had compassion."

You see how the focus has shifted. The question about what kind of man is dying is not even in the story anymore. The whole focus is now on the kind of people who are walking by. The first two felt no compassion. The Samaritan was a different kind of person. So when

2   The Levites were descendants of the tribe of Israel named after Levi (Exod. 6:25; Lev. 25:32; Num. 35:2). The name however, is, generally used as the part of the tribe that assisted the priests in the service of the temple (1 Kings 8:4; Ezra 2:70).

you get to the end, what's the question that Jesus asks? Was it, "So was the wounded man a neighbor?" No. That is not the question. Jesus asked the lawyer, "Which of these three do you think proved to *be* a neighbor to the man who fell among the robbers?"(Luke 10:36). The lawyer answered, "The one who showed him mercy." And Jesus said to him, "You go, and do likewise" (Luke 10:37). Jesus does not give an answer to his question, "Who is my neighbor?" Instead, he says in effect, go become a new kind of person. Go get a compassionate heart.

### The Death of Jesus: Purchase and Pattern

This is exactly what Jesus died for. This is the promise of the new covenant in Ezekiel 36:26, "I will give you a new heart, and a new spirit I will put within you." And Jesus said at the Last Supper, "This cup that is poured out for you is the new covenant in my blood" (Luke 22:20). Those who follow Jesus all the way to the cross will see him there paying for their new heart with his own blood.

Which brings us to one final point in this chapter: the relationship between Jesus's command that we love our neighbor as ourselves and his command that we love each other as he has loved us. Jesus's death is both guilt-bearing and guidance-giving. It is a death that forgives sin and a death that models love. It is the purchase of our life from perishing and the pattern for a life of love. I close with this focus because of the seeming tension between the two commandments: "Love your neighbor as yourself" and the "new commandment."

In John 13:34–35 Jesus said, "A new commandment I give to you, that you love one another: just as I have loved you, you also are to love one another. By this all people will know that you are my disciples, if you have love for one another" (see also John 15:12). Jesus makes the connection between his love and his death when he says, "Greater love has no one than this, that someone *lay down his life* for his friends" (John 15:13). So it is important that we see the connection between the death of Jesus and our fulfillment of the commandment, "Love your neighbor as yourself." On the one hand, the death of Jesus models how we should love, and on the other hand the death of Jesus purchases for us the very transformation that enables us to love.[3] We have discussed the purchasing work of Jesus in previous chapters (see *Commands #10, 23*). Here we need to ponder how the pattern of Jesus's love relates to the command "Love your neighbor as yourself."

Jesus called the commandment to love as he loved "a new commandment" (John 13:34). But the commandment "Love your neighbor as yourself" is an old commandment from Leviticus 19:18. Does that mean that the command to love our neighbor as we love ourselves is now passé and we have a new one—to love as Jesus loved? I don't think so.

What's new is that we had never seen the old commandment of love lived out for us perfectly by the Son of God. Before Jesus, no one had ever been able to say without qualification, "Love as I have loved." Not only that, the newness seems to relate to the purpose of Jesus to have a new people whose mark in the world would be allegiance to him (and his Father) and to each other in love. So he says, "By this all people will know that you are my disciples, if you have love for one another" (John 13:35). "Love like mine is the badge of belonging to the new people that I am gathering."

## Jesus Loved Us Perfectly in Loving Himself Perfectly

But the essence of what love is—what we have unfolded earlier in this chapter—is not different from what Jesus commands here. When Jesus died for us, he loved us as he loved himself. He perfectly fulfilled the command "Love your neighbor as yourself." Jesus loved himself perfectly in that he desired his happiness with perfectly holy desire. That is, he found his happiness from all eternity in his fellowship with his

---

3 See *Commands #20, 21, 27* for the relationship between the transformation that Jesus's death purchases and the location or justification that it purchases. The point there is that Jesus is the basis of a new "location" in God's favor that becomes the basis and hope of the demonstration of that favor through a transformed heart and life.

Father and in being one with the Father (John 10:30). When he laid down his life for us, he did not deny or discard that desire for his own infinite happiness in God; he expressed it. He pursued it.

When Jesus died he purchased for sinners like us everything needed for us to find our joy in God. Since our joy in God magnifies the worth of God, this is exactly what Jesus has delighted in for all eternity. Therefore, in dying for our joy in God, he is dying to display and preserve his fullest joy in God's glory. That glory is reflected in our blood-bought joy in God. Therefore, Jesus's love is a perfect expression and fulfillment of the command to "Love your neighbor as yourself."

So whether he says to us, "Love God and love your neighbor as yourself, because on these two hang all the Law and the Prophets," or whether he says, "Love one another as I have loved you so that all will know you are my disciples," he is commanding essentially the same thing. It is a radical command. We must make our own passion for happiness the measure of our passion for the good of others. And we must make the measure of Jesus's suffering and the perfection of his happiness in God the standard of our sacrifice and the focus of the joy we pursue for ourselves and others.

*Do not lay up for yourselves treasures on earth, where moth*
*and rust destroy and where thieves break in and steal, but*
*lay up for yourselves treasures in heaven, where neither moth*
*nor rust destroys and where thieves do not break in and steal.*
*For where your treasure is, there your heart will be also.*

MATTHEW 6:19–21

*You received without paying; give without pay.*

MATTHEW 10:8

*One who is faithful in a very little is also faithful in*
*much, and one who is dishonest in a very little is also*
*dishonest in much. If then you have not been faithful in*
*the unrighteous wealth, who will entrust to you the true*
*riches? And if you have not been faithful in that which is*
*another's, who will give you that which is your own?*

LUKE 16:10–12

# Lay Up for Yourselves Treasures in Heaven by Giving Sacrificially and Generously

THE MORE SACRIFICIALLY GENEROUS you are on earth, the greater will be your enjoyment of heaven. Therefore, since Jesus loves us and summons us to maximize our eternal joy in heaven, he demands radical freedom from the love of money and radical generosity, especially toward the poor.

### Sacrifice Is the Measure of a Gift's Size

The reason I say, "the more *sacrificially* generous you are" is because of what Jesus said about the widow's offering. Here's the story:

> [Jesus] sat down opposite the treasury and watched the people putting money into the offering box. Many rich people put in large sums. And a poor widow came and put in two small copper coins, which make a penny. And he called his disciples to him and said to them, "Truly, I say to you, this poor widow has put in more than all those who are contributing to the offering box. For they all contributed out of their abundance, but she out of her poverty has put in everything she had, all she had to live on." (Mark 12:41–44)

The point here is that the value of a gift is not measured by its size but by its sacrifice. She put in "more" than all, Jesus said. Not more in quantity but more in sacrifice. The reason is that sacrifice is a better measure of where your heart is. If you are rich and give much, you have so much left over that your heart may easily rest in the remainder. But if you sacrifice for Jesus and have little left, then the heart has less to rest in. The heart is more likely to be resting in the hope of heaven. It is more likely to be depending on Jesus than on money.

### Why Such a Huge Concern with Our Money and Possessions?

It is astonishing how much Jesus deals with money and what we do with it. Randy Alcorn reckons that "15 percent of everything Christ said relates to this topic—more than his teachings on heaven and hell combined."[1] Consider just a sampling of the kinds of things Jesus says about money and related lifestyle issues:

> You lack one thing: go, sell all that you have and give to the poor, and you will have treasure in heaven; and come, follow me. (Mark 10:21)

> Blessed are you who are poor, for yours is the kingdom of God. . . . But woe to you who are rich, for you have received your consolation. (Luke 6:20, 24)

> Any one of you who does not renounce all that he has cannot be my disciple. (Luke 14:33)

> It is easier for a camel to go through the eye of a needle than for a rich person to enter the kingdom of God. (Luke 18:25)

---

1   Randy Alcorn, *The Treasure Principle* (Sisters, Ore.: Multnomah, 2001), 8. I highly recommend this small book as a way to help people live out the radical call of Jesus concerning money.

One's life does not consist in the abundance of his possessions. (Luke 12:15)

Seek first the kingdom of God and his righteousness, and all these things will be added to you. (Matt. 6:33)

Sell your possessions, and give to the needy. Provide yourselves with moneybags that do not grow old. (Luke 12:33)

Zacchaeus . . . said to the Lord, "Behold, Lord, the half of my goods I give to the poor." . . . And Jesus said to him, "Today salvation has come to this house." (Luke 19:8–9)

The kingdom of heaven is like treasure hidden in a field, which a man found and covered up. Then in his joy he goes and sells all that he has and buys that field. (Matt. 13:44)

Jesus . . . saw a poor widow put in two small copper coins. And he said, "Truly, I tell you, this poor widow has put in more than all of them." (Luke 21:1–3)

But God said to [the man who built even bigger barns], "Fool! This night your soul is required of you, and the things you have prepared, whose will they be?" So is the one who lays up treasure for himself and is not rich toward God. (Luke 12:20–21)

Foxes have holes, and birds of the air have nests, but the Son of Man has nowhere to lay his head. . . . Follow me. (Luke 9:58–59)

Why does Jesus express such a remarkable concern with what we do with our money? The reason for this, it seems, is the basic principle that Jesus laid down: "Where your treasure is, there your heart will be also"

(Matt. 6:21; Luke 12:34). In other words, the reason money is so crucial is that what we do with it signals where our heart is. "Where our heart is" means where our worship is. When the heart is set on something, it values it, cherishes it, treasures it. That is what worship means.

### You Cannot Serve Two Masters: God and Money

You can see this in Jesus's warning that "no one can serve two masters, for either he will hate the one and love the other, or he will be devoted to the one and despise the other. You cannot serve God and money" (Matt. 6:24). The idea of "serving" here is peculiar. It relates more to worshiping than to providing a service. Jesus said, "You cannot serve God and *money*." How do we serve money?

The answer is not: Provide a service for money. Or, provide help to money, or meet money's needs. Just the opposite: Serving money means looking to money to provide you a service and to provide your help and meet your needs. Serving money means planning and dreaming and strategizing and maneuvering to be in a position to maximize our wealth and what money can provide for us. Money is the giver and the benefactor in this servant-master relationship. You don't do any good for money. You look to money to do good for you.

Now Jesus says, "You cannot serve God and money." The meaning of "serve" would, presumably, be the same in these two relationships. So what Jesus is saying is that we should serve God *not* in the sense of providing a service or giving him help, but the opposite: we look to God to be our helper, benefactor, and treasure. To serve him would be to plan and dream and strategize and maneuver to be in a position to maximize our enjoyment of God and what he alone promises to be for us. God then, not money, becomes the giver and the benefactor in this servant-master relationship. You don't meet God's needs (he has none!). You look to God to meet yours.

So the reason money is so crucial for Jesus is that across all cultures and all ages it represents the alternative to God as the treasure of our hearts, and therefore the object of our worship. It becomes the great threat to our obedience to the first and last of the Ten Commandments: "You shall have no other gods before me" (Exod. 20:3), and "You shall not covet" (Exod. 20:17). Money represents all the other material things and securities and pleasures that it can buy. Therefore, it represents the great alternative to God in our hearts. This is why what we do with our money is so crucial to Jesus.

## Selfishness Separates from Heaven, and Sacrifice Heightens Joy in It

Let's return to the main point I made in the first paragraph of this chapter: the more sacrificially generous you are on earth, the greater will be your enjoyment of heaven. There are two things being said here. One is that a selfish spirit will keep us out of heaven. And the other is that there are degrees of reward, or degrees of joy, in heaven, depending on how sacrificially generous we were on earth. Both of these claims are controversial. But in view of what we have seen in the previous chapters, they should not come as a complete surprise. In the next chapter I will take them one at a time and give some evidence from the words of Jesus.

*How difficult it is for those who have wealth to enter the kingdom of God! For it is easier for a camel to go through the eye of a needle than for a rich person to enter the kingdom of God.*

LUKE 18:24–25

*One who is faithful in a very little is also faithful in much, and one who is dishonest in a very little is also dishonest in much. If then you have not been faithful in the unrighteous wealth, who will entrust to you the true riches? And if you have not been faithful in that which is another's, who will give you that which is your own?*

LUKE 16:10–12

# Lay Up for Yourselves Treasures in Heaven and Increase Your Joy in Jesus

EMERGING IN THE PREVIOUS CHAPTER were two controversial claims that I will try to support from Jesus's teaching in this chapter. First, the claim that a selfish spirit will keep us out of heaven. Second, the claim that there are degrees of reward, or degrees of joy, in heaven, depending on how sacrificially generous we were on earth.

First, Jesus implies, again and again, that a selfish spirit will keep us out of heaven. Here are five examples to show this truth.

### The Rich Ruler and Eternal Life

First, when the rich ruler asked Jesus what he must do to inherit eternal life, Jesus responded, "Sell all that you have and distribute to the poor, and you will have treasure in heaven; and come, follow me" (Luke 18:18, 22). This seems to make eternal life dependent on being free from the love of money and being generous to the poor. This is indeed what Jesus is saying, as we can see from the fact that when the man who was "extremely rich" (Luke 18:23) turns away, Jesus says, "How difficult it is for those who have wealth to *enter the kingdom of God!* For it is easier for a camel to go through the eye of a needle than for a rich person to *enter the kingdom of God*" (Luke 18:24–25).

As we can imagine, the disciples are surprised by this statement and ask, "Then who can be saved?" (Luke 18:26). They see that "inheriting eternal life" and "entering the kingdom of God" are terms that refer to "being saved." Jesus's answer is *not* to say, "Salvation is not at stake in this man's selfishness." Rather he says, "What is impossible with man is possible with God" (Luke 18:27). In other words, only God can change the selfishness that keeps a man out of heaven. But it is clear that this man's love for his money kept him out of heaven: "He went away sorrowful, for he had great possessions" (Mark 10:22). (For how this relates to justification by faith alone see *Command #20*.)

### The Rich Man, the Beggar, and Two Destinies

A second example is the story of the rich man and the beggar at his gate. Jesus said, "There was a rich man who was clothed in purple and fine linen and who feasted sumptuously every day. And at his gate was laid a poor man named Lazarus, covered with sores" (Luke 16:19–20). The poor man wanted just a crumb from the rich man's table, but the picture we get is that the rich man was oblivious or disdainful to the poor at his very door. So Jesus describes the death and afterlife of both men: "The poor man died and was carried by the angels to Abraham's side. The rich man also died and was buried, and in Hades, being in torment, he lifted up his eyes and saw Abraham far off and Lazarus at his side" (Luke 16:22–23). In other words, Jesus is saying that the selfish indifference of the rich has landed him in hell.[1]

---

1   The point is not that poverty lands someone in heaven. The spiritual condition of the poor man is not the focus of the parable. It goes unmentioned. There is no reason to assume he was not a genuine believer. But the focus is on the rich man who perished. The parable is a warning of the danger of riches.

## Failure to Love and Final Judgment

Third, similarly, in Matthew 25:31–46 Jesus warns that a professing follower of Jesus who is indifferent to the needs of the poor will endure "eternal punishment." When the king (representing Jesus in the story) pronounces this dreadful sentence over the selfish "disciples," they say, "Lord, when did we see you hungry or thirsty or a stranger or naked or sick or in prison, and did not minister to you?" And the king answers, "Truly, I say to you, as you did not do it to one of the least of these, you did not do it to me." And Jesus gives the final word: "And these will go away into eternal punishment, but the righteous into eternal life" (Matt. 25:44–46). In other words, a selfish spirit will keep us out of heaven.

## The Rich Fool Who Loses His Soul

Fourth, again Jesus tells a parable of a rich fool. The man's fields prosper, and he has more than he can use. Instead of thinking generously, he says, "I will tear down my barns and build larger ones, and there I will store all my grain and my goods. And I will say to my soul, Soul, you have ample goods laid up for many years; relax, eat, drink, be merry" (Luke 12:18–19). To this selfish decision Jesus says that God responds with these words: "Fool! This night your soul is required of you, and the things you have prepared, whose will they be?" (Luke 12:20). In other words, his selfish spirit led to the loss of his soul.

## How to Lose True and Lasting Riches

Fifth, here is one last illustration of how a selfish spirit keeps us out of heaven. After the parable of the dishonest manager (Luke 16:1–9), Jesus draws out these conclusions:

> One who is faithful in a very little is also faithful in much, and one who is dishonest in a very little is also dishonest in much. If then you have not been faithful in the unrighteous wealth, who will

entrust to you the true riches? And if you have not been faithful in that which is another's, who will give you that which is your own? (Luke 16:10–12)

It is fairly clear that "true riches" and "that which is your own" refer to the treasures of heaven—the pleasures of the age to come when we enjoy unbroken fellowship with Jesus. Therefore, Jesus is saying that we will not get these *true riches* if we have not been faithful with what we were given to use in this fallen world. He is referring to our money—that is, the material resources at our disposal here. If we have been stingy rather than using our money to lead people to faith (Luke 16:9), we will not enter heaven with its true riches of fellowship with Jesus.

### The Ground of Our Acceptance with God

That is one implication of what I said in the first sentence of this chapter: a selfish spirit will keep us out of heaven entirely. I hope it is plain by now in this book that I do not believe a sacrificially generous spirit is the ground of our acceptance with God. When Jesus says that a selfish spirit keeps us out of heaven, he does not mean that God watches to see if we show ourselves to be generous before he accepts us into his everlasting favor. Before we can be generous, God receives us into his favor through faith in Jesus (John 3:16). He takes us into his family as his children (John 1:12). He counts us righteous (Luke 18:14); he forgives our sins (Matt. 26:28); he gives us eternal life (John 5:24). None of these is obtained in this life by first overcoming our selfish spirit. It is the other way around. We recognize our selfish spirit and despair of overcoming it on our own and turn to Jesus as our only hope. In this turning to Jesus, we are justified, forgiven, adopted, secured in his care forever (John 10:28–30). On that basis we now make progress in overcoming our selfish spirit.

## Greater Sacrifices of Love Lead to Greater Joy in Heaven

The other controversial claim emerging in the previous chapter and mentioned in the first paragraph of this chapter is that the degree to which we overcome our selfishness determines, in some measure, the degree of our reward—our joy—in heaven. The more sacrificially generous you are on earth, the greater will be your enjoyment of heaven. The first indication that Jesus means this is found in his Parable of the Ten Minas.[2] Jesus compares his departure from this earth to a nobleman who goes to a far country to receive a kingdom and gives his ten servants (representing the followers of Jesus) one mina each, saying, "Engage in business until I come" (Luke 19:13). I take this "business" to include the kind of loving generosity that Jesus repeatedly commanded.

When the king returns, he calls his servants to give an account of how they used their mina. The first came and said he had made ten more minas with his mina. The second said he had made five more. The third made none. To the first Jesus said, "Well done, good servant! Because you have been faithful in a very little, you shall have authority over ten cities." To the second he said, "And you are to be over five cities" (Luke 19:17, 19). I take these two different rewards to represent diversity of rewards in heaven. My point is not how literally to take the promise of cities. My point is simply that this is an indication that in the kingdom there will be different rewards.

## The Measure You Use Will Be Used to Measure You

Another indication that Jesus thinks this way about heaven is the way he speaks in Luke 6:37–38: "Judge not, and you will not be judged; condemn not, and you will not be condemned; forgive, and you will be forgiven; give, and it will be given to you. Good measure, pressed down, shaken together, running over, will be put into your lap. For with

---

2  A mina is an amount of money, namely, about three months' wages for a laborer.

the measure you use it will be measured back to you." What does Jesus mean, "With the measure you use it will be measured back to you"?

First, he confirms what we saw before, that a selfish spirit will rob us of all blessing: "Give, and it will be given to you." He is not speaking of mere human relations here. He is speaking of the final reckoning with God. That is the context of judgment and condemnation and forgiveness. It is also implied in the gracious promise that our reward will be "pressed down, shaken together, running over." This is a picture of God's overflowing grace. If we give, God will super-reward. If we do not, we will be condemned for our selfish, unbroken, unredeemed heart.

But what about "the measure" that we use in giving? "With the measure you use it will be measured back to you." This is where I get the idea that there will be varying rewards in heaven for different measures of sacrificial generosity on earth. R. C. H. Lenski seems to me to be especially insightful on this text. He says:

> Jesus explains this return measure by stating the principle on which it is given: "for with what measure you go on measuring it shall be measured to you in return," ἀντί in the verb [*anti*metrēthēsetai] means in turn or back. In other words, by our giving we build the measure that will be used for giving back to us. Our own measure is used to measure back to us. By using it ourselves we declare that we want God to use it for us at the end. . . . It is the measure we bring to God, and all he can do is to fill it. And fill it overflowing he will ["pressed down, shaken together, running over"]. . . . Thus they who give nothing will receive even less, and they who give much their lifelong will receive vastly more. This is both justice and grace.[3]

I assume that by "justice" he does not speak strictly, since even our best generosity is imperfect and deserves nothing from God. I take him to

---

3   R. C. H. Lenski, *The Interpretation of St. Luke's Gospel, 1–11* (Minneapolis: Augsburg, 1946), 374–75.

mean that it is *fitting* and *proper* and *just* that there be a correspondence between our giving and God's giving to us—not an exact one, but a real one. So God uses the same measure, but he fills it more overflowingly than we ever did for anyone here.

The point I am stressing here is that there are differences in the fullness of delight that each of us enjoys in heaven. Each will be full in heaven, for there are no frustrations there. But the fullness of each will not be the same since the measure that we used to bless others on earth, and that God will use to bless us in heaven, is different for different people. Therefore I say again, the more sacrificially generous we are on earth, the greater will be our enjoyment of heaven.

### "Lay Up for Yourselves Treasures in Heaven"

Because of this, I take Jesus's command, "Lay up for yourselves treasures in heaven" (Matt. 6:20), to mean: strive to make the measure of your generosity as large as you can. This is clearly the way Jesus means it in Luke 12:33, "Sell your possessions, and give to the needy. Provide yourselves with moneybags that do not grow old, with a treasure in the heavens that does not fail, where no thief approaches and no moth destroys." In other words, the way you provide yourselves with "moneybags that do not grow old" and with "treasure in the heavens" is to "give to the needy." *Ageless moneybags* and *treasure in heaven* are metaphors for heavenly reward—the fullness of the measure of joy we will be given in heaven. Their measure is determined by the positive command, "Give to the needy." We lay up treasure in heaven by not hoarding here on earth, but by using our possessions sacrificially and generously—that is, lovingly.

We will see in the next chapter that this kind of sacrificial generosity is grounded in the goodness of God to us *before* and *while* we are generous to others. We are able to love and give because he has already given freely to us and promises to meet every need we have in a lifetime of generosity (Matt. 6:33; 7:7–12; Luke 12:32).

*Fear not, little flock, for it is your Father's good pleasure to give you the kingdom. Sell your possessions, and give to the needy. Provide yourselves with moneybags that do not grow old, with a treasure in the heavens that does not fail, where no thief approaches and no moth destroys. For where your treasure is, there will your heart be also.*

LUKE 12:32–34

# Lay Up for Yourselves Treasures in Heaven—"It Is Your Father's Good Pleasure to Give You the Kingdom"

BEFORE LOOKING AT THE GROUND of our giving in the goodness of God, there is a pressing question that rises whenever the motivation of rewards is mentioned. I turn first to that question and then to the goodness of God beneath all our giving.

### Why Is This Not Prudential Self-Regard?

Why would this motivation for giving—to enlarge the measure of our joy in heaven—not turn our giving from an act of love into an act of prudential self-regard? The reason is that in all our giving our aim is that the beneficiaries—whether enemies or brothers—will be helped, by our giving, to see more of the beauty of Jesus so that they are drawn with us into the heavenly reward. No genuine follower of Jesus wants to enjoy Jesus alone. That is not the kind of Jesus who exists. He cannot be enjoyed alone. He lived and died to be "a ransom for *many*" (Mark 10:45). The joy that we want to increase for ourselves is a shared joy. Giving sacrificially and generously enlarges the measure of our joy in heaven not only by the size of our *heart* toward others, but—to shift the emphasis—by the size of our heart toward *others*. We aim that they share our joy and that we share theirs, so that both joys are larger because of being shared.

Or to turn the problem around: What sort of love would it be if in giving generously to others we did not want to share in the joy we want for them? Disinterested giving would send the signal that the gift I am giving you is not worth having. If I have no passion to enjoy what I offer you, then how can my offer be seen as valuable? I think some people entangle themselves in a contradiction here because they think it is loving to give to the needy without regard to the eternal joy of the needy. They think that simply giving to the poor without aiming at their conversion, so that Jesus becomes their treasure, is a loving thing to do. It is not. If we are indifferent to whether our generosity leads the beneficiary to love Christ, we are not acting in love. I do not mean we must succeed in order for our generosity to be love. Our aim may not be attained. They may reject Jesus while accepting our generosity. We will not stop loving them for that—as long as they live. But not to *aim* at their eternal joy in Jesus is not a loving way to give.

## Giving Sacrificially Shows Our Freedom from Bondage to Things

The giving that Jesus has in mind is as diverse as the possible ways to bless others with what we have and do and say. His command is that we use what we have to bless others. It may be money (Matt. 19:21) or healing (Matt. 10:8) or a cup of cold water (Mark 9:41) or time and effort like the Good Samaritan (Luke 10:34–35) or your home and hospitality (Luke 14:13–14). The point of Jesus's command is that we be radically free from the love of money and what it can buy, and from the fear of losing the security and comforts it affords.

Money enslaves either by greed or fear. We are greedy for more of it and fearful of losing what we have. Jesus wants us free. Sacrificial giving is one evidence that we have been liberated from the idols that money provides. It is also evidence that we have begun to love other people the way we should—that is, we are focusing outwardly on the joy of making others glad, not just the private pleasures that putrefy in the small world of selfishness.

We can see how Jesus thinks about our liberation by the way he links the promise of God's provision with the demand for sacrificial generosity. Here's the link: "Fear not, little flock, for it is your Father's good pleasure to give you the kingdom. Sell your possessions, and give to the needy" (Luke 12:32–33). Surely Jesus intends for us to understand a "therefore" between the promise and the command: "Fear not, little flock, for it is your Father's good pleasure to give you the kingdom. *Therefore*, sell your possessions, and give to the needy."[1]

Luke 12:32 is the key to being liberated from our fearful slavery to possessions. It is the dynamite that can demolish the house of materialism that we live in. Luke 12:32 is a powerful word from Jesus about the nature of God. It's about what kind of heart God has—what makes God glad, not merely what he has or does. Indeed, it is about what *delights* to do, what he *loves* to do and *takes pleasure* in doing. "Fear not, little flock, for it is your Father's good pleasure to give you the kingdom." These are the words that set us free to sell our possessions and give sacrificially and generously.

## The Goodness of God Is the Ground of Our Giving

Notice every amazing part of this extravagantly gracious verse: "It is your Father's *good pleasure* to give you the kingdom." In other words, God is not acting in this generous way in order to cloak and hide some malicious motive. The words "good pleasure" utterly rule that out. He

---

1   The same logic is found in numerous places in the teachings of Jesus. For example, Jesus says, "When you give a feast, invite the poor, the crippled, the lame, the blind, and you will be blessed, because they cannot repay you. [*For*] you will be repaid at the resurrection of the just" (Luke 14:13–14). And: "If you then, who are evil, know how to give good gifts to your children, how much more will your Father who is in heaven give good things to those who ask him! *So* whatever you wish that others would do to you, do also to them" (Matt. 7:11–12). And: "Therefore do not be anxious, saying, 'What shall we eat?' or 'What shall we drink?' or 'What shall we wear?' *For* . . . your heavenly Father knows that you need them all" (Matt. 6:31–32).

is not saying inside, "I will have to be generous for a while even though I don't want to be, because what I really want to do is bring judgment on sinners."

Jesus's meaning is inescapable: God is acting here in freedom. He is not under constraint to do what he doesn't really want to do. At this very point, when he gives his flock the kingdom, he is acting out of his deepest delight. This is what the word means: God's joy, his desire, his want and wish and hope and pleasure and gladness and delight, is to give the kingdom to his flock.

*recognize who is our father*

Then consider the phrase "your Father's." "Fear not, little flock, it is *your Father's* good pleasure to give you the kingdom." Jesus does not say, "It is your employer's good pleasure to pay you your salary." He does not say, "It is your slavemaster's good pleasure to provide your lodging." He does not even say, "It is your king's good pleasure to bestow the kingdom." He chooses every word in this sentence to help us get rid of the fear that God is ill-disposed toward us. So he calls God our "Father."

### God Is the Best of Fathers—Far Better Than the One You Had!

Now, not all of us have had fathers who patterned their lives after God. And so the word *father* may not be full of peace and security the way Jesus means it to be. So let me try to fill the word *father* with two of the meanings Jesus intended it to carry.

First, if the King is our Father, then we are heirs of his kingdom. There is something natural about our receiving it—it's our inheritance. Matthew 25:34 says that in the last day King Jesus will say, "Come, you who are blessed of my Father, *inherit* [note the word!] the kingdom prepared for you from the foundation of the world." Before the beginning of the world God prepared a kingdom for his children. It is theirs by the right of inheritance. And God does not begrudge his children coming into their inheritance. It is his good pleasure to give them the kingdom.

Second, if the King is our Father, then we are free from being taxed. In Matthew 17:25, Peter wondered if the disciples had to pay the temple tax. Jesus says, "What do you think, Simon? From whom do kings of the earth take toll or tax? From their sons or from others?" And when he said, "From others," Jesus said to him, "Then the sons are free." God does not levy taxes against his children. It is those outside the palace who feel the burden of law, not the children within. The children are free! The fatherhood of God means freedom.

The list of implications of what it means to have God as our Father could go on—and all of them would serve to overcome the fear that God is begrudging in his kindness to us. He is not begrudging. He is eager. He delights to give to his children. He is our Father, and if we who are evil know how to give good things to our children, how much more will our Father in heaven give the kingdom to those who ask him (Matt. 7:7–11).

## The Lavish and Tender Generosity and Care of God

Then consider the word "give." "It is your Father's good pleasure to give you the kingdom." Jesus does not say sell you the kingdom. He does not say trade you the kingdom. He says it is the Father's good pleasure to give you the kingdom. God is a mountain spring and not a watering trough. He wells up self-replenishingly. He delights to overflow. It is the nature of an eternal fountain of life to give, give, give. The good news is that God does not need a bucket brigade or sweaty pumpers. He demands water drinkers, not water haulers. Following Jesus means getting down on our faces and satisfying our soul-thirst with his perfect love.

He gives the kingdom! It cannot be bought or bartered for or earned in any way. There is only one way to have it, and it is the easiest way of all—the way of Luke 18:17: "Truly, I say to you, whoever does not receive the kingdom of God like a child shall not enter it." It is God's good pleasure to give us the kingdom. (See Luke 8:10.)

Then consider the word "flock." "Fear not, little *flock*, for it is your Father's good pleasure to give you the kingdom." Jesus is piling up the metaphors. God is our Father. And since he gives us a kingdom, he must be a King. And since we are his flock, he must be a Shepherd. Jesus is at pains to choose every word he can to make his point clear: God is not the kind of God who begrudges his blessings.

Calling us his "flock" or his "sheep" reminds us that Jesus said that the good shepherd lays down his life for the sheep. Does he do it begrudgingly or under constraint? No. "No one takes [my life] from me, but I lay it down of my own accord" (John 10:18). The Father did not begrudge the gift of his Son, and the Son did not begrudge the gift of his life. It is the *Shepherd's* good pleasure to give the kingdom to his *flock*.

Then ponder the word "little." "Fear not, *little* flock, for it is your Father's good pleasure to give you the kingdom." Why does he say "*little* flock"? I think this has two effects. First, it's a term of affection and care. If I say to my family when they are in danger, "Don't be afraid, little family," what I mean is, I know you are in danger and that you are small and weak, but I will use all my power to take care of you because you are precious to me. So "*little* flock" carries the connotation of affection and care.

It also implies that God's goodness to us is not dependent on our greatness. We are a little flock—little in size, little in strength, little in wisdom, little in righteousness, little in love. If God's goodness to us depended on our greatness, we would be in big trouble. But that's the point. It doesn't. So we aren't. "Fear not, *little* flock, it is the Father's good pleasure to give us the kingdom."

### The Gift of God's Sovereign Rule on Our Behalf

Finally, consider the word "kingdom." There might be one little foothold left for the feeling that God is begrudging and ill-disposed toward us. Someone might say, "OK, God is our Father and not our slavemaster; he enjoys giving instead of selling; he treats us the way a good shepherd treats his flock; he has an affection and pity toward us in our littleness. But what, after all, does he promise to give?"

He doesn't promise to give money. In fact, he says, "It is easier for a camel to go through the eye of a needle than for a rich man to enter the kingdom of God" (Luke 18:25). He doesn't promise popularity or fame or admiration among men. In fact, he says, "Blessed are you when men hate you and when they exclude you and revile you and spurn your name as evil, on account of the Son of Man!" (Luke 6:22). He doesn't even promise security in this life. Instead, he says, "You will be delivered up even by parents and brothers and relatives and friends, and some of you they will put to death. You will be hated by all for my name's sake" (Luke 21:16–17).

What does he promise to give to his little flock—to prove once and for all that it is not only his good pleasure to give, but that it is his good pleasure to give big? He promises to give them the *kingdom of God*. And what does it mean to be given the sovereign reign and rule of God?

It means simply and staggeringly and unspeakably that the omnipotent rule and authority of the King of the universe will be engaged forever and ever on behalf of the little flock of God. Who can describe what it will be like when that saying comes to pass that Jesus spoke at the Last Supper, "I assign to you as my Father has assigned to me a kingdom, that you may eat and drink at my table in my kingdom" (Luke 22:29–30)?

Jesus knows that the flock of God struggles with fear about selling what we don't need and giving sacrificially and generously to the poor. He knows that one of those fears is that God is the kind of God who is basically angry and delights most of all to judge sinners and only does good out of a sense of constraint and duty, not delight. Therefore, the Lord is at pains in Luke 12:32 to free us from this fear by telling us the truth about God. He has chosen every word to help liberate us from the love of money and satisfy us with all that God promises to be for us in Jesus. Every word counts. Always read it slowly.

> Fear not,
> little
> flock,
> for it is your Father's
> good pleasure
> to give you
> the kingdom!

## The Simplicity and Generosity of William Carey

What kind of life will this promise produce for those who really believe it? I close this chapter with one illustration from the life of the missionary to India, William Carey. In October 1795, Carey received a packet of letters in India from his homeland, England. One of the letters criticized him for "engaging in affairs of trade," instead of devoting himself full-time to his missionary work (which would go on to last for over thirty years of amazing fruitfulness, without a furlough). Carey was hurt and angered by the accusation. If he had not worked, he and his family would probably have starved, since the support from England was so slow and small and sporadic in arriving. He wrote back these words that describe the kind of life that I pray you and I will live:

> It is a constant maxim with me that, if my conduct will not vindicate itself, it is not worth vindicating. . . . I only say that, after my family's obtaining a bare allowance, my whole income, and some months, much more, goes for the purposes of the gospel, in supporting persons to assist in the translation of the Bible, write copies, teach school, and the like. . . . I mention . . . [this] to show that the love of money has not prompted me to pursue the plan that I have engaged in. I am indeed poor, and shall always

be so till the Bible is published in Bengali and Hindosthani, and the people [lack] no further instruction.[2]

That is the kind of sacrificial, generous devotion to the cause of his kingdom that Jesus meant when he commanded, "Lay up for yourselves treasures in heaven."

2  Mary Drewery, *William Carey: A Biography* (Grand Rapids, Mich.: Zondervan, 1984), 91.

*Again you have heard that it was said to those of old, "You shall not swear falsely, but shall perform to the Lord what you have sworn." But I say to you, Do not take an oath at all, either by heaven, for it is the throne of God, or by the earth, for it is his footstool, or by Jerusalem, for it is the city of the great King. And do not take an oath by your head, for you cannot make one hair white or black. Let what you say be simply "Yes" or "No"; anything more than this comes from evil.*

MATTHEW 5:33–37

# Do Not Take an Oath—Cherish the Truth and Speak It Simply

JESUS TEACHES THAT TRUTH IS PRECIOUS. All of us agree with this when we are being lied about. The most relativistic professor in the university, who scoffs at the concept of truth in the classroom, will be indignant if his electricity bill is false to his disadvantage. He will call the utility company and complain that there is some mistake. He will not think it funny if the voice on the other end says, "It's a mistake in *your* view but not in *our* view."

### For Ordinary People Truth Is Precious

Truth is precious. Did the baby swallow the missing needle or didn't she? Is this water drinkable or isn't it? Are you a friend or a spy? Will you keep your marriage vows to love and cherish me, or are you only interested in money and sex? Do we have enough fuel on this airplane to reach our destination, or should we turn back? Will this surgery leave me worse or better than I was before? Did the desperate 911 caller say 11th Avenue or 11th Street?

Those who mock the concept of truth are people with power who do not (at the moment) need to appeal to truth for their lives. Totalitarian despots do not care about truth because they have power to create the reality they want—for a fleeting moment in history. Tenured professors may not care about truth in the classroom because they have the power and security to entertain their students with academic games without being forced to apply their foolishness to their own real lives after they go home at night. But for most of the world, truth matters. And they know it. It matters ultimately. Their lives depend on it.

### "I Have Come to Bear Witness to the Truth"

Jesus loved truth and hated deceit. He confirmed the ninth commandment, "Do not bear false witness" (Mark 10:19). He warned that "deceit" comes out of the heart and defiles a person (Mark 7:21–22). He considered religious hypocrisy a hellish form of lying (Matt. 23:15). He said that those who use their piety to cloak their evil are sons of the devil. "You are of your father the devil, and your will is to do your father's desires. He was a murderer from the beginning, and does not stand in the truth, because there is no truth in him. When he lies, he speaks out of his own character, for he is a liar and the father of lies" (John 8:44). Lying originates with the devil, and those who turn away from speaking truth join forces with Satan.

Over against this, Jesus came into the world to reveal the truth about God and man and salvation and what is right and wrong. At the end of his ministry, when he was on trial for his life, he said to Pontius Pilate, "For this purpose I was born and for this purpose I have come into the world—*to bear witness to the truth*. Everyone who is of the truth listens to my voice" (John 18:37). Like many modern cynics, Pilate responded, "What is truth?" and turned to go without waiting for an answer.

### "I Am the Truth"

But we know the answer he would have received. Jesus would have said what he had already said, "I *am* . . . the truth" (John 14:6). Jesus himself—in all that he is and all that he does and all that he says—is the criterion of what is real and true and right and beautiful. When he speaks, there is no error or falsehood. He said of himself, "The one who seeks the glory of him who sent him is true, and in him there is no falsehood" (John 7:18). Therefore, when others did not believe what he said, he did not consider changing the message to win a better hearing. If truth was met with unbelief, the problem lay with the unbelieving heart, not the truth. "Because I tell the truth, you do not believe me" (John 8:45). Jesus said that people turn away from the light not because they think it's false but because they love darkness (John 3:19).

When Jesus left the earth he promised to send a Helper. He called him "the Spirit of truth." "When the Helper comes, whom I will send to you from the Father, the *Spirit of truth*, who proceeds from the Father, he will bear witness about me" (John 15:26). This Spirit of truth will help us know the truth and be changed by the truth. So Jesus prays before he leaves and asks the Father to make the truth effective in our lives: "Sanctify them in the *truth*; your word is truth" (John 17:17). So we can see how supremely important truth is to Jesus, and how destructively evil is the impulse to deceive and mislead and speak in devious ways.

## The Folly of Crossing Your Fingers and Crossing Your Heart

Therefore, it is not surprising that in the Sermon on the Mount Jesus overturned one of the subtle practices used in his day to avoid truth-telling and promise-keeping. When a promise is not kept, it becomes a lie. And when a promise made with a public oath is not kept, we call it perjury. When I was growing up we joked that if you had your fingers crossed when you made a promise, you didn't have to keep it. We also had our own youthful ways of reinforcing our distrusted word: we said, "Cross my heart and hope to die." What we meant was: I am speaking from my heart, not just my lips, and if what I say is not true let me die.

Jesus was not happy about either of these devices—the crossing of the fingers to escape a promise and the crossing of the heart to reinforce a promise. Here is what he said:

> Again you have heard that it was said to those of old, "You shall not swear falsely, but shall perform to the Lord what you have sworn." But I say to you, Do not take an oath at all, either by heaven, for it is the throne of God, or by the earth, for it is his footstool, or by Jerusalem, for it is the city of the great King. And do not take an oath by your head, for you cannot make one hair white or black. Let what you say be simply "Yes" or "No";[1] anything more than this comes from evil. (Matt. 5:33–37)

Jesus is commanding two things here: First, he commands that we not use verbal evasions to escape promise-keeping; second, he commands that we be so truthful that oaths are superfluous.

### Technical Evasions of Promise-Keeping

The verbal evasions Jesus cites are in reference to heaven and earth and Jerusalem and the head. Evidently some people assumed that as long as their oath did not directly call upon God as witness, it was not binding. So if they said, "I swear by heaven" or "I swear by earth" or "I swear by Jerusalem" or "I swear by my head," then they could break their word because they had not said, "I swear by *God*." This devious logic says something like this: "Heaven and earth and Jerusalem and my head cannot really take vengeance on me if I break my word—only God can. But I did not call God to witness my words and to hold me accountable, so I am not really in trouble."

Jesus rejects that kind of evasion. He points out that everything you swear by has God behind it one way or the other. Heaven is his throne.

---

1   Or more literally: "Let your word be yes, yes/no, no; and what is more than these is from evil (or the evil one)."

Earth is his footstool. Jerusalem is his city. And your head is under his control, not yours, because only under his providence does our hair change color. Therefore, your problem is your small view of God and truth. You think truth is insignificant and can be manipulated to your liking. And you think God is off in a corner with little concern for your truthfulness until his name is mentioned. In these two things you are wrong. Truth is precious beyond your ability to imagine, and God is behind every molecule in the universe and is always concerned that his creatures be truthful.

**Truth Evasion by Belittling God**

Jesus encountered this evasive strategy in the Pharisees in Matthew 23:16–22. His indignation is unmistakable:

> Woe to you, blind guides, who say, "If anyone swears by the temple, it is nothing, but if anyone swears by the gold of the temple, he is bound by his oath." You blind fools! For which is greater, the gold or the temple that has made the gold sacred? And you say, "If anyone swears by the altar, it is nothing, but if anyone swears by the gift that is on the altar, he is bound by his oath." You blind men! For which is greater, the gift or the altar that makes the gift sacred? So whoever swears by the altar swears by it and by everything on it. And whoever swears by the temple swears by it and by him who dwells in it. And whoever swears by heaven swears by the throne of God and by him who sits upon it.

It is almost incredible that the Pharisees not only use evasions like this, but *teach* them. Jesus says that the blind guides "*say* [that is, they teach others], 'If anyone swears by the temple, it is nothing.'" Perhaps it is not a direct quote but rather the upshot of what they say. In either case, Jesus is furious at the way truth and God are belittled here. Gold is esteemed above God's temple. Sacrifices are esteemed above God's altar. Heaven is esteemed above God who dwells there. All this evasiveness ignores the fact that the holiness of heaven, altar, and temple come from their connection with God. But this means little to those who are bent on finding ways to make peace with falsehood.

What alternative did Jesus command to these manifold ways of evading the binding claims of truth on our lives? To that we turn in the next chapter.

*And do not take an oath by your head, for you cannot make one hair white or black. Let what you say be simply "Yes" or "No"; anything more than this comes from evil.*

MATTHEW 5:36–37

*But Jesus remained silent. And the high priest said to him, "I adjure you by the living God, tell us if you are the Christ, the Son of God." Jesus said to him, "You have said so."*

MATTHEW 26:63–64

COMMAND #39

# Do Not Take an Oath—Let What
# You Say Be Simply "Yes" or "No"

### A New Standard of Truthfulness

Over against the creative and corrupt ways people find to evade telling
the truth (which we saw in the previous chapter), Jesus says, "But I
say to you, Do not take an oath at all. . . . Let what you say be simply
'Yes, yes' or 'No, no'; anything more than this comes from evil" (Matt.
5:34, 37, at). In other words, Jesus now goes beyond the Old Testament
standard of keeping our oaths to not using any. His reason seems to
be that with the arrival of the kingdom of God in his ministry (Luke
11:20; 17:21) and the presence of the King himself (Matt. 21:15–16)
and the sending of the Spirit of truth (John 15:26) and the inauguration
of the new covenant (Luke 22:20; see *Command #23*), the standards
of truthfulness should rise, and the measure of compromise with evil
in this world should decrease.

He argues, "Do not take an oath at all . . . anything more than [yes,
yes, and no, no] comes from evil." Evil in the human heart has created
lying and deceit. Jesus said it originated with the "father of lies" (John
8:44) and gains strength from the on-going evil of the human heart.
Therefore, truth is in jeopardy all the time. But life in community

cannot survive without truth. There must be some measure of trust in marriages and businesses and schools and governments and in the vast realm of contractual agreements, not to mention the precious fabric of personal friendships. Therefore, the evil of lying and falsehood and deceit that pervades the human heart and society has been restrained by devices called oaths.

## We Look to Oaths to Do What Love Does Not Do

The evil that ruined trust is essentially selfishness and ill will. We distort the truth to get what we want, even if it hurts others. Which implies that, for truth to hold sway, love must hold sway. If we were not selfish or unloving to others, we would not break our word or tell lies or act hypocritically. Truth would hold sway.

But love does not hold sway in the world, and so oaths have arisen to compensate for what love should do. Oaths are born out of the necessities created by lovelessness. Since we do not love, and so secure the reliability of our word, we take oaths to assure people we mean what we say. We put ourselves under the threat of deity for breaking our word. Which means we make our own self-regard the measure of our truthfulness. We do not want to be struck down by God. This self-regard we share with all people (even if they don't believe in God). Therefore, this kind of oath carries weight in guaranteeing our truthfulness.

Jesus says in effect, "I am calling you to a different level of truthfulness. I am calling you to witness to the inbreaking of my kingdom and the kind of integrity I have brought into the world. Yes, you still live in a fallen world. There is lying and deceit. Oaths may be necessary among those who do not know my saving power. They may still help fallen society hang together. They are a kind of dam against the river of human falsehood."[1]

---

1 I borrowed this image from Adolf Schlatter, *Erläuterungen zum Neuen Testament, Das Evangelium nach Matthäus*, Erster Band (Stuttgart: Calwer Vereinsbuchhandlung, 1928), 76. "Against this flood of sins we seek with the oath to erect a dam; but it does not reach its goal, because it only enlarges the power of the lie" (my translation).

*James 5:12*
*John 8:31-32*
*John 12:13*
*Prov 12:13*
*Ps 51:6*
*Num 30:2*
*John 17:17*

## Jesus Simply Said, "You Have Said So"

Jesus was saying, "But for you—you who know me and follow me and are forgiven and transformed by me—let your yes and no be as good as an oath. Let your integrity be unimpeachable. Look the court clerk in the eye when she asks you, 'Do you swear to tell the truth, the whole truth, and nothing but the truth, so help you God?' and say, 'I will tell the truth.'" When Jesus was adjured by the high priest at his court appearance the night before he died, the priest said, "I adjure you by the living God, tell us if you are the Christ, the Son of God" (Matt. 26:63). In other words, he commanded that Jesus call God to witness with an oath as he made his claim to messiahship.

Jesus would not yield. He answered, in accord with his own command in Matthew 5:37, "You have said so." This is Jesus's simple yes: "You have said it, and you are right" (Matt. 26:64; see Mark 14:62). There was no need for an oath. His yes is as good as an oath. The high priest felt the full force of it and did not need to press for an oath. He tore his robe and said, "He has uttered blasphemy. What further witnesses do we need? You have now heard his blasphemy" (Matt. 26:65).

## Should the Followers of Jesus Ever Take an Oath?

Even though Jesus's main point in his radical command concerning oaths is that we be people of utter integrity and complete truthfulness, we must still ask the question, should the followers of Jesus, then, ever use an oath? To answer this it may be helpful to note that the question can be asked another way. Not only did Jesus say, "Do not take an oath at all" (Matt. 5:34), he also said the positive counterpart, "Let what you say be simply 'Yes' or 'No'"—or literally, "Let your word be 'yes, yes,' 'no, no'" (Matt. 5:37). So the question of application can also be put this way: Should the followers of Jesus ever make a promise or answer a question or make an assertion with any other words than "yes" and "no"?

The reason it may be helpful to consider this second question is that there are exceptions in Jesus's ministry that would warn us against saying followers of Jesus may not add any words to "yes" and "no" to emphasize the speaker's truthfulness. The most prevalent is Jesus's use of the phrase, "Truly" or "Truly, truly." Over fifty times in the Gospels Jesus says something like, "Truly, I say to you," or "Truly, I tell you." And over twenty-five times he uses the even stronger phrase "Truly, truly, I say to you."

D. A. Carson says of the phrase, "Jesus uses it before an utterance to confirm and emphasize its trustworthiness and importance."[2] If anyone in the world ever existed whose integrity did not demand added words to emphasize his truthfulness, it was Jesus. Yet he did so. Evidently the use of reinforcing words do not have to flow from the speaker's lack of integrity, but from an impulse of love that the listeners need to be awakened to the absolute trustworthiness of what is being said because they might not know how reliable the speaker is.

This gives me pause, therefore, that I should be slow to say that a follower of Jesus may have such integrity that there is no situation in which love may not demand some reinforcing expression for the sake of the listeners. Add to this that Jesus knew that God himself, who is the essence of integrity, confirmed his word at times with oaths. This was not to make up for untrustworthiness on his part, but to give multiple encouragements to help us believe him (see Luke 1:73; Gen. 22:16). It seems, then, that Jesus's argument aims at absolute integrity and truthfulness but does not intend to stipulate absolutely the wording that expresses this truthfulness.

### Some Oaths May Be Permitted

Returning then to the seemingly absolute prohibition, "Do not take an oath at all," should we infer from these thoughts that there are

---

2   D. A. Carson, *The Gospel According to John* (Grand Rapids, Mich.: Eerdmans, 1991), 162.

exceptions to the prohibition? I am inclined to think we should be open to the possibility that the wording of an oath (like, "I call God to witness that what I say is true") could be one way that we show love to someone who does not know us (and whether we are trustworthy) and whose cultural situation would give credit to our account if we used this form of speech. In other words, Jesus's absolute prohibition relates to the abuses of oaths referred to in Matthew 5:35–36 and 23:16–22, and the principle that is absolute across all time and culture is the command that we be people of absolute truthfulness and honesty.

## But Beware of Taking the Edge Off of Jesus's Radical Demand for Truth

This would imply that we use an oath or some other formula *not* to make up for lack of trustworthiness in us but only to help others embrace the unvarnished truth that we speak. But even as I write this I feel some of the edge being taken off of what Jesus said. He really was lifting us to a higher level than "You shall not swear falsely, but shall perform to the Lord what you have sworn" (Matt. 5:33). His aim was greater than, keep your promises. There is a call away from oaths.

Our new inclination should be, my oath is not necessary. I should be slow to use an oath. An oath will very likely (if not necessarily) communicate something about the weakness of my trustworthiness that may dishonor Jesus. One of the glories of Jesus is that he frees me from the need to lie and from the need to prove that I don't lie.

The followers of Jesus are not just honest, they are moving toward a condition in which protections against being thought dishonest will not be necessary. Therefore, they will find countercultural ways of declaring the lordship of Christ over their minds and mouths. In the end Jesus aims to be known as the way, the *truth*, and the life. He commands that we live and speak in a way that will make that glory known.

*Have you not read that he who created them from the beginning made them male and female, and said, "Therefore a man shall leave his father and his mother and hold fast to his wife, and they shall become one flesh"? So they are no longer two but one flesh. What therefore God has joined together, let not man separate.*

MATTHEW 19:4–6

*Your Maker is your husband, the* LORD *of hosts is his name.*

ISAIAH 54:5

**Judicial Watch**
Because no one
is above the law!®

Father-may we have ears
to hear & hearts to
obey that all we
think & do & say may
be to your glory

Tiny
Theologians

gideons Trumpet
Tell no lies

# What God Has Joined Together Let No Man Separate, for Marriage Mirrors God's Covenant with Us

JESUS COMMANDS THAT husbands and wives be faithful to their marriages. He does not assume this is easy. But he teaches that it is a great thing because marriage is the work of God himself whereby he creates a new reality of "one flesh" that surpasses human comprehension and portrays to the world in human form the covenant union between God and his people. Marriage is sacred beyond what most people imagine, because it is a unique creation of God, a dramatic portrayal of God's relation to his people, and a display of God's glory. Against all the diminished attitudes about marriage in our day, Jesus's message is that marriage is a great work of God and a sacred covenant breakable only by death.

## Marriage: The Mirror of God's Covenant with His People

Jesus knew his Jewish Scriptures and saw them as coming to fulfillment in himself and his work (Matt. 5:17–18). This includes his awareness of what God had said about his relationship with his people when he portrayed it as marriage. For example, God said, "Your Maker is your husband, the Lord of hosts is his name" (Isa. 54:5). And "In that day, declares the Lord, you will call me 'My Husband.' . . . And I will betroth you to me forever. I will betroth you to me in righteousness and in justice, in steadfast love and in mercy. I will betroth you to me in faithfulness. And you shall know the Lord" (Hos. 2:16, 19–20). And "When I passed by you again and saw you, behold, you were at the age for love, and I spread the corner of my garment over you and covered your nakedness; I made my vow to you and entered into a covenant with you, declares the Lord God, and you became mine" (Ezek. 16:8). And "Surely, as a treacherous wife leaves her husband, so have you been treacherous to me, O house of Israel, declares the Lord" (Jer. 3:20).

With these Scriptures as the backdrop, it is inevitable that Jesus would see God's creation of marriage in the beginning as a means of portraying his relationship with his people. So Jesus read in Genesis 2:24, "Therefore a man shall leave his father and his mother and hold fast to his wife, and they shall become one flesh." When God said this—and Jesus explicitly says that *God* said this, not just Moses, the writer of Genesis (Matt. 19:4–5)—he had in view (as he has all things in view) that he would call his people his wife and himself her husband. Therefore, the union between a man and a woman is uniquely God's creation with a view to portraying the relationship between himself and his people.

## God Creates the Union of Each Marriage for His Glory

Jesus is explicit about marriage as God's creation. He does not leave us to figure this out from the Scriptures, and he does not limit the creation to the first marriage between Adam and Eve. He says, "What therefore *God* has joined together, let not man separate" (Matt. 19:6). God, not man, is the decisive creator of the marriage union. And the point is that *each* marriage is "joined" this way by God, because he tells us not to "separate," and the only marriage we can decisively separate is the one we are in. So this marriage—this particular marriage, not just the concept of marriage or the general ordinance of marriage or the first marriage—is God's work. God has acted in the union of this husband and this wife. These two are one flesh by God's work, not just by their choice.

And as a God-created union of "one flesh" this man and this woman are in a covenant analogous with God's covenant with Israel. Their marriage portrays God's relationship with his people. Through marriage God fills the earth with (mostly unwitting) witnesses to the relationship between him and his covenant people. This is one of the main reasons that divorce and remarriage are so serious. They tell a lie about God's relationship to his people. God never divorced his wife and married another. There were separations and much pain, but he always took her back. The prophet Hosea is a testimony to God's radical love for his wayward spouse. God never abandons his wife. And when he has to put her away for her adulterous idolatry, he goes after her in due time. This is what marriage is meant to portray: God's invincible and gracious commitment to his covenant people—his wife.

In this way marriage is meant to glorify God. In Jeremiah 13:11 God says, "As the loincloth clings to the waist of a man, so I made the whole house of Israel and the whole house of Judah cling to me, declares the Lord, that they might be for me a people, a name, a praise, and a *glory*." God freely chose and married Israel so that they would display his glory. Therefore, marriage is the work of God's creation, the portrayal of his covenant love, and the display of his glory.

### But What about Moses's Permission of Divorce?

This gives some sense of why Jesus's demand for marital faithfulness astonishes the Pharisees. They can hardly believe he would raise the bar so high. They had come to him with a question: "Is it lawful to divorce one's wife for any cause?" (Matt. 19:3). Jesus answers them not by reference to the Mosaic law but by reference to the Mosaic creation account. In other words, he intends to root the meaning of marriage in its original design, not in the way marriage is managed by the law in view of sin.

Jesus says, "Have you not read that he who created them from the beginning made them male and female, and said, 'Therefore a man shall leave his father and his mother and hold fast to his wife, and they shall become one flesh'? So they are no longer two but one flesh. What therefore God has joined together, let not man separate" (Matt. 19:4–6). So the answer to their question is: God made marriage to last, so don't treat it as breakable.

Now the Pharisees think they have Jesus trapped. He seems to have just taken a position contrary to the Law of Moses. So they ask, "Why then did Moses command one to give a certificate of divorce and to send her away?" (Matt. 19:7). In other words, they hear correctly in Jesus's answer the implication that one should never break the marriage covenant. But that is not the way they understand Moses. So they ask, why did Moses make a provision for divorce if, you say, the covenant is not to be broken?

Jesus responds, "Because of your hardness of heart Moses allowed you to divorce your wives, but from the beginning it was not so" (Matt. 19:8). So Jesus takes his stand with Moses in the creation account and says that just as in the beginning the marriage covenant was not meant to be breakable, so now in the kingdom that he is bringing on earth, this original intention is to be rediscovered and reasserted. In other words, Jesus is raising the standard of his disciples above what Moses allowed. He puts it like this: "And I say to you: whoever divorces his wife, except for sexual immorality, and marries another, commits adultery" (Matt. 19:9).

## The Devastation of Divorce

We are now at a point where we need to tackle the question, did Jesus make provision for his disciples to divorce and remarry? Are there situations in which he would sanction this? There is no consensus on the answer to this question today among his followers. I want to say clearly from the beginning that I am aware that men more godly than I have taken views different from the one I will give here. I do not claim to have seen or said the last word on this issue, nor am I, I pray, above correction should I prove to be wrong. What follows is an attempt to show why I believe Jesus considered the marriage covenant breakable only by death and therefore forbade remarriage while a spouse is living.

I realize that simply saying this will feel devastating to some, adding more misery to the injury of what they did not want to happen. Divorce is painful. It is often more emotionally wrenching than the death of a spouse. It is often long years in coming and long years in the settlement and in the adjustment. The upheaval of life is immeasurable. The sense of failure and guilt and fear can torture the soul. Like the psalmist, night after night a spouse falls asleep with tears (Ps. 6:6). Work performance is hindered. People draw near or withdraw with uncertain feelings. Loneliness can be overwhelming. A sense of a devastated future can be all-consuming. Courtroom controversy compounds the personal misery. And then there is often the agonizing place of children. Parents hope against hope that the scars will not cripple them or ruin their own marriages someday. Tensions over custody and financial support deepen the wounds. And then the awkward and artificial visitation rights can lengthen the tragedy over decades.

Because of these and many other factors, people with sensitive hearts weep with those who weep. They try not to increase the pain. And sometimes this care is confused with compromise. People think that loving care is incompatible with confrontation—that the tenderness of Jesus and the toughness of his commands cannot both be love. But surely this is not right.

### The Challenge to Love Biblically

Jesus was an extraordinarily caring person. His teaching on divorce and remarriage was also firm: "What . . . God has joined together, let not man separate." In fact, firm and loving confrontation with the commands of Christ *is* a form of caring, because a sinful decision is just as harmful to a person as the emotional pain. This is true individually, and it is true for the church and society. Compassionate compromises on the sanctity of marriage that weaken the solidity of the covenant of marriage look loving in the short run but wreak havoc over decades. Preserving the solid framework of the marriage covenant with high standards feels tough in the short run but produces ten thousand blessings the future generations take for granted.

The great challenge to Jesus's followers in the face of divorce and remarriage is to love biblically. The great challenge is to mingle the tears of compassion with the tough love of obedience. This alone will honor Christ and preserve the spiritual health and power of the marriage and the church Jesus founded.

In Matthew 19:3–9 and Mark 10:2–12 Jesus rejected the Pharisees' justification of divorce from Deuteronomy 24 and reasserted the purpose of God in creation that no human being separate what God has joined together. He said that Moses's handling of divorce was owing to the hardness of the human heart and then implied that he had come to do something about that. His aim was that the standard of his followers would be higher than what the Law allowed.

How high? That's the question I try to answer in the next chapter.

*Whoever divorces his wife and marries another commits
adultery against her, and if she divorces her husband
and marries another, she commits adultery.*

MARK 10:11–12

*Everyone who divorces his wife and marries another
commits adultery, and he who marries a woman
divorced from her husband commits adultery.*

LUKE 16:18

*It was also said, "Whoever divorces his wife, let him
give her a certificate of divorce." But I say to you that
everyone who divorces his wife, except on the ground
of sexual immorality, makes her commit adultery. And
whoever marries a divorced woman commits adultery.*

MATTHEW 5:31–32

*And I say to you: whoever divorces his wife, except for sexual
immorality, and marries another, commits adultery.*

MATTHEW 19:9

# What God Has Joined Together Let No Man Separate, for Whoever Divorces and Marries Another Commits Adultery

JESUS SET A HIGHER STANDARD FOR marital faithfulness than Moses or the Jewish teachers of his day. He did not affirm the permission for divorce found in Deuteronomy 24. He said it was owing to the hardness of the human heart (Matt. 19:8) and implied that he was here to change that. In this chapter we will try to discern just how high Jesus's standard of marital faithfulness is.

### Clues in Moses That Divorce Did Not Destroy God's Union

I suspect that Jesus saw a higher standard for marriage implied not only in the creation account of Genesis 2:24 but also in the very wording of Deuteronomy 24:1–4, which shows that the *one-flesh* relationship established by marriage is not completely nullified by divorce or even by remarriage. Consider what Moses wrote:

> When a man takes a wife and marries her, if then she finds no favor in his eyes because he has found some indecency in her, and he writes

her a certificate of divorce and puts it in her hand and sends her out
of his house, and she departs out of his house, and if she goes and
becomes another man's wife, and the latter man hates her and writes
her a certificate of divorce and puts it in her hand and sends her out
of his house, or if the latter man dies, who took her to be his wife,
then her former husband, who sent her away, may not take her again
to be his wife, after she has been defiled, for that is an abomination
before the Lord. And you shall not bring sin upon the land that the
Lord your God is giving you for an inheritance. (Deut. 24:1–4)

The remarkable thing about these four verses is that while divorce is
taken for granted, nevertheless the woman who is divorced becomes
"defiled" by her remarriage (v. 4). Therefore, it may well be that when
the Pharisees asked Jesus if divorce was legitimate, he based his negative answer not only on God's original intention expressed in Genesis
1:27 and 2:24, but also on the implication of Deuteronomy 24:4, that
remarriage after divorce, while permitted, nevertheless *defiles* a person.
In other words, there were clues in the writings of Moses that the divorce
concession was on the basis of the hardness of man's heart and did not
make divorce and remarriage the most God-honoring path.

Moses's prohibition of a wife returning to her first husband even after
her second husband dies (because it is an "abomination," v. 4) suggests
that today no second marriage should be broken in order to restore a
first one. I will return to this issue later on. But for now I would say
that even a disobedient second or third marriage should not be broken,
but confessed as less than ideal and yet sanctified by God's mercy. It is
better in God's eyes than more broken covenants.

### The Prohibitions without Exception

Twice in the Gospels Jesus expresses with no exceptions his prohibition
of divorce followed by remarriage. In Luke 16:18 he says, "Everyone
who divorces his wife and marries another commits adultery, and he

who marries a woman divorced from her husband commits adultery." Here Jesus seems to call all remarriage after divorce adultery. These are strong words. Evidently the reason a second marriage is called *adultery* is because the first one is considered to still be valid. So Jesus is taking a stand against the Jewish culture at the time in which all divorce was considered to carry with it the right of remarriage.[1]

Luke 16:18 carries another implication: the second half of the verse ("he who marries a woman divorced from her husband commits adultery") shows that not only the divorcing man is guilty of adultery when he remarries, but also *any* man who marries a divorced woman commits adultery. This is all the more remarkable because the woman in view here is presumably the innocent party in the divorce, because when her husband divorces her he commits adultery in marrying another. Apparently this is because he had no right to divorce his wife. That is, she has

---

1   It puzzles me that so many commentators take the opposite approach. They observe that since "any Jewish reader would have taken for granted" that divorce opened the door to remarriage, therefore Jesus agrees with this assumption and does not need to say it in Mark 10:11–12 and Luke 16:18. Hence Andreas Köstenberger, for example, writes, "Rather than concluding that Jesus did not allow for any divorce in sexually consummated marriages, it is much more likely that he did not elaborate on points at which he agreed with the commonly held view in his day." *God, Marriage, and Family: Rebuilding the Biblical Foundation*, 2nd ed. (Wheaton, IL: Crossway, 2010), 281. I am inclined to say that Jesus's explicit, unqualified rejection of remarriage in Mark 10 and Luke 16 is a direct repudiation of this cultural assumption as a compromise with the hardness of man's heart. How could he have more clearly addressed and rejected the cultural assumption of the legitimacy of remarriage after divorce? David Instone-Brewer's arguments that (1) the short form of Jesus's saying in Luke 16:18 is a reference to Herod Antipas's marriage of his brother's wife (160–61), and (2) that the omission of any exception clause is explained on the analogy of rabbinic abbreviations (161–67), and (3) that the exception clause, "except for *porneia*," should be "except for indecency," referring to the phrase "some indecency" in Deuteronomy 24:1 and expressing the more conservative Rabbi Shammai's position all seem unlikely to me. David Instone-Brewer, *Divorce and Remarriage in the Bible: The Social and Literary Context* (Grand Rapids, Mich.: Eerdmans, 2002). If one objects that Jesus did not endorse or forbid remarriage after the death of a spouse because he shared the commonly accepted view, my response would be: (1) None of Jesus's discussions of remarriage are aimed at answering the question about what is legitimate in the death of a spouse, but only what is legitimate in the divorce of a spouse. (2) In one place where Jesus comes close to the issue of the death of a spouse (in the question of the Sadducees about the wife who was widowed seven times, Matt. 22:23–32), Jesus finds no fault in her remarriage after a spouse's death.

done nothing to make his divorce legitimate. Nevertheless, any man who marries this abandoned woman, Jesus says, "commits adultery."

This is a hard saying. The woman who is forsaken by a man who leaves to marry another is called by Jesus to display the holiness of her marriage vows and the nature of the marriage covenant by not marrying another. Since there are no exceptions mentioned in the verse, and since Jesus is evidently rejecting the common cultural conception of divorce as including the right of remarriage, the first readers of Luke's Gospel would have been hard-put to see any exceptions on the basis that Jesus shared the cultural acceptance of divorce.

The other instance of Jesus's unqualified rejection of remarriage after divorce is found in Mark 10:11–12. He said, "Whoever divorces his wife and marries another commits adultery against her, and if she divorces her husband and marries another, she commits adultery." These two verses repeat the first half of Luke 16:18 but go further and say that not only the man who divorces, but also a woman who divorces and then remarries is committing adultery. And as in Luke 16:18, there are no exceptions mentioned to this rule.

What we have so far is two seemingly absolute prohibitions of remarriage after divorce in Luke 16:18 and Mark 10:11–12 since Jesus sees marrying a second time as adultery, even if you are the innocent party in the divorce. And we have a strong statement in Matthew 19:6 and Mark 10:9 that God has joined married couples together and therefore no man should separate them.

## Is There a Permission for Divorce in Matthew 5:32?

But what makes the matter more controversial is that in Matthew 5:32 and 19:9 there seems to be an exception to the rule of no remarriage after divorce. In Matthew 5:32 Jesus says, "Everyone who divorces his wife, *except on the ground of sexual immorality*, makes her commit adultery, and whoever marries a divorced woman commits adultery." Again in Matthew 19:9 he says, "Whoever divorces his wife, *except for sexual immorality*, and marries another, commits adultery." Both these verses are generally interpreted to say that Jesus allowed divorce and remarriage where there has been "sexual immorality" by one of the partners. Is that what the "exception clauses" mean?

According to the wording of Matthew 5:32 (". . . *makes* her commit adultery"), Jesus assumes that in most situations in that culture a wife who has been put away by a husband will be drawn into a second marriage. Nevertheless, in spite of these pressures on the divorced woman to remarry, Jesus still forbids this second marriage. His words imply that the remarriage of an innocent wife who has been put away is nevertheless adultery: "Everyone who divorces his wife, *except on the ground of sexual immorality*, makes her [the innocent wife who has not committed sexual immorality] commit adultery." This would mean that remarriage is wrong not merely when a person is *guilty* in the process of divorce, but also when a person is *innocent*. In other words, Jesus's opposition to remarriage seems to be based on the unbreakableness of the marriage bond, not on the conditions of the divorce.

So Matthew 5:32 does not teach that remarriage is lawful in some cases. Rather, it reaffirms that to remarry after divorce is to commit adultery, even for those who have been divorced innocently, and that a man who divorces his wife is guilty of the adultery of her second marriage, and that a man who marries a woman who is put away by her husband, even innocently, commits adultery. Hence the final clause of the verse: "And whoever marries a divorced woman commits adultery." Before we tackle what the exception clause means, let's put the similar text from Matthew 19:9 before us.

## The Exception Clause in Matthew 19:9

The other place where Jesus seems to express an "exception clause" to the prohibition of divorce and remarriage is Matthew 19:9, "And I say to you: whoever divorces his wife, *except for sexual immorality*, and marries another, commits adultery." Does this exception mean that there are situations in which a married person may be free to remarry after divorce? That is what most commentators see and what most followers of Jesus think. In my understanding of Jesus's command this is not what it means. It may help if I describe my pilgrimage to another understanding.

All of my adult life I assumed that adultery and desertion were two legitimate grounds for divorce and remarriage. This was the air I breathed, and I saw a confirmation of this in the exception clause in Matthew 19:9, even though, as I see it now, the rest of the New Testament pointed in the other direction.[2] But there came a point when this assumption began to crumble.

I was initially troubled that the absolute form of Jesus's denunciation of divorce and remarriage in Mark 10:11–12 and Luke 16:18 is not expressed by Matthew, if in fact his exception clause is an opening for divorce and remarriage. I was bothered by the assumption so many writers make, namely, that Matthew is simply making explicit something that would have been implicitly understood by the hearers of Jesus or the readers of Mark 10 and Luke 16 (see footnote 1).

2    A fuller statement of my understanding of the rest of the New Testament may be found under the topic "Divorce and Remarriage" at www.desiringGod.org, specifically, "Divorce and Remarriage: A Position" (1986). A survey of three views is offered in *Remarriage After Divorce in Today's Church*, ed. Mark L. Strauss (Grand Rapids, Mich.: Zondervan, 2006), in which Gordon Wenham represents the position of no marriage after divorce, William A. Heth (who no longer holds his view represented in his book coauthored with Wenham, *Jesus and Divorce*, updated ed. [Carlisle, U.K.: Paternoster, 1997; orig. ed. 1984] represents the position of two grounds for divorce and remarriage, and Craig S. Keener represents the position that various other grounds are allowed for divorce and remarriage. In addition, see Craig S. Keener, *And Marries Another: Divorce and Remarriage in the Teaching of the New Testament* (Peabody, Mass.: Hendrickson, 1991); and Carl Laney, *The Divorce Myth: A Biblical Examination of Divorce and Remarriage* (Minneapolis: Bethany, 1981), who argues for no divorce after remarriage. David Instone-Brewer, *Divorce and Remarriage in the Bible: The Social and Literary Context* (Grand Rapids, Mich.: Eerdmans, 2002) and *Divorce and Remarriage in the Church* (Carlisle, U.K.: Paternoster, 2003) argues for a range of grounds for divorce and remarriage including abuse and neglect. Geoffrey W. Bromiley, *God and Marriage* (Grand Rapids, Mich.: Eerdmans, 1980) and Andreas Köstenberger, *God, Marriage, and Family*, offer good overviews of the wider biblical vision of marriage and defend a limited divorce and remarriage position.

Would they really have assumed that the absolute statements included exceptions? I began to have serious doubts. Therefore, my inclination was to inquire whether or not, in fact, Matthew's exception clause conforms to the absoluteness of Mark and Luke, not the other way around.

The second thing that began to disturb me was the question, why does Matthew use the Greek word πορνεία (*porneia,* "sexual immorality") instead of the word μοιχεία (*moicheia*) which means adultery? Sexual immorality in marriage would naturally be adultery. But the word Matthew uses to express Jesus's meaning is one that usually means *fornication* or *sexual immorality without reference to marital unfaithfulness.* Almost all commentators seem to make the assumption again that *porneia* refers to adultery in this context. The question nagged at me why Matthew would not use the word for adultery (*moicheia*), if that is in fact what he meant.

Then I noticed something very interesting. The only other place besides Matthew 5:32 and 19:9 where Matthew uses the word *porneia* is in Matthew 15:19 where it is used *alongside moicheia.* Therefore, the primary contextual evidence for Matthew's usage is that he conceives of *porneia* as, in some sense, *different* from adultery. Could this mean, then, that in Matthew's record of Jesus's teaching he is thinking of *porneia* in its more usual sense of fornication or incest or prostitution that does not denote marital unfaithfulness, that is, adultery?[3]

3    Abel Isaksson agrees with this view of πορνεία and sums up his research as follows:

> Thus we cannot get away from the fact that the distinction between what was to be regarded as *porneia* and what was to be regarded as *moicheia* was very strictly maintained in pre-Christian Jewish literature and in the N.T. *Porneia* may, of course, denote different forms of forbidden sexual relations, but we can find no unequivocal examples of the use of this word to denote a wife's adultery. [Giving Isaksson the benefit of the doubt here in what may be a technical overstatement, he may mean this (which is what I would say): If a wife sells herself into a life of prostitution, the way Israel did in Jeremiah 3:6 and Hosea 2:2, her acts may be called both *porneia* and *moicheia.* But the fact that the same act may be described in these two ways does not make the words interchangeable. *Moicheia* still denotes the covenant-breaking of marital unfaithfulness, while *porneia* denotes illicit sexual immorality that does *not* denote marital unfaithfulness, but may involve married people.]

The next clue in my search for an explanation came when I noticed the use of *porneia* in John 8:41 where Jewish leaders indirectly accuse Jesus of being born of *porneia*. In other words, since they don't accept the virgin birth, they assume that his mother Mary had committed *fornication* and that Jesus was the result of this act. On the basis of that clue, I went back to study Matthew's record of Jesus's birth in Matthew 1:18–20.

### The Relevance of the Exception Clauses for Joseph's Betrothal to Mary

In these verses Joseph and Mary are referred to as husband (ἀνήρ) and wife (γυνή). Yet they are described as only being *betrothed* to each other. This is probably owing to the fact that the words for husband and wife are simply *man* and *woman* in the Greek, and to the fact that betrothal was a more significant commitment at that time than engagement is today. In Matthew 1:19 Joseph resolves to "divorce" Mary though they were only betrothed and not yet married. The word for divorce (ἀπολῦσαι) is the same as the word in Matthew 5:32 and 19:9. But most important of all, Matthew says that Joseph was "just" in making the decision to divorce Mary, presumably on account of her assumed *porneia*, fornication. In other words, this "divorce" was permitted according to Matthew.

Only Matthew has told that story of the crisis Joseph faced in whether to marry his betrothed even though she, as far as he knew at first, had committed fornication (πορνεία). In handling this crisis he called

---

Under these circumstances we can hardly assume that this word means adultery in the clauses in Matthew. The logia on divorce are worded as a paragraph of the law, intended to be obeyed by the members of the Church. Under these circumstances it is inconceivable that in a text of this nature the writer would not have maintained a clear distinction between what was unchastity and what was adultery: *moicheia* and not *porneia* was used to describe the wife's adultery. From the philological point of view there are accordingly very strong arguments against this interpretation of the clauses as permitting divorce in the case in which the wife was guilty of adultery. (Abel Isaksson, *Marriage and Ministry in the New Temple*, trans. Neil Tomkinson and Jean Gray [Lund, Sweden: Gleerup, 1965], 134–35).

Joseph "just" in the plan to "divorce" her. That means that Matthew, as a follower of Jesus, would not consider this kind of "divorce" wrong. It would not have prevented Joseph (or Mary) from marrying another. Since only Matthew had told this story and raised this question, he was the only Gospel writer who would feel any need to make clear that Jesus's absolute prohibition of divorce followed by remarriage did not include a situation like Joseph and Mary's. That is what I think he does with the exception clauses. He records Jesus saying, "Whoever divorces his wife—not including, of course, the case of fornication [πορνεία] between betrothed couples—and marries another, commits adultery."[4]

A common objection to this interpretation is that both in Matthew 19:3–9 and in Matthew 5:31–32 the issue Jesus is responding to is marriage, not betrothal. The point is pressed that "except for fornication" is irrelevant to the context of marriage. My answer is that this irrelevancy is precisely the point of the exception clause. Whether it sounds irrelevant in the context depends on how you hear it. I don't think it sounds pointless if you hear it the way I just suggested or if Matthew 5:32 goes like this: "But I say to you that everyone who divorces his wife—*excluding, of course, the case of fornication* [πορνεία] *during betrothal*—makes her commit adultery." In this way Jesus makes clear that the action his earthly father almost took—to "divorce" Mary because of πορνεία—would not have been unjust. It would have been right. That is the kind of situation the exception clause is meant to exclude.[5]

This interpretation of the exception clause has several advantages:

4   I do not know all the words Jesus may have used to express this prohibition over the time of his ministry. Therefore, I am slow to say that Matthew created this exception clause and put it in Jesus's mouth. It is likely that Jesus taught in Aramaic, and so in one sense Matthew and the other Gospel writers, who were writing in Greek, decided what exact wording to use in our Gospels. My own conviction is that these Gospel writers were inspired by the Holy Spirit and that what they wrote in Greek accurately represented what Jesus taught.

5   Andreas Köstenberger arrays seven arguments against this view in *God, Marriage, and Family*, pp. 280–82. Though I don't find them compelling, I have tried to take them into account in my thinking and conclusions.

- It does not force Matthew's Gospel to disagree with the seemingly plain, absolute meaning of Mark and Luke.
- It provides an explanation for why the word *porneia* is used in Matthew's exception clause instead of *moicheia*.
- It squares with Matthew's own use of *porneia* (for fornication) in distinction from *moicheia* (for adultery) in Matthew 15:19.
- It fits Matthew's wider context concerning Joseph's contemplated "divorce" from Mary (Matt. 1:19).

What are the implications of this high standard of marriage? To this we turn in the next chapter.

*The disciples said to him, "If such is the case of a man with his wife, it is better not to marry." But he said to them, "Not everyone can receive this saying, but only those to whom it is given. For there are eunuchs who have been so from birth, and there are eunuchs who have been made eunuchs by men, and there are eunuchs who have made themselves eunuchs for the sake of the kingdom of heaven. Let the one who is able to receive this receive it."*

MATTHEW 19:10–12

# What God Has Joined Together Let No Man Separate—One Man, One Woman, by Grace, Till Death

## If Such Is the Case, Better Not to Marry?

Not surprisingly, when Jesus had finished teaching on marriage and divorce in Matthew 19:3–9, his disciples were bewildered by how strict Jesus's standards were. So they said, "If such is the case of a man with his wife, it is better not to marry" (Matt. 19:10). This response confirms that we are on the right track when we hear Jesus setting the bar very high. The disciples assume that this standard is so high it is better not to marry. In other words, if there is no back door to marriage, it is better not to walk through the front door. This response would not make as much sense if Jesus had just prescribed a back door as large as infidelity.

Jesus's response is not to lower the bar so that marriage becomes less risky. Instead, he says, in essence, that the ability to remain single if necessary and the ability to stay in a hard marriage if necessary are both a gift of God. In other words, flourishing in singleness and flourishing in marriage are a work of divine grace. "Not everyone can receive this saying [the saying that marriage is permanent], but only those to whom it is given" (Matt. 19:11). The point is not that some disciples are given the grace and some are not. The point is that this grace (or faithfulness in singleness and marriage) is the mark of a disciple. "Those to whom it is given" are followers of Jesus.[1] God gives the grace for what he commands.

## Eunuchs for the Kingdom

Then Jesus illustrates that such grace has actually been given to those who for various reasons have not been permitted to marry. "For there are eunuchs who have been so from birth, and there are eunuchs who have been made eunuchs by men, and there are eunuchs who have made themselves eunuchs for the sake of the kingdom of heaven. Let the one who is able to receive this receive it" (Matt. 19:12). The point here is that if you do not marry or if you are divorced and must remain single, you are not alone but are in the company of some who have had singleness forced on them and some who have chosen it for the sake of the kingdom. In all cases God gives grace.

The words "Let the one who is able to receive this receive it" are like the words "He who has ears, let him hear" (Matt. 13:9, 43; 11:15). That is, whether you have ears to hear—or whether you have grace to receive this call to radical respect for marriage—is the mark of being a follower of Jesus. "My sheep hear my voice, and I know them, and they follow me" (John 10:27).

## The Folly of Homosexuality

Marriage is a great work of God. It is a great gift to the world. It is worthy of books and songs and poetry and life and sacrifice, not just a little chapter like this. Jesus would grieve over the cavalier way that marriage is treated in our day. He would be appalled at any thought of two men or two women calling their homosexual union *marriage*. He

---

1    Compare the parallel wording between Matthew 19:11 and 13:11, the parallels between Matthew 19:12 and 13:9, 43; 11:15, and the parallel between Matthew 19:11 and 19:26.

would not call it marriage. As much pity as he may feel for the sexual brokenness, he would call the practice of homosexuality sin and the attempt to sanctify it with the word *marriage* folly.

He would respond to this folly the same way he responded to the Pharisees' justification of divorce with Moses's teaching. He would go back to the beginning. Only this time he would underline the words *male* and *female*. "Have you not read that he who created them from the beginning made them *male* and *female*, and said, 'Therefore a *man* shall leave his father and his mother and hold fast to his *wife*, and they shall become one flesh'?" (Matt. 19:4–5). Jesus would root heterosexual marriage in the creation of man as male and female and in the original union of man and woman into one flesh. He would count it a great sadness that the glory of marriage and all that it stands for is so debased as to make it a covering for the sin of homosexuality.

### Are Divorce and Remarriage the Unforgivable Sins?

But as great as marriage is, divorce followed by remarriage is not the unforgivable sin. Sometimes I am asked whether my understanding of Jesus implies that divorce is the unforgivable sin. The answer is no. Jesus said that his blood will be the basis of forgiveness for all sins (Matt. 26:28). Therefore he is able to say, "Truly, I say to you, all sins will be forgiven the children of man, and whatever blasphemies they utter, but whoever blasphemes against the Holy Spirit never has forgiveness, but is guilty of an eternal sin" (Mark 3:28–29).

From these wonderful promises we learn that forgiveness for sins is available on the basis of the shed blood of Jesus. Forgiveness is available for all sins, without exception. Forgiveness is received freely through trusting Jesus to forgive our sins. This implies that we see sin as sin and hate it as a dishonor to Jesus. The only unforgivable sin is the sin that we refuse to confess and forsake. We commit unforgivable sin when we cleave to a sin so long and so tenaciously that we can no longer confess it as sin and turn from it. What Jesus calls "the blasphemy against the

Holy Spirit" (in Matthew 12:31–32) and "eternal sin" (in Mark 3:29) is the resistance against the Holy Spirit's convicting work to the point where he withdraws, leaving the sinner in helpless hardness of heart, unable to repent.

Neither divorce nor remarriage is in itself the unforgivable sin any more than is murder, stealing, lying, coveting, adultery, or homosexual behavior. "All sins will be forgiven the children of man" (Mark 3:28). God is faithful and just to forgive—he will honor the worth of his Son's sacrifice for all who confess their sin and bank their hope on the saving work of Jesus.

Marital sin is in the same category as lying and killing and stealing. If someone has lied, killed, stolen, or illegitimately left a marriage, the issue is not, can they be forgiven? The issue is, do they admit that what they did was sin? Do they renounce it? And do they do what they can in order to make it right if possible?

What usually causes the conflict is not whether divorce and remarriage are unforgivable sins, but whether they are sins at all—to be confessed (from the past) and to be avoided (in the future). If a person has stolen things in his past, no one would say that we are treating stealing as the unforgivable sin if we insist that this person confess his sin and begin to make amends to those he defrauded. A sin is not unforgivable because it must be confessed as sin, renounced as an option, and its effects made right (as far as possible).

So it is with divorce or remarriage. It should not keep anyone out of fellowship with the followers of Jesus any more than a past life of robbery. But there should be a heartfelt confession of the sin committed and a renouncing of it and an affirming of what is right, just as with all other sins of the past.

## What Does a Follower of Jesus Do Who Has Divorced and Remarried?

What then would Jesus expect from one of his followers who has sinned and is divorced and remarried? He would expect us to acknowledge that the choice to remarry and the act of entering a second marriage was sin and to confess it as such and seek forgiveness. He would also expect that we not separate from our present spouse. I base this on at least five observations.

First, Jesus seemed to regard multiple marriages as wrong but real. He said to the woman at the well in John 4:18, "You have had five husbands, and the one you now have is not your husband." She is living with a man now, but there has been no marriage—no covenant-making. The others he calls "husbands," but the one she is with now is not her husband.

Second, Jesus knew that Deuteronomy 24:4 spoke against going back to a first husband after marrying a second. He did not go out of his way to qualify this provision.

Third, covenant-keeping is crucial to Jesus as we saw in the previous chapter (also see *Command #23*). Therefore, even though the current covenant is adulterous in the making, it is real and should be kept. Its beginning in sin does not have to mean that it is continuously sinful and without hope of purification.

Fourth, there are illustrations of God taking acts of disobedience and turning the result into God-ordained plans. One example is the fact that it was sin for the people of Israel to ask for a king to be like the nations (1 Sam. 12:19–22). Nevertheless, God turned the sinfully instituted kingship into the origin of the Messiah and the kingship of Jesus. Another example would be the sinful marriage of David to Bathsheba. The adultery with her, the murder of her husband, and the marriage "displeased the Lord" (2 Sam. 11:27). So the Lord took the life of the first child of this union (2 Sam. 12:15, 18). But the second child, Solomon, "the Lord loved" and chose him as ruler over his people (2 Sam. 12:24).

Fifth, through repentance and forgiveness on the basis of the blood of Jesus and through the sanctifying work of the promised Holy Spirit, a marriage that was entered sinfully can be consecrated to God, purified from sin, and become a means of grace. It remains less than ideal, but it is not a curse. It may become a great blessing.

## Marriage: Great and Precious but Not Ultimate or Permanent

There is no doubt that Jesus's demand for faithfulness in marriage is a radical word to our modern culture. Here is a test for his lordship over our lives. His standards are high. They do not assume that this earth is our final home. He makes it very clear that marriage is an ordinance for this age only. "For in the resurrection they neither marry nor are given in marriage, but are like angels in heaven" (Matt. 22:30). Therefore, marriage is a brief blessing. A great one but not an ultimate one. A precious one but not a permanent one.

This eternal perspective explains why Jesus can be so radical. Never to have married is not a tragedy. Otherwise Jesus's life is a tragedy. Tragedy is craving the perfect marriage so much that we make a god out of being married. Jesus's standards are high because marriage does not and should not meet all our needs. It should not be an idol. It should not and cannot take the place of Jesus himself. Marriage is but for a moment. Jesus is for eternity. How we live in our marriages and our singleness will show if Jesus is our supreme treasure.

*Then the Pharisees went and plotted how to entangle [Jesus] in his words. And they sent their disciples to him, along with the Herodians, saying . . . "Tell us, then, what you think. Is it lawful to pay taxes to Caesar, or not?" But Jesus, aware of their malice, said, "Why put me to the test, you hypocrites? Show me the coin for the tax." And they brought him a denarius. And Jesus said to them, "Whose likeness and inscription is this?" They said, "Caesar's." Then he said to them, "Therefore render to Caesar the things that are Caesar's, and to God the things that are God's."*

MATTHEW 22:15–21

# Render to Caesar the Things That Are Caesar's and to God the Things That Are God's

JESUS WAS JEWISH. He was part of a people who lived in their home-land under the totalitarian rule of Rome. The Caesar was absolute and claimed even divine status as emperor of Rome. Caesar Augustus was the emperor when Jesus was born (Luke 2:1), and his son, Tiberius Caesar, ruled from AD 13–37 during the rest of Jesus's life (Luke 3:1). So when Jesus asked the Pharisees for a coin with Caesar's picture on it, the coin very likely pictured Tiberius.[1]

## The Trap

When the Pharisees asked Jesus if it was lawful to pay taxes to Caesar, they were trying to hang him on the horns of a politically supercharged

---

1    "The silver denarius of Tiberius, including a portrait of his head and minted especially at the Lyon, circulated there in this period; although an earlier coin might be in view, this imperial denarius is most likely. . . . The coin related directly to pagan Roman religion and to the imperial cult in the east: the side bearing his image also included a superscription, namely, 'TI. CAESAR DIVI AVG.F.AVGVSTVS'— "Tiberius Caesar, son of the Divine Augustus"; the other side bore a feminine image (perhaps of the Empress Livia personified as the goddess Roma) and read "PONTIF. MAXIM," referring to the high priest of Roman religion. The Empire actively used such coins to promote the worship of the emperor." Craig S. Keener, *A Commentary on Matthew* (Grand Rapids, Mich.: Eerdmans, 1999), 525.

dilemma. The Jews were oppressed and were indignant that the promised land where they lived was ruled by pagan Romans. Paying taxes to Rome was a religious offense. But not to pay them would be suicidal. The Pharisees were manifestly making an effort to entangle Jesus in a trap. "Either he will support taxes to Rome, undercutting his popular, messianic support, or he will challenge taxes. . . . [Then] the Herodians could charge him with being a revolutionary—hence that he should be executed, and executed quickly."[2]

So they ask him, "Tell us, then, what you think. Is it lawful to pay taxes to Caesar, or not?" Jesus exposes their hypocrisy and then gives an answer that penetrates deep into the meaning of how his followers should live as dual citizens of his kingdom and the kingdom of this world. He says, "Why put me to the test, you hypocrites? Show me the coin for the tax." So they brought him a denarius. And Jesus said to them, "Whose likeness and inscription is this?" They said, "Caesar's." Then he said to them, "Therefore render to Caesar the things that are Caesar's, and to God the things that are God's" (Matt. 22:17–21).

I don't think Jesus dodged the question. I think he answered it in a way that forces us to think, and in the end the answer demands radical allegiance to God's supreme authority over all things. The first command, "Render to Caesar the things that are Caesar's" gets its meaning from the second one, "Render to God the things that are God's." It's the juxtaposition of these two commands that gives the first one its proper scope.

### The Unexpected, Penetrating Answer

One can picture his hearers holding their breath as he says, "Render to Caesar the things that are Caesar's." Perhaps a smile of devious success began to come over the faces of his adversaries. This sounds very much like a capitulation to the supremacy of Rome. I wonder how long Jesus paused between the two commands. Perhaps long enough to let the

2    Ibid., 524.

words work their way into the mind: "Caesar has a scope of ownership and authority. Comply with that." As that begins to sink in, Jesus
adds one short but massive qualification: "Render to God the things
that are God's." The smiles that were forming on the adversaries' faces
pause. This is not what they were expecting. It is not what anybody was
expecting. Jesus has called for a kind of allegiance in two directions: to
Caesar according to his ownership and authority, and to God according
to his ownership and authority.

Jesus wisely left the scope of these two ownerships and authorities for
the listener to answer. Whether this is a compromise with Rome will
depend on how a person understands the scope and nature of God's
ownership and authority in relation to Caesar's scope of ownership and
authority. That is what he forces us to think about.

The starting point for this thinking is the unmistakable assumption
of the second command, "Render to God the things that are God's."
That assumption is: *Everything* is God's. If a person does not hear that
in Jesus's command, he would say, "Hearing they do not hear. They
have ears, but they do not hear." In other words, the all-important fact
is unspoken and obvious to all who are willing to hear the obvious.
By being unspoken, it accomplishes more than getting Jesus out of a
trap; it leads to an answer to the question that is far deeper and more
far-reaching than what his adversaries were asking.

## Rendering to Caesar Is Rendering to Jesus, or It Is Treason

The fact that God owns everything and has all authority in the universe puts the first command under the second: "Render to Caesar the
things that are Caesar's" becomes a subcategory of "Render to God
the things that are God's." All is God's. Therefore what is Caesar's is
God's. Therefore rendering to Caesar what is his must be seen as an
expression of rendering to God what is God's. This is all-important in
understanding how one can be utterly devoted to Jesus as Lord and
live in a world with Caesar—or any other authority.

Even though the power of Caesar stood behind the crucifixion of Jesus, Jesus is the supreme Lord over Caesar. Jesus knows this. He is consciously abstaining during his earthly life from exercising the right and power to subdue his enemies. He is choosing to lay down his life. "I lay down my life that I may take it up again. No one takes it from me, but I lay it down of my own accord. I have authority to lay it down, and I have authority to take it up again" (John 10:17–18). Therefore, when he had risen from the dead he said, "All authority in heaven and on earth has been given to me" (Matt. 28:18). That means that he is above all of Caesar's authority. "Render to Caesar the things that are Caesar's" means, therefore: in all your rendering to Caesar, render to Jesus the full honor of the absolute authority that he has over Caesar.

It was fitting during Jesus's earthly ministry that he not draw excessive attention to his universal ownership and authority. He was here to suffer and die. He knew that the day would come when he would rule openly over the nations. That's why he said, "When the Son of Man comes in his glory, and all the angels with him, then he will sit on his glorious throne. Before him will be gathered all the nations" (Matt. 25:31–32). But during his earthly ministry Jesus did not exert this kind of open power. Hence when it came time to express how his followers should relate to Caesar, he called attention to God, not explicitly to himself. He did not say, "Render to Caesar the things that are Caesar's, and to me the things that are mine."

But that is, in fact, what he does call for. He and the Father are one (John 10:30). "The Father judges no one, but has given all judgment to the Son, that all may honor the Son, just as they honor the Father" (John 5:22–23). At his weakest hour the high priest asked him if he was the Messiah, the Son of the Blessed. Jesus answered, "I am, and you will see the Son of Man seated at the right hand of Power, and coming with the clouds of heaven" (Mark 14:62). In other words, "Even though I am weak and despised in your eyes now, very shortly I will sit in the place of absolute authority over you and Pilate and Herod and

Caesar." Therefore, "Render to God the things that are God's" means also, render to Jesus the honor of absolute ownership and authority over everything, including all that is Caesar's.

## There Is No Authority Except What Is Given from Above

Therefore, Jesus is demanding absolute allegiance to himself and his ownership and authority. All other allegiances are relativized by this supreme allegiance. All other allegiances are *warranted* and *limited* and *shaped* by this first allegiance.

They are *warranted* because the subordinate authorities in the world, like Caesar, are owing to God's authority. Jesus said to Pilate, who seemed to have authority over Jesus at his trial, "You would have no authority over me at all unless it had been given you from above" (John 19:11). Pilate has authority because God has given it to him. Therefore, such human authority is warranted because it is indirectly God's. When Jesus said, "Render to God the things that are God's," the term "the things that are God's" included Pilate's authority, because it was, indirectly, God's. God had given it to him. He would not have it without God. Therefore, Jesus acknowledges the legitimacy of human authority. It is legitimate but not absolute. It is *from* God, but it is not God.

It is risky for Jesus to say, "Render to Caesar the things that are Caesar's." That puts a high premium on obedience to the demands of Caesar. One of the realities that warrants this risk is that the heart of rebellion is more dangerous in us than the demands of Caesar outside of us. Jesus wants us to see that the danger to our soul from unjust, secular governments is nowhere near as great as the danger to our soul from the pride that kicks against submission. No mistreatment from Caesar or unjust law from Rome has ever sent anyone to hell. But pride and rebellion are what send to hell everyone who doesn't have a Savior. Therefore, the subordinate authorities of the world are warranted by God's will in two senses. On the one hand, he wills that we recognize that these authorities are indeed subordinate and that we glorify him as the only supreme sovereign. On the other hand, he wills that we recognize these authorities as God-ordained and that we not proudly kick against what he has put in place.

All our earthly allegiances are not only *warranted* by the supreme authority of God but also *limited* and *shaped* by that authority. For these functions of God's authority we pass now to the next chapter.

*Then the Pharisees went and plotted how to entangle [Jesus] in his talk. And they sent their disciples to him, along with the Herodians, saying . . . "Tell us, then, what you think. Is it lawful to pay taxes to Caesar, or not?" But Jesus, aware of their malice, said, "Why put me to the test, you hypocrites? Show me the coin for the tax." And they brought him a denarius. And Jesus said to them, "Whose likeness and inscription is this?" They said, "Caesar's." Then he said to them, "Therefore render to Caesar the things that are Caesar's, and to God the things that are God's."*

MATTHEW 22:15–21

# Render to Caesar the Things
# That Are Caesar's as an Act of
# Rendering to God What Is God's

I SAID IN THE PREVIOUS CHAPTER that Jesus commands absolute allegiance to himself and his ownership and authority. All other allegiances are *warranted* and *limited* and *shaped* by this supreme allegiance to Jesus as the King of kings. We have seen how they are warranted. Now we turn to see how they are limited and shaped.

## When Caesar Demands What God Forbids

All our earthly allegiances are *limited* by what God's supreme authority accomplished through Jesus (see John 5:27; Matt. 28:18).

We should do what Caesar says since he has his authority by God's design. But we should not do all that he says. If Caesar says, "Caesar is Lord!" we do not imitate him. If he commands us to bow under his lordship, we do not do it. *Jesus* is Lord. His followers bow to him as supreme and to no one else. Even though human authority is ultimately from God, it does not always act according to God's word. Therefore, it may demand what God forbids.

This is why Jesus warns of impending conflict. He tells his disciples they will have to choose between allegiance to him and allegiance to

Caesar's state. This will cost some of them their lives. "They will lay their hands on you and persecute you, delivering you up to the synagogues and prisons, and you will be brought before kings and governors for my name's sake. . . . Some of you they will put to death" (Luke 21:12, 16). The only way this warning makes sense is if Jesus is telling us not to render to Caesar everything that Caesar thinks is Caesar's. Rendering to Caesar the things that are Caesar's does not include rendering obedience to Caesar's demand that we not render supreme allegiance to God. God's supreme authority limits the authority of Caesar and the allegiance we owe to him.

## We Submit to Caesar to Acknowledge the Supreme Lordship of Jesus

All our earthly allegiances are not only warranted and limited by the supreme authority of God but are also *shaped* by that authority. In other words, even the duty we properly render to Caesar is rendered differently because Caesar is not absolute. We render obedience to Caesar where we can, not because he is Lord, but because our Lord Jesus bids us to. In other words, all our obedience to Caesar dethrones Caesar by expressing the lordship of Jesus. We view all our serving of Caesar as serving his owner and Lord, Jesus. There is, therefore, no whiff of worship toward Caesar. He is stripped of his claim to divinity in the very act of submitting to his laws. Even our submission is therefore seditious toward rulers with pretensions of deity.

Jesus illustrates this shaping of submission by the supremacy of God's authority in Matthew 17:24–27.

> When they came to Capernaum, the collectors of the two-drachma tax went up to Peter and said, "Does your teacher not pay the tax?" He said, "Yes." And when he came into the house, Jesus spoke to him first, saying, "What do you think, Simon? From whom do kings of the earth take toll or tax? From their sons or from others?" And

when he said, "From others," Jesus said to him, "Then the sons are free. However, not to give offense to them, go to the sea and cast a hook and take the first fish that comes up, and when you open its mouth you will find a shekel. Take that and give it to them for me and for yourself."

This "two-drachma tax" probably refers to a temple tax that the Jewish people paid annually for the upkeep of the temple. The exact identity of the tax is not crucial for the point that is relevant here. The question was, will Jesus and his disciples pay it? The answer is yes. But the way Jesus justifies the payment is what is crucial for us.

He compares the payment to the way a secular king taxes his empire: Does he demand taxes from his children? No. So the children are free. "Now," Jesus says, "that's the way it is with me and my disciples; we are the children of God who has all authority and owns everything, and therefore we do not have to pay this temple tax. But will we? Yes. Why? Not to give an offense."

The principle is this: there are at times reasons to submit to an authority that arise not from the intrinsic right of the authority but from a principle of freedom and what would be for the greater good. So, applying this to Caesar, the principle would go like this: God owns Caesar. God has absolute authority over Caesar. This all-authoritative God is our Father. We are his children. Therefore, the demands of Caesar to fund his government are not absolutely binding on us. Our Father owns the government. We are free. In fact, the whole earth is ours as heirs of our Father, and we will one day inherit it completely (Matt. 5:5). Nevertheless, in this freedom, should we pay Caesar's taxes? Yes, because that would lead to the greatest good for now and because our Father bids us, "Render to Caesar the things that are Caesar's." In this way we can see how God's supreme ownership over all things not only warrants and limits but also shapes the way we express our earthly allegiances.

## How Jesus's Authority Shapes Our Disobedience to Caesar

That shaping effect of Jesus's supreme authority extends even to the way we disobey Caesar. That is, even our disobedience, when it must be, is not indifferent to the proper authority of Caesar. Even our disobedience will be shaped by Jesus's supremacy over, and endorsement of, the perverted authority of Caesar. We saw above that Jesus's authority limits Caesar's authority. We saw this in Jesus's command that we should die rather than submit to Caesar's demand that we deny Jesus. Jesus himself did not comply with Herod's demands (Luke 23:9) or Pilate's demands (Mark 15:5) or the demands of the high priest (Matt. 26:62–63). Jesus modeled and demanded some civil disobedience. And it is his life and teaching and authority that shape what that disobedience looks like.

We have already devoted whole chapters to Jesus's commands concerning servanthood (*Command #15*) and love of our enemies (*Command #20*) and care of our neighbors (*Command #21*). These and other commands will shape profoundly the way Jesus's followers engage in civil disobedience. It may be helpful here to apply these commands again to this situation and give some direction.

## Shaping Civil Disobedience by the Commands of Jesus

Matthew 5:38–48 contains strong words about non-resistance and active love for your enemy (see *Command #30*). What we saw, and now see again, is that non-resistance and active love are not always the same. On the non-resistance side, Jesus said,

> You have heard that it was said, "An eye for an eye and a tooth for a tooth." But I say to you, Do not resist one who is evil. But if anyone slaps you on the right cheek, turn to him the other also. . . . And if anyone forces you to go one mile, go with him two miles. Give to the one who begs from you, and do not refuse the one who would borrow from you. (Matt. 5:38–42)

All of those commands call for compliance to one who mistreats you or asks you for something. This looks like the opposite of resistance. But then, in the flow of Jesus's sermon, comes something a little different in verses 43–48, namely, more active love rather than non-resistance.

> You have heard that it was said, "You shall love your neighbor and hate your enemy." But I say to you, Love your enemies and pray for those who persecute you, so that you may be sons of your Father who is in heaven; for he makes his sun rise on the evil and on the good, and sends rain on the just and on the unjust. . . . You therefore must be perfect, as your heavenly Father is perfect.

Here a different note is struck. The emphasis falls on seeking the good of the enemy. Love your enemy. Pray for your enemy—presumably that he would be saved and find hope and life in Jesus. Do good to your enemy the way God does with rain and sunshine. So in verses 38–42 the note of compliance is struck (don't resist, turn the other cheek, go the extra mile). But in verses 43–48 Jesus strikes the note of positive actions for the good of our enemies with a view to their blessing.

Now this raises the question of whether the non-resistance and compliance of verses 38–42 is always the best way to love others and do them good as prescribed in verses 43–48. One focuses on passivity—don't retaliate, be willing to suffer unjustly. The other focuses on activity—seek to do good for your enemy. Is passivity always the best way to do good?

### When Love for One Demands Resistance to Another

The answer becomes clearer when we realize that in most situations of injustice or persecution we are not the only person being hurt. For example, how do you love two people if one is the criminal and the other is the victim—if one is hurting and the other is being hurt? Is love passive when it is not only *your* cheek that is being smacked but someone else's—and repeatedly?

Or what about the command to give to the one who asks? Is it love to give your coat to a person who will use it to strangle an infant? And how do you go the extra mile (lovingly!) with a person who is taking you along to support his bloodshed? Do you go the extra mile with a person who is making you an active accomplice to his evil?

The point of these questions is this: in these verses Jesus is giving us a description of love that cuts to the depth of our selfishness and fear. If selfishness and fear keep us from giving and going the extra mile, then we need to be broken by these words. But Jesus is not saying that passive compliance in situations of injustice is the only form of love. It can be a form of cowardice. When love weighs the claims of justice and mercy among all the people involved, there can come a moment, a flash point, when love may go beyond passive, compliant non-resistance and drive the money-changers from the temple (Mark 11:15).

## The Greatest Battle Is to Be Brokenhearted in Our Resistance

What guidelines are there, then, for how a follower of Jesus will perform civil disobedience? The words of Jesus rule out all vindictiveness and all action based on the mere expediency of personal safety. The Lord cuts away our love for possessions and our love for convenience. That's the point of Matthew 5:38–42. Don't act merely out of concern for your own private benefit, your clothes, your convenience, your possessions, your safety.

Instead, by trusting Jesus, become the kind of person who is utterly free from these things to live for others (both the oppressed and the oppressors; both the persecuted and the persecutors; both the dying children and the killing abortionists; both the racists and the races). The tone and demeanor of this civil disobedience will be the opposite of strident, belligerent, rock-throwing, screaming, swearing, violent demonstrations.

We are people of the cross. Our Lord submitted to crucifixion willingly to save his enemies. We owe our eternal life to him. We are forgiven sinners. This takes the swagger out of our protest. It takes the arrogance out of our resistance. And if, after every other means has failed, we must disobey for the sake of love and justice, we will first remove the log from our own eye, which will cause enough pain and tears to soften our indignation into a humble, quiet, but unshakable no. The greatest battle we face is not overcoming unjust laws, but becoming this kind of people.

"Render to Caesar the things that are Caesar's, and to God the things that are God's." Let this command exalt the supremacy of God and his Son Jesus over all earthly powers. Let it bind our hearts in absolute allegiance to the kingship of Jesus. Let it warrant and limit and shape the way we render allegiance to "Caesar." And let it free us to live in this world as citizens of another kingdom—not escaping, not conforming, but living out the radical difference that King Jesus makes in every relationship, including our relationship with the state.

*[Jesus] said to them, "But who do you say that I am?"*
*Simon Peter replied, "You are the Christ, the Son of the*
*living God." And Jesus answered him, "Blessed are you,*
*Simon Bar-Jonah! For flesh and blood has not revealed*
*this to you, but my Father who is in heaven. And I tell*
*you, you are Peter, and on this rock I will build my*
*church, and the gates of hell shall not prevail against it.*

MATTHEW 16:15–18

*Make disciples of all nations, baptizing them in the name*
*of the Father and of the Son and of the Holy Spirit.*

MATTHEW 28:19

*And behold, I am sending the promise of my*
*Father upon you. But stay in the city until you*
*are clothed with power from on high.*

LUKE 24:49

# Do This in Remembrance of Me, for I Will Build My Church

THE COMMAND OF JESUS, "Do this in remembrance of me" comes from the institution of the Lord's Supper in Luke 22:19. But it assumes something, namely, that there would be a church worshiping Jesus when he was gone. Did Jesus plan for that and provide for the church? That is what this chapter addresses. It is foundational for the next.

## "I Will Build My Church"

Jesus promised to build his church. By "church" he did not mean a building. That is never the meaning of church (ἐκκλησία) in Greek. He means he will build a people. He will gather a people who trust him as their Lord (John 13:13; 20:28) and Savior (John 3:17; 10:9) and who love each other (John 13:34–35) and their enemies (Matt. 5:44). Jesus describes himself as "the good shepherd" who gathers his sheep into a flock. "I am the good shepherd. I know my own and my own know me, just as the Father knows me and I know the Father; and I lay down my life for the sheep. And I have other sheep that are not of this fold. I must bring them also, and they will listen to my voice. So there will be one flock, one shepherd" (John 10:14–16).

The words "I must bring them also" and "they will listen to my voice" carry the same authority as the words "I will build my church" (Matt. 16:18). "I *must* bring them." "They *will* hear my voice." "I *will* build my church." This is what the power of the kingdom does. Jesus compares the kingdom of God to a net that was cast into the sea of humanity and "gathered fish of every kind" (Matt. 13:47). The kingdom of God, as Jesus presents it, is not a realm or a people but a rule or a reign. Therefore, it brings a people into being the way a net gathers fish. Some skeptics have tried to find a contradiction between Jesus's message of the kingdom of God and the subsequent rise of the church. But there is no contradiction. The kingdom creates the church. Or, to say it another way, the King, Jesus, builds his church.

Jesus knew and taught that between his first and second coming to earth there would be a lapse of time. For example, Jesus's parable of the wicked tenants is a story of what will happen between his first and second coming. It begins, "A man planted a vineyard and let it out to tenants and went into another country *for a long while*" (Luke 20:9). This is one of the clearest statements indicating that Jesus expected the time before his second coming to be substantial. He knew that he would be away from his "flock," and therefore he made provision for them while he is gone.

### Jesus Took Care to Provide for the Church though the Holy Spirit

This provision includes the sending of the Holy Spirit, the preservation of inspired truth in the writings of his apostles and their close associates, guidelines for how to handle sin in the flock, and the ordinances of baptism and the Lord's Supper.

Jesus was keenly aware of what it would mean to leave his "little flock" (Luke 12:32) in a hostile world and return to the Father. How were they to live without his physical presence? He had been the literal center of their lives for three years, and now he was going to leave. Who would teach them? Who would guide and protect them? How were they to live in his absence? These and many other questions would come when Jesus was gone. Therefore he assured them, "I will not leave you as orphans; I will come to you" (John 14:18).

What he meant by this promise was that he would send the Holy Spirit and that this Spirit of God would be his own presence among them. "I will ask the Father, and he will give you another Helper, to be with you forever, even the Spirit of truth, whom the world cannot receive, because it neither sees him nor knows him. You know him, for he dwells with you and will be in you" (John 14:16–17). "He dwells *with* you, and will be *in* you." Jesus is saying that he himself is now *with* his disciples—physically present—and when the Spirit comes he himself will be *in* them. Jesus comforts his followers with the truth that he himself will be present in the church by the Spirit whom he sends in his place.[1]

### "Let Not Your Hearts Be Troubled"

Jesus intends for these promises to give strong encouragement to his followers when he leaves. "Peace I leave with you; my peace I give to you. Not as the world gives do I give to you. Let not your hearts be troubled, neither let them be afraid" (John 14:27). Therefore, even though the church is destined for trouble in a hostile world of unbelief (John 15:20), they should be encouraged because Jesus promises to send the Holy Spirit who will help them and will, in fact, prove to be a manifestation of the presence of Jesus himself.

Jesus promised at the end of his earthly life, "Behold, I am with you always, to the end of the age" (Matt. 28:20). Jesus himself promises to be with his followers even after he is gone from them. This can be true because of the Holy Spirit, who also is the Spirit of Jesus. Therefore, because of Jesus's past work on the cross (Matt. 20:28) and his present

---

1  I should make explicit that in describing the coming of the Spirit this way I do not mean to imply that the Person of the Spirit and the Person of the Son are not distinct persons. They are. That the Spirit can manifest the Son and mediate an experience of the presence of the Son is part of the mysterious unity that they have, not a contradiction of their distinct persons.

work by the Spirit (John 10:16; 12:32) and his future work in coming again in triumph (Matt. 16:27), his church may be confident in a hostile world. "In the world you will have tribulation," Jesus says. "But take heart; I have overcome the world" (John 16:33). "I will build my church, and the gates of hell shall not prevail against it" (Matt. 16:18).

Therefore, in view of this crucial role of the Holy Spirit in Jesus's absence, Jesus commands that his followers wait for the Spirit and not blunder ahead into ministry without this gift. Just before his ascension into heaven, Jesus said, "Behold, I am sending the promise of my Father upon you. But stay in the city until you are clothed with power from on high" (Luke 24:49). All subsequent generations of the followers of Jesus are to receive this Spirit and in this way enjoy the power and presence of the risen King.

### Jesus Provides a New Testament for His Church

Jesus provides for his flock after his departure not only by sending them the Holy Spirit but also by preparing for the preservation of inspired truth in the writings of his apostles. Jesus does not refer to the writings of the apostles but puts in place both apostles and the Holy Spirit as the guarantee of their teaching for the foundation of his church.

At a crucial juncture in his earthly ministry Jesus chose twelve apostles from all the disciples who were following him. He did not make these choices lightly. He prayed all night. "In these days he went out to the mountain to pray, and all night he continued in prayer to God. And when day came, he called his disciples and chose from them twelve, whom he named *apostles*" (Luke 6:12–13). The word "apostle" means "someone who is 'sent' (ἀποστέλλειν) and who shares the authority of the one who sends, as his representative."[2] Not all whom Jesus sent were

---

2   Donald Hagner, *Matthew 1–13, Word Biblical Commentary*, Vol. 33a (Dallas: Word, 1993), 265. Norval Geldenhuys defines an apostle as "one chosen and sent with a special commission as the fully authorized representative of the sender." Geldenhuys, *Supreme Authority: The Authority of the Lord, His Apostles and the New Testament* (Grand Rapids, Mich.: Eerdmans, 1953), 53–54.

appointed as apostles. For example, he sent out seventy-two ahead of him and said to them, "I am sending you out as lambs in the midst of wolves. . . . Heal the sick . . . and say to them, 'The kingdom of God has come near to you'" (Luke 10:3, 9). But these were not called apostles.

The fact that there were twelve apostles—just as there were twelve tribes of Israel—and that the word *apostle* carries the implication of special authority to represent him suggests that Jesus intended for the apostles to be the foundation for the true Israel, the church. He had said concerning the old Israel that, at least temporarily, they were being replaced. "I tell you, the kingdom of God will be taken away from you [Israel] and given to a people producing its fruits [Jesus's followers, the church]" (Matt. 21:43; see also *Command #28*). This new "Israel" would have its foundation in the twelve apostles. They will represent Jesus's authority as they lay the foundation for this new people.

To secure the future truthfulness of the teaching of the Twelve, Jesus promised to send the Spirit of truth to preserve his teaching and lead them into crucial truth that he had not yet given them. Speaking to the eleven apostles, after Judas had left them on the night before he was crucified, Jesus said:

> I still have many things to say to you, but you cannot bear them now. When the Spirit of truth comes, he will guide you into all the truth, for he will not speak on his own authority, but whatever he hears he will speak, and he will declare to you the things that are to come. He will glorify me, for he will take what is mine and declare it to you. (John 16:12–14)

> He will teach you all things and bring to your remembrance all that I have said to you. (John 14:26)

This is Jesus's way of caring for his flock after he is gone. He provides an authoritative band of representatives and then gives them the assurance that in their teaching office they will have divine assistance to provide the church with the truth it needs for all of life and godliness. He intends that the teaching of these authoritative spokesmen be preserved for later generations.

We know this because Jesus says to his Father in prayer at the end of his life, "I do not ask for these [twelve] only, but also for those who will believe in me *through their word*, that they may all be one" (John 17:20–21). All subsequent generations of the church will come to faith in Jesus "through their word." This implies that their word should be preserved. This is the origin of what we call the New Testament. The foundation of the church today is the Spirit-guided teaching of the apostles, preserved for us in the writings of the New Testament.[3]

---

3   There is a controversial passage from Jesus's teaching about the place of Peter in relationship to the foundation of the church. Jesus asked the disciples, "Who do you say that I am?" Simon Peter replied, "You are the Christ, the Son of the living God." Jesus responded, "Blessed are you, Simon Bar-Jonah! For flesh and blood has not revealed this to you, but my Father who is in heaven. And I tell you, you are Peter, and on this rock I will build my church, and the gates of hell shall not prevail against it. I will give you the keys of the kingdom of heaven, and whatever you bind on earth shall be bound in heaven, and whatever you loose on earth shall be loosed in heaven" (Matt. 16:15–19).

   Some take this passage to teach that Peter and his successors (such as the bishops of Rome and the popes), have a unique authority and administrative role in the church throughout history. The "keys of the kingdom" would be in their hands and would refer to the unique role of decision-making for what the church believes and does. The direction of my own understanding is given by George Ladd in the following interpretation:

   > Another interpretation lies nearer at hand. Jesus condemned the scribes and the Pharisees because they had taken away the key of knowledge, refusing either to enter into the Kingdom of God themselves or to permit others to enter (Luke 11:52). The same thought appears in the first Gospel. "Woe to you, scribes and Pharisees, hypocrites! Because you shut the kingdom of heaven against men; for you neither enter yourselves nor allow those who would enter to go in" (Matt. 23:13). In biblical idiom, knowledge is more than intellectual perception. It is "a spiritual possession due to revelation." The authority entrusted to Peter is grounded upon revelation, that is, spiritual knowledge, which he shared with the twelve. The keys of the Kingdom are therefore "the spiritual insight which will enable Peter to lead others in through the door of revelation through which he has passed himself" [Anthony Flew, *Jesus and His Church*, 1943, p. 95]. The authority to bind and loose involves the admission or exclusion of men from the realm of the Kingdom of God. Christ will build his *ekklesia* [i.e., church] upon Peter and upon those who share the divine revelation of Jesus' messiahship. To them also is committed by virtue of this same revelation the means

### The Spirit and the Word Are Inseparable

In this way Jesus has provided for his church both the Spirit and the word. His Spirit and his teaching are inseparable. He would be critical of any who try to separate the word and the Spirit. The objective teachings of Jesus, brought to memory by the Spirit and recorded for following generations, are the standard for the church. Any attempt to abandon or distort this objective, historical, once-for-all deposit of teaching will go astray from what Jesus commands and teaches and promises.

But it is also true that without the Spirit, no one will receive, or properly grasp, these historical teachings. By nature we are all simply human with no spiritual life. But without spiritual life we do not have eyes to see truly what Jesus taught. The remedy for this blindness and spiritual deadness is to be born again by the Spirit. "Unless one is born again he cannot see the kingdom of God" (John 3:3). This new birth is the work of the Spirit. "That which is born of the flesh is flesh, and that which is *born of the Spirit* is spirit" (John 3:6). If we are going to have the spiritual life and sight that enable us to see what Jesus really teaches, we must be born of the Spirit. (To see more on this important work of the Spirit see *Command #1*.)

Jesus also made three other noteworthy provisions for his church. In the next chapter we take up Jesus's commands regarding church discipline and the two ordinances of baptism and the Lord's Supper.

---

of permitting men to enter the realm of the blessings of the Kingdom or of excluding men from such participation. (George Ladd, *The Presence of the Future* [Grand Rapids, MI: Eerdmans, 1974], 274–75)

This view fits with what I have said about Jesus providing a foundation for the church in the teaching of the apostles. Peter had a prominent role to play in that, but his founding authority was shared by the others and is found today in the New Testament, not in the office of the pope.

*If your brother sins against you, go and tell him his fault,*
*between you and him alone. If he listens to you, you have*
*gained your brother. But if he does not listen, take one or two*
*others along with you, that every charge may be established by*
*the evidence of two or three witnesses. If he refuses to listen to*
*them, tell it to the church. And if he refuses to listen even to*
*the church, let him be to you as a Gentile and a tax collector.*

MATTHEW 18:15–17

*And [Jesus] said to them, "I have earnestly desired to eat this*
*Passover with you before I suffer. For I tell you I will not eat*
*it until it is fulfilled in the kingdom of God." And he took a*
*cup, and when he had given thanks he said, "Take this, and*
*divide it among yourselves. For I tell you that from now on*
*I will not drink of the fruit of the vine until the kingdom*
*of God comes." And he took bread, and when he had given*
*thanks, he broke it and gave it to them, saying, "This is my*
*body, which is given for you. Do this in remembrance of me."*
*And likewise the cup after they had eaten, saying, "This cup*
*that is poured out for you is the new covenant in my blood."*

LUKE 22:15–20

# Do This in Remembrance of Me—Baptize Disciples and Eat the Lord's Supper

## How Jesus Commands That We Handle Sin in the Church

In addition to providing his church with the Spirit and the word (which we saw in the previous chapter), Jesus also provided guidelines for how to handle sin in the flock. In one sense, all of his teachings do this. They are the charter for how his followers are to live in the church and in the world. But he gave more specific guidelines for what has come to be called church discipline in Matthew 18:15–17.

> If your brother sins against you, go and tell him his fault, between you and him alone. If he listens to you, you have gained your brother. But if he does not listen, take one or two others along with you, that every charge may be established by the evidence of two or three witnesses. If he refuses to listen to them, tell it to the church. And if he refuses to listen even to the church, let him be to you as a Gentile and a tax collector.

The word "church" signals the fact that Jesus is preparing his followers for the ongoing fellowship of his band of followers in his absence. The implication of the teaching is that persistent, unrepented sin—a refusal to take sin seriously and make war against it in our own lives—will mean we are not really followers of Jesus. In other words, even though Jesus knew that the church would always have false believers in it (Matt. 13:30, 48), nevertheless he made provision for a kind of careful, loving, patient discipline that would not tolerate blatant unwillingness to repent.

Treating an unrepentant "brother" like a "Gentile and tax collector" did not mean treating him with hostility. Jesus had said plainly that such people are to be loved: "And if you greet only your brothers, what more are you doing than others? Do not even the Gentiles do the same?" (Matt. 5:47). What it means to "let him be to you as a Gentile and a tax collector" is to no longer share the unique fellowship of Jesus with him—not to relate with him as if there is no barrier in the fellowship. This would include not sharing, for example, in the Lord's Supper together.

### Go, Make Disciples, Baptizing Them

Which brings us now to the ordinances that Jesus prepared for his church before he left, namely, baptism and the Lord's Supper. Just before he departed into heaven, Jesus gave the command that we should "make disciples of all nations, baptizing them in the name of the Father and of the Son and of the Holy Spirit" (Matt. 28:19). In other words, part of becoming a disciple or a follower of Jesus is being baptized. This is the outward mark of the inward change that has happened to bring one under the lordship of Jesus as a forgiven sinner.

John the Baptist had baptized people as a call to repentance in preparation for the coming of the Messiah (Mark 1:4). This was in one sense amazing. He was calling on Jewish people to undergo a special sign of repentance as a sign of being part of Messiah's people. But some of the leaders were indignant at this and protested that they were already the people of the Messiah. They were Abraham's offspring. To this John replied, "Do not presume to say to yourselves, 'We have Abraham as our father,' for I tell you, God is able from these stones to raise up children for Abraham" (Matt. 3:9). In other words, "The baptism I demand is a sign that a true people of Israel is being formed. It is not coextensive with the physical offspring of Abraham. It is made up of those who repent and who will very soon meet and believe in the Messiah, Jesus. Do not think," he says to the Jewish leaders, "that if you are rejected for unbelief, God will be unable to fulfill his covenant promises; he can raise up from stones beneficiaries of his promises."

Therefore, already in John's baptism we see how it functioned to distinguish true believers from mere descendants of believers. Now Jesus chooses this sign as the mark of his own followers in his absence. When they are converted from unbelief to belief, they are to be baptized. That is, they are to demonstrate in their obedience to this command that they are truly his.[1] My simple point here is that this act, practiced by almost all Christian churches today, was not invented by the churches. Jesus put this in place before he left and commanded that we do it. Therefore a follower of Jesus should be baptized in the name of the Father, the Son, and the Holy Spirit, as Jesus said. This is part of becoming his disciple and becoming a part of his church.

### "Do This in Remembrance of Me"

The other ordinance that Jesus provided for his church is the Lord's Supper. I am calling baptism and the Lord's Supper *ordinances* to signify that Jesus *ordained* them. That is, he established the pattern of

---

1 I don't intend to go into the controversial issues surrounding infant baptism versus believer's baptism. I would recommend Paul K. Jewett, *Infant Baptism and the Covenant of Grace: An Appraisal of the Argument That as Infants Were Once Circumcised, So They Should Now Be Baptized* (Grand Rapids, Mich.: Eerdmans, 1978), which defends the truth of believer's baptism. For my own more extended treatment see "Brothers, Magnify the Meaning of Baptism," in *Brothers, We Are Not Professionals* (Nashville: Broadman & Holman, 2002).

their observance. This is clear with regard to baptism because he commanded it as a more or less formal act in the name of the Father, Son, and Holy Spirit. It is also clear in regard to the Lord's Supper because, in the context of a very solemn declaration about the bread and the cup, Jesus commands us to "do this." "'This is my body, which is given for you. *Do this* in remembrance of me.' And likewise the cup after they had eaten, saying, 'This cup that is poured out for you is the new covenant in my blood'" (Luke 22:19–20).

Jesus did not give this ordinance a name. He called the entire meal that he was eating with his disciples that last night the Passover and described it in relationship to his own sacrifice. "I have earnestly desired to eat this *Passover* with you before *I suffer*" (Luke 22:15). The Passover marked the event in Egypt when God spared the Jewish sons from the angel of death because their doorposts and lintel were marked with blood from a sacrificial lamb (Exod. 12:13, 23). Since everything about Jesus's last evening and the following trial and crucifixion was planned by God and followed obediently by Jesus, it would be folly to think his last supper was only coincidentally a Passover meal. "The Son of Man goes as it is written of him" (Matt. 26:24).

Therefore, it is not surprising that the earliest Christian document that refers to this ordinance not only calls it "the Lord's Supper" (κυριακὸν δεῖπνον; 1 Cor. 11:20), but also refers to Jesus as "our Passover lamb" (τὸ πάσχα ἡμῶν; 1 Cor. 5:7). That was surely what Jesus meant to say: "I am instituting a sacred supper for my people when I am gone, and in it they should see a sacred sign of the Passover sacrifice that I will perform tomorrow morning when I die for their sins."

### How Are the Cup and Bread the Blood and Body of Jesus?

Of course using the word *sign* in that last sentence is controversial. There have been several different understandings of what Jesus meant by taking the bread and saying, "*This is* my body, which is given for you" (Luke 22:19) and by taking the cup and saying, "*This is* my blood of the covenant, which is poured out for many for the forgiveness of sins" (Matt. 26:28). Was he saying that the cup and the bread were signs of his body and blood or that they somehow were transformed into the very body and blood of Jesus?

It was natural then, and it is natural today, to point to a representation of something and say that the representation is the thing. For example, I look at a photograph of our house and say, "This is our house." It would not enter anyone's mind to think I mean that the photograph was transformed into my house. If Jesus stooped down and drew a camel in the sand, he would say, "This is a camel." The drawing doesn't become a camel. It represents a camel.

We know he used language this way because in the parable of the four soils, he interprets the images of four kinds of people with these words: "As for what was sown on rocky ground, *this is the one who hears* the word and immediately receives it with joy" (Matt. 13:20). He means the rocky ground *represents* a kind of person. There is nothing modern or strange about this way of thinking, and it is the most natural way to understand Jesus's words. The cup and the bread represent his blood and body.

Moreover, if we insist on saying that "this is my body" and "this is my blood" must refer to the physical body and blood of Jesus, what becomes of the statement, "This cup . . . is the new covenant in my blood" (Luke 22:20)? Are we to say that the cup is the new covenant in the same way that the cup is the blood? Surely, "this cup . . . is the new covenant" means "this cup represents the new covenant that will be purchased and inaugurated by my blood-shedding tomorrow morning." Therefore, it seems wise to understand the words "this is my body" and "this is my blood" to mean: "The cup and bread represent my physical body and blood offered up for you in death as a sacrifice for your sins."

## "The Words That I Have Spoken to You Are Spirit and Life"

Sometimes another saying of Jesus is used as a support for seeing the cup and bread as literally transformed into the blood and body of Jesus.

In John 6:53–54 Jesus said, "Truly, truly, I say to you, unless you eat the flesh of the Son of Man and drink his blood, you have no life in you. Whoever feeds on my flesh and drinks my blood has eternal life." But Jesus wants us to see this language as a vivid expression of *spiritual* feeding, not physical feeding. He tells us this ten verses later when he makes sure that we understand that the life promised in verses 53–54 is not mediated through flesh but through the Spirit: "It is the Spirit who gives life; the flesh is no help at all. The words that I have spoken to you are spirit and life" (John 6:63). This verse is a warning against taking the words "this is my body" and "this is my blood" in a way that makes eternal life flow through physical eating and drinking.

Therefore, Jesus commands that his followers celebrate the Lord's Supper as a commemoration of his death and an anticipation of his coming again in the glory of his kingdom (Luke 22:18). Knowing that this cup and bread represent the most wonderful act of love in history and that it accomplished the purchase and inauguration of the new covenant—that is, the purchase of forgiveness and a new heart (Jer. 31:31–34)—makes the Lord's Supper a matchless act of communion with the risen Jesus. He draws near by his Spirit and his word and makes himself known to us for our enjoyment in a way that is uniquely shaped by this solemn act.

### The Command of Jesus: Be the Church

What we have seen in this chapter is that the church is not an afterthought created by the followers of Jesus because his message of the coming kingdom did not materialize. No, the church did not replace the kingdom. The church is created and sustained by the kingdom. The church was planned by Jesus, and he provided for her in every way.

"I will build my church" is the banner that flies over the gatherings of Jesus's followers today. He is building his people. He is gathering his flock. He is fulfilling his promise to be with her to the end of the age. He is teaching her by his Spirit and through his word. And he is marking her off from the world through the sign of baptism and by making himself remembered and known and enjoyed in the Lord's Supper. "Do this" is a command of the Lord that calls us today to be not just individual followers but a flock, a gathering, a community, and a church.

*You are the salt of the earth, but if salt has lost its taste, how shall its saltiness be restored? It is no longer good for anything except to be thrown out and trampled under people's feet.*

*You are the light of the world. A city set on a hill cannot be hidden. Nor do people light a lamp and put it under a basket, but on a stand, and it gives light to all in the house. In the same way, let your light shine before others, so that they may see your good works and give glory to your Father who is in heaven.*

MATTHEW 5:13–16

*Salt is good, but if the salt has lost its saltiness, how will you make it salty again? Have salt in yourselves, and be at peace with one another.*

MARK 9:50

# Let Your Light Shine before Others That They May Glorify Your Father Who Is in Heaven

THE COMMAND THAT WE LET OUR LIGHT SHINE before the world has a goal: that people might give glory to our Father who is in heaven. So ultimately, the command is that we seek to glorify God by letting our light shine. It is fitting then that we devote this chapter to the importance of this goal: the glorifying of God. Then in the following chapter we will turn to what it means to let our light shine.

## Jesus's First Passion and Supreme Value

The first thing that Jesus commands that we pray is that our Father's name be hallowed. "Pray then like this: 'Our Father in heaven, hallowed be your name'" (Matt. 6:9). In saying this, Jesus signals that his first passion is—and our first passion should be—the manifest holiness of God. I choose the phrase "manifest holiness of God" for three reasons. First, the Greek word behind "hallowed be" (ἁγιασθήτω) is built on the word for "holy" (ἅγιος). Second, when you turn the word "holy" into a verb like this, it means to "show yourself holy"—hence

381

the idea of *manifest* holiness. Third, another way to speak of the manifest holiness of God is to speak of his glory.[1]

The reason it is important to see the connection between the *hallowing* of God's name and the *glory* of God is that numerous sayings of Jesus (as we will see in a moment) show that the glory of his Father and his own glory are supremely important. Nothing in the universe is more valuable than the glory of God. Seeing the connection between the hallowing of God's name as the first passion of Jesus and the glory of God as the supreme value in the universe shows that there is no conflict between these two. Hallowing God's name and glorifying God are largely the same act.

**What Is the Glory of God?**

God's glory is the radiance of his manifold perfections. Those are poor words for the richest reality of all. But though words are inadequate, we must try. God's glory is the outshining of the infinite value of all that God is. It is his moral beauty. It is visible to the physical eye only as the glorious created world points to its invisible but more glorious Maker. "Consider the lilies of the field. . . . Even Solomon in all his *glory* was not arrayed like one of these. . . . God so clothes the grass of the field" (Matt. 6:28–30). The glory of the lilies is the work of God. It is meant to get our attention and waken us to a glory of which lily-glory is only a likeness.

We love to look at glory. We were made to enjoy seeing it. This is why Jesus came into the world. He came to reveal the glory of God more fully than nature ever had (John 1:14) and to die in our place so that we

---

1   One way to think of the holiness of God in relation to his glory is that his holiness is the infinite worth of his intrinsic perfection and purity, and his glory is the manifestation or the radiance of that worth. One textual pointer toward this relationship is Leviticus 10:1–3, "Now Nadab and Abihu, the sons of Aaron, each took his censer and put fire in it and laid incense on it and offered unauthorized fire before the Lord, which he had not commanded them. And fire came out from before the Lord and consumed them, and they died before the Lord. Then Moses said to Aaron, 'This is what the Lord has said, "Among those who are near me I will be *sanctified* [ἁγιασθήσομαι], and before all the people I will be *glorified* [δοξασθήσομαι].""" The priests must treat God as holy in their sacrifices, and the result will be that God will be manifested as holy to the people—that is, he will be glorified.

could be saved from God's wrath in order to enjoy forever the glory of God's grace (John 3:14–15, 36; 17:24) and to awaken in us a desire for that glory so that we do not perish in our blind love affair with the glory of sin (John 3:19). Jesus consciously aimed to reveal the glory of God. His actions and words were designed to fulfill prophecies like this: "The people dwelling in darkness have seen a great light, and for those dwelling in the region and shadow of death, on them a light has dawned" (Matt. 4:16). He said, "As long as I am in the world, I am the light of the world" (John 9:5; cf. 8:12). That is, he revealed the brightness of God's glory as never before and by this light put everything in truthful perspective.

### How Jesus Glorified God

Jesus displayed the glory of God in accomplishing what God had given him to do. So he prayed to his Father at the end of his life, "I glorified you on earth, having accomplished the work that you gave me to do" (John 17:4). That work included many miracles during his life and the great final work of redemption when he died and rose again.

For example, when Jesus did his first public miracle by turning water into wine, John says, he "manifested his glory" (John 2:11). When Jesus healed a paralytic and forgave his sins, "the crowds saw it [and] were afraid, and they *glorified* God" (Matt. 9:8). When the people saw "the mute speaking, the crippled healthy, the lame walking, and the blind seeing . . . they *glorified* the God of Israel" (Matt. 15:31). When ten lepers were cleansed, one grateful man "turned back, *glorifying* God with a loud voice" (Luke 17:15, NASB). When a woman who was bent over for eighteen years was touched and straightened, "she *glorified* God" (Luke 13:13). And when Jesus was about to raise Lazarus from the dead, he said to his sister, "Did I not tell you that if you believed you would see the *glory* of God?" (John 11:40). Everything Jesus did was done with a view to making God look great. His work was to display the greatness and the beauty of the full range of God's perfections.

But the greatest miracle of all was Jesus's death and resurrection so that we might be redeemed from the guilt and power of sin (Mark

10:45) and have forgiveness (Matt. 26:28) and eternal life (John 3:14–15). In this great act of substitution—the guiltless for the guilty—Jesus displayed the glory of the wrath of God and the glory of the love of God. God's wrath is a glorious wrath (Luke 21:23; John 3:36). He could have no other kind. And God's love is a glorious love. When Jesus came to die, as the climax of his earthly work, there was a huge sense that this was the moment of greatest groaning and greatest glory.

In those last hours he said, "The hour has come for the Son of Man to be *glorified*. Truly, truly, I say to you, unless a grain of wheat falls into the earth and dies, it remains alone; but if it dies, it bears much fruit" (John 12:23–24). The glory of Jesus was manifested both in the suffering and in the triumphal resurrection afterward. Jesus said, "Was it not necessary that the Christ should suffer these things and enter into his *glory*?" (Luke 24:26). The sufferings were the pathway to glory.

### The Father and the Son Glorify Each Other

But they were not just the path. They were an essential part of his glory. "Now [in this very hour of suffering] is the Son of Man *glorified*, and God is *glorified* in him. If God is *glorified* in him, God will also *glorify* him in himself, and *glorify* him at once" (John 13:31–32). God is shown to be gloriously worthy in Jesus's willingness to die so that God would be just to remove the wrath that rightly falls on sinners. And when the Father is thus glorified in the Son, he then undertakes to glorify the Son with a mighty display of approval in the resurrection.

Back and forth goes the work of the Father and the Son in glorifying each other in the act of salvation. If we have seen that the Son glorifies the Father, and the Father responds by glorifying the Son, the reverse is also true. "Father," Jesus says, "the hour has come; *glorify* your Son that the Son may *glorify* you" (John 17:1; 12:27–28). When Jesus is glorifying the Father in his death, it is the Father at work glorifying the Son as well; and when the Father glorifies the Son in his resurrection and exaltation, it leads to the Son glorifying the Father as well. This mutual display of the glory of God in the work of the Father and of the Son is the supreme passion of their hearts.

## No Greater Love Than God's Glorifying Himself in Jesus for Us

And the good news is that this is the very essence of their love for us. They are displaying their glory not only to make it visible for the enjoyment of soul-hungry creatures like us who were made to find ultimate satisfaction in it but also in a way that pays for our failures to treasure God's glory so that we can escape judgment (John 5:29). In other words, God's passion to glorify himself and his Son is an act of love because of the preciousness of what he gives and the price that he pays to give it. He gives us his glory, and he pays for it with his Son's life. There is no greater gift than God himself in all his glory. There is no greater price than the death of God's Son. Therefore, there is no greater love than God's glorifying himself in the death and resurrection of Jesus.[2]

When that great work of redemption is done in the crucifixion and resurrection, Jesus sets about, over the centuries, to gather a people for himself by sending the Holy Spirit whose central work is to glorify Jesus and draw people to him in faith. So he promised, "When the Spirit of truth comes, he will guide you into all the truth. . . . *He will glorify me, for he will take what is mine and declare it to you*" (John 16:13–14). The central work of the Spirit is to continue the great work of glorifying the Father and the Son. He does that by opening our spiritual eyes to see the truth and beauty of who Jesus is and what he has already done in his life and death and resurrection (John 3:3, 8; Matt. 16:17). When we see him for who he is, we are drawn to receive him and trust him and worship him and obey him.

Now, in view of the passion for God's glory, what does it mean to "let your light shine" for the glory of God? That's the focus of the next chapter.

---

2  To see this point unfolded in greater detail and with more texts, see John Piper, *God Is the Gospel: Meditations on God's Love as the Gift of Himself* (Wheaton, Ill.: Crossway, 2005).

*Blessed are you when others revile you and persecute you
and utter all kinds of evil against you falsely on my account.
Rejoice and be glad, for your reward is great in heaven,
for so they persecuted the prophets who were before you.*

*You are the salt of the earth, but if salt has lost its taste, how
shall its saltiness be restored? It is no longer good for anything
except to be thrown out and trampled under people's feet.*

*You are the light of the world. A city set on a hill cannot be
hidden. Nor do people light a lamp and put it under a basket,
but on a stand, and it gives light to all in the house. In the
same way, let your light shine before others, so that they may see
your good works and give glory to your Father who is in heaven.*

MATTHEW 5:11–16

# Let Your Light Shine before Others—the Joyful Sacrifice of Love in Suffering

IN THE PREVIOUS CHAPTER WE FOCUSED on the supreme passion of Jesus, his Father, and the Holy Spirit—namely, that they be glorified in the work of our salvation. Which brings us now to the command, "Let your light shine before others, so that they may see your good works and give glory to your Father who is in heaven" (Matt. 5:16). After seeing that Jesus's and the Father's and the Spirit's supreme passion is to display the glory of God, it should not be surprising that the followers of Jesus should be drawn into this passion. Live in such a way that people look at your life and make much of your God. That is what Jesus commands.

## Shine with the Light That You Are

The light that we let shine is the light that we are. Jesus said, "You *are* the light of the world" (Matt. 5:14). So there is a movement from the inside to the outside. What people see from the outside is our "good works." But that is not who we *are*. The good works have a light source from inside. The key to understanding the light that shines out through good works is the aim of the works, namely, that people see and *give glory to God.* Why do they give glory to God and not to us? Because the light that is shining out is the light of God, or the light of Jesus who is the revelation of the glory of God.

### What Actually Is the Light That People See?

So what does it mean then that we *are* the light of the world? How do good deeds grow from who we are in such a way that they make God look glorious? Here it would be wise to stay close to the context of Jesus's words. He has just spoken the Beatitudes: Blessed are the poor in spirit, those who mourn, the meek, those who hunger and thirst for righteousness, the merciful, the pure in heart, the peacemakers, and those who suffer for righteousness' sake (Matt. 5:3–10). Here is a kind of identity that is very unusual in the world. It is like savory salt when things are tasteless and flat,[1] and it is like hope-filled light when people are stumbling around in the dark.

But the closest beatitude to the command to let your light shine for the glory of God is that you are blessed when you are reviled. "Blessed are you when others revile you and persecute you and utter all kinds of evil against you falsely on my account. Rejoice and be glad, for your reward is great in heaven, for so they persecuted the prophets who were before you" (Matt. 5:11–12). Immediately following this command to rejoice in persecution comes the statement: "You are the salt of the earth. . . . You are the light of the world" (Matt. 5:13–14). Therefore, I conclude that what is most salty and bright in this insipid and dark world is the almost incomprehensible joy of Jesus's followers in the midst of persecution and the hardships of life.

---

1 W. D. Davies and Dale Allison give eleven possible meanings for "you are the salt of the earth" (Matt. 5:13), and then conclude that perhaps that's the point: the many uses of salt. *A Critical and Exegetical Commentary on the Gospel According to Saint Matthew*, International Critical Commentary, Vol. 1 (Edinburgh: T & T Clark, 1988), 472–73. But I follow those who think that the savor of salt is the most natural thing referred to. There is a kind of radical life rooted in the promises of the Beatitudes that has a rare and wonderful taste in a world gone flat with an excess of superficial titillation.

It is a joy that is meek and merciful and pure and peaceable, but these things alone do not awaken people to the glory of God. In order to waken people to consider God as an explanation for our good works there generally must be an obstacle of suffering that would ordinarily cause them to be angry or despairing but does not have that effect on us. Rather they see us "rejoice" in hardship. They see that this hardship does not make us self-centered and self-pitying and mean-spirited. Instead they see our joy and wonder what we are hoping in when ordinary props for hope have been knocked away. The answer, Jesus says, is that we have great reward in heaven (Matt. 5:12). That is, Jesus has become a treasure for us that is more precious than what the world offers. Therefore, when persecution or calamity take natural pleasures away, we still have Jesus, and we still have joy.

Now when our good works get their flavor from this salt and glow with this light, the world may well be awakened to taste something they have never tasted before and to see something they have never seen before, namely, the glory of God in Jesus. If we give a word of testimony concerning the truth and beauty of Jesus,[2] and if the Spirit mercifully blows on the hearts of those who see the evidence of that beauty in our lives, then people will "give glory to [our] Father who is in heaven" (Matt. 5:16).

### Is the Glory of God an "Ulterior Motive" for Love?

The supremacy of the value of the glory of God is seen in the way Jesus makes the command of Matthew 5:16—"Let your light shine

---

2  Jesus would consider it a great mistake if we took his words to mean that a person could come to a saving sight of the glory of God in our deeds without some verbal testimony as to who Jesus is and what he has done for us and promised to us. This is why Jesus sent his disciples out to *preach* and to *do* good works (Matt. 10:7–8; Luke 9:2; 10:9). Not either-or, but both-and. The great saving task of the followers of Jesus is to speak the gospel along with a life of salt-like, light-like love: "And this gospel of the kingdom will be proclaimed throughout the whole world as a testimony to all nations, and then the end will come" (Matt. 24:14).

before others, so that they may see your good works and give glory to your Father who is in heaven." He explicitly says that our aim in doing good works for others is that they might glorify God. Sometimes people who talk much of love but are not God-centered the way Jesus is say things like, "If you do good to people to get them to glorify your God, you are not loving them, for you have ulterior motives."

This kind of criticism results from a failure to experience the glory of God as the greatest gift and highest joy imaginable. How could it not be love to lay down your life for someone (in doing good for them) specifically with a view to satisfying them with the glory of God forever? This motive is not ulterior; it is open and front and center. It is the very essence of love: followers of Jesus are not do-gooders with no eternal aims for those they love. They know exactly what the greatest and highest and most joyful good is: seeing and savoring God in Jesus forever. This is their aim and they are unashamed of it. They think any lesser aim is a failure of love.

### Jesus Loved Us by Obtaining for Us at the Cost of His Life God's Glory

We have seen it already, but it is so important we should see it again from different texts: Jesus loved like this. In his darkest hour he let his light shine most brightly in a "good work." As he did the greatest "good work" that has ever been done, he pondered out loud, "And what shall I say? 'Father, save me from this hour'?" His answer is no. Instead he described the ultimate reason why he came to the hour of his death: "But for this purpose I have come to this hour. Father, glorify your name" (John 12:27–28). D. A. Carson rightly calls this "nothing other than an articulation of the principle that has controlled his life and ministry (John 7:18; 8:29, 50)."[3] From beginning (John 2:11) to

---

3   D. A. Carson, *The Gospel According to John* (Grand Rapids, Mich: Eerdmans, 1991), 440.

end (John 12:28) Jesus let his light shine—did his good works—to vindicate and display the glory of God.

The way he thought of this as the supreme act of love was not only that it cost him his life (John 15:13) but that it obtained freely for sinners the greatest gift possible. He prayed for it in John 17:24, "Father, I desire that they also, whom you have given me, may be with me where I am, *to see my glory*." This was the final, greatest, and most satisfying gift obtained by Jesus in the "good work" that he did on the cross.

This will make no sense at all to a person who does not see and savor the glory of God above all other gifts. But for those who have renounced all that this world offers (Luke 14:33) and set their heart on the "great reward" in heaven, namely, the enjoyment of the glory of Jesus, Jesus's purchase of this reward at the cost of his life will be the greatest act of love imaginable.

## Letting Our Light Shine, like Jesus, in the Way We Die

When Jesus calls us to let our light shine that others may see our good deeds and glorify God, he is calling us to join him in the work he came to do. And just as he pursued the glory of his Father through his final act of dying, he expects that we will do the same. Therefore, he said to Peter, "'Truly, truly, I say to you, when you were young, you used to dress yourself and walk wherever you wanted, but when you are old, you will stretch out your hands, and another will dress you and carry you where you do not want to go.' (This he said to show *by what kind of death he was to glorify God*)" (John 21:18). Jesus simply takes it for granted that his disciples will make God look good in the way they die.

The only question is, how will we die? That decision lies in the hands of God, as Jesus makes clear with the words, "Are not two sparrows sold for a penny? And not one of them will fall to the ground apart from your Father. But even the hairs of your head are all numbered. Fear not, therefore; you are of more value than many sparrows" (Matt. 10:29–31). In other words, if God rules over how the birds die, how much more surely will he govern your death.

### Jesus's Light and Ours at His Second Coming

The final great historical display of Jesus's shining light—and ours—happens at his second coming. He tells us how it will be both for him and for us. For him, he says, "The Son of Man is going to come with his angels in the *glory* of his Father. . . . All the tribes of the earth will mourn, and they will see the Son of Man coming on the clouds of heaven with power and *great glory*. . . . Then shall he sit upon the throne of *his glory*" (Matt. 16:27; 24:30; 25:31, KJV). He came the first time to display the glory of his Father. He will come the second time to complete that revelation and "gather out of his kingdom all causes of sin and all law-breakers" (Matt. 13:41).

What about for us? What will his second coming mean for us? It turns out that letting our light shine will be our *eternal* vocation. We will never cease to have this calling. This is why we were created: to be so satisfied with our great reward, the glory of God in Jesus, that we reflect his infinite worth in acts of love that cause others to see and savor and show more of the glory of God. We can see our eternal shining in Matthew 13:43 where Jesus describes what becomes of his followers at his second coming: "The righteous will *shine* like the sun in the kingdom of their Father."

This is our final destiny. Beholding the glory of Jesus (John 17:24), we will shine with the beauty and the love that he has. The church that he promised to build (Matt. 16:18, see *Command #45*) will find its final destiny in reflecting to one another the glory of Jesus, so that our enjoyment of him will be all the greater because of the manifold manifestations of it in the shining members.

## The Bright Command

Jesus's command for all the world is that all human beings find in him the all-satisfying glory for which we were made. Then he commands that we turn from trusting in anything else, and bank our hope on the "great reward" of everlasting joy in him. And then, in that hope and joy, he commands that we let that light shine in sacrificial good deeds of love, so that others will see and savor and spread the glory of God.

*All authority in heaven and on earth has been given to me.*
*Go therefore and make disciples of all nations, baptizing them*
*in the name of the Father and of the Son and of the Holy*
*Spirit, teaching them to observe all that I have commanded*
*you. And behold, I am with you always, to the end of the age.*

MATTHEW 28:18–20

*The harvest is plentiful, but the laborers are few;*
*therefore pray earnestly to the Lord of the harvest*
*to send out laborers into his harvest.*

MATTHEW 9:37–38

*Go out to the highways and hedges and compel*
*people to come in, that my house may be filled.*

LUKE 14:23

*I tell you, there will be more joy in heaven over*
*one sinner who repents than over ninety-nine*
*righteous persons who need no repentance.*

LUKE 15:7

*As the Father has sent me, even so I am sending you.*

JOHN 20:21

# Make Disciples of All Nations,
# for All Authority Belongs to Jesus

BEFORE JESUS COMMANDED THAT his followers go make disciples of all nations, he gave the justification for this seemingly presumptuous mission. He said, "All authority in heaven and on earth has been given to me" (Matt. 28:18). The basis today of any follower of Jesus telling a follower of another lord to repent and turn and follow Jesus is that Jesus has all authority in the universe.

## What Is Authority?

*Authority* refers to the right and the power to hold sway in a given relationship. So a father has authority over his children but not necessarily over his neighbor. An army lieutenant has authority over his platoon but not over the company commander. A teacher has authority over the students in the classroom but not over their parents. An office manager has authority over the secretaries but not over the CEO.

We see a picture of the meaning of authority in the story of Jesus's encounter with the Roman centurion. This officer wanted Jesus to heal his servant but did not feel worthy to have Jesus come into his home. So he said to Jesus, "Lord, I am not worthy to have you come under my roof, but only *say the word*, and my servant will be healed. For I too am a man under *authority*, with soldiers under me. And I say to one, 'Go,' and he goes, and to another, 'Come,' and he comes, and to my servant, 'Do this,' and he does it" (Matt. 8:8–9). In other words, authority is the right and power to have your subordinates do what you choose for them to do.

That is the authority Jesus has over everyone and everything. "*All* authority in heaven and on earth has been given to me." The phrase "heaven and earth" is meant to include everything. Therefore, everyone and everything is subordinate to Jesus. Every human. Every angel. Every demon. The devil himself. And all the natural world and what happens in it.

## The Total Authority of Jesus

We see this illustrated even during Jesus's earthly ministry. He has authority to forgive sins, which only God can do, and so he was accused of blasphemy (Mark 2:7–12). We see it in the way he taught the people and the way he handled the Jewish Scriptures: "They were astonished at his teaching, for he taught them as one who had authority, and not as the scribes" (Mark 1:22; Matt. 5:17–18). We see it in the way he rebuked the devil (Matt. 4:10) and commanded unclean spirits: "He commands even the unclean spirits, and they obey him" (Mark 1:27). We see it in the way he commanded the forces of nature by healing all kinds of diseases (Matt. 4:23) and turning water into wine (John 2:9; 4:46) and calming the storm: "He awoke and rebuked the wind and said to the sea, 'Peace! Be still!' And the wind ceased, and there was a great calm" (Mark 4:39).

We see Jesus's authority in the matter of life and death, both his own and other's—and ultimately in the matter of eternal life. He raised people from the dead (Mark 5:41–42; Luke 7:14–15; John 11:43–44) and ruled over his own death and resurrection: "No one takes [my life] from me, but I lay it down of my own accord. I have authority to lay it down, and I have authority to take it up again" (John 10:18). And he holds full sway in the final judgment. He said that God the Father "has given him authority to execute judgment, because he is the Son of Man" (John 5:27). And God has "given him authority over all flesh, to give eternal life to all whom [God has] given him" (John 17:2).

## How Jesus Lays Claim on the World

There is nothing outside the authority of Jesus. He has the right and the power to command allegiance from every soul that exists. As the Lord of the universe, Jesus commands that everyone from every nation and every religion become his disciple. The way Jesus pursues this universal claim on every soul is by sending his followers to make disciples from all the nations. After saying that all authority in heaven and earth is his, he says, "therefore . . . ." This word shows not only that his universal authority is the *basis* of his universal claim on every person but also that the *way* he lays claim to those persons follows in the next verse.

What follows is a commission that his followers go and make disciples. "Go therefore and make disciples of all nations" (Matt. 28:19). In other words, Jesus does not lay claim on a person directly from heaven. He lays claim on people through his followers. He laid down the principle while he was still here: "Truly, truly, I say to you, whoever receives the one I send receives me, and whoever receives me receives the one who sent me" (John 13:20; Matt. 10:40). It is true that he said, "*I* will build my church" (Matt. 16:18), and "I have other sheep that are not of this fold. *I* must bring them also, and they will listen to my voice" (John 10:16). Yes, he is doing it himself. But he did not mean that he would do it *directly* from heaven without emissaries. We know this because when he prayed for the future church in John 17:20, he described them as "those who will believe in me through their word."

## The Mission Lasts as Long as This Age Lasts

In other words, Jesus builds his church and gathers his flock from the nations of the world *through the word* of those he sends. So the universal authority of Jesus issues in a mission that lasts as long as history and extends as far as humanity: "Go therefore and make disciples of all nations. . . . And behold, I am with you always, *to the end of the age*" (Matt. 28:19–20). The words "to the end of the age" show that the mission should last till Jesus comes back. The command is not given only to the first generation of disciples. The mission lasts as long as the mission-sustaining promise lasts. And that promise is: the all-authoritative Jesus will be with us "to the end of the age." As long as there is time, and as long as there are nations to reach, Jesus's command to go make disciples is valid.

### The Followers of Jesus Speak on His Behalf

This implies several things. First, it implies that Jesus's exclusive claim will be made not just by him but by his followers. He claimed that he is the one and only Lord of the universe and that every person from every nation and every religion or non-religion should be his disciple. This claim is now given to his emissaries to make disciples among all the nations and all the religions of the world. Jesus sends his followers to go make disciples of all nations, no matter what their religion is—Jews, Hindus, Buddhists, Muslims, animists, atheists, agnostics. He sends his followers, backed by his universal authority, to go and call all people in every nation and every religion to turn to become the disciples of Jesus.

This means that in times of relativism (like our own), when people do not cherish objective, unchanging truth, followers of Jesus will be accused of arrogance. They will proclaim that Jesus has all authority—because it is true—and that everyone should repent and believe in him and become his disciple. They will warn everyone that to reject Jesus as the eternal Son of God who came into the world to redeem sinners by his death and who rose again as Lord of the universe is to forfeit eternal life. Jesus said, "Whoever believes in the Son has eternal life; whoever does not obey the Son shall not see life, but the wrath of God remains on him. . . . Whoever does not honor the Son does not honor the Father who sent him" (John 3:36; 5:23; cf. 15:23).

This is the mandate and promise that sustains Jesus's emissaries: "The one who hears you hears me, and the one who rejects you rejects me, and the one who rejects me rejects him who sent me" (Luke 10:16). The followers of Jesus will be scorned for saying that all authority belongs to Jesus and that everyone must become his disciple or forfeit eternal life. But Jesus knew that would happen: "If the world hates you, know that it has hated me before it hated you" (John 15:18). That is why he enclosed this radical command to make disciples between the double assurance (1) that all authority really is his and (2) that he will be with his emissaries till the end of the age.

### Jesus Commands That We Pursue Ethnic Diversity in His Kingdom

A second implication of Jesus's universal mission is that Jesus cares for all ethnic groups and intends to have disciples from every "nation." When he says, "Go therefore and make disciples of all *nations*," the meaning of the word "nations" is not political states. "Nations"—or its synonym, "peoples" (Luke 2:31; Ps. 117:1)—in the Bible does not refer to political states like America, Spain, Brazil, China, etc., but to ethnic or language or cultural groupings within these political states. For example, within the political state of China there are dozens of "nations"—Dulong, Li, Lisu, Shui, Salar, Yao, etc. And in the Jewish Scriptures that Jesus knew, we read about "the Jebusites, the Amorites, the Girgashites, the Hivites, the Arkites, the Sinites, the Arvadites, the Zemarites, and the Hamathites" (Gen. 10:16–18).

So in our day the command of Jesus to make disciples of all nations would mean, for example, to make disciples among the Baloch of Pakistan, the Maninka of Guinea, the Bugis of Indonesia, the Wa of China, the Somali and Dakota of Minneapolis. These are the kinds of groups Jesus was referring to when he said, "Go therefore and make disciples of *all nations*." Wherever there is a distinct people group[1] that has no disciples of Jesus, the command of Jesus is resoundingly clear: "Go as my emissaries with my authority and my word and my love and my power and make disciples there." There is no partiality with Jesus in this mission. He is not western, and he is not eastern. He is utterly committed to ethnic diversity and unity in the truth of his supremacy. In fact, the word from which we get "ethnic" is the word for "nations" in Matthew 28:19, ἔθνος.

It has not always seemed as though God were pursuing all the nations. At times he seemed to be committed to his people Israel but not the nations. His way has been indirect and at times inscrutable. How shall we understand this roundabout way toward a global church of worshipers from all the nations? That is what we turn to in the final chapter.

---

[1] For a more complete defense and explanation of what "all nations" means in a biblical and missiological perspective, see John Piper, *Let the Nations Be Glad: The Supremacy of God in Missions*, revised and expanded edition (Grand Rapids, Mich.: Baker, 2003), 155–200.

*I tell you, many will come from east and west and
recline at table with Abraham, Isaac, and Jacob in
the kingdom of heaven, while the sons of the kingdom
will be thrown into the outer darkness. In that place
there will be weeping and gnashing of teeth.*

MATTHEW 8:11–12

*But before all this they will lay their hands on you and
persecute you, delivering you up to the synagogues and prisons,
and you will be brought before kings and governors for my
name's sake. This will be your opportunity to bear witness.*

LUKE 21:12–13

*They will fall by the edge of the sword and be led captive
among all nations, and Jerusalem will be trampled underfoot
by the Gentiles, until the times of the Gentiles are fulfilled.*

LUKE 21:24

# Make Disciples of All Nations, for The Mission Cannot Fail

## God's Roundabout Way of Pursuing the Nations: Focusing on Israel

We must not stumble over God's unusual way of pursuing the nations for the glory of his Son. It is true that Jesus taught that God chose to work in a unique way with the people of Israel instead of the nations. Jesus called the Jews of his day "the sons of the kingdom" (Matt. 8:12), that is, those to whom God gave a unique first privilege to be the focus of his saving deeds in history—like the deliverance from Egypt at the Red Sea, and miracles of provision in the wilderness, and the gift of the promised land, and many victories in battle (see Psalm 105 for a narrative of these blessings).

And it is also true that when Jesus came, he came as the *Jewish* Messiah, announcing the coming of the long-expected kingdom of triumph over the enemies of Israel. But he did not intend to bring the kingdom the way they thought. His intention was to suffer and die for their sins before he would reign as their king. This was their only hope of eternal life. Jesus focused his mission on the Jews, giving them every opportunity to know him and believe in him. He even said to the twelve apostles as he sent them out during his lifetime, "Go nowhere among the Gentiles and enter no town of the Samaritans, but go rather to the lost sheep of the house of Israel" (Matt. 10:5–6). And at one point he said, "I was sent only to the lost sheep of the house of Israel" (Matt. 15:24). We may think this a roundabout way to reach the nations. But God has his reasons.

### Jesus's Focus Was Rejected, and He Turned to the Nations

There are lessons the nations must learn from the failure of Israel to trust God and welcome a suffering Messiah. During his lifetime on earth most Jews did not believe that Jesus was the Messiah (Matt. 21:39; Mark 15:11–13; John 5:47; 6:36; 8:45; 12:37). They did not expect a suffering servant. Jesus upbraided this failure: "O foolish ones, and slow of heart to believe all that the prophets have spoken! Was it not necessary that the Christ should suffer these things and enter into his glory?" (Luke 24:25–26).

Not only did God intend for his Son, the Messiah, to suffer before he enters his glory, but God also intended all along that this would be the way the door of salvation would be opened to the nations. In the Jewish Scriptures that Jesus knew and loved, the prophecy was clear: the Son of God would one day inherit the nations. God said in Psalm 2 that he would establish his Royal Son in Jerusalem, and then this Son speaks: "I will tell of the decree: The Lord said to me, 'You are my Son; today I have begotten you. Ask of me, and I will make the nations your heritage, and the ends of the earth your possession'" (Ps. 2:7–8).

Again and again in these Scriptures we read the promise that all the nations would one day bow down and worship the true God, and that his Servant-Son would be a light to the nations. "All the ends of the earth shall remember and turn to the Lord, and all the families of the nations shall worship before you. . . . I will make you as a light for the nations, that my salvation may reach to the end of the earth" (Ps. 22:27; Isa. 49:6; cf. Gen. 49:10; Deut. 32:43; Ps. 66:4; 67:3–4;

68:32; 72:8; 86:9; 97:1; 138:4–5; Isa. 11:10; 42:10–12; 45:22; 49:12; Jer. 16:19; Dan. 7:14; Mic. 4:1–4).

When Jesus came as the light of the world, though his focus was on Israel, he began to make it clear that the kingdom he was bringing through suffering would bless the nations and that Israel herself would be, for a season, left to the side. For example, when a Gentile centurion believed in him and the Jewish leaders didn't, Jesus said, "I tell you, many will come from east and west and recline at table with Abraham, Isaac, and Jacob in the kingdom of heaven, while the sons of the kingdom will be thrown into the outer darkness. In that place there will be weeping and gnashing of teeth" (Matt. 8:11–12). The meaning is clear: the natural heirs of the kingdom (Israel) are not going to inherit its blessings because of unbelief, but the Gentile nations, that is, those who come from east and west, will enter the kingdom.

The mystery is opening. Gentiles—the nations—are going to inherit the blessings of Israel. Jesus had signaled this in his very first sermon in his hometown of Nazareth. He said that "there were many widows in Israel in the days of Elijah, when the heavens were shut up three years and six months, and a great famine came over all the land, and Elijah was sent to none of them but only to Zarephath, in the land of Sidon, to a [Gentile!] woman who was a widow. And there were many lepers in Israel in the time of the prophet Elisha, and none of them was cleansed, but only Naaman the [Gentile!] Syrian" (Luke 4:25–27). What was the response among the Jewish hometown people? "When they heard these things, all in the synagogue were filled with wrath" (Luke 4:28).

## The Times of the Gentiles

More and more it became clear, for those who had ears to hear, that Jesus had come to save all the nations as well as Jews. For example, he told his disciples, "You will be dragged before governors and kings for my sake, to bear witness before them and the *Gentiles* [i.e., the nations]" (Matt. 10:18). When he drove the money-changers out of the temple he said, "Is it not written, 'My house shall be called a house of prayer *for all the nations*'?" (Mark 11:17). He said that in the last judgment "before him will be gathered *all the nations*, and he will separate people one from another as a shepherd separates the sheep from the goats" (Matt. 25:32), and the criterion of judgment will *not* be Jewishness but how people have related to him in the ministry of his messengers. He said that the judgment of God was going to fall on Jerusalem and that "Jerusalem will be trampled underfoot by the Gentiles, until *the times of the Gentiles* are fulfilled" (Luke 21:24). In other words, there is an appointed time for the mission to the Gentiles when Israel is passed over, until the day comes when Israel will say, "Blessed is he who comes in the name of the Lord" (Matt. 23:39).

During this time—the times of the Gentiles—the sovereign promise of Jesus stands firm: "And this gospel of the kingdom *will* be proclaimed throughout the whole world as a testimony to all nations, and then the end will come" (Matt. 24:14). There is no *maybe* here. The mission that he gives to his followers to go and make disciples of all nations *will* come to pass. "I *will* build my church" (Matt. 16:18). "I have other sheep that are not of this fold. I *must* bring them also, and they *will* listen to my voice" (John 10:16). "Thus *it is written* [and cannot be broken!], that the Christ should suffer and on the third day rise from the dead, and that repentance and forgiveness of sins *should be proclaimed in his name to all nations*" (Luke 24:46–47). The mission to make disciples of all nations *will* succeed.

### The Blessings of Abraham Are for the Nations

So even though God focused his redeeming work on Israel for many centuries, everything was preparation for the global mission to the nations. This was there from the first promise to Abraham: "Now the LORD said to Abram, 'Go from your country and your kindred and your father's house to the land that I will show you. . . .

I will bless those who bless you, and him who dishonors you I will curse, and *in you all the families of the earth shall be blessed*" (Gen. 12:1–3). This is the promise that is coming true in Jesus's command, "Go therefore and make disciples of all nations." When the nations become disciples of Jesus, they receive the Messiah of Israel. And when they receive the Messiah of Israel, they receive the God of Abraham. And when they receive the God of Abraham, they become heirs of all the promises God made to Israel. This is what Jesus meant in Matthew 21:43 when he said, "Therefore I tell you, the kingdom of God will be taken away from you [Israel] and given to a people producing its fruits." That new "people" is the church gathered from all the nations.

### His Final Command: "Make a Global Claim on My Behalf"

Jesus's final command is that we never lose sight of the global scope of his claim on the human race. He is not a tribal deity. He is the Lord of the universe. Every knee will one day bow either willingly or unwillingly (Matt. 25:31–32). All judgment is given to him (John 5:22). The command is that his followers reach the nations with "all that he has commanded." "Go therefore and make disciples of all nations[1] . . . *teaching them to observe all that I have commanded you*" (Matt. 28:19–20). The mandate is that everything I have tried to set forth in this book (and it is not exhaustive) be taken to the nations. This is what it means to make disciples—not just that they make a profession of faith, but that they "observe all that I have commanded you."

### By Prayer, Word, and Suffering

The certainty of success is guaranteed (Matt. 24:14). Jesus will see that it gets done. But it is in our hands to do it. We do it by prayer

---

1   I omit the command to baptize here ("Go therefore and make disciples of all nations, *baptizing* them in the name of the Father and of the Son and of the Holy Spirit") not because it is an unimportant part of becoming a disciple of Jesus, but because I have dealt with this command in *Command #46.*

and by the word and by suffering for others. Jesus said, "The harvest is plentiful, but the laborers are few. Therefore pray earnestly to the Lord of the harvest to send out laborers into his harvest" (Luke 10:2). We must earnestly pray that God will do what he promised he would do. Promises do not make prayer superfluous; they make the answer certain.

Then we must open our mouths and speak the truth of Jesus to all nations. "What I tell you in the dark, say in the light, and what you hear whispered, proclaim on the housetops" (Matt. 10:27). "Go out to the highways and hedges and compel people to come in, that my house may be filled" (Luke 14:23). "I tell you, there will be more joy in heaven over one sinner who repents than over ninety-nine righteous persons who need no repentance" (Luke 15:7). And don't be ashamed, Jesus says, because "Everyone who acknowledges me before men, I also will acknowledge before my Father who is in heaven, but whoever denies me before men, I also will deny before my Father who is in heaven" (Matt. 10:32–33).

Finally, in all our praying and speaking we must be ready to suffer. "As the Father has sent me, even so I am sending you" (John 20:21). Jesus was sent to suffer. We will not be able to make disciples of all nations without taking up our cross and following Jesus on the Calvary road of sacrificial love (Mark 8:34). This is the light of Jesus that the world can most clearly see (*Command #48*).

### He Is Worth It

Jesus does not call us to an easy life or an easy mission. "They will lay their hands on you and persecute you, delivering you up to the synagogues and prisons, and you will be brought before kings and governors for my name's sake. This will be your opportunity to *bear witness*" (Luke 21:12–13). There will be no wasted suffering. In the short run, it will always be an occasion to speak and show the reality of Jesus. In the long run, it will lead to eternal life. "For whoever would save his life will lose it, but whoever loses his life for my sake and the gospel's will save it" (Mark 8:35). Therefore, in all your suffering for the advance of Jesus's mission you are increasingly rewarded. "Blessed are you when others revile you and persecute you and utter all kinds of evil against you falsely on my account. Rejoice and be glad, for your reward is great in heaven" (Matt. 5:11–12). That reward is the enjoyment of the inexhaustibly glorious Jesus forever and ever.

# A Word to Biblical Scholars
# (and Those Who Wonder
# What They Are Doing)

IT REQUIRES LITTLE IMAGINATION to hear a New Testament scholar say, "Good heavens, Piper totally ignores two hundred years of critical quests for the historical Jesus!" I would understand the response. It isn't quite right, however. "Ignores" is not the right word. It would be more accurate to say that I estimate most of the fruit of those quests to be unreliable and unusable to accomplish what Jesus aims to accomplish in the world.

## What Fruit from the Quests for the Historical Jesus?

In this regard little has changed since 1931 when Edwyn Hoskyns and Noel Davey wrote, "There are no 'assured results' of New Testament Criticism."[1] What this means in regard to the Quest for the Historical Jesus is not that nothing sure can be said about Jesus, but that the effort

---

1  Sir Edwyn Hoskyns and Noel Davey, *The Riddle of the New Testament* (London: Faber and Faber Limited, 1931), 259.

to go behind the four New Testament Gospels launches one onto a sea of speculation that has arrived at no island that could be called a reliable portrait of Jesus.[2]

Scholars speak of three Quests for the Historical Jesus. The First Quest was rooted as far back as Benedict Spinoza (1632–1677) and then worked out through Hermann Reimarus (1694–1768), David Friedrich Strauss (1808–1874), William Wrede (1859–1906), and others. It came to an end under the double attack of Albert Schweitzer (1875–1965), who argued that it wasn't radical enough, and Martin Kähler (1835–1912), who argued that the historical Jesus, as reconstructed by the critics, was not the "historic biblical Christ" and was therefore useless for the faith of the church.[3]

The Second Quest for the Historical Jesus was awakened in 1953 by a student of Rudolf Bultmann, Ernst Käsemann. These were the German giants whom I felt I had to come to terms with in my graduate school days in Munich in the early 1970s. Interestingly, both Bultmann and Käsemann lived to be ninety-two years old. But Bultmann was no longer active in the early 1970s. He died in 1976. Käsemann was in his sixties when I was studying in Germany, but I met him only briefly at a seminar in Paris. Along with Günther Bornkamm these three were

2   Ben Witherington III renders the following assessment of the first two Quests: "The upshot of the first two quests, as much as anything else, was to reveal the frustrating limitations of the historical study of any ancient person. . . . Nothing is as fleeting as many of the latest trends in New Testament scholarship, including studies of the historical Jesus. This is easily seen simply by reviewing the trends and impact of the Second Quest for the historical Jesus, which offered us, among other things, an existentialist Jesus. The historical Jesus and the Jesus that can be reconstructed by the historical-critical method are not one and the same. More to the point, the Jesus that is reconstructed by an idiosyncratic use of the historical-critical method or is based on reducing the field of focus to a few passages may have only minimal connections with the real Jesus." *The Jesus Quest: The Third Search for the Jew of Nazareth* (Downers Grover, Ill.: InterVarsity Press, 1995), 247.

3   All the relevant documents by these and other authors are gathered helpfully into one volume: *The Historical Jesus Quest: Landmarks in the Search for the Jesus of History*, ed. Gregory W. Dawes (Louisville: Westminster John Knox, 1999). Another helpful collection of historic essays on the quests for the historical Jesus is *The Historical Jesus in Recent Research*, ed. James D. G. Dunn and Scot McKnight, *Sources for Biblical Theological Study*, Vol. 10 (Winona Lake, Ind: Eisenbrauns, 2005).

the guardians of critical history with whom I had to reckon no matter what saying of Jesus I quoted in my doctoral dissertation on Jesus's love command.

## The Roots of Disillusionment

The upshot of those days in Germany was a growing disillusionment with the historical effort to reconstruct a Jesus of history behind the unified portrayal of Jesus in the New Testament Gospels. I detected a good bit of what seemed to be scholarly disingenuousness. Scholarly articles would begin with a healthy dose of "perhaps," "probably," "possibly," and other nuanced qualifiers, but by the end of the article there had emerged (out of nowhere it seemed to me) a confidence that something reliable and useful had been found. For my part I saw massive minds assembling, with great scholarly touch, a house of cards.

It helps to be over seventy-five years old. I have watched the cards collapse over and over. For example, who of us today can give any serious account of the reconstructions of the historical Jesus by Milan Machoveč (*Jesus für Atheisten*, 1972), Herbert Braun (*Jesus*, 1969), or Kurt Niederwimmer (*Jesus*, 1968)? But these were the cutting-edge reconstructions that, by the standards of the guild, I had to come to terms with. The first two argued with Bultmann that the kingdom of God in Jesus's ministry was a mythological construct that could be dispensed with today as we find the political (Machoveč was a Marxist) and existential "meaning" of Jesus for us. Niederwimmer exploited, as the book jacket said, "the assured results of depth psychology" to find in the kingdom of God "the objectification of a collective process of consciousness." I was not impressed with the fruit of the Second Quest. I had seen glorious things in the Jesus of the Gospels, and the Quest was offering me husks and ashes.

I found myself at home in these amazing words of Adolf Schlatter as he defined what he believed scholarship (*die Wissenschaft*) should be.

I keep myself as free as possible from conjectures and avoid therefore the effort to overturn them. This does not seem like a fruitful business to me. For conjectures are not overturned by producing more of the same. They sink away when one sees that observation is more fruitful than conjecture. . . . I call *Wissenschaft* [scholarship] the observation of what exists (*des Vorhandenen*), not the attempt to imagine what is not visible. Perhaps one will object that the guesswork of conjecture excites and entertains while observation is a hard and difficult work. That's true; play is easier than work. But the Gospel is misunderstood when one makes a plaything out of it.[4]

The conviction was growing in me that life is too short and the church is too precious for a minister of the Word to spend his life trying to recreate a conjectured Jesus. There was work to be done—very hard work—to see what is really there in the God-given portrayal of Jesus in the New Testament Gospels.

## What Hope for the Third Quest?

The Third Quest for the Historical Jesus "began in the early 1980s, fueled by some new archaeological and manuscript data, some new methodological refinements, and some new enthusiasm that historical research did not need to lead to a dead end."[5] It is still in process, and there are surveys available of what is happening.[6] Ben Witherington observes, "The desire to say something new and fresh characterizes almost all of the [Third Quest] works examined in this study, sometimes to the extreme of preferring the new over the probable."[7] My own

---

4   Adolf Schlatter, *Der Evangelist Matthäus*, 6th ed. (Stuttgart: Calver Verlag, 1963), xi. My translation.
5   Witherington, *The Jesus Quest*, 12–13.
6   Besides Witherington's overview cited in the previous footnote, see Larry Hurtado, "A Taxonomy of Recent Historical-Jesus Work," in *Whose Historical Jesus?* ed. William E. Arnal and Michel Desjardins (Waterloo, Ontario: Wilfrid Laurier University Press, 1997), 272–95; Jonathan Knight, *Jesus: An Historical and Theological Investigation* (London: T&T Clark International, 2004), 15–56; *The Historical Jesus in Recent Research*, ed. Dunn and McKnight.
7   Witherington, *The Jesus Quest*, 247.

assessment of what is happening is this: to the degree that the present reconstructions of the historical Jesus depart from the portrayal found in the Gospels of the New Testament, they will be forgotten the same way Machoveč, Braun, and Niederwimmer are forgotten.

There are reasons why this is so.

First, no reliable or lasting portrait of Jesus has ever been reconstructed from going behind what the four Gospels portray. There is no reason to think this will change. The reason is at hand: When you abandon *das Vorhandenen* (what exists at hand) for conjectures, you turn scholarship into an academic game. What is needed to give the game life is toys. And everybody knows the market and the academy demand new toys every generation. They cannot last. The tragedy is how much damage they do to people who do not have roots in the Gospels—and do not have the benefit of being as old as I am.

## The Gospels Have Not Been Overthrown

Second, the portrayal of Jesus in the four Gospels has not been overthrown by scholarship. The appearance of overthrow arises from the unwarranted creation of criteria of authenticity that by definition will rule out aspects of the New Testament portrayal. Thankfully, God has raised up several generations of careful, rigorous, and faithful scholars who are not cowed by the radical critics and who patiently go about their work establishing the historical credibility of the four Gospels. I thank God for them. I don't mean that they provide proof of the Gospels. I mean they show that the attacks on the historical validity of the portrayal of Jesus in the Gospels are not compelling.[8]

8   In this connection, the following books offer counterarguments to the Third Quest and the Quest in general: Craig L. Blomberg, *The Historical Reliability of the Gospels*, 2nd ed. (Downers Grove, Ill.: InterVarsity Press, 2007); Blomberg, *Jesus and the Gospels* (Nashville: Broadman & Holman, 1997); Blomberg, *The Historical Reliability of John's Gospel* (Downers Grove, Ill.: InterVarsity Press, 1998); D. A. Carson, *The Gospel According to John* (Grand Rapids, Mich.: Eerdmans, 1991), 40–68; *Jesus Under Fire*, ed. Michael J. Wilkins and J. P. Moreland (Grand Rapids, Mich.: Zondervan, 1995); Paul Barnett, *The Truth about Jesus: The Challenge of the Evidence* (Sydney: Aquila Press, 1994); Luke Timothy Johnson, *The Real Jesus: The Misguided Quest for the Historical Jesus and the*

### Fragments Lead to Arbitrary Reconstructions

Third, the attempt to reconstruct a reliable, compelling portrait of Jesus behind the Gospels is an illusion because by definition the method adopted only offers fragments without immediate context. Floating sayings and events can only be connected arbitrarily. That means the mind of the scholar, not the reality of Jesus, is governing the reconstruction. Luke Timothy Johnson has made this point effectively:

> When the compositions are fragmented, chopped into small pieces, and arranged in arbitrary sequences, they do not work at all. The literary compositions of the New Testament are analyzed best when their literary integrity is respected and appreciated. Approached in this fashion, they can be appreciated as witnesses and interpretations of religious experience and convictions.[9]

### Only the Gospels Remain

Fourth, the portrayal of Jesus in the Gospels of the New Testament is the only portrayal that has any chance of shaping the church and the world over the long haul. This is because it is the only one that people have access to. Whatever the Questers may construct, it will usually be read by only a handful of people. And even if they turn it into a blockbuster movie, seen by millions, that will pass without so much as a memory in ten years, while the Gospels will still be in the hands of the masses. I will wager my life that this was God's idea and that it will be worth all my remaining breath to try to understand what is actually there and teach it faithfully.

---

*Truth of the Traditional Gospels* (San Francisco: HarperSanFrancisco, 1996); Gregory Boyd, *Cynic, Sage or Son of God? Recovering the Real Jesus in an Age of Revisionist Replies* (Grand Rapids, Mich.: Baker, 1995); Gary Habermas, *The Historical Jesus: Ancient Evidence for the Life of Christ* (Joplin, Mo.: College Press, 1996); Lee Strobel, *The Case for Christ: A Journalist's Personal Investigation of the Evidence for Jesus* (Grand Rapids, Mich.: Zondervan, 1998).

9  Johnson, *The Real Jesus*, 167.

## My Approach in This Book

In addition to what I said about method under the subheading, "A Word about Method" in the Introduction, it may be helpful to point out here that the process of selecting which commands to discuss was complex. I gathered and recorded all the commands by reading the Gospels. This included implied commands (for example, "Blessed are the merciful" implies "Be merciful"). This list was over five hundred, counting the multiple restatements among the Gospels. The next step was to distinguish commands that would have abiding significance for faith and life. That is, I excluded commands like "Pick up your bed, and go home" (Mark 2:11). Finally there was a process of grouping and categorizing. After several passes, I was able to include all the commands in about thirty categories. These groupings formed the initial structure of the chapters. Some expanded, and the chapters were divided into two or more. Hence the round number of fifty chapters. I do not claim to have commented on every command. My hope is that enough categories and enough specific commands are handled to give help even for those I may have passed over.

## The Jesus of the Gospels Is the Most Radical

The fifth and final reason why reconstructions of Jesus that attempt to go behind the Gospels will not last and will fail to shape the church long-term is that the most radical Jesus is the one portrayed in the Gospels. So many of the reconstructions of Jesus behind the Gospels are motivated by the desire to liberate Jesus from the domesticated traditions of the church that fit Jesus into this world in predictable and compromising ways. That is a good desire. But their approach accomplishes the very opposite of what is hoped for. To the degree that the church is trained to distrust the Jesus of the Gospels and to look for ever-new human creations of Christ, the real Jesus is blurred, and his power to break free from the unbiblical traditions that bind him is blunted.

This is the point that Luke Timothy Johnson makes so well: the critical need in the church and the world is the "real Jesus" of the Gospels. Johnson's words are a fitting conclusion to this word to biblical scholars for *All That Jesus Commanded.*

Does the church act triumphalistically, or treat its people arrogantly? Is it an agent for the suppression of human needs and aspirations? Does it foster intolerance and small-mindedness? Does the church proclaim a gospel of success and offer Jesus as a better business partner? Does it encourage an ethos of prosperity to the neglect of the earth's good, or an individualistic spirituality to the neglect of the world's needy? Are its leaders corrupt and coercive? Such distortions of Christianity can find no harsher critic, no more radical rejecter, than the Jesus found *only* in the pages of the New Testament, the Jesus who was himself emptied out for others and called his followers to do the same.

The Jesus to whom Saint Francis of Assisi appealed in his call for a poor and giving rather than a powerful and grasping church was not the Historical Jesus but the Jesus of the Gospels. One must only wonder why this Jesus is not also the "real Jesus" for those who declare a desire for religious truth, and theological integrity, and honest history.[10]

---

10  Johnson, *The Real Jesus*, 177.

# General Index

# Scripture Index

**⧱ desiringGod**

Everyone wants to be happy. Our website was born and built for happiness. We want people everywhere to understand and embrace the truth that *God is most glorified in us when we are most satisfied in him.* We've collected more than thirty years of John Piper's speaking and writing, including translations into more than forty languages. We also provide a daily stream of new written, audio, and video resources to help you find truth, purpose, and satisfaction that never end. And it's all available free of charge, thanks to the generosity of people who've been blessed by the ministry.

If you want more resources for true happiness, or if you want to learn more about our work at Desiring God, we invite you to visit us at desiringGod.org.